CONTESTING
THE MIDDLE AGES

Contesting the Middle Ages is a thorough exploration of recent arguments surrounding nine hotly debated topics: the decline and fall of Rome, the Viking invasions, the Crusades, the persecution of minorities, sexuality in the Middle Ages, women within medieval society, intellectual and environmental history, the Black Death, and, lastly, the waning of the Middle Ages.

The historiography of the Middle Ages, a term in itself controversial among medieval historians, has been continuously debated and rewritten for centuries. In each chapter, John Aberth sets out key historiographical debates in an engaging and informative way, encouraging students to consider the process of writing about history and prompting them to ask questions even of already thoroughly debated subjects, such as why the Roman Empire fell, or what significance the Black Death had in the late Middle Ages and beyond.

Sparking discussion and inspiring examination of the past and its ongoing significance in modern life, *Contesting the Middle Ages* is essential reading for students of medieval history and historiography.

John Aberth is an independent scholar and medieval historian. He received his Ph.D. in Medieval History from the University of Cambridge, UK, and has taught, both full and part-time, at various colleges and universities in Vermont, New York, and Nebraska. He is the author of numerous books on the Black Death and European culture during the late Middle Ages.

CONTESTING THE MIDDLE AGES

Debates that are Changing
our Narrative of Medieval History

John Aberth

Routledge
Taylor & Francis Group

LONDON AND NEW YORK

First published 2019
by Routledge
2 Park Square, Milton Park, Abingdon, Oxon OX14 4RN

and by Routledge
711 Third Avenue, New York, NY 10017

Routledge is an imprint of the Taylor & Francis Group, an informa business

© 2019 John Aberth

British Library Cataloguing-in-Publication Data
A catalogue record for this book is available from the British Library

Library of Congress Cataloging-in-Publication Data
A catalog rcord for this book has been requested

ISBN: 978-0-415-72929-1 (hbk)
ISBN: 978-0-415-72930-7 (pbk)
ISBN: 978-1-315-71282-6 (ebk)

Typeset in Bembo and Stone Sans
by Florence Production Ltd, Stoodleigh, Devon

CONTENTS

FIGURES

MAPS

FOREWORD

In the original conception for this book, I was asked to write a survey of the Middle Ages, that period of history from about 500 to 1500 A.D. This was to be one of many such medieval history survey texts currently on the market, which provide a litany of dates, names, and other useful facts and information. Obviously, I decided not to write that kind of book. The simple reason is that, over the course of many years of teaching, I have found that my students almost never read those kinds of texts. They are useful for looking up things, but they hardly make for the most riveting read.

So instead, I decided to write a different kind of book: One that focuses on the recent and raging debates about what medieval history should be, rather than simply stating what it is. Most historians would therefore call my book a work of historiography, or the history of the writing of history. Rather than provide definitive statements about the period, this book actually tries to pose more questions than it answers, in the hope that this will stimulate thoughtful discussion or introspection. Above all, it seeks to pose the burning questions of history that every student or general reader should be asking when making a study of the Middle Ages. Some of these questions, such as the reasons for the decline and fall of the Roman Empire, or the significance of the Black Death of the late Middle Ages, are questions that have been debated for a very long time; even if these debates are close to being settled, they still generate a veritable industry of academic literature and commentary, and this will not likely change for the foreseeable future. If one can't always provide the answers to these questions, they are still worth the asking because they make history relevant to our own times; more simply put, they are downright interesting and make history "come alive". It is my hope that they will also make this book intriguing enough to read.

I have intentionally written this book with the aim of making it controversial, subversive, eccentric, and, as one can tell just by glancing at the chapter headings, even whimsical at times. More seriously, I try in this book to illuminate the side alleyways and dimly-lit passages that some have opened up on the single, standard narrative thread too often imposed on our past. Always remaining within the realms of possibility, I hope to showcase some different interpretations by which history can be provocative and, indeed, life-changing. While some of these interpretations certainly can be contested, it is essential that they receive an airing, because they are changing the way we view the medieval world. However, one thing that I do not do here is speculate on what might have been if history had happened a little differently, part of the genre known as "alternate history" and which I reserve for another book.[1] All of the scenarios that I discuss in this book, therefore, are purported to have really happened, although some revisionist interpretations of history go so far as to change the standard narrative of the actual course of events, which is particularly true if the sources in question are murky and indistinct. My main goal in all of this has been to get you, the reader, thinking about the past and about its significance for us here in the present. If this book has done that, then it will have served its purpose. If you disagree with it, even violently perhaps, it will have served its purpose better still.

John Aberth
Roxbury, Vermont

Note

1 For my excursions into alternate history, see my forthcoming, *How Harold Won Hastings: The Middle Ages that Might Have Been*. For this reason, I avoid using the terms "alternate" or "alternative" in this book, even when describing radically revisionist interpretations of the past.

PREFACE

One of the more memorable lines from Quentin Tarantino's cult film, *Pulp Fiction* (1994), is when the mob hit man, Marsellus (played by Samuel Jackson), taunts his victim by saying, "I'm gonna git Medieval on your ass," just before he whacks him. Like much of the film's dialogue (which won an Academy Award for best screenplay), the line both references a popular consciousness and itself has become a touchstone in popular culture. It both testifies to the widely-held notion (at least here in the United States) that medieval is synonymous with a violent, cruel, backward, and generally barbaric age of human history, and it helps to perpetuate that notion. Indeed, so iconic is the line that it has since entered the online *Oxford English Dictionary* as one of the standard definitions (number 3b) of the term. Its influence will also be recognized by any instructor or graduate student who must correct student essays for a medieval history survey course, where he or she will inevitably find the misspelling, "midevil," on any number of papers or exams.[1] These students are simply committing the Freudian slip of spelling out what they really think of this period and all that it implies. To correct such errors, we must not only improve our students' command of the English language but also their understanding of history.

And yet, it can be legitimately asked, what do historians really mean by the term, "medieval"? According to most textbooks, the Middle Ages generally designates that period of European history that begins with the end of the Roman Empire sometime in the fifth century, and ends with the dawn of the Early Modern period sometime in the fifteenth century. But the thousand years of history encompassed by these dates are by no means easy to categorize or describe. This is, in fact, one of the more difficult periods of European history for students and readers to comprehend, standing, as it does, with one foot in the ancient world, and the other in the modern. Some texts do attempt to treat the Middle Ages as a coherent civilization unto itself, with a "making" and a "waning" to its culture.[2] Even so, the very term, "Middle Ages," was coined by Renaissance humanists writing at the end of the medieval period and beyond, and thus, this was not a term that would have occurred to the vast majority of the people living during the era covered by this book. (The Latin term, medium aevum, only achieved widespread currency towards the end of the seventeenth century.) Moreover, the Renaissance authors who were the first to conceive of the Middle Ages as a distinct period did so only in order to distinguish their own culture from what had come before, not to study their immediate predecessors on their own terms. Rather, they were simply dismissing an inconvenient era that had intervened between the glories of ancient Greek and Roman civilization and their own reinvention, rediscovery, and "rebirth" of that civilization. To understand the Middle Ages, therefore, one must understand that those who lived in those times never saw it as a "Middle Age".

How, then, should we approach this rather elusive era in Europe's past? Some scholars would prefer to do away with the term "medieval" altogether, arguing that it is a "tyrannous construct," generally used to designate a "feudal" society, but one that does not clearly define a coherent social formation or stage of development, particularly in an extra-European context.[3] One alternative approach is to adopt the periodization known as "Old Europe," in which at least the entire second half of the Middle Ages is subsumed into a larger, more continuous block of time extending from about 1000 to 1800.[4] One of the arguments for adopting this new division of history is that it is more organic to the contemporary mindset. It seems to assume that for most medieval people, the year 1000 was a key marker of time, one that was fraught with apocalyptic expectations. This outsized significance attached to the year 1000, however, is itself subject to considerable debate, with most historians these days downplaying the idea of the millennium as a convenient marker of key transitions or transformations in medieval society.[5] On the other hand, the notion of a "Late Antiquity" that extended from c. 200 to 800 A.D., put forward by the historian Peter Brown starting in 1971, in preference to the hoary old "decline and fall" of the Roman Empire championed by Edward Gibbon in 1776, is now almost a standard feature of most medieval history textbooks (Chapter 1). In the Late Antiquity scenario, Europeans up until about 1000 still saw themselves as living in the long shadow of the Roman Empire: An early medieval person, then, would say that he was not witnessing a birth or "making" to a new civilization so much as keeping alight the flame of a still vital ancient culture in the midst of, what in retrospect, was to be the twilight of the Roman past. This past, after all, included not only the venerable pagans of old, but also the upstart religion of Christianity, which had served as the dominant cultural milieu of the empire for at least the last hundred years of its official existence, down to 476, when the last Roman emperor, Romulus Augustulus, was usurped by the Germanic military leader, Odoacer.

After 1000, to continue this line of reasoning, Europeans shed their ancient skin and began to talk about themselves as "moderns". Perhaps crucial to this new outlook was the emergence of "Europe" as a new, coherent entity in place of the cosmopolitan internationalism of Rome at its height, which may have already begun by the reign of Charlemagne (768–814).[6] It was also then that we begin to see the first glimmerings of the typical medieval institutions of feudalism and manorialism, which represented a decisive break from the old Roman administrative and economic systems that most likely did not survive into the Carolingian period, despite its "renaissance" recovery of ancient Latin texts.[7] Nor does the emergence of Europe under Charlemagne seem to have much to do with the concurrent rise of Islam as a world empire, which according to the "Pirenne Thesis" (named after the early twentieth-century Belgian historian, Henri Pirenne), had been responsible for the commercial and cultural isolation of the northern and western regions of the former Roman Empire, an idea that now can no longer be sustained on archaeological grounds.[8] Instead, the "idea of Europe" seems to have emerged from Charlemagne's educational and missionary program to create a unified Latin Christian culture within his domains stretching from the Spanish march to Saxony.[9] Perhaps a tragic footnote to this creation of a new European identity is that it swept away, or else in the process of assimilation transformed beyond recognition, the last vestiges of a pagan, Celtic culture that had somehow managed to survive the Roman Empire.[10]

Adopting Old Europe in place of the Middle Ages forces us not only to rethink the intrinsic value and integrity of the former divisions into ancient, medieval, and modern, but also of the divisions of the Middle Ages itself into early, high, and late. One often hears, for example, that the thirteenth century was the high watermark of a high Middle Ages, the so-called "greatest of centuries".[11] It is so named in deference to the order imposed by national monarchies and their parliaments, to the impressive synthesis achieved of pagan philosophical rationalism with the mystical Christian faith, to the soaring heights attained by the Gothic cathedral spires, and to the relentless expansion of population, agricultural production, town settlements, and commercial enterprise. But the high Middle Ages may not have been quite so "high". The achievements of these centuries were significant, but for an increasing number of textbooks, celebrating them is paradoxically bound up with acknowledging a dark underside to the high Middle Ages, such as the brutal oppression of marginal groups including Jews, heretics, and homosexuals (Chapters 4 and 5), or the environmental degradation that was an inevitable by-product of population expansion and increasing arable land use.[12]

At one time, I found the periodization of Old Europe attractive because it would strike a blow against the popular perception of the late Middle Ages (c. 1300–1500) as a period of decline or "waning" of civilization and culture, a perception which I believe is fundamentally wrong (Chapter 9).[13] The "waning" thesis was first popularized by the Dutch historian, Johan Huizinga, in a famous book that was translated as *The Waning of the Middle Ages* in 1924 (with the original Dutch edition, *Herfsttij der Middeleeuwen*, published in 1919). Some would argue that the concept of a waning to the Middle Ages is almost necessitated by the mere acceptance of this time period as an organic unit all unto itself, which naturally would have had a birth, a maturation, and finally a decline. Just like a human being, the Middle Ages would then inevitably have slipped in its final stages into senility, decadence, and decrepitude, when it was subjected to one "crisis" after another to which it could not have helped but succumb.[14] Or to use another metaphor, which is perhaps closer to the original Dutch title of Huizinga's work, the late Middle Ages was like the "autumn" of the seasons, a time of dying and decay after the spring and summer of origins and growth.[15] It should be noted that this depressing outlook on the late Middle Ages could equally well apply to the *fin de siècle* environment of late nineteenth-century Europe in which Huizinga grew up, or the era of "Lost Generation" disillusionment in between the two world wars when he actually came out with his magnum opus.[16]

I now believe that to adopt "Old Europe" as a new periodization of history would be a great mistake, mainly because it would paper over an event that was perhaps the most momentous in all of European history, if not of the world: the Black Death. Indeed, the Black Death, the greatest natural disaster and disease event of all time, inaugurated some fundamental changes in European society that signaled a transition away from the Middle Ages and ushered in the Early Modern era (Chapter 8). Since these changes entailed the end of some key markers of medieval civilization and culture, such as serfdom,[17] historians are entirely justified in closing the chapter on one era of history and opening another, even if this may not have been clear to people living at the time. In other words, the term "medieval" is not some "tyrannous" construct arbitrarily imposed by historians upon their hapless students, but an organic one that emerges out of some very real transformations taking place in society. This transition from the Middle Ages to the Early Modern period may have been gradual, but it nonetheless had a definite beginning and end: namely, from 1348 up to c. 1450.[18] For it was at this time that Europe suffered a catastrophic drop in population with the first outbreak of the Black Death of *at least* 50 percent (i.e., the population was suddenly cut in half), where it then remained for at least a century due to regular and frequent recurrences of the plague, with the disease striking broadly across Europe once a decade.[19] Only in the mid-fifteenth century do we see the European population slowly begin to rise again from its demographic deadlock of the previous century.[20] It was this enormous and sustained population loss that was largely responsible for the transformative changes that, eventually but inevitably, brought the medieval era to a close.

With new arguments now championing, once again, a definitive decline and fall of ancient Rome, and therefore a true beginning to the Middle Ages (Chapter 1), we have a clear demarcation of medieval times that is pretty close to what traditional historiography said it had been all along. What is different, though, is that now it no longer makes sense to talk about a decline, or "waning," to medieval culture similar to what happened to ancient Rome (Chapter 9). This is because the Black Death, through its massive demographic impact, inaugurated perhaps the greatest windfall of wealth and income in history, creating a new class of patrons who, in turn, stimulated a dynamic resurgence in art and culture. Instead of a society supposedly obsessed with death and guilt, it was the "Plague Economy" that helped society make the transition to capitalism and thus made possible patronage of the Renaissance, while the plague's deprivation of so many parishes of their priests forced a rethinking of laymen's relationship with the Church, which laid the groundwork for the Reformation.[21] While the Black Death may have been a demographic disaster, it was the means by which the people of the late Middle Ages were able to reinvent themselves as moderns.

Thus, there is a very good reason why we still study the Middle Ages, and why we still use the term, "medieval". It is because this was a time that was very different from our own, but one that has made us who we are today.

Notes

1 The misspelling is also noted by John M. Riddle in his textbook, *A History of the Middle Ages, 300–1500* (Lanham, MD.: Rowman and Littlefield, 2008), p. 2, where he writes, "In every set of examinations I find some students, even on the final examination, make this error".

2 Richard Southern, *The Making of the Middle Ages* (New Haven, CT.: Yale University Press, 1953); Johan Huizinga, *The Waning of the Middle Ages: A Study of the Forms of Life, Thought and Art in France and the Netherlands in the Fourteenth and Fifteenth Centuries*, trans. Jan Hopman (London: Edward Arnold, 1924).

3 Jacques Heers, *Le Moyen Âge: une imposture* (Paris: Perrin, 1992); Timothy Reuter, "Medieval: Another Tyrannous Construct?" *Medieval History Journal* 1 (1998):25–45; Toby Burrows, "Unmaking 'the Middle Ages'," *Journal of Medieval History*, 7 (1981):127–34.

4 Dietrich Gerhard, *Old Europe: A Study of Continuity, 1000–1800* (New York: Academic Press, 1981); Gerhard first proposed this idea in an article, "Periodization in European History," *American Historical Review* 61 (1956):903.

5 See, in particular, Dominique Barthélemy, "The Year 1000 Without Abrupt or Radical Transformation," in *Debating the Middle Ages: Issues and Readings*, eds. Lester K. Little and Barbara H. Rosenwein (Oxford: Blackwell Publishers, 1998), pp. 134–47.

6 Denys Hay, *Europe: The Emergence of an Idea* (Edinburgh: Edinburgh University Press, 1957); Alessandro Barbero, *Charlemagne: Father of a Continent*, trans. Allan Cameron (Berkeley, CA.: University of California Press, 2004); Rosamond McKitterick, *Charlemagne: The Formation of a European Identity* (Cambridge: Cambridge University Press, 2008).

7 Chris Wickham, "The Fall of Rome Will Not Take Place," in *Debating the Middle Ages: Issues and Readings*, eds. Lester K. Little and Barbara H. Rosenwein (Oxford: Blackwell Publishers, 1998), pp. 45–57.

8 Henri Pirenne, *Mohammed and Charlemagne* (Cleveland, OH. and New York: Meridian Books, 1957); Richard Hodges and David Whitehouse, *Mohammed, Charlemagne and the Origins of Europe: Archaeology and the Pirenne Thesis* (Ithaca, NY.: Cornell University Press, 1983), esp. pp. 169–76; Michael McCormick, *Origins of the European Economy: Communications and Commerce, A.D. 300–900* (Cambridge: Cambridge University Press, 2001), pp. 115–19.

9 Chris Wickham, *The Inheritance of Rome: Illuminating the Dark Ages, 400–1000* (New York: Viking Penguin, 2009), p. 555.

10 Ramsay MacMullen, *Christianity and Paganism in the Fourth to Eighth Centuries* (New Haven, CT.: Yale University Press, 1997).

11 From the book by James Joseph Walsh, *The Thirteenth, Greatest of Centuries* (New York: Catholic Summer School Press, 1907).

12 See John Aberth, *An Environmental History of the Middle Ages: The Crucible of Nature* (London: Routledge, 2013); Richard C. Hoffmann, *An Environmental History of Medieval Europe* (Cambridge: Cambridge University Press, 2014).

13 I briefly comment on "Old Europe" as a response to the waning thesis in John Aberth, *From the Brink of the Apocalypse: Confronting Famine, War, Plague, and Death in the Later Middle Ages*, 2nd edn. (London: Routledge, 2010), p. 5.

14 Howard Kaminsky, "From Lateness to Waning to Crisis: The Burden of the Later Middle Ages," *Journal of Early Modern History*, 4 (2000):85–125.

15 This is, in fact, the title of a new English translation of Huizinga's book by Robert Payton and Ulrich Mammitz, *The Autumn of the Middle Ages* (Chicago, IL.: Chicago University Press, 1996). However, it seems that the translation is actually from the German edition of 1923 rather than the original Dutch of 1919.

16 For Huizinga's contemporary context that may have influenced his work, see Peter Burke, "The History of Johan Huizinga," *Times Literary Supplement* (13 December 1974):1423; and Norman F. Cantor, *Inventing the Middle Ages: The Lives, Works, and Ideas of the Great Medievalists of the Twentieth Century* (New York: Morrow, 1991), pp. 377–81.

17 Mark Bailey, *The Decline of Serfdom in Medieval England: From Bondage to Freedom* (Woodbridge, UK: Boydell Press, 2014).

18 Ole Benedictow, "New Perspectives in Medieval Demography: The Medieval Demographic System," in *Town and Countryside in the Age of the Black Death: Essays in Honour of John Hatcher*, eds. Mark Bailey and Stephen Rigby (Turnhout, Belgium: Brepols, 2012), pp. 20, 28.

19 For a summary of the latest demographic evidence on the Black Death, see: Ole J. Benedictow, *The Black Death, 1346–1353: The Complete History* (Woodbridge, UK: Boydell Press, 2004), pp. 245–384; John Aberth, *The Black Death: A New History of the Great Mortality*, forthcoming with Oxford University Press.

20 John Hatcher, "Understanding the Population History of England, 1450–1750," *Past and Present* 180 (2003):102–4.

21 These arguments are developed more in-depth in John Aberth, *The Black Death: A New History of the Great Mortality*, forthcoming with Oxford University Press.

1

IF A GERMAN MIGRATES INTO YOUR EMPIRE, DO NOT BE ALARMED

The decline and fall of Rome

It was a dark, cold night in March. I was stranded at the four corners intersection in the sleepy little town of East Warren, Vermont. I was locked out of my car, which was still running (don't ask me why or how). I knocked at the only house on the corner, but no one answered. In my desperation, I decided to flag down the next car that came along, which happened to be some tourists from Massachusetts.

"Help me," I said, "I'm an absent-minded history professor, and I've locked myself out of my car!"

"How do we know you're a history professor?" they asked, eyeing me suspiciously.

"Test me on anything you like".

"Explain the decline and fall of the Roman Empire in five minutes!" A half hour later, I was back at the intersection, breaking into my car with the help of a professional locksmith from Waitsfield, where I had been dropped off by my new friends from Massachusetts.

The above is a true story that really happened to me, and I retell it on occasion to demonstrate the practical utility of the subject of history. "So history can actually save your life," is the concluding punch-line of my story. But it also illustrates another truism: The enduring fascination that people have with the decline and fall of the Roman Empire. A large part of the reason for this fascination, I believe, is that it serves as a bellwether for our own, more modern empires.

Did Rome fall or was it transformed?

Attempts to explain the decline and fall of Rome are legion and ancient, to pardon a pun. The most famous remains the classic work by the English antiquarian, Edward Gibbon, *The History of the Decline and Fall of the Roman Empire*, published in six volumes between 1776 and 1788. Gibbon's fame, however, rests entirely on his prose, for his explanation that Christianity sapped the martial spirit, vigor, and personnel of Rome is almost universally rejected these days by historians. Since Gibbon's time, plenty of other contenders have stepped forward to answer this age-old question. Two and a half decades ago, a German scholar, Alexander Demandt, compiled no less than 210 explanations, arranged from A-Z, in his book, *The Fall of Rome*.[1] Some of the more silly, outrageous, or even offensive (at least to our modern sensibilities) of the reasons cited include: "abolition of gods," "bolshevization," "communism," "decline of Nordic character," "excessive freedom," "female emancipation," "gout," "homosexuality," "hyperthermia," "impotence," "Jewish influence," "lack of male dignity," "lead-poisoning," "moral decline," "negative selection," "orientalization," "prostitution," "public baths," "racial degeneration," "socialism," "tiredness of life," "useless diet," and "vulgarization". Indeed, if I had attempted to reel off all 210 of these explanations to my saviors from Massachusetts, I very much doubt if I would be here today.

But in recent years, many historians have sidestepped altogether the question of when Rome fell and why by challenging whether Rome fell at all. Instead, most historians these days speak of a "transformation" or "slow transition" from classical to medieval sensibilities and generally avoid the terms "fall" or "decline," which, if they use at all, they put into quotation marks to emphasize their reservations.[2] Therefore, the question nowadays is no longer why Rome declined and fell, but, did it in fact do so? This is obviously a fundamental rethinking of the very terms of the debate.[3]

Perhaps the first historian to question the decline and fall of the Roman Empire was the great Belgian medievalist, Henri Pirenne, whose *Mohammed and Charlemagne* was published posthumously in 1935. In this seminal and summative book, Pirenne argued that the Germanic successor kingdoms set up after the fall of the Roman Empire in the West in the late fifth century preserved much of Roman culture and institutions, so that there was a great deal of continuity extending down until at least the seventh century. Thereafter, however, the rise of Islam severed most of the Mediterranean world—including Spain, North Africa, Egypt, and Palestine—from its connections with the rest of the former Roman Empire to the north, so that by necessity the great Germanic ruler, Charlemagne (reigned 768–814), was forced to reconstitute the empire as an exclusively European state, confined by physical boundaries that hold true almost to this day, with a center of gravity that naturally shifted northward and westward to fall along France, Germany, and northern Italy, reaching its terminus in Rome. If Charlemagne had indeed given birth to Europe, then it was the founder of Islam, Muhammad, who had served as midwife: To quote perhaps the most famous phrase from Pirenne's book, "without Mohammed Charlemagne would have been inconceivable".[4] Pirenne also claimed that it was not until Charlemagne that the real break with Roman antiquity occurred and the Middle Ages truly began, with a genuine assimilation now emerging of Roman and Germanic cultures.

These days, Pirenne's thesis has been challenged and replaced, largely owing to advances in archaeology. Much of this evidence seems to indicate that the rise and expansion of Islam beyond the Arabian peninsula in the seventh century was a symptom, rather than the cause, of the collapse of the Roman Empire, which was largely complete by the end of the sixth century.[5] But an interesting variation on Pirenne's thesis is that Islam, far from cutting off Europe from international trade, actually stimulated its revival (particularly in slaves) during the reign of Charlemagne, whose commerce with the Abbasid dynasty based in Baghdad was evidenced by the importation of silver and the issuance of a heavier, silver *denarius* or penny as the standard currency. Only with the decline of Charlemagne's empire after his death in the ninth century do we see the real beginnings of economic stagnation in Europe and therefore the catalyst for an inward-looking, decentralized feudal-manorial system that heralded the dawn of the Middle Ages.[6] Recent evidence for the ongoing demographic impact of the First Pandemic of plague between 541 and 750 (made possible by a continuing trade, especially in grain, which transferred infected rats and fleas) has tended to reinforce this view.[7]

Even though the Pirenne thesis no longer dominates academic debates, its argument for a long transformation, rather than the decline and fall, of ancient Rome into early medieval society has been taken up wholesale by the supplanting concept of "Late Antiquity," which argues for the gradual evolution of Europe independent of the concurrent rise of Islam. This term was first introduced by early twentieth-century German historians as *Spätantike*, but the label was popularized in English since the 1970s by the Irish historian, Peter Brown. Brown was able to fashion Late Antiquity, generally defined as extending from c. 200 to c. 800, as its own distinct period by emphasizing the vitality of the early Christian Church.[8] In the latest edition of his textbook, Brown emphasized "micro-Christendoms" and "symbolic goods" to make the point that "applied Christianity" at this time continued to thrive in spite of the fall of Rome as a center of empire and in spite of the economic collapse of its trade and industry.[9] He also stressed the dynamic interplay between Christian institutions and the emerging "barbarian" kingdoms, as well as the fluid cultural and ecological integrity of the Mediterranean world, even in the midst of its political and economic fragmentation. All this was meant to counter Gibbon's portrayal of late classical Rome as a decadent phase of history, or of the early medieval period as a "primitive" time or a "Dark Ages" of cultural decline and despair. It should be obvious by now that in Brown's schema, religious, and cultural considerations were paramount and were accorded priority above all other factors, an approach that he owed ultimately to a French method of historical enquiry known as the *Annales* school of "cultural anthropology".[10] The acceptance of the Late Antiquity thesis, at least in academic circles, is indicated by the title given to a major research project funded by the European Science Foundation, "The Transformation of the Roman World".[11]

What this means is that typically in a history course today, students are taught that a range of long-term social, political, and economic problems were responsible for the empire being transformed into something that would have been unrecognizable in the time of Augustus, Rome's first emperor (r. 31 B.C.–14 A.D.), or indeed even during Rome's golden age of the Five Good Emperors (r. 96–180 A.D.). Therefore, Rome's decline and fall is itself transformed into a gradual, lengthy process that took as long as two centuries to complete. It very much implies that the empire's fragmentation into "successor kingdoms" ruled by "barbarian" or Germanic tribal chieftains was an inevitable outcome, something that no Roman could have done anything about. It turns the Germans who took over the empire into rather inoffensive occupiers who, instead of invading or sacking Rome (as they most assuredly did in 410 and 455), are now shown to have been invited in as part of an accommodation process that would produce military allies (*foederati*), who were badly needed as Rome began to suffer manpower shortages at this time. Instead of rampaging, pillaging, and plundering across the empire, Germans *migrated*, which is usually shown on maps complete with routes supposedly taken by each tribe, whether this be the Vandals (down into North Africa), Visigoths and Suevi (to Spain), Ostrogoths (Italy), Saxons (Britain), or Burgundians, Franks, and Alamanni (France, southern Germany, and Switzerland).

However, it must be emphasized that scholars these days argue that the German migrations and identities were far less coherent and chronologically hide-bound than these rather outdated maps, as well as modern myths of national formation, would suggest. Instead, tribes that poured across the borders of the Roman Empire such as the Goths, Franks, and the Alamanni, "were composed of groups speaking a variety of languages, following various customs, and identifying themselves with varying traditions".[12] Moreover, such tribal identities inevitably changed over time, so that it makes no sense to speak as if "the Franks of 700 were exactly the same as the Franks of 350".[13] Those tribes that endured and were successful in setting up successor states in the fifth and sixth centuries, such as the Franks, assimilated much of Roman culture in terms of law, religion, and administration.

It is even argued that Germans did not actually take over Romans' land when they appropriated various parts of the empire, but rather only their tax revenues, which Roman curiales, or upper-class denizens of the cities, no longer wanted to collect anyway.[14] In addition to emphasizing continuity and gradual change, the modern version of the migration thesis is certainly a more politically correct way to portray Germans than as berserk-eyed, invariably destructive "barbarians".

Historians are also attracted to Late Antiquity's theme of transformation because, while it may not be the dawn yet of a fully-fledged Middle Ages, it does encourage tracing some typically medieval institutions, such as feudalism and manorialism, back into earlier centuries, when they first put down their roots. For example, the *comitatus* (meaning "company" or "armed group") of Germanic warrior chiefs and their followers, such as were described by the Roman historian Tacitus in his *Germania* (written c. 98 A.D.), are here portrayed as leading eventually to the feudal bond between a lord and his vassal, particularly in terms of the loyalty and military service that was expected. The withdrawal of wealthy Roman senators and aristocrats to their manor houses and country estates, where they provided

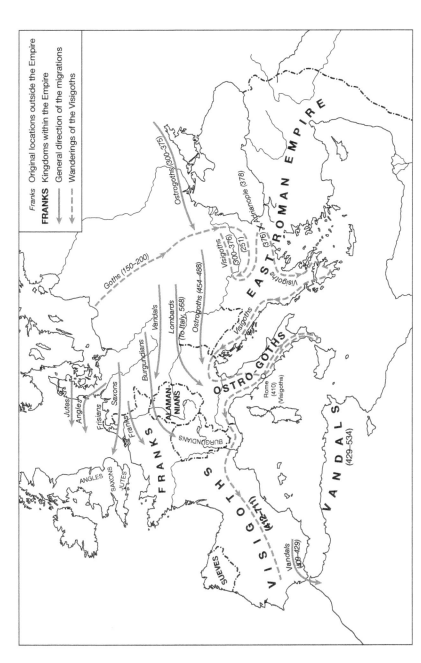

MAP 1.1 An often-reproduced map of the supposed migrations of the Germanic tribes, now considered too neat and pat to reflect reality

protection from both German marauder and Roman tax collector alike to the *coloni* (meaning "farmers" or "cultivators") at the cost of their land and liberty, is seen as the precursor of serfdom or villeinage, whereby medieval peasants became bound by all sorts of legal customs and duties to the manor.[15] In order to establish these foundations, most history surveys of the Middle Ages start somewhere around 300 A.D., with the reigns of the emperors Diocletian (284–305) and Constantine (312–337).[16] These are seen as crucial for imposing a rigid social hierarchy and establishing the dominance of Christianity, both key features of almost any definition of the Middle Ages. However, it also should be pointed out that there was considerable regional variation in terms of the formation of aristocratic and peasant social structures in the early medieval period.[17]

The concept of Late Antiquity is an appealing one, not only because it avoids the pejorative connotations of "Dark Ages" and "medieval," but also because it seems more in line with the thought world of most contemporaries, who certainly would not have recognized themselves yet as living in an early Middle Ages. Recently, however, its notion of a long, drawn-out transformation has been challenged, at least in political and economic terms, by historians bent on resurrecting the idea of a dramatic, violent, and relatively sudden "fall of Rome". Bryan Ward-Perkins, for example, has raised the rather obvious point that Rome did, in fact, fall. For many Romans, the collapse of their empire meant the end of a very sophisticated and "civilized" way of life, at least in material terms, one that was not to be recaptured in Europe until perhaps at the very end of the Middle Ages.[18] The Dutch historian, Willem Jongman, agreed with this assessment, arguing that, at its height in the early second century, "Rome had created perhaps the most prosperous and successful pre-industrial economy in history," with the reign of Antoninus Pius (138–61) "probably the best age to live in pre-industrial history".[19]

This demise of "comfort" can be measured archaeologically through the physical evidence of changes in household construction and amenities as well as in the quality and quantity of industrial products, such as pottery and tableware. Roof tiles, for example, used in the construction of solid buildings made of brick or stone, were very prevalent throughout the Roman world, being used even for humble structures such as farm sheds. By the fifth and sixth centuries, however, archaeological evidence for these materials began to disappear, as they apparently were now reserved for only the grandest structures, such as churches. Production of good quality pottery, whose distribution and quantity at archaeological sites would indicate its availability to even the very humble, also started to fall off dramatically at this time. Human and animal stature both began to decline, as measured by femur bone length. Fewer shipwrecks indicated a decline in shipping and trade. One could even trace the collapse of Roman industry in the Greenland ice caps that have trapped within their cores the higher levels of metallic pollution (such as lead) that were released into the atmosphere during Rome's productive period.[20]

Secondly, Ward-Perkins emphasized that there was little love lost between the Romans and the Germanic "barbarians".[21] Other historians have begun placing the Germans front and center once again behind Rome's decline and fall.[22] This also is much more in accord with what popular culture still conceives to be a decline and fall of Rome at the hands of Germanic marauders, as evidenced by the film, *The Last Legion* (2007), which imagines what happened to the last Roman emperor, the adolescent Romulus Augustulus ("little Augustus"), when he was deposed in 476 by the Germanic chieftain, Odoacer. (In the film, Odoacer and his Germans are shown to be besieging and sacking Rome, when in fact the transfer of power took place in Ravenna; but it also shows, quite correctly, that Odoacer, who had been *magister militum*, or master of the soldiers, under the previous emperor, Julius Nepos, felt betrayed when he was not rewarded by Romulus' father, Orestes, for leading the revolt that helped put his son on the throne, and that he afterwards came to a *modus operandi* with the Roman senate.)

Ever since Quinctilius Varus lost three legions, totaling 20,000 men, in the Teutoburg forest of northwest Germany in 9 A.D., the detritus of which lay strewn about the battlefield for years afterward and which the Emperor Augustus mourned for the remainder of his reign, the area known as Germania was never incorporated into the Roman Empire, one of those events that may have seemed insignificant at the time but which was to have enormous consequences later. While the Roman historians, the pagan Tacitus (c. 56–117 A.D.) and the Christian Salvian (fifth century), did give somewhat flattering depictions of the Germans, the purpose of this was primarily to shock their civilized readers by holding up the better moral behavior of the "barbarians". Salvian's comment from *The Governance of God* that poor yet well-born and well-educated Roman widows and orphans now "seek among the barbarians the dignity of the Roman because they cannot bear barbarous indignity among the Romans," is often quoted in textbooks as evidence of a decrepit empire whose oppressions were driving its own citizens into the arms of a more vibrant Germanic invader. Nevertheless, one has to remember that in the very next sentence Salvian highlighted the desperation of this act by pointing to all the ways in which the two peoples were different, including their religious beliefs, language, and even personal hygiene. To get a truer picture of how difficult life could be living with the Germans, one should read Eugippius's *Life of Severinus*, about the saintly bishop of Noricum in present-day western Austria and his doomed efforts to defend his diocese against a host of Germanic invaders, including the Rugi, Alamanni, Thuringians, Ostrogoths, and Herules.

Some Germans, such as Theodoric the Ostrogoth (ruler of Italy from 493 to 526 who was brought up as a hostage at the court of Constantinople), were clearly enamored of Roman culture and wanted to share in its benefits rather than destroy it completely. According to the *Variae* (i.e., official correspondence) of Theodoric's chief administrator, Cassiodorus, his Gothic master "delighted" in the law of the Romans, which he saw as a moderating influence on the "barbarian" turmoil and cruelty of his own people, and assured the eastern emperor, Anastasius, that his Italian kingdom was "an imitation of yours, modeled on your good purpose, a copy of the only empire". Yet there still could be an unbridgeable divide of suspicion and distrust between the Romans and the Goths, such as when Theodoric had his *magister officiorum* (master of the offices), Boethius, who came from an old Roman family and was a Catholic rather than an Arian Christian, executed in 524 on a charge of treason. (Boethius' one consolation was that he was to go on to become arguably more famous than his persecutor, as a result of the celebrated work he wrote in prison while awaiting his death, the *Consolation of Philosophy*.) For all his imitation of Roman ways, Theodoric's "Gothicness" was given away by his depiction on coins with a very un-Roman moustache.[23]

Roman hostility to and contempt for their "barbarian" neighbors was, in turn, underscored by the way in which even German allies, or *foederati*, were treated by the empire.[24] The Roman Christian apologist, Orosius, congratulated the Emperor Theodosius for winning a double victory at the Frigid River in 393, not only against his rival emperor in the West, Eugenius, but also over his own Gothic soldiers, who largely perished in the battle. This indeed seems to support Ward-Perkins' claim that, to the Romans, "the best barbarian was a dead barbarian".[25] Roman abuse of German refugees settled across the Danube River led to an uprising and humiliating defeat at Adrianople in 378, where the Emperor Valens met his death, while the murder of the half-Vandal Roman general Stilicho in 408, accompanied by a pogrom against the wives and children of German-born Roman soldiers in northern Italy, helped swell the army of the Visigothic chieftain, Alaric, that was to go on to sack Rome in 410. Scenes of Germans' brutal execution and enslavement upon defeat in battle were prominently displayed on the Column of Marcus Aurelius in the Piazza Colonna of Rome that was erected towards the end of the second century A.D.[26]

Last but not least, some of the causal explanations for Rome's transformation, as opposed to sudden fall, are now shown to be without secure foundation. For example, textbooks often recite that Rome's economy and trade, and hence its tax base needed to finance its large army, began shrinking as early as the third century, but the latest archaeological evidence on this is quite mixed and by no means conclusive.[27] A definitive economic decline throughout the Mediterranean world only seems to have set in after the first outbreak of plague in 541.[28] Assertions about declining population throughout the empire at this time are also in reality sheer guesses at best. Rome did have a census (the most useful records of which survive from the province of Egypt), but there are numerous limitations in utilizing this and other evidence.[29] There were periodic epidemics and pandemics of disease, or mortality crises, which may have caused "severe disruptions of the rhythms of life" and therefore contributed to the decline of the late empire.[30] But their demographic impact, owing to a dearth of statistically-valid archival data, is extremely hard to pin down,[31] and hence their role in the ultimate fate of the empire is still being debated (see below).

Instead, scholars like Ward-Perkins argue that the Roman Empire was quite viable as late as the early fifth century and that its fall, which could have been averted for some time, was then relatively rapid and unpredictable. Rather than being preordained by a long, slow decline, a series of fortuitous circumstances (for the end of Rome) just happened to coincide at this particular moment. These included the more frequent coalescing of various Germanic tribes, normally divided against each other (a circumstance that Rome was able to consistently rely upon until now), into larger aggregates or confederacies and, at the same time, a disastrous series of civil wars and social unrest in the empire (at the hands of the mysterious *Bacaudae*, or peasant brigands and "fighters") that divided Roman leadership in the West and severely weakened its ability to resist and counter foreign incursions. In self-destructive fashion, the imperial government showed a disturbing propensity to sacrifice and surrender provinces like Aquitaine, northern Gaul, and areas of present-day Switzerland in order to accommodate "allies" such as the Visigoths, Burgundians, and Alans, who were able to eventually leverage these land settlements by treaty into independent kingdoms. This kind of political maneuvering, for example, led to the loss of perhaps Rome's richest tax base, North Africa, to the Vandals in 429–30. Even leadership of the regular Roman army itself was now handed over to Germanic warlords, who since 457 began appointing emperors at will, until one of them, Odoacer, concluded that he was powerful enough to simply dispense with the emperor altogether and rule in his own right.

Such arguments on behalf of a true decline and fall of the Roman Empire seem to have persuaded even the *doyen* of Late Antiquity, Peter Brown, to at least partially concede the point. Brown began his most recent book by acknowledging that, after 430, the Roman Empire did indeed enter a period of profound crisis, one in which "we are now dealing with an impoverished society in the aftermath of violent dislocation," so that, by 600 at the latest, "we have come to stand on the threshold of another world, one very different from the ancient world with which we began our story". Brown still emphasized the local nature of this process, such that some regions fared "a lot better than others," and he eschewed any specific dates for Rome's fall, such as 476; in addition, he argued for at least some continuity, particularly in terms of the communal wealth of the Roman state, which was now transferred to the Christian Church. But Brown did concede that this had been his "most difficult book to write," in terms of maintaining his thesis that the continuity of the Church also meant the continuity of Late Roman culture and society. Living in the midst of a "dam burst" of scholarship on the period has persuaded Brown that, "a dramatic turn in the study of the concrete circumstances of the Roman world has come to alter our image of late Roman society as a whole and, consequently, of the role of Christianity in this society".[32]

If Rome did truly decline and fall, then what were the consequences of that earth-shaking event? There is a case to be made that, at least in much of the western half of the Roman Empire, the material well-being and overall economic status of the population suffered a catastrophic blow with the end of Rome, falling to prehistoric levels not seen since Europe's Iron Age, or to before the start of the Roman Republic in c. 509 B.C. Other historians would point out, of course, that the eastern half of the empire fared much better (which is, not coincidentally, where most scholars of Late Antiquity prefer to focus their studies), but even here there was probably a steep drop from higher levels of sophistication than known in the West.[33] Even those historians who opt for a "continuist" rather than "catastrophist" interpretation of the transformation of the Roman world must admit that by the end of the fifth century, there was a loss of cultural, administrative, and economic unity and sophistication throughout the former domains of the empire in favor of greater regional diversity and simplification, especially in terms of a classical Latin education, fiscal system of tax collection, and commercial exchange.[34]

This does not mean, of course, that regional differences did not also exist even at the height of the Roman Empire, or that everyone was enamored of the *Pax Romana*, or Roman Peace. The inexorable march of Rome was particularly destructive of Celtic culture stretching from the British Isles to Germany.[35] On the eastern borders of the empire, the Jews in Palestine also perennially rebelled against the Romans, with major revolts occurring in 66–70 and 132–35 A.D. And, as Seneca (4 B.C.–65 A.D.) so eloquently pointed out, throughout the history of the empire, even at its height, enslavement of conquered peoples and other unfortunates gave the lie to much of Rome's claims of establishing a universal brotherhood, or "commonwealth", of humanity. Perhaps the end of the empire did liberate some of these conquered cultures and allowed them to be recaptured by modern historians of Late Antiquity. But the rising dominance of Christianity at this time could be an equally, if not more, oppressive influence than pagan Rome's. Ward-Perkins has made the case that the Roman Empire, at least in its late incarnation, was uniquely tolerant in the history of civilization and was quite different from modern empires bent on domination and exploitation. Among all the reasons for the fall of Rome, a putative desire by its subjects for freedom and liberty is not high on the list.[36] A lament for the Roman Empire can be both a siren call for greater international cooperation in this day and age and a warning of just how fragile and easily lost is the interconnected peace and prosperity that the Romans had worked so hard to achieve.

The ecological decline and fall of Rome—Part I

Among the most enthusiastic supporters of the revived thesis of a decline and fall of the Roman Empire are environmental historians.[37] Partly, this is because much of the "proxy data" that historians rely upon to inform them of what was going on in the environment of the past—such as tree ring measurements (dendrochronology), ice core readings, analysis of speleothems or mineral deposits in caves, etc.—indicate that the climate of the empire was undergoing abrupt transitions at this time. A "Roman Climate Optimum," extending from about 200 B.C. to 150 A.D., when the weather in the empire was generally "warm, wet, and stable," gave way to the "Roman Transitional Period," from 150 to c.450, when the climate became cooler and drier as well as far less stable and predictable, and which finally culminated in the "Late Antique Little Ice Age," from 450 to about 700, when temperatures entered a severe cooling trend that started with a "dust veil" event in 536 (the "year without a summer"), caused by volcanic eruptions releasing aerosol particulates into the atmosphere that blocked the warming energy of the sun.[38]

But in addition to climate, the late empire also faced repeated bouts with disease, which for the first time reached the level of global pandemics owing to the interconnected reach of Rome's far-flung trading networks. First came the "Antonine Plague," probably smallpox, from 165 to as late as 191 A.D.; then, the mysterious "Plague of Cyprian," perhaps viral hemorrhagic fever, from c.249 to 262; finally, there arrived the greatest killer of them all, the First Pandemic of plague, from 541 to 750.[39] While disease certainly had a causal connection with climate, it is also believed that human impacts upon the environment, particularly in terms of urbanization, created lethal "ecologies within which deadly microbes live". It is also argued that disease, rather than climate change, was the more forceful factor "deciding the fate of Rome".[40] All this sets up a humbling dramatic tale for the would-be conquerors of the world, in which the fall of the Roman Empire represents, in Kyle Harper's words, "the triumph of nature over human ambitions".[41]

Historians of Rome often talk of a "first fall" of the empire, or the "crisis of the third century," when the empire nearly collapsed under the weight of foreign invasion, disease, drought, civil war, political instability, and economic depression. Of all these, climate change and disease were arguably the precipitating or forcing factors, in that they created at least temporary manpower and food shortages that had a "cascading" or domino effect on other aspects of Roman life, whether economic, social, political, military, etc.[42] This was the age of the "barracks emperors," when Roman emperors were made and unmade by the army at an alarming rate, with no less than 26 emperors proclaimed in 33 years, between 235 and 268, averaging a new candidate every one and a half years or less. Obviously, this created enormous political unrest, which was but one of many interconnected problems during the crisis.

The prelude to that crisis was the Antonine Plague of the previous century, whose advent coincided almost precisely with the end of the Roman Climate Optimum.[43] Originating in Africa from one of the poxviruses endemic to rodents, the smallpox virus, or *Variola major*, first struck Rome in 166, and, even though he had fled the capital, the famous Roman physician, Galen of Pergamum (129–c.210), described symptoms that seem to match modern diagnoses of the disease, including fever, a "black pustular rash," and ulcerous lesions in the throat.[44] The pandemic overrode the usual chronic disease background to Roman life, when diseases struck seasonally, typically peaking in the late summer-early autumn (owing largely to the local presence of malaria), but it amplified existing age patterns of normal mortality, carrying away especially the very young and the very old.[45] Communicated directly from person-to-person, smallpox spread to the four corners of the empire, from Britain and Spain in the west to Syria and Egypt in the east, perhaps aided by troop movements during the Marcomannic Wars (166–80), as well as by trade.[46] Credible estimates as to the pandemic's overall mortality range from 10–20 percent: enough to make a demographic impact, to be sure, but perhaps not enough to set off an irreversible population decline.[47]

Historians have debated the Antonine Plague's long-term impacts.[48] If there is a consensus, it seems to be that, while smallpox was a "shock to the system" of virgin-soil populations, the empire did recover, but to a state of health that was no longer endowed with the same "unchallengeable hegemony". Challenges of recruitment to the army, stabilization of the currency, price inflation, impacts upon agriculture and building programs, provincialization of power structures, and religious explanations for the mortality were all to presage even graver tests yet to come. While the empire survived, it perhaps used up its reserves of resilience that set the stage for the third-century crisis, when the empire had far less margin for error in the face of stresses from both climate and disease.[49]

After the Severan recovery from 193–235 (i.e., the rule of Emperor Septimius Severus and his descendants), there came the mid-century crisis. The real years of anarchy began after the Plague of Cyprian, the "forgotten pandemic" that first struck Egypt in 249 and Rome in 251 and then raged at various points in the Mediterranean for a total of 15 years. This was a disease characterized by rapid onset of diarrhea, fever, vomiting, bleeding from the eyes, gangrene in the limbs, weakness, and deafness and blindness. Originating, like the Antonine Plague, in Africa, the Plague of Cyprian (named after the Carthaginian bishop who spearheaded the Christian response to the disease) was fast-spreading, apparently highly contagious from person-to-person, and had a high case fatality rate resulting in large mortalities numbering in the thousands wherever it struck. It also was indiscriminate of social class, struck in both large cities and small villages, and, like the Antonine Plague, disregarded the typical seasons of chronic illnesses, running rampant in the winter months when perhaps people were clustered together in their households.[50] At the same time, the Roman province of Egypt, the "bread basket" of the empire, suffered a severe drought during the unstable climate pattern known as the Roman Transitional Period. In the 240s, the yearly flooding of the Nile failed in successive years, resulting in poor harvests and therefore enormous increases in the price of grain.[51] Altogether, this comprised what Harper estimated to have been "the severest environmental crisis detectible at any point in the seven centuries of Roman Egypt".[52]

These shocks were now delivered to an empire that was far less resilient than before, under the Antonine Plague, and which now stressed it "beyond a sustainable threshold, triggering cascading change and systemic re-organization".[53] This was a multi-faceted crisis, comprising a monetary collapse owing to severe debasement of the silver currency, resulting in an inflation spiral; an overturning of the social/political order, with the army no longer controlled by the Senate, but now in the hands of a professional military elite almost all hailing from a frontier region along the Lower Danube River, in present-day Croatia and Serbia; a collapse in the frontier defenses of the empire on two fronts, with Germanic tribes pouring over the Rhine-Danube border into Gaul and Italy in the West, and Persians overwhelming the provinces of Armenia and Syria in the East; and finally, the advance of Christianity, at the expense of civic polytheism, perhaps owing to the Christians' more effective spiritual response to the existential challenges posed by the deadly Cyprian plague.[54] When the empire was finally reconstituted, under the Emperor Diocletian (r. 284–305), this was under radically different terms, with the empire now effectively split between an eastern and western theater, each under its own Augustus and a designated successor, or Caesar, with the four co-rulers comprising what was called the "Tetrarchy". Subsequently, the Emperor Constantine (r. 306–37) took the equally radical step of adopting the Christian religion and relocating the capital to Constantinople, at the mouth of the Bosphorus, a narrow strait separating Europe from Asia.[55] Impelled by a severe drought lasting two decades, from 350–70, described by climate historians as the worst drought event in the last 2,000 years, the Huns of the Eurasian steppes sought greener pastures to the west during the late fourth and early fifth centuries.[56] Thus commenced, in a kind of domino effect, the Migration Period of the Germanic tribes, whose end result was the fall of the empire in the West.[57]

The ecological decline and fall of Rome—Part II

The fourth century was a time of recovery and restoration for the empire, after being set on this path by the Emperors Diocletian and Constantine. But the climate also cooperated in this effort, being generally warmer and more stable than in the previous century, although with some exceptions and differences between the western and eastern provinces.[58] In the fifth century, of course, the western provinces succumbed to the Germanic and Hunnish invasions, while the eastern half of the empire, based at Constantinople (formerly Byzantium), weathered the storm far more gracefully than Rome.[59] Its army, economy, and political leadership emerged in a far more robust state than those of her western counterpart.

Consequently, when an emperor came along whose ambitions were as large as the empire at its height, the machinery was in place to act on his commands. Justinian came to the throne in 527, and it seems that no one told him that the Roman Empire was dead. Even though the eastern empire was a complex mix of Latin, Greek, and Asiatic influences, throughout the Middle Ages it was known in Europe as "Romania" and among the Arabs as Rūm, or "Rome," and its inhabitants called themselves Romaioi, or "Romans". Clearly, the Byzantines saw themselves as the true heirs of a far from defunct Roman Empire and the ones most qualified to carry on its legacy. So it is no surprise that Justinian aimed at nothing less than the complete restoration of the empire, with Constantinople as its center. After an inconsequential war with Persia, Byzantium's most dangerous and powerful rival, Justinian turned his attention to the west, where he had his formidably talented general, Belisarius, invade the Vandal kingdom in North Africa. No sooner were the Vandals defeated in 534 than Justinian ordered a new invasion, this time of the Ostrogothic kingdom of Italy (technically a subject state of the empire). Belisarius took Sicily in 535 and then Rome the next year. But since the Goths put up more of a fight than the Vandals, it took another twenty years, until 554, before all of Italy was finally pacified. In that same year, Byzantine armies occupied southern Spain. Except for the northern provinces, Justinian had achieved his dream of recovering the furthest limits of the empire in the West.

But it was not to last. By the seventh and eighth centuries, Byzantium was increasingly isolated by the rising power of Islam and by a split with her fellow Christians in the West—chiefly represented by the pope in Rome—over Emperor Leo III's iconoclastic policies, which ordered the destruction of religious images, or icons. But even in the midst of Justinian's reign (527–65), it is clear that all was not as well as it seemed. One man, in particular, Procopius of Caesarea (c. 500–54), who could be considered the official historian of Justinian's court, lamented the devastation that his emperor wrought, both at home and abroad, by the seemingly endless wars. In his *Secret History*—one that was never meant for the eyes of the emperor or his censors—Procopius accused Justinian of turning all of Libya and Italy into a "desert," and it is true that Rome was simply abandoned at this time, and the Senate, the heart and symbol of the old Republic, ceased to meet. Ironically, in trying to revive the glory of the former empire, Justinian, by this account, actually hastened its tragic demise. So much contempt did Procopius have for the man he held responsible for this state of affairs that he called him a "wicked demon" in human guise, a fiend and a monster who killed "a trillion people," when you reckoned all the "Roman soldiers" dead, along with their even more numerous victims, which included men, women, and children.[60] Procopius was being quite literal when he identified Justinian as a demon. He cited as evidence the testimony of the emperor's own mother, who claimed that she was impregnated by an incubus, or demon in male form. Moreover, several attendants of the emperor testified that his head would suddenly disappear from his body or else change into a "shapeless lump" and that he was invariably restless at night and never ate regular meals.

Some might object that all this is too harsh an assessment of the man. It leaves out arguably Justinian's greatest achievement—the *Corpus Juris Civilis* (Body of Civil Law), a collection of Roman legal precedents, both old and new, that were preserved and handed down to posterity—which perhaps did the most to ensure some degree of continuity between the Roman world and the coming Middle Ages. However much historians like to trace the origins of nation states as far back as the Germanic "successor kingdoms" of the late fifth and early sixth centuries— the Franks under Clovis (r. 481–511) come to mind, as do the Ostrogoths under Theodoric (r. 475–526)—one has to remember that Justinian proved these early medieval kingdoms to be quite fragile. Moreover, much of their population, such as the Gallo-Romans in Clovis' Frankish realm, did not see themselves as members of any proto-national tribe at all, but rather, as part of a cosmopolitan world empire, and to this idea they still gave their allegiance. Most scholars and historians would agree that, at the very least, Justinian exhausted the resources of his empire— resources it would desperately need later against other enemies—and that he did lay waste to much of what he conquered, which made it close to impossible to maintain his conquests by taxing them.[61]

Leaving aside the internal causes of Byzantium's decline, if not fall (Constantinople remained in Greek hands until the Fourth Crusade of 1204 and then was permanently lost to the Ottoman Turks in 1453), debate now mostly centers around external influences upon that decline. One very important factor was the changing climate. Around 450, the Transitional Period gave way to what has been called the Late Antique Little Ice Age, which, as the name implies, inaugurated a dramatically cooling trend. Just before the arrival of the First Pandemic of plague in 541, two volcanic eruption events occurred in 536 and 539–40, releasing sulfate particles that acted as a "dust veil" blocking the warmth of the sun. Temperatures, based on proxy data, plunged by over 5°F as a result of these events, making the decade from the mid-530s to the mid-540s one of the coldest in 2000 years.[62]

Considering the timing of this climate anomaly, one is naturally tempted to connect it in some way to the other great ecological crisis, the arrival of plague. But how? If this ice age was accompanied by extraordinarily wetter weather, as seems to be the case in much of the Caucasus, or region between the Black and Caspian Seas,[63] which served as a terminus of Silk Road routes across Central Asia and was itself (and remains to this day) an enzootic center of plague, then this could have facilitated plague's eruption out of its endemic focus. How it did that is called the "trophic cascade" model of disease precipitation, whereby increased rains and moisture stimulated plant growth, which in turn stimulated explosions in populations of rodents and fleas, the hosts and vectors of bubonic plague.[64] By the same token, flooding or severe cold could have triggered wild rodents to seek shelter near human habitations and their commensal rodents, which facilitated the communication and spread of plague, engineering its transition from epizootic (i.e., outbreak among rodents) to panzootic (outbreak among both rodents and humans).[65] A directly parallel event that may have triggered the late medieval Black Death was the Little Ice Age (LIA), which likewise inaugurated a period of colder and wetter weather beginning in the 1340s.[66]

The first pandemic of plague

Plague is a disease caused by *Yersinia pestis*, characterized as "one of the most deadly bacteria" known to man.[67] In humans, plague can appear in three forms—bubonic, pneumonic, and septicemic—depending on how the bacteria invade and spread in the body. Bubonic plague has a case fatality rate of around 80 percent, while pneumonic and septicemic plague cause 100 percent mortality; these are among the highest fatality rates of any disease known to have afflicted humans.[68]

In 541 A.D., plague struck the Egyptian port city of Pelusium on the eastern Nile Delta (near the present-day Suez Canal), and then, by late 541 or early 542, it had come to the Byzantium capital of Constantinople on the Bosphorus.[69] This was the start of the First Pandemic of plague, or the first world-wide occurrence of the disease, which was to recur in at least 17 further outbreaks during the next two centuries, until c. 750, whereupon it then simply disappeared from the scene until the arrival of the Black Death, or Second Pandemic, in the middle of the fourteenth century.[70] (A Third Pandemic of plague emerged in the nineteenth century in China and India and remains active to this day.) Descriptions by contemporary observers, such as Procopius and the Syriac-speaking deacon, John of Ephesus, provide a clear diagnosis of bubonic plague—the most common form of the disease, which was spread by rats and their fleas and whose signature symptom were the *boubones*, or swellings, principally on the groin, armpit, and neck.[71] Nonetheless, Procopius also described symptoms, such as "black pustules" and blood-spitting, that are strongly suggestive of septicemic and pneumonic plague, respectively.[72] A couple of scholars have championed a greater role for pneumonic plague—spread person-to-person via airborne droplets—on the grounds that this would account for the disease's rapid early spread in Constantinople and that the population density of the city would facilitate its spread.[73] Yet the consensus of most scholarship on the First Pandemic seems to argue against it.[74]

Plague produced astounding mortalities in the capital, according to the chroniclers. Procopius reported 10,000 dying a day at the epidemic's peak, while John of Ephesus reported 16,000. According to John, men posted at the harbors, crossroads, and gates counted a total of 230,000 dead, after which they stopped counting, although he estimated that over 300,000 died by the time the epidemic had run its course. In addition, John described mass grave pits, where up to 70,000 were buried at a time, with the gravediggers trampling down the bodies "like spoiled grapes" in a winepress, as some of the bodies sank into the 5–10-day old, pus-filled victims underneath. The living took to going out with name tags, in case they should drop dead and be left in the streets or consigned, nameless, to a mass grave.[75] While John's figures might yield a death rate of 60 percent (assuming a total pre-plague population in Constantinople of half a million), most modern historians view his testimony as highly anecdotal and impressionistic, and therefore unreliable.[76] We simply lack for this time period the hard data from archival material, such as is plentifully available for the Black Death, that can give us a firm handle on actual mortality figures, which is essential for assessing the true impact of the plague.[77]

There is no longer any question that the Justinianic plague was caused by *Yersinia pestis*, thanks to recent advances in paleomicrobiology, or the science of isolating and identifying ancient microbes in the excavated remains of disease victims of the past. In the case of the First Pandemic, ancient *Yersinia pestis* DNA has been successfully isolated and identified from samples at four sites: Aschheim and Altenerding in Bavaria, dating to the sixth century; Vienne in France, dating to the seventh to ninth centuries; and Sens in France, dating to the fifth to sixth centuries.[78] All these samples were taken from the dental pulp encapsulated by the teeth of excavated plague victims, which would test positive for the bacterium provided that it entered the bloodstream, and therefore the blood supplying the teeth. In the words of one research team, "These findings confirm that *Yersinia pestis* was the causative agent of the Justinianic Plague and should end the controversy over the etiologic agent of the first plague pandemic".[79] What they also prove is that the strain or strains of *Yersinia pestis* responsible for the First Pandemic of plague were genetically distinct from those that caused the second and third pandemics. In fact, the First Pandemic strains became extinct—judging from their complete absence in modern reservoir samples—which implies that completely new strains emerged in rodent reservoirs in order to give rise to the late medieval Black Death.[80]

Were the strains that caused the Justinianic Plague less virulent than those that caused the later Black Death? *Yersinia pestis* exhibits remarkable genetic stability over time, but mutations do occur, usually by means of neutral processes such as genetic drift, particularly when the disease breaks out of its enzootic and endemic foci and infects large populations of rodents and humans (i.e., epizootics and epidemics).[81] Plague probably contained all the genetic elements necessary for its extraordinary virulence and spread as a zoonotic disease by the beginning of the first millennium B.C., yet analysis of a reconstructed genome from a victim at Altenerding reveals that genetic mutations did occur in genes relating to virulence shortly before the First Pandemic, and even a single mutation can result in tweaks that greatly enhance plague's "deadly potential".[82] Since an even bigger genetic "big bang" occurred shortly before the Black Death (Chapter 8), and since plague usually selects for ever higher virulence in order to secure the rodent septicemia that can infect its flea vectors,[83] it is likely that plague was deadlier still during the Second Pandemic of the late Middle Ages. The Bavaria finds also show how paleomicrobiology can add to the historical record about plague, since no written sources recorded the disease in this region during the First Pandemic.[84]

Two more epidemiological questions remain open to debate with regard to the First Pandemic: Where did the First Pandemic begin, and why did it end? The historical evidence, including the testimony of contemporary chroniclers writing in Greek, such as Procopius and Evagrius Scholasticus, seems to favor an origin in Africa, specifically Egypt or Ethiopia, with whom the Byzantine Empire had much closer diplomatic and trading relations at this time than with China or India to the east.[85] Arabic sources from the ninth century onwards also point to an endemic center of plague in Ethiopia.[86] At the same time, it is argued that there is no historical evidence for the presence of plague in China, Central Asia, or India at the time of the outbreak in 541–42.[87]

Nonetheless, paleomicrobiological studies show that the strain or strains of *Yersinia pestis* that killed victims during the First Pandemic originated in Asia.[88] One strain that is hypothesized to have originated in Africa, the "Angola" strain, is old enough to have caused the Justinianic Plague, but so far, no *Yersinia pestis* aDNA isolated from plague victims matches it.[89] Of course, it is possible that *Yersinia pestis* migrated from Asia to Africa and formed an endemic center there long before the First Pandemic, but it's also equally possible that endemic centers in Asia directly gave rise to the plague outbreak in Constantinople and in Egypt and Africa simultaneously.[90] Until more information is forthcoming, such as from paleomicrobiology, we have no way of knowing for sure.[91]

As for why a pandemic arose at this time in the Mediterranean, scholars have pointed to three factors that came together at this moment in time to make the First Pandemic possible. First, a new, more lethal version of the pathogen was bred, probably in the Central Asian steppes that was the disease's original homeland, shortly before the pandemic's arrival in 541. Next, the empire itself had prepared the ground for plague's rapid dispersal, at least in the Mediterranean basin, by its increased traffic and trade as the result of Justinian's wars in both North Africa and Italy. Third, there was the climatic trigger of the Late Antique Little Ice Age, discussed in the previous section, which may have caused a "trophic cascade" incident leading to the rapid increase and eventual dispersal of rat and flea populations.[92] However, some believe that the concatenation of factors that produced plague are so complex that we can never truly know precisely why an outbreak occurred at any given time.[93]

Then there is the need to explain why plague suddenly disappeared in the mid-eighth century, only to reappear six centuries later.[94] There are basically two, not necessarily exclusive, solutions to the problem. One is exogenous in nature, or in other words, outside of human awareness or control. This would include that, somehow, rats and/or humans became permanently, that is, genetically, immune to this particular strain of plague. Such a conclusion would explain why this strain became extinct and is no longer found in modern populations.[95] The assumption here also is that plague became endemic to rodent populations in Europe and would have persisted indefinitely, causing occasional flare-ups in the human population (every 11.6 years, on average), had not a genetic mutation in the bacterium or in the host caused its extinction.[96] Other scholars also point to climate change as being a factor, when the Late Antique Little Ice Age gave way to a warmer and drier trend known as the Medieval Climate Anomaly, or Medieval Warm Period, which may not have been as favorable to the activity of flea vectors or rodent hosts.[97]

The endogenous explanation sees the disappearance of plague as originating within human culture and behavior. Here, however, the options are rather limited: Unlike during the Black Death, there were no quarantine measures or trade embargos enacted (that we know of) in order to contain the disease and halt its spread. Nor were there any significant changes made to the man-made environment, such as building construction, that would affect rat and flea infestations. No new rodent species were introduced that could have displaced the black rat. This leaves trade as the only possible candidate for how humans could have altered their disease trajectory during the First Pandemic. This explanation assumes that no endemic reservoirs of *Yersinia pestis* existed in Europe, but that trade, or some other means, had to periodically re-introduce the bacterium to the region, and that when this cycle of re-introduction stopped, plague disappeared.[98]

But what possibly could have halted trade, such as from Asia to Europe, in the mid-eighth century? Curiously, the date of 750 coincides with the rise of the Abbasid Caliphate, which overthrew the Ummayyad Dynasty, at the Battle of the Zab in present-day Iraq on January 25. Almost immediately thereafter, the new Abbasid caliph, As-Saffāh (r. 750–54), inflicted a crushing defeat on the Tang Dynasty of China at the Battle of Talas in July 751. This ended Chinese control of Central Asia, and thereby of the Silk Road that linked East to West (which the Tang had re-opened in 639) and introduced a much more contested and unstable period in which various powers, including the Arabs, vied for dominance. It was not until the rise of the Mongol Empire in the thirteenth century that a reliable trade route carrying goods, and germs, through the endemic centers of plague in Central Asia, could be re-opened once again.

What was the overall impact of the First Pandemic on the eastern Roman Empire? This almost entirely depends on what one accepts as a mortality percentage: Since hard data are lacking, this comes down to an educated guess. It is not enough to simply plug in the better documented numbers of the Black Death, on the assumption that the two occurrences of the disease were the same, and therefore would have had the same mortality effects.[99] Both pandemics cannot have been "the greatest disease event human civilization had ever experienced"![100] The bottom line is that there just isn't much hard data available to work with for the First Pandemic.

Consequently, with this much uncertainty over the true mortality of the First Pandemic, the debate over its impact has swung wildly back and forth over the years. An older generation of scholars, perhaps reacting to the neglect their subject had received, argued for an outsized influence of the plague. Assuming a cumulative mortality of 50–60 percent, equivalent to the impact of the later Black Death, these scholars argued that the Justinianic Plague caused a manpower shortage, or vacuum, that allowed for an Arab invasion on the eastern frontier and invasion by the Slavs and Lombards in the West. In short, the plague swept away the last vestiges of the Roman Empire (the second, or final, "fall"), to be replaced by the much smaller Byzantine Empire, and ushered in the early Middle Ages, marked by a gravitational shift from the Mediterranean to the north of Europe and the rise of fledging nation-states facing an emergent Islamic empire.[101]

Predictably, a reaction set in that swung the pendulum the other way, minimizing the plague's impact. This argued that the testimony of contemporary literary sources, such as by Procopius, John of Ephesus and Evagrius, was "hysterical" in tone and thus exaggerated the importance of the First Pandemic. If, instead, one turned to archaeological, or at least non-literary, evidence, such as funerary inscriptions or the record of coinage production (i.e., numismatics), then the impact of epidemic mortality, particularly in the countryside, appeared limited.[102] However, critics pointed out that much of this evidence was fragmentary, and thus unreliable, largely because the plague itself was so disruptive that it curtailed production.[103] Thus, silence of the sources could be made to advocate both for and against influence of the plague, and from an outsider's vantage point, it's hard to see any way to referee such circular arguments.

Recently, the pendulum has now swung back again to the thesis of an over-mighty influence for the plague (some might say "monocausal," but this is currently unfashionable) as the agent of transition from Late Antiquity to early Middle

Ages.[104] Once again, there is an assumption (apparently based on Procopius) that the population of the *entire* eastern empire, not just that of the capital, was halved, from around 30 million to 15 million, with periodically recurring, smaller mortality events keeping the population at this low level until at least 600.[105] This is pure speculation, at best. It could well be true that the First Pandemic did match the "astounding" mortality of the Black Death, at 50–60 percent. It is equally likely that it did not. Some make arguments for economic and religio/cultural transformations that paralleled those for the Black Death, but this still does not mean that the impacts were equally as great. Certain trends, such as collapse in grain prices, rise in wages, and recruitment shortfalls to the army, can easily be traced to a severe demographic crisis such as that imposed by the plague. But other, more existential changes, like the rise of a Marian cult, iconolatry, apocalypticism, and the "liturgification" of society, likely had a multitude of causes.[106] Nor it is easy to quantify all these changes, since hard data is, again, lacking. Nonetheless, this school would argue that "there is a relatively uncomplicated line from demographic collapse to the failure of the eastern empire".[107]

Then there is the argument to take a midway point between these two extremes, on the basis of an average mortality rate for the First Pandemic of, at most, 40 percent.[108] This is still quite a bit lower than the 50–60 percent mortality currently argued for the first outbreak of the Second Pandemic, in 1346–53 (Chapter 8).[109] In addition to possibly having a lower virulence, the Justinianic Plague may also have had a smaller geographical scope than the Black Death. The First Pandemic undoubtedly did penetrate the rural areas as well as the cities, as John of Ephesus' testimony makes clear.[110] But it probably did not invade everywhere all at once in the first great pandemic "wave" of 541–44, despite Procopius' claim that it "overlooked no island or cave or mountain peak".[111] Indeed, the notion that plague would invade Italy, Gaul, Spain, Britain, Egypt, Palestine, Syria, and Mesopotamia (i.e., all points east and west) all within one year, 543, as the literary sources claim, stretches credulity.[112] Moreover, as the sixth century progressed, more and more trading links were severed and communities became isolated and localized, further limiting the potential reach of plague.[113] Local sources for England and Spain indicate that plague did not arrive until the seventh century and then only in limited, sporadic outbreaks.[114] And while plague certainly made regular, repeated appearances in Syria and Mesopotamia, at least according to literary sources, its presence was far more spotty in Egypt and Palestine and throughout the West.[115] Plague at this time therefore may not have enjoyed as rapid and diffuse a spread as it did centuries later during the Black Death, when European commerce and trade was far more developed and advanced.[116] Rats were also probably more numerous and dispersed in the late Middle Ages than they had been in the empire, although archaeological evidence does place them at this time throughout Britain, Gaul, the Rhineland, Italy, and Upper Egypt, with a presence in Germany, eastern Europe, the Balkans, Anatolia, northern Syria, North Africa, and southern Spain.[117]

This third way would therefore conclude that plague did contribute *something* to the decline of the eastern Roman Empire, but also that it did not dominate the stage of history to the same degree as did the Black Death during the late Middle Ages. Obviously there was depopulation, in both city and countryside, and this affected tax revenues and recruitment for the army, which made it harder to defend borders and resist invaders.[118] Economically, plague ushered in a period of contraction, as evidenced by lack of new building inscriptions, debasing of coinage, and more expensive labor costs—owing to demands for higher wages and better lease terms.[119] At the very least, plague reduced the resources available to Justinian and his successors to maintain his conquests and perpetuate the power and glory of the empire.[120] But credit must also be given to other actors, such as the newly converted Arabs, who stood ready to take advantage of opportunities opened up by the plague.[121]

The rise of Islam

If plague delivered the body blow that dashed Justinian's dreams of reviving the old Roman Empire, then the rise of a new power in the east, in Arabia, that appropriated much of Byzantium's former territory, such as Syria and Egypt, delivered the *coup d'grace*. Islam was founded by a man named Muhammad, who was born in 570 A.D. in a town called Mecca near the western coast of the Arabian peninsula, where it borders the Red Sea. By the time of Muhammad's death in 632, Muslims (meaning, those who "submit" to the one god, Allah) were poised to commence their explosive expansion outside Arabia into Syria, Iraq, Egypt, Persia, and beyond, even though initial probing raids into Byzantine-ruled Syria during Muhammad's lifetime had been inauspicious. Yet the story of the "Islamic Conquests" in the century or more after the death of Muhammad has been roiled by debate over the very origins of Islam itself. In the latest reincarnation of this revisionism, Islam, instead of emerging fully-formed as its own distinct religion during Muhammad's lifetime, was instead a "believers' movement" (from *mu'min* or "believer" in Arabic, which occurs 1000 times in the *Qu'ran*, as opposed to only 60 occurrences of *Muslim*). Like Muslims, "believers" adhered to a strict mono-theism or a belief in the oneness of God, as well as to the idea of prophecy or that God revealed his word to a series of messengers, the last, and best (or "seal"), of them was Muhammad. But believers were not exclusionary of Jews or Christians, since they included anyone who accepted its rigorous monotheism and righteous code of conduct. In other words, Muhammad never set out to form his own, new religion distinct from other monotheistic confessions such as Judaism and Christianity, as the traditional Muslim school would have it, but rather was only founding "a monotheistic reform movement" that gradually became Islam by the end of the seventh century, during the reign of Caliph 'Abd al-Malik (685–705).[122]

In the context of Islam's extremely rapid and impressive expansion, from the borders of India in the Sind valley along the Indus River in the East to the Iberian peninsula in the West (see Map 1.2), the believers' movement explains this expansion as motivated, above, all by a religious imperative to usher in a righteous new world order, against what was perceived as the sinful rule and less rigorous monotheism of the Byzantine and Sassanid Persian empires. In this interpretation, the expansion was not so much a violent "conquest" that imposed Islam upon a resistant non-Muslim population as, rather, a more or less peaceful "occupation"—punctuated by the occasional pitched battle or raid—in which the largely heterodox, Christian inhabitants and, to a lesser extent, Jewish and Zoroastrian subjects as well, acquiesced in paying their customary taxes to new masters, who were much more accommodating in terms of religious policy than the Byzantine or Persian rulers.[123] For instance, many of the Christian subjects in Syria, Egypt, and Iraq were Monophysites or Nestorians, who believed either in one, divine nature to Christ or who stressed his more human side, both of which could easily have slotted in with the anti-Trinitarian, strictly monotheistic dogma of the Arabian believers but who were regularly persecuted by the Byzantine emperor and orthodox church based at Constantinople.

All this necessitates a critical re-examination, and often rejection, of the traditional Muslim sources in favor of more contemporary ones, such as archaeological evidence or Greek and Syriac literature. For example, up to about 685, the coins that survive from regions ruled by the Arabian "believers" closely followed Byzantine or Persian designs and were inscribed with only a "single" *shahada*, namely, "There is no god but [the one] God," with the second part mentioning Muhammad as God's "apostle" left out; this appeared only later when believers following *Qur'anic* law seemed to wish to draw a "line in the sand" between themselves, now identified as "Muslims," and Jews and Christians. There is also archaeological evidence of new Christian churches being built at the very same time that their cities were being "conquered" during the seventh century and of collective worship of *Qur'anic* and Christian believers taking place in some of these churches, such as the Cathisma Church in Palestine, where a *mihrab* or prayer niche facing south (towards Mecca) was installed in its final phase of construction. By the same token, there is the negative evidence of a complete lack of any destructive layer in the excavation of most towns and churches in Syria, with a few exceptions such as Caesarea, a port city along the coast of Palestine that was subjected to a siege, which suggests peaceful occupation rather than conquest. We also have the testimony of contemporary Christian observers such as the monk John bar Penkāyē and the Nestorian Patriarch Isho'yahb III of Mesopotamia and of Bishop Sebeos of Armenia. These authors noted that the Arab believers respected and even honored their faith and left them alone, provided they paid "tribute", and that fellow Christians participated in Arab raids and that a Jew served as the believers' first governor of Jerusalem.[124]

Such integration among the believers tends to contradict the usual evidence presented in the Muslim tradition, such as the "Pact of Umar," a staple of many textbooks that feature it as a "primary source" of the Islamic Conquests. Supposedly

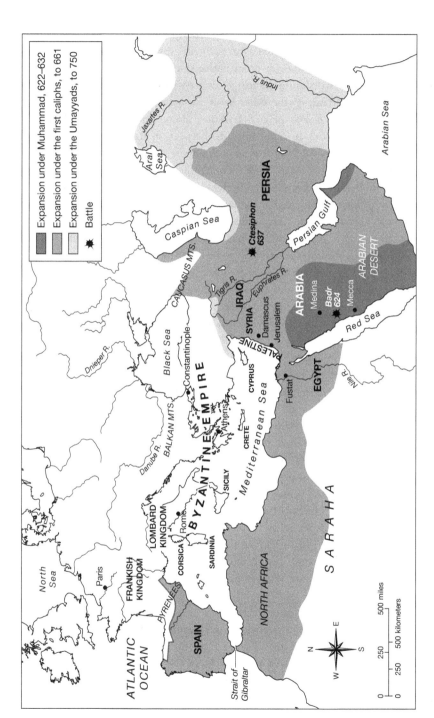

MAP 1.2 Map of the expansion of the believers' movement, later known as Islam, to 750

a treaty or peace accord drawn up by Caliph Umar ibn al-Khattab (r. 634–44) with the Christians or *dhimmis* of Jerusalem when he conquered the city in 636, the "Pact of Umar" is usually cited as an authentic document demonstrating precocious Islamic tolerance towards other faiths, since by its terms Christians were granted freedom of worship in exchange for payment of the *jizya* or "poll tax". For revisionist historians, on the other hand, the pact is instead a prime example of the way that the *hadith*, or oral tradition about the Prophet Muhammad, projected its agenda back in time. Instead, the pact, in this view, really dates to the eighth century, when Muslims were engaging in an act of "cultural apartheid," or drawing of clear boundaries between Muslims and Christians in order to prevent acculturation or assimilation and when Islam was just beginning to define itself vis-à-vis other religions. (For instance, the pact states that Christians can no longer build new churches, carry or display crosses, adopt Muslim dress or recite the *Qur'an*, all of which would not have been forbidden to "believers" during what skeptics argue was the pre-Islamic phase of Islam, or in other words, for most of the first/seventh century.) However, some skeptics have also read too much, perhaps, into the silence of the archaeological and literary record of the Islamic Conquests. It has been argued, for instance, that not only did the Arabs occupy Syria, Egypt, and other former provinces of the Byzantine Empire more peacefully than was previously thought, but that this occupation was actually official policy on the part of the Greeks, whereby they invested their Arab neighbors as *foederati* or allies to help defend the eastern frontier. Likewise, it is hypothesized that Christian heresies were deliberately fostered in local churches in order to wean these off their dependence on Constantinople.[125] Needless to say, most find this theory of an empire choosing to destroy itself extremely far-fetched.

Finally, it also can be argued that Islam was much less heavily devastated by the plague than was the Byzantine Empire at this stage of the conquests. The first major outbreak to be mentioned in the Islamic tradition is the Plague of 'Amwâs, named after the town in Palestine where Islamic troops first contracted the disease. This was an epidemic of bubonic plague, which struck Syria and Mesopotamia beginning in the spring of 638, and which did not burn itself out until the autumn of 639.[126] At this stage, Islam had basically completed the conquest of Palestine and was pushing northwards into Anatolia and Armenia (modern-day Turkey). Because Arabs only encountered the plague outside their homeland in 638–39, they perhaps had greater reserves of manpower than those available to the Byzantines. In a way, the Plague of 'Amwâs may actually have helped consolidate Arabic leadership: By taking out a whole generation of Muslim leaders, known as Companions of the Prophet, the plague paved the way for the rise of Mu'awiya (r. 661–80), the founder of the Umayyad dynasty of caliphs that ruled until 750. The Plague of 'Amwâs also gave rise to the Islamic tradition—"If you hear of [plague] in a land, do not approach it; but if it breaks out in a land and you are already there, then do not leave in flight from it".[127] This both ensured quarantine of Arabia against incursions of the plague, and assured those abroad caught up by the disease that they would be attended to in their illness, by Muslims fulfilling their social duty towards fellow believers as part of the *umma*, or community of the faithful.

Notes

1 Alexander Demandt, *Der Fall Roms: Die Auflösung des römischen Reiches im Urteil der Nachwelt* (Munich: C.H. Beck, 1984).

2 John M. Riddle, *A History of the Middle Ages, 300–1500* (Lanham, MD.: Rowman and Littlefield, 2008), pp. 19–20.

3 The origins of this rethinking can perhaps be traced back to Lynn White, Jr.'s seminal book, *The Transformation of the Roman World* (Berkeley, CA.: University of California Press, 1966).

4 Henri Pirenne, *Mohammed and Charlemagne* (Cleveland, OH. and New York: Meridian Books, 1957), p. 234.

5 Richard Hodges and David Whitehouse, *Mohammed, Charlemagne and the Origins of Europe: Archaeology and the Pirenne Thesis* (Ithaca, NY.: Cornell University Press, 1983), esp. pp. 169–76; Richard Hodges and David Whitehouse, "The Decline of the Western Empire," in *Debating the Middle Ages: Issues and Readings*, eds. Lester K. Little and Barbara H. Rosenwein (Oxford: Blackwell Publishers, 1998), pp. 58–71.

6 Michael McCormick, *Origins of the European Economy: Communications and Commerce, A.D. 300–900* (Cambridge: Cambridge University Press, 2001), pp. 115–19.

7 *Plague and the End of Antiquity: The Pandemic of 541–750*, ed. Lester K. Little (Cambridge: Cambridge University Press, 2008).

8 Brown's ideas about Late Antiquity were originally put forward in *The World of Late Antiquity: From Marcus Aurelius to Muhammad* (New York: Harcourt Brace Jovanovich, 1971) and *The Making of Late Antiquity* (Cambridge, MA.: Harvard University Press, 1978). Brown somewhat modified and expanded his views in later works, such as: *Society and the Holy in Late Antiquity* (Berkeley, CA.: University of California Press, 1982); *The Body and Society: Men, Women, and Sexual Renunciation in Early Christianity* (London: Faber and Faber, 1989); and "The World of Late Antiquity Revisited," *Symbolae Osloenses* 72 (1997): 5–30.

9 Peter Brown, *The Rise of Western Christendom: Triumph and Diversity, A.D. 200–1000*, 2nd edn. (Oxford: Blackwell, 2003).

10 In *The Rise of Western Christendom*, Brown also acknowledged his intellectual debts to Christopher Dawson, Henri Pirenne, and Ferdinand Braudel. See Brown, *The Rise of Western Christendom*, pp. 5–12.

11 The same title was earlier given to a prescient essay collection edited by Lynn White Jr., *The Transformation of the Roman World: Gibbon's Problem after Two Centuries* (Berkeley, CA.: University of California Press, 1966). Even though White claimed that his generation of scholars were less polemical than Gibbon, perhaps the orthodoxy has now gone too far the other way. While the Science Foundation project is advertized as a "scientific programme," its axe to grind is given away by the title of the first volume published in the series: *Kingdoms of the Empire: The Integration of Barbarians in Late Antiquity*, ed. Walter Pohl (Leiden, Netherlands: Brill, 1997).

12 Patrick J. Geary, *The Myth of Nations: The Medieval Origins of Europe* (Princeton, NJ.: Princeton University Press, 2002), p. 58. Readers will also want to consult Guy Halsall, *Barbarian Migrations and the Roman West, 376–568* (Cambridge: Cambridge University Press, 2008).

13 Chris Wickham, *The Inheritance of Rome: A History of Europe from 400 to 1000* (New York: Viking Penguin, 2009), p. 100.

14 This is argued by Walter Goffart in *Barbarians and Romans, A.D. 418–584: The Techniques of Accommodation* (Princeton, NJ.: Princeton University Press, 1980); he then "revisits"

the argument in *Barbarian Tides: The Migration Age and the Later Roman Empire* (Philadelphia, PA.: University of Pennsylvania Press, 2006). See also Goffart's essay collection, *Rome's Fall and After* (London: Bloomsbury, 1989) and debate about his thesis in *Kingdoms of the Empire*, ed. Walter Pohl (Leiden, Netherlands: Brill, 1997).

15 Chris Wickham, "The Other Transition: From the Ancient World to Feudalism," *Past and Present* 103 (1984):3–36.

16 See, for example, Matthew Innes, *The Sword, the Book, and the Plough: An Introduction to Early Medieval Western Europe, 300–900* (London: Routledge, 2006).

17 Chris Wickham, *Framing the Early Middle Ages* (Oxford: Oxford University Press, 2006), especially Chapters 6 and 9.

18 Bryan Ward-Perkins, *The Fall of Rome and the End of Civilization* (Oxford: Oxford University Press, 2005).

19 Willem M. Jongman, "Gibbon was Right: The Decline and Fall of the Roman Economy," in *Crises and the Roman Empire: Proceedings of the Seventh Workship of the International Network, Impact of Empire, (Nijmegen, June 20–24, 2006)*, eds. Olivier Hekster, Gerda de Kleijn, and Daniëlle Slootjes (Leiden, Netherlands: Brill, 2007), p. 199.

20 Ward-Perkins, *Fall of Rome*, pp. 87–168; Jongman, "Gibbon was Right," pp. 187–95; Kyle Harper, *The Fate of Rome: Climate, Disease, and the End of an Empire* (Princeton, NJ.: Princeton University Press, 2017), pp. 263–66, 299–303; R.P. Duncan-Jones, "Economic Change and the Transition to Late Antiquity," in *Approaching Late Antiquity: The Transformation from Early to Late Empire*, eds. Simon Swain and Mark Edwards (Oxford: Oxford University Press, 2004), pp. 27–42; Hodges and Whitehouse, "Decline of the Western Empire," pp. 58–71; David Brown, "Problems of Continuity," in *Anglo-Saxon Settlement and Landscape: Papers presented to a Symposium, Oxford 1973*, ed. Trevor Rowley (*British Archaeological Reports*, 6, 1974), pp. 16–19.

21 Ward-Perkins, *Fall of Rome*, pp. 13–31.

22 Peter Heather, *The Fall of the Roman Empire: A New History of Rome and the Barbarians* (Oxford: Oxford University Press, 2006).

23 Ward-Perkins, *Fall of Rome*, pp. 63–83.

24 There is considerable debate about the "barbarization" thesis of the Roman army and its consequent decline of discipline. Some scholars have pointed out that Rome had always incorporated "barbarian" elements into its army and that criticism of this practice was nothing new. One could also argue that the Roman Army was reconstituted and operated effectively throughout the fourth century, after the "crisis" of the third century. See: Arthur Ferrill, *The Fall of the Roman Empire: The Military Explanation* (London: Thames and Hudson, 1986); A.D. Lee, "The Army," in *The Cambridge Ancient History, vol. 13: The Late Empire, A.D. 337–425*, eds. Alan Cameron and P. Garnsey (Cambridge: Cambridge University Press, 1997), pp. 211–37; Hugh Elton, *Warfare in Roman Europe, A.D. 350–425* (Oxford: Clarendon Press, 1996); Michael Whitby, "Emperors and Armies, A.D. 235–395," in *Approaching Late Antiquity*, pp. 156–86.

25 Ward-Perkins, *Fall of Rome*, p. 24.

26 Ward-Perkins, *Fall of Rome*, pp. 25–27.

27 Duncan-Jones, "Economic Change," pp. 20–52.

28 McCormick, *Origins of the European Economy*, pp. 114–16; Harper, *Fate of Rome*, pp. 259–71.

29 Walter Scheidel, "Progress and Problems in Roman Demography," and Bruce W. Frier, "More is Worse: Some Observations on the Population of the Roman Empire," in *Debating Roman Demography*, ed. Walter Scheidel (Leiden, Netherlands: Brill, 2001), pp. 1–81, 139–59; Walter Scheidel, *Death on the Nile: Disease and the Demography of Roman Egypt* (Leiden, Netherlands: Brill, 2001); Roger S. Bagnall and Bruce W. Frier, *The Demography of Roman Egypt* (Cambridge: Cambridge University Press, 1994), pp. 1–11, 40–52.

30 Scheidel, "Progress and Problems," p. 31; Harper, *Fate of Rome*, pp. 72–115, 136–49, 206–45.

31 It is telling that, in order to give an impression of the demographic impact of ancient pandemics, such as the First Pandemic of plague of 541–750, historians often resort to the much better documented mortalities of the Black Death of the late Middle Ages. See, for example, Harper, *Fate of Rome*, pp. 232–34.

32 Peter Brown, *Through the Eye of the Needle: Wealth, the Fall of Rome, and the Making of Christianity in the West, 350–550 A.D.* (Princeton, NJ.: Princeton University Press, 2012), pp. xx–xxvi. Brown's last comment, in particular, seems a concession to Ward-Perkin's argument, based on archaeological evidence, for a demise of material comfort after the fall of Rome, as outlined above.

33 Ward-Perkins, *Fall of Rome*, pp. 117–20; Harper, *Fate of Rome*, pp. 263–64, 266.

34 Wickham, *Framing the Early Middle Ages*, pp. 825–31; Wickham, *Inheritance of Rome*, pp. 553–55; Chris Wickham, "The Fall of Rome Will Not Take Place," in *Debating the Middle Ages*, p. 57.

35 Tacitus perhaps said it best, when he put into the mouth of the Caledonian leader, Calgacus, as he was inciting a revolt against Rome in 83 A.D.: "To robbery, slaughter, plunder, they [the Romans] give the lying name of empire; they create a desert and call it peace". See Tacitus, *Agricola*, Chapter 30, in *Complete Works of Tacitus*, ed. Sara Bryant (New York: Random House, 1876, repr. 1942).

36 Ward-Perkins, *Fall of Rome*, pp. 169–83.

37 Kyle Harper, "The Environmental Fall of the Roman Empire," *Dædelus, the Journal of the American Academy of Arts and Sciences* 145 (2016):101–11.

38 Harper, *Fate of Rome*, pp. 14–15, 39–54, 129–36, 167–75, 249–59; Michael McCormick, et al., "Climate Change during and after the Roman Empire: Reconstructing the Past from Scientific and Historical Evidence," *Journal of Interdisciplinary History* 43 (2012):174–99; *The Years without Summer: Tracing A.D. 536 and Its Aftermath*, ed. J.D. Gunn (Oxford: Archaeopress, 2000).

39 Harper, *Fate of Rome*, pp. 72–115, 136–49, 206–45; Kyle Harper, "Pandemics and Passages to Late Antiquity: Rethinking the Plague of c.249–270 described by Cyprian," *Journal of Roman Archaeology* 28 (2015):223–60; Kyle Harper, "Another Eyewitness to the Plague described by Cyprian, with Notes on the 'Persecution of Decius'," *Journal of Roman Archaeology* 29 (2016):473–76; Sergio Sabbatini and Sirio Fiorino, "The Antonine Plague and the Decline of the Roman Empire," *Le Infezioni in Medicina* 17 (2009):261–75; Christer Bruun, "The Antonine Plague and the 'Third-Century Crisis'," in *Crises and the Roman Empire*, pp. 201–17; R.P. Duncan-Jones, "The Impact of the Antonine Plague," *Journal of Roman Archaeology* 9 (1996):108–36; *Plague and the End of Antiquity*.

40 Harper, *Fate of Rome*, pp. 15–16.

41 Harper, *Fate of Rome*, p. 4.

42 Harper, *Fate of Rome*, pp. 122, 136.

43 Harper, *Fate of Rome*, p. 72.

44 Harper, *Fate of Rome*, pp. 103–7; Duncan-Jones, "Impact of the Antonine Plague," p. 118.

45 Harper, *Fate of Rome*, pp. 72–91, 172–73; Kyle Harper, "A Time to Die: Preliminary Notes on Seasonal Mortality in Late Antique Rome," in *Children and Family in Late Antiquity: Life, Death and Interaction*, eds. Christian Laes, Katariina Mustakallio, and Ville Vuolanto (Leuven: Peeters, 2015), pp. 15–33; Walter Scheidel, "Measuring Sex, Age and Death in the Roman Empire: Explorations in Ancient Demography" (*Journal of Roman Archaeology*, Supplementary Series, 21, 1996), pp. 139–63; Walter Scheidel, "Germs for Rome," in *Rome the Cosmopolis*, eds. Catharine Edwards and Greg Woolf (Cambridge: Cambridge University Press, 2003), pp. 158–76; Robert Sallares, *Malaria and Rome: A History of Malaria in Ancient Italy* (Oxford: Oxford University Press, 2002). The same mortality patterns were found for victims of a smallpox epidemic in Martigues, France, in 1705. See Michel Signoli, Isabelle Séguy, Jean-Noël Biraben, and Oliver Dutour, "Paleodemography and Historical Demography in the Context of an Epidemic: Plague in Provence in the Eighteenth Century," *Population* 57 (2002):838–42.

46 Harper, *Fate of Rome*, p. 102; Duncan-Jones, "Impact of the Antonine Plague," pp. 134–36. The pandemic may have reached the frontier provinces of Dacia and Moesia along the Lower Danube. See Dragos Mitrofan, "The Antonine Plague in Dacia and Moesia Inferior," *Journal of Ancient History and Archaeology* 1 (2014):9–13.

47 Estimates of the mortality of the Antonine Plague have ranged widely, from as low as 1–2 percent to as high as 50 percent. See: Harper, *Fate of Rome*, p. 115; Brunn, "Antonine Plague and the 'Third-Century Crisis'," p. 203; J.N. Hays, *Epidemics and Pandemics: Their Impacts on Human History* (Santa Barbara, CA.: ABC-Clio, 2005), pp. 17–20; J.F. Gilliam, "The Plague under Marcus Aurelius," *American Journal of Philology*, 82 (1961):250; R.J. Littman and M.L. Littman, "Galen and the Antonine Plague," *American Journal of Philology* 94 (1973):254. A useful comparison is with the Great Famine of northern Europe from 1315–22, which caused an estimated mortality of 10–15 percent, but from which population seems to have recovered quickly to its former numbers in the decades prior to the Black Death. See William Chester Jordan, *The Great Famine: Northern Europe in the Early Fourteenth Century* (Princeton, NJ: Princeton University Press, 1996), pp. 184–85. Nonetheless, an alternative view does see the Antonine Plague as the beginning of a long-term population decline culminating in the Justinianic Plague, or First Pandemic of true plague, in 541. See Robert Sallares, "Ecology, Evolution, and Epidemiology of Plague," in *Plague and the End of Antiquity*, p. 288.

48 Brunn, "Antonine Plague and the 'Third-Century Crisis'," pp. 202–9. For example, arguments for an infrastructure collapse based on the silence of the record with regard to building inscriptions or public works projects, championed by Duncan-Jones and Scheidel (who even made comparisons with the Black Death of the late Middle Ages), have been disputed by Greenberg and Brunn. See: James Greenberg, "Plagued by Doubt: Reconsidering the Impact of a Mortality Crisis in the 2nd c. A.D.," *Journal of Roman Archaeology* 26 (2003): 413–25; Christer Brunn, "The Antonine Plague in Rome and Ostia," *Journal of Roman Archaeology* 16 (2003):426–34; Brunn, "Antonine Plague and the 'Third-Century Crisis'," pp. 209–14; Walter Scheidel, "A Model of Demographic and Economic Change in Roman Egypt after the Antonine Plague," *Journal of Roman Archaeology* 15 (2002):97–114; Duncan-Jones, "Impact of the Antonine Plague," pp. 120–34;

49 Harper, *Fate of Rome*, pp. 112–18; Kyle Harper, "People, Plagues, and Prices in the Roman World: The Evidence from Egypt," *Journal of Economic History* 76 (2016):815–16; Duncan-Jones, "Impact of the Antonine Plague," pp. 120–34.

50 Harper, *Fate of Rome*, pp. 136–45; Harper, "Pandemics and Passages to Late Antiquity," pp. 241–48.

51 Harper, *Fate of Rome*, pp. 129–36; Harper, "People, Plagues and Prices," pp. 816–17.

52 Harper, *Fate of Rome*, p. 134.

53 Harper, "Pandemics and Passages to Late Antiquity," p. 249.

54 Harper, "Pandemics and Passages to Late Antiquity," pp. 248–59; Harper, *Fate of Rome*, pp. 145–49; Duncan-Jones, "Economic Change," pp. 43–49.

55 Harper, *Fate of Rome*, pp. 163–67.

56 Harper, *Fate of Rome*, pp. 191–92; E. Cook, "Megadroughts, ENSO, and the Invasion of Late-Roman Europe by the Huns and Avars," in *The Ancient Mediterranean Environment between Science and History*, ed. William V. Harris (Leiden, Netherlands: Brill, 2013), pp. 89–102; McCormick, et al., "Climate Change," p. 190.

57 Harper, *Fate of Rome*, pp. 163, 188–95; Peter Heather, "The Huns and Barbarian Europe," in *The Cambridge Companion to the Age of Attila*, ed. M. Maas (Cambridge: Cambridge University Press, 2015), pp. 209–29; Peter Heather, "Goths and Huns, c. 320–425," in *Cambridge Ancient History, vol. 13*, pp. 487–515; Peter Heather, "The Huns and the End of the Roman Empire in Western Europe," *English Historical Review* 110 (1995):4–41.

58 Harper, *Fate of Rome*, pp. 167–75; McCormick, et al., "Climate Change," pp. 186–88.

59 Harper, *Fate of Rome*, pp. 196–98.
60 Procopius of Caesarea, *Secret History*, Chapter 18, available online at https://sourcebooks.fordham.edu, accessed December 25, 2017.
61 For assessments of Justinian's reign, see: James Joseph O'Donnell, *The Ruin of the Roman Empire* (New York: Harper Perennial, 2008); M. Maas, "Roman Questions, Byzantine Answers: Contours of the Age of Justinian," in *The Cambridge Companion to the Age of Justinian*, ed. M. Maas (Cambridge: Cambridge University Press, 2005), pp. 3–27; John Morehead, *Justinian* (London and New York: Longman, 1994).
62 Harper, *Fate of Rome*, p. 253; McCormick, et al., "Climate Change," p. 195.
63 Harper, *Fate of Rome*, p. 258.
64 Sharon K. Collinge, et al., "Testing the Generality of a Trophic-Cascade Model for Plague," *EcoHealth* 2 (2005):102–4, 109–10; Tamara Ben Ari, et al., "Interannual Variability of Human Plague Occurrence in the Western United States Explained by Tropical and North Pacific Ocean Climate Variability," *American Journal of Tropical Medicine and Hygiene* 83 (2010):627–30; Tamara Ben Ari, et al., "Plague and Climate: Scales Matter," *PLoS Pathogens* 7 (2011): online: e1002160; Kyrre Linné Kausrud, "Climatically Driven Synchrony of Gerbil Populations Allows Large-Scale Plague Outbreaks," *Proceedings of the Royal Society B* 274 (2007):1967–68; Hau V. Pham, et al., "Correlates of Environmental Factors and Human Plague: An Ecological Study of Vietnam," *International Journal of Epidemiology* 38 (2009):1639; Robert R. Parmenter, et al., "Incidence of Plague Associated with Increased Winter-Spring Precipitation in New Mexico," *American Journal of Tropical Medicine and Hygiene* 61 (1999):818–20; Russell E. Ensore, et al., "Modelling Relationships between Climate and the Frequency of Human Plague Cases in the Southwestern United States, 1960–1997," *American Journal of Tropical Medicine and Hygiene* 66 (2002):191–94; Lei Xu, et al., "Nonlinear Effect of Climate on Plague during the Third Pandemic in China," *Proceedings of the National Academy of Sciences* 108 (2011): 10217; T. Snäll, R.E. Benestad, and N.C. Stenseth, "Expected Future Plague Levels in a Wildlife Host under Different Scenarios of Climage Change," *Global Change Biology* 15 (2009):505–6; Kenneth L. Gage, et al., "Climate and Vectorborne Diseases," *American Journal of Preventive Medicine*, 35 (2008):444.
65 Bruce M.S. Campbell, *The Great Transition: Climate, Disease and Society in the Late-Medieval World* (Cambridge: Cambridge University Press, 2016), p. 236; Xu, et al., "Nonlinear Effect of Climate," p. 102–17.
66 Campbell, *Great Transition*, pp. 335–44; John Aberth, *An Environmental History of the Middle Ages: The Crucible of Nature* (London: Routledge, 2013), pp. 49–51.
67 Simon Rasmussen, et al., "Early Divergent Strains of *Yersinia pestis* in Eurasia 5,000 Years Ago," *Cell* 163 (2015):575.
68 Lawrence I. Conrad, *The Plague in the Early Medieval Near East* (Princeton, NJ., Princeton University Ph.D. thesis, 1981), p. 488; Ole J. Benedictow, *Plague in the Late Medieval Nordic Countries: Epidemiological Studies*, 2nd edn. (Oslo, Norway: Middelalderforlaget, 1993), pp. 146–49; Ole J. Benedictow, *The Black Death, 1346–1353: The Complete History* (Woodbridge, UK: Boydell Press, 2004), p. 9; Ole J. Benedictow, *What Disease was Plague? On the Controversy over the Microbiological Identity of Plague Epidemics of the Past* (Leiden, Netherlands: Brill, 2010), p. 9.
69 Mischa Meier, "The 'Justinianic Plague': The Economic Consequences of the Pandemic in the Eastern Roman Empire and its Cultural and Religious Effects," *Early Medieval Europe* 24 (2016):274; Harper, *Fate of Rome*, p. 226. Procopius reported plague at Constantinople in the spring of 542. See Procopius of Caesarea, *History of the Wars*, II:22.6, 9, trans. H.B. Dewing (London: W. Heinemann and Macmillan, 1914–40), pp. 454–55.
70 Dionysios Stathakopoulos, *Famine and Pestilence in the Late Roman and Early Byzantine Empire: A Systematic Survey of Subsistence Crises and Epidemics* (Burlington, VT.: Ashgate, 2004), pp. 113–24, 278–386; Dionysios Stathakopoulos, "Crime and Punishment: The

Plague in the Byzantine Empire, 541–749," in *Plague and the End of Antiquity*, pp. 99–105. As proven by paleomicrobiology, plague did occur prior to the First Pandemic, going back as far as the Bronze Age (third–first millennium B.C.), but only in isolated outbreaks. See: Rasmussen, et al., "Early Divergent Strains," p. 572; Sallares, "Ecology, Evolution, and Epidemiology of Plague," p. 251.

71 Procopius of Caesarea, *History of the Wars*, II:22.17, 29, 32–34; Pseudo-Dionysius of Tel-Mahre, *The Chronicle of Zuqnīn, Parts III and IV*, trans. A. Harrak (Toronto: Pontifical Institute of Mediaeval Studies, 1999), p. 104. Procopius even reported that local physicians dissected plague patients and cut open the *boubones*, revealing a "carbuncle" that would correspond to the shriveled lymph node where the body was trying to fight off the disease. See Timothy L. Bratton, "The Identity of the Plague of Justinian, Part I," *Transactions and Studies of the College of Physicians of Philadelphia*, ser. 5, 3 (1981):120.

72 Procopius of Caesarea, *History of the Wars*, II:22, 30–31.

73 Sallares, "Ecology, Evolution, and Epidemiology of Plague," pp. 240–45; T.H. Hollingsworth, *Historical Demography* (Ithaca, NY.: Cornell University Press, 1969), pp. 357, 367. In addition, Sallares argued that throat swellings, or "tonsillar plague," could likewise have been spread "by the respiratory route".

74 Bratton, "Identity of Plague of Justinian, Part I," pp. 113–14, 118–19, 122–24, and n. 1; Harper, *Fate of Rome*, p. 223. Bratton argued that pneumonic plague presented a narrow window for infectivity, emerging as a secondary symptom in only a small minority of bubonic plague patients, while most people even in the sixth century would have taken precautions against infection, and that chroniclers like Procopius devoted little space to, and seemed to evince little interest in, the pneumonic variety. In addition, see Timothy L. Bratton, "The Identity of the Plague of Justinian, Part II," *Transactions and Studies of the College of Physicians of Philadelphia*, ser. 5, 3 (1981):175–78, where he argued that the population density of Constantinople was much lower than previously thought.

75 Pseudo-Dionysius of Tel-Mahre, *Chronicle of Zuqnīn*, pp. 86–87, 93, 99–100, 105, 108–11; Procopius of Caesarea, *History of the Wars*, II:23.2.

76 Harper, *Fate of Rome*, p. 226; Meier, "'Justinianic Plague'," p. 277; Bratton, "Identity of Plague of Justinian, Part II," pp. 174–75; J.-N. Biraben and Jacques Le Goff, "The Plague in the Early Middle Ages," in *Biology of Man in History*, eds. Robert Forster and Orest Ranum and trans. Elborg Forster and Patricia M. Ranum (Baltimore, MD.: Johns Hopkins University Press, 1975), p. 62. Meier, despite arguing for an outsized influence for the First Pandemic, admitted that Ephesus' figures were "suspicious," "overstated," and probably not intended "to provide a precise quantitative record in the modern sense," but rather to convey the "monstrousness" of the plague's dimensions. Modern demographers have come up with more sober totals and percentages for the Justinianic plague mortality than those based on John of Ephesus. For example, Hollingsworth hypothesized that 244,000 died out of 508,000 in total, or a mortality rate of 48 percent, while Bratton supplied a much more conservative estimate of 57,660 dead out of 288,300, or a mortality rate of 20 percent. See: Hollingsworth, *Historical Demography*, p. 367; Bratton, "Identity of Plague of Justinian, Part II," pp. 178–79.

77 Harper, *Fate of Rome*, pp. 228, 232; Jo N. Hays, "Historians and Epidemics: Simple Questions, Complex Answers," in *Plague and the End of Antiquity*, p. 36.

78 To date, I have counted a total of seven paleomicrobiological studies, four of which focus on the sixth-century grave-site in Aschheim in Bavaria, that relate to the First Pandemic of plague. See: Christina Garrelt and Ingrid Wiechmann, "Detection of *Yersinia pestis* DNA in Early and Late Medieval Bavarian Burials," in *Deciphering Ancient Bones: The Research Potential of Bioarchaeological Collections* (*Documenta archaeobiologica*, 1, 2003), pp. 247–54; Michel Drancourt, et al., "Genotyping, Orientalis-like *Yersinia pestis*, and Plague Pandemics," *Emerging Infectious Diseases*, 10 (2004):1585–

92; Ingrid Wiechmann and Gisela Grupe, "Detection of *Yersinia pestis* DNA in Two Early Medieval Skeletal Finds from Aschheim (Upper Bavaria, sixth century A.D.)," *American Journal of Physical Anthropology* 126 (2005):48–55; Michel Drancourt, et al., "*Yersinia pestis* Orientalis in Remains of Ancient Plague Patients," *Emerging Infectious Diseases* 13 (2007):332–33; Michaela Harbeck, et al., "*Yersinia pestis* DNA from Skeletal Remains from the 6th Century A.D. Reveals Insights into Justinianic Plague," *PLoS Pathogens* 9 (2013):online, e1003349; David M. Wagner, et al., "*Yersinia pestis* and the Plague of Justinian, 541–543 A.D.: A genomic analysis," *The Lancet* 383 (2014):319–26; Michal Feldman, et al., "A High-Coverage *Yersinia pestis* Genome from a Sixth-Century Justinianic Plague Victim," *Molecular Biology and Evolution* 33 (2016):2911–23.

79 Harbeck, et al., "*Yersinia pestis* DNA," online, e1003349.

80 Wagner, et al., "*Yersinia pestis* and the Plague of Justinian," pp. 323–25; Stephanie Haensch, et al., "Distinct Clones of *Yersinia pestis* Caused the Black Death," *PLoS Pathogens* 6 (2010): online, e1001134; Kirsten I. Bos, et al., "A Draft Genome of *Yersinia pestis* from Victims of the Black Death," *Nature* 478 (2011): 508–9; Kirsten I. Bos, et al., "*Yersinia pestis*: New Evidence for an Old Infection," *PLoS One* 7 (2012):online, e49803; Verena J. Schuenemann, et al., "Targeted Enrichment of Ancient Pathogens Yielding the pPCP1 Plasmid of *Yersinia pestis* from Victims of the Black Death," *Proceedings of the National Academy of Sciences* 108 (2011):751. The strains that caused the medieval Black Death are thought to have emerged in a genetic "big bang" around 1268 (Chapter 8).

81 Yujun Cui, et al., "Historical Variations in Mutation Rate in an Epidemic Pathogen, *Yersinia pestis*," *Proceedings of the National Academy of Sciences* 110 (2013):580–81; Wagner, et al., "*Yersinia pestis* and the Plague of Justinian," p. 324.

82 Rasmussen, et al., "Early Divergent Strains," p. 577; Feldman, et al., "A High-Coverage *Yersinia pestis* Genome," p. 2919; Daniel L. Zimbler, Jay A. Schroeder, Justin L. Liddy, and Wyndham W. Lathem, "Early Emergence of *Yersinia pestis* as a Severe Respiratory Pathogen," *Nature Communications* 6 (2015): online, ncomms8487.

83 B. Joseph Hinnebusch, "The Evolution of Flea-Borne Transmission in *Yersinia pestis*," *Current Issues of Molecular Biology* 7 (2005):206; Rebecca J. Eisen and Kenneth L. Gage, "Adaptive Strategies of *Yersinia pestis* to Persist during Inter-Epizootic and Epizootic Periods," *Veterinary Research*, 40 (2009): online, vetres:2008039.

84 Harbeck, et al., "*Yersinia pestis* DNA," online, e1003349; Wagner, et al., "*Yersinia pestis* and the Plague of Justinian," p. 324; Feldman, et al., "High-Coverage *Yersinia pestis* Genome," p. 2919.

85 Peter Sarris, "Bubonic Plague in Byzantium: The Evidence of Non-Literary Sources," in *Plague and the End of Antiquity*, pp. 120–23.

86 Michael W. Dols, "Plague in Early Islamic History," *Journal of the American Oriental Society* 94 (1974):372–73.

87 Sarris, "Bubonic Plague in Byzantium," pp. 121–22; William Rosen, *Justinian's Flea: Plague, Empire, and the Birth of Europe* (New York: Viking, 2007), pp. 194–95.

88 Harbeck, et al., "*Yersinia pestis* DNA," online, e1003349; Wagner, et al., "*Yersinia pestis* and the Plague of Justinian," p. 323.

89 Cui, et al., "Historical Variations in Mutation Rate," pp. 581–82; Harbeck, et al., "*Yersinia pestis* DNA," online, e1003349. Indeed, Harbeck questioned whether the Angola strain is native to Africa at all, since it is not known where this genome was isolated in modern sampling of *Yersinia pestis* DNA.

90 Giovanna Morelli, et al., "Phylogenetic Diversity and Historical Patterns of Pandemic Spread of *Yersinia pestis*," *Nature Genetics* 42 (2010):1140–43; Mark Achtman, et al., "Microevolution and History of the Plague Bacillus, *Yersinia pestis*," *Proceedings of the National Academy of Sciences* 101 (2004):17841–42; Wagner, et al., "*Yersinia pestis* and the Plague of Justinian," p. 323.

91 Meier, "'Justinianic Plague'," p. 275.

92 Harper, *Fate of Rome*, pp. 218–20; Sarris, "Bubonic Plague in Byzantium," p. 123; Wagner, et al., "*Yersinia pestis* and the Plague of Justinian," p. 325; Michael McCormick, "Rats, Communications, and Plague: Toward an Ecological History," *Journal of Interdisciplinary History* 34 (2003):20–21.

93 Rosen, *Justinian's Flea*, pp. 290–91; Harper, *Fate of Rome*, p. 220.

94 Most contend that the epidemic of 743–50 was the last outbreak of the First Pandemic, although others point to an outbreak in Naples in 767, but the dating here is contested. See Stathakopoulos, "Crime and Punishment," pp. 104–5.

95 Wagner, et al., "*Yersinia pestis* and the Plague of Justinian," pp. 324–25.

96 M.J. Keeling and C.A. Gilligan, "Metapopulation Dynamics of Bubonic Plague," *Nature*, 407 (2000):903–6; M.J. Keeling and C.A. Gilligan, "Bubonic Plague: A Meta-population Model of a Zoonosis," *Proceedings of the Royal Society of London B*, 267 (2000):2219–30; Stathakopoulos, "Crime and Punishment," p. 105; Wagner, et al., "*Yersinia pestis* and the Plague of Justinian," p 324.

97 Harper, *Fate of Rome*, p. 244; McCormick, et al., "Climate Change," p. 200.

98 Boris V. Schmid, et al., "Climate-driven Introduction of the Black Death and Successive Plague Reintroductions into Europe," *Proceedings of the National Academy of Sciences*, 112 (2015):3020–25. For an alternative view that sees the First Pandemic as driven by recirculating enzootic centers within Europe, see; Harper, *Fate of Rome*, p. 236; Meier, "'Justinianic Plague',", p. 274. This makes it even more challenging, however, to explain how plague suddenly disappeared in 750.

99 Harper, *Fate of Rome*, pp. 232–34; Little, "Life and Afterlife," and Sallares, "Ecology, Evolution, and Epidemiology of Plague," in *Plague and the End of Antiquity*, pp. 18–21, 233–45.

100 As quoted from Harper, *Fate of Rome*, p. 201, with reference to the Justinianic Plague. For similar assertions made for the late medieval Black Death, see Chapter 8.

101 Josiah C. Russell, "That Earlier Plague," *Demography* 5 (1968):180–84; Biraben and Le Goff, "Plague in the Early Middle Ages," pp. 62–63; Allen, "'Justinianic' Plague," p. 20.

102 Mark Whittow, *The Making of Byzantium, 600–1025* (Berkeley, CA.: University of California Press, 1996), pp. 66–68; J. Durliat, "La peste du VIᵉ siècle: Pour un nouvel examen des sources byzantines," in *Hommes et Richesses dans l'Empire Byzantin*, eds. V. Kravari, C. Morrison, and J. Lefort, 2 vols. (Paris: Lethielleux, 1989–91), 1:107–19; Clive Foss, "Syria in Transition, A.D. 550–750," *Dumbarton Oaks Papers* 51 (1997):189–270; Hugh N. Kennedy, "Justinianic Plague in Syria and the Archaeological Evidence," and Sarris, "Bubonic Plague in Byzantium," in *Plague and the End of Antiquity*, pp. 87–88, 125.

103 Sarris, "Bubonic Plague in Byzantium," pp. 126–27.

104 Harper, *Fate of Rome*, pp. 220–45; Meier, "'Justinianic Plague',", pp. 267–92; Sarris, "Bubonic Plague in Byzantium," pp. 124–25.

105 Harper, *Fate of Rome*, pp. 232, 244–45.

106 Meier, "'Justinianic Plague',", pp. 182–92; Harper, *Fate of Rome*, pp. 234, 276–82.

107 Harper, *Fate of Rome*, pp. 235, 271–75. See also Meier, "'Justinianic Plague',", p. 270.

108 Wagner, et al., "*Yersinia pestis* and the Plague of Justinian," p. 324.

109 Benedictow, *Black Death*, p. 383; John Aberth, *From the Brink of the Apocalypse: Confronting Famine, War, Plague, and Death in the Later Middle Ages*, 2nd edn. (London: Routledge, 2010), p. 93; P.J.P. Goldberg, *Medieval England: A Social History, 1250–1550* (London: Arnold, 2004), p. 164.

110 It is a defining feature of bubonic plague that it has an inverse relationship with population density, owing to the fact that it is spread primarily by rats, not humans. See: Wagner, et al., "*Yersinia pestis* and the Plague of Justinian," p. 325; Benedictow, *Black Death*, pp. 33, 233; Benedictow, *What Disease was Plague*, pp. 34–38, 389–11.

111 Harper, *Fate of Rome*, p. 225.

112 Harper, *Fate of Rome*, pp. 241–42, 304–15.

113 Harper, *Fate of Rome*, pp. 261–71. The impression here is that collapse in trade in the late empire was more severe than in late medieval Europe in the wake of the Black Death.

114 M. Kulikowski, "Plague in Spanish Late Antiquity," and John Maddicott, "Plague in Seventh-Century England," in *Plague and the End of Antiquity*, pp. 150–70, and 173–79. Maddicott argued that, even though we lack definitive descriptions of symptoms, the outbreaks in Britain were part of a geographical and chronological advance of plague from the Mediterranean northwards, leaving "virtually no doubt" as to the identity of the disease.

115 Harper, *Fate of Rome*, pp. 241–42.

116 Harper flatly denied this argument, asserting that the idea that "the degraded systems of connectivity in the west could have slowed the dispersal of the plague bacillus . . . cannot carry too much conviction". He cited in support the fact that paleomicrobiology uncovered plague victims at Aschheim and Altenerding in Bavaria, despite these being a "remote, rural outpost in the west". Yet this still does not establish *when* plague arrived here and if it was during the first, great outbreak of the pandemic. Moreover, Harper's conclusion that the plague's presence in Bavaria proves that it was also present in "many other places which lie in the dark zones on our map" is a kind of argument from silence in reverse, namely, that the silence of the record *cannot* be used to prove that something did not exist. See Harper, *Fate of Rome*, p. 230.

117 McCormick, "Rats, Communications, and Plague," pp. 19–23; Harper, *Fate of Rome*, p. 214; Philip L. Armitage, "Unwelcome Companions: Ancient Rats Reviewed," *Antiquity* 68 (1994):233–34. It is argued that rats disappeared from Britain during the "Dark Ages" (sixth to eighth centuries), based on the absence of rat bones in archaeological sites during this period, but the presence of bubonic plague in Britain during the seventh century confirms that black rats were, in fact, on the island. For an update on McCormick's survey, see his database available online at http://darmc. harvard.edu, accessed January 7, 2018.

118 Sarris, "Bubonic Plague in Byzantium," pp. 131–32; Rosen, *Justinian's Flea*, pp. 309–11; Angeliki E. Laiou, "The Byzantine Empire in the Fourteenth Century," in *The New Cambridge Medieval History, Volume VI: c. 1300–c. 1415*, ed. Michael Jones (Cambridge: Cambridge University Press, 2000), p. 821; Harper, *Fate of Rome*, pp. 234–35; Meier, "'Justinianic Plague'," pp. 280–81.

119 Kennedy, "Justinianic Plague in Syria," and Sarris, "Bubonic Plague in Byzantium," in *Plague and the End of Antiquity*, pp. 87–95, 127–31; Harper, *Fate of Rome*, p. 234; Meier, "'Justinianic Plague'," pp. 279–80.

120 Harper, *Fate of Rome*, pp. 271–75.

121 There is some debate as to how much credit or influence is to be accorded to Islam in the fall of the eastern empire. Harper, for example, preferred to see the rising power of Islam as simply delivering the *coup d'grace* to an empire already laid prostrate by the plague and climate change. Moreover, Harper viewed Islam itself as an apocalyptic movement responding to the impact of the plague. See Harper, *Fate of Rome*, pp. 283–87.

122 Fred Donner, *Muhammad and the Believers: At the Origins of Islam* (Cambridge, MA.: Harvard University Press, 2010), pp. 56–89.

123 Donner, *Muhammad and the Believers*, pp. 90–144. For more traditional accounts of the Islamic conquests, see: Fred Donner, *The Early Islamic Conquests* (Princeton, NJ.: Princeton University Press, 1981); Ira M. Lapidus, *A History of Islamic Societies* (Cambridge: Cambridge University Press, 1988); Hugh Kennedy, *The Great Arab Conquests: How the Spread of Islam Changed the World We Live In* (Cambridge, MA.: Da Capo Press, 2007).

124 Donner, *Muhammad and the Believers*, pp. 112–15.

125 Yehuda D. Nevo and Judith Koren, *Crossroads to Islam: The Origins of the Arab Religion and the Arab State* (Amherst, NY.: Prometheus Books, 2003), pp. 27–65, 155–68.

126 Conrad, "Plague," pp. 167–246.
127 Conrad, "Plague," pp. 169–76; Lawrence I. Conrad, "Umar at Sargh: The Evolution of an Umayyad Tradition on Flight from the Plague," in *Story-Telling in the Framework of Non-Fictional Arabic Literature*, ed. S. Leder (Wiesbaden, Germany: Harrassowitz, 1998), pp. 488–528; Michael W. Dols, *The Black Death in the Middle East* (Princeton, NJ.: Princeton University Press, 1977), pp. 21–25.

2

FROM THE OBSCURANTISM OF THE NORTHMEN, O LORD, DELIVER US!

The Viking invasions

At the Seljord Folkehøgskole ("Folk High School") in the picturesque town of Seljord in central Norway, students can now enroll in a nine-month-long "craftscourse" on how to live like a tenth-century Viking. This includes how to build an authentic Viking house, how to sail in a Viking longship, how to make authentic Viking clothes, armor, and other handicrafts, etc. What students are *not* taught, is how to pillage and plunder like a true Viking. The course is entirely peaceful. As the school's website puts it, "The Viking culture was much more than just warriors raiding and plundering the rest of Europe ... Most were farmers, fishermen, and craftsmen". Accordingly, the course, as part of its mission of "celebrating the crafts of the Viking Age," attempts to have students recreate or reconstruct artifacts that have been recovered by modern archaeology.[1]

However, not everyone is entirely enamored of Seljord's "revisionist" approach to Viking culture. Some activities that might be deemed legitimate reconstructions of Viking life—such as animal sacrifices, swordplay, and the taking of hallucinogenic plants to make one go "beserk"—are ruled "inappropriate" and strictly "off limits". No doubt some potential enrollees are bitterly disappointed that these elements are missing from the curriculum. As one dissenter puts it, the "politically correct Viking" may be so far removed from the complete picture of a true, medieval Viking that "he does not really appeal to anybody".[2] Indeed, the latest histories of the Vikings try to strike a balance between unrelievedly portraying them as heartlessly cruel pillagers and rapists—which is all too easily sourced in contemporary chronicles of the Christian monks who were their victims—and presenting only their peaceful and positive activities, such as trade, cultural achievements, and above all, exploration and settlement, to the exclusion of their incredibly destructive raids. The consensus these days dares to suggest that the Vikings could be both, and that neither image is mutually exclusive of the other.[3] In this chapter, we will focus on two of the most popular, and controversial, strands of the Viking story:

their raids and reputation for violence; and their seafaring exploits, particularly their voyages to North America.

The reasons for the raids

Why did the Vikings burst so violently, and so suddenly, upon the European scene when they did? The earliest appearances of Viking raiders, at least as recorded by their victims, was toward the end of the eighth century off the coasts of northeastern and southern England, western Scotland, and northern and eastern Ireland in the British Isles, and off the western coast of France. Thereafter, raids began in earnest both in Britain and on the Continent during the 830s and continued on and off for some decades down into the tenth and early eleventh centuries. Shifting from random raids to strategic settlements, Vikings from Norway and Denmark eventually established a permanent presence in the duchy of Normandy in northern France by 911 and through a swath of territory known as the Danelaw in England, which was later to be converted for a brief time into a Viking kingdom under Canute the Great (1016–35), who ruled it as part of a pan-Scandinavian empire. Vikings also established a kingdom in Ireland around their new capital city of Dublin (which had close connections with the kingdom of York in England) and settled in the Orkney, Shetland, and Hebrides islands of Scotland and on the Isle of Man and Anglesey off the coast of Wales. In the meantime, Vikings raided further afield to Muslim Spain, southern France, and Italy in the Mediterranean, while in the East, the Rus, or Swedish Vikings, established principalities based at Novgorod and Kiev. Sailing west to the limits of the known world, Vikings set up colonies in Iceland and Greenland and, in around 1000 A.D., explored the northeastern coast of North America, spending several winters in a place they called "Vinland," which has been variously identified with Newfoundland, Nova Scotia, or New England.[4]

One popular, time-honored explanation for the Viking raids, which continues to be favored by some textbooks, is that the Vikings were driven by overpopulation in Scandinavia, accompanied by a lack of good farming or pasture land and perhaps poor weather, in order to seek their fortunes elsewhere. This is an idea that can be traced all the way back to the Norman chronicler, Dudo of St. Quentin, who in the early eleventh century attributed the Viking overflow to shameful practices of polygamy and promiscuous sexual intercourse that bred "innumerable progeny," an observation that seems to be more the product of Christian prejudices towards a pagan culture than any verifiable fact.[5] Other Christian chronicles that speak of Viking invasions numbering thousands upon thousands of people are also not likely to be free of exaggeration. There is simply no hard evidence that Vikings were motivated to make their raids from overpopulation, especially as the initial attacks were all about pillage and plunder, not settlement and land.[6]

Yet another popularly-received explanation for the Viking raids is that this was an expression of pagan hostility, indeed of a pagan war or crusade, against Christianity. Again, this can be traced back to contemporary Christian chronicles, such

MAP 2.1 The raids of the Vikings, as well as of the Magyars and Muslims, during the ninth and tenth centuries

as the annals of St. Vaast, which in 884 bemoaned the bodies of Christian men, women, and children, both clergy and laity, that lay strewn along all the roads after being slain by the Vikings, who also "without ceasing destroy churches and dwellings and burn towns". But if we are to judge on this basis that the Vikings had something against Latin Christianity, then by the same measure of their violence we must also accept that they were targeting Islam and the Greek Orthodox Church: At Algeciras in Spain, for example, they burned down the grand mosque, while in Constantinople the patriarch Photius described a Viking attack in 860 in lurid terms that rival any hyperbolic plaint in the West. Typically, the Viking "heathens" were cast in Christian accounts as the agents of divine wrath sent down to correct a sinful Christian society, but one must remember that the authors also had their own agenda, which was to advance the cause of the Church and promote a renewal of the Christian religion among their readers.[7]

Looking at it from the other side of the coin, Viking paganism, albeit recorded by later Christianized writers such as the thirteenth-century Icelandic historian, Snorri Sturluson, reveal none of the missionary fervor and bias towards other religions such as we see in Christianity. Instead, pagan Viking religious attitudes were mainly characterized by an air of eminent practicality and flexibility, some might say in contrast to Christian intolerance of rival beliefs.[8] In this way, whole Viking communities could convert to Christianity quite easily and rapidly, although there is some question as to how deep and enduring such changes of heart actually were.

An excellent illustration of the eminently practical approach of the Vikings towards religion is the story of how, in the year 1000 in Iceland, the *althing* or representative parliament asked a pagan, Thorgeir the Lawspeaker, to adjudicate over whether the country should become Christian or remain heathen. Contrary to what one might expect, Thorgeir decided, after spending a day and a night on the Law Rock, that Iceland should become Christian. His reasoning was that there could be only one law and one faith and that, after all, Christianity was a "reasonable religion"; yet, by way of compromise, Thorgeir also provided that pagan practices, such as sacrifices to the gods, eating horsemeat, and even infanticide, could still go on if conducted in private. Likewise, Vladimir, the Viking prince of Kiev, supposedly had some very down-to-earth motives when he opted for Greek Orthodox Christianity after considering, in turn, Islam, Judaism, and Latin Christianity. Despite being tempted by Islam, since it allowed for polygamy (Vladimir was notorious for maintaining hundreds of concubines), the prince in the end balked at becoming a Muslim because he would have to give up alcohol, and he reasoned that "drinking is the joy of the Rus and we cannot live without this pleasure".[9] Archaeological excavations have uncovered Thor hammer amulets lying side-by-side with Christian crosses in Viking graves, while at Repton in England, remains of the Danish great army wintering there in 873–74 have been found in both a Christian burial mound associated with the Mercian royal monastery and in a charnel deposit where traditional pagan cremations took place, complete with animal sacrifices.[10] It is clear that even "hostile" Vikings bent on conquering the land were quite willing to accommodate themselves to a plurality of beliefs and had no inherent aversion or prejudice against Christianity. Indeed, the only time Viking kings attempted to impose a religion upon their subjects was when they were attempting to convert them to Christianity as part of cementing their political rule over the country, as evidenced by the reigns of Olaf Trygvasson (995–1000) and Olaf Haraldsson (1016–28) of Norway, both of whom died violent deaths at the hands of their own people.[11]

Nevertheless, the pagan rationale behind the Viking attacks recently has been resurrected in an intriguing new theory. This sees the initial raids as pagan payback for Charlemagne's three decades long war against the heathen Saxons, which finally ended in c. 800. There is some evidence for rising tensions between Gudfred, king of Denmark, and Charlemagne in the aftermath of the Saxon war, which culminated in a Danish attack on the Frisian coastline of Charlemagne's empire in 810. A further escalation into outright war between the Danes and the Franks was only narrowly averted by Gudfred's murder later that year, but it is not clear that religious differences were behind hostilities between the two realms.[12] Most of the early Viking raids that took place contemporaneously with the Saxon war are thought to have been carried out by Norwegians and took place in the British Isles, which was not part of Charlemagne's empire and which actually contained descendants of Saxons who had come over in the fifth century. Nor can we assume that the pagan religions of the Germanic Saxons and of the Scandinavian Vikings were one and the same: They undoubtedly had their parallels and similarities in terms of their pantheon and mythology, but an attack on one would not necessarily have been seen as an attack on the other. When the main Viking attack on Francia did come, it was more than three decades after the end of the Saxon war and was apparently in response to a divided Frankish leadership that actually invited such outside interference as part of its political rivalry.

The chief virtue of paganism for understanding the Viking raids is as a reflection of the unique Viking culture that was quite different from its Christian counterpart in Europe and that explains much of the Vikings' success. We've already mentioned the flexibility and practicality of Viking pagans that allowed for a relatively easy conversion to Christianity around the year 1000 (except for Sweden, which converted about 100 years later).[13] This same flexibility extended to morality, which is to say that Viking mythology was distinctly amoral: The gods did not serve as moral exemplars for human worshippers, in contrast to the Christian approach to Jesus. On the contrary, the chief Viking god, Odin, was portrayed by the sagas as a master of cunning, deceit, and trickery (such as by using shapeshifting) in order to overcome his adversaries and gain his powers, including magic and wisdom.[14] It is this low cunning and moral blindness that is exactly what we get in the many tales of human Viking behavior when interacting with foreigners.

Three entertaining examples will suffice by way of illustration. In 845 the Moorish poet, al-Ghazal, undertook an embassy on behalf of the Umayyad emir of Córdoba, Abd ar-Rahman II (822–52), to a Viking ruler called the king of the "Majus," or "fireworshippers". (It seems the Muslims may have confused the Vikings with Zoroastrians.) This was one year after a Viking fleet sailing into the Mediterranean had temporarily seized Seville, which apparently impressed the emir, even as he hanged and decapitated all his Viking prisoners. Al-Ghazal had insisted before his audience with the Viking king that he not be required to kneel before him. However, the Viking king thought of a clever way to get around this stipulation, by constructing an entrance to the audience hall so low that the ambassador would be required to enter on his knees. Al-Ghazal was only able to solve this problem by dragging himself in feet first on his bottom![15]

Our second example comes from Dudo of St. Quentin, who relates how in 860 a Viking chieftain called Hastein, in the course of raiding southern France and the western coast of Italy, mistook the white walls of Luna for those of Rome and devised a ruse to take the former capital of the civilized world. He hid himself in a coffin and sent a message to the bishop and duke of the city that a Viking chieftain wished to be buried as a Christian, but once inside the walls Hastein rose from the dead to slay them both and seize control of the town. Once informed that he had taken Luna, not Rome, Hastein allegedly ordered the massacre of every male inhabitant.[16]

Our third example, perhaps the most famous, tells of how a Danish or Norwegian Viking chieftain called Hrolf, latinized to Rollo, converted a raiding expedition up the Seine to Rouen into a noble title with a claim to the duchy of Normandy. According to the Norman historian, William of Jumièges, writing in the eleventh century, Rollo or his representative was required to kiss the foot of the Carolingian Frankish king, Charles the Simple (or more euphemistically, Charles the Straightforward) in order to receive his duchy, but at the last moment the Viking simply lifted the king's foot from the horse's stirrup up to his mouth, rather than bending down to kiss it, thus catapulting his highness onto the horse's back, much to the amusement of the crowd.[17] All these examples illustrate, in an amusing but also, in the case of Hastein, in a chilling way, how the apparent lack of expectations of ethical behavior in Viking pagan culture allowed the Vikings to adapt at will to circumstances as they arose, which gave them a distinct advantage over their enemies, especially when the latter expected their adversaries to play by the same "civilized" rules.

It is perhaps in this same spirit of flexibility or opportunism that we are to find the best explanation for the Viking raids.[18] Leaving aside the problematical and polemical theories of overpopulation and pagan hostility mentioned above, a unique combination of circumstances in both Scandinavia and Europe meant that the time of the ninth century was simply right for the Vikings. Three main factors are alleged to have been at work here. One was trade, which, like raiding, seemed to come naturally to the Vikings and which existed in a symbiotic relationship with the raids, the two often reinforcing and leading into each other, since wealth was the basis for chieftains' ability to retain warriors and reward them.[19] Danish trade with Frisia, for example, had been going on for a long time before the first raids in 834 and seems to have made Vikings aware of the wealth that was there for the taking. In turn, we have already seen how a Viking raid upon Moorish Spain in 844 led to al-Ghazal's embassy to the Vikings in 845 that sought a trading relationship, mainly in the commodity of slaves. Long-distance trade in luxury items had revived under Charlemagne, especially along the North Sea routes, but even when this trade declined in the ninth century under the later Carolingians, regional networks between Europe and Scandinavia continued to carry high volumes of lower value goods, and although Viking raids might indeed have disrupted this trade, it quickly resumed once peace was made, with the Vikings often putting back into circulation the spoils that they stole.

A second factor was the political chaos and disintegration in Europe that created opportunities for the Vikings to exploit. This occurred, of course, in the former empire of Charlemagne, even before it was formally split into France, Germany, and Lotharingia by the Treaty of Verdun of 843. But it was also true of England and Ireland, which were likewise divided into separate and competing kingdoms.

At the same time, there seemed to be a complementary process of political consolidation going on in Denmark and Norway, so that it is possible that politically thwarted nobles and minor chieftains were forced to seek their fortunes elsewhere, and hence became Vikings.[20]

The third factor is the Viking ship (of which there was a great variety), perfectly suited to the Viking strategy of flexibility, raiding anywhere and at any time. Clinker-built of strakes or planks split for strength along the grain of the wood and fastened to cross-frames with spruce roots for great flexibility and hydro-dynamics, the Viking ships had very little draw-weight in the water (as little as 3–5 feet) and at the same time great stability, allowing the Vikings to sail up the shallowest rivers and across the deepest oceans. They were also light enough to be transported overland, if necessary, in order to bypass fortified bridges or for portage between headwaters; they could even be placed on wheels, as was done in a *Rus* attack on Constantinople in 907.[21]

On the other side of this debate, it is argued that none of these three factors were especially unique to the Vikings. Almost everyone conducted trade, experienced political divisions (most of the attacks on Viking homelands came from within Scandinavia), and had ships powered by both sail and oar. The Vikings' navigational abilities were not especially advanced for their times, nor did their warrior ethos—the desire for glory, riches, and renown—set them apart from their enemies. In this scenario, then, the Vikings' raids and expeditions were simply the product of accident or chance—the lucky payoff of a daring gamble undertaken for any number of reasons—as opposed to being the weighty consequence of some far-planned goal or coordinated strategy.[22]

How violent (and fearsome) were the Vikings?

From a modern point of view, it is all too easy to think of the Vikings as the "bad asses" of their day, whose violent propensity to pillage and plunder can be either a source of condemnation, or, indeed, of tacit admiration. (Think of the "What's in Your Wallet" commercials for the Capital One Bank credit card that featured Vikings, which flooded the television airwaves in 2003 and 2009.) Yet it is important to place the Vikings' reputation for violence in context. The Vikings were violent in a violent age.[23] Raiding the lands of one's enemies and rivals was a standard tactic employed by the Christian kings of Ireland and of Anglo-Saxon England, and, indeed, even by that most heroic and renowned of leaders, Charlemagne. The "father of Europe" acquired his vast empire by methodically and successively raiding his neighbors, including the Avars in what is now Hungary, the Basques in northeastern Spain, the Lombards in Italy, and, above all, the Saxons in Germany. His 30+-year war against Saxony, raging from about 772 to 804, was particularly bloodthirsty and ruthless, with no less than 4,500 Saxons perishing at the "blood court" (*Blutgericht*) of Verden in October 782, on a charge of practicing paganism (which was equated here with political treason). Thousands more were exiled or displaced. Yet Charlemagne is fondly remembered, and commemorated, to this day as "a symbol of the unification of Europe," while the Vikings are vilified. No less than the Vikings, Charlemagne used the loot from his pillaging raids, as well as the tribute he extracted from various subjects, in order to pay his army and reward his followers.[24]

In terms of military weaponry and tactics, the Vikings had much in common with their adversaries. They all fought with swords, spears and arrows; wore mail and leather armor and carried shields; and tried to attack when conditions were most favorable and husband their resources when vulnerable. Yet there were certain features that did distinguish the Vikings and make them unique in the annals of war. They used the battle-axe and made it their signature weapon, which required a degree of strength and dexterity to wield effectively; they perhaps had a "roguish warrior spirit," which allowed them to quickly adapt, change course, and do the unexpected and sometimes surprise and outfox the enemy; finally, they had their ships, although there is some debate as to how much of an advantage this really gave the Vikings over their neighbors.[25] Most ships of the time were well adapted to sailing along the coast; where the Vikings may have had an advantage was out on the open seas, owing to their deeper-keeled boats.[26] It is noteworthy, however, that when the Vikings did fight ship-to-ship, they usually lashed their vessels together in an effort to make the battle conditions as much like those on land as possible. (In other words, they did not have a uniquely naval strategy that differed substantially from what they did on land.)[27] It is also remarked upon that Vikings usually did not face threats of invasion from without; when attacks did come, it was most often from rival chieftains or raiding parties within Scandinavia.[28] One can speculate on the reasons for this: Partly, it may have been because the Vikings did not have anything of great value, such as rich lands or wealthy monasteries, that tempted invaders; partly, it may have been because other Europeans simply did not have the ship-building skills of the Vikings in order to launch far-flung raids.[29] This, of course, was to change as Vikings assimilated with the cultures they raided and, sometimes, conquered.

In some respects, the Vikings' reputation for savage violence may not be wholly deserved. Indeed, the popular stereotype of a "Hagar the Horrible" Viking can take on a life of its own, due to the continued, wilful misreading of the sources. For example, one of the most popular legends about the Vikings is that certain warriors were "berserks," who went on uncontrolled rampages in battle by working themselves up into a frenzy, perhaps with the aid of psychotropic mushrooms (*fly agaric* being one such contender).[30] The original meaning of *berserkir* in Old Norse was "bear shirt" (the term, *ulfhednar*, or "wolf skin," was also used); in its original reference in a ninth-century Norwegian poem, *berserkir* seems to have been a "poetic circumlocution" for the chain-mail armor that warriors wore, akin to the Old English *byrnie*. This was then fancifully elaborated by later, thirteenth-century authors, including the Danish historian, Saxo Grammaticus, and saga writers from Iceland, into warriors who went "berserk," fighting wildly like wolves or with the strength of bears.[31]

A similar misreading is responsible for the legend of the "blood eagle," said to have been a particularly gruesome form of execution torture in which the Vikings either cut the image of an eagle onto the backs of their victims, or else hacked away their ribs from the backbone in order to expose the lungs, which were then spread out in the shape of eagle's wings, all while the victims were still alive. Yet the original meaning of the "blood eagle" was most likely far more prosaic. It was the eleventh-century *skald* or court poet, Sigvat Thoradson, who seems to have first given birth to the "blood eagle," with a line from his poem about how Ivar the Boneless avenged the death of his father, Ragnar Lodbrok or Hairybreeches, by killing his murderer, King Ælla of Northumbria, in the battle of York in 866. In the original Old Norse, Sigvat can be read as saying either that "Ivar caused the eagle to cut the back of Ælla," or that "Ivar cut the eagle on the back of Ælla"; both meanings are possible owing to the "cryptic" and "easily misunderstood" style of skaldic poetry (a style that the poets deliberately cultivated). The former interpretation, that Ivar left his enemy's body to be eaten by carrion scavengers like eagles, requires far less imaginative convolutions in order to make sense of the poem.[32] Yet, for many Viking enthusiasts, perhaps the latter interpretation is simply too attractive to be abandoned for the sake of historical accuracy.

If Vikings did win their battles, then we have to remember that they lost the war—the war of words, that is, over what image of themselves they would leave for posterity. Vikings may be remembered for their deeds in songs and sagas, but, as we have seen, many of these in the Old Norse are obscure and difficult to read, even for native speakers. On the other hand, the Christian monks who wrote in Latin and bemoaned their fate at the hands of Viking marauders have undoubtedly received more "air time" in most modern historical accounts of the Vikings.[33] We can perhaps say that this is an unusual instance of history being written by the vanquished, rather than the victors, except that Christianity did eventually triumph over pagan Viking culture.

When one reads of how the nuns of Coldingham in England mutilated their own faces in order to avoid being raped or enslaved by Ivar the Boneless, but were then burnt alive anyway, or of how the peaceful fairgoers of Nantes in France were massacred by Norwegian Vikings on St. John's Day, June 24, in 843, one can't help but be appalled at Viking behavior. How can it be called courage, in any way to boast of, when armed brutes slew or enslaved defenseless men, women, and children? But if one looks a little closer, a more nuanced picture comes into view. This is possible in the case of the massacre at Nantes, which was recorded by an eyewitness, a monk from Indre monastery, lying about 5½ miles downstream on the River Loire from Nantes. Ironically, the Indre monks fled to Nantes to seek refuge within the city walls from a Viking attack they saw coming as the Vikings rowed up the Loire. Here, the author supplied far more details than are usually available in the terse annals that record most Viking attacks. What emerges is that the Vikings clearly timed their attack well, a month after the local count, Rainald of Nantes, was killed in battle against a rival Breton army. Nantes was therefore defenseless, and ripe for plunder, because of local power politics. More specifically, the Vikings attacked on St. John's Day, a holy day, not because they were targeting Christians per se, but because they knew many people would be gathered in the city in their best finery, which would mean more booty, both in terms of gold and silver valuables and in terms of wealthy human hostages. Thus, despite the chronicler's claim that "the heathens mowed down the entire multitude" of inhabitants, many survived the massacre and were deliberately spared by the Vikings, if only for the sake of ransom, which the chronicler, a few lines later, freely admitted did, in fact, happen. We can only wonder how many more quali-fications need to be made in other accounts of Viking raids that do not supply as much information as this one does.[34]

We therefore shouldn't be completely taken in by the monastic chroniclers, who taught us to pray, "From the fury of the Northmen, O Lord, deliver us" (*A furore normannorum, libera nos, domine*). Even the alleged berserker, Egil Skallagrimsson, who lived in Iceland during the ninth century and who celebrated in his poems how "red flames ate up men's roofs" and how spears and swords "skewered bodies sprawled sleepy in town gate-ways," was not incapable of finer feelings, such as when he mourned the death by drowning of his favorite son by locking himself in a closet, refusing to eat or drink, until his daughter offered to share his fate. Vikings were human beings, after all, sharing in the marvelous complexity of the human experience. They were not invincible, nor superhuman. We must remember that they didn't always win their battles (in fact, by one estimate they lost more often than they won the average encounter), and the Muslims and the Greeks, with their organized defenses and advanced technological weaponry, such as "Greek fire," showed what could be done when a unified state trained its full resources on a ragtag Viking army.[35] There is just the possibility that the Vikings were deliberately brutal and ruthless, so that next time they could gain their land or plunder by more peaceful, less strenuous means, such as payment of "danegeld" tribute. Despite their portrayal in contemporary accounts as strange, foreign heathen who struck suddenly and randomly like a bolt from the blue, we have to remember that the Vikings and their raids were not inexplicable. They were, in fact, part of a network of trade and power politics in Europe that made them fully part of the European scene.[36]

Nor do historians of today accept the raids as entirely senseless, a wasteful orgy of destruction and mayhem. While it is true that books were burned or lost as monastic libraries were sacked, not all of the intellectual decline after the Carolingian Renaissance is to be laid at the feet of the Vikings. Moreover, a silver lining can always be found in the most catastrophic raids, such as spurring the money economy by putting gold and silver hoarded in monastic and Arab treasuries back into circulation, or encouraging stronger state institutions such as country-wide taxation, standing armies, and fortified towns in order to ward off the Vikings or pay danegeld.[37] Without the Vikings, there probably would have been no Capetian dynasty in France descended from the Viking fighter, Robert the

Strong, or no Alfred the Great or William the Conqueror in England. It is hard to imagine strong monarchies emerging in these two countries during the high Middle Ages without these forebears. In the words of the historian, Donald Logan, the exuberant, if at times destructive, energies of the Vikings revitalized a "decaying civilization" in Europe, which under the Normans eventually found expression in the expansive movement of the crusades and the advanced legal and state systems devised in England and Sicily.[38] For many, it is perhaps too much to ask that we be grateful to the Vikings. But of one thing we can be sure: If we are to accept the Vikings for who they were, on their own terms, then we must accept both the good and the bad, like in any human nature.

The Vikings in North America

There is no longer any debate that the Vikings did indeed land in North America around the year 1000 and that they spent some time there, even if they did not establish a permanent settlement. The timing of these voyages was probably not by chance, as this era coincided with the Medieval Warm Period or Medieval Climate Anomaly (c.950–c.1250), when warmer temperatures around the globe reduced the duration and extent of the northern ice pack, freeing up the Northwest Passage through the Arctic Ocean.[39] Until about fifty years ago, the only evidence for the Viking exploration of North America were two Icelandic sagas written in the early thirteenth century. The *Grænlendinga saga* (Greenlanders' Saga) and *Eiriks saga rauða* (Erik the Red's Saga) both testify to expeditions led by Leif Ericson (also known as Leif the Lucky), his brothers Thorvald and Thorstein, and Thorfinn Karlsefni, the husband of Thorstein's widow, Gudrid. After sailing west from Greenland, the Vikings first spied "Helluland" (i.e., "flat-stone land"), then traveling south put ashore at "Markland" ("wood land"), before finally overwintering at a base camp from where they made further explorations in "Vinland" ("wine land," i.e., where wild grapes were found).[40] Most scholars identify Helluland with modern-day Baffin Island, and Markland with the eastern coast of Labrador.[41] However, there is still some debate as to where Vinland corresponds. The consensus of scholarship these days seems to have settled on Newfoundland, the Gulf of St. Lawrence, and the Bay of Fundy in New Brunswick.[42] However, older scholarship favored Nova Scotia and Cape Cod, with some intrepid Vikings possibly even making their way as far south as New York.[43]

In the 1960s, new evidence emerged of an archaeological nature that took Vinland out of the realm of "myth and conjecture" and, supposedly, proved that the sagas' account of Viking voyages to North America had a basis in reality.[44] A Viking settlement of at least eight buildings, whose foundations can still be seen in the grass, was discovered at L'Anse aux Meadows, located on the northern tip of Newfoundland. (Anse refers to "bay" or "cove" in French, while Meadows is derived from *méduses*, or "jellyfish," and does not refer to the landscape, which was originally forested.) Radiocarbon dating of Norse artifacts found on the site confirms that it was settled sometime between 980 and 1020 A.D. The buildings, which included three large halls of Icelandic design, indicate that this was a year-round, if not permanent, settlement that could accommodate as many as 90 people. Each building had a timber frame covered by thick sod walls and roofs, while the halls had wooden paneling inside. The three large halls alone would have required 35,000 cubic feet of sod and 86 large trees for their construction, an undertaking that seems possible only for a good-size colony of about 100 settlers, which would have been no small investment for Greenland, whose total population numbered no more than four or five hundred. This was primarily a working site, where smithies forged iron nails from locally-found bog iron ore and a carpentry shop churned out spruce planks, both of which were used for boat repair. A weaving hut containing loom weight stones and other textile implements indicate that some women were present in this mostly adult male community. The existence of butternuts, which are not native to Newfoundland but grow only further south, such as the St. Lawrence River valley, prove that the inhabitants of this site explored further afield. Finally, the absence of expensive equipment and tools and the firing of two of the halls, perhaps set intentionally, indicate that the Anse aux Meadows settlement was evacuated in an orderly and deliberate fashion. Scholars think that this site corresponds to the Straumfjörd (Current Fjord) settlement mentioned in *Erik the Red's Saga* or to the *Leifsbuðir* (Leif's Camp) described in the *Greenlanders' Saga*.[45]

The Vikings are simply the best documented, and most widely accepted, of many postulated pre-Columbian visitors to American shores. Among the "ancient mariners" to the Americas are said to have been the Phoenicians, Greeks, Romans, Celts, Sumerians, Minoans, Egyptians, Hebrews, and Libyans.[46] In medieval times, voyagers who arrived in North America before, during, and after the Vikings supposedly included St. Brendan of Ireland (c. 545 A.D.), Madoc of Wales (c. 1170), and Prince Henry Sinclair of Scotland (1398).[47] None of these non-Viking theories have any definitive archaeological or literary proof, despite claims for over 3000 inscriptions in North America allegedly written in ancient Ogham, Hebrew, Phoenician, and Iberic scripts.[48] Within my home state of Vermont, there are over 50 stone chambers, which some allege to be of ancient Celtic construction, but which the Vermont state archaeologist, in a survey conducted during the 1970s, determined to be root cellars dating back no further than colonial times.[49] In addition, there are those who argue for a more expansive dispersal—both geographically and temporally—of the Vikings in North America beyond the Vinland exploration based at L'Anse aux Meadows around the year 1000. However, the "artifacts" that serve as the foundation for this theory, which include the Vinland Map, the Newport Tower in Rhode Island, and the Kensington Stone in Minnesota, are all now proved to be forgeries or misinterpretations, the product of a romantic revival of interest in the Vikings during the nineteenth and early twentieth centuries.[50] Yet even today debate still rages between the "diffusionists," who argue for an impressive diffusion of Old World cultures in the Americas prior to Columbus, and the "inventionists," who declare that the only confirmed pre-

Columbian visitors were the Vikings, whose presence was, nonetheless, not permanent nor of any lasting consequence.[51]

The inventionist-diffusionist debate has broader implications for the politics
surrounding American prehistory and for attitudes towards Amerindian achievements and culture. If the diffusionists are right, then "any and all sophisticated
artifacts" found in the Americas can plausibly be attributed to "more advanced
ancient arrivals," rather than to native civilizations. If the inventionists are right,
then authentic North American artifacts, such as the "mounds" of the Ohio River
Valley, are evidence of an accomplished and progressive Amerindian culture.
Features such as the alignment of stone chamber openings with the solstice or the
equinox can be taken either as proof of one culture influencing another, or of
cultures independently developing a shared quality, such as fascination with
astronomical phenomena. Ironically, both views were used to justify removal and
reeducation efforts directed against Amerindian tribes in the United States during
the nineteenth century.[52]

With regard specifically to contacts between the Norse and Native Americans,
we mainly have to rely on the saga evidence. Both the *Greenlanders' Saga* and *Erik
the Red's Saga* tell of peaceful trading relations between the Vikings, led by
Thorfinn Karlsefni, and the *skraelings* or natives they encountered, as well as of
bloody pitched battles between them. At first, the Vikings were able to trade milk
and red cloth in exchange for the fur pelts offered by the *skraelings*, but later,
misunderstandings led to violent confrontations, in which the Vikings, despite
being outnumbered, were able to drive off their attackers, but not without loss of
life and the realization that they could no longer safely remain in the land, despite
all that it "had to offer there". Before the Vikings left, however, Thorfinn and his
wife, Gudrid, sired the first white man born on North American soil, whom they
named Snorri, and who spent three winters, or years, in the land of his birth.[53]

The sagas must be interpreted with caution, however, because they were not
contemporaneous with the year 1000, but were written down in the twelfth or
thirteenth century as part of an oral tradition or distant memory of events. They
thus reflect the historical context of their own times, just as much as of the original
time period, and cannot be taken as a universally accurate record of the voyages.
A good example is the *einfœtingr* or "uniped" reported in *Erik the Red's Saga*,
which was a common feature of natural histories or encyclopedias as a marvelous
wonder in Africa, which was here transferred to the Americas.[54] Moreover, there
are archaeological finds that indicate that "the sagas do not tell the whole story"
about Norse-Amerindian encounters in the North Atlantic.[55] Amerindian artifacts,
such as arrow points and a soapstone lamp, found on Norse sites in Greenland,
and Norse artifacts, such as metal fragments and a minted coin, found at Amerindian
sites, point to a more complex relationship than simple raiding of abandoned
settlements or other chance encounters.[56]

Based on other archaeological data that allow us to map the prevailing tribes in
various parts of North America, it is likely that the Vikings encountered ancestors
of the Micmac in New Brunswick, and ancestors of the Innu and Dorset peoples

in Labrador.[57] Judging just from the term, *skraeling* (perhaps meaning "little wretches" or "people who screech"), that the Vikings used to refer to the natives of North America, it is evident that they held a derogatory view of people described in *Erik the Red's Saga* as "short in height with threatening features and tangled hair".[58] This is aside from the fact that the Vikings killed or took prisoner any stray *skraelings* they happened to find on beaches hiding under their hide canoes. In turn, the Thule Innuit of the Canadian Artic referred to the Norse as *qadlunat*, or "white people".[59] Clearly, both sides, who were roughly equal in terms of military capabilities, viewed the other with mistrust, even to the point of killing each other, but they also viewed each other as resources to be exploited. The Norse saw the *skraelings* as sources of furs and walrus ivory, in addition to the natural bounty of timber and grapes to be found in Vinland; the Amerindians seem to have coveted the iron or metalwork that the Norse could provide (assuming they were willing to do so), as well as the manufactured cloth and domestic animal products that appeared to be unfamiliar to them.[60]

The first contacts between Europeans and Native Americans, although ephemeral and perhaps inconsequential, have nonetheless been the subject of much romantic speculation in literature and film.[61] The dark underside of this picture is the cruelty, misunderstanding, distrust, and exploitation that characterized the Norse relationship with the Native Americans, which is evident even from the brief and vague descriptions of natives in the sagas. While we may celebrate the Viking voyages to the New World for their daring boldness and adventurous curiosity, this is tinged with a touch of sadness, a foreboding of far greater tragedies yet to come.

FIGURE 2.1 The author investigating a stone chamber, known locally as "Calendar II," in South Woodstock, Vermont

Notes

1 Course description available at www.seljord.fhs.no/english, accessed on September 17, 2015.
2 Anders Winroth, *The Age of the Vikings* (Princeton, NJ.: Princeton University Press, 2014), pp. 8–12; Andrew Higgins, "Norway Again Embraces the Vikings, Minus the Violence," *The New York Times*, September 17, 2015.
3 Martin Arnold, *The Vikings: Culture and Conquest* (London and New York: Hambledon Continuum, 2006), p. 2; Robert Ferguson, *The Vikings: A History* (New York: Viking Penguin, 2009), p. 6; Magnus Magnusson, "The Vikings—Saints or Sinners?" in *Vinland Revisited: The Norse World at the Turn of the First Millennium*, ed. Shannon Lewis-Simpson (St. John's, NL.: Historic Sites Association of Newfoundland and Labrador, 2000), pp. 155–64.
4 For more detailed discussion of these events, see: Arnold, *The Vikings*, pp. 79–214; Paddy Griffith, *The Viking Art of War* (London: Greenhill Books, 1995), pp. 49–72; Martin Arnold, *The Vikings: Wolves of War* (Lanham, MD: Rowman and Littlefield, 2007), pp. 51–138; Martina Sprague, *Norse Warfare: The Unconventional Battle Strategies of the Ancient Vikings* (New York: Hippocrene Books, 2007), pp. 9–29; F. Donald Logan, *The Vikings in History*, 3rd edn. (New York and London: Routledge, 2005), pp. 21–187; *Vikings: The North Atlantic Saga*, eds. William W. Fitzhugh and Elisabeth I. Ward (Washington, DC.: Smithsonian Institution Press, 2000), pp. 99–279.
5 Logan, *Vikings in History*, pp. 10–12; William F. McNeil, *Visitors to Ancient America: The Evidence for European and Asian Presence in America Prior to Columbus* (Jefferson, NC.: McFarland and Co., 2005), pp. 44–45; Annette Kolodny, *In Search of First Contact: The Vikings of Vinland, the Peoples of the Dawnland, and the Anglo-American Anxiety of Discovery* (Durham, NC.: Duke University Press, 2012), p. 45.
6 Griffith, *Viking Art of War*, pp. 42–46, 122–26; *Vikings: The North Atlantic Saga*, p. 29; Anders Winroth, *The Conversion of Scandinavia: Vikings, Merchants, and Missionaries in the Remaking of Northern Europe* (New Haven, CT.: Yale University Press, 2012), pp. 33–40. However, colonization seems to have been the main motive for the Norwegian exploration of the Orkney, Shetland, and Hebrides islands off the coast of Scotland.
7 Matthew Innes, *Introduction to Early Medieval Western Europe, 300–900: The Sword, the Plough and the Book* (London and New York: Routledge, 2007), pp. 516–17; Arnold, *The Vikings*, p. 14.
8 Arnold, *The Vikings*, pp. 47–48.
9 Logan, *Vikings in History*, pp. 54, 177–78.
10 Julian D. Richards, "Pagans and Christians at a Frontier: Viking Burial in the Danelaw," in *The Cross Goes North: Processes of Conversion in Northern Europe, A.D. 300–1300*, ed. Martin Carver (York: York Medieval Press, 2003), pp. 383–95.
11 Winroth, *Conversion of Scandinavia*, pp. 115–16.
12 Ferguson, *The Vikings*, pp. 47–57; Arnold, *The Vikings*, pp. 13–14.
13 Recent scholarship, however, has suggested that informal Viking conversions to Christianity were taking place earlier than previously thought, primarily through missionary work beginning in the early ninth century. However, "conversion" can be variously defined, either as a "slow seepage" or infiltration of Christian beliefs, or as an "institutional conversion" of an entire region under the patronage of a king. See: Winroth, *Conversion of Scandinavia*, pp. 102–20; *Vikings: The North Atlantic Saga*, p. 102.
14 Kirsten Wolf, *Daily Life of the Vikings* (Westport, CT.: Greenwood Press, 2004), pp. 152–53; Winroth, *Age of the Vikings*, pp. 181–98; Sprague, *Norse Warfare*, p. 11. A thorny problem in recapturing Viking-age pagan religious beliefs is separating out the later prejudices of Christian writers, who provide much of our information about pagan Viking religion. This is no truer than in what to make of descriptions of pagan sacrifices (which allegedly included humans), such as Adam of Bremen's account of the sacred grove in Uppsala, Sweden. Winroth concludes that Viking pagan cults evinced "great variation and diversity," which cannot easily be characterized, nor,

unfortunately, can these be easily recovered, since they were ultimately suppressed by Christianity.

15 *Al-Ghazal y la Embajada Hispano-Musulmana a Los Vikingos en el Siglo IX*, ed. Mariano G. Campo (Madrid: Miraguano Ediciones, 2002); W.E.D. Allen, *The Poet and the Spae-Wife. An Attempt to Reconstruct al-Ghazal's Embassy to the Vikings* (Kendal, UK: Titus Wilson and Sons, 1960).

16 Dudo of St. Quentin, *History of the Normans: Translation with Introduction and Notes*, ed. Eric Christiansen (Woodbridge, UK: Boydell Press, 1998), pp. 18–20.

17 Logan, *The Vikings*, pp. 109–10; Arnold, *The Vikings*, pp. 157, 162; *The Gesta Normannorum Ducum of William of Jumièges, Orderic Vitalis, and Robert of Torigni*, 2 vols. ed. Elisabeth M.C. van Houts (Oxford: Oxford University Press, 1992–95), pp. 9–28.

18 Griffith, *Viking Art of War*, p. 50; Winroth, *Conversion of Scandinavia*, pp. 32–33.

19 Winroth, *Conversion of Scandinavia*, pp. 85–101.

20 Griffith, *Viking Art of War*, p. 49; *Vikings: The North Atlantic Saga*, pp. 72–75.

21 Sprague, *Norse Warfare*, pp. 87–100; Griffith, *Viking Art of War*, pp. 89–98; *Vikings: The North Atlantic Saga*, pp. 143–45; Winroth, *Age of the Vikings*, pp. 44, 71–97; Innes, *Introduction to Early Medieval Western Europe*, pp. 450–56; Arnold, *The Vikings*, pp. 10–14, 50–51; Ferguson, *The Vikings*, pp. 44–45.

22 Griffith, *Viking Art of War*, pp. 46–50, 73–82, 105–26; Innes, *Introduction to Early Medieval Western Europe*, pp. 450–56; Arnold, *The Vikings*, pp. 10–14, 50–51; Ferguson, *The Vikings*, pp. 44–45; Winroth, *Age of the Vikings*, pp. 44, 71–97; Sprague, *Norse Warfare*, pp. 33–82, 117–34; John Haywood, *Dark Age Naval Power: A Re-Assessment of Frankish and Anglo-Saxon Seafaring Activity* (London: Routledge, 1991).

23 This view is sometimes known as the "war and society" thesis, i.e., that warfare and violence were an integral part of nearly all cultures at this time, so that it makes no sense to speak of separate military and civilian aspects of society. Even though this view has held sway since the 1990s, some scholars propose that the Vikings had unique military skills that can help explain the success of their raiding ventures. See Griffith, *Viking Art of War*, pp. 24–25.

24 Winroth, *Age of the Vikings*, pp. 41–43; Winroth, *Conversion of Scandinavia*, pp. 33, 38–40; Griffith, *Viking Art of War*, pp. 62–63; William R. Short, *Viking Weapons and Combat Techniques* (Yardley, PA.: Westholme, 2009), pp. 1–2.

25 Sprague, *Norse Warfare*, pp. 26–27, 139–89; Winroth, *Age of the Vikings*, pp. 24–34; Winroth, *Conversion of Scandinavia*, p. 32; Griffith, *Viking Art of War*, pp. 73–126, 162–208; Short, *Viking Weapons*, pp. 29–125. Sprague and Griffith characterized the Vikings as the "Special Forces" or "counter-terrorists" of their day, owing to their ability to wage "unconventional" or "small scale guerrilla" warfare.

26 Griffith, *Viking Art of War*, pp. 82–98; Haywood, *Dark Age Naval Power*, p. 69.

27 Sprague, *Norse Warfare*, pp. 177–79; Griffith, *Viking Art of War*, pp. 79–80, 197–98.

28 Sprague, *Norse Warfare*, pp. 171, 188.

29 Sprague, *Norse Warfare*, p. 27.

30 Sprague, *Norse Warfare*, pp. 80–82.

31 Winroth, *Age of the Vikings*, pp. 38–39; Griffith, *Viking Art of War*, pp. 134–36.

32 Roberta Franks, "Viking Atrocity and Skaldic Verse: The Rite of the Blood-Eagle," *English Historical Review* 99 (1984):336–39; Winroth, *Age of the Vikings*, pp. 35–37; Griffith, *Viking Art of War*, pp. 35–37.

33 Short, *Viking Weapons*, pp. 1–2.

34 Winroth, *Age of the Vikings*, pp. 15–21.

35 Arnold, *The Vikings*, p. 58; Innes, *Introduction to Early Medieval Western Europe*, p. 522; Sprague, *Norse Warfare*, p. 21; Griffith, *Viking Art of War*, pp. 49–58, 68–72.

36 Innes, *Introduction to Early Medieval Western Europe*, pp. 519–21; *Vikings: The North Atlantic Saga*, pp. 99–101.

37 Arnold, *The Vikings*, pp. 5–6; Innes, *Introduction to Early Medieval Western Europe*, pp. 520–22; *Vikings: The North Atlantic Saga*, p. 29.

38 Logan, *Vikings in History*, pp. 2–3. Logan is here building upon the views of the early twentieth-century medievalist, Charles Homer Haskins.

39 *Vikings: The North Atlantic Saga*, p. 153. Correspondingly, the advent of the Little Ice Age by the early fourteenth century would have shut the Northwest Passage down, and eventually forced the abandonment of settlements in Greenland itself.

40 *Vikings: The North Atlantic Saga*, pp. 218–24; Frederick J. Pohl, *The Viking Settlements of North America* (New York: Clarkson N. Potter, 1972), pp. 259–305; James Robert Enterline, *Viking America: The Norse Crossings and their Legacy* (Garden City, NY.: Doubleday and Co., 1972), pp. 13–28, 49–71; Tryggvi J. Oleson, *Early Voyages and Northern Approaches, 1000–1632* (Toronto: McClelland and Stewart, 1963), pp. 18–30. There is some debate as to whether the Vinland referred to the sagas should be *Vínland* ("wine land") or *Vinland* ("pasture land"). Scholarly consensus seems to favor *Vínland*. See Magnús Stefánsson, "Vínland or Vinland?" and Alan Crozier, "Arguments Against the *＊Vinland* Hypothesis," in *Vínland Revisited*, pp. 319–37.

41 *Vikings: The North Atlantic Saga*, pp. 228–29, 233; Enterline, *Viking America*, pp. 14–27; Oleson, *Early Voyages*, p. 19. However, Mats Larsson favored southern Labrador for Helluland and Newfoundland for Markland. See Mats G. Larsson, "The Vínland Sagas and the Actual Characteristics of Eastern Canada—Some Comparisons with Special Attention to the Accounts of the Later Explorers," in *Vínland Revisted*, p. 392.

42 *Vikings: The North Atlantic Saga*, pp. 227–28, 232–37; Enterline, *Viking America*, pp. 49–71; George M. Shendock, "A Core Condensation of My Ideas Concerning the Locations of Sites Mentioned in the Voyages of Leifr Eiríksson, Þorvaldr Eiríksson and Þorfinnr Karlsefni," in *Vínland Revisited*, pp. 403–5.

43 *Vikings: The North Atlantic Saga*, p. 233; Pohl, *Viking Settlements*, pp. 165–255; Oleson, *Early Voyages*, pp. 31–35; Larsson, "Vínland Sagas," pp. 394–98.

44 Kolodny, *In Search of First Contact*, p. 43. For a contrarian's argument that Vinland was never a real place, see Magnus Magnusson, "Vinland: The Ultimate Outpost," in *Vínland Revisited*, pp. 83–96.

45 *Vikings: The North Atlantic Saga*, pp. 208–16; Kolodny, *In Search of First Contact*, pp. 95–98; Birgitta Linderoth Wallace, "The Later Excavations at L'Anse aux Meadows," in *Vínland Revisited*, pp. 165–80. The Norwegian explorer, Helge Ingstad, who, along with his wife and archaeologist, Anne Stine, originally discovered the Viking site at L'Anse aux Meadows, told his story in *Westward to Vinland: The Discovery of Pre-Columbian Norse House-sites in North America*, trans. Erik J. Friis (New York: St. Martin's Press, 1969).

46 McNeil, *Visitors to Ancient America*, pp. 115–35.

47 McNeil, *Visitors to Ancient America*, pp. 104–14.

48 McNeil, *Visitors to Ancient America*, pp. 202–35; Eugene R. Fingerhut, *Explorers of Pre-Columbian America? The Diffusionist-Inventionist Controversy* (Claremont, CA.: Regina Books, 1994), pp. 12–19, 23–50. McNeil was far more sympathetic to the "diffusionist" evidence, while Fingerhut was more even-handed, in that he briefly summarized the literature on both sides.

49 McNeil, *Visitors to Ancient America*, pp. 159–201; Joseph A. Citro and Diane E. Foulds, *Curious New England: The Unconventional Traveler's Guide to Eccentric Destinations* (Hanover, NH: University Press of New England, 2003), pp. 302–3; Fingerhut, *Explorers of Pre-Columbian America*, pp. 10–12; Giovanna Neudorfer, "Vermont's Stone Chambers: Their Myth and Their History," *Vermont History: Proceedings of the Vermont Historical Society* 47 (1979): 79–147. Other stone artefacts or "megalithic" structures allegedly built in North America include dolmens, menhirs, cairns, and stone circles. A sort of compromise theory is that the stone chambers were built by modern Irish immigrants, who were imitating the ancient Celtic construction techniques of their homeland. See Robert R. Gradie, III, "Irish Immigration to 18th Century New England and the Stone Chamber Controversy," *Bulletin of the Archaeological Society of Connecticut* 44 (1981):30–38.

50 Kolodny, *In Search of First Contact*, pp. 103–50; McNeil, *Visitors to Ancient America*, pp. 64–88; James Robert Enterline, *Erikson, Eskimos and Columbus: Medieval European Knowledge of America* (Baltimore, MD.: Johns Hopkins University Press, 2002), pp. 61–70; *Vikings: The North Atlantic Saga*, pp. 354–84; Fingerhut, *Explorers of Pre-Columbian America*, pp. 67–84.

51 Fingerhut, *Explorers of Pre-Columbian America*, pp. ix–xvi, 1–6, 169–217; *Vikings: The North Atlantic Saga*, p. 205.

52 Kolodny, *In Search of First Contact*, pp. 19–43, 103–212; Fingerhut, *Explorers of Pre-Columbian America*, pp. xiv, 8.

53 *Vikings: The North Atlantic Saga*, pp. 220–24; Kolodny, *In Search of First Contact*, pp. 49–93; Ingstad, *Westward to Vinland*, pp. 39–59.

54 Shannon Lewis-Simpson, "Introduction: Approaches and Arguments," in *Vinland Revisited*, p. 21.

55 Kolodny, *In Search of First Contact*, p. 99.

56 *Vikings: The North Atlantic Saga*, pp. 203–7, 238–47; Kolodny, *In Search of First Contact*, pp. 97–98.

57 *Vikings: The North Atlantic Saga*, pp. 193–205, 238–47; Kolodny, *In Search of First Contact*, pp. 98–99. In addition, there were other tribes in the area that the Vikings do not seem to have encountered, at least on the Vinland voyages. These include the Thule Inuit in Greenland and Baffin Island, the Beothuk peoples in Labrador and Newfoundland, and perhaps the Maliseet and Abenaki tribes in Nova Scotia, New Brunswick, and New England.

58 Kolodny, *In Search of First Contact*, pp. 3, 58; *Vikings: The North Atlantic Saga*, p. 223.

59 *Vikings: The North Atlantic Saga*, p. 247.

60 *Vikings: The North Atlantic Saga*, pp. 243, 200, 242–45.

61 *Vikings: The North Atlantic Saga*, p. 205; Kolodny, *In Search of First Contact*, pp. 151–212; John Aberth, *Knight at the Movies: Medieval History on Film* (New York: Routledge, 2003), pp. 60–61; *The Vikings on Film: Essays on Depictions of the Nordic Middle Ages*, ed. Kevin J. Harty (Jefferson, NC.: McFarland and Co., 2011). A less than romantic, and indeed quite violent, vision of the meeting of Norse and Amerindians is the 2007 film, *Pathfinder*, which in turn is a remake of a 1987 Norwegian film of the same title, depicting the Sami people native to Finnmark in Norway.

3

GOD WILLS IT!
(OR AT LEAST THE POPE DOES)

The crusades

A crusade can be defined in many ways. The modern definition of crusade is that it was "a sustained effort to achieve something,"[1] or that it was "an aggressive movement or enterprise against some public evil" (*OED* definition), which imply that almost anything could be a crusade. In a medieval context, crusade obviously had a more specific meaning, but what this was has generated considerable debate among scholars.[2] "Pluralist" historians take an expansive view and see a crusade as any enterprise "initiated and organized" by the papacy, while "traditionalist" scholars consider a true crusade as one that had the specific goal of liberating Jerusalem and the Holy Sepulcher, or the tomb where Christ was said to have been buried and resurrected. "Popularists" see a crusade as only that which captured the original, popular excitement and spirit of the First Crusade and is perhaps the most narrowly defined or "restrictive" of the definitions; "generalist" historians, on the other hand, are the most expansive, defining a crusade as any holy war fought in defense of the faith and inspired by God.[3]

Even during the Middle Ages, it is clear that the meaning of crusade and crusading began to shift, as crusades began to be called for a growing variety of motives, including ones that had more to do with politics than religion, and against a growing variety of targets, including fellow Christians themselves.[4] Therefore, at the very time during the thirteenth century when the term "crusade" began to emerge into the light of day, derived from the Latin, *cruce signati*, meaning "signed with the cross," crusading already was beginning to be diluted of its highly charged religious origins.[5] Yet it is also true that to this day, there are some, particularly those who adhere to a "Pan-Islamism" within the Muslim community, for whom crusade still has as its primary meaning that of a religious holy war.[6] Former U.S. President George W. Bush discovered this to his cost when, in the immediate aftermath of the September 11, 2001 terrorist attacks on the World Trade Center and the Pentagon, he referred to his declared "war on terrorism" as a "crusade".[7] For Al-Qa'ida ("the base"), the terrorist organization responsible for the World Trade Center attacks, as well as for other radical Islamic groups, the crusades indeed have never ended since the end of the Middle Ages.[8]

More recently, in March of 2011, Colonel Muammar el-Qaddafi of Libya invoked the crusades as part of his propaganda against the air strikes and no-fly zone imposed by the Allies—led by the United States, France, and Britain—in fulfillment of U.N. Resolution 1973. However, Qaddafi's portrayal of himself as an anti-imperialist, counter-crusade hero dates back to the 1980s, when his government churned out defensive pamphlets in response to a West perceived as hostile to his regime, such as the *Nationalist Documents to Confront the Crusader Attack on the Arab Homeland*.[9] But others besides Qaddafi also got on board to express their concerns about the Allied air strikes in crusader terms. Prime Minister Vladimir Putin of Russia, for example, compared U.N. Resolution 1973 to "medieval calls for crusades", as his nation was joined by China, Brazil, Germany, and India in abstaining from voting on the resolution. Crusade-inspired propaganda, such as equating modern political leaders with Saladin, the self-proclaimed defender of Islam during the Third Crusade, has also been employed in Iraq and Syria, which have likewise faced Western—specifically, U.S.—intervention in recent times.[10]

All these anecdotes remind us of the continued relevance of the crusades for our understanding of the strategically vital, and perennially volatile, present-day Middle East. Perhaps the most fruitful development in crusade historiography in recent years has been the recovery, and greater accessibility, of Islamic sources on the crusade and the presentation of the Islamic perspective in new histories of crusading.[11] This chapter will therefore focus on that part of medieval crusading history that can best illustrate the contrasting perspectives of the European Christian and Eastern Islamic worlds. Some attention also will be paid to aspects of crusading that had nothing to do with Muslims or the Middle East—such as crusader attacks upon Jews, pagans, and fellow Christians in Europe. But our focus is intended to give insights into the misunderstandings that continue to plague the West's fraught relationship with Islam (which many see as originating with the crusades), and into how the meaning and scope of crusades morphed into a modern, more expansive conception beyond religious war.

It should be obvious by now that there are two ways of looking at the crusades, one from the point of view of the still largely Christian West, the other from that of the Islamic East. This was certainly true during the Middle Ages, when Muslim and Christian chroniclers had radically different perspectives on the same events. Occasionally, a chronicle like the *Gesta Francorum* (Deeds of the Franks), written by an anonymous knight in the retinue of Bohemond of Antioch, tried to tell the story from the other side (i.e., from the Muslim point of view), even though the author must, by necessity, have relied almost entirely on his imagination, and his bias still showed through.[12] Nonetheless, one can draw a straight line from views promulgated by contemporary chroniclers of the First Crusade, all the way to modern-day histories of the crusades.[13]

A striking trend in the West these days among popular accounts of the crusades—as represented by works such as Karen Armstrong's bestselling book, *Holy War* (1988), Terry Jones' television series, *The Crusades* (1995), and Ridley Scott's film, *Kingdom of Heaven* (2005)—is that they are very much in sympathy with the Islamic point of view. This is that the crusades were an unprovoked act of aggression by barbarically violent Westerners whose religion was merely a cloak for their greedy lust for land and wealth; their Muslim adversaries, by contrast, were mostly peaceful, devout, and far more culturally advanced than those invading their native soil. Naturally, this is likewise the picture we get from popular versions of the crusades coming out of the Middle East, such Youssef Chahine's film, *Saladin* (1963) and Amin Maalouf's book, *The Crusades Through Arab Eyes* (1989).[14] Sometimes professional historians from Western academies have colluded with this distorted and one-sided version of the crusades. Sir Steven Runciman, whose three volume *A History of the Crusades* (1951–54) remains enormously influential, famously summed up the crusades in the last sentence of his book thus: "High ideals were besmirched by cruelty and greed, enterprise and endurance by a blind and narrow self-righteousness; and the Holy War itself was nothing more than a long act of intolerance in the name of God, which is the sin against the Holy Ghost".[15]

Recently, these views have come in for considerable revision by crusade scholars, who are far more empathetic with the original aims and motives of the medieval Christian crusaders, insofar as these can be gleaned from the sources available. From this perspective, the crusades were in fact a defensive enterprise, undertaken against a relentlessly expanding Islamic empire that enfolded Europe on both its western and eastern flanks and that had conquered areas such as Syria, Egypt, North Africa, and Spain, that had been firmly part of the Christian Roman Empire and later of the Byzantine Empire for centuries.[16] Moreover, the Islamic Aghlabid dynasty of North Africa had undertaken the conquest of Sicily and southern Italy during the ninth and tenth centuries which threatened the very heart of Catholic Europe itself, namely Rome (which was sacked by the Aghlabids in 846); indeed, it was not until 1091, on the very eve of the First Crusade, that the Muslims were completely driven from Sicily by the Normans, who also formed one of the leading crusading contingents. Europe therefore had good reason to feel that it was being besieged by the forces of Islam, rather than the other way around, at the time that the First Crusade was called by Pope Urban II in 1095. In addition, genuinely-felt religious motives played a far greater role than previously thought among the participants in the crusading enterprise, especially during the First Crusade.[17] And finally, Europe was not so far removed from the Islamic Middle East when it came to cultural achievement and sophistication, a fact that became ever more evident as the crusades progressed, even though each culture did, naturally enough, have its own particular strengths. Islam's rediscovery of classical Greek philosophy and learning was a shared common inheritance with the West, albeit Islam also benefitted from the further eastern contributions of ancient Persia and India, which it generously passed on to Europe. What each culture did with this ancient legacy of wisdom could, of course, differ, but it should not be surprising that there was also much overlap and similarity between them.[18]

Despite being firmly grounded in the primary sources, many of which have only recently become available or brought to light, and in spite of a laudable effort to avoid the most egregious sins of historical anachronism, this revision of the crusades has so far made frustratingly little headway into the popular consciousness of the majority of the educated public, insofar as this can be judged on a purely anecdotal level.[19] The outdated, stereotypical image of the crusades as the emblem of medieval Europe's violent aggression and ignorant barbarism lives on against the academic odds, in spite of scholars' best efforts to dispel it. Why? Part of the answer may be that it is too great a leap for most people to stomach to argue that the crusades were, at least initially, a defensive rather than offensive enterprise, which arguably has always been the weakest link in the revisionist argument. While this may accurately reflect contemporary perception by the majority in medieval Europe, it is not so certain at this stage that the territories of Islam— which in any case were characterized by tremendous regional diversity—had aggressive intentions or capabilities towards the West. Spain and Sicily, for example, were already well on their way to a Christian *Reconquista* long before the crusades, despite the temporary setback of the arrival on the scene of a new power from North Africa, the Almoravids. It is true that the Byzantine Empire had been hard-pressed by the Turks ever since the disaster at the battle of Manzikert in 1071, but, as will be more fully explained below, Muslim Syria and Egypt were severely divided and demoralized on the eve of the First Crusade, and the Byzantine emperor's plea for help from the West in 1095 may just as well have been motivated by a desire to take advantage of such weakness. Other scholars have pointed to alternative explanations for the origins and motivations of crusading, including social/psychological factors, economic and environmental forces, and disaster theory, or that the crusades were a response to an "inflammatory millenarian force". For the moment, this debate seems inconclusive.[20]

I strongly suspect, however, that the main reason crusade revisionism encounters such headway has to do with the West's self-loathing over its legacy with nineteenth-century colonialism, when European imperialist powers dominated much of the globe and only disgorged their gains in the aftermath of World War II. Many western crusade historians would argue that it was during the colonial era, when nineteenth-century Romantics were enchanted with all things medieval, that the West also introduced the Muslim inhabitants of its Middle Eastern colonies to the history of the crusades (on perhaps the mistaken assumption that it would reflect gloriously upon the mother country), which until then had been apparently forgotten in the Islamic world.[21] Only then did Muslims take up the crusades as a symbol of their supposed superiority and victory over the West, which was a natural enough response at the very time when they had to endure the humiliating spectacle of the imperialist powers picking over the corpse of the once mighty Ottoman Empire (the so-called "sick man" of Europe).[22] But one can argue that this very view is itself yet another example of Western colonial imperialism—on an intellectual plane—in that it assumes that it was up to Europeans to reacquaint the Muslim world with its "own memory of the crusades," thus assuming a cultural superiority in comparison to "Muslims' ignorance and apathy". An alternative interpretation sees the memory of the crusades—particularly fears of Western interference in Syria and Palestine—as being kept alive in lesser known (at least in the West) literary and historical Islamic works written during the sixteenth and seventeenth centuries.[23]

While it is currently the fashion in the popular mindset, and among some medievalists, to claim that the present conflict between Christianity and Islam, which has arguably grown only worse since the September 11 terrorist attacks, can be traced back to its "roots" in the medieval crusades, from the point of view of crusade historians, nothing could actually be further from the truth.[24] Instead, one can argue that it is nineteenth-century colonialism that has been projected back onto the Middle Ages, so that even in some introductory texts, the crusades are portrayed as essentially colonial enterprises on behalf of the West, a view that many see as grossly anachronistic and that greatly distorts the crusader presence in the Middle East.[25] By the latter half of the twentieth century, the Islamist view of the crusades meshed well with Western shame and guilt over its former colonial domination, which had become an embarrassing relic of the past. But it's high time now that both the West and the Islamic world face up to the reality of the crusades.

The First Crusade

Most historians would probably agree that it was the First Crusade of 1096–99 that was the most important of all the crusades, at least in terms of establishing the standard protocols and mythological ethos of crusading, and that it was the most successful in terms of achieving its original goals, at least from the Western perspective.[26] The First Crusade therefore fully merits the outsized attention it has received from crusade scholars, even if it is the Third Crusade of 1189–92, which pitted against each other the heroic figures of Richard the Lionheart and Saladin, that claims the attention of most popular renderings of the crusades.[27] It was also during the First Crusade that Islam was first forced to confront head-on the growing challenge from Christianity and the West and to set the parameters for its attitude and relationship with another culture with which it was to coexist for the next two centuries in Palestine.

The First Crusade began with the famous sermon preached by Pope Urban II at Clermont in France on November 27, 1095, in which he called for an armed pilgrimage to the East to "liberate" Jerusalem from Muslim occupation and to bring succor to embattled orthodox brethren residing in both the Holy Land and Byzantium. Whereas traditionally scholars have emphasized that Urban's sermon was in response to an appeal he had received the previous March from the Byzantine emperor, Alexius Comnenus (r. 1081–1118), who had requested aid against the Seljuq Turks pressing in upon Byzantium's eastern flank in Asia Minor, nowadays most historians view the pope as developing his own agenda, one that focused instead upon Jerusalem, not Constantinople, as the ultimate goal of the enterprise.[28] This allowed the pope to draw upon the deep emotional appeal that the city where Christ had been crucified and entombed (on a site commemorated by the Church of the Holy Sepulcher) would inevitably have for his Christian listeners.[29] Even the Byzantine emperor, Alexius, himself appealed to Christians' duty to defend Jerusalem, and all other holy places, in his letters to King Zvonimir of Croatia and Count Robert of Flanders in order to recruit military assistance against the Pechenegs prior to the First Crusade.[30]

It has often been said that Urban in his call for crusade merely synthesized a number of pre-existing ideas and institutions: pilgrimage, just war, indulgence, feudalism, chivalry, and so on.[31] But the First Crusade is still a testament to Urban's breathtaking scope of vision, one that went far beyond anything dreamed of by his predecessor, Pope Gregory VII (1073–85). Whereas Gregory conceived of a knighthood of St. Peter (*militia Sancti Petri*) led and loyal to himself, Urban called into being a knighthood of Christ that would serve the entire Church; and where Gregory sought to bend to his will one particular layman, Emperor Henry IV, during the Investiture Controversy of 1076–77, Urban succeeded in having thousands wage his war! Urban achieved this by making a revolutionary, radical appeal for penitential war, which allowed knights to participate more fully in the religious life by doing what they did best, fighting, but which had never before assumed "a permanent place in the theology and practice of Christian violence".[32] Undoubtedly, the ultimate triumph of the First Crusade also vastly increased the power and prestige of the papacy relative to that of the Holy Roman Empire, whose epic struggle with each other had so marked the reign of Pope Gregory VII during the Investiture Controversy.[33] But while it may be easy to cynically maintain that the political agenda comprised Urban's main motive for calling the First Crusade, one has to keep in mind that the new enterprise was also a considerable gamble for the pope, who cannot have foreseen the tremendous response that probably far exceeded anything he imagined. In any case, medieval people did not readily separate the secular and the holy as we do today, but in their minds the two were inextricably linked.

Two further points of revision need to be raised before we leave Urban's sermon at Clermont. One is the claim that the pope and his audience saw his appeal in 1095 as an act of peace or love, not war. It is argued, for example, that contemporaries viewed the crusade as fulfilling the Christian duty of charity and as the logical culmination and continuation of the Peace and Truce of God movements that began on either side of the year 1000.[34] Urban may have preached his sermon on the basis of Christ's call in the Gospels to leave everything and follow him and take up the cross, while according to Fulcher of Chartres, Urban appealed for a renewal of the Truce of God at the same time as he delivered his sermon at the council of Clermont.[35] On the other hand, there are those who argue that the peace movement was "peripheral" to the calling of the First Crusade.

If the Peace of God had been successful, this argument goes, then contemporaries would not have had to justify the crusade as a means of redirecting the martial energies of European knights elsewhere.[36]

One also can argue that peace was essential to the ideas of the "knighthood of Christ" and "warrior monk" that were interwoven into appeals to crusade. As enunciated by churchmen from Pope Urban to St. Bernard of Clairvaux, the knighthood of Christ topos made the distinction between fighting undertaken by crusaders and fighting for purely secular motives, and between holy war and just war. From this perspective, only the former was truly peaceful and did not need any kind of justification or forgiveness as a sinful act; rather, the whole enterprise of crusading itself was viewed as one long act of repentance and not just as a campaign of conquest.[37] Therefore, warfare on behalf of Christ was really the only acceptable call to arms because it was the only one to truly fulfill the Augustinian concept of charitable warfare undertaken out of love for one's enemy, an idea that had been expounded even before the First Crusade by a succession of popes from Leo IX (1049–54) to Gregory VII and by St. Anselm of Lucca (1036–86). Even so, some churchmen still objected to sanctioning violence or fighting of any sort, so that the crusading vow was far from being a free license to kill on the Church's behalf; instead, acts of atonement had to be performed all throughout the crusade.[38]

Secondly, many have made much of Urban's lurid depictions of supposed Muslim tortures, desecrations, and other atrocities committed against Christians and Christian holy sites in the holy land; according to Robert the Monk, who provides the most explicit catalogue of such outrages that Urban used to justify the crusade, these included destruction of churches and altars, forcible circumcision of Christians, disembowelment, beheading, and rape.[39] What are we to make of such accusations? Assuredly they contain no small element of exaggeration for effect, in order to heighten the audience's sense of righteous indignation and perceived need for urgent action. But at the same time, this does not mean that such stories are entirely without foundation. The Church of the Holy Sepulcher in Jerusalem was razed to the ground on the orders of the so-called "mad caliph" of Egypt, al-Hakim, in September 1009, a sacrilege that became widely known and was long remembered in the West, largely through native Christian accounts, some of which were incorporated by European chroniclers into their own works.[40] In subsequent years, a number of Christian pilgrims suffered martyrdom at Muslim hands in the Holy Land, including Gerald of Thouars, abbot of Saint-Florent-lès-Saumur in 1022; Richard of Saint-Vanne in 1026–27; and Ulrich of Breisgau in 1040.[41] Then in 1064–65, a large group of between 7,000–12,000 German pilgrims led by the archbishop of Mainz and three other bishops was waylaid by Muslim bandits at Caesarea on their way to Jerusalem, when it is estimated that only a third survived to complete the journey; it is of this group that Guibert of Nogent may have been thinking when he has Urban claim that Muslims cut open the calloused heels of Christian pilgrims to look for hiding places for their money, or induced vomiting or even cut open their stomachs in case they had swallowed coins.[42]

On the eve of the First Crusade, Jerusalem had an unsettled history under Islamic control. In 1073, the Seljuq Turks, who had recently converted to Sunni Islam, captured Jerusalem from their Fatimid Shi'ite rivals based in Egypt. Twenty-five years later, in 1098, the Fatimids retook Jerusalem from the Artuqids, a Turkish tribe associated with the Seljuqs. Nonetheless, according to a Moorish traveler from Spain, Ibn al-'Arabī, Jerusalem in the 1090s was a teeming, harmonious melting pot of Muslim, Christian, and Jewish visitors and scholars, where local Christians and Jews suffered no evident oppression and were free to practice their religion and maintain churches and temples in good repair.[43] However, we should not omit to mention the contradictory observation of another Muslim writer, the Syrian chronicler al-'Azimi, who wrote in c. 1160 with considerable hindsight that in 1093–94, "the people of the Syrian ports prevented Frankish and Byzantine pilgrims from crossing to Jerusalem. Those of them who survived spread the news about that to their country. So they prepared themselves for military invasion".[44] It is entirely possible that indigenous Christians in the Holy Land—feeling persecuted under their Muslim masters—sent their own appeal for aid to the West, via such figures as Peter the Hermit, who had made a pilgrimage to Jersualem prior to the First Crusade.[45]

The main events of the First Crusade are too well known to need repeating in detail here. After the "first wave," or People's Crusade, led by the preacher Peter the Hermit, was annihilated outside Civetot near Nicaea along the northwest coast of Asia Minor in October 1097, the "second wave," or the Lords' or Princes' Crusade, had considerably better success, even if it faced some truly horrendous hardships and trials of its own. Its main highlights included the conquest and subsequent defense of the city of Antioch on the northwest coast of Palestine in June and July 1098 after an eight-month siege, followed a year later by the conquest and defense of Jerusalem, this time against Fatimid Shi'ite Muslims, between June and August of 1099. With the successful conclusion of the First Crusade, those Latins remaining in Palestine set up the four crusader territories: the County of Edessa in the northeast; the Principality of Antioch in the northwest; the County of Tripoli midway down the coast; and the Kingdom of Jerusalem in the south.

One of the main issues of debate on the First Crusade are the motivations of the some 40,000–60,000 crusaders in the "second wave" that took Jerusalem, who together represented anywhere from a third to a half of the approximately 136,000 people who took a vow to go on crusade in response to Urban's appeal, but of whom another third probably never even left for Palestine.[46] The assumption has always been that these were the landless "second sons" of noble families who had been cut out of inheritances and for whom the Holy Land beckoned as a kind of safety valve for their restless and inchoate energies.[47] Instead, the exact opposite was usually the rule. One look at the leaders of the "second wave"—Godfrey of Bouillon, duke of Lower Lorraine; Hugh the Great, count of Vermandois, brother to the king of France; Raymound IV of St. Gilles, count of Toulouse; and Bohemond I, prince of Taranto—will tell you that here was the crème de la crème of feudal society, not a rag-tag bunch of ruffian adventurers. A detailed examination of crusade charters—which, relatively speaking, survive in good number and which were drawn up by the participants prior to departure—reveal that major financial sacrifices were being made that invested the entire family, including its women, in the crusading enterprise for years to come.[48] Either patrimonial land was being mortgaged or sold, or territorial claims of long-standing were being renounced in exchange for a cash settlement, and such business was most often conducted with neighboring monastic houses with whom local families had long-standing ties and that had the disposable wealth and the obvious incentive to contribute to so holy a venture.[49] An expedition of this kind, like any long trip abroad, was not to be entered into lightly, especially given that it was being made in the aftermath of ecological crises, such as a pestilence and famine in northern Europe between 1093 and 1095.[50] It is estimated that for the average knight a crusade might cost him four or five times his annual income; for the greater nobles, the cost was even more, since they were usually expected to finance a retinue of feudal vassals who accompanied them, and, rather than waste their money, noble leaders certainly weeded out the more disorderly and less genuinely committed elements.[51]

Thus, the knightly contingent who went on the First Crusade drew upon some of the most stable and prestigious members of the allegedly "anarchic" feudal aristocracy of the eleventh century, and these first crusaders then established a chain of familial commitment to crusading that spanned generations.[52] With some notable exceptions that included Godfrey of Bouillon, Bohemond of Taranto, and Raymond of Toulouse, who stayed on in Palestine to become, respectively, the king of Jerusalem, Prince of Antioch, and Count of Tripoli, most of the first crusaders returned home poorer than when they had set out, and not a few, including Stephen II, count of Blois, deserted the crusade even sooner.[53] Of course, this is not to deny that materialistic motivations played a role in the First Crusade, especially in terms of expectations before realities set in. Such motivations are transparent enough in the clauses inserted into charters providing for contingencies in case crusaders settled in the East; in addition, the pope and other crusade preachers tacitly acknowledged these motivations, both by appealing to them in their sermons, and by making them a disqualification for remission of sins.[54]

It is also true that the charter evidence represents only a small, elite fraction of crusaders, and that these were drawn up by churchmen who were concerned to put the best religious spin on such documents.[55] But charters are also the best window we have onto crusader motivations because, even if the crusaders were illiterate and did not draft the charters themselves, they had a stake in the formulation of their terms and how their preambles portrayed them for posterity; no doubt, charters were read out to patrons and reflected at least their general outlook. Other kinds of evidence that can be brought to bear on the question, such as letters written back home by crusaders and pilgrim miracle stories that date to the time of the First Crusade, confirm that Jerusalem was indeed the main goal of its participants and that the journey was commonly viewed as a dangerous and difficult one, not for the faint-hearted. On balance, the consensus is that the origins and execution of the First Crusade in the West were securely grounded in idealistic and religious motives, which best explain how it succeeded against great odds.[56]

One other issue that needs to be addressed is the massacres and other atrocities alleged to have been committed by the crusaders in their march across Palestine. Perhaps the most famous of these is the sack of Jerusalem that immediately ensued upon its capture on July 15, 1099.[57] From the very beginning, the eyewitness accounts—which included the *Gesta Francorum*, chronicles by Peter Tudebode and Raymond of Aguilers, and a letter written to the pope by the crusade leaders in September 1099—contained "considerable discrepancies" between them. These included whether the massacre of the Muslim enemy was a total or partial one; whether it lasted one day or two (i.e., July 15–16); how much blood the conquerors waded in at the Al-Aqsa Mosque (up to men's ankles, knees, or horses' knees and bridles); and, perhaps most important in terms of how the massacre was judged by contemporary standards, whether commanders ordered killings at the mosque after granting "banners of protection".[58]

Other contemporary authors—including Fulcher of Chartres, William of Tyre, Albert of Aachen, Guibert of Nogent, Baudri of Bourgueil, and Robert the Monk—were not eyewitnesses, but may have gathered their information from first-hand participants whom they met during visits to Jerusalem or when the participants returned home from crusade. Despite the fact that they were writing months or years after the event, these authors added many new details. These included that men, women, and children were massacred, even when they were begging for their lives; that crusaders committed horrible atrocities, such as ripping babes from mothers' arms and cradles and dashing their brains against the wall, or slaughtering whole families in their homes; that crusaders inflicted indignities upon their enemies even when dead, such as splitting open or burning corpses in order to extract swallowed bezants or gold coins from the intestines; that as many as 10,000 Saracens were killed at the Al-Aqsa mosque; and that "waves" of blood in the mosque not only reached the conquerors' ankles, calves, or knees, but that they also carried in their wake cut-off hands and arms, which then joined up with amputated corpses rolling on the floor.[59] With the exception of Ibn al-'Arabī, Muslim chroniclers of the crusades inflated the number of residents killed well beyond any figure supplied by their Christian counterparts, to as many as 70,000–100,000. In addition, Muslims claimed that the crusaders burned Jewish residents in their synagogue, something that no Christian author recounted, nor, for that matter, any Jewish witnesses writing from Egypt. al-'Arabī, who resided in Jerusalem in the years just prior to the First Crusade, provided what is today regarded as the most reliable figure for the massacre, namely, 3,000 killed, out of a total estimated population of 20,000–30,000.[60]

As one might expect, medieval Christian authors justified the slaughter at Jerusalem as a just retribution upon the Saracens for their own outrages or "pollution" committed against Christians and their holy places, a theme that meshed well with Pope Urban's sermon that originally called for the crusade. In addition, there was a strategic reason for the massacre, namely, that it would preclude having to fight a second, home front of Muslim survivors should the Fatimids of Egypt choose to attack, and indeed, a month later the crusaders had to defend their conquest at the Battle of Ascalon on August 12, 1099. Yet chroniclers also pointed out that the Jerusalem massacre was unprecedented in terms of its near total slaughter of the defending population. Moreover, a few authors, particularly Albert of Aachen and William of Tyre, evinced a visceral disgust both at the amount of blood and the way that it was shed during the massacre. Albert described the crusaders as behaving with "excessive cruelty," who were so "incensed with rage" that they committed a "pitiable carnage" on the Saracen "wretches". Likewise, William characterized the crusaders as "thirsting for the infidels' blood and utterly prone to carnage," and he suggested that even the victors themselves, drenched in blood "from the soles of their feet to the tops of their heads," may have been filled with "disgust and horror" at what they had done. But the fact that Albert and William appeared to condemn the massacre does not preclude them providing justifications for it as well.[61]

As crusade histories entered the late medieval and early modern era, Albert of Aachen and William of Tyre proved to be particularly influential sources, since their chronicles were reprinted or redacted into other versions numerous times. Thus, Albert's and William's condemnatory stance towards the Jerusalem massacre was adopted by other authors, although criticism of, as well as apologies for, the crusades could arise independently of them, since their accounts were embroidered or watered down at will.[62] Enlightenment authors were almost universally critical of the massacre, parading it as an emblem of a barbaric age, but as we move into the nineteenth century, a more nuanced picture emerged as historians began to scrutinize and evaluate the relative reliability of sources.[63] Finally, in modern times, source criticism of the Jerusalem massacre, and of the crusades in general, has come into full swing.

Modern historians are especially anxious to avoid the charge of anachronism that plagued the judgmental histories of earlier authors (particularly during the Enlightenment), and to that end they seek to judge the massacre strictly within the context of contemporary rules of war. In this view, even a wholesale slaughter of a castle or town was justified if the enemy refused to surrender and the fortifications had to be taken by assault. This certainly applied to the first day of the Jerusalem massacre, July 15, when the Muslim defenders continued to fight even after the crusaders had entered the city, making a last stand at the Al-Aqsa mosque. But it did not necessarily apply to the second day, July 16, when 300 Muslim survivors on the roof of the mosque were slaughtered, even though they had been granted banners of protection the previous day. (At the same time, the Muslim defenders of David's Tower, who had surrendered to Raymond of Saint Gilles, were allowed to depart for Ascalon.) The alleged third day of the massacre, on July 17, when all remaining Muslims—men, women, and children—were killed despite having been ransomed or taken into prison custody, would also have been a war crime by contemporary standards, although Albert of Aachen is the only source for this incident. It also stands to reason that, while the massacre on the first day could have been excused as a "crime of passion," since it was committed in the heat of battle, those on the second and third were premeditated, when cooler heads prevailed, and therefore were more egregious, akin to what nowadays is termed "ethnic cleansing".[64]

In addition, many modern historians of the crusades privilege eyewitness accounts, such as the *Gesta Francorum*, over second-hand reports, such as by Albert of Aachen, even though it is not clear how "eyewitness" should be defined. The author of the *Gesta*, for example, may not even have tried or intended to write from an eyewitness perspective, while Albert's chronicle seems to be solidly based on genuine eyewitness accounts reported second-hand.[65] Modern historians also want to argue that the Jerusalem massacre was not exceptional, in the context of other atrocities committed by crusaders and Christians at other places, and of massacres committed by Muslims of Christian-held towns, both before and after the First Crusade. However, this ignores the testimony of contemporary chroniclers that the Jerusalem massacre *was* extraordinary, if only because it was the product of the calling of the crusade itself, an unprecedented event with possibly eschatological implications.[66] Some modern historians are apparently unaware of a crucial piece of third-party evidence: the so-called Geniza letters, written by Jews based in Egypt concerning the fate of their co-religionists in Jerusalem, dated to less than a year after the crusader conquest. These attest to the possibility that the massacre was both more and less severe than previously imagined: More, because the letters suggest that the massacre did extend to a third day, as Albert of Aachen originally claimed; and less, because the letters also speak of the ransoming of at least a few Jews, which would obviate a total slaughter of inhabitants.[67] If the Jerusalem massacre can no longer be held up as emblematic of the crusade's inherently barbaric and violent nature, neither can it be dismissed or rationalized as simply another casualty of war.

There are any number of medieval Muslim authors who commented on the First Crusade from the Islamic perspective, despite claims that the crusaders were ignored by the *Dar al-Islam* as beneath its notice or were confused with Byzantines.[68] However, many of these sources were written decades later, when Muslim attitudes towards the Franks had evolved considerably compared to the time of first contact.[69] The most important authors include the religious lawyer and scholar from Damascus, 'Ali ibn Tahir al-Sulami, who wrote the earliest after the First Crusade, in 1105; the Syrian chroniclers, al-'Azimi and Ibn al-Qalanisi, both writing in c. 1160; and the Iraqi historian, Ibn al-Athir, who wrote his *Universal History* sometime in the early decades of the thirteenth century.[70] A major theme of the Muslim accounts of the First Crusade is that Islamic defeats at the hands of the *Franj*, above all the loss of Jerusalem in 1099, were entirely the Muslims' fault, due mainly to their political and religious disunity in the face of a sudden and inexplicable incursion from the West.[71] (A parallel disunity to that in Syria and Egypt was likewise at work among the *taifa* Moorish states of Spain during the Christian *Reconquista*.) It is an undeniable fact that the years 1092–94 made a clean sweep of nearly the entire leadership of the Islamic world from Cairo to Baghdad, which included both the Seljuq sultan and the Fatimid caliph, as well as their respective viziers.[72]

Compounding the sense of crisis was an ongoing religious schism and fundamental distrust between the Sunni Turks of Syria and the Fatimid Shi'ites of Egypt; anticipations of the apocalypse with the imminent arrival of a new Islamic century—the sixth from the *hijra* of 622—in 1106; and succession disputes and infighting among local *emirs* almost everywhere, including Egypt, Syria, and Anatolia. As if all this was not enough, a breakaway Persian sect of the Fatimid Isma'ilis established itself in the mountains of northwest Syria around 1100 and, pursuing its own agenda, would go on to wreak havoc in the Holy Land among Muslims and Christians alike under the derogatory name of the Assassins (or *Hashishiyya* in Arabic, intended as a slander of its supposed use of hashish or marijuana to drug its adherents). Meanwhile, the attention of the Seljuq sultanate, described as the only power capable of arresting the Frankish advance, was focused very much to the east, in Iran and Iraq, not in Syria and Palestine. There truly could have been no more auspicious time for the Franks to invade the Holy Land than in 1096, and it was probably not mere coincidence that they did so.[73] Indeed, al-Sulami observed that, at the very least, crusaders took advantage of Muslim disunity once they encountered it in the Holy Land in order to extend their conquests beyond what they had originally planned.[74] While it may be too much to expect the courts of Europe to be conversant with the intimate internal affairs of the Middle East, this was certainly not beyond the ken of Constantinople, whose rulers still laid claim to territories in northern Syria and who maintained diplomatic relations with their Fatimid counterparts in Cairo.[75] If this interpretation is correct, then Byzantium played a key role as the nexus between Islam and the West, even as it was left behind in the victorious march of the First Crusade.[76]

Muslim authors did not so much debate the motivations of European crusaders as offer differing explanations for why they came.[77] Most obviously, the crusaders were seen as motivated by greed for conquest, an explanation favored by the well-known twelfth-century memoirist, Usama ibn Munqidh, and which he shared with contemporary Byzantine observers of the Franks. Other explanations, favored by al-'Azimi and the Syrian poet, Ibn al-Khayyat, were that the First Crusade was an act of revenge for Muslim obstruction of Christian pilgrims, or that the crusaders were simply out to destroy Islam, having a penchant for "evil-doing" and "injustice".[78]

Perhaps the most perceptive observer was al-Sulami, whose analysis of why the Franks came to the East has been described as being the "most accurate" out of all the other explanations of his contemporaries. In his *Kitab al-Jihad* (Book of the Holy War), al-Sulami recognized that the crusaders were focused on Jerusalem, whose conquest was their "dearest wish," and that they were waging their own version of *jihad* or religious war equivalent to that of the Muslims. But al-Sulami's insights didn't exclude him endorsing other explanations, such as that the crusaders were greedy for territory or out to destroy Islam, which were later taken up by other writers. [79]

Nonetheless, al-Sulami was practically the only Muslim to acknowledge that the crusaders had a religious motivation behind their crusade and that their presence in the Holy Land was intended to be permanent.[80] Clearly, al-Sulami was taking a risk here, as he seemed to give the crusaders a legitimate reason to launch their invasion of Islamic lands and to have a long-term stake in their conquests. One possible explanation as to why he took this risk was that he became privy to information that other authors did not have, such as from a Frankish prisoner of war. In this scenario, al-Sulami was simply being more accurate than other writers. Another, and frankly more likely, explanation is that al-Sulami was willing to boldly go where no other Muslim would, because this suited the propaganda purposes of his work.[81] Al-Sulami's main objective was to cajole and browbeat his Muslim listeners—specifically, the "politico-military classes" charged with defending the lands of the faithful—into setting aside their differences and uniting in the cause of *jihad* in order to expel the crusader presence. Portraying the crusaders as inspired by a *jihad* comparable to their own may have been part of his strategy to shake Muslims out of their slumber and grasp the urgency of the situation facing them in the Levant. If anything, al-Sulami exaggerated the crusader threat, depicting the Franks as both more coordinated in their attacks on Moorish Spain and Palestine, and more opportunistically aware of Muslim disunity, than they probably were.[82] Yet al-Sulami deflected any potential criticism of such a portrayal of the enemy by presenting the crusaders as instruments of God's design: sent both to chastise Muslims for their "sluggish" prosecution of *jihad*, and to present them the opportunity of fulfilling a *hadith* prophecy, whereby the Muslims would lose Jerusalem for a time, only to reconquer it and go on to conquer Constantinople, the long-coveted capital of Christendom in the East.[83]

Over a century later, the Mosuli historian, Ibn al-Athir, likewise noted that the first crusaders waged their own version of *jihad* and that their true goal was conquering Jerusalem, not coming to the aid of the Byzantines.[84] However, al-Athir refused to acknowledge that the Christians waged a true *jihad*; rather, theirs had more to do with "political maneuvering" and a greedy desire for material gain than with a sincere religious motivation. In this regard, al-Athir invented a set-piece, wherein a fictional Western king, Baldwin, was distracted from conquering North Africa by the Norman king of Sicily, Roger II, who proposed Jerusalem as a consolation prize. This also gave al-Athir an opportunity to entertain and titillate his Muslim listeners, namely, by having Roger reject his courtiers' advice to aid Baldwin when he "raised his leg and gave a loud fart".[85] Much like Usama's memoirs,[86] al-Athir's anecdote aimed to reinforce pre-existing Muslim stereotypes of the Franks as rude and crude Westerners, whose culture was far inferior to that of the East.

In addition, al-Athir followed other Muslim authors in giving more credit to Muslim failings—specifically, their lack of unity—than to crusader abilities as an explanation for Christian victories. In this case, al-Athir blamed the religious schism between the Fatimid Shi'ites of Egypt and the Sunni Turks of Syria. He speculated, for example, that the Fatimids actually invited the Franks to invade because "they saw the strength and power of the Seljuq state, that it had gained control of Syrian lands as far as Gaza, leaving no buffer state between the Seljuqs and Egypt to protect them".[87] Some modern scholars dismiss al-Athir's explanation as a "slur" against the Fatimids, an opportunity to score a propaganda coup against the Shi'ite rivals to his Sunni masters in Mosul. But another interpretation is that al-Althir was fundamentally correct: The Fatimids did seek to make common cause with the Franks, perhaps using the Byzantines as intermediaries, and seized Jerusalem in 1098 from the Seljuqs in the expectation that the crusaders would let them keep their spoils. But if this is so, then the Fatimids badly misjudged their would-be allies.[88] Another point of debate is whether al-Athir was correct in seeing the First Crusade as part of a broader front embracing Spain, North Africa, and Italy, where the Christians were currently seeking, or had done so in the recent past, to dislodge a Muslim presence. Either al-Athir was remarkably perceptive about the geopolitical scope of the crusades, or else he was overreaching in drawing connections between discrete events.[89]

One could say that, for all their prescient insights into their own failings and shortcomings, the Muslim authors writing about the First Crusade, with perhaps the exception of al-Sulami, fatally underestimated and denigrated their Frankish foe.[90] Not only did they fail to appreciate the sincere religious motivations underlying the Frankish cause, but Muslim authors also displayed a singular lack of curiosity about the superior Frankish navy, siege technology, fortification construction, and military formation and equipment, all of which played significant roles in the crusaders' success.[91] It is as if there was a stubborn determination not to give the Westerners any credit for fear of endangering Islam's overweening sense of superiority.[92]

On the other hand, one also could say that Muslims—at least those among the politico-military elite—were not overly exercised about the Frankish intrusion into Palestine, viewing the invaders simply as one more power to negotiate and make alliances with in the rather byzantine politics of the eastern Mediterranean.[93] This can be seen in the failure of the Seljuq "counter-crusade" of 1110–15, when local Muslim emirs preferred to make common cause with Christian crusaders than answer the call to *jihad* of Sultan Muhammad of Baghdad (r. 1105–18). In the end, political considerations trumped the religious scruples indulged in by al-Sulami and other authors.[94] It was not until the latter half of the twelfth century that al-Sulami's call for a revival of *jihad* ideology that could unite the Islamic world was, according to their contemporary biographers, taken up by Nūr al-Dīn, ruler of Aleppo and Damascus (1146–74) and Saladin, sultan of Egypt and Syria (1174–93), who were the banes of, respectively, the Second and Third Crusades.[95] But among ordinary Muslims, popular resistance to the Franks had been taking place from the very beginning of the crusades and took many forms, both active and passive; one can certainly consider such activities as part of the "counter-crusade" movement and to have demonstrated popular support for jihad.[96] Meanwhile, the crusaders had fully insinuated themselves into the local power politics, and even into some of the cultural observances, of the Holy Land, from which they proved stubbornly hard to dislodge.

The later crusades

It was perhaps inevitable that later crusades could never match the intensity of religious motivation and the miraculous success (from the Christian point of view) of the first one.[97] But later crusades did see a revival of fortunes in both Islamic jihad and Muslim political unity, and they also brought about at least an expansion of crusading activity and participation in the West, as well as a regularization of crusade preaching and logistics. It was during the Second Crusade, which was called in 1145 in response to the fall of the crusading state of Edessa to the Muslim ruler of Mosul and Aleppo, Imad al-Din Zengi (r. 1127–46), that we see the first papal bull issued that laid out the standard crusading privileges that were to be granted in all subsequent crusades, as well as the first participation by European monarchs, namely Louis VII of France (r. 1137–80) and Conrad III of Germany (r. 1138–52), which was also to become a regular feature of later crusades.[98] Moreover, the Second Crusade was perhaps originally conceived as a war against Muslims and pagans to be fought on a broad front that went far beyond Syria: Other theaters of operation included the Baltic, Spain, and Portugal.[99] But the failure of the Second Crusade to recapture Edessa, or, for that matter, to capture its new target of Damascus, had political and spiritual ramifications for the papacy and the cause of crusading that some regard as a turning point.[100]

On the Muslim side, the Second Crusade's diversion to Damascus, formerly an ally of the Latin kingdom of Jerusalem, was also a turning point, in this case in the cause of jihad and the "counter-crusade" against the infidel, which had been kept alive by scholars such as Ibn 'Asakir in his Forty Hadiths.[101] In addition, many Islamic holy men were in the vanguard of the defense of Damascus and became its martyrs, while Nūr al-Dīn, younger son and heir of Zengi, became the new mujahid or jihad champion and, by the time of his death in 1174, was well on his way to uniting all of Muslim Syria under his rule.[102] However, according to Ibn al-Athir, the ruler of Damascus, Mu'īn al-Dīn, not only sought alliances with fellow Muslims like Nūr al-Dīn in order to defend against the Second Crusade, but he also made common cause with native Franks, seeking to drive a wedge between them and new crusader arrivals, such as Conrad III, who was allegedly persuaded to abandon his siege of Damascus in exchange for Banyas. This shows that Muslims were becoming more familiar with the Frankish presence, cultivating alliances and a detailed knowledge of their internal politics.[103] After the Second Crusade, Nūr al-Dīn cemented his influence and ultimate control over Damascus, while both the Franks and Muslims shifted their focus to Egypt, where the Fatimid state was in collapse.[104]

To this day, there is considerable debate over Nūr al-Dīn's legacy. Traditionally, Nūr al-Dīn has been seen as a genuine champion of *jihad* and of Sunni Islam, as evidenced by his personal leadership of his armies, his personal alliance with religious scholars, and his patronage of *madrasas* (legal and preaching colleges), *maristans* (hospitals), mosques, and other religious buildings and institutions. Numerous architectural inscriptions attest to Nūr al-Dīn's deliberate cultivation of this image, and a *minbar* (preaching pulpit) he commissioned for the Al-Aqsa mosque in Jerusalem indicates that his ultimate aim was to capture this third most important city for Islam, which became the lifetime achievement of Saladin.[105] But other, mostly Western, scholars take a more critical view of Nūr al-Dīn, seeing many of his actions as mere propaganda and politically motivated, as evidenced by his willingness to attack fellow Muslims in order to consolidate his rule and achieve a unified front facing the crusaders. It may well be that, in the eyes of Nūr al-Dīn himself and of other contemporaries, the two motivations—religious and political— were seen as not incompatible but mutually reinforcing and justified.[106]

Of all the crusades, the Third Crusade of 1189–92 is perhaps the most famous, owing to the participation of the towering figures of Richard the Lionheart, king of England (1189–99), and Saladin, sultan of Egypt and Syria (1174–93).[107] Although the Third Crusade may represent the height of the crusading movement in the West, it represents a low point in the fortunes of the Latin crusading states in Palestine. Indeed, the reason the crusade was called at all was because of the disastrous defeat for the Latins at the battle of the Horns of Hattin on July 4, 1187, when the kingdom of Jerusalem not only lost its army but also most of its garrison forces that had been conscripted in order to man the army.[108] As a consequence, Saladin was able to go on to conquer Jerusalem as well as nearly all the important cities in the crusading states, with almost the sole exception of Tyre. This situation was the culmination of a reversal of fortunes compared to just half a century earlier, with the Latin leadership now bitterly divided between rival candidates for the throne of Jerusalem, and the Muslims now united and highly motivated behind their leader, Saladin, and motivated by a rejuvenated *jihad* program that encompassed both Sunni adherents in Syria and Shi'ite believers in Egypt.

Like all the other crusades, there is a Christian and a Muslim side to the Third Crusade, but here the Muslim point of view is greatly enriched by an abundance of Arab sources, particularly biographies of Saladin written by contemporaries who knew him personally, such as his army judge, Bahā' al-Dīn, and his private secretary, Imad al-Dīn. Saladin is the pivotal figure of the Third Crusade, as he is the one who set it in motion, was its target, and had the most at stake in its outcome. There is much debate over Saladin's true motivations, not only during the Third Crusade but throughout his career. While his contemporary biographers were most anxious to portray him as a true *mujahid*, modern revisionist scholars (as well as some Muslim contemporaries) note that he came to the cause of *jihad*, particularly that of liberating Jerusalem and expelling the Frankish presence in Palestine, rather late. Up until 1185, when he fell victim to a serious illness that contemporaries say had a transformative effect on his religious outlook, the evidence suggests that Saladin pursued a ruthlessly political agenda of consolidating his dynastic power base in Syria and Egypt against rival Muslims, while being content to make truces with the Franks. If one were being less cynical about Saladin's motives, one could say that his political strategy was simply a tool in order to accomplish the *jihad* goal: Saladin did what was necessary in order to unite Muslims and field the massive army with rotating units that had to remain in the field for months at a time. And even though Saladin remains to this day a potent symbol of Arab unity and resistance to foreign incursions—Gamal Abdul Nasser of Egypt, Saddam Hussein of Iraq, and Hafez al-Assad of Syria all cultivated leadership cults identified with him—there remains an ambivalence towards Saladin among some Muslims, particularly Shi'ites, who hold him responsible for the fall of Fatimid rule in Egypt in 1171.[109]

Saladin has had almost equal significance for Westerners. Even though contemporary Latin sources were hostile, Saladin quickly acquired among Christians a reputation as a chivalrous, generous, and tolerant leader, so much so that he served as a model for princes in the West.[110] By the thirteenth and fourteenth centuries, Saladin's praises were being sung by German minnesingers and by early Renaissance authors such as Dante and Boccaccio, and it was rumored that in his youth he was inducted into an order of chivalry and knighted by a Christian nobleman from the kingdom of Jerusalem.[111] Saladin's Muslim biographers also emphasized his benevolent qualities, although for them these came second to the need to establish his reputation as a religious leader on a par with Nūr al-Dīn, Saladin's predecessor as ruler of Syria. There is ample evidence that Saladin's gallant reputation was deserved. His release from captivity of the Christian inhabitants of Jerusalem upon his conquest of the city in 1187 is but the most famous example. But one also should emphasize that this gallantry was in accordance with medieval standards, not modern ones: Saladin's biographers noted that 16,000 Jerusalemites were still unable to ransom themselves and so were enslaved, while Saladin personally executed his prisoner from Hattin, Reynald de Châtillon, and ordered the execution of all 200 Templars and Hospitallers captured in the battle.[112]

Nonetheless, Saladin's chivalry was reputed among Christians as all the greater precisely because they held the religion of Islam in such low esteem.[113] Thus, Saladin was the great exception, the "noble heathen" who was the perfect knight because he was a closet Christian instead of the devoted Muslim his Arab biographers so assiduously portrayed him as.[114] Once again, this exposes medieval Christians' woeful ignorance of Islam, which contains express commands in the Qu'ran to show tolerance towards resident Christians and Jews (*dhimmis*), to not compel men of other faiths to convert, to honor treaties made with the enemy, to be generous in the giving of alms, etc. Yet even to this day, Saladin is celebrated in the West as a symbol of the honorable Muslim to whom it is okay to lose once in a while, and who will play by the rules of civilized behavior. From the West's point of view, it was Western scholars who in the eighteenth century undertook the first serious, academic studies of Saladin, using Latin translations of his Arab biographies, while in the Muslim world comparable works on Saladin were not produced until 1920. Allegedly, it was also Westerners like Wilhelm II of Germany (r. 1888–1918) who re-introduced Saladin to the popular consciousness of the Middle East, largely as an act of self-aggrandizement. Wilhelm, for example, styled himself Saladin's successor as "emperor of all the Arabs," much to the chagrin of the Ottoman Turkish sultan, Abdulhamid II (r. 1876–1909), who saw himself as the "politico-spiritual leader" of a pan-Islamic movement and as a kind of "caliph" of all Sunni Muslims.[115] But this view that ascribes European responsibility for "rediscovering" Saladin can be contested, especially from an Islamic perspective. Saladin was never forgotten in the Middle East: His memory was kept alive in works such as the seventeenth century poem by Shaykh Muhammad al-'Alami, who portrayed his son, 'Abd al-Samad, the new administrator of the Salahiyya Khanqah, which included Jerusalem, as "a new Saladin ... in a new age".[116] Nonetheless, Kaiser Wilhelm did view Saladin differently from Muslims, as an almost purely secular figure and as an exemplar of core Western values. Thus, when Wilhelm paid a state visit to Saladin's tomb in Damascus in 1898, he extolled Saladin as "a knight without fear or blemish, who often had to instruct his opponents in the art of chivalry". These days, however, it is not so clear that what the West values most about Saladin is at all the same as how he is viewed in his very homeland in the Middle East.[117]

The Fourth Crusade of 1202–4 is perhaps the least popular among crusade historians, largely because of its perceived "perversion" of crusading ideals and its "disastrous" and "criminal" results, namely, the sack of Constantinople.[118] The Fourth Crusade marks the first time that an army that took the cross dared attack fellow Christians, first the Hungarian city of Zara in November 1202, and then the Greek Orthodox capitol city of Constantinople in July 1203 and April 1204. Nonetheless, some would argue that Constantinople was still a legitimate target of crusade: The Greeks had a long-standing history of hostility and perceived obstructionism towards the Latins; Constantinople was of strategic significance for expeditions to the East; and Constantinople was a city of great religious significance and attraction for Christian pilgrims, chiefly in the form of its many relics.[119] Historians of Byzantium, however, argue that Greek relations with the Latins were complex and that the crusaders would have had no preordained attitudes towards Constantinople.[120]

Without getting too much into the convoluted and "insoluble" reasons for the diversion to Constantinople,[121] suffice it to say that from the very start, the Fourth Crusade was overwhelmed by financial necessity. The simple fact that the crusading barons overestimated the number of men likely to take ship for the journey (33,500), when in fact only a third actually showed up at the port of embarkation in Venice (11,000), resulted in a debt to the tune of 34,000 silver marks that was owed the Venetians who had arranged a specially-constructed fleet to transport the crusaders. Diversions to Zara (a former colony of Venice) and Constantinople were undertaken, not without objections from some members of the army, because by this means the crusaders hoped to postpone or pay off their debt to the Venetians, who accompanied them perhaps as surety for payment.

Nonetheless, some would argue that the crusaders, including the Venetians, were still inspired by sincere religious motivations. From a contemporary point of view, the miraculous conquest of such a defensible city was the work of God, while afterwards many crusaders still went on to Egypt and Palestine in fulfillment of their vows.[122]

Although this aspect has received considerably less attention in histories, it does seem that from the very beginning of the Fourth Crusade, the leaders planned to sail not directly to Palestine, but rather to Egypt in order to attack the center of Ayyubid power there, perceiving this as the best way to re-conquer Jerusalem. This was not an entirely new strategy, as Egypt had long been a target of the kings of Jerusalem going back to King Baldwin I (r. 1100–18), who died on campaign there and was embalmed in true Egyptian fashion for the return journey home, and Richard the Lionheart also envisioned an attack on Egypt during the Third Crusade. But the Fourth Crusade set a precedent that, despite being aborted, was to form the blueprint for the strategy of nearly all subsequent crusades.[123]

There are many possible perspectives on the Fourth Crusade, which even in its own time was controversial.[124] Pope Innocent III (r. 1198–1216) staked much of the authority and prestige of his papacy on the crusade, which he was determined to see through to its completion, whatever that may have been. Much debate focuses on the extent of his role in the diversion of the crusade to Constantinople. While most historians are not prepared to absolve Innocent of any blame for the diversion, they are divided as to how much responsibility should be laid at his door. Equally intriguing is how much control Innocent ever really had over events as they unfolded. The forcible reunion of the Greek and Latin churches was perhaps his only consolation for an enterprise that strayed far from his original aims.[125]

Then there were the "magnates" or leading nobles of the Fourth Crusade, whose viewpoint was best presented in Geoffrey of Villehardouin's *Chronicle*.[126] They seemed to have operated from a position of expediency, that the overarching goal of Jerusalem could be sacrificed to more immediate concerns, such as fulfillment of their contract with Venice. Meanwhile, the point of view of crusaders who departed directly for the Holy Land from other ports, whom Villehardouin roundly condemned as trying to sabotage the entire enterprise, remained unrepresented.[127] Villehardouin's focus on the high diplomacy of the crusade contrasts with the more mundane perspective of the ordinary foot-soldiers, as presented in the chronicle of Robert of Clari.[128] Then there were the Venetians, who were often portrayed, particularly by the Greeks, as the conniving villains of the Fourth Crusade, led by their doge, Enrico Dandalo (r. 1192–1205), but who were depicted in their own chronicles as playing a heroic and central role, and who perhaps were the most autonomous actors in the crusade.[129]

The Greeks could be said to have been fatally undermined by their own divisions, and by their overconfidence in the formidable defenses of their triple walls, which nonetheless proved only as strong as the courage and willingness of the defenders who manned them.[130] The Latin takeover of the Byzantine Empire, which lasted barely half a century, could be said to have fatally weakened the Greeks even after their restoration in 1261, thus paving the way for Constantinople's second, final fall to the Ottoman Turks in 1453. Meanwhile, the Latin's three-day sack of the city in 1204, albeit exaggerated by both Greek and Latin sources, opened an irreparable rift between Orthodox believers and Catholics (whose relationship was already strained by the experience of previous crusades and by the schism of 1054) that persists to the present day and which was hardly helped by a forced, temporary union of the two churches through the appointment of a Latin patriarch in Constantinople. From the Greek point of view, the sack of the city in 1204 and the forced union with Rome were never forgiven and represented a turning point from simple "mistrust and dislike" of the Latins to "open hatred". Even after the Greek recovery of Constantinople in 1261, alliances between the Greeks and Latins in the face of the Turkish threat, even on the very eve of the Ottoman conquest of the capital in 1453, were precluded by an absolute refusal of the Greek populace, both religious and lay, to countenance another forced union with the Roman Church, which the emperors regarded as mere political expediency.[131]

From the Muslim perspective, the capture of Constantinople by the crusaders was not nearly so important as the arrival of remnants of the army in Acre, who proceeded to raid enemy territory. This forced concessions from al-Adil, the hard-pressed sultan of Egypt (r. 1200–18), which arguably could be presented as a success for the original focus of the crusade in Palestine and Egypt, although Muslim chroniclers hardly admitted the fact. This was an aspect of the Fourth Crusade that was barely mentioned in Latin and Greek chronicles.[132]

The rest of the thirteenth century is a sordid tale of the last gasp of Latin possessions in Palestine, despite no less than four major crusades called in its defense. Nearly all of these, however, targeted Egypt and the Ayyubid sultanate of Saladin's descendants. Both the Fifth Crusade of 1218–21 and the Seventh Crusade of King Louis IX of France in 1249–54 enjoyed initial successes, such as the capture of Damietta, an important port city on the coast of the Nile Delta, but both eventually foundered and frittered away their gains to nothing. The Seventh Crusade, in particular, ended disastrously with the capture of the French king and his ignominious ransom, despite the fact that the enterprise was well financed, well organized, and generally well-led by Louis. Perhaps the most important issue from this crusade was the rise to prominence of the Mamluk commander, Baybars, who was to go on to topple the Ayyubid dynasty of Egypt and expel the crusader presence in Palestine by 1291. The Sixth Crusade of Emperor Frederick II of 1228–29 was an anomaly, a bloodless return of Jerusalem to Christian control that had been negotiated by Frederick with the Ayyubid sultan, al-Kamil (r. 1218–38), by the terms of a ten-year treaty; nonetheless, the truce was highly unpopular among both native Christians and Muslims. What may look to modern eyes as enlightened policy was viewed as a betrayal by contemporaries, although some loyal to Frederick blamed the papacy for sapping the morale of crusaders by excommunicating the emperor just as he was about to embark on crusade. It all ended with the "unedifying spectacle" of a papal army bearing the keys of St. Peter fighting Frederick's crusading army bearing the cross for control of southern Italy. The Eighth Crusade of St. Louis in 1270 was an aborted affair abruptly cut short by the king's death in Tunis.[133]

As "pluralist" historians now like to emphasize, the idea and importance of crusading by no means ended with the fall of Acre in 1291 to the Mamluks.[134] Particularly under Baybars (r. 1260–77), the Mamluks pursued a policy of complete extermination of the Latin presence in Palestine, largely because of their concerns that the West might make common cause with the even graver threat posed by the Mongols from the East. [135] As crusading entered its post-Palestine era, enthusiasm was kept alive by alternative theaters in Spain and Prussia, by strategic treatises such as the *De Acquisitione Terrae Sanctae* (Concerning the Acquisition of the Holy Land) of 1309 by Raymond Lull, and, above all, by papal taxation of the Church, which ensured a steady supply of funds for various enterprises. Despite setbacks such as the Hundred Years War between England and France (1337–1453), the Black Death (1346–53), and the Great Schism in the papacy (1378–1417), the focus on crusading was revived by the new threat on Europe's doorstep posed by the Ottoman Turkish Empire. While land campaigns against the Turks often met with defeat, such as the Nicopolis fiasco of 1396, naval operations in the eastern Mediterranean met with much greater success, culminating in the crusaders' victory at Lepanto in 1571. Meanwhile, the Protestant Reformation could be said to have dealt a blow to further crusades by rending the unity of Christendom, but historians still debate whether crusading went into terminal decline at this stage.[136]

Meanwhile, much of the wind was taken out of the sails of the annual *Reisen*, or Prussian Crusades led by the Teutonic knights against Lithuanian pagans, with the conversion of the Lithuanian grand duke, Jagiełło, in 1386 (who at the same time married Queen Jadwiga to become King Władisław II of Poland) and with the subsequent defeat of the Teutonic knights by a combined Lithuanian-Polish army at Tannenberg in 1410. The Spanish national *Reconquista* or crusade crowned its victories with a ten-year war against the last Moorish state on the peninsula, the emirate of Granada, which capitulated to King Ferdinand (r. 1479–1516) and Queen Isabella (r. 1474–1504) of a united Aragon and Castile in 1492. This, of course, paved the way for the western voyages of Christopher Columbus, who viewed his discovery of islands and inhabitants of what later turned out to be the New World as a continuation of a crusade to expand the territories of Christendom.[137] It could be said that the Reformation and the Enlightenment of the modern era finally killed off popular enthusiasm for, and participation in, crusading in the West, even if individual examples of crusade indulgences, preaching, and taxes can still be found.[138] That the spirit of crusading nonetheless could still live on even after all practical applications of holy war had long since died can be seen in the oath administered to inductees of the Knights of Columbus, a Roman Catholic fraternal organization founded in the United States in 1882. Brothers had to promise to "make and wage relentless war, secretly and openly, against all heretics, Protestants and Masons" until they were extirpated "from the face of the whole earth," sparing "neither age, sex or condition" of the victims, and using whatever methods at hand against them, including that they would "hang, burn, waste, boil, flay, strangle, and bury alive these infamous heretics, rip up the stomachs and wombs of the women, and crush their infants' heads against the walls in order to annihilate their execrable race".[139]

A reconquest of al-Andalus?

Just as "crusade" was not contemporary with the origins of the movement and has had a fraught history of meaning, so the "Reconquest" or *Reconquista*—referring to the 770 years of warfare between Spanish Christians and Muslims, or Moors— is mired in controversy and debate.[140] Reconquest is considered by most scholars to be a modern term, dating to the nineteenth century, to express a nationalist, Catholic identity for Spain as defined by its centuries-long conflict with Muslims, dating all the way back to the original Umayyad conquest of the Iberian peninsula in 711.[141] The flip side of this exalting of Reconquest was the banishment of al-Andalus from having anything to do with Spanish national identity. Spain's rich, and arguably superior, Moorish culture was not allowed to play its allotted role in the country's medieval history. This holds true even to this day in Spain's right-wing, conservative politics and religious agenda.[142]

Arguably, the wars in Spain did not acquire a "crusading character," in the sense that these were perceived as part of a broad-front religious or holy war against Islam, until the twelfth century. Up until then, historians argue, any conflicts in Spain between Christians and Moors should not really be considered part of a "Reconquest" so much as part of regional power struggles between local kings and emirs. More often than not, Christians allied with Moors against their co-religionists in order to advance their mutual strategic interests. The acceptance of Spain as a theater of crusade seems to have been due in no small part to outside influences, particularly from France.[143]

Perhaps the most famous figure from the Reconquest was Rodrigo Díaz de Vivar, better known as "El Cid," (c.1043–99). Basically a mercenary or soldier-for-hire (what later became known in fourteenth-century Italy as a *condottiere* or *capitanus*), El Cid became, from 1094, de facto ruler of Valencia on the eastern coast. For sheer fame, El Cid was equivalent to Saladin or Richard the Lionheart, who received his own cinematic treatment with *El Cid* (1961), starring Charlton Heston in the leading role. In his own time, El Cid was celebrated in a Latin prose work, the *Historia Roderici* (History of Rodrigo), written probably in the early twelfth century, shortly after the Cid's death. The *Historia* makes it clear that the Cid was his own man, raiding the Rioja region of the Christian kingdom of Castile in order to distract King Alfonso VI (r. 1072–1109) from a conquest of Valencia, and for a time faithfully serving the Muslim emir of Zaragoza, al-Mu'tamin (r. 1081–85), as the guardian of his *taifa* or territory. By contrast, contemporary Muslim accounts paint a portrait of the Cid as a ruthless conqueror and ruler of Valencia, conducting hit and run raids, levying oppressive taxes, and burning a man alive in order to discover the whereabouts of some hidden treasure.[144]

In the *Poema de Mio Cid* (Poem of My Cid), a Spanish verse epic written over a century after the Cid's death, the Cid emerged as a fully-fledged hero of the Reconquest, or crusade.[145] Here, the Cid was uncompromisingly Christian; supremely loyal to his king, Alfonso VI; and always fought against the Moors, never alongside them. This became the basis for the modern biography of the Cid by the Spanish philologist, Ramón Menéndez Pidal, in 1929.[146] Pidal, who rather uncritically accepted that the *Poema* preserved an authentic, contemporary oral tradition of the Cid that was then written down much later, purveyed the Cid as the great unifer of Spain and the soul of Spanish nationalism, in which the Reconquest was "a collective project of national liberation" from the Moorish yoke.[147] By the time of the Spanish Civil War (1936–39), the Cid was recruited as a fascist and Catholic revanchist figure by Generalísimo Francisco Franco, the *Caudillo* or leader of the Nationalist forces, in his *cruzada* to unify Spain, which he subsequently ruled until 1975.[148]

To this day, there are two contrasting views on the Reconquest in Spain. To right-wing conservatives, the Reconquest is to be celebrated or exalted as not only a nation-building or re-unification exercise, but also as one that purged Spain of its undesirable elements, namely, the Moors who threatened Spain's Catholic identity, now compounded by the threat of radical Islamic terrorism.[149] To liberals, the Reconquest is to be lamented, or at least critically re-examined, as an event that eventually deprived Spain of its rich cultural diversity and *convivencia*, or "coexistence," of different faiths (i.e., Christianity, Judaism, and Islam). This debate was born out of the evolving attitudes towards the crusades in medieval Spain as it was living through the Reconquest itself.

Crusades against Jews, Pagans, and fellow Christians

Even as the First Wave of the First Crusade departed in the spring of 1096 for the East, already the tremendous outpouring of religious enthusiasm occasioned by Pope Urban's sermon resulted in violence closer to home, in the form of bloody persecutions against several Jewish communities along the Rhine River in Germany, with the largest massacres allegedly taking place at Worms and Mainz, where a total of 2100 Jews died, according to one contemporary Hebrew chronicler, Rabbi Eliezer bar Nathan, in May of 1096. Traditionally, historians of the crusades have treated the Jewish massacres as either emblematic of the violent and "sinister" nature of the crusades themselves, or else as a "reprehensible aberration" from what was otherwise a heroic and glorified enterprise. More recently, historians have aimed for a more objective, and less moralizing, approach by accessing the Hebrew narratives that provide a view of the massacres from the victims' perspective, to balance out the Latin Christian accounts. Debate has instead focused on the crusaders' motivations for the massacres. Just as some works saw the crusade itself as motivated by greed or the desire for gain, one school of thought opted for a materialistic/economic motive—that the crusaders were look-ing to loot the Jews' wealth, or else targeted the Jews because they engaged in the sin of usury, or lending at interest. A less popular interpretation was that the Jews were caught up in the politics of the Investiture Controversy, namely, that because secular rulers such as the Holy Roman emperor, Henry IV (r. 1084–1105), protected the Jews, a movement inspired by the reform papacy naturally denied them such protection. Another interpretation plumbed for a spiritual explanation: that the crusaders aimed for a forcible conversion of the Jews in fulfillment of the prophecy of the end of days. But perhaps the most convincing explanation is one that encompasses a combination of motives to include looting, forcible conversion, and, above all, vengeance, in that the crusaders saw the massacres as revenge for the Jews' alleged role in the crucifixion of Christ, which paralleled their justification of the crusade itself as an act of revenge against Muslims' alleged persecution of Christians in the Holy Land.[150]

Both Jewish and Christian crusade narratives testified to the crusaders' stated desire to take vengeance upon a perceived enemy of Christ right here at home—the Jews, who were blamed for the crucifixion—by forcing them to convert or else exterminating them, although material motives, like the greedy appropriation of the Jews' wealth and possessions also undoubtedly played a role.[151] Thus, the enemy within, at the very heart of Europe, a definition that was gradually extended to fellow Christians themselves, was already a target from the very beginning of the crusades. But it is not the tragic interactions that Jews had with Christians—even though some Christians, such as the bishops of Speyer, Worms and Mainz as well as the burghers of Mainz, did try to shelter the Jews—that is the most heartrending aspect of these massacres. Rather, it is the Jews' slaughter of themselves—part of a ritualistic act of martyrdom known as *kiddush ha-Shem*, or "sanctification of the divine name"—that is the distinguishing feature of the crusaders' attacks upon the Jews, witnessed in both Hebrew and Christian accounts.

Kiddush ha-Shem, from the Jewish perspective, was a righteous confession of faith in the Hebrews' monotheistic belief in one god, as opposed to the trinitarian concept of the Christians, a point of view that the Jews shared with the Muslims. Even though homicide and suicide were forbidden under Talmudic law, martyrdom under conditions of duress, such as the threat of forced conversions, was allowed as a sacrificial offering to God in imitation of Abraham's intended sacrifice of Isaac on Mount Moriah (Genesis 22), among other biblical examples, some of which were actually quoted in support of the 1096 martyrs by the Hebrew chronicler, Solomon bar Samson.[152] Such horrific scenes of self-imposed slaughter, described by the Christian chronicler Albert of Aachen as well as by Hebrew authors like Samson, whereby fathers and mothers slit the throats of their sons and daughters, brother slew brother and sister slew sister, husbands and bridegrooms their wives and brides, teachers their students, deacons their scribes, and so on, certainly made an indelible impression upon the crusaders who witnessed them.[153] For some Jewish scholars, this was the start of the infamous blood libel accusations—that Jews supposedly kidnapped and tortured Christian children—

since Christians reasoned that, "If yearning for their redemption and our punishment led them to kill their own children, how can we expect them to behave toward our children?"[154] Many other historians also see the 1096 martyrdoms and massacres as the start of a long decline in the status and treatment of Jews, since it marks "the first major outbreak of anti-Jewish violence in medieval Christian Europe," that extends not just through the Middle Ages, but even down to the modern tragedy of the Holocaust.[155]

Hebrew chronicles of the First Crusade usually have been treated by most historians as straightforward, trustworthy narratives of the tragic events of 1096, since, even though they may have been written down during the twelfth century, a generation or two removed from the actual incidents in question, it was assumed that they were based on first-person, eyewitness accounts of survivors of the massacres whose testimony was preserved orally or in written form. Authenticity and factual accuracy were taken for granted because of the detailed descriptions of the massacres (especially by Solomon bar Samson, who provided by far the longest account compared to those by the "Mainz Anonymous" and Eliezar bar Nathan, complete with extended anecdotes of individual martyrs); because of the diversity of reactions recorded among both Jewish and Christian participants; and because of the close correspondence among the three accounts. (For example, the crusaders' speech justifying a detour to attack the Jews is nearly identical, word for word, in the accounts by Samson and Eliezar bar Nathan.) It also was assumed that the Hebrew First Crusade narratives evinced a new concern for accuracy in Jewish historical writing, because sometimes various outcomes were given for individual martyrs based on differing sources of information, which were cited in the chronicles, and because the narrators were alleged to have had a "reverence" for the martyrs' actions, in which these should be allowed to "speak for themselves".[156] In addition, all this presupposed a history of mutual hostility or distrust between the Jewish communities and their Christian counterparts, whereby the Jews preferred martyrdom at their own hands as an act of defiance towards their Christian persecutors, since the exact timing and manner of their deaths was of their own choosing, and since such public and dramatic spectacles advertized the Jews' absolute faith in their own religion and their extreme contempt for that of their rivals.[157] If it was any consolation to the Jews, such extreme demonstrations of the rectitude of their beliefs—even to the point of slaying their own children rather than allow them to be brought up in the religious confession of another—cannot help but have sown doubts in the minds of the Christian tormentors who drove them to such desperate measures.

However, it was only natural that the Hebrew chroniclers of the 1096 massacres had their own agenda and sought to integrate the First Crusade martyrdoms into the Hebrews' self-justifying view of history, particularly in terms of their relationship with the one god.[158] But a truly different and even radical re-interpretation of the Hebrew First Crusade chronicles has been taken up by the Israel-based scholar, Jeremy Cohen. Cohen wanted to argue that there was far greater interaction and empathy than previously assumed between Christians and the Ashkenazic Jewish community of Germany, something that was normally reserved only for the Sephardic Jews of Spain, who supposedly enjoyed a *convivencia* or peaceful "coexistence" with their Catholic counterparts on the peninsula.[159] But in order to soften the hard-line attitudes that the Ashkenazic Jews seem to have taken towards their Christian persecutors in the Hebrew First Crusade narratives— where Solomon bar Samson, for example, referred to Jesus Christ and the Virgin Mary as, respectively, the "bastard son of a menstruating and wanton mother"[160]— Cohen had to drastically alter the story-line of the Jewish martyrdoms. While not disputing the numbers of those massacred or indeed the fact that the massacres actually took place, Cohen argued that most of the victims prevaricated about converting to Christianity rather than immediately submitted to *kiddush ha-Shem*, as Solomon bar Samson says 1100 Jews did at Mainz. Using the methods of post-modernist literary criticism, Cohen "re-read" the Hebrew First Crusade narratives, especially some of Solomon bar Samson's anecdotes about the "martyrs," as mainly cultural insights into what the Ashkenazic community wished to collectively remember about the events of 1096, rather than as objective, veridical statements of what actually occurred.[161]

Perhaps the classic example in this regard is Samson's searing tale of "Mistress Rachel," a mother who sacrificed her two daughters and two sons, even after one of them, her youngest child, Aaron, hid under a box after witnessing the death of his elder brother, Isaac, and who was then drawn out by his feet to have his throat slit, after which Rachel greeted the crusaders with her four children gathered 'round her, "two children on one side and two on the other, beside her stomach, and they quivered beside her, until finally the enemy captured the chamber and found her there sitting and lamenting over them". For Cohen, Rachel became a symbolic, apocryphal figure rather than a real person, who evoked not only biblical figures from the Old Testament but also the Virgin Mary and Ecclesia, or Holy Mother Church, lamenting over the death of Jesus and receiving his sacrificial blood except that in Samson's account Mistress Rachel was herself sacrificed when the crusaders struck her down after seeing that she had no money up her sleeves and had slaughtered her own children. This is part of Cohen's wider point that both medieval Jews and Christians shared a common cultural appreciation for martyrdom and sacrifice, which was indeed central to the Christian faith in the form of Jesus and was embodied in the call to go on crusade and the crusaders' battle cry of "God wills it!" Other of Samson's stories received the same treatment: That of Isaac, the *parnas* or community warden of the Mainz Jews, who converted to Christianity but then repented, slaughtering his children and burning himself alive in the synagogue, was declared by Cohen to be too full of contradictions and ironic passages to be believable; meanwhile, that of Kalonymos, another *parnas* of Mainz, who led 53 Jews to take refuge in the bishop's wardrobe under his pro-tection, only embracing *kiddush ha-Shem* when informed by the bishop that they must convert or die, was pronounced to be a more accurate and realistic reflection of the "limbo of indecisiveness" that characterized the natural human reaction when faced with the ultimate crisis.[162]

The problem with Cohen's interpretation, as he himself readily admitted, is that it is based on pure speculation. Cohen's response, however, was to argue that it more realistically reflects the "different and ambivalent reactions" of the Jews who were attacked as well as their cultural context, whereby they were influenced by Christian and even crusading ideology, instead of springing ready-made from a "long dormant idealism". Only in this way, Cohen said, can we "narrow the distance between the *event of the compilation of the chronicle* and the *event of the persecution*," which naturally assumes that the two are far apart, or in other words, that the Hebrew First Crusade narratives are not true accounts of what happened.[163] In light of other heated debates over Jewish history, such as the Holocaust Denial controversy, this was quite a controversial position to take, but I would also argue that, in the end, it was an unnecessary innovation on Cohen's part when faced with the alleged "conundrums" of the Hebrew First Crusade chronicles. I think Cohen was surely right to say that Jews and Christians had some kind of interactions with each other on the eve of the First Crusade. But by the time that the Hebrew chronicles were written, the bitter disruption of the crusade massacres had occurred, which the chroniclers made clear were unprecedented, so that it is certainly a stretch to think that the Hebrew authors were consciously imitating Christian models when writing of the events, or that even at the time the martyrs themselves were doing so. Cohen asked us to believe that Solomon bar Samson was making up stories when writing of Mistress Rachel or Isaac, but telling the straight truth when writing of Kalonymos, when the simple answer might be that they all reflected the complexity of Jewish responses to the crusaders. If indeed Samson had an agenda, one would expect him to be more consistent: If his intent was to showcase the inflexible martyrdoms of the Jews when faced with the crusaders, then why include the wavering responses of Isaac and Kalonymos at all? If the generation that lived to tell the tale of the massacres had "survivors' guilt," and most Jews had indeed initially flirted with conversion, then would it not have been better from the point of view of assuaging that guilt to admit to this in the chronicles and keep the few, uncompromising hold-outs as examples to which the rest of the community could aspire?

But there is yet one more objection which Cohen has not considered, which is that during the Black Death of 1348–51, when Jewish pogroms stalked many Jewish communities in Germany on the basis of a spurious charge of poisoning wells in order to communicate the plague to Christians, Jews allegedly exhibited once again such self-sacrificing behaviors as marked the *kiddush ha-Shem* martyrdoms of 1096.[164] Only here, all these heroic acts were exclusively described by Christian chroniclers: Authors from France, Flanders, and Germany, including Jean de Venette, Jean le Bel, Heinrich of Herford, and Heinrich of Diessenhofen, universally reported that Jews went to their deaths in mass executions, where they were burnt alive at the stake, by processing to the flames, all the while "dancing," "singing," and otherwise "rejoicing," which Le Bel explained was their way of expressing that "the souls of those who were to die should go gladly in their firm faith in [winning] paradise".[165] Another German chronicler, Konrad of Megenberg, wrote that "sometimes in some places they shut themselves up in a house with the doors barred and, after setting the house on fire, they died by their own hands by slitting the throats of their children, along with their own".[166] Indeed, Diessenhofen told an anecdote that was remarkably similar to the story of Isaac in Samson's chronicle, in which a Jew from Constance called Terasson, who had accepted Christian baptism and even taken on the Christian name of Ulrich, later repented and shut himself and his family up in his house and set it on fire, crying out to the Christian onlookers as his dwelling burned down around him: "I have burnt my own house, so that I, along with my boys, may die a Jew, not a Christian!" And yet, Diessenhofen, a Christian, was completely mystified by the Jew's actions, attributing them to Terasson's desire to burn down the whole street of Mordergass, "paying these dwellings back like a rat in a bag [of grain], a fire in a pit, and a serpent in a bosom are accustomed to show to their hosts".[167] Are we to credit the testimony of Diessenhofen and not Samson, or of Samson and not Diessenhofen, or of neither? Rather, the fact that Jewish communities in nearly the same region of Germany but separated in time by two centuries and a half were said to have engaged in the same demonstrative martyrdoms argues for this being an ingrained and enduring part of their culture. Applying the principle of Occam's Razor, that the simplest solution is the best, it seems likely that the Hebrew First Crusade chroniclers were simply telling the truth about all the *kiddush ha-Shem* martyrdoms, the memory of which they undoubtedly felt obliged to preserve as best they could, and which the community of Mainz in particular would have girded themselves for as they heard of the fate of their brethren in Speyer and Worms in the weeks leading up to their own tragedy.[168]

Europe's crusades against its other internal enemies were no less ferocious as that against the Jews. In 1147, at the same time as the expedition to Syria was getting underway, a crusade against the pagan Wends or Slavs, who lived in present-day eastern Germany and the Baltic states, was also preached by the Cistercian monk, St. Bernard of Clairvaux.[169] This really could be considered a continuation of the brutal campaign of Charlemagne against the pagan Saxons of the eighth century, now taken up once again after an interlude of some three and a half centuries (during which Europe had been mostly preoccupied with the Vikings) and extended further east against a new enemy.[170] The Wends, like the Saxons before them, believed in a pantheon of gods worshipped in walled-off sacred groves that contained their temples. From the very beginning, the Baltic crusade was bedeviled by the conundrum of converting pagans by force or violence, which normally was judged inimical to Christianity's missionary ethos.[171] Even as St. Bernard was dissuading the crusaders from repeating the Jewish massacres of the First Crusade, on the grounds that Jews needed to be preserved to bear witness to the ultimate triumph of Christianity, he was nonetheless apparently merciless in his approach to the Wends, urging that "either their rite be destroyed [*deleatur*], or their people [*natio*]".[172] Moreover, Pope Eugenius promised the same indulgence to Baltic crusaders as to those who journeyed to the Holy Land.[173] But was Bernard to be taken literally? Friedrich Lotter argued that Bernard's exhortation should be taken to mean that the Wends' tribal communities or identity should be destroyed, not the people themselves, after which missionary work could more easily take place under German patronage.[174] But other scholars are inclined to take Bernard at his word.[175]

Even though the Baltic crusade of 1147 was a dismal failure, it set an important precedent that ensured regular campaigning for years to come. In 1202, Bishop Albert von Buxhövden of Riga founded the "Swordbrothers," whose ranks after their crushing defeat in 1236 at the battle of Saule in present-day Lithuania were folded into the military order of the Teutonic Knights (founded in c.1190 in Acre).[176] These early years of the Baltic crusades were marked by several features that differentiated them from regular crusading to the East. The Baltic crusades were primarily missionary in focus, aiming to convert the heathen, rather than kill them outright (especially as new settlers relied on them as a labor force); often the crusaders fought fellow Christians, as well as pagans; and, despite being called "pilgrims," crusaders to the Baltic had no Christian holy places to visit or "liberate". Added to this the fact that the Baltic theater was far from the main action in Palestine and that conquest and colonization seemed more of a motivating factor than religion, there always has been skepticism among some scholars as to whether the Baltic crusades qualified as true crusades at all, but rather as "missionary" or "border" wars.[177] On the other hand, if one adopts a pluralist or expansive definition of crusade as "a holy war fought against those perceived to be the external or internal foes of Christendom for the recovery of Christian property or in defense of the Church or Christian people," then the Baltic crusades certainly seem to qualify.[178]

Nonetheless, ambivalence towards the Baltic crusades was evident even in the Middle Ages. Christian chroniclers like Adam of Bremen noted how crusaders and Wends alike were "only intent on loot," while Bernard of Clairvaux himself testified to the material motives of crusaders by peremptorily forbidding them to make truces with the Wends "either for money or for tribute" until they were all converted or destroyed.[179] The fact that crusaders against the Wends did not believe in or had doubts about the righteousness of their enterprise and were at "cross purposes" owing to competing claims for land in the Baltic can go a long way to explaining why the crusade was such a failure.[180] Yet some scholars argue that the crusaders did indeed have a sincere religious motive to convert the heathen, in addition to acquiring land, as evidenced by the fact that church-men accompanied them on crusade.[181] Others, however, point out that no contemporary documentation exists that reveals a plan for mass conversion of the Wends.[182] Even such mass conversions as did occur, as celebrated by Adam of Bremen, were ephemeral and sacrificed depth for breadth. Assuming such conversions were forcibly achieved at the point of the sword, they could even be considered a violation of true Christian principles.[183] Not surprisingly, the Wends and Livonians came off as hardly more "Christian" after conversion, especially when compared with their German neighbors, while the heathens, despite their polytheism and idolatry, were able to achieve some accommodation with the predominant Christian culture and were at least admired for their bravery in battle.[184] In the later Middle Ages, the Teutonic Knights organized pagan crusades as annual *Reisen* (meaning, "to set out on a journey") in the manner of aristocratic hunting parties, hounding the Lithuanians who dwelled on the borders of the Baltic Sea, Poland, and Russia.[185] In modern times, historiography on the Baltic crusades has been heavily politicized by Nazi, Communist, and nationalist historians which, to some degree, continues to the present day.[186]

Crusades against fellow Christians have traditionally been viewed as perversions or distortions of the original ideals of crusading, but recent scholarship, especially with the advent of the pluralist school, has integrated the so-called "political" or "internal" crusades into the mainstream of crusading history.[187] These crusades are assumed to have begun with the political war waged by Pope Innocent III in 1199 against a German imperial official, Markward of Anweiler, who had invaded Sicily, and with the Albigensian Crusade beginning in 1209 against the so-called Cathar heretics in the south of France.[188] Yet, some historians would argue that the origins of Christian-on-Christian crusades go back even further, to the reform papacy of Gregory VII (r. 1073–85), when the pope and his allies, in an effort to enforce the peace and truce of God, proved more than willing to sanction violence and grant absolution to those who waged war against their political enemies and against "robber barons".[189] During the Albigensian Crusade, crusaders were promised the exact same indulgences and privileges as those fighting the Saracens in the Holy Land, and heresy was portrayed as an even graver threat to Christendom than Islam, since it struck at the Christian fabric from within, targeting the very heart of the Church, like a disease, and endangering the integrity of Christian souls, as well as their bodies. Yet contemporary critics of the Albigensian Crusade pointedly asked why such a just cause did not meet with immediate victory, and they also questioned the motives of its crusaders and whether it was not "siphoning off men and money needed for the Holy Land". If the papacy hoped that, by defeating heresy, it might redirect energies to the East in what had been a ripe recruiting ground for past crusades, then an unintended consequence of the Albigensian Crusade was the absorption of southern France by the French crown, thus arguably eviscerating the independent nobility that had traditionally manned the crusades.[190]

The Albigensian Crusade, which lasted until the Peace of Paris of 1229, was particularly brutal, as epitomized by the sack of Béziers on July 22, 1209, when the entire population was put to the sword. Allegedly, the papal legate, the Cistercian abbot of Cîteaux, Arnaud-Amaury, urged on the massacre on the grounds that the only way to distinguish between Catholic and Cathar in the city was to: "Kill them all! God will recognize his own".[191] Yet it could be argued that the Albigensian Crusade never really achieved its stated objective, which was to stamp out the Cathar heresy (if indeed this heresy ever existed); instead, this was only achieved by the long, dogged work of the Inquisition down into the early fourteenth century. Although evidence of skepticism and disillusionment can perhaps be detected in criticisms of crusading during the thirteenth century, this doesn't seem to have affected enthusiasm for and participation in the later crusades, and the response could very much depend on the perceived intent of the crusaders.[192] Indeed, Pope Gregory IX (r. 1227–41), the man who established the Inquisition, continued to expand crusading against fellow Christians by authorizing crusades during the 1230s against heretics in Germany, Bosnia, and Italy, granting the same plenary indulgences as to those campaigning in the East.[193] Ultimately, the most far-reaching impact of the expansion of crusading targets in later crusades was to expand the scope of what it meant to go on crusade, anticipating the modern Western definition of the term.

Notes

1 Niall Christie, *Muslims and Crusaders: Christianity's Wars in the Middle East, 1095–1382, from the Islamic Sources* (London: Routledge, 2014), p. 114.
2 Giles Constable, "The Historiography of the Crusades," in *The Crusades from the Perspective of Byzantium and the Muslim World*, eds. Angeliki E. Laiou and Roy Parviz Mottahedeh (Washington, DC.: Dumbarton Oaks, 2001), pp. 12–15; Giles Constable, *Crusaders and Crusading in the Twelfth Century* (Farnham, UK: Ashgate, 2008), pp. 18–22; Norman Housley, *Contesting the Crusades* (Oxford: Blackwell, 2006), pp. 2–13; Jean Flori, "Pour une redéfinition de la croisade," *Cahiers de civilization médiévale* 47 (2004):329–50; Jonathan Riley-Smith, "The Crusading Movement and Historians," in *The Oxford History of the Crusades*, ed. Jonathan Riley-Smith (Oxford: Oxford University Press, 1999), pp. 9–10; Jonathan Riley-Smith, *What were the Crusades?*, 3rd edn (Basingstoke, UK and New York: Palgrave Macmillan, 2002), pp. 1–8; Jonathan Phillips, *The Crusades, 1095–1204*, 2nd edn. (London: Routledge, 2014), pp 6–7; Helen J. Nicholson, "Introduction: Definition and Scope," in *Palgrave Advances in the Crusades* (Basingstoke, UK: Palgrave Macmillan, 2005), pp. 3–9; Jason T. Roche, "The Second Crusade: Main Debates and New Horizons," in *The Second Crusade: Holy War on the Periphery of Latin Christendom*, eds. Jason T. Roche and Janus Møller Jensen (Turnhout, Belgium: Brepols, 2015), pp. 25–26.
3 Jean Flori and Hans Eberhard Mayer are classified among the "traditionalist" crusade historians, while Jonathan Riley-Smith and Giles Constable are classed as "pluralists" (although Constable himself expressed some sympathy with the popularist approach). Housley concluded that a true definition of crusade that captured "what crusading meant to contemporaries" would include an amalgamation of each of the four definitions. See: Housley, *Contesting the Crusades*, pp. 18–23; Constable, *Crusaders and Crusading*, p. 19.
4 Rebecca Rist, *The Papacy and Crusading in Europe, 1198–1245* (London: Continuum, 2009).
5 The thirteenth century is generally seen as marking a "watershed" in crusade preaching, organization, and implementation, largely due to the influence and leadership of Pope Innocent III (r. 1198–1216). In line with the emergence of the actual term, "crusade," Christopher Tyerman has argued that no expeditions prior to the thirteenth century can be legitimately called crusades. However, in a more recent work, he seems to have changed his position and adopted the pluralist definition of crusades. See: Christopher J. Tyerman, *The Invention of the Crusades* (Toronto: University of Toronto Press, 1998), pp. 8–29; Christopher J. Tyerman, *Fighting for Christendom: Holy War and the Crusades* (Oxford: Oxford University Press, 2004), pp. 30–32; Housley, *Contesting the Crusades*, pp. 49–58; Phillips, *The Crusades*, pp. 7–8, 203–4.
6 Jonathan Riley-Smith, "Islam and the Crusades in History and Imagination, 8 November 1898–11 September 2001," *Crusades* 2 (2003):164.

7 Christie, *Muslims and Crusaders*, p. 114; Paul E. Chevedden, "The Islamic View and the Christian View of the Crusades: A New Synthesis," *History: The Journal of the Historical Association* 93 (2008):181. President Bush made his remarks in an address to a joint session of the U.S. Congress on September 20, 2001. The full quote was as follows: "This crusade, this war on terrorism, is going to take a while".

8 Riley-Smith, "Islam and the Crusades," pp. 165–66; Carole Hillenbrand, *The Crusades: Islamic Perspectives* (New York: Routledge, 2000), p. 602; Christie, *Muslims and Crusaders*, pp. 115–17, 163–66; Richard Bonney, *Jihad: From Qu'ran to bin Laden* (New York: Palgrave Macmillan, 2007), pp. 357–60; Chevedden, "Islamic View and the Christian View of the Crusades," pp. 181–82. The former leader of Al-Qaeda and the man held responsible for the September 11, 2001 terrorist attacks, Osama Bin Laden, was heavily influenced by a thirteenth to fourteenth century Islamic theologian, Ibn Taymiyya, who preached *jihad* not only against Western crusaders, but also against fellow Muslims deemed insufficiently committed to the global struggle against Islam's enemies.

9 Hillenbrand, *Crusades: Islamic Perspectives*, pp. 609–11.

10 Hillenbrand, *Crusades: Islamic Perspectives*, pp. 595–600; Christie, *Muslims and Crusaders*, p. 117.

11 Leading examples of this scholarship include: Christie, *Muslims and Crusaders*; Hillenbrand, *Crusades: Islamic Perspectives*; *Crusades from the Perspective of Byzantium*; Jonathan Riley-Smith, *The Crusades, Christianity, and Islam* (New York: Columbia University Press, 2008). However, Paul Chevedden argued that, even with the recovery and translation of Islamic sources, the Muslim perspective has still not been fully incorporated into crusade studies, no matter whether this perspective originated in the West or in the Islamic world. His main argument was that the crusades began not in 1095, with Pope Urban's sermon, but in 1060, with the Norman invasion of Muslim Sicily. See Chevedden, "Islamic View and the Christian View of the Crusades," pp. 182–200.

12 Yuval Noah Harari, "Eyewitnessing in Accounts of the First Crusade: the *Gesta Francorum* and Other Contemporary Narratives," *Crusades* 3 (2004):87–90. The anonymous author especially exhibited his bias in his imaginary account of a dialogue between Kerbogha, ruler of Mosul, and his mother, a sorceress, who predicted disaster for her son on the eve of the battle outside Antioch on June 28, 1098.

13 This is especially evident in chronicle accounts of the massacre in Jerusalem that ensued upon its capture by the crusaders on July 15, 1099. Even among contemporary Western observers, views and justifications of the massacre ranged from celebratory to horror-stricken, as recounted by Benjamin Z. Kedar, "The Jerusalem Massacre of July 1099 in the Western Historiography of the Crusades," *Crusades* 3 (2004):15–75. For general overviews of crusade historiography, see: Riley-Smith, "Crusading Movement and Historians," pp. 1–12; Constable, "Historiography of the Crusades," pp. 1–22; Constable, *Crusaders and Crusading*, pp. 3–43; Housley, *Contesting the Crusades*, pp. 1–23.

14 Helen J. Nicholson, "Muslim Reactions to the Crusades," in *Palgrave Advances in the Crusades*, pp. 281–82.

15 Steven Runciman, *A History of the Crusades*, 3 volumes (Cambridge: Cambridge University Press, 1951–54), 3:480; Riley-Smith, "Crusading Movement and Historians," p. 7. Runciman's view has also been endorsed by Geoffrey Barraclough and John Ward. See Constable, "Historiography of the Crusades," p. 3; Constable, *Crusaders and Crusading*, pp. 5–6.

16 Constable, *Crusaders and Crusading*, pp. 6–8.

17 Constable, *Crusaders and Crusading*, pp. 24–25.

18 This revised view of the crusades is most accessible in the following texts: Jonathan Riley-Smith, *The Crusades: A Short History* (New Haven: Yale University Press, 1987); Thomas F. Madden, *The New Concise History of the Crusades*, updated student edition (Lanham, MD.: Rowman and Littlefield, 2006); Housley, *Contesting the Crusades*; Rodney Stark, *God's Battalions: The Case for the Crusades* (New York: HarperCollins, 2009).

19 Constable denoted a "fourth period" of crusade historiography, the most recent and present one, when "there has been a growing division between scholarly and popular views of the crusades". See Constable, *Crusaders and Crusading*, p. 5.

20 Thomas Asbridge, *The Crusades: The Authoritative History of the War for the Holy Land* (New York: HarperCollins, 2010), pp. 26–29; Philip Slavin, "Crusaders in Crisis: Towards the Re-Assessment of the Origins and Nature of the 'People's Crusade' of 1095–1096," *Imago Temporis* 4 (2010):175–99; Constable, "Historiography of the Crusades," p. 18; Constable, *Crusaders and Crusading*, pp. 25–26; Jean Flori, "Ideology and Motivations in the First Crusade," in *Palgrave Advances in the Crusades*, pp. 15–36.

21 Riley-Smith, "Islam and the Crusades," pp. 151–52. According to Riley-Smith, the West's reintroduction of the crusades to Islamic consciousness dates to the well-publicized visit by Kaiser Wilhelm II of Germany to Jerusalem and other crusader sites in the Levant in 1898.

22 Riley-Smith, "Islam and the Crusades," pp. 160–67. Riley-Smith argued that Islam took away two lessons from Western presentations of crusade history. In the "critically romantic" approach, "barbarous, primitive and destructive crusaders" had appropriated the "civilized, liberal and modern-looking" values of Islam, which Muslims characterized as a kind of "rape" of their culture. In the "imperialistic" view, it was the crusaders who "brought enlightenment to a heathen world," which modern Muslims took as a sign that the West's continued assault upon the Arab world had to be resisted. Neither, of course, reflected well upon the West, in Arab eyes.

23 Diana Abouali, "Saladin's Legacy in the Middle East before the Nineteenth Century," *Crusades*, 10 (2011):178–82; Christie, *Muslims and Crusaders*, pp. 113–14; Paul M. Cobb, *The Race for Paradise: An Islamic History of the Crusades* (Oxford: Oxford University Press, 2014), pp. 277–78.

24 Riley-Smith, "Islam and the Crusades," p. 160.

25 Riley-Smith," Islam and the Crusades," pp. 159–60; Riley-Smith, *Crusades, Christianity, and Islam*, pp. 45–78; Constable, *Crusaders and Crusading*, pp. 28–29; Elizabeth Siberry, "Nineteenth-Century Perspectives of the First Crusade," in *The Experience of Crusading*, eds. Marcus Bull and Norman Housley, 2 vols. (Cambridge: Cambridge University Press, 2003), 1:281–93; Elizabeth Siberry, "Images of the Crusades in the Nineteenth and Twentieth Centuries," in *Oxford History of the Crusades*, pp. 363–84; Hillenbrand, *Crusades: Islamic Perspectives*, pp. 590–92; Stark, *God's Battalions*, pp. 172–73. For the portrayal of crusades as colonial enterprises in textbooks, see: Joshua Prawer, *The Latin Kingdom of Jerusalem: European Colonialism in the Middle Ages* (London: Weidenfeld and Nicolson, 1972); Joshua Prawer, "The Roots of Medieval Colonialism," in *The Meeting of Two Worlds: Cultural Exchange between East and West during the Period of the Crusades*, eds. Vladimir P. Goos and Christine Verzár Bornstein (Kalamazoo, MI.: Medieval Institute Publications, Western Michigan University, 1986), pp. 22–38; Wim Blockmans and Peter Hoppenbrouwers, *Introduction to Medieval Europe, 300–1550*, trans. Isola van den Hoven (London: Routledge, 2007), pp. 191–95; Nikolas Jaspert, *The Crusades*, trans. Phyllis G. Jestice (New York: Routledge, 2006), pp. 100–102; Barbara H. Rosenwein, *A Short History of the Middle Ages*, 4th edn. (Toronto: University of Toronto Press, 2014), pp. 170–73.

26 Housley, *Contesting the Crusades*, p. 24.

27 For texts that focus exclusively on the First Crusade, see: Peter Frankopan, *The First Crusade: The Call from the East* (Cambridge, MA.: Belknap Press of Harvard University Press, 2012); Thomas Asbridge, *The First Crusade: A New History* (Oxford: Oxford University Press, 2004); Jonathan Riley-Smith, *The First Crusaders, 1095–1131* (Cambridge: Cambridge University Press, 1997); *The First Crusade: Origins and Impact*, ed. Jonathan Phillips (Manchester, UK: Manchester University Press, 1997); John France, *Victory in the East: A Military History of the First Crusade* (Cambridge: Cambridge University Press, 1994); Jonathan Riley-Smith, *The First Crusade and the Idea of Crusading* (Philadelphia, PA.: University of Pennsylvania Press, 1986). A good collection of

primary sources on the First Crusade is available in *The First Crusade: The Chronicle of Fulcher of Chartres and Other Source Materials*, ed. Edward Peters (Philadelphia, PA.: University of Pennsylvania Press, 1971). For the crusades as rendered in popular culture, particularly on film, see: John Aberth, *A Knight at the Movies: Medieval History on Film* (New York: Routledge, 2003), pp. 63–147; Nickolas Haydock and Edward L. Risden, *Hollywood in the Holy Land: Essays on Film Depictions of the Crusades and Christian-Muslim Clashes* (Jefferson, NC.: Mcfarland, 2009).

28 The consensus opinion, that the origins of the First Crusade are to be found in Europe rather than in Byzantium, has been enunciated recently by: Housley, *Contesting the Crusades*, pp. 32–33, 36–37; Andrew Jotischky, "The Christians of Jerusalem, the Holy Sepulchre, and the Origins of the First Crusade," *Crusades*, 7 (2008):35. One may contrast especially Carl Erdmann's thesis in *The Origin of the Idea of Crusade*, trans. Marshall W. Baldwin and Walter Goffart (Princeton, NJ.: Princeton University Press, 1977), pp. 319–34 and 355–71, with H.E.J. Cowdrey, "Pope Urban II and the Idea of Crusade," *Studi Medievali*, 3rd ser. 36 (1995):721–42, reprinted in H.E.J. Cowdrey, *The Crusades and Latin Monasticism, 11th–12th Centuries* (Aldershot, UK: Ashgate, 1999). Nonetheless, a recent attempt to revive the importance of the appeal from Alexius for the origins of the First Crusade was made by Frankopan, *First Crusade*, pp. 13–100. It is likely that Alexius was shocked by the appearance of the First Crusade, when he was expecting merely mercenary aid. See Sakellariou, "Byzantine and Modern Greek Perceptions of the Crusades," pp. 246–48.

29 Sylvia Schein, *Gateway to the Heavenly City: Crusader Jerusalem and the Catholic West (1099–1187)* (Aldershot, UK: Ashgate, 2005), pp. 125–26; Jotischky, "Christians of Jerusalem," pp. 35–36.

30 Peter Frankopan, "Co-operation between Constantinople and Rome before the First Crusade: A Study of the Convergence of Interests in Croatia in the late Eleventh Century," *Crusades* 3 (2004):4–8.

31 Jotischky, "Christians of Jerusalem," p. 35; Phillips, *The Crusades*, pp 17–18.

32 Jonathan Riley-Smith, "The State of Mind of Crusaders to the East, 1095–1300," in *Oxford History of the Crusades*, pp. 78, 89.

33 Erdmann, *Origin of the Idea of Crusade*, pp. 333–34; Riley-Smith, *The First Crusade*, p. 30; John France, *The Crusades and the Expansion of Catholic Christendom, 1000–1714* (London: Routledge, 2005), pp. 34–44.

34 H.E.J. Cowdrey, "The Peace and Truce of God in the Eleventh Century," *Past and Present* 46 (1970):42–67; Georges Duby, "Laity and the Peace of God," in Georges Duby, *The Chivalrous Society*, trans. C. Postan (London: Edward Arnold, 1977), pp. 123–33; Jean Flori, "De la paix de Dieu à la croisade? Un réexamen," *Crusades* 2 (2003):1–23.

35 Jonathan Riley-Smith, "Crusading as an Act of Love," in *Crusades: The Essential Readings*, p. 33. For a good overview of each version of the sermon and their authors, see Penny J. Cole, *The Preaching of the Crusades to the Holy Land, 1095–1270* (Cambridge, MA: Medieval Academy of America, 1991), pp. 8–33; H.E.J. Cowdrey, "Pope Urban II's Preaching of the First Crusade," *History* 55 (1970):117–88.

36 Housley, *Contesting the Crusades*, pp. 27–29; Riley-Smith, *The First Crusade*, pp. 25–26, 30; France, *Crusades and the Expansion of Catholic Christendom*, pp. 34–51; Jean Flori, *Croisade et chevalerie XIe–XIIe siècles* (Paris-Bruxelles: De Boeck Université, 1998); Marcus Bull, *Knightly Piety and the Lay Response to the First Crusade: The Limousin and Gascony, c.970–c.1130* (Oxford: Clarendon Press, 1993), pp. 21–69; Erdmann, *Origin of the Idea of Crusade*, pp. 333–34. Housley also pointed to a chronological as well as geographical "disjuncture" between the peace and truce of God movements and Urban's preaching and recruitment on behalf of the First Crusade.

37 Tomaž Mastnak, *Crusading Peace: Christendom, the Muslim World, and Western Political Order* (Berkeley, CA.: University of California Press, 2002), pp. 154–66; James A. Brundage, "Crusades, Clerics and Violence: Reflections on a Canonical Theme," in

The Experience of Crusading, eds. Marcus Bull and Norman Housley, 2 vols. (Cambridge: Cambridge University Press, 2003), 1:147–56; Flori, "Ideology and Motivations," pp. 19–22.

38 H.E.J. Cowdrey, "Christianity and the Morality of Warfare during the First Century of Crusading," in *The Experience of Crusading*, 1:175–92; Norman Houseley, "Crusades against Christians: Their Origins and Early Development, c. 1000–1216," in *Crusade and Settlement: Papers read at the first conference of the Society for the Study of the Crusades and the Latin East and presented to R.C. Smail*, ed. P.W. Edbury (Cardiff: University College Cardiff Press, 1985), pp. 17–19; France, *Crusades and the Expansion of Catholic Christendom*, pp. 42–43; Riley-Smith, *Crusades, Christianity, and Islam*, pp. 29–44; Jean Flori, *La guerre sainte: La formation de l'idée de croisade dans l'Occident chrétien* (Paris: Aubier, 2009).

39 The idea of vengeance as a motivating factor was not just used for the First Crusade, but was widespread and even gained in significance throughout the twelfth century, although it did not always specify atrocities committed by Muslims against Christians in the Holy Land. See Susanna Throop, "Vengeance and the Crusades," *Crusades*, 5 (2006):21–38.

40 Jotischky, "Christians of Jerusalem," pp. 44–48.

41 Jotischky, "Christians of Jerusalem," p. 52.

42 Stark, *God's Battalions*, p. 92.

43 Joseph Drory, "Some Observations During a Visit to Palestine by Ibn al-'Arabī of Seville in 1092–1095," *Crusades* 3 (2004):101–24.

44 Hillenbrand, *Crusades: Islamic Perspectives*, p. 50.

45 Jotischky, "Christians of Jerusalem," pp. 35–57.

46 For the debate on numbers of those who went on the First Crusade, see: Housley, *Contesting the Crusades*, p. 39; Riley-Smith, *The Crusades: A Short History*, p. 11; John France, "Patronage and the Appeal of the First Crusade," in *First Crusade: Origins and Impact*, p. 6; France, *Victory in the East*, pp. 122–42.

47 This idea has been traced to an off-hand remark backed up with little evidence that was made by Georges Duby in *La Société aux XIe et XIIe siècles dans la region mâconnaise* (Paris: S.E.V.P.E.N., 1953), p. 435. See also: Jonathan Riley-Smith, "The Motives of the Earliest Crusaders and the Settlement of Latin Palestine, 1095–1100," *English Historical Review* 389 (1983):723; Hans Eberhard Mayer, *The Crusades* (Oxford: Oxford University Press, 1996), pp. 21–23.

48 Giles Constable, "Medieval Charters as a Source for the History of the Crusades," in *Crusade and Settlement*, pp. 73–89; Constable, *Crusaders and Crusading*, pp. 93–116; Riley-Smith, *The First Crusade*, pp. 35–49; Riley-Smith, *The First Crusaders*, pp. 15–22, 33–39, 83–105; Bull, *Knightly Piety*, pp. 250–81; Marcus Bull, "The Diplomatic of the First Crusade," in *First Crusade: Origins and Impact*, pp. 35–47; Nikolas Jaspert, "Eleventh-Century Pilgrimage from Catalonia to Jerusalem: New Sources on the Foundations of the First Crusade," *Crusades*, 14 (2015):1–47. Bull emphasized that the charter evidence for the First Crusade may be underrepresented, since some documents make no explicit mention of crusade, even when discussing evident preparations for departure or when the patrons were known crusaders.

49 Bull, *Knightly Piety*, pp. 258–74; Constable, *Crusaders and Crusading*. pp. 117–41.

50 Slavin, "Crusaders in Crisis," pp. 177–91; Riley-Smith, "State of Mind of Crusaders," p. 73.

51 For a detailed look at the composition of one crusade contingent, that led by Godfrey of Bouillon, see Alan V. Murray, "The Army of Godfrey of Bouillon: Structure and Dynamics of a Contingent on the First Crusade," *Revue Belge de Philologie et d'Histoire*, 70 (1992):301–29. See also Riley-Smith, "Motives of Earliest Crusaders," pp. 724–36.

52 Of course, there also were some important nobles who evidently refused to go on the First Crusade, such as Fulk IV, count of Anjou, and William IX, duke of Aquitaine. See: France, "Patronage and the Appeal of the First Crusade," pp. 9–10; Riley-Smith, "State of Mind of Crusaders," p. 81; Riley-Smith, *First Crusaders*, pp. 81–105; Housley, *Contesting the Crusades*, pp. 89–90.

53 Riley-Smith, "Motives of the Earliest Crusaders," pp. 723–24.

54 Riley-Smith, "Motives of the Earliest Crusaders," pp. 722–23. Materialistic motivations for the First Crusade continue to be emphasized by scholars like John France, who has viewed the knightly participants as a "grasping, aspirant group" operating within a "theatre of ambitions," in which they competed for patronage and experienced considerable social "fluidity" at all levels. Jean Flori also pointed out that, even if the first crusaders returned home poorer than when they set out, they could not have known that this would happen and probably hoped for something better when they first departed. See: France, "Patronage and the Appeal of the First Crusade," pp. 13–16; Flori, "Ideology and Motivations," pp. 28–29; Housley, *Contesting the Crusades*, pp. 90–91.

55 France, "Patronage and the Appeal of the First Crusade," p. 8; Flori, "Ideology and Motivations," p. 19; Housley, *Contesting the Crusades*, p. 81.

56 Constable, "Medieval Charters," pp. 73–89; Housley, *Contesting the Crusades*, pp. 29–30, 90–91; Riley-Smith, *The First Crusade*, pp. 35–49; Riley-Smith, *The First Crusaders*, pp. 15–22, 33–39, 83–105; Bull, *Knightly Piety*, pp. 250–81; Bull, "Views of Muslims and of Jerusalem," 1:13–38; Bull, "Diplomatic of the First Crusade," p. 47; Jaspert, "Eleventh-Century Pilgrimage," pp. 13–16, 30–31; Susan Edgington, "The First Crusade: reviewing the evidence," in *First Crusade: Origins and Impact*, pp. 58–59; France, *Crusades and the Expansion of Catholic Christendom*, pp. 52–60; Housley, *Contesting the Crusades*, pp. 75–98. Some medievalists still dispute the charter evidence on the grounds that individual motivations for any enterprise are complex and can never be fully ascertained. See, in particular, France, "Patronage and the Appeal of the First Crusade," pp. 5–17.

57 The most authoritative treatment of the Jerusalem massacre is Kedar's "Jerusalem Massacre," pp. 15–75.

58 Kedar, "Jerusalem Massacre," pp. 16–19.

59 Kedar, "Jerusalem Massacre," pp. 19–30.

60 Kedar, "Jerusalem Massacre," pp. 48, 63, 73–74; Christie, *Muslims and Crusaders*, pp. 127–28; Hillenbrand, *The Crusades: Islamic Perspectives*, pp. 63–68; Stark, *God's Battalions*, pp. 155–60.

61 Kedar, "Jerusalem Massacre," pp. 19–26.

62 Kedar, "Jerusalem Massacre," pp. 30–42.

63 Kedar, "Jerusalem Massacre," pp. 42–54.

64 Kedar, "Jerusalem Massacre," pp. 30, 67–73; Stark, *God's Battalions*, pp. 157–60; Asbridge, *The First Crusade*, pp. 274–75, 316–19.

65 Harari, "Eyewitnessing," pp. 85–91; Kedar, "Jerusalem Massacre," pp. 64–65; Edgington, "First Crusade," pp. 61–63.

66 Kedar, "Jerusalem Massacre," pp. 67–73. Perhaps the only incident that can compare in notoriety to the Jerusalem massacre is the cannibalism alleged to have been committed by crusaders when they took the north Syrian town of Ma'arrat al-Nu'man in December 1098, which was retailed by Fulcher of Chartres. But significantly, such lurid tales of cannibalism were omitted altogether by contemporary Muslim observers of the First Crusade, including Ibn al-'Adim, who was writing from nearly Aleppo and was in the best position to know about it. See Hillenbrand, *The Crusades: Islamic Perspectives*, pp. 59–63.

67 S. Goitein, "Contemporary Letters on the capture of Jerusalem," *Journal of Jewish Studies*, 3 (1952):162–77; Kedar, "Jerusalem Massacre," pp. 59–64.

68 Edgington, "First Crusade," p. 74; Carole Hillenbrand, "The First Crusade: the Muslim perspective," in *First Crusade: Origins and Impact*, pp. 130–31; Niall Christie, "Religious Campaign or War of Conquest? Muslim Views of the Motives of the First Crusade," in *Noble Ideals and Bloody Realities: Warfare in the Middle Ages*, eds. Niall Christie and Maya Yazigi (Leiden, Netherlands: Brill, 2006), pp. 65–66; Niall Christie, "Motivating Listeners in the *Kitab al-Jihad* of 'Ali ibn Tahir al-Sulami (d. 1106)," *Crusades*, 6 (2007):9–10.

69 Christie, *Muslims and Crusaders*, pp. 20–21.
70 Christie, "Religious Campaign," pp. 57–59, 63, 69; Hillenbrand, "First Crusade: the Muslim perspective," p. 131. For Muslim sources on the First Crusade in English translation, see: Christie, *Muslims and Crusaders*, pp. 127–35; *Arab Historians of the Crusades*, trans. Francesco Gabrieli and E.J. Costello (Berkeley, CA.: University of California Press, 1984).
71 Hillenbrand, "First Crusade: the Muslim perspective," pp. 131–34. This perspective also has been adopted by modern histories of the crusades. See, for example: Jaspert, *The Crusades*, pp. 72–73; Asbridge, *The Crusades*, pp. 20–29; Asbridge, *The First Crusade*, pp. 113–16; Robert Irwin, "Islam and the Crusades, 1096–1699," in *Oxford History of the Crusades*, pp. 213–18.
72 Hillenbrand, "First Crusade: the Muslim perspective," p. 132.
73 Hillenbrand, "First Crusade: the Muslim perspective," pp. 132–35.
74 Christie, "Motivating Listeners," p. 7; Christie, *Muslims and Crusaders*, p. 133.
75 Hillenbrand, *Crusades: Islamic Perspectives*, pp. 32–48. Muslim authors were generally more conversant and knowledgeable about the Byzantines, given that they were both closer and more often in conflict with Islam, to the point that they frequently "confused or conflated" them with European crusaders. See Christie, "Motivating Listeners," p. 10.
76 Ralph-Johannes Lilie, *Byzantium and the Crusader States, 1096–1204*, trans. J.C. Morris and Jean E. Ridings (Oxford: Clarendon Press, 1994).
77 Christie, "Religious Campaign," pp. 59–70; Christie, *Muslims and Crusaders*, pp. 21–24.
78 Christie, "Religious Campaign," pp. 59–63; Christie, *Muslims and Crusaders*, pp. 22, 130–31.
79 Christie, "Religious Campaign," pp. 63–64; Christie, *Muslims and Crusaders*, pp. 21–22; Irwin, "Islam and the Crusades," p. 220; Chevedden, "Islamic View and the Christian View of the Crusades," pp. 184–85. For a full text and translation of the *Kitab al-Jihad*, see: *The Book of the Jihad of 'Ali ibn Tahir al-Sulami (d. 1106): Text, Translation and Commentary*, trans. and ed. Niall Christie (London: Routledge, 2017); and Niall Christie and Deborah Gerish, *Preaching Holy War: Crusade and Jihad, 1095–1105* (London: Routledge, 2017).
80 Nikita Elisséeff, "The Reaction of the Syrian Muslims after the Foundation of the First Latin Kingdom of Jerusalem," in *Crusaders and Muslims in Twelfth-Century Syria*, ed. Maya Shatzmiller (Leiden, Netherlands: Brill, 1993), p. 163.
81 Christie, "Religious Campaign," pp. 66–67; Christie, *Muslims and Crusaders*, pp. 22–23.
82 Christie, "Motivating Listeners," pp. 4–8.
83 Christie, "Religious Campaign," pp. 64–67; Christie, "Motivating Listeners," pp. 8–13; Christie, *Muslims and Crusaders*, p. 22; Irwin, "Islam and the Crusades," p. 220.
84 Elisséeff, "Reaction of the Syrian Muslims," p. 163.
85 Christie, "Religious Campaign," pp. 68–70; Christie, "Motivating Listeners," p. 7; Christie, *Muslims and Crusaders*, pp. 23, 132. Hillenbrand, "First Crusade: the Muslim perspective," p. 136.
86 A good, recent translation of Usama's memoirs is available in Usama Ibn Munqidh, *The Book of Contemplation: Islam and the Crusades*, trans. Paul M. Cobb (London: Penguin Books, 2008).
87 Christie, *Muslims and Crusaders*, p. 132; Gabrieli, *Arab Historians of the Crusades*, pp. 4, 10.
88 Christie, "Religious Conquest," p. 70; Christie, *Muslims and Crusaders*, pp. 23–24; Hillenbrand, *The Crusades: Islamic Perspectives*, pp. 46–47, 52–54. According to al-'Azimi, in 1096 the Byzantines sent a letter about the coming crusade to an unnamed Muslim ally, which most interpret to have been the Fatimids of Egypt.
89 Christie, "Religious Campaign," pp. 64, 67–68; Christie, *Muslims and Crusaders*, p. 21; Irwin, "Islam and the Crusades," p. 221; Hillenbrand, *The Crusades: Islamic Perspectives*, pp. 51–54; Chevedden, "Islamic View and the Christian View of the Crusades,"

pp. 185–86. One also should note that other Muslim observers, including al-'Azimi, al-Sulami, and al-Nuwayri, also set the First Crusade in a broad geopolitical context.

90 Hillenbrand, "First Crusade: the Muslim perspective," p. 136.

91 Stark, *God's Battalions*, pp. 70–76. For re-assessments of crusader military tactics and strategy, see: David Nicolle, *Crusader Warfare*, 2 vols. (London: Hambledon Continuum, 2007); Hugh Kennedy, *Crusader Castles* (Cambridge: Cambridge University Press, 2001); R.C. Smail, *Crusading Warfare, 1097–1193*, 2nd edn. (Cambridge: Cambridge University Press, 1995); Christopher Marshall, *Warfare in the Latin East, 1192–1291* (Cambridge: Cambridge University Press, 1992). Similarly, Piers D. Mitchell, in *Medicine in the Crusades: Warfare, Wounds and the Medieval Surgeon* (Cambridge: Cambridge University Press, 2004), argued that, by the time of the crusades, Western medicine had caught up to Islamic standards through translation of Arabic mediators of the ancient Hippocratic-Galenic corpus.

92 In a remarkable parallel, Greek authors from Byzantium, such as Anna Komnene, sister to Emperor Alexius, also failed to understand or appreciate the crusaders' religious motivations and dismissed them as "barbarians," greedy and treacherous. See Sakellariou, "Byzantine and Modern Greek Perceptions of the Crusades," p. 247.

93 Michael Köhler, *Alliances and Treaties between Frankish and Muslim Rulers in the Middle East*, trans. Peter M. Holt and ed. Konrad Hirschler (Leiden, Netherlands: Brill, 2013); Hillenbrand, *Crusades: Islamic Perspectives*, pp. 76–84.

94 Christie, *Muslims and Crusaders*, p. 24; Irwin, "Islam and the Crusaders," pp. 218–20; Yaacov Lev, "The *Jihād* of Sultan Nūr al-Dīn of Syria (1146–1174): History and Discourse," *Jerusalem Studies in Arabic and Islam* 35 (2008):231–32.

95 Hillenbrand, *Crusades: Islamic Perspectives*, pp. 71–74; Lev, "*Jihād* of Sultan Nūr al-Dīn," pp. 233–40, 264–69. The earlier figure of Imad al-Din Zangi, conqueror of Edessa and Nur al-Din's father, presents a much harder case as a true *mujahid*, or *jihad* fighter. Even in Muslim sources, Zengi was remembered almost exclusively for his conquest of Edessa and as a fearsome military figure rather than as a religious or political leader. See: Christie, *Muslims and Crusaders*, pp. 27–28; Lev, "*Jihād* of Sultan Nūr al-Dīn," pp. 243–51; Irwin, "Islam and the Crusades," pp. 226–27; Hillenbrand, *Crusades: Islamic Perspectives*, pp. 112–16; Carole Hillenbrand, "'Abominable Acts': The Career of Zengi," in *The Second Crusade: Scope and Consequences*, eds. Martin Hoch and Jonathan Phillips (Manchester, UK: Manchester University Press, 2006), pp. 118–27.

96 Alex Mallett, *Popular Muslim Reactions to the Franks in the Levant, 1097–1291* (Farnham, UK: Ashgate, 2014), pp. 27–30.

97 Constable, *Crusaders and Crusading*, pp. 29–30; Housley, *Contesting the Crusades*, pp. 58–60. While Throop emphasized how criticism sapped the enthusiasm and morale of later crusades, Siberry questioned how much impact criticism really had on crusade's enduring popularity. Housley, perhaps taking a middle view, insisted that "fundamental questioning of the validity of crusading existed from the start of the movement," but that the thirteenth century saw fewer doubts expressed about crusading due to the "armor plating" of a just war framework created by the canonists. See: Palmer A. Throop, *Criticism of the Crusade: A Study of Public Opinion and Crusade Propaganda* (Amsterdam, Netherlands: Swets and Zeitlinger, 1940); Elizabeth Siberry, *Criticism of Crusading, 1095–1274* (Oxford: Clarendon Press, 1985); Norman Housley, *The Later Crusades, 1274–1580: From Lyons to Alcazar* (Oxford: Oxford University Press, 1992), p. 377.

98 Giles Constable, "The Second Crusade as Seen by Contemporaries," *Traditio* 9 (1953): 216–20, 244–56; Constable, *Crusaders and Crusading*, pp. 231–35, 264–71; Roche, "Second Crusade," and Ane L. Bysted, "The True Year of Jubilee: Bernard of Clairvaux on Crusade and Indulgences," in *Second Crusade: Holy War on the Periphery*, pp. 10–11, 38–43; Jonathan Phillips, *The Second Crusade: Extending the Frontiers of Christendom* (New Haven, CT.: Yale University Press, 2007), pp. 37–60; Phillips, *The Crusades*, pp. 79–82. There is some debate as to whether Pope Eugenius III offered a new indulgence that promised remission of divine, as well as ecclesiastical, punishments for sin, based on

interpretations of the phrase, *remissio peccatorum* ("remission of sins"); according to Bysted, these issues have yet to be resolved. Aside from Bernard's preaching contribution, which was central to recruitment but which arguably oversold the crusade, there is debate over the relative contributions of the lay contingents, led by Louis VII and Conrad III. While some have argued that it was improved relations between Louis and Eugenius that made the Second Crusade possible, other scholars have emphasized the importance of the contributions made by Conrad and his contingent. See: Ane L. Bysted, *The Crusade Indulgence: Spiritual Rewards and the Theology of the Crusades, c. 1095–1216* (Leiden, Netherlands: Brill, 2015); Mayer, *The Crusades*, pp. 23–37, 293–95; Riley-Smith, *Crusades: A History*, pp. 13, 133–34; Riley-Smith, *What were the Crusades*, 4th edn., pp. 60–65; Monique Amouroux, "Louis VII, Innocent II et la Seconde Croisade," in *La papauté et les croisades*, ed. Michel Balard (Farnham, UK: Ashgate, 2011), pp. 55–65; Jonathan Phillips, "Papacy, Empire and the Second Crusade" and Rudolf Hiestand, "The Papacy and the Second Crusade," in *The Second Crusade: Scope and Consequences*, pp. 15–53; John G. Rowe, "The Origins of the Second Crusade: Pope Eugenius III, Bernard of Clairvaux and Louis VII of France," in *The Second Crusade and the Cistercians*, ed. M. Gervers (New York: St. Martin's Press, 1992), pp. 79–89; A. Grabois, "The Crusade of Louis VII: A Reconsideration," in *Crusade and Settlement*, pp. 94–104.

99 Constable, "Second Crusade," pp. 213–15, 221–39, 256–60; Constable, *Crusaders and Crusading*, pp. 236–53, 271–81; Phillips, *Second Crusade*, pp. 136–67, 228–68; Phillips, *The Crusades*, pp. 85–89; Roche, "Second Crusade"; Luis García-Guijarro, "Reconquest and the Second Crusade in Eastern Iberia: The Christian Expansion in the Lower Ebro Valley," Susan B. Edgington, "The Capture of Lisbon: Premeditated or Opportunistic?" and Jay T. Lees, " 'Why Have You Come with Weapons Drawn? The Leaders of the Wendish Campaign of 1147," in *Second Crusade: Holy War on the Periphery*, pp. 21–32, 219–99. Some scholars argue that the campaigns in Scandinavia at this time should also be considered part of the Second Crusade, although no evidence is forthcoming that Pope Eugenius sanctioned these expeditions or that their participants took a formal crusading vow. Alan Forey argued that the simultaneous theaters in Syria, the Baltic, and the Iberian peninsula were not all planned as a concerted Christian campaign against pagans, as Constable averred, but rather must be considered separately. See: Alan J. Forey, "The Second Crusade: Scope and Objectives," *Durham University Journal* 86 (1994):165–75; Roche, "Second Crusade," Janus Møller Jensen, "The Second Crusade and the Significance of Crusading in Scandinavia and the North Atlantic Region," and John H. Lind, "The 'First Swedish Crusade' against the Finns: A Part of the Second Crusade?," in *Second Crusade: Holy War on the Periphery*, pp. 4, 26, 155–82.

100 Martin Hoch, "The Price of Failure: The Second Crusade as a Turning-Point in the History of the Latin East?" in *Second Crusade: Scope and Consequences*, pp. 180–200; Phillips, *Second Crusade*, pp. 269–79; Constable, "Second Crusade," pp. 266–76; Constable, *Crusaders and Crusading*, pp. 281–92; Hiestand, "Papacy and the Second Crusade," pp. 46–47. Hoch concluded that the failure of the Second Crusade and criticism resulting from it discredited crusading and hindered major activities for four decades, until the Third Crusade was called in response to the fall of Jerusalem to Saladin in 1187, but that it had little impact on the Latin Kingdom of Jerusalem itself. Apparently, Damascus was chosen as a target because of its recent alliance with Aleppo, ruled by Nūr ad-Dīn, which replaced the city's former alliance with the Latin kingdom of Jerusalem. It is also argued that the pull of Jerusalem for the second crusaders made the shift in focus from Edessa to Damascus "all but inevitable". See: Martin Hoch, "The Choice of Damascus as the Objective of the Second Crusade: A Re-evaluation," in *Autour de la première croisade: Actes du Colloque de la Society for the Study of the Crusades and the Latin East (Clermont-Ferrand, 22–25 Juin 1995)*, ed. Michel Balard (Paris: Publications de la Sorbonne, 1997), pp. 359–69; Graham A. Loud, "Some Reflections

on the Failure of the Second Crusade," *Crusades*, 4 (2005): 9–14; Roche, "Second Crusade," p. 19.

101 Suleiman A. Mourad and James E. Lindsay, "Rescuing Syria from the Infidels: The Contribution of Ibn 'Asakir of Damascus to the *Jihad* Campaign of Sultan Nur al-Din," *Crusades*, 6 (2007):49–54; Suleiman A. Mourad and James E. Lindsay, "A Muslim Response to the Second Crusade: Ibn 'Asākir of Damascus as Propagandist of Jihad," in *Second Crusade: Holy War on the Periphery*, pp. 91–111. For an edition and translation of the *Forty Hadiths*, see Sulaymān 'Alī Murād and James E. Lindsay, *The Intensification and Reorientation of Sunni Jihad Ideology in the Crusader Period: Ibn 'Asākir of Damascus (1105–1176) and his Age, with an Edition and Translation of Ibn 'Asākir's The Forty Hadiths for Inciting Jihad* (Leiden, Netherlands: Brill, 2013).

102 Hillenbrand, *Crusades: Islamic Perspectives*, pp. 112–41; Lev, "*Jihād* of Sultan Nūr al-Dīn," pp. 233–36, 274–75; Christie, *Muslims and Crusaders*, p. 31.

103 Christie, *Muslims and Crusaders*, pp. 33–35, 136–37; Köhler, *Alliances and Treaties*.

104 Christie, *Muslims and Crusaders*, pp. 31–32; Phillips, *The Crusades*, pp. 113–16.

105 Yasser Tabbaa, "Monuments with a Message: Propagation of *Jihad* under Nūr al-Dīn (1146–1174)," in *The Meeting of Two Worlds: Cultural Exchange between East and West during the Period of the Crusades*, eds. Vladimir P. Goss and Christine Verzár Bornstein (Kalamazoo, MI.: Medieval Institute Publications, Western Michigan University, 1986), pp. 223–40; Hillenbrand, *Crusades: Islamic Perspectives*, pp. 119–61; Lev, "*Jihād* of Sultan Nūr al-Dīn," pp. 269–76; Elisséeff, "Reaction of the Syrian Muslims," pp. 167–71. Lev argued that Nūr al-Dīn's inscriptions testified more to the sultan's "inner religious world," particularly his "militant piety," than to his desire to unify Syria and wage *jihad*. Lev also noted that even when titles did refer to Nūr al-Dīn's waging of holy war, his religious enemies could just as well have been internal ones within Islam (such as the Shi'ites), as the infidel Christian crusaders.

106 Christie, *Muslims and Crusaders*, pp. 35–40; Hillenbrand, *Crusades: Islamic Perspectives*, pp. 117–19, 193–95; Irwin, "Islam and the Crusades," p. 226; Geoffrey Hindley, *Saladin* (New York: Harper and Row, 1976), pp. 34–45; Lev, "*Jihād* of Sultan Nūr al-Dīn," pp. 252–64, 274–77; Elisséeff, "Reaction of the Syrian Muslims," pp. 165–67; Mourad and Lindsay, "Muslim Response to the Second Crusade," pp. 108–10. Indeed, *jihad* itself had this dual, intertwined nature—the greater *jihad* was entirely spiritual in nature and concerned with religious renewal, while the lesser *jihad* was the worldly duty to wage war on the infidel, or enemies of Islam. Both al-Sulami and Ibn 'Asākir stressed this two-fold nature of *jihad* and argued that the greater *jihad* was an essential prerequisite for the lesser one. However, Lev argued that, practically speaking, Nūr al-Dīn's *jihad* policy was constrained by his military capabilities and resources.

107 Although there have been many modern biographies of Saladin, Richard has received comparatively less attention, until recently. Aside from John Gillingham' standard biography, *Richard the Lionheart* (London: Weidenfeld and Nicolson, 1978), there is now Michael Markowski's "Richard Lionheart: Bad King, Bad Crusader?" *Journal of Medieval History* 23 (1997):351–65, which argued that Richard failed to take Jerusalem because he was overly-cautious and lacked the religious conviction of the first crusaders.

108 Benjamin Z. Kedar, "The Battle of Hattin Revisited" in *The Horns of Hattin*, ed. Benjamin Z. Kedar (Jerusalem and London: Yad Izhak Ben-Zvi and Variorum, 1992); Michael Ehrlich, "The Battle of Hattin: A Chronicle of a Defeat Foretold?" *Journal of Medieval Military History* 5 (2007):16–32.

109 *Arab Historians of the Crusades*, pp. 87–93, 99–105, 139–75; Hillenbrand, *Crusades: Islamic Perspectives*, pp. 171–92; Hannes Möhring, *Saladin: The Sultan and His Times, 1138–1193*, trans. David S. Bachrach (Baltimore, MD.: The Johns Hopkins University Press, 2005), pp. 103–4; Anne-Marie Eddé, *Saladin*, trans. Jane Marie Todd (Cambridge, MA.: Harvard University Press, 2011), pp. 169–86, 496–500; Andrew S. Ehrenkreutz, *Saladin* (Albany, NY.: State University of New York Press, 1972), pp. 233–38; Christie, *Muslims and Crusaders*, pp. 40–45, 48–54; Irwin, "Islam and the Crusades," pp. 228–29;

Yaacov Lev, *Saladin in Egypt* (Leiden, Netherlands: Brill, 1999), pp. 45–94; Malcolm Cameron Lyons and D.E.P. Jackson, *Saladin: The Politics of the Holy War* (Cambridge: Cambridge University Press, 1982), pp. 365–74. For a more positive approach to Saladin than most biographies in English, see P.H. Newby, *Saladin in his Times* (London: Faber and Faber, 1983).

110 The so-called "dark legend" of Saladin, in which the sultan was variously portrayed as a bastard, pimp, murderer, and sorcerer, was later superseded by more positive portrayals. See Eddé, *Saladin*, pp. 470–77.

111 Margaret Jubb, "The Crusaders' Perceptions of their Opponents," in *Palgrave Advances in the Crusades*, pp. 225, 238–39; Eddé, *Saladin*, pp. 465–69. The story of Saladin's knighting is told in the mid-thirteenth century French poem, *Ordene de Chevalerie* (Order of Chivalry). Saladin was said to have been knighted by either Hugh of Tiberias or Humphrey of Toron, with the knighting ceremony devoid of Christian elements. Another mid-thirteenth century French work, *La Fille du Comte de Ponthieu*, proposed that Saladin was descended from the counts of Ponthieu, on his mother's side.

112 *Arab Historians of the Crusades*, pp. 93–99, 105–13, 124–25, 142–43, 158; Christie, *Muslims and Crusaders*, pp. 47, 51, 142–45.

113 Saracens were portrayed in contemporary works as godless pagans, despite the fact that many authors surely knew that they followed a monotheistic faith, worshipping the same god as the Hebrews and Christians. Several theories have been proposed—ranging from political to psychoanalytical—as to why Christian authors pushed such grossly inaccurate and negative stereotypes of Islam. See: Jubb, "Crusaders' Perceptions," pp. 228–33; Nicholas Morton, "Encountering the Turks: The First Crusaders' Foreknowledge of their Enemy; Some Preliminary Findings," in *Crusading and Warfare in the Middle Ages: Realities and Representations. Essays in Honour of John France*, eds. Simon John and Nicholas Morton (Farnham, UK: Ashgate, 2014), pp. 51–56.

114 In these legends, Saladin had himself secretly baptized on his deathbed, or else hosted a debate among the leaders of the three religions—Islam, Christianity, and Judaism—without choosing one. See: Eddé, *Saladin*, pp. 486–91; Jubb, "Crusaders' Perceptions," p. 239; Newby, *Saladin*, p. 13.

115 Riley-Smith, "Islam and the Crusades," pp. 152, 160; Hillenbrand, *Crusades: Islamic Perspectives*, pp. 592–600; Christie, *Muslims and Crusaders*, p. 152; Möhring, *Saladin*, pp. 91–103; Abouali, "Saladin's Legacy in the Middle East," pp. 176–78; Eddé, *Saladin*, pp. 493–96.

116 Abouali, "Saladin's Legacy in the Middle East," pp. 181–82.

117 Riley-Smith noted that, in addition to harboring suspicions over his true *mujahid* credentials, most Arabs remembered Saladin as a Kurd, and thus of a different ethnicity than theirs. However, Eddé argued that Saladin was easier to "Arabize" than Baybars, a Turk and thus a representative of the Ottoman dynasty, because as a Kurd, Saladin presented a more "neutral" figure. See: Riley-Smith, "Islam and the Crusades," p. 152; Eddé, *Saladin*, p. 496.

118 Constable, *Crusaders and Crusading*, pp. 321–24; Housley, *Contesting the Crusades*, p. 64.

119 Constable, *Crusaders and Crusading*, pp. 332–47.

120 Michael Agnold, *The Fourth Crusade: Event and Context* (Harlow, UK: Pearson Longman, 2003); Harris, *Byzantium and the Crusades*.

121 Scholars have postulated either the "chance" theory, that the crusade was diverted simply by accident, or the "intrigue" theory, that the crusade was deliberately and premeditatively diverted to Constantinople, especially by the Venetians. Then there is the "modified" accidents theory, namely, that the Fourth Crusade was diverted by chance, but that "some participants took advantage of events to promote their own interests, but without a prior plot or conspiracy". See Constable, *Crusaders and Crusading*, pp. 324–25; Housley, *Contesting the Crusades*, pp. 64–68.

122 Constable, *Crusaders and Crusading*, pp. 325–32.

123 For accounts of the Fourth Crusade, see: Donald E. Queller and Thomas F. Madden, *The Fourth Crusade: The Conquest of Constantinople*, 2nd edn. (Philadelphia, PA.:

University of Pennsylvania Press, 1997); Michael Agnold, *The Fourth Crusade: Event and Conquest* (London: Pearson/Longman, 2003); Jonathan Phillips, *The Fourth Crusade and the Sack of Constantinople* (New York: Viking, 2004); Phillips, *The Crusades*, pp. 183–201; Constable, *Crusaders and Crusading*, pp. 321–47.

124 Marcho Meschini, "The 'Four Crusades' of 1204," in *The Fourth Crusade: Event, Aftermath, and Perceptions*, ed. Thomas F. Madden (Aldershot, UK: Ashgate, 2008), pp. 27–42.

125 Meschini, "'Four Crusades'," pp. 28–32; Aphrodite Papyianni, "The Papacy and the Fourth Crusade in the Correspondence of the Nicaean Emperors with the Popes," in *Papauté et les croisades*, pp. 157–63; Alfred J. Andrea and John C. Moore, "A Question of Character: Two Views on Innocent III and the Fourth Crusade," in *Innocent III: Urbis et Orbis*, ed. Andrea Sommerlechner (Rome: Presso de la Società alla Biblioteca Vallicelliana, 2003), pp. 525–85.

126 Geoffrey of Villehardouin and Jean de Joinville, *Chronicles of the Crusades*, trans. Caroline Smith (London: Penguin Books, 2008).

127 Meschini, "'Four Crusades'," pp. 32–38; Housley, *Contesting the Crusades*, pp. 91–92.

128 Robert of Clari, *The Conquest of Constantinople*, trans. Edgar Holmes McNeal (New York: Columbia University Press, 1936). Clari's hard-headed perspective is illustrated when he observed that the Venetians kept the crusaders cooped up on the Lido in order to pressure the leaders to come to terms, whereas Villhardouin displayed naivety (or at least feigned to) in that he praised the Venetians' sudden rush to assume the cross as motivated by pure religious feeling. Nonetheless, Housley argued that poor knights shared a great deal of the same motivations as their superiors, namely, a mixture of spiritual "anxiety" and devotion, tempered by an acquisitive desire for booty. See Housley, *Contesting the Crusades*, pp. 68, 93.

129 Meschini, "'Four Crusades'," pp. 36–37, 39–40; Serban Marin, "Between Justification and Glory: The Venetian Chronicles' View of the Fourth Crusade," in *Fourth Crusade*, pp. 113–21.

130 Meschini, "'Four Crusades'," pp. 38–39.

131 Sakellariou, "Byzantine and Modern Greek Perceptions of the Crusades," pp. 253–61; David Jacoby, "The Greeks of Constantinople under Latin Rule, 1204–1261," in *Fourth Crusade*, pp. 53–73.

132 Taef El-Azhari, "Muslim Chroniclers and the Fourth Crusade," *Crusades*, 6 (2007):107–16; William J. Hamblin, "Arab Perspectives on the Fourth Crusade," in *Fourth Crusade*, pp. 167–78.

133 Housley, *Contesting the Crusades*, pp. 68–74; Madden, *New Concise History of the Crusades*, pp. 143–86; Caroline Smith, *Crusading in the Age of Joinville* (Aldershot, UK: Ashgate, 2006); G.A. Loud, "The Papal 'Crusade' against Frederick II in 1228–1230," in *Papauté et les croisades*, pp. 91–103; Christie, *Muslims and Crusaders*, pp. 88–98.

134 For a history of these later crusades, see: Housley, *Later Crusades*; Housley, *Contesting the Crusades*, pp. 122–43.

135 Christie, *Muslims and Crusaders*, pp. 99–110; Madden, *New Concise History of the Crusades*, pp. 181–2; Hillenbrand, *Crusades: Islamic Perspectives*, pp. 227–30; Irwin, "Islam and the Crusades," p. 239.

136 Housley, *Contesting the Crusades*, pp. 122–43; Norman Housley, "The Crusading Movement, 1274–1700," in *Oxford History of the Crusades*, pp. 258–90; Housley, *The Later Crusades*.

137 Indeed, the "forgotten crusades" to Greenland in the early decades of the sixteenth century likewise had the goal of finding a western passage to the Indies. See Janus Møller Jensen, "The Forgotten Crusades: Greenland and the Crusades, 1400–1523," *Crusades*, 7 (2008):199–215.

138 Housley, *Later Crusades*; Housley, "Crusading Movement," pp. 258–90; Housley, *Contesting the Crusades*, pp. 122–43.

139 The text of the oath is entered into the Congressional Record of the U.S. House of Representatives, House Bill 1523, February 15, 1913.

140 The Reconquest is generally dated between the battle of Covadonga of 718 or 722, and the siege of Granada of 1492.

141 Apparently, "Reconquest" can be shown to have a possible medieval origin, dating to a late twelfth-century Latin text describing how King Alfonso II of Asturias (r. 791–842) "reconquered [*recunquisierat*] the greater part of Spain". See Alejandro García-Sanjuán, "Rejecting al-Andalus, exalting the Reconquista: historical memory in contemporary Spain," *Journal of Medieval Iberian Studies* 10 (2018):129 and n. 12.

142 García-Sanjuán, "Rejecting al-Andalus," pp. 128–41.

143 R.A. Fletcher, "Reconquest and Crusade in Spain, c. 1050–1150," *Transactions of the Royal Historical Society*, 5th ser. 37 (1987):31–47.

144 *The World of El Cid: Chronicles of the Spanish Reconquest*, trans. Simon Barton and Richard Fletcher (Manchester, UK: Manchester University Press, 2000); Richard Fletcher, *The Quest for El Cid* (New York: Knopf, 1990).

145 María Eugenia Lacarra, *El Poema de Mio Cid: Realidad Histórica e Ideología* (Madrid: J. Porrúa Turanzas, 1980); Colin Smith, *The Making of the Poema de Mio Cid* (Cambridge: Cambridge University Press, 1983).

146 Pidal's *La España del Cid* was translated into English as *The Cid and His Spain*, trans. H. Sunderland (London: Frank Cass, 1934).

147 García-Sanjuán, "Rejecting al-Andalus," p. 131.

148 García-Sanjuán, "Rejecting al-Andalus," p. 130; John Aberth, *A Knight at the Movies: Medieval History on Film* (New York: Routledge, 2003), pp. 135–47.

149 García-Sanjuán, "Rejecting al-Andalus," pp. 132–41.

150 Benjamin Z. Kedar, "Crusade Historians and the Massacres of 1096," *Jewish History*, 12 (1998):11–31; Jonathan Riley-Smith, "The First Crusade and the Persecution of the Jews," *Studies in Church History*, 21 (1984):51–72.

151 *The Jews and the Crusaders: The Hebrew Chronicles of the First and Second Crusades*, trans. and ed. Shlomo Eidelberg (Hoboken, NJ.: KTAV Publishing, 1996), pp. 22, 25–26, 80, 99; *Chronicles of the Crusades: Eye-Witness Accounts of the Wars between Christianity and Islam*, ed. Elizabeth Hallam (New York: Welcome Rain, 2000), p. 68.

152 *Jews and the Crusaders*, pp. 32–33; Jeremy Cohen, *Sanctifying the Name of God: Jewish Martyrs and Jewish Memories of the First Crusade* (Philadelphia, PA.: University of Pennsylvania Press, 2004), pp. 13–22; Kenneth R. Stow, *Alienated Minority: The Jews of Medieval Latin Europe* (Cambridge, MA.: Harvard University Press, 1992), p. 117.

153 *Jews and the Crusaders*, pp. 32–33; Cohen, *Sanctifying the Name of God*, pp. 5–6; Kenneth Stow, "The Cruel Jewish Father: From Miracle to Murder," in *Studies in Medieval Jewish Intellectual and Social History: Festschrift in Honor of Robert Chazan*, eds. David Engel, Lawrence H. Schiffman, and Elliot R. Wolfson (Leiden, Netherlands: Brill, 2012), pp. 245–57.

154 Cohen, *Sanctifying the Name of God*, p. 40.

155 Cohen, *Sanctifying the Name of God*, pp. 1, 31–33, 40; Robert Chazan, *European Jewry and the First Crusade* (Berkeley, CA.: University of California Press, 1987); Gavin I. Langmuir, *Toward a Definition of Antisemitism* (Berkeley, CA.: University of California Press, 1990), p. 99; David Nirenberg, "The Rhineland Massacres of Jews in the First Crusade: Memories Medieval and Modern," in *Medieval Concepts of the Past: Ritual, Memory, Historiography*, eds. Gerd Althoff, Johannes Fried, and Patrick J. Geary (Cambridge: Cambridge University Press, 2002), pp. 299–303. For a dissenting view, see Stow, *Alienated Minority*, p. 103. The argument for the connection between the 1096 martyrdoms and the blood libel accusations was more fully developed in an article (in Hebrew) by the Israeli scholar, Israel Jacob Yuval, "Vengeance and Damnation, Blood and Defamation: From Jewish Martyrdom to Blood Libel Accusations," *Zion* 58 (1993):33–90. For a critical review of Yuval's arguments, see David Berger, *From Crusades to Blood Libels to Expulsions: Some New Approaches to Medieval Antisemitism* (New York: Touro College, 1997), pp. 16–22.

156 Chazan, *European Jewry*, pp. 40–49; Robert Chazan, *God, Humanity, and History: The Hebrew First Crusade Narratives* (Berkeley, CA.: University of California Press,

2000); Robert Chazan, *In the Year 1096: The First Crusade and the Jews* (Philadelphia, PA.: Jewish Publication Society, 1996).

157 Chazan, *European Jewry*, pp. 27–37.

158 Ivan G. Marcus, "From Politics to Martyrdom: Shifting Paradigms in the Hebrew Narratives of the 1096 Crusade Riots," *Prooftexts* 2 (1982):40–52; Nirenberg, "Rhineland Massacres," p. 283.

159 It should be pointed out that Chazan also believed that there were sometimes amicable interactions between Christians and the Ashkenazic Jews, but he argued that ultimately their relationship suffered from anti-Jewish stereotypes in Christian society, as well as from the special political and economic status that the Jews were perceived to have held.

160 *Jews and the Crusaders*, p. 32.

161 This was also the approach of Ivan Marcus, who saw the Hebrew crusade chronicles as primarily literary works or fictions, that is, "imaginative reorderings of experience within a cultural framework and system of symbols". More generally, Marcus rejected both the "positivist" and "literary folklorist" approaches to Ashkenazic history in favor of an "anthropological" approach, which he described as assuming that "the narrative presents a set of symbolic expressions of experiences or events that can be known only as mediated through the narrative". See: Marcus, "From Politics to Martyrdom," p. 42; Ivan G. Marcus, "History, Story, and Collective Memory: Narrativity in Early Ashkenazic Culture," *Prooftexts* 10 (1990):366.

162 Cohen, *Sanctifying the Name of God*, pp. 55–69, 91–141.

163 Cohen, *Sanctifying the Name of God*, pp. 139–40.

164 Samuel K. Cohn, Jr. "The Black Death and the Burning of the Jews," *Past and Present* 196 (2007):3–36; Alfred Haverkamp, "Die Judenverfolgungen zur Zeit des Schwarzen Todes im Gesellschaftsgefüge deutscher Städte," in *Zur Geschichte der Juden im Deutschland des späten Mittelalters und der frühen Neuzeit*, eds. Alfred Haverkamp and Alfred Heit (Stuttgart, Germany: Hiersemann, 1981), pp. 217–93. There is some debate as to whether the "mass suicides" alleged to have occurred in towns like Würzburg during the Black Death actually occurred. It is argued that, since the citizens of Würzburg had both past and present agreements to protect their Jews, any breach of these oaths would have been seen as an embarrassing "loss of credibility," and therefore native Christian chroniclers recording the events would have felt it "necessary to launch the fiction of the collective suicide of the Jewish community". See Hans-Peter Baum, "Die Vernichtung der jüdischen Gemeinde in Würzburg 1349," in *Strukturen der Gesellschaft im Mittelalter: Interdisziplinäre Mediävistik in Würzburg*, eds. Dieter Rödel and Joachim Schneider (Wiesbaden: Dr. Ludwig Reichert Verlag, 1996), pp. 379–80.

165 *Corpus Documentorum Inquisitionis Haereticae Pravitatis Neerlandicae*, ed. Paul Fredericq, 3 vols. (Ghent, 1889–1906), 2:123.

166 John Aberth, *The Black Death: The Great Mortality of 1348–1350: A Brief History with Documents* (Boston, MA. and New York: Bedford/St. Martin's, 2005), p. 156.

167 *Fontes Rerum Germanicarum*, ed. Johann Friedrich Böhmer, 4 vols. (Stuttgart, Germany: J.G. Cotta'scher Verlag, 1843–68), 4:72.

168 Solomon bar Samson indeed related that when the Mainz Jews heard of what happened to the communities of Speyer and Worms and that the "sword" of the crusaders "would soon reach them, their hands became faint and their hearts melted and became as water". Their leaders then "gathered together and discussed various ways of saving themselves," which included trusting in (and buying) the protection of the bishop. Only when that failed, after an armed confrontation in the bishop's courtyard, did the Jews of Mainz resort to *kiddush ha-Shem*. Samson in his full account thus gave much more of a sense of prevarication in the Jews' response to, and consideration of, their dilemma than Cohen gave him credit for. See *Jews and the Crusaders*, pp. 23–30.

169 Burnam W. Reynolds, *The Prehistory of the Crusades: Missionary War and the Baltic Crusades* (London: Bloomsbury, 2016); Lees, "Leaders of the Wendish Campaign," pp. 273–99; Phillips, *Second Crusade*, pp. 228–43; Iben Fonnesberg-Schmidt, *The Popes*

and the Baltic Crusades, 1147–1254 (Leiden, Netherlands: Brill, 2007); William Urban, *The Baltic* Crusade, 2nd edn. (Chicago, IL: Lithuanian Research and Studies Center, 1994); Eric Christiansen, *The Northern Crusades: The Baltic and the Catholic Frontier, 1100–1525* (Minneapolis, MN.: University of Minnesota Press, 1980).

170 Reynolds, *Prehistory of the Crusades*, pp. 19–22; *Chronicles of the Crusades*, pp. 83–94.

171 Housley, *Contesting the Crusades*, p. 110.

172 Christiansen, *Northern Crusades*, pp. 48–69; Reynolds, *Prehistory of the Crusades*, pp. 19–22; *Chronicles of the Crusades*, pp. 126–27. Hans-Dietrich Kahl suggested that one reason Bernard may have taken such an uncompromising stance towards the Wends was that he subscribed to "Sibylline prophecies" of the imminent end to the world featuring "heathen inhabitants of areas beyond the River Elbe". See Hans-Dietrich Kahl, "Crusade Eschatology as Seen by St. Bernard in the Years 1146 to 1148," in *Second Crusade and the Cistercians*, pp. 35–47.

173 However, the successive popes, Alexander III (r. 1159–81) and Innocent III (r. 1198–1216), apparently relegated the Baltic crusade down to "penitential warfare," implying that it did not share the same spiritual rewards as crusading to the Holy Land, which were only restored by Pope Honorius III (r. 1216–27). See: Fonnesberg-Schmidt, *Popes and the Baltic Crusades*; Housley, *Contesting the Crusades*, p. 112.

174 Friedrich Lotter, "The Crusading Idea and the Conquest of the Region East of the Elbe," in *Medieval Frontier Societies*, eds. Robert Bartlett and Angus McKay (Oxford: Clarendon Press, 1989), pp. 286–92. Housley, *Contesting the Crusades*, pp. 110–11, found Lotter's argument convincing.

175 Roche, "Second Crusade," and Lees, "Leaders of the Wendish Campaign," *in Second Crusade: Holy War on the Periphery*, pp. 22, 286, 288; Phillips, *Second Crusade*, pp. 236–38.

176 Reynolds, *Prehistory of the Crusades*, pp. 23–25.

177 Reynolds, *Prehistory of the Crusades*, pp. 26–38, 142–78. Particularly as conceived as "missionary war," the Baltic crusades present some interesting points of comparison with the later European "discovery" of lands and people in the New World. See Reynolds, *Prehistory of the Crusades*, pp. 179–94.

178 Reynolds, *Prehistory of the Crusades*, pp. 43–52; Roche, "Second Crusade," pp. 25–26.

179 Lees, "Leaders of the Wendish Campaign," pp. 280–81, 286–88. Lees also argued that Bernard resorted to desperate extremes in his letter calling for the Wendish crusade, both urging destruction of an implacable enemy and providing assurances that the campaign would be easy. In Lees' view, this was because Bernard had to convince an audience with a variety of motives: "men who were not interested in a campaign against the Wends, others unsure about such a campaign's purpose, and others willing to turn it to their own advantage".

180 Lees, "Leaders of the Wendish Campaign," pp. 297–99.

181 Pegatha Taylor, "Moral Agency in Crusade and Colonization: Anselm of Havelberg and the Wendish Crusade of 1147," *International History Review* 22 (2000):757–84; Christiansen, *Northern Crusades*, pp. 250–51; Housley, *Contesting the Crusades*, p. 115.

182 Lees, "Leaders of the Wendish Campaign," pp. 293, 299.

183 Reynolds, *Prehistory of the Crusades*, pp. 69–119; Roche, "Second Crusade," and Lees, "Leaders of the Wendish Campaign," in *Second Crusade: Holy War on the Periphery*, pp. 22, 279–82.

184 Alan V. Murray, "Heathens, Devils and Saracens: Crusader Concepts of the Pagan Enemy during the Baltic Crusades (Twelfth to Fifteenth Centuries)," in *Crusading on the Edge*, pp. 199–223; Shami Ghosh, "Conquest, Conversion, and Heathen Customs in Henry of Livonia's *Chronicon Livoniae* and the *Livländische Reimchronik*," *Crusades*, 11 (2012):90–108; Reynolds, *Prehistory of the Crusades*, pp. 120–41. Not surprisingly, it was "pagan war tactics" that were most commonly assimilated into the Christian milieu.

185 Christiansen, *The Northern Crusades*, pp. 132–70.

186 Sven Ekdahl, "Crusades and Colonization in the Baltic," in *Palgrave Advances in the Crusades*, pp. 179–94.

187 Housley, *Contesting the Crusades*, pp. 115–21.

188 For the crusades waged by the papacy against its perceived political enemies in Italy, see Norman Housley, *The Italian Crusades: The Papal-Angevin Alliance and the Crusades against Christian Lay Powers, 1254–1343* (Oxford: Oxford University Press, 1982). For works on the Albigensian crusade, see n. 190 below.

189 Norman Housley, "Crusades against Christians: Their Origins and Early Development, c. 1000–1216," in *Crusade and Settlement*, pp. 17–36.

190 Mark Gregory Pegg, *A Most Holy War: The Albigensian Crusade and the Battle for Christendom* (Oxford: Oxford University Press, 2008), pp. 187–91; Jessalyn Bird, "Paris Masters and the Justification of the Albigensian Crusade," *Crusades*, 6 (2007):124, 136–39; Karl Borchardt, "Casting out Demons by Beelzebul: Did the Papal Preaching against the Albigensians Ruin the Crusades?" in *Papauté et les croisades*, pp. 77–89; Walter L. Wakefield, *Heresy, Crusade and Inquisition in Southern France, 1100–1250* (Berkeley, CA.: University of California Press, 1974), pp. 96–129; A.P. Evans, "The Albigensian Crusade," in *A History of the Crusades*, ed. K.M. Setton, 6 vols, 2nd edn. (Madison, WI.: University of Wisconsin Press, 1969–89), 2: 277–324. Pegg argued that the declared enemy of the Albigensian Crusade, the so-called "Cathar" heretics, never in fact existed as "a discrete religion with an organized heretical 'Church'". Yet, Pegg undercut his own argument by calling the crusade a "genocide," a term usually used to refer to the attempted elimination of a discrete ethnic, racial, national, or religious group. The debate over whether Catharism actually existed is addressed in the next chapter.

191 The actual quote in Latin, as reported by Caesar of Heisterbach, is: "*Caedite eos! Novit enim Dominus qui sunt eius*". Arnaud-Amaury's own report to the pope, however, only stated that the crusaders' rallying cry was "To arms, to arms!" See *Chronicles of the Crusades*, p. 232.

192 Siberry, *Criticism of Crusading*, pp. 190–216; Housley, *Contesting the Crusades*, pp. 120–21.

193 Rebecca Rist, "Pope Gregory IX and the Grant of Indulgences for Military Campaigns in Europe in the 1230s: A Study in Papal Rhetoric," *Crusades*, 10 (2011):83–102.

4

I'M A JEWISH, HERETIC, LEPER, BUT DON'T HOLD THAT AGAINST ME

Persecution of minorities

In the spring of 1997, I was teaching at a private military college, when I received a hand-addressed letter in my faculty mailbox. The letter was addressed to me in blue marker, and inside was a flyer of a talk I had given the previous semester. On the flyer, in the same blue marker, were two swastikas (drawn backwards) and underneath were written the words: "Fucker, will get you". To this day, the image of that hateful message is burned into my memory, but I still have no idea why anyone would have sent it to me. I am part Jewish, on my grandmother's side of the family, who hailed from Strasbourg (her maiden name was Fuchs); but I never advertized this fact. I did, however, make a point of emphasizing the Holocaust as a historical topic in my World Civilization classes: Every year, I brought in an ex-Army ranger and veteran of the Second World War in order to talk about his experiences liberating some of the death camps in Nazi Germany, which never failed to make a great impression on my students. Then again, it could simply have been the rantings of a student disgruntled over his grade. But then, why the swastikas? These usually signify a racial hatred of Jews and of anything to do with Jewishness.

But this is not the most shocking part of the story. Obviously, I was greatly unnerved by what I took to be a threat against my life. That whole day, I felt as if I was walking over my grave. This was doubly true, in that I was teaching at a military school, where every cadet was issued with an M-1 semi-automatic rifle. This was an armed campus, where there were ample opportunities and means to carry out a death threat. But when I took my concerns and showed the flyer to my department head, and to the associate vice-president of academic affairs, their response was the verbal equivalent of a shrug. One of them actually said, "Boys will be boys," and there was nothing they could, or would, do about the situation. I was invited to conduct my own investigation, but I was not to receive any help or support from the administration.

I recite this incident merely as a reminder of how, even in this day and age and in some sectors of our society, including institutions of higher learning, not only is there prejudice against minority groups, which should hardly be surprising, but even the teaching of minority history can be a risky enterprise. Nevertheless, the study of the history of minority or fringe populations in the Middle Ages—Jews, prostitutes, homosexuals, heretics, lepers, etc.—has come a long way in the past half century or so, ever since the publication of Bronislaw Geremek's *The Margins of Society in Late Medieval Paris*.[1] But what was once on the margins, has now become mainstream, as minority history has graduated to a veritable academic industry, complete with its own sourcebook.[2] This really should not be surprising, as the recovery of the lost voices of medieval society was long overdue.

But even with a supportive administration, doing minority medieval history is something of a challenge, in that available sources and a coherent narrative are not always immediately obvious. One attempt to make sense of it all has been to explain exactly how and why persecution of minorities emerged in medieval Europe when it did. This has been the work of Robert I. Moore, a historian of heretics who first came out with his *Formation of a Persecuting Society* in 1987, updated twenty years later in a second edition in 2007.[3] Moore's thesis is that, contrary to past assumptions, a persecuting mentality was not natural or innate to medieval society, but was actually "born," or emerged in Europe, in the course of the twelfth and thirteenth centuries; not coincidentally, this was also the time that saw the rise of centralized governments, both in terms of secular nation-states and of ecclesiastical institutions, particularly the papal monarchy and the Inquisition. Therefore, the driving motivation behind medieval persecution of minorities was simply the will to power, both among the authorities who ordered the persecution, and among their "functionaries," or literate clerks and courtiers, who enabled their masters to carry it out. This was very much a persecution planned and directed "from above," rather than spontaneously erupting from below through mob violence or passions. It also means that there was little real difference among marginal groups where persecution was concerned, because any real or perceived threat from these groups—such as a proliferation in their numbers, wealth, or influence—was not really a factor in the desire to persecute. Rather, the main urge was to make people conform, no matter who or what was responsible for the offending deviance. It was thus the formation of state systems, and their enforcement of self-appointed cultural norms, which laid the foundations for a medieval "persecuting society".[4]

This is a rather revolutionary way of looking at medieval history in general and has had broad implications that go far beyond just the history of minorities in the Middle Ages. An older generation of medieval scholars, such as Sir Richard Southern in England and Joseph Strayer in the United States, had chronicled the high Middle Ages, from c. 1000–1300, as a period of great intellectual and cultural progress, one that saw the rise of cathedral schools and universities; the formation of centralized state and feudal bureaucracies; the development of syncretic philosophical systems; the expansion of population, agriculture, and commerce;

the flourishing of the arts, particularly in terms of Gothic architecture and courtly literature; and energetic reform of the Church, including the proliferation of new religious orders.[5] To many, it seemed that the thirteenth century, when the high Middle Ages reached its apogee, was the "greatest of centuries".[6] What Moore did was turn this heady celebration of high medieval achievement on its head.[7] If the middle centuries of the Middle Ages were indeed the "greatest" that the era had to offer, then Moore was determined to show how great it was in every, unflattering respect. And in truth, it was high time that someone lifted up the rug of history and exposed the dark underbelly of high medieval life for all to see. Moore's thesis was part of a larger vision, which saw this as a time not only of the formation of a persecuting society, but also, inextricably, of the formation of a consciousness and identity that was truly European, or when the "idea" of Europe was born.[8] Inevitably, the social groups and communities that came out of this process, i.e., the three orders of *oratores*, *bellatores*, and *laboratores*—those who prayed, fought, and worked—were defined just as much by who was *excluded* as much as by who was included.[9]

A natural objection to Moore's thesis is that it is too general, eliding some real differences among the various marginal or minority "outgroups" of medieval society, which can be shown to have evolved in substantially different contexts as persecuted targets of ruling authorities, and who presented quite different challenges to medieval cultural norms. Thus, Moore risks seeing too much of the forest instead of the trees, ignoring particular local contexts that gave rise to persecution. This, at least, has been the main criticism leveled at Moore by David Nirenberg, a scholar of medieval Jewish-Christian relations in medieval Spain. Instead of taking the "long view" (*longue durée*) that seeks to trace the history of "collective mentalities" of persecution and that tends to find continuities of attitudes towards minorities between the past and the present, Nirenberg argued that the minority experience in the Middle Ages could only be truly understood when examined with reference to the specific "social, political and cultural contexts" within which these minorities moved. This necessarily implied that persecution of minorities was fundamentally different in medieval times than it is today, and that perhaps it doesn't even make sense to talk about a cultural norm to "persecuting discourse," since this was constantly evolving and changing in accordance with the dictates of particular times and places. [10] Nirenberg applied his localist approach to minority history by trying to show how a normative "community of violence" underlay the celebrated *convivencia* (literally, "coexistence") used to describe a supposedly tolerant and peaceful polyglot society in medieval Spain. This implies that violent persecution of minorities could be entirely rational in its approach and was intertwined, and indeed interdependent, with toleration and acceptance, which in turn would seem to argue that we can never talk about a "tolerant," non-persecuting society, as opposed to an intolerant, persecuting one. [11]

Obviously, Nirenberg's ideas run counterintuitive to how many historians have explained the history of persecution of minorities, namely, as one of steady and inevitable progress from intolerance to enlightened acceptance as we move from the Middle Ages to modern times. Moore didn't exactly buy into this history either, but, in at least the original formulation of his thesis, he would certainly have disagreed with Nirenberg that persecution could be "a normal component of the human condition," which he regarded as unwarrantedly "pessimistic".[12] Nevertheless, in the second, 2007 edition of his book, Moore did acknowledge Nirenberg's criticisms and tried to paint a more nuanced picture of his thesis, arguing that it was never his intent to override "differences between particular groups of victims and the contexts and circumstances of their persecution," only to show how "persecution in Europe since the twelfth century" was in general "more likely to happen" and when it did, to be "more severe" and long lasting.[13] Yet Moore still retained two elements of his original thesis, namely, that the persecution history of various minority groups, including Jews, heretics, and lepers, was interconnected, on the grounds that "the coincidences are simply too many to be credible," and that it was the literate elite class of clerical and lay "functionaries" that were responsible for implementing this persecution, largely to serve their own interests.[14]

But even this, more narrowly-defined thesis can be shown to not always apply to persecuting incidents of the Middle Ages. For example, during the Black Death of the mid-fourteenth century, a series of pogroms was directed against Jewish communities, mainly in Germany and Switzerland, on the pretext that the victims were alleged to have spread the plague by dispersing poison in wells and springs used by Christians. But the traditionally accepted pattern of this persecution is that it was the literate elites in the papal court of Avignon, and among the nobles and burghers who ran the town councils of the imperial free cities, who consistently tried to *protect* the Jews, and that most of the impetus to burn or kill Jews instead came from below, from the pressure of the mob.[15] What is more, one can argue that the persecution of the Jews in this instance was not primarily related to, or motivated by, their Jewishness; in other words, the Jews were not being persecuted because they were Jews. Rather, it was the belief that plague was caused by a poisoning of the air or water—a belief grounded in contemporary medical theory and natural philosophy—that was chiefly behind the Black Death pogroms.[16]

One thus can make a good case that each minority in the Middle Ages had a unique history in terms of its persecution at the hands of the majority; in order to determine if there is any unifying theme in that persecution, it could equally well be argued that one should first approach the history of each minority separately. This will be the approach adopted in this chapter. Our focus will be on medieval Christian persecution of Jews, heretics, and lepers, marginal groups that, Moore argued, were intertwined in terms of how they were viewed and treated by the persecuting society.[17] In presenting a brief history of each minority's persecution, I make no pretensions to covering all of the complex issues involved or of surveying the entire scholarly literature on the subject. Our main question here is a very basic one: How and why was each minority persecuted during the Middle Ages? In this, there is plenty of room for debate, if not for definitive answers.

Persecution of the Jews: The variety of Jewish experience

How did the experience of being a Jew play itself out across the various countries of medieval Europe? Were these experiences uniquely different in each country or region? Were there any similarities that one can trace across borders and time-frames?

The oldest Jewish communities in Europe were established in ancient Roman times after Roman intervention in, and eventual conquest of, Judea as a Roman province during the two centuries on either side of the birth of Christ. These communities were located in the southern Mediterranean region, namely, in Spain, southern France, and Italy. Spain's "Sephardic" Jews experienced a rather unique, polyglot culture in which, for much of the Middle Ages, they lived under Muslim rulers before the country was largely "reconquered" by Catholic Christians by the mid-thirteenth century. During the *Reconquista*, Jews played important roles as settlers, farmers, moneylenders, traders, and professionals (i.e., doctors, lawyers, administrators) as part of the *repoblación* of conquered lands. This *convivencia* or "coexistence" only definitively came to an end with the complete expulsion of the Jews from Spain in 1492, while around the same time those families that had converted—the *conversos*—became subject to the feared Spanish Inquisition.[18] In Italy, Jewish communities were subject to a wide diversity of experiences, reflecting the diverse political, social, and economic make-up of the peninsula. Communities in the south were among the largest in the country and, in the case of Sicily, lived among various masters, including Muslim, Byzantine, and Norman rulers. The Jews of the north were rather small in number and highly mobile. Those in Rome, the center, comprised perhaps the most stable community, surviving without interruption from 1000 to 1500, in large degree due to the protection of the papacy.[19] Finally, the Jews of southern France were among the most culturally sophisticated communities in Europe, home to a number of schools devoted to study of the Talmud and to philosophical and mystical speculation. With the expulsions of 1306–94, Jews in southern France, specifically, Languedoc, could either take refuge in the east, in the county of Provence, or to the west, in the county of Rousillon and northeast Spain.[20]

In northern France and England, the Jewish communities mirrored each other, in that both were closely allied with the centralized monarchy, whose guarantees of loans made with landed property as collateral, which technically the Jews could not confiscate and own, facilitated the expansion of Jewish endeavors in banking and moneylending. The downside of this arrangement for the Jews was that their profits could be subject to crippling taxation—in a sense, "our Jews" were a means for the monarchy to access the wealth of Christian subjects—and the royal policy of protection could all too quickly change to persecution. France was particularly fickle towards its Jews: They were expelled from the royal domain in 1182, recalled in 1198, expelled in 1306, readmitted (in limited numbers) in 1315, and expelled a final time in 1394. French policy was also deeply affected by the monarchy's self-stylized reputation as the "most Christian kings of France," which did not always sit well with toleration of another religion. During the reign of Louis IX (r. 1226-70), later canonized as a saint, Jews were forbidden, upon pain of expulsion, from practicing their main livelihood—"usury," or lending at interest; the Talmud, the main source of Rabbinic interpretation of Judaism, was put on "trial" in Paris, found guilty of blasphemy against Christianity, and condemned to be burned; and Jews were subject to intensive conversion efforts, such as staged "debates" in which the parameters were set in favor of the Christian position— such as that the Talmud actually supported "Christian truth claims"—rather than allowing the Christian position to be challenged directly.[21]

In England, where Jews were expelled in 1290, after at least a century and a half in the country, having come over sometime in the late eleventh or first half of the twelfth centuries, Jews were subject to perhaps the most bureaucratically intensive management of any country in Europe. In the twelfth century, England established a separate administrative department solely to manage Jewish affairs, entitled the Exchequer of the Jews, whose records from the thirteenth century still survive and form one of the most voluminous archives on medieval Jewry. The sponsorship of such a powerful monarchy as England's allowed many English Jews to become successful bankers and moneylenders and to amass large fortunes: Aaron of Lincoln, who died in c. 1186, is said to have been "the wealthiest person in England," and the English crown set up a special office within the Exchequer— the *Scaccarium Aaronis*—just to track down and collect all debts owed to him upon his death. But this also meant that the Jews could be ruthlessly exploited and squeezed for tax revenue, which reached its apogee during the long reign of Henry III, from 1216 to 1272, when the English Jewish community was finally ground down into poverty. England's Jews were also subjected to some extraordinary popular animosity. The first "blood libel," or accusation of ritual murder and crucifixion, arose in England in connection with the discovery of the mutilated body of a twelve-year-old boy, William, at Norwich in 1144; further accusations were made at Gloucester in 1168, Bury St. Edmunds in 1181, and Bristol in 1183. Then, in 1189–90, riotous attacks took place against Jewish communities in London, King's Lynn, Norwich, Stamford, Lincoln, Bury St. Edmunds, and York—the last culminating in an act of self-martyrdom as 150 Jews immolated themselves in the royal castle where they had taken refuge—which coincided with the coronation and departure on the Third Crusade of King Richard I (r. 1189–99). Further blood libel accusations arose at Winchester in 1192, 1225, and 1232; at Norwich in 1230; London in 1244 and the late 1260s; Lincoln in 1255; and Northampton in 1277. At Lincoln, 90 Jews were accused of murdering a nine-year-old boy named Hugh and throwing his body down a well. While the Jew, Copin, was tortured into confessing to the crime, 18 others who refused to submit to trial by an all-Christian jury were also executed, leaving the rest to be pardoned after a formal trial and conviction. This set another, important precedent, marking the first time Jews were tried and convicted for the "crime" of ritual murder.[22]

The fate of the Jews in Germany, who, along with those of England and northern France were known as the "Ashkenazic" Jews, somewhat mirrors that in

Italy, especially in terms of the political fragmentation of the country, which necessarily resulted in a varied experience within the country. But German Jewry (which perhaps first migrated to the country from Italy in the tenth to eleventh centuries) was both more successful than in Italy in terms of numbers, forming several large communities, especially in the Rhineland, and more liable to persecution in all the ways that were possible in the Middle Ages. From the very beginning, Jews—labeled by their aristocratic patrons as "serfs of our chamber," or treasury—were settled in Germany for the express purpose of helping to develop the economic and mercantile interests of their communities, largely as traders and merchants, with moneylending only emerging as a vested activity later. The charters of foundation for some of these Jewish communities could be quite generous, which is perhaps how they were enticed to settle there. That for Speyer, drawn up by Bishop Rudiger Huozmann in 1084, granted them their own residential area in town encircled by a protective wall; their own cemetery; freedom to buy and sell anywhere in town; right to govern themselves, through an *archisynagogus*, equivalent to a mayor; and freedom from the usual restrictions imposed by the Church, such as might forbid them from hiring Christian wet-nurses and servants or from selling to Christians of un-kosher meats. But such privileges were more than balanced out by the many and assorted persecutions that assailed German Jews over the centuries. These included the 1096 massacres in several Rhineland communities (Mainz, Worms, Speyer, and Cologne) during the First Crusade; blood libel accusations in Würzburg in 1147, Cologne in 1180, Neuss in 1186, Speyer in 1196, Fulda in 1235, Mainz in 1283, and Oberwesel in 1287; the Rindfleisch and Armleder massacres of 1298 and 1336–38; and the well-poisoning accusations and pogroms during the Black Death in 1348–51. The final act for many Jewish communities in Germany was their expulsion between c. 1290 and c. 1520, which occurred in many cities and territories, leaving only Frankfurt, Friedberg, and Worms with a significant Jewish presence by the end of the Middle Ages.[23]

In eastern Europe, primarily Poland and Hungary, Jews both benefitted from a relatively primitive, backward economy and suffered from relocating (mostly from Germany) to the extreme periphery of medieval Europe. Charters granted to the Jews by King Bela IV of Hungary in 1251 and by Duke Boleslav of Kalisch in Poland in 1264 illustrate these themes: The charters were granted in the wake of Mongol invasions and widespread destruction in both countries earlier in the century, in an evident attempt to reconstruct the economy. Consequently, Jews in both Hungary and Poland were allowed more leeway in terms of their legitimate activities than simply moneylending, to include trade, minting of coins, tax collection, and governmental positions. And despite frontier-like conditions, the central authorities in both Hungary and Poland were more successful than those in the West in protecting Jews from both Church interference and popular persecution, particularly with regard to the blood libel accusations and the pogroms during the Black Death. But Jews were also more limited in their business and cultural opportunities in the East as opposed to the West, with the Yiddish language of the Polish Jews just one symbol of their earlier, Ashkenazic origins.

Nonetheless, the Jews of eastern Europe were to emerge as the center of Jewish life and population after 1500, which was only brought to an end by the Holocaust of the twentieth century.[24]

Finally, the experience of the Jews in the regions of Islam—namely, in parts of Spain, North Africa, Egypt, Palestine, and other parts of the Middle East—can serve as a useful baseline of comparison with the Christian milieu. However, this debate is necessarily caught up in the modern politics of Jewish-Arab relations. Originally, the myth of an "interfaith utopia" between medieval Muslims and Jews was taken up by nineteenth-century Jewish writers in order to provide a "historical precedent for a more tolerant attitude toward Jews" in their own times. Then, Arab authors writing in the aftermath of the Six-Day War of 1967 themselves adopted the interfaith utopia myth, as part of their narrative in which "historical Islamic tolerance gave way in the twentieth century to Arab hostility in reaction to Zionist encroachment" in Palestine. This, in turn, provoked a "countermyth" among Jewish historians, who now did an about-face and proposed a "neo-lachrymose conception of Jewish-Arab history". Here, the focus was on documented cases of "Islamic persecution," such as under the "mad" caliph of Egypt, al-Hakim (r. 996–1021), and during the Almohad rule of North Africa and Spain beginning in the 1140s. One can interpret these instances of persecution either as indicative of a broader pattern throughout the history of Muslim-Jewish relations, or else as isolated exceptions to a more tolerant norm.[25]

The scholarly consensus these days seems to favor the latter view. Compared to their situation in Christian Europe, Jews in Islamic countries seem to have suffered far less persecution, and were correspondingly more "embedded," or integrated, into mainstream society. A number of factors were responsible for this disparity. In Islamic law, Jews, like all *dhimmis* or non-Muslims, were subject to a relatively stable and enduring arrangement dating back to the seventh-century "Pact of Umar," while in Christian lands, Jews were subject to ever-shifting regulations depending on local conditions, encompassing both Church canon law and secular laws of the state.[26] In economics, Jews occupied a more prestigious and respected position in Islam as merchants, since this had been the occupation of the Prophet Muhammad, a town dweller, whereas in Christian Europe, the Jew as merchant, or more frequently, as moneylender, was held in greater contempt and suspicion.[27] Because Jews under Islam had more opportunities for social interactions, such as commercial partnerships and intellectual exchanges, and because Muslims were less "self-defined" in relation to the Old Testament, the interreligious polemics between Jews and Muslims were less adversarial or acrimonious. The lower level of persecution in Islam is likewise indicated by the fact that, when persecution did occur, Jews responded in more measured ways, such as temporary conversion, as opposed to self-sacrifice and martyrdom (*kiddush ha-Shem*). All this lends support to the idea that Jews in medieval Christian Europe faced some uniquely adverse circumstances, namely, a persecuting/irrational society.[28]

Yet, the varied experience of Jewry across Europe suggests that the motivations and dynamics of their persecution were extraordinarily complex. If a generalization must be made, it is that Jewish circumstances in Christian Europe began to deteriorate in the twelfth century, and then persecution picked up steam in the thirteenth and fourteenth centuries, largely owing to a Christian "aggressiveness" towards perceived and real enemies, both without and within. The crusades beginning in 1096 obviously marked the start of Christian aggression and expansion at the expense of Islamic foes in the Holy Land and Spain. The eleventh and twelfth centuries also saw the rise of heresies and the beginning of Christian concern with internal enemies that threatened a universal, Catholic orthodoxy and unity. Jews could be, and were, considered both external and internal enemies: Those of another faith alien to Christendom, but who also lived among Christians and threatened their aspirations towards a "monolithic" homogeneity from within. In terms of timing, persecution of Jews and heretics did coincide during the high Middle Ages and suggests some interchangeability in terms of majority perceptions, which would validate Moore's thesis of the emergence of a persecuting society.[29]

But in terms of who was responsible for their persecution and why, the Jewish experience does not fit Moore's "trickle down" model well at all. Rather, persecution of Jews percolated up from below as well as down from above, and was really the product of a complex interplay among the three "orders" of medieval society.[30] These included the common folk and their popular perceptions of Jews; the Church and its policies; and secular governments, both at a national and local level. But the Jews themselves also had a role to play, as a minority society interacting with a domineering and oppressive majority culture.[31] Most alarming, from the viewpoint of the Jews and their defenders, was the growing popular acceptance of the blood libel, the idea that Jewish enmity towards Christians was such that Jews would seek to murder and torture innocent, defenseless Christian boys. At the very least, this evinces a deepening Christian mistrust of the Jews, while at a certain point, the accusations of the blood libel began to take on "a reality all their own, convincing many in western Christendom of the profound dangers posed by the Jews".[32] It is simply not enough to state that this was an irrational majority fantasy that should never have taken root in the minds of reasonable Christians. We don't have to accept that there was any truth to the accusations to say that such a broad-based and visceral reaction was triggered, in part, by some unique characteristics of the Jews as Jews, that were not shared by any other minority culture.[33]

Traditionally, three explanations have been offered as to why majority perceptions of Jews deteriorated so markedly at this time.[34] First, ecclesiastical policies towards the Jews became more restrictive in a number of areas—the most notorious of which was the "Jewish badge" to be worn on clothing—designed to segregate Jews and thereby limit the potential "harm" they were now perceived to be causing Christians. This seemed to arise out of the Church's growing familiarity with the Talmud and its alleged "blasphemies" against Christianity, as well as a growing concern with the "sin" of usury, or moneylending, particularly when religious or sacred objects were used as collateral.[35] Second, the integration and synthesis of rational philosophical reasoning into the Christian faith, as embodied in the works of such schoolmen as Thomas Aquinas, generated, counter-intuitively, even greater intolerance of Jews, who were now portrayed as non-rational and unreasonable in their unbelief.[36] Third, there were the growing "anxieties" and "doubts" within the majority Christian culture, despite its over-whelming superiority compared to the position of the minorities in its midst. Some of the anxieties concerning both internal and external enemies were undoubtedly imagined, but some were quite real—while the existence of heretics may be disputed (see below), the power of Islam *was* resurging to the point that the Latin presence in the Holy Land was untenable by the end of the thirteenth century. Adding to all this anxiety was the rapid pace of change within European society itself during the high Middle Ages, change that, no matter whether it was positive or negative, was deeply unsettling to those invested in the status quo. The Jews, owing to their unique religious and economic status in Christian society, could be associated with every single one of these threats.[37]

For much of the Middle Ages, authorities in both Church and state generally assumed a protective stance towards the Jews, largely because it was in their own economic and religious self-interest to do so. These positions seemed to have changed, however, as we move into the high and late medieval periods. The Church had long taken the position that Jews must be protected as living witnesses in the here and now to the superiority of the Christian faith, and as future witnesses to the triumph of Christianity during the end times. Secular authorities sponsored Jewish immigrants as agents of economic progress, particularly in trade and banking, and as a backdoor access to their subjects' wealth through taxation. The tipping point—towards segregation and expulsion—came when Jewish liabilities, particularly in terms of moneylending, were seen to outweigh these vested interests.[38]

The Church began to view the Jews as more harmful, and less seemly subservient, with its growing awareness of the Talmud and the sin of usury during the thirteenth century. Even without this development, Church policy always contained an inherent tension between its emphasis upon Jews' sinful misdeeds—which explained their current, humiliating subservience to Christians—and its demand that Christians not act upon feelings of outrage or vengeance for those misdeeds. It was a tall order to expect the Christian populace to absorb and con-sistently abide by this complex reasoning, particularly when Jewish animosity seemed to extend not only from the time of Christ but to the here and now in the form of the blood libel. Although the Church generally rejected such accusations, it made an exception in the case of the charge of host desecration, perhaps because it touched upon popular veneration of the consecrated host, which was a boon to the Church's prestige and that of its clergy.[39] For the secular powers, the turning point was whenever Jewish usefulness in terms of exploitable wealth and economic innovation was exhausted, or when ecclesiastical and popular pressures overwhelmed economic considerations.[40] Again, we must emphasize here that Jewish persecution was the result of a complex interplay of forces, not one of which can really be isolated from the others. When the end came, the fears and prejudices of both elite and popular cultures intermingled and fed off each other, creating a toxic brew that no minority, not even one as resourceful and resilient as the Jews, could possibly resist.[41]

Anti-Semitism vs. Anti-Judaism

It goes without saying that the Jews were one of the most persecuted minorities of the Middle Ages. But how do we characterize the hostility and prejudice towards them among medieval Christians? The two most popular terms of choice among historians are anti-Semitism and anti-Judaism. Anti-Semitism, a term coined towards the end of the nineteenth century (specifically, in 1879), is usually associated with a racial or ethnic hatred of Jews with particularly virulent overtones.[42] The alternative term, anti-Judaism (also dating to the late nineteenth century), usually relates this hatred as a function of the religious conflict between Christians and Jews, particularly in terms of Jews' alleged responsibility for Jesus' crucifixion and death (the "deicide" or "Christ-killer" accusation).[43] Both words have their adherents in writings about the history of gentiles' relations with Jews.

Anti-Semitism, when used to refer to anti-Jewish feelings during the Middle Ages, naturally presupposes a historical continuity, or connection, with modern prejudice and hatred towards Jews, despite the racial or ethnic overtones of the latter. In this "long view" of the Jewish minority experience in Europe, the murder of six million Jews by Nazi Germany during World War II—commonly referred to as the "Holocaust"—becomes the endpoint, or the final catastrophe, towards which all previous history of the Jews must lead as a way of understanding this ultimate tragedy. This naturally implicates Christianity as playing a major role in anti-Jewish atrocities and massacres, committed not just during the Middle Ages, but in modern times as well.

The champion of this approach has been Gavin Langmuir, a Canadian scholar who served (and was wounded) in World War II, was married to a Holocaust survivor, and taught at Stanford University for most of his career.[44] Langmuir sought to "free anti-Semitism from its racist, ethnocentric implications" and instead made its leading characteristic the irrational thoughts, fantasies, or delusions of the persecuting majority about Jews. In doing this, Langmuir was departing from the approach of an older generation of scholars, who had used anti-Semitism quite loosely as "a catch-all designation for anti-Jewish sentiment over the ages".[45] Instead, Langmuir tried to make the parameters of anti-Semitism, at least as it applied to the Middle Ages, far more specific and subtle. He defined anti-Semitism as the irrational attribution to Jews of menacing, subhuman "characteristics or conduct that no Jews have been observed to possess or engage in".[46] Jews were thus hated not for what they actually were, but as symbols onto which medieval Christians projected all "their own weaknesses, guilt, doubts and fears" about their faith, which was central to their identity as both individuals and as a collective people.

The Christian faith, Langmuir argued, required its adherents to subscribe to a "non-rational" belief system that conflicted with a rational, empirical approach that began to come into vogue during the high Middle Ages with the recovery of the pagan philosophical legacy of ancient Greece and Rome.[47] For example, of particular concern to Christians, according to Langmuir, was the conundrum of the sacrament of the Eucharist, namely, how the bread and wine blessed by the priest could embody the real presence of Christ's flesh and blood, even though it still retained the "accidents," or physical appearance, of bread and wine.[48] This self doubt was then internalized until it found outward expression by scapegoating a living reminder of that doubt: the Jews. After the year 1000, irrational fantasies about Jews began to be expressed in terms of the "blood libel," which included accusations of ritual murder, crucifixion, and cannibalism; these, along with the accusation of host desecration, were said to have culminated in the mid-fourteenth century with the well poisoning charge that became the basis for the widespread Jewish pogroms during the Black Death.[49]

One problem with Langmuir's argument is that the application of his new definition of anti-Semitism seems rather limited. As he himself admitted, the supposedly irrational accusations against Jews were "made by psychologically troubled people who were poorly integrated in their societies," and who internalized some deep-rooted tensions between good and evil, Christian and Jew, within themselves.[50] Did he mean to suggest that this characterized every Christian who believed or adhered to anti-Jewish accusations that he deemed irrational, which comprised thousands, perhaps millions, of people? We can readily believe this of one or two individuals who showed themselves to be especially virulent in their anti-Jewish feelings and beliefs: people like Thomas of Monmouth, the monk who started the ritual murder and crucifixion libel surrounding William of Norwich, a twelve-year-old boy found dead on Easter Sunday in 1144, or Peter the Venerable, the abbot of Cluny who wrote a hate-filled letter against the Jews to King Louis VII in 1146, as well as a whole treatise against the Jews (*Against the Inveterate Obduracy of the Jews*).[51] But the vast majority of medieval people who subscribed to anti-Jewish beliefs probably did so by force of cultural habituation that was devoid of thought—irrational or otherwise—unless we are to believe it was the product of a mass sublimated angst about their faith.[52]

Perhaps the main objection to Langmuir's thesis is that not all the examples he cited of medieval anti-Semitism can be shown to have been irrational. The historian Robert Stacey has argued this to be the case with the ritual murder charge, in particular regarding the incident surrounding "Little Saint" Hugh, a nine-year-old boy whose body was discovered down a well in Lincoln and whose death was laid at the door of over 90 Jews who had gathered at Lincoln at around the same time to celebrate a wedding. Hugh's "murder" was investigated with all the legal trappings of the medieval English judicial system, and one Jew, named "Copin," actually confessed to the murder, albeit under torture. Even without this legal imprimatur, medieval people had very different standards of what they regarded as rational, empirical evidence than we do today; for them, definitive proofs could include supernatural miracles, such as those that quickly began to associate themselves with Hugh's body, which we today would find inadmissible.[53] An Italian scholar based in Israel, Ariel Toaff, has recently made an even more direct, and far more controversial, challenge to the Langmuir Thesis, arguing that the ritual murder and cannibalism charges may have had an actual basis in reality, albeit limited to an extreme, "fundamentalist" Jewish sect in Italy that enacted a Passover ritual using dried blood from "paid and willing donors who remained 'alive and well'".[54] Such historians have challenged Langmuir's insistence upon a strict "moral boundary" around the blood libel accusation, whereby any suggestion that that the libel might have been anything other than an irrational or "chimerical" fantasy is to be considered out of bounds and taboo.[55]

My own research into the medical response to the Black Death suggests a similarly rational approach behind the well poisoning accusation against the Jews during the plague pogroms of 1348–50.[56] The accusation that Jews poisoned wells in order to give the plague to Christians can be considered an extension of the medical explanation of the disease—developed in accordance with contemporary principles of natural philosophy—that many doctors subscribed to throughout the entire history of the Black Death in the later Middle Ages.[57] This was that plague was caused by a natural poisoning of the air, water, or food by bad vapors created either by planetary conjunctions (the higher cause) or by more local sources of infection, such as swamps, rotting corpses, refuse, or anything giving rise to a foul stench (the near cause). If patients were being warned by their doctors to be on their guard against poisoned air, food, or drink, then it was but a small step to conclude that humans could be behind such *artificial*, as opposed to natural, poisoning conspiracies. Indeed, the first artificial poison accusation to emerge during the Black Death did so in the region of Languedoc, at Narbonne and Carcassonne, where the accused were described as "poor men and beggars of diverse nations," while Jews were not mentioned at all[58]; nor could they have been, for Jews were expelled from this region, as well as from the rest of the kingdom of France, by 1327, although they were readmitted to the autonomous county of Provence (ruled by Queen Joanna of Sicily) in c.1345.[59] I also seriously question Langmuir's assumption that flagellants played a role in Jewish pogroms during the Black Death, which for him illustrates once again the irrationality of the charge, since flagellants in the course of their travels were made "more aware than most that Jews were dying of the plague like Christians".[60] It's quite clear that in most towns, the flagellants arrived long after Jewish pogroms had occurred, thus making any connection impossible. Indeed, the attribution of responsibility for attacks upon Jews was one of the spurious charges leveled against the flagellants by their critics.[61]

The opposing case, that anti-Judaism rather than anti-Semitism is a more appropriate term to describe persecution of Jews during the Middle Ages, was made by Steven Katz. Katz based his argument on the grounds that anti-Semitism, a primarily racial concept associated with Nazism, viewed Jews as "inherently corrupt and nonredeemable," for whom the only solution, indeed, the "Final

Solution" (*Endlösung*), was mass execution and extermination. By contrast, medieval Christianity, spearheaded by the pope, adopted as its official policy that Jews must be preserved as living proofs of Christian superiority and as final witnesses to Christian triumph at the end times, when the Jews would finally be redeemed and convert to the one, true religion. Such an approach, dating back to the Church father, St. Augustine of Hippo (354–430), was enshrined in the papal bull, *Sicut judaeis,* first issued in 1120 by Pope Calixtus II and re-issued no less than 22 times over the ensuing centuries. This Augustinian tradition, for example, provided the theological justification for Bernard of Clairvaux's defense of the Jews during the Second Crusade of 1147–49, which was credited, by both Jews and Christians, with preventing a repeat of the infamous massacres of a half century earlier, during the First Crusade in 1096. Jews were also protected by secular leaders, even if largely out of economic self-interest, until royal policy switched to expulsion. Katz's observation, that anti-Jewish violence as a rule "wells up from the lower and middle echelons of the sociopolitical order," is also a major challenge to Moore's "persecuting society" thesis, that intolerance of minorities was born during the twelfth and thirteenth centuries out of centralized governments and their administrative elites.[62]

Even though Katz's differentiation between anti-Semitism and anti-Judaism— the one demanding the death of all Jews, the other, their survival—may appear stark and unbridgeable, the gulf may not have been as wide as he made it seem. This is especially true when Katz detailed how Christian anti-Judaism demonized Jews, turning them into a subhuman, or superhuman, other. Particularly in the incarnation of the "wandering Jew," Katz argued that the Jew was "made so uncanny, so abnormal, so monstrous that all possibility for human empathy, for charity and sympathy, is destroyed". Moreover, from the twelfth century, the demonized Jew became a pervasive motif through dramatic representations in the "plastic and graphic arts," such that the Jew's "presence, though tolerated, is intolerable".[63] Here, then is a flagrant contradiction: How could a people so thoroughly de-humanized be allowed to live? Is this not exactly how the Nazis perpetrated the Holocaust?

Another inconsistency is that Katz wanted to say that "Christian anti-Judaism is a necessary precondition" for the Holocaust, yet at the same time he insisted upon maintaining that anti-Judaism was not equivalent to the "novel racial anti-Semitism" that caused our modern tragedy. One way that Katz tried to resolve this contradiction was to argue that, beginning in the fourth century, when Christianity became the state religion of the Roman Empire, "anti-Jewish prejudice" entered upon a deadly tradition whereby it was "supported by the police apparatus of the state," which Katz cited as a "decisive turn in the history of Christian anti-Judaism, a turn whose ultimate disfiguring consequence was enacted in the *political* anti-Semitism of Adolf Hitler".[64] However, I think Katz would be the first to point out that a "police state" never really existed in the Middle Ages, certainly not in the fragmented and weakly centralized collection of territories known as the German kingdom. And if medieval royal governments generally protected and supported Jews, until it become more economically and politically expedient not to do so, then how was a state-supported tradition of intolerance towards Jews continuously and consistently maintained in order to be a formative influence upon anti-Semitic Nazism? Unfortunately, Katz never fully grappled with these paradoxes.

Another historian who favored anti-Judaism over anti-Semitism was David Nirenberg. For Nirenberg, anti-Judaism was the preferred term because it allowed him to range broadly and expansively over the entire course of the Western tradition, exploring the history of anti-Jewish attitudes not just in religious terms, i.e., how Christians viewed the "Jewish other," but also as an ideational concept, or in other words, how "non-Jews can make sense of and criticize their world". By contrast, anti-Semitism, Nirenberg felt, was too limited, both "historically and conceptually".[65] A good example of Nirenberg's method is his chapter on anti-Judaism's medieval phase. Because European monarchies allied themselves with Jews as a means of increasing their power and wealth, anti-Judaism in the Middle Ages became a kind of shorthand for expressing political resistance and dissatisfaction with the state in general.[66] But Nirenberg did not really engage in the debate about the relative virtues of the terms, anti-Judaism and anti-Semitism, or whether a historical connection was to be drawn between the medieval and modern versions of anti-Jewish sentiment and thinking.

Then there is the third way of the prolific New York University scholar, Robert Chazan. Chazan rejected the use of both terms, anti-Judaism and anti-Semitism. He regarded the former as "too flaccid," in that it obscured the historical tendency to conflate the religious outlook of Judaism, with the people who espoused that religion, namely, the Jews. In other words, Chazan did not believe that anti-Judaism made it clear enough how closely Jews were identified with their religion, in the eyes of those who were hostile towards them. Certainly, Nirenberg would agree with Chazan on this score, although for him the ambiguity of anti-Judaism was precisely what attracted him to the term. Nor did Chazan generally use anti-Semitism, since he regarded this as too restricted to the modern era, a problem given his focus on medieval Jewish history; nonetheless, Chazan still aimed to show that there were "lines of influence between the Middle Ages and the more recent centuries" with regard to "anti-Jewish sentiment". His preferred term would be *sin'at Yisra'el*, a Hebrew term meaning "hatred of Israel," although even this fails to convey the full complexity of the original, since *Yisra'el* "connotes both Judaism and the Jewish people". Chazan was therefore forced to fall back on simply using variations of the descriptor, "anti-Jewish".[67] This allowed him to go on to describe the variations, or "gradations," in historical anti-Jewish sentiment, which provided the basis for his own criticisms of Langmuir's thesis. For Chazan, it did not really matter whether anti-Jewish hostility during the Middle Ages was irrational or not, but rather, how dangerous the Jew was perceived to be and how grave a threat he appeared to pose to the Christian community. Chazan argued that by the mid-twelfth century, "a new stage in the history of Christian anti-Jewish sentiment" emerged with the blood libel accusation, in that many Christians became convinced that Jews were capable of "the here-and-now murder" of Christian neighbors—not just of deicide in the distant past—that arose out of Jews' "elemental hatred of the Christian faith". In this way, the "Christian legacy" of medieval anti-Jewish thinking could evolve and change over the succeeding centuries into modern anti-Semitism, without ever being quite the same thing.[68]

A lachrymose history of medieval Jewry?

The history of the Jews of medieval Europe can all too easily descend into one long, dreary and depressing litany of persecution and oppression.[69] Indeed, there is no shortage of violent and bloody incidents against the Jews to relate: the Rhineland massacres during the First Crusade in 1096; various blood libel accusations and trials throughout the twelfth and thirteenth centuries; the Rindfleisch and Armleder massacres in Germany in 1298 and 1336–38; the Black Death pogroms associated with the charge of well poisoning in 1348–51; the 1391 pogroms in Spain; etc. Continuing the efforts of Salo Baron early in the twentieth century, some recent scholars, particularly Robert Chazan, have sought to produce a more balanced picture of Jewish life during the Middle Ages, emphasizing some of the Jewish community's positive achievements, as well as its capacity to determine its fate instead of simply falling victim to it. In addition, Jews could relate to their Christian neighbors in peaceful, even friendly, ways, and not just through violence and hostility.[70]

Chazan argued that the mere fact that Jews lived for centuries in Europe—albeit rather longer in the south than in the north—indicated that peaceful coexistence with Christian neighbors was the norm, and that violent eruptions, such as outlined above, were the exception. Moreover, throughout the high and late Middle Ages, from 1000 to 1500, Jewish population in Europe continued to grow, setting the stage for a resurgence of European Jewry in the Early Modern period.[71] This argument is a little disingenuous, in that, by the end of the Middle Ages, Jewish population in the vast majority of Europe—including England, France, Spain, and parts of Germany and Italy—was either non-existent, owing to previous expulsions, or was stagnant, experiencing no "real growth or expansion".[72] An overall growth in European Jewry can then only be explained by the fact that, in certain, restricted parts of Europe—namely, Poland and, to a lesser extent, northern and central Italy—Jewish population did indeed expand, to a large degree by means of immigration from other areas.[73] More properly, therefore, we might say that European Jewry experienced a dramatic shift in population focus at this time, from west to east. Nonetheless, Chazan deemed it significant that Jews still preferred to stay within the confines of Europe, despite heavy persecution, rather than migrate back to ancient, ancestral homelands in Palestine and Mesopotamia under Islamic rule. This is not entirely true, as some émigrés from Spain and its possessions in Sicily and Sardinia did make their way to Palestine and other parts of the Ottoman Empire in Greece, Egypt, and North Africa after the mass expulsion of 1492.[74] But Chazan's larger point was that much of Jewish migration, even when initiated by forces beyond the Jews' control, such as forcible conquest or dislocation, nonetheless entailed an independent choice of where to live, which was largely voluntary. Even if the Jewish center of gravity within Europe changed during the Middle Ages, world Jewish population and culture had largely transferred itself from the eastern Mediterranean to points north and west, from the Muslim sphere of influence to the Christian one, which mirrored the overall shift in military power and cultural dynamism in this direction as well.[75]

Modern scholarship, almost by necessity, has heavily invested in the lachrymose history of the Jews by way of explaining the Holocaust of the mid-twentieth century. Only by tracing the long history of Jewish suffering at the hands of Christians was it felt possible to explain how such a terrible tragedy could occur in Western civilization.[76] But a lachrymose history of Jewry also seems to naturally emerge from the records, as few instances of positive or peaceful relations between Christians and Jews as they went about their normal, everyday lives were explicitly stated in the chronicles and other sources.[77] One should be aware, however, that contemporary authors, on both the Jewish and Christian sides, had a vested interest in, or bias towards, the lachrymose portrayal. From the Jewish perspective, medieval misfortunes were fully in line with Jews' sense of the legacy of their biblical history, in which it was prophesied that Jews, owing to their sins, were destined to experience a "middle period" of exile and displacement before the restoration of their former political independence and religious worship in the Promised Land, specifically, Jerusalem. From the Christian point of view, Jewish misfortune was also emphasized as evidence of the breaking of God's covenant with the Jews, here envisioned as a permanent rupture, which could be traced to one Jewish sin in particular: Jews' rejection of Jesus Christ as messiah, and indeed, their complicity in his crucifixion and death. For the Christians, the long Jewish exile could only end with the Jews' conversion to Christianity and the disappearance of Judaism as an independent religion.[78]

One can point to two main areas of Jewish achievement during the medieval period. One was in the economic sphere. Jews seem to have drifted into the economic activity that is classically associated with them, moneylending, as an outgrowth of their trading and merchant activities. Although a negative, "Shylock" image often comes to mind at the mention of moneylending,[79] one has to remember that, by making investment capital available, Jews fulfilled an important and necessary function in the rapidly expanding economies of high medieval Europe, one that was fully recognized by rulers who were glad to have the Jews in their domains. In turn, Jews migrated to northern Europe because they recognized that this was a dynamic, growing society where business opportunities abounded and money was to be made. And since the Church had proscribed lending at interest to fellow Christians as part of the sin of usury, Jews filled a niche that was mutually beneficial to both borrower and lender, ruler and subject, alike. Although their lending activities later aroused popular hostility and opposition from the Church, the fact that the Jews fulfilled the same function in the developing

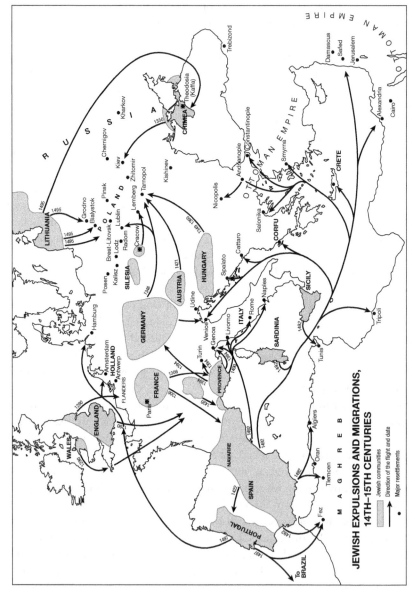

MAP 4.1 Expulsions and migrations of Jews within and outside Europe, 1290–1495.

cconomies of eastern Europe as they had in the West proves just how essential and necessary they were. Jewish success in business is also indicated by the fact that some joined the ranks of the wealthiest and most influential citizens of Europe.[80]

In the spiritual and cultural sphere, Jews made creative advances centered mainly around study and commentary of the Hebrew Bible (i.e., the written tradition, corresponding to the Christian Old Testament) and the Babylonian Talmud (i.e., the oral tradition). This educational program was carried out chiefly in the synagogue, supplemented by the rabbinic *responsum*, or answers to difficult questions, and manuals or guides to Jewish law. Other, "alternative" enterprises included translations of works by Judeo-Arabic authors, such as Maimonides (1135–1204); philosophical enquiry, which generated much controversy in the Jewish community owing to non-literal and relativist readings of biblical texts; mystical speculations; and historical narratives, such as Jewish chronicles of the First Crusade.[81] Much of this intellectual and creative activity was, ironically enough, stimulated by Christian persecution; indeed, one could almost say that without the goad of its rivalry with Christianity, medieval Jewish culture might have been poorer as a result.[82]

But there was another side to this creativity, which was that Christian persecution could inspire a tragic response from the Jews. We have already seen in Chapter 3 how Jews responded to Christian attacks in the Rhineland during the First Crusade with very public displays of self-martyrdom, the *kiddush ha-Shem*, celebrated by Hebrew chroniclers as a re-enactment of Abraham's intended sacrifice of Isaac and an affirmation of Jewish commitment to monotheism, its covenant with the one god. Such a response by the Jews could be considered analogous to the heightened rhetoric and propaganda indulged in by the crusaders, who considered themselves to be undertaking a sacrificial, perhaps apocalyptic, journey in imitation of Christ's passion by the very act of going on crusade. The one kind of martyrdom was almost a mirror image of the other.[83]

Another line of Christian attack that put Jews on the defensive was to put the Talmud "on trial" and to step up conversion efforts, which were largely undertaken in the thirteenth century with the collaboration of Jewish converts to Christianity, such as Nicholas Donin and "Friar Paul". The missionary work of Friar Paul and another, Christian-born Dominican, Raymond Martin, took a new, "innovative" tack by utilizing recently-translated rabbinic texts to argue that Jewish exegesis of the Hebrew Bible itself validated Christian truth claims, namely, that Jesus was the long-awaited and prophesied messiah. Jews responded to such claims, as they had done to Christian interpretations of the Old Testament, by pointing to the inaccuracy of Latin translations, as opposed to the Hebrew original, and by arguing that Christians took their biblical and rabbinic readings out of context and resorted to figurative instead of literal interpretations of such texts. A second line of argument that required a Jewish response were Christian claims that the rational legacy of ancient pagan philosophy validated Christian doctrine, such as the trinity and God made flesh. In response, Jewish polemicists built upon Christians' own doubts about such articles of faith and pointed to their utter incompatibility with logic and their idolatrous blasphemy. Third, Jews had to respond to Christian claims of superiority and ascendancy viz-a-viz the degraded and inferior Jewish position in their society. This was perhaps the most disturbing and difficult argument for Jews to grapple with, since it seemed to be so self-evident, borne out by material realities. The Jewish response, naturally, was to emphasize their spiritual achievements as a small but steadfast and ethically moral community, in contrast to a decadent, belligerent, and morally corrupt Christian majority. Jews were aided in this response by their sense of history, both in terms of the ancient past—when Jews had outlasted "great and successful empires" such as those of the Babylonians, Persians, Greeks, and Romans—and in terms of the present, when Christians began to suffer reversals at the hands of Muslims in the Holy Land. In all this, Jews not only adopted a defensive posture but also went on the offensive as well, attacking Christianity directly in Hebrew polemical works obviously meant for Jewish eyes only.[84]

Finally, there is the evidence of cordial relations between Christians and Jews, not just antagonistic ones. Admittedly, this evidence is rather sparse, but it must speak to many more instances that were simply left unrecorded. One of the more obvious examples of such cordial relations is the *convivencia* of medieval Spain. Here, Jews and Christians intermingled in a host of ways, with Jews living in Christian neighborhoods, owning land and properties normally reserved for Christians, bringing cases before Christian courts, taking administrative positions in Christian governments, adopting Christian dress, and having sexual relations with Christians. Even after major disruptions in this relationship, such as the massacres or riots against the Jews of 1391, Jewish communities like that in Morvedre (modern-day Sagunto), just north of Valencia, could experience a "Renaissance" of renewed peaceful relations with Christians as well as reintegration into the economy as wine merchants, money lenders, tax farmers, and artisans.[85] Such interactions were not only a concern for Christian authorities, but for Jewish ones as well. Rabbis actually petitioned for greater separation out of fear of the greatest comingling of all: conversion. Thus, the allure of a vital and seductive Christian material culture for Jews seems to have had some basis in reality.[86]

It may be instructive to explore a remarkable testimonial to inter-faith friendship that to date has gone almost unnoticed,[87] which comes from the register of Richard de Swinfield, bishop of Hereford (1282–1317). The incident occurred in the cathedral city of Hereford at the end of August 1286, just four years before all the Jews in England were expelled in 1290 on the orders of King Edward I. At issue was the fact that "several Christians" in Hereford had been invited to attend a Jewish wedding celebrated on August 28, 1286, a Wednesday. Remarkably, the Christians had received a formal, open invitation from the Jews, rather than being invited "secretly," as one might expect given the taboos, both written and unwritten, against such familiarity, which dates back to at least the fourth century.[88] On August 26, a Monday, two days before the wedding, the bishop wrote to his chancellor, also acting as dean of the cathedral, instructing him to publicly announce his prohibition against attendance at the wedding in all the churches of the city, as well as to publicly cry it in all the streets so that no one could plead ignorance, on both Tuesday, the day before the wedding, and on Wednesday, the day of the wedding itself.[89] Swinfield's justification for his action, while receiving little sympathy from modern observers, was fully in line with the Church's growing concern throughout the thirteenth century about the possible "harm" Jews could commit through their interactions with Christians (which we have seen was a concern for Jewish authorities as well). Earlier in the century, in 1222, the Oxford synod had prohibited any relations whatsoever between Christians and Jews in the province of Canterbury. Although the decree was nullified by the crown, since it would have brought all Jewish lending activities to an end, the government of Henry III did support the wearing of the "Jewish badge" and sponsor missionizing and conversion efforts by Dominican and Franciscan friars among the Jews.[90] One should therefore not be surprised when Bishop Swinfield portentously claimed that disapproval of "intercourse" between Christians and Jews, as embodied in the wedding invitation, came not just from himself, but "down from the very heights of heaven to the depths of this world".[91]

It seems obvious that the Jews intended to do their Christian guests great honor by inviting them to their wedding, and such an act, given the circumstances, must have required great courage and testifies to the warmth and depth of feeling that the Jews had towards their Christian friends. But what is perhaps even more remarkable, is that the Christians, in defiance of their bishop, accepted the Jews' invitation and attended the wedding. On September 6, Swinfield wrote again to the dean of Hereford, complaining that "several sons of iniquity or rebellion presumed to attend the impious nuptials of the said enemies of the cross of Christ [i.e., the Jews], holding intercourse with them and manifoldly honoring and gracing them [with their presence], to the disparagement of [all other] Christians".[92] From this second letter, we learn a little more about what attendance at the Jewish wedding entailed: Christian guests were said to have been "eating, drinking, playing games, jesting, or taking part in any kind of dramatic entertainment whatsoever" with their Jewish hosts. In other words, these were all the things one might expect to happen at a typically raucous "reception" of the wedding party after the taking of vows. In addition, Christians, dressed in their finest in "silken or gilded cloth," rode on horseback or in a carriage alongside Jews, which was presumably the wedding party going to or from the *chuppah*, or bridal canopy just outside the synagogue, or to or from the reception.[93] On a purely polemical level, there was no cause for concern: Jews were not attempting to proselytize to Christians, and indeed, the only danger perceived by Swinfield seems to have come from the camaraderie and bonhomie evidently indulged in by both Christians and Jews during the wedding celebrations.

While it must have taken courage for the Christians to defy the bishop by attending the wedding, just as it took courage for the Jews to invite them, there is also the distinct possibility that the dean of Hereford failed to fully publish the bishop's bans on attendance at the wedding. This much is indicated by the fact that the bishop had to repeat his command to the dean to censure the attendees, urging him to "stand firm in whatever you do in the aforementioned matter," and reserving to himself the power of granting absolution. Moreover, Swinfield warned the dean at the end of his letter that he intended "to demand from others the proper execution" of a sentence of excommunication against the attendees, "should you be negligent in the aforesaid matter".[94] All this points to the dean sympathizing with what must have appeared to many, even during the Middle Ages, as a harmless social occasion between Christians and Jews. But we can't close this case without also pointing to the fact that there must have been many others who disapproved of this fraternization between Christians and Jews. There is no other way to explain how the bishop found out about the wedding, and about the Christian attendance at it. He himself says that he received "frequent reports" about the matter from certain, "trustworthy men".[95] One has to wonder, however, just how accurate these reports were. While any street walker could see Jews and Christians riding to or from the wedding ceremony, only an invitee could observe the one activity missing from the bishop's description of the festivities: dancing.

The long-time Jewish history scholar, Joseph Shatzmiller, has illuminated another revealing instance of cordial relations between Christians and Jews, this time from Marseilles in France. At the trial in 1317 of a Jewish moneylender, Bondavid, a flood of Christian witnesses—which included two noblemen, a clergyman, three public notaries, and various other citizens—came forward to testify both to Bondavid's overall good character and to specific instances of his generosity in his business transactions. The latter included postponement of debt repayments, remittance of interest, and waiving of any securities for loans. While he was just one individual, Bondavid nonetheless provides a powerful antidote to the typical "Shylock" image of the grasping, unrelenting Jewish moneylender.[96] Other anecdotal evidence of friendly relations between Christians and Jews includes the fact that Jews turned to their Christian fellow citizens for protection during the crusader attacks of 1096 at Worms and Cologne, and that a Christian laundrywoman helped rescue a Jewess accused of ritual murder at Würzburg in 1147.[97] In southern France and Spain, there seems to have been a free sharing of information between Christian and Jewish scholars.[98] There also was a steady stream of conversions of Jews to Christianity, which, as already mentioned, was a concern to Jewish rabbis urging greater separation, but which apparently was not enough to impact the growth of Jewish communities in Europe.[99] On the other hand, recorded instances of medieval Christians converting to Judaism were few and far between, understandably enough given the severe penalties involved, but this doesn't mean that it didn't happen. Two such conversions occurred in England: In 1222, a young deacon studying Hebrew at Oxford converted, had himself circumcised, and married a Jewess, with the result that he was degraded from his office and then burnt at the stake. Then, in 1274, an English Dominican, Robert of Reading, converted in the course of his biblical studies, which perhaps he was conducting in order to better debate the Jews, and ended up marrying a Jewess and took the Jewish name of "Haggai," but nothing else is known of his fate.[100]

In the end, what is most impressive is how Jews managed to retain their identity in the face of great challenges and pressures from the majority Christian environment. This is testimony to the cohesiveness, adaptability, and tenacity of medieval Jewry. But also, one cannot explain how and why Jews migrated, stayed, and thrived in Europe except that, for most of the time, they experienced a safe, peaceful, and "normal" environment among their Christian neighbors.[101]

Defining heresy

Almost from the very beginning of Christianity, there was heresy. Derived from the Greek, *haeresis*, meaning "choice," heresy posed a different sort of challenge to mainstream society than Jewry or leprosy.[102] Since heretics chose to deviate from the norm, their marginal status was bound to give greater offense, even if, at the same time, it was also more tenuous, easily reversed by the conversion of the heretic back to orthodoxy. And yet, heretics also had this in common with Jews, lepers, and homosexuals, that they were considered "unclean" by the persecuting majority, a disease of the body and of the soul, and a threat to ideological, biological, and social purity and unity.[103]

It was the apostle, Paul, writing in his first letter to the Corinthians, who perhaps first bore witness to the existence of "heresies," or dissensions, among the earliest Christians (1 Corinthians 11:19). Subsequently, some of the early leaders of the Church, including Tertullian (155–240 A.D.), Augustine of Hippo (354–430), and Theodoret (393–457), wrestled with how to identify heretics, who they were, and how far to compel them to submit.[104] With the conversion of the emperor, Constantine (r. 306–37), to Christianity, as well as with his declaration of toleration of Christians by the Edict of Milan of 313 and his intervention in the Arian controversy at the Council of Nicaea in 325, the relationship between the defenders of "orthodoxy" and dissenters changed. Already under Constantine, heretics were excluded from privileges granted to Christians, and by the time of Emperor Theodosius (r. 379–95), when Christianity became the official religion of the state, it was decreed that all heresies were hereafter forbidden and "shall forever cease". Those "demented and insane" followers of "heretical dogmas," which were explicitly named, were to suffer exclusion from public office and the right of public worship, although if they were to return to the Catholic faith they were to be speedily and simply "absolved of all guilt".[105] The persecution of heretics had begun.

Heresy at this early stage was mainly defined in terms of specific dissenting groups and their beliefs. Thus, the Manichaeans, a dualist sect founded by the Persian, Mani (216–74 A.D.), attracted to its ranks Augustine of Hippo, before he converted to orthodox Christianity.[106] The Arians, inspired by Arius (256–336), a Christian presbyter in Alexandria, taught that Jesus Christ, although divine, was not "co-equal" or "co-eternal" with God the Father, and claimed the adherence of several Germanic tribes, including the Ostrogoths of Italy and the Visigoths of Spain. The Donatists, who originated during the persecutions of the Christians under the emperor, Diocletian (r. 284–305), held that only clergy who were faultless could administer the sacraments. Many of these early heresies corresponded with, if not actually influenced, later heresies during the high Middle Ages.

There was then thought to have been a long hiatus, roughly from the end of the sixth century until the end of the tenth, when heresy disappeared from the European scene.[107] When it re-emerged, in the eleventh century, heresy was largely associated with the reform movement in the Church, which was sometimes led by the popes themselves, such as Pope Gregory VII (1073–85). Thus, the Patarenes of Milan, and the followers of Henry of Lausanne and Arnold of Brescia (the "Arnoldists"), who were active from the mid-eleventh to the mid-twelfth centuries, were popular anti-clerical movements that attacked real abuses in the Church, such as simony, clerical marriage, and worldliness.[108] The question then became, how to distinguish between a genuine heresy, and a good-faith effort to reform the Church?[109]

It was around the mid-twelfth century that a new type of heresy supposedly emerged in the West, but one that had old roots in Christian culture. This was the dualist heresy of the "Cathars," or "Catharism," which has been described as the heresy most feared by the Church in the Middle Ages. Rather than simply attacking the authority of the Church and of its priesthood, the Cathars challenged the very belief system of Catholicism and the social mores of medieval society. According to contemporary observers like Ranier Sacconi, a Dominican inquisitor and allegedly a former Cathar himself, the Cathars believed that everything in this world—the material realm—was the product of Satan (in "mitigated" dualism a fallen angel, but in "absolute" dualism a deity in his own right). The realm of the spirit was ruled by the good god; the goal of Cathars was therefore to free souls from their material prison. Since everything of the flesh was evil, the sacraments of baptism, eucharist and marriage (i.e., to procreate and create more "flesh") were especially anathema to Cathars. Moreover, the Cathars supposedly set up their own church hierarchy and their own rites to rival those of Catholicism. Much of the debate about the origins of Catharism has revolved around whether it arose independently in the Rhineland, southern France, and northern Italy, or whether it was imported from the East harboring older dualist beliefs, particularly Bogomilism, which arose in the tenth century in Bulgaria and other parts of the Byzantine Empire.[110]

Now, however, this debate has been entirely superseded by another that goes right to the heart of the historical investigation of heresy: Did Catharism even exist at all?

Catharism: The heresy that never was?

One of the more hotly debated, or "controversial," topics in medieval history these days is Catharism.[111] This debate pits two sides that have very little common ground, or room for compromise, between them.[112] On one side is the revisionist view (also characterized as "radical skeptic," "inventionist" or "deconstructionist"), that claims Catharism is an "historians' illusion" or myth, a made-up heresy or straw man that was the product of the "persecuting society" of the twelfth century, which, later in the thirteenth century, became a self-fulfilling prophecy of the Albigensian Crusade and the Inquisition.[113] On the other side is the "traditionalist" view that Catharism was a real religion, with its own belief system, or doctrine, and organizational structure, or ecclesiology.[114] Although there seems to be no middle ground in between these two poles, some have tried to stake out intermediate positions.[115] These include that a dualist heresy did exist in southern France but was not called Catharism, or, at least, that the term is inadequate to sum up all the local variations, or "catharisms," that existed on the ground.[116] Here, however, we will focus on the main debate over the very existence of Catharism.

The case against Catharism largely comes down to the fact that there are no sources from the heretics' point of view that lay out what exactly they believed in, or that even attest to their very existence. (In this view, literacy was a weapon wielded by the Church against heretics.[117]) Instead, we have to rely on hostile sources written by Church authorities, or, at best, sources that allow us to reconstruct the "spiritual landscape" within which heretics were accused.[118] The one possible Cathar source, an account of a Cathar assembly at Saint-Félix-de-Caraman in 1167, exists only in a seventeenth-century copy and is marred by controversy as a possible forgery.[119] Otherwise, there are tantalizing second-hand references to a whole putative library of Cathar texts—including charters, wills and other notarial documents; sermons, conciliar decrees, and letters; and service books, bibles, and other theological texts—but no surviving primary sources to confirm their actual existence.[120]

As a name, Catharism hardly exists in the medieval record.[121] It was used by Eckbert of Schönau to refer to the *Catharistae*, a branch of the ancient Manichaean heresy active in the 1160s in the Rhineland, which was really separate from the Cathar movement proper in southern France.[122] The historical term "Cathar"—used to refer to a broad dualist heresy across Europe—was not coined until the nineteenth century by the historian, Charles Schmidt, as an alternative to "Albigensian".[123] Contemporary inquisitors referred to Cathars as simply "heretics" (*heretici*), or else as the "perfect" or "perfected" (*heretici perfecti*), terms that did not necessarily imply dualist connotations.[124] What the so-called Cathars called themselves were "good men" (*boni homines* or *bons omes*), "believers" (*credentes* or *crezens*), and "good Christians" (*boni christiani* or *bos crestias*).[125] "Good man" and "good woman" were titles of respect or deference in southern France, akin to "prudent man" (*prudome* or *probi homines*), which was used to address men who embodied "courtliness, honor, and holiness". This could be considered part of the social customs of "courtesy" (*cortezia*), or courtly manners and chivalry, that was a renowned aspect of culture in southern France during the high Middle Ages.[126] In this light, the "adoration" or "melioration" (*melioramentum*) with which believers in the village routinely greeted the good men, and the "consolation" or "comforting" (*consolamentum*) that good men dispensed to believers on their death bed as a kind of blessing by the laying on of hands, could simply be part of this "courtly ethos celebrated by the troubadours," as opposed to defining acts of heresy according to the inquisitors.[127] Good men, by this account, were not antithetical to the Church, but rather complemented it as those to whom people turned in default of good priests, or simply in default of any priests available in the isolated rural parishes far from civilization. Far from being marginal figures, the good men, it is argued, were part of the "very familiar, distinctly mundane, rhythms of medieval existence," which therefore deprived the medieval Church and society of much of its *raison d'être* to persecute.[128] By the thirteenth century, good men were forced underground into the role of heretics by a paranoid institution, determined to root out internal enemies and whose crusading ideology turned inwards against the very society it was supposed to protect.[129]

On the other side, scholars claim that Catharism comprised a coherent religion with dualist tenets (which either arose independently or were derived from eastern influences); established an elaborate body of ritual or rites (e.g. *consolomentum*, *meliormentum*, *apparellamentum*, etc.); and had its own hierarchical Church structure (i.e., bishops, elder sons, younger sons, deacons, believers).[130] This picture relies almost entirely on accounts by establishment Church figures, such as Eberwin of Helfenstein, abbot of the Premonstratensian house of Steinfeld; Peter of Vaux-de-Cernay, the monastic author of the *Historia Albigensis*; Ranier Sacconi, a former Cathar "bishop" or heresiarch who converted to Catholicism and became a Dominican inquisitor; and Moneta of Cremona, a Dominican inquisitor and professor of philosophy at Bologna.[131] Some "new" sources are cited in support of Catharism, such as the *Paenitenciae* kept by the Dominican inquisitor, Peter Sellan, from 1241, which lists in brief form the depositions, or confessions, of suspected heretics, followed by their assigned penances.[132] However, one will note that this still is a source from the victors' perspective, and brings us no closer to the Cathars' own point of view. Some modern defenders of Catharism complain that skeptics are too dismissive of "positivist" sources that attest to the existence of Catharism, even when these are relatively unbiased and credible.[133] But traditionalists may not always be pleased with a renewed scrutiny of their preferred sources. Such is the case for a letter written by Eberwin of Steinfeld to Bernard of Clairvaux in 1143–47, which described a heretical group that most scholars assume were Cathars (although Eberwin never named them as such). Yet it has recently been pointed out that some of Eberwin's criticisms of the sect—such as their adherence to strict apostolic poverty and their keeping company with women—also were charged against schismatics within the Premonstratensian movement, with whom Eberwin had been contending for decades.[134] Far from being an unimpeachable, dispassionate witness to Catharism, Eberwin's testimony is now "subject to the same doubts and difficulties" as any other source text read in its contemporary context. This inevitably puts all other positivist sources on Catharism—particularly those arising from the inquisition that was determined to root out and identify heretics—in question.[135]

There is much at stake in this debate. Even though this is not the first time that an alleged heresy has been debunked—half a century ago, Robert Lerner proved the non-existence of the so-called Heresy of the Free Spirit[136]—Catharism has traditionally been viewed as the quintessential heresy of the Middle Ages. If Catharism goes, then the viability of all other heresies, and the very *raison d'etre* of the Inquisition itself, are now at risk. Personally, I am inclined to side with the skeptics. I say this based on my own research into the flagellant movement during the Black Death of the mid-fourteenth century.[137] Until the discovery of a "flagellant scroll" that was written and used by the flagellants themselves as the basis for their penitential performances,[138] we had to rely on hostile chronicle sources written mostly by clerical observers, who almost universally portrayed the flagellants as hysterical fanatics who believed their extraordinary penance absolved them of all sin. In actual fact, the scroll demonstrates that the flagellants were highly choreographed and disciplined performers, who aimed to imitate the passion of Christ as a means to appease God's anger in order to take away the plague. The prejudices of the sources on the flagellants became those of modern historians who relied on them to construct a history of the movement. Unless new sources are discovered that tell the story of the "Cathars" from their own perspective, we will never be able to counterbalance the weight of the Church's prosecution against them. This same bias also worked, until relatively recently, against the women and men accused of witchcraft throughout the Early Modern period. As it stands, it seems unlikely that a fair trial of the evidence concerning the "Cathars" will ever be possible. In the meantime, I am inclined to judge the "good men" as innocent of heretical Catharism, until proven guilty.

Leprosy: The living death?

Leprosy was the most feared disease in the Middle Ages, that is, until plague arrived in the mid-fourteenth century, killing about half of Europe's population in one fell stroke. Like plague, leprosy is caused by a bacterium, in this instance, *Mycobacterium leprae*, which is related to the bacterium causing tuberculosis, which accords immunity to leprosy. (A milder form of the disease is known as "tuberculoid" leprosy.) These days, leprosy is also known as "Hansen's disease," named after a Norwegian physician, Gerhard Armauer Hansen (1841–1912), who discovered the bacterium. Leprosy is non-hereditary and not highly contagious, but it is spread person-to-person through close contact with the bodily fluids, particularly nasal discharges, of infected patients. Its classic symptoms, especially in the more severe form known as lepromatous or "leonine" leprosy, is disfigurement of the face caused by granulomas, or nodular swellings, of the peripheral nerves, accompanied by anesthesia of the nerve endings and resorption of bone tissue, often resulting in stunted extremities, blindness, and loss of speech. Of course, the medical understanding of leprosy in the Middle Ages was quite different, based on the ancient humoral conception of disease, but its diagnosis could be quite elaborate and sophisticated, based on as many as 50 telltale "signs," perhaps because the consequences of a positive diagnosis could be so severe. Moreover, the medieval approach to leprosy always included a "moral" element, in addition to a purely epidemiological understanding of the disease, although this may have been de-emphasized in the later Middle Ages as the "medicalization" of leprosy proceeded apace, and as society's preoccupation with leprosy—insofar as this can be judged—went into decline after a high point had been reached in the twelfth or mid-thirteenth centuries.[139]

One of the main debates or points of revision that has emerged about leprosy in recent years is whether it constituted a "living death" for victims, who were thereby shunned by medieval society, forced to wander with bell or rattle to announce their approach, or even physically "walled off" in separate enclosures known as leprosaria (which became a common feature in many medieval towns, with over 300 in England alone[140]). Perhaps the most notorious popular misconception about lepers was the "Leper Mass," or rite of separation of the leper from the rest of society, with the leper supposedly standing in a grave while the rite of the dead was said over him and dirt actually thrown onto his misshapen head. This is a dramatic image worthy of any portrayal in literature or film, but it seems to have been a fiction, with no evidence that it was actually enacted in real life.[141] Leprosaria were either prisons to contain the lepers' infection (communicated primarily through their uncontrollable lust), or monastic-type institutions that channeled the lepers' spiritual power through prayer on behalf of all the faithful.[142] The contrasting views of leprosy either as a punishment for sin or as the "holy disease" that cleansed the fortunate victim, like Job, seemed to reflect the ambivalence and changing attitudes towards the disease in medieval society. If lepers were marginalized by their fellow men and women, then they were both persecuted for the threat they posed to the body, and venerated for the salvation they promised for the soul.[143]

It is instructive to compare leprosy with plague, in order to illustrate some of the most salient aspects of either disease. Like plague, leprosy was viewed as highly contagious and a punishment for sin. Both were seen as spread by poison, either naturally or through human artifice: In 1321, the "Lepers' Plot" in southern France and northeastern Spain targeted lepers as part of an alleged conspiracy in league with Jews and Muslims to poison wells to communicate leprosy, just as Jews and others were accused during the Black Death of poisoning wells to spread the plague.[144] Leprosy was grouped with plague as among the "incurable diseases," for which no remedy could be found.[145]

However, there also were some important differences. Because plague had such a high mortality and morbidity, medieval responses to plague were less forgiving than towards leprosy. From the very beginning of the Black Death, town ordinances, such as enacted by Pistoia, Florence, and Milan, attempted to enforce strict quarantine and segregation of actual and potential plague victims, and by the fifteenth century, plague control measures were coordinated by town health boards across Europe.[146] Even caretakers of plague patients had to wear special distinguishing "signs" on their garments and not frequent certain public spaces while they fulfilled their tasks, while hospital attendants and disinfection personnel were liable to be accused of deliberately spreading the plague if the epidemic was not contained, as happened at Geneva in the sixteenth century.[147] Leprosy, on the other hand, took years for an infection to emerge after first contact, and, with proper treatment, milder cases of the disease could be managed on a chronic basis. This led to doubts as to whether leprosy was truly contagious or instead was hereditary, and whether the disease could, in fact, be cured.[148] Those who attended lepers, which could include the great and powerful, such as King Louis IX of France (r. 1226–70), were seen as performing a divine and holy act, in imitation of Christ's cleansing of a leper (Matthew 8:1–4).[149] The difference between leprosy and plague might be summed up as that, whereas leprosy was the living death, plague was death to the living.

One can also compare how different cultures in the medieval world treated lepers. As in the Latin West, Byzantium established leprosaria as its main response to leprosy, with the Greeks founding some of the earliest known leper hospitals, dating to the fourth century A.D.[150] These tried to balance the sometimes contrary agendas of charity and public health, but their existence did not necessarily indicate a higher incidence of leprosy. Other religions, such as Islam and Judaism, shared with Christianity a belief that leprosy was contagious from person-to-person, despite their strict adherence to the direct agency of the one god.[151] While Muslims had the Prophetic tradition that there was no contagion, the Prophet Muhammad had also commanded to "Flee the leper as you would from a lion," which is perhaps a pun on the appearance of the leper. This was traditionally explained as more a command to protect the faith rather than the health of the believer, who might be tempted to revert back to pagan *Jahiliyya* beliefs in contagion.[152] Islam also had the tradition that disease, especially the plague, was a mercy and martyrdom for the faithful; while a similar belief was not held with respect to plague in the Christian world, there was with respect to leprosy, in that the disease represented a chance for the Christian to purge his soul here on earth.[153] Both Islam and Judaism shared with Christianity the belief that lepers must be separated or excluded from the community for the sake of self-preservation, with the Hebrew texts of the Old Testament serving as the basis for a shared set of cultural assumptions among both Jews and Christians.[154] The crusades also undoubtedly brought the Latins into contact with Muslim and Greek views on leprosy and perhaps acted as a moderating influence.[155] Yet despite these similarities, Islamic and Jewish cultures were assumed to be more tolerant of lepers, on the grounds that they lacked institutional responses to leprosy in the form of official leprosaria, and that therefore lepers in Islamic and Jewish communities were allowed greater freedom of movement and intermingling with the healthy.[156] This must be revised in light of recent research, particularly on leprosy in Christian Europe. After all, Christ himself sought to re-integrate marginal figures such as the leper and the prostitute back into mainstream society, and his example was further emphasized in iconographic images in art as well as literature.[157] If there is a common thread among all these cultures with respect to leprosy, it is that society's attitudes towards lepers were conflicted, a mixture of fear and pity, condemnation and toleration.

Notes

1 Originally published in Polish in 1971 and in French in 1976. The English version, translated by Jean Birrell (from the French), was published in 1987 by Cambridge University Press. For a spirited defence of minority history, see John Boswell, "Revolutions, Universals, and Sexual Categories," in *Hidden from History: Reclaiming the Gay and Lesbian Past*, eds. Martin Duberman, Martha Vicinus, and George Chauncey, Jr. (New York: Meridian, 1989), p. 17.

2 *Other Middle Ages: Witnesses at the Margins of Medieval Society*, ed. Michael Goodich (Philadelphia, PA.: University of Pennsylvania Press, 1998).

3 R.I. Moore, *The Formation of a Persecuting Society: Power and Deviance in Western Europe, 950–1250* (Oxford: Basil Blackwell, 1987); R.I. Moore, *The Formation of a Persecuting Society: Authority and Deviance in Western Europe, 950–1250*, 2nd edn. (Oxford: Blackwell Publishing, 2007). For a reevaluation of Moore's work on heresy, see: *Heresy and the Persecuting Society in the Middle Ages: Essays on the Work of R.I. Moore*, ed. Michael Frassetto (Leiden, Netherlands: Brill, 2006).

4 Moore, *Formation of a Persecuting Society*, 2nd edn., pp. 144–45.

5 R.W. Southern, *The Making of the Middle Ages* (New Haven, CT.: Yale University Press, 1953); Joseph R. Strayer, *On the Medieval Origins of the Modern State* (Princeton, NJ.: Princeton University Press, 1970).

6 This comes from the title of a book by James J. Walsh, *Thirteenth, Greatest of Centuries* (New York: Catholic Summer School Press, 1907).

7 Particularly revealing are Moore's comments on the work of Sir Richard Southern, his former teacher at Oxford, in *Formation of a Persecuting Society*, 2nd edn., p. 3.

8 R.I. Moore, *The First European Revolution, c. 950–1215* (Oxford: Blackwell, 2000); Edward Peters, "Moore's Eleventh and Twelfth Centuries: Travels in the Agro-Literate Polity," in *Heresy and the Persecuting Society in the Middle Ages*, pp. 15–16. Moore argued that once the genie of popular revolution had served its purpose and created European power structures, it needed to be put back in the bottle through persecution.

9 The idea of the three orders of medieval feudal society can be traced back to the eleventh century, but in modern times, the idea has been explored by the French historian, Georges Duby. See: R.I. Moore, "Duby's Eleventh Century," *History* 69 (1984):42–46; Peters, "Moore's Eleventh and Twelfth Centuries," pp. 18–19.

10 David Nirenberg, *Communities of Violence: Persecution of Minorities in the Middle Ages* (Princeton, NJ.: Princeton University Press, 1996), pp. 3–7; Mark R. Cohen, *Under Crescent and Cross: The Jews in the Middle Ages* (Princeton, NJ.: Princeton University Press, 1994), pp. 162–63; Peters, "Moore's Eleventh and Twelfth Centuries," pp. 14–15; David Berger, *From Crusades to Blood Libels to Expulsions: Some New Approaches to Medieval Antisemitism* (New York: Touro College, 1997), pp. 6–8. Cohen defined persecution during the Middle Ages as "unwarranted violence against persons or property," which included individual and mass murder, forced conversion, and physical expulsion. Other kinds of "mistreatment," such as discriminatory bias and negative attitudes and speech, which we today might classify as persecution, Cohen argued were simply part of normal medieval discourse. For more on the debate over the definition of "persecution" as applied to medieval Jews, see Jörg R. Müller, "Judenverfolgungen und -vertreibungen zwischen Nordsee und Südalpen im hohen und späten Mittelalter," in *Geschichte der Juden im Mittelalter von der Nordsee bis zu den Südalpen*, ed. Alfred Haverkamp (Forschungen zur Geschichte der Juden, 14/1, 2002), pp. 189–90.

11 One reassessment of Moore's thesis did argue that a degree of toleration was displayed towards Muslims, Jews, and even heretics, or religious non-conformists, by members of the medieval Church throughout the Middle Ages. See Cary J. Nederman, "Introduction: Discourses and Contexts of Tolerance in Medieval Europe," in *Beyond the Persecuting Society: Religious Toleration before the Enlightenment*, eds. John Christian Laursen and Cary J. Nederman (Philadelphia, PA.: University of Pennsylvania Press, 1998), pp. 13–24.

12 Moore, *Formation of a Persecuting Society*, 2nd edn., p. 5.

13 Moore, *Formation of a Persecuting Society*, 2nd edn., p. 145.

14 Moore, *Formation of a Persecuting Society*, 2nd edn., p. 144.

15 Recently, however, this thesis has been challenged by Samuel Cohn, Jr., "The Black Death and the Burning of the Jews," *Past and Present* 196 (2007):3–36.

16 For this reason, I refer to the Black Death pogroms as the "artificial poisoning conspiracy," rather than identifying them specifically as the "Jewish pogroms". I discuss this approach in far more detail in Chapter 6 of John Aberth, *The Black Death: A New History of the Great Mortality*, forthcoming with Oxford University Press.

17 Moore, *Formation of a Persecuting Society*, 1st edn., pp. 62–65. One marginal group that we do not address in this chapter are blacks in the Middle Ages: Much of the reason for this is that medieval people understood skin color differences so very differently than we do today, seeing these more in terms of religious and cultural differences than of race or ethnicity. See: T. Hahn, "The Difference the Middle Ages Makes: Color and Race before the Modern World," *Journal of Medieval and Early Modern Studies* 31 (2001):8–9; Margaret Jubb, "The Crusaders' Perceptions of their Opponents," in *Palgrave Advances in the Crusades*, ed. Helen J. Nicholson (Basingstoke, UK and New York: Palgrave Macmillan, 2005), p. 227.

18 Robert Chazan, *The Jews of Medieval Western Christendom, 1000–1500* (Cambridge: Cambridge University Press, 2006), pp. 90–115; Jonathan Ray, *The Sephardic Frontier: The Reconquista and the Jewish Community in Medieval Iberia* (Ithaca, NY.: Cornell University Press, 2006); Eliyahu Ashtor, *The Jews of Moslem Spain*, trans. Aaron Klein and Jenny Machlowitz Klein, 3 vols. (Philadelphia, PA.: Jewish Publication Society, 1973–84); Yitzhak Baer, *A History of the Jews in Christian Spain*, trans. Louis Schoffman, et al., 2 vols. (Philadelphia, PA.: Jewish Publication Society, 1961–66). Nirenberg, in *Communities of Violence*, made the unconventional argument that Spain's *convivencia* was predicated on the ritualized violence acted out on a regular basis by Christians upon Jews.

19 Chazan, *Jews of Medieval Western Christendom*, pp. 115–27; Cecil Roth, *A History of the Jews of Italy* (Philadelphia, PA.: Jewish Publication Society of America, 1946).

20 Chazan, *Jews of Medieval Western Christendom*, pp. 78–90; William Chester Jordan, "Home Again: The Jews in the Kingdom of France, 1315–1322," in *The Stranger in Medieval Society*, eds. F.R.P. Akehurst and Stephanie Cain Van D'Elden (Minneapolis, MN.: University of Minnesota Press, 1997), pp. 27–45; Mark R. Cohen, *Under Crescent and Cross: The Jews in the Middle Ages* (Princeton, NJ.: Princeton University Press, 1994), pp. 124–25.

21 Chazan, *Jews of Medieval Western Christendom*, pp. 131–53; Robert Chazan, *Medieval Jewry in Northern France: A Political and Social History* (Baltimore, MD.: Johns Hopkins University Press, 1973); William Chester Jordan, *The French Monarchy and the Jews: From Philip Augustus to the Last of the Capetians* (Philadelphia, PA.: University of Pennsylvania Press, 1989); Jordan, "Home Again," pp. 27–39; Cohen, *Under Crescent and Cross*, pp. 86–87; Robert Bonfil, "Aliens Within: The Jews and Antijudaism," in *Handbook of European History, 1400–1600: Late Middle Ages, Renaissance and Reformation. Volume I: Structures and Assertions*, eds. Thomas A. Brady, Jr., Heiko A. Oberman, and James D. Tracy (Leiden, Netherlands: Brill, 1994), p. 275.

22 Chazan, *Jews of Medieval Western Christendom*, pp. 154–67; H.G. Richardson, *The English Jewry under Angevin Kings* (London: Methuen, 1960); Cecil Roth, *A History of the Jews in England* (Oxford: Clarendon Press, 1964); R.B. Dobson, *The Jews of York and the Massacre of 1190* (York: York University Press, 1974); Robert C. Stacey, *Politics, Policy and Finance under Henry III: 1216–1245* (Oxford: Oxford University Press, 1987); Zefira Entin Rokéah, "The State, the Church, and the Jews in Medieval England," in *Anti-semitism Through the Ages*, ed. Shmuel Almog and trans. Nathan H. Reisner (Oxford: Pergamon Press, 1988), pp. 99–125; Robin R. Mundill, *The King's Jews: Money, Massacre and Exodus in Medieval England* (London: Continuum, 2010).

23 Chazan, *Jews of Medieval Western Christendom*, pp. 170–98; Cohen, *Under Crescent and Cross*, pp. 45–48; *Germania Judaica*, 2 vols. (Breslau: M. and H. Marcus, 1934–68); Jeffrey Richards, *Sex, Dissidence and Damnation: Minority Groups in the Middle Ages* (London: Routledge, 1991), p. 99; Jörg R. Müller, "*Erez gezerah*—'Land of Persecution': Pogroms against the Jews in the regnum Teutonicum from c. 1280 to 1350," in *The Jews of Europe in the Middle Ages (Tenth to Fifteenth Centuries): Proceedings of the International Symposium held at Speyer, 20–25 October 2002*, ed. Christoph Cluse (Turnhout, Belgium: Brepols, 2004), pp. 248–58; Müller, "Judenverfolgungen," pp. 210–21; David Malkeil, *Reconstructing Ashkenaz: The Human Face of Franco-German Jewry, 1000–1250* (Stanford, CA.: Stanford University Press, 2009).

24 Chazan, *Jews of Medieval Western Christendom*, pp. 198–208; Bonfil, "Aliens Within," p. 268.

25 Cohen, *Under Crescent and Cross*, pp. 3–14, 163–69.

26 Cohen, *Under Crescent and Cross*, pp. 30–74.

27 Cohen, *Under Crescent and Cross*, pp. 77–136.

28 Cohen, *Under Crescent and Cross*, pp. 139–94. I do, however, think that Cohen accepted the Moore and Langmuir theses rather too uncritically.

29 Moore, *Formation of a Persecuting Society*, 1st edn., pp. 29–45; Chazan, *Jews of Medieval Western Christendom*, pp. 210–11, 240–41; Robert Chazan, *Medieval Stereotypes and Modern Antisemitism* (Berkeley, CA.: University of California Press, 1997), pp. 78–85; Richards, *Sex, Dissidence, and Damnation*, pp. 94–95.

30 Chazan, *Jews of Medieval Western Christendom*, pp. 239–40.

31 Chazan, *Jews of Medieval Western Christendom*, p. 216.

32 Chazan, *Jews of Medieval Western Christendom*, p. 214; Bonfil, "Aliens Within," pp. 272–73.

33 Hannah R. Johnson, *Blood Libel: The Ritual Murder Accusation at the Limit of Jewish History* (Ann Arbor, MI.: University of Michigan Press, 2012), pp. 59–90.

34 Chazan, *Jews of Medieval Western Christendom*, p. 240. See also Shmuel Ettinger, "Jew-Hatred in its Historical Context," in *Antisemitism Through the Ages*, pp. 1–12.

35 Chazan, *Jews of Medieval Western Christendom*, pp. 211–15; Chazan, *Medieval Stereotypes*, pp. 95–109; Kenneth R. Stow, *Alienated Minority: The Jews of Medieval Latin Europe* (Cambridge, MA.: Harvard University Press, 1992), pp. 247–59; Bonfil, "Aliens Within," pp. 270–71; Richards, *Sex, Dissidence, and Damnation*, pp. 106–11; Jeremy Cohen, *The Friars and the Jews: The Evolution of Medieval Anti-Judaism* (Ithaca, NY.: Cornell University Press, 1982); Cohen, *Under Crescent and Cross*, pp. 40–42; Joseph Shatzmiller, *Shylock Reconsidered: Jews, Moneylending, and Medieval Society* (Berkeley, CA.: University of California Press, 1990), pp. 43–55; Lester K. Little, *Religious Poverty and the Profit Economy in the Middle Ages* (Ithaca, N.Y.: Cornell University Press, 1978), pp. 54–56; Berger, *From Crusades to Blood Libels to Expulsions*, pp. 9–13.

36 Chazan, *Medieval Stereotypes*, pp. 85–88; Chazan, *Jews of Medieval Western Christendom*, p. 240; Anna Sapir Abulafia, "Twelfth-Century Renaissance Theology and the Jews," in *From Witness to Witchcraft: Jews and Judaism in Medieval Christian Thought*, ed. Jeremy Cohen (Wolfenbütteler Mittelalter-Studien, 11, 1996), pp. 128–32.

37 Chazan, *Medieval Stereotypes*, pp. 88–94; Chazan, *Jews of Medieval Western Christendom*, p. 240.

38 Cohen, *Under Crescent and Cross*, pp. 42–49; Shatzmiller, *Shylock Reconsidered*, pp. 62–67; Kenneth R. Stow, "Hatred of the Jews or Love of the Church: Papal Policy Toward the Jews in the Middle Ages," in *Antisemitism Through the Ages*, pp. 71–89.

39 Robert Chazan, *Reassessing Jewish Life in Medieval Europe* (Cambridge: Cambridge University Press, 2010), pp. 165–66, 177.

40 Cohen, *Under Crescent and Cross*, pp. 50–51.

41 Chazan, *Jews of Medieval Western Christendom*, pp. 210–31, 239–42; Chazan, *Medieval Stereotypes*, pp. 95–124; Richards, *Sex, Dissidence, and Damnation*, p. 100.

42 Gavin I. Langmuir, *History, Religion, and Antisemitism* (Los Angeles, CA.: University of California Press, 1990), pp. 21–23; Chazan, *Medieval Stereotypes*, pp. 126–27.

43 Langmuir, *History, Religion, and Antisemitism*, pp. 23–24, 275–76; Gavin I. Langmuir, *Toward a Definition of Antisemitism* (Berkeley, CA.: University of California Press, 1990), pp. 57–62; Chazan, *Medieval Stereotypes*, p. 128; Guido Kisch, *The Jews in Medieval Germany: A Study of their Legal and Social Status* (Chicago, IL.: University of Chicago Press, 1949), pp. 305–16, 323–41.

44 Johnson, *Blood Libel*, p. 81.

45 Chazan, *Medieval Stereotypes*, p. 126.

46 Langmuir, *History, Religion, and Antisemitism*, pp. 245, 297, 304; Langmuir, *Toward a Definition of Antisemitism*, pp. 301–2, 351–52. The forerunner of this approach was Joshua Trachtenberg, who argued that medieval anti-Semitism had an irrational basis in the subconscious association between Jews and the Devil, black magic, and heresy. See Joshua Trachtenberg, *The Devil and the Jews: The Medieval Conception of the Jew and its Relation to Modern Antisemitism* (New Haven, CT.: Yale University Press, 1943).

47 Langmuir, *History, Religion, and Antisemitism*, pp. 271, 304; Langmuir, *Toward a Definition of Antisemitism*, pp. 102–3, 308–9.

48 Langmuir, *History, Religion, and Antisemitism*, p. 259; Langmuir, *Toward a Definition of Antisemitism*, p. 306.

49 Langmuir, *History, Religion, and Antisemitism*, pp. 298–301; Langmuir, *Toward a Definition of Antisemitism*, pp. 61–62, 263–98, 302–6.

50 Langmuir, *Toward a Definition of Antisemitism*, pp. 62, 306.

51 Langmuir, *Toward a Definition of Antisemitism*, pp. 197–236; Chazan, *Medieval Stereotypes*, pp. 47–52; Johnson, *Blood Libel*, pp. 30–58.

52 In *Toward a Definition of Antisemitism*, p. 308, Langmuir admitted that "chimerical fantasies" about Jews were developed by a "minority of anxious Christians" restricted to northern Europe, namely, England, northern France, and Germany. However, in *History, Religion, and Antisemitism*, p. 263, Langmuir claimed that the few examples of medieval Christians who openly expressed, through their virulent attitudes towards Jews, how they "wrestled with doubts they wanted to repress" was "only the tip of an iceberg". Nonetheless, Langmuir did not explain why such fantasies about Jews, such as the blood libel, were developed in northern but not southern Europe.

53 Robert C. Stacey, "History, Religion, and Medieval Antisemitism: A Response to Gavin Langmuir," *Religious Studies Review* 20 (1994):99; Robert C. Stacey, "1240–60: A Watershed in Anglo-Jewish Relations?" *Historical Research* 61 (1988):147–50. For other reviews and criticisms of Langmuir's thesis, see: Marc Saperstein, "Medieval Christians and Jews: A Review Essay," *Shofar* 8 (1990):1–10; Berger, *From Crusades to Blood Libels to Expulsions*, pp. 14–16. In spite of his criticisms, Stacey agreed with Langmuir that anti-Semitism did indeed exist in the Middle Ages, and that it formed the basis for its modern version in the twentieth century, although what the new basis should be for a working definition of anti-Semitism that would justify such a position has yet to emerge. For Langmuir's treatment of the Hugh of Lincoln case, see Langmuir, *Towards a Definition of Antisemitism*, pp. 237–62.

54 Ariel Toaff, *Pasque di Sangue: Ebrei d'Europa e omicidi rituali* (Milan: Il Mulino, 2007). Toaff based his argument on the ritual murder trial in 1475 of Jews in connection with the death of a young boy, Simon of Trent, and whose "confessions" were extracted by torture. The whole "Toaff affair" and controversy is discussed extensively in Johnson, *Blood Libel*, pp. 129–64.

55 Johnson, *Blood Libel*, p. 77.

56 My argument is presented more fully in two forthcoming books: John Aberth, *Doctoring the Black Death: Europe's Late Medieval Medical Response to Epidemic Disease* (forthcoming with Rowman and Littlefield); and John Aberth, *The Black Death: A New History of the Great Mortality* (forthcoming with Oxford University Press). But see also, John Aberth, *From the Brink of the Apocalypse: Confronting Famine, War, Plague, and Death in the Later Middle Ages*, 2nd edn. (London: Routledge, 2010), pp. 156–91.

57 Although isolated incidents against Jews in relation to well poisoning occurred prior to the Black Death—at Troppau in 1163, Wrocław in 1226, Vienna in 1267, and southern

France in 1321—the Black Death pogroms were unique in that Jews were charged with participation in a widespread, international conspiracy that mirrored the universal spread of the plague itself. See Richards, *Sex, Dissidence, and Damnation*, p. 103.

58 Christian Guilleré, "La Peste Noire a Gérone (1348)", *Annals Institut d'Estudis Gironins* 27 (1984):141; *The Black Death*, trans. and ed. Rosemary Horrox (Manchester, UK: Manchester University Press, 1994), p. 223.

59 Jordan, "Home Again," pp. 38–39.

60 Langmuir, *History, Religion, and Antisemitism*, p. 305.

61 For example, the Jews were slaughtered in Strasbourg on February 14, 1349, but the flagellants did not arrive there until mid-June or early July later that year; at Würzburg, the Jews were burned on April 20–21, but the flagellants did not arrive until May 2; and at Konstanz, the Jews were burnt on March 3, but the flagellants did not arrive until May 9 of that year. See Chapter 5 in my forthcoming, *The Black Death: A New History of the Great Mortality*, with Oxford University Press. Also see: Aberth, *From the Brink of the Apocalypse*, 2nd edn., pp. 133–56; Christoph Cluse, "Zur Chronologie der Verfolgungen zur Zeit des 'Schwarzen Todes'," in *Geschichte der Juden im Mittelalter*, pp. 240–41; František Graus, *Pest-Geissler-Judenmorde: das 14. Jahrhundert als Krisenzeit* (Göttingen: Vandenhoeck and Ruprecht, 1994), pp. 220–22; Alfred Haverkamp, "Die Judenverfolgungen zur Zeit des Schwarzen Todes im Gesellschaftsgefüge deutscher Städte," in *Zur Geschichte der Juden im Deutschland des Späten Mittelalters und der Frühen Neuzeit*, ed. Alfred Haverkamp (Stuttgart: Anton Hiersemann, 1981), pp. 43–46.

62 Steven T. Katz, *The Holocaust in Historical Context. Volume I: The Holocaust and Mass Death before the Modern Age* (New York: Oxford University Press, 1994), pp. 227, 235, 250, 260–62, 315–17, 322–24, 330–33, 338–40, 346–62.

63 Katz, *Holocaust in Historical Context*, pp. 263–64, 269–98, 309–14. See also Trachtenberg, *Devil and the Jews*; Robert Bonfil, "The Devil and the Jews in the Christian Consciousness of the Middle Ages," in *Antisemitism Through the Ages*, pp. 91–98.

64 Katz, *Holocaust in Historical Context*, pp. 227, 264, 268–69.

65 David Nirenberg, *Anti-Judaism: The Western Tradition* (New York: W.W. Norton and Company, 2013), p. 3.

66 Nirenberg, *Anti-Judaism*, pp. 183–216.

67 Chazan, *Medieval Stereotypes*, pp. 128–29.

68 Chazan, *Medieval Stereotypes*, pp. 129–40; Chazan, *Jews of Medieval Western Christendom*, pp. 158, 184, 191, 214.

69 This "lachrymose school" of historiography dates back to the sixteenth century. See David Nirenberg, "The Rhineland Massacres of Jews in the First Crusade: Memories Medieval and Modern," in *Medieval Concepts of the Past: Ritual, Memory, Historiography*, eds. Gerd Althoff, Johannes Fried, and Patrick J. Geary (Cambridge: Cambridge University Press, 2002), p. 297.

70 Chazan, *Reassessing Jewish Life*, pp. ix–xx. Chazan claimed in his prologue to be merely following in the footsteps of his teacher, Salo Baron, who first mounted a challenge to the "lachrymose" narrative of Jewish history in 1928, but whose "innovative" approach had been largely ignored in popular and academic culture. See: Salo W. Baron, "Emphases in Jewish History," *Jewish Social Studies* 1 (1939):37; David Engel, "Salo Baron's View of the Middle Ages in Jewish History: Early Sources," in *Medieval Jewish Intellectual and Social History: Festschrift in Honor of Robert Chazan*, eds. David Engel, Lawrence H. Schiffman, and Elliot R. Wolfson (Leiden, Netherlands: Brill, 2012), p. 299.

71 Chazan, *Reassessing Jewish Life*, pp. 85–106.

72 Anna Foa, *The Jews of Europe after the Black Death*, trans. Andrea Grover (Berkeley, CA.: University of California Press, 2000), p. 8; Bonfil, "Aliens Within," pp. 266–67.

73 Bonfil, "Aliens Within," pp. 268–69.

74 Bonfil, "Aliens Within," pp. 264, 268.

75 Chazan, *Reassessing Jewish Life*, pp. 85–106.

76 Chazan, *Reassessing Jewish Life*, pp. 225–27.

77 Chazan, *Reassessing Jewish Life*, p. 159.

78 Chazan, *Reassessing Jewish Life*, pp. 19–51.

79 This image is reevaluated in Shatzmiller, *Shylock Reconsidered*.

80 Chazan, *Reassessing Jewish Life*, pp. 107–32.

81 Chazan, *Jews of Medieval Western Christendom*, pp. 257–83.

82 For example, it is argued that Christian missionary efforts and forced sermons in Jewish synagogues gave Jewish polemicists ammunition for their anti-Christian works, by providing them with one of their few sources of information about Christianity. See Daniel J. Lasker, "Jewish Knowledge of Christianity in the Twelfth and Thirteenth Centuries," in *Studies in Medieval Jewish Intellectual and Social History*, pp. 103–9; Bonfil, "Aliens Within," p. 276.

83 Chazan, *Medieval Stereotypes*, pp. 76–77; Chazan, *Reassessing Jewish Life*, pp. 168–71, 199; Stow, *Alienated Minority*, p. 117.

84 Chazan, *Jews of Medieval Western Christendom*, pp. 247–57; Chazan, *Reassessing Jewish Life*, pp. 193–221.

85 Mark D. Meyerson, *A Jewish Renaissance in Fifteenth-Century Spain* (Princeton, NJ.: Princeton University Press, 2004).

86 Jonathan Ray, "Beyond Tolerance and Persecution: Reassessing Our Approach to Medieval *Convivencia*," *Jewish Social Studies*, 11 (2005):5–12.

87 Kenneth Stow included a very brief and generalized reference to Christian attendance at "Jewish feasts and wedding celebrations" in the 1280s in England, without mentioning that this referred specifically to the incident at Hereford in 1286. See Stow, *Alienated Minority*, p. 232.

88 James Parkes, *The Conflict of the Church and the Synagogue: A Study in the Origins of Antisemitism* (New York: Jewish Publication Society, 1934) p. 381.

89 *Registrum Ricardi de Swinfield, Episcopi Herefordensis, A.D. 1283–1317*, ed. William W. Capes (Hereford: Wilson and Phillips, 1909), pp. 120–21.

90 Chazan, *Jews of Medieval Western Christendom*, pp. 55–56, 163; Rokéah, "The State, the Church, and the Jews," pp. 112–13.

91 *Registrum Ricardi de Swinfield*, pp. 120–21.

92 *Registrum Ricardi de Swinfield*, p. 121.

93 *Registrum Ricardi de Swinfield*, p. 122.

94 *Registrum Ricardi de Swinfield*, p. 122.

95 *Registrum Ricardi de Swinfield*, p. 121.

96 Shatzmiller, *Shylock Reconsidered*, pp. 107–18; Chazan, *Reassessing Jewish Life*, pp. 131–32, 186–87. Nonetheless, David Berger wryly commented that the Jews' profession of moneylending "was not conducive to feelings of warmth and amity." See Berger, *From Crusades to Blood Libels to Expulsions*, pp. 12–13.

97 Chazan, *Reassessing Jewish Life*, pp. 187–88.

98 Lasker, "Jewish Knowledge of Christianity," pp. 101–3. A rabbinic scholar from Perpignan, Menachem Meiri, even proposed that Jews and Christians shared a "fundamental affinity" in terms of their religious beliefs, a sentiment that was rare for its times. See Bonfil, "Aliens Within," pp. 274–75.

99 Chazan, *Reassessing Jewish Life*, pp. 198–200, 221; Bonfil, "Aliens Within," pp. 275–76. The most widespread Jewish conversions to Christianity took place in Spain in 1391, although this is problematic in that it occurred in the aftermath of a very violent pogrom throughout much of the country.

100 Israel Abrahams and Frederic Maitland, "The Deacon and the Jewess," *Transactions of the Jewish Historical Society* 16 (1908–10):254–76; Roth, *History of the Jews in England*, pp. 76, 83; Stow, *Alienated Minority*, p. 289; Rokéah, "The State, the Church, and the Jews," p. 114.

101 Chazan, *Reassessing Jewish Life*, pp. 191–92, 220–21.

102 *Heresy and Authority in Medieval Europe: Documents in Translation*, ed. Edward Peters (Philadelphia, PA.: University of Pennsylvania Press, 1980), p. 1; Moore, *Formation of a Persecuting Society*, 1st edn., p. 68; Jennifer Kolpacoff Deane, *A History of Medieval Heresy and Inquisition* (Lanham, MD.: Rowman and Littlefield, 2011), pp. 2–4;

Walter L. Wakefield, *Heresy, Crusade and Inquisition in Southern France, 1100–1250* (Berkeley, CA.: University of California Press, 1974), p. 16.

103 Moore, *Formation of a Persecuting Society*, 1st edn., pp. 62–64, 67, 97–98; Robert I. Moore, "Heresy as Disease," in *The Concept of Heresy in the Middle Ages (11th–13th C.): Proceedings of the International Conference of Louvain, May 13–16, 1973*, eds. W. Lourdaux and D. Verhelst (Louvain, Belgium: Leuven University Press, 1976), pp. 1–11; Gordon Leff, *Heresy in the Later Middle Ages: The Relation of Heterodoxy to Dissent, c.1250–c.1450*, 2 vols. (Manchester, UK: Manchester University Press, 1967), 1:1–2; Wakefield, *Heresy, Crusade and Inquisition*, p. 16.

104 *Heresy and Authority*, pp. 29–41.

105 *Heresy and Authority*, pp. 41–47; Moore, *Formation of a Persecuting Society*, 1st edn., p. 12.

106 For the theory that the Manicheans influenced the later Cathars, see Heinrich Fichtenau, *Heretics and Scholars in the High Middle Ages, 1000–1200*, trans. Denise A. Kaiser (University Park, PA.: Pennsylvania State University Press, 2000), pp. 105–10.

107 Moore, *Formation of a Persecuting Society*, 1st edn., pp. 13–14; *Heresy and Authority*, p. 3; Wakefield, *Heresy, Crusade and Inquisition*, pp. 17–18.

108 R.I. Moore, *The Origins of European Dissent* (New York: St. Martin's Press, 1977), pp. 46–136; Moore, *Formation of a Persecuting Society*, 1st edn., pp. 19–22; Wakefield, *Heresy, Crusade and Inquisition*, pp. 18–25; Malcolm Lambert, *Medieval Heresy: Popular Movements from the Gregorian Reform to the Reformation*, 3rd edn. (Oxford: Blackwell, 2002), pp. 43–62.

109 Deane, *History of Medieval Heresy*, p. 28.

110 Malcolm Barber, *The Cathars: Dualist Heretics in Languedoc in the High Middle Ages* (Harlow, UK: Pearson, 2000), pp. 6–33; Malcolm Lambert, *The Cathars* (Oxford: Blackwell, 1998), pp. 19–44; Lambert, *Medieval Heresy*, 3rd edn., pp. 52–69, 133–37; Fichtenau, *Heretics and Scholars*, pp. 70–104, 111–14, 155–71; R.I. Moore, *The Birth of Popular Heresy* (London: Edward Arnold, 1975), pp. 132–38; Moore, *Origins of European Dissent*, pp. 139–96; Deane, *History of Medieval Heresy*, pp. 30–36; Leff, *Heresy in the Later Middle Ages*, 2: 445–48; Wakefield, *Heresy, Crusade and Inquisition*, pp. 27–43. For the case for an Eastern origin to Catharism, see: Steven Runciman, *The Medieval Manichee: A Study of the Christian Dualist Heresy* (Cambridge: Cambridge University Press, 1969), pp. 63–93; Bernard Hamilton, "Wisdom from the East: The Reception by the Cathars of Eastern Dualist Texts," in *Heresy and Literacy, 1000–1500*, eds. Peter Biller and Anne Hudson (Cambridge: Cambridge University Press, 1994), pp. 38–60; Bernard Hamilton, "Cathar Links with the Balkans and Byzantium," in *Cathars in Question*, ed. Antonio Sennis (Woodbridge, UK and York, UK: Boydell Press and York Medieval Press, 2016), pp. 131–50; Daniel F. Callahan, "Adhemar of Chabannes and the Bogomils," and Bernard Hamilton, "Bogomil Influences on Western Heresy," in *Heresy and the Persecuting Society*, pp. 31–41, 93–114.

111 A good sense of this debate may be obtained from: *Cathars in Question; L'Histoire du Catharisme en Discussion: Le "Concile" de Saint-Félix (1167)*, ed. Monique Zerner (Collection du Centre d'Études Médiévales de Nice, 3, 2001); *Inventer l'Hérésie? Discours Polémiques et Pouvoirs avant l'Inquisition*, ed. Monique Zerner (Collection du Centre d'Études Médiévales de Nice, 2, 1998).

112 Robert Moore summed up the 2013 conference on Catharism at the University College, London, as that "the differences between the contested views have proved not to be susceptible of resolution by the ordinary procedures of historical method alone". Yet John Arnold optimistically observed that, "part of the irony of the debate is just how much shared ground there actually is". See John H. Arnold, "The Cathar Middle Ages as a Methodological and Historiographical Problem" and R.I. Moore, "Principles at Stake: The Debate of April 2013 in Retrospect," in *Cathars in Question*, pp. 77, 273.

113 Mark Gregory Pegg, "The Paradigm of Catharism; or, the Historians' Illusion," Julien Théry-Astruc, "The Heretical Dissidence of the 'Good Men' in the Albigeois (1276–1329): Localism and Resistance to Roman Clericalism," and Moore, "Principles

at Stake," in *Cathars in Question*, pp. 21–52, 79–111, 257–73; R.I. Moore, *The War on Heresy* (Cambridge, MA.: Harvard University Press, 2012), pp. 332–36; *Inventer l'Hérésie*, ed. Zerner.

114 Arnold, "Cathar Middle Ages," Jörg Feuchter, "The *Heretici* of Languedoc: Local Holy Men and Women or Organized Religious Group? New Evidence from Inquisitorial, Notarial and Historiographical Sources," and Peter Biller, "Goodbye to Catharism?" in *Cathars in Question*, pp. 53–79, 112–30, 274–304.

115 Deane, *History of Medieval Heresy*, pp. 7–8; Arnold, "Cathar Middle Ages," p. 77–78.

116 Claire Taylor, "Looking for the 'Good Men' in the Languedoc: An Alternative to 'Cathars'?" in *Cathars in Question*, pp. 242–56; Pilar Jiménez-Sanchez, *Les catharismes: Modèles dissidents du christianisme médiéval (xiie -xiiie siècles)* (Rennes: Presses Universitaires de Rennes, 2014); Jean-Louis Biget, *Hérésie et inquisition dans le Midi de la France* (Paris: Picard, 2007).

117 James B. Given, *Inquisition and Medieval Society: Power, Discipline, and Resistance in Languedoc* (Ithaca, NY.: Cornell University Press, 1997), pp. 25–51; Peter Biller, "Heresy and Literacy: Earlier History of the Theme," and R.I. Moore, "Literacy and the Making of Heresy, c.1000–c.1150," in *Heresy and Literacy, 1000–1530*, eds. Peter Biller and Anne Hudson (Cambridge: Cambridge University Press, 1994), pp. 3–10, 19–37.

118 Deane, *History of Medieval Heresy*, pp. 5–6; Claire Taylor, "Authority and the Cathar Heresy in the Northern Languedoc," in *Heresy and the Persecuting Society*, pp. 141–46.

119 Pegg, "Paradigm of Catharism," pp. 46–47; Moore, *Birth of Popular Heresy*, pp. 99–101; *L'Histoire du Catharisme en Discussion*, pp. 57–102; Bernard Hamilton, "The Cathar Council of S. Félix Reconsidered," *Archivum Fratrum Praedicatorum* 48 (1978): 23–53.

120 Peter Biller, "The Cathars of Languedoc and Written Materials," in *Heresy and Literacy*, pp. 63–70; Wakefield, *Heresy, Crusade and Inquisition*, pp. 34–36.

121 R.I. Moore, "The Cathar Middle Ages as an Historiographical Problem," in *Christianity and Culture in the Middle Ages: Essays to Honor John van Engen*, eds. David C. Mengel and Lisa Wolverton (Notre Dame, IN.: Notre Dame University Press, 2015), p. 59.

122 Moore, *Origins of European Dissent*, pp. 176–82; Mark Pegg, "Heresy, Good Men, and Nomenclature," in *Heresy and the Persecuting Society*, p. 229; Uwe Brunn, *Des contestaires aux 'Cathares': Discours de réforme et propagande antihérétique dans le pays du Rhin et de la Meuse avant l'inquisition* (Paris: Institut d'Études Augustiniennes, 2006); Taylor, "Looking for the 'Good Men'," p. 243.

123 Pegg, "Paradigm of Catharism," pp. 31–32; Moore, "Cathar Middle Ages," p. 59; Wakefield, *Heresy, Crusade and Inquisition*, p. 30.

124 Pegg, "Paradigm of Catharism," pp. 42; Pegg, "Heresy, Good Men, and Nomenclature," p. 233; Feuchter, "*Heretici* of Languedoc," pp. 118–25; Moore, "Cathar Middle Ages," p. 59; Wakefield, *Heresy, Crusade and Inquisition*, p. 31. Even when the accused referred to themselves as "good men" or "good women," inquisitorial scribes "relabeled" or rewrote these terms as "heretics," which obviously begs the question of their bias.

125 Deane, *History of Medieval Heresy*, pp. 28–30; Pegg, "Paradigm of Catharism," p. 39; Pegg, "Heresy, Good Men, and Nomenclature," pp. 229–31; Moore, "Cathar Middle Ages," p. 59; Wakefield, *Heresy, Crusade and Inquisition*, p. 31.

126 Pegg, "Paradigm of Catharism," pp. 39–41; Pegg, "Heresy, Good Men, and Nomenclature," pp. 230–31.

127 Pegg, "Paradigm of Catharism," pp. 40–42; Pegg, "Heresy, Good Men, and Nomenclature," pp. 233–34.

128 Pegg, "Paradigm of Catharism," pp. 42–45; Pegg, "Heresy, Good Men, and Nomenclature," pp. 238–39.

129 Pegg, "Paradigm of Catharism," pp. 45–46; Mark Gregory Pegg, *The Corruption of Angels: The Great Inquisition of 1245–1246* (Princeton, NJ.: Princeton University Press, 2001); Wakefield, *Heresy, Crusade and Inquisition*, pp. 82–94.

130 Deane, *History of Medieval Heresy*, pp. 34–36; Lambert, *Medieval Heresy*, 3rd edn., 116–21; Wakefield, *Heresy, Crusade and Inquisition*, pp. 31–39. For a detailed picture of

one Cathar community, the Cathar "diocese" of the Agenais in France during the first half of the thirteenth century, see Claire Taylor, *Heresy in Medieval France: Dualism in Aquitaine and the Agenais, 1000–1249* (Woodbridge, UK: Boydell Press, 2005), pp. 225–60.

131 Caterina Bruschi, "Converted-Turned-Inquisitors and the Image of the Adversary: Ranier Sacconi Explains Cathars," and Lucy J. Sackville, "The Textbook Heretic: Moneta of Cremona's Cathars," in *Cathars in Question*, pp. 185–228; Deane, *History of Medieval Heresy*, pp. 26–28.

132 Feuchter, "*Heretici* of Languedoc," pp. 112–30. In addition, Feuchter adduces a notarial charter from 1189 which mentioned a woman who "gave herself to the men whom they call heretics," and to a chronicle account by the Syrian Patriarch Michael the Great from c. 1179 that referred to the "bishops" of the Cathars. None of these sources is definitive as to the Cathars' actual existence as a heresy.

133 Biller, "Goodbye to Catharism," pp. 278–82.

134 Brunn, *Contestaires aux "Cathares"*; Moore, "Principles at Stake," pp. 262–67; Moore, "Cathar Middle Ages," p. 74.

135 Moore, "Principles at Stake," p. 267. For the debate on how far to take the "deconstruction" of contemporary texts attesting to heresy, see: L.J. Sackville, *Heresy and Heretics in the Thirteenth Century: The Textual Representations* (Woodbridge, UK and York, UK: Boydell Press and York Medieval Press, 2011), pp. 1–11; *Texts and the Repression of Medieval Heresy*, eds. Caterina Bruschi and Peter Biller (Woodbridge, UK and York, UK: Boydell Press and York Medieval Press, 2003). For a case study of how depositions of suspected Cathars should be reexamined in the context of the operating power of the Inquisition, see John H. Arnold, *Inquisition and Power: Catharism and the Confessing Subject in Medieval Languedoc* (Philadelphia, PA.: University of Pennsylvania Press, 2001).

136 Robert E. Lerner, *The Heresy of the Free Spirit in the Later Middle Ages* (Berkeley, CA.: University of California Press, 1972).

137 See Chapter 5 of my forthcoming book, *The Black Death: A New History of the Great Mortality*, with Oxford University Press. Coincidentally, many Cathars in Italy joined flagellant confraternities, despite their focus on the body as the means of salvation (through discipline), because they saw in them kindred spirits interested in religious devotion and perfection. For them, the line "between heresy and orthodoxy was based not upon theology or doctrine but upon practice and aspect". See Susan Taylor Snyder, "Cathars, Confraternities, and Civic Religion: The Blurry Border between Heresy and Orthodoxy," in *Heresy and the Persecuting Society*, pp. 241–51.

138 Ria Jansen-Sieben and Hans van Dijk, "Un slaet u zeere doer Cristus eere! Het flagellantenritueel op een Middelnederlandse tekstrol," *Ons Geestelijk Erf* 77 (2003): 139–213.

139 Timothy S. Miller and John W. Nesbitt, *Walking Corpses: Leprosy in Byzantium and the Medieval West* (Ithaca, NY.: Cornell University Press, 2014), pp. 38–47, 65–71, 100–6, 110–17; Ephraim Shoham-Steiner, *On the Margins of a Minority: Leprosy, Madness, and Disability among the Jews of Medieval Europe*, trans. Haim Watzman (Detroit, MI.: Wayne State University Press, 2014), pp. 21–71; Luke Demaitre, *Leprosy in Premodern Medicine: A Malady of the Whole Body* (Baltimore, MD.: Johns Hopkins University Press, 2007), pp. 34- 74, 103–23; Christine M. Boeckl, *Images of Leprosy: Disease, Religion, and Politics in European Art* (Kirksville, MO.: Truman State University Press, 2011), pp. 8–66; Carol Rawcliffe, *Leprosy in Medieval England* (Woodbridge, UK: Boydell Press, 2006), pp. 44–204; Moore, *Formation of a Persecuting Society*, 1st edn., pp. 45–65; Saul Nathaniel Brody, *The Disease of the Soul: Leprosy in Medieval Literature* (Ithaca, NY.: Cornell University Press, 1974), pp. 21–106. This moral element of leprosy included the accusation that lepers were extraordinarily lustful, which put them into a similar category with prostitutes. See Moore, *Formation of a Persecuting Society*, 1st edn., pp. 97–98.

140 Rawcliffe, *Leprosy in Medieval England*, pp. 106–7.

141 Rawcliffe, *Leprosy in Medieval England*, pp. 19–23; Moore, *Formation of a Persecuting Society*, 1st edn., pp. 58–60.
142 Miller and Nesbitt, *Walking Corpses*, pp. 72–95, 118–38; Rawcliffe, *Leprosy in Medieval England*, pp. 104–54. Thus, Rawcliffe emphasized how lepers had to apply for entry to the leprosarium and could be evicted for failing to follow the rules, while some actually tried to mimic the symptoms of leprosy to obtain entry, as opposed to trying to hide their symptoms to avoid incarceration.
143 This represents a major revision of Brody's more simplistic interpretation of medieval leprosy as simply a "disease of the soul". See: Miller and Nesbitt, *Walking Corpses*, pp. 38–43, 100–6; Rawcliffe, *Leprosy in Medieval England*, pp. 48–64, 104–54; Demaitre, *Leprosy in Premodern Medicine*, pp. 34–74; Brody, *Disease of the Soul*, pp. 60–106.
144 Malcolm Barber, "Lepers, Jews, and Moslems: The Plot to Overthrow Christendom in 1321," *History* 66 (1981):1–17; Nirenberg, *Communities of Violence*, pp. 43–68, 93–124.
145 Karl Sudhoff, "Pestschriften aus der ersten 150 Jahren nach der Epidemie des 'schwarzen Todes' von 1348," *Archiv für Geschichte der Medizin* 17 (1925):54–55.
146 *The Black Death*, trans. and ed. Rosemary Horrox (Manchester, UK: Manchester University Press, 1994), pp. 27, 194–203; Neil Murphy, "Plague Ordinances and the Management of Infectious Diseases in Northern French Towns, c.1450-c.1560," in *The Fifteenth Century XII: Society in an Age of Plague*, eds. Linda Clark and Carole Rawcliffe (Woodbridge, UK: Boydell Press, 2013), pp. 139–59; Carole Rawcliffe, *Urban Bodies: Communal Health in Late Medieval English Towns and Cities* (Woodbridge, UK: Boydell Press, 2013); Kristy Wilson Bowers, *Plague and Public Health in Early Modern Seville* (Rochester, NY.: University of Rochester Press, 2013), pp. 30–88; C. de Backer, "Maatregelen Tegen de Pest te Diest in de Vijftiende en Zestiende Eeuw," *Koninklijke Academie voor Geneeskunde van Belgie* 61 (1999):273–99; Ann G. Carmichael, *Plague and the Poor in Renaissance Florence* (Cambridge: Cambridge University Press, 1986), pp. 98–126; Carlo M. Cipolla, *Public Health and the Medical Profession in the Renaissance* (Cambridge: Cambridge University Press, 1976), pp. 11–66; Carlo M. Cipolla, *Faith, Reason, and the Plague in Seventeenth-Century Tuscany*, trans. M. Kittel (Ithaca, NY.: Cornell University Press, 1979), pp. 1–14.
147 De Backer, "Maatregelen Tegen de Pest," pp. 275–76; William G. Naphy, *Plagues, Poisons, and Potions: Spreading Conspiracies in the Western Alps, c. 1530–1640* (Manchester, UK: Manchester University Press, 2002).
148 Miller and Nesbitt, *Walking Corpses*, p. 111; Rawcliffe, *Leprosy in Medieval England*, pp. 93–95.
149 Miller and Nesbitt, *Walking Corpses*, pp. 40–43, 103–6; Rawcliffe, *Leprosy in Medieval England*, pp. 55–64, 135–47.
150 Miller and Nesbitt, *Walking Corpses*, pp. 72–95.
151 Shoham-Steiner, *On the Margins of a Minority*, pp. 21–43; Elinor Lieber, "Old Testament 'Leprosy,' Contagion and Sin," in *Contagion: Perspectives from Pre-Modern Societies*, eds. Lawrence I. Conrad and Dominik Wujastyk (Aldershot, UK: Ashgate, 2000), pp. 99–136; Michael W. Dols, "The Leper in Medieval Islamic Society," *Speculum* 58 (1983):891–917; Russell Hopley, "Contagion in Islamic Lands: Responses from Medieval Andulasia and North Africa," *Journal for Early Modern Cultural Studies* 10 (2010):46–50; Justin K. Stearns, *Infectious Ideas: Contagion in Premodern Islamic and Christian Thought in the Western Mediterranean* (Baltimore, MD.: Johns Hopkins University Press, 2011), pp. 112–13.
152 Dols, "Leper in Medieval Islamic Society," pp. 895–97.
153 Michael W. Dols, *The Black Death in the Middle East* (Princeton, NJ.: Princeton University Press, 1977), pp. 109, 112–14; Miller and Nesbitt, *Walking Corpses*, pp. 40–43; Rawcliffe, *Leprosy in Medieval England*, pp. 55–64.
154 Shoham-Steiner, *On the Margins of a Minority*, pp. 25–42; Lieber, "Old Testament 'Leprosy,'" pp. 107–31; Dols, "Leper in Medieval Islamic Society," pp. 897–912.
155 Shoham-Steiner, *On the Margins of a Minority*, pp. 69–70.

156 Shoham-Steiner, *On the Margins of a Minority*, pp. 43, 70–71; Dols, "Leper in Medieval Islamic Society," pp. 912–16.

157 Boeckl, *Images of Leprosy*, pp. 92–106; Marcia Kupfer, *The Art of Healing: Painting for the Sick and the Sinner in a Medieval Town* (University Park, PA.: Pennsylvania State University Press, 2003), pp. 104, 107; Rawcliffe, *Leprosy in Medieval England*, pp. 60–63.

5

NO SEX PLEASE, WE'RE MEDIEVAL

Sexuality in the Middle Ages

Once upon a time, when I was giving a guest lecture to some elementary-school students, I was asked, "Did anyone fall in love in the Middle Ages?" I answered that, yes, people did fall in love in the Middle Ages, just like people do today, but that the context in which they might fall in love was quite different. Ironically, aristocratic women, despite their high status, may have had less leeway to fall in love and choose their partners, because of familial obligations and pressures to make a good match. Peasant women, by contrast, were in some senses liberated by their relative poverty to marry whom they liked.[1]

A similar question might be asked (of a strictly adult audience), whether people ever had sex in the Middle Ages? We know that, of course they did, since that is how they propagated the species. Yet, imagining how people so long ago had sex, and whether they enjoyed it, is something that may give some the puzzled, queasy feeling they get when imagining their parents having sex. We know that they did it, but how they did so seems to require a large and rather passionless effort of pornographic fantasy.

Sex may be universal, but the Middle Ages is not really known for its sexual foreplay. In the popular consciousness, this was an age dominated by the Church, with its strictures against sexual pleasure, or "fornication". Sex was to take place strictly within marriage, and was strictly for the sake of procreation. Such may be the popular stereotype. The reality, of course, was quite different. Not only did medieval men and women have sex, both within and outside marriage, and enjoy it, but also those considered at the "margins" of society, such as homosexuals and prostitutes, were fully part of the medieval sexual landscape. All these aspects of medieval sexuality will be explored in this chapter.

The medieval theory of sex

Medieval attitudes towards sexuality were derived from a number of sources that included: medical treatises and works of natural philosophy; "popular" works of literature, such as the *fabliaux*; and legal and religious texts.[2] In general, our medieval forebears seem to have viewed sex as "something done by someone to someone else"; in other words, sex was about who penetrated whom, or who was the "active" partner and who the "passive," with the former classified as "masculine" and the latter as "feminine" (even in the case of homosexual relations).[3] This implies that the sexual experience was quite different for men as opposed to women, and is far from the ideal in today's society, at least in the West, where sex is supposed to be a mutually pleasurable and fulfilling act.[4] However, scholars working with medical texts contend that, especially by the late Middle Ages, "medieval views of sex difference are much richer and more complex than the stereotypical dichotomies of active/passive, soul/body, superior/inferior sometimes imputed to them".[5] Such complexity suggests that our modern and medieval views on sex have more in common than is apparent at first glance.

Despite being "theoretical" in nature, medical and scientific texts, it is argued, genuinely reflect contemporary attitudes towards sex because there was very little authoritative commentary for medieval authors to fall back on, and so they were forced to participate "in the broader culture's assumptions about gender".[6] Beginning with Constantine the African, an eleventh-century Benedictine doctor based at Monte Cassino, there arose the assumption that women, despite being the passive partners in intercourse, experienced the greater pleasure in sex because theirs was a "twofold pleasure": both in receiving men's sperm and in ejaculating their own.[7] (This assumes the "two seed" theory of procreation, that both men and women contributed seminal emissions in order to form a fetus.) By the late Middle Ages, scientific/medical texts that addressed intercourse paid greater attention to female pleasure than ever before, but the results were not always liberating for women. Reflecting misogynist themes that coincided with women's exclusion from universities and medical schools, some authors declared women to be the most sexually voracious of creatures, surpassing both men and animals. Women's desire for sex continued even after they became pregnant, i.e., when sex had lost its functionality, and the fact that some women became pregnant as a result of rape implied that they ultimately had pleasure in the encounter, since women could not emit their seed without it (an opinion that can be traced to the second-century physician, Soranus). The only way around this odious conclusion was to revert to the Aristotelean position that female emission of seed was not essential to reproduction (i.e., the "one-seed" theory), which likewise obviated the necessity of female pleasure in intercourse and men's obligation in sexually satisfying them.[8] Thus, it seems that medieval women could not be both sexually safe and sexually fulfilled.

Late medieval authors continued the debate about which of the sexes had the greater pleasure in sex. Women were declared to have less control over their sexual appetite, as evidenced by their weaker intellect and moral character, but men had the more powerful sexual urges. A compromise of sorts was that women had the greater amount of pleasure, extended over a longer period of time, but that men's pleasure was qualitatively greater or more intense. If anything, this appreciated that women experienced sexual pleasure "on a different scale" than men. Certainly, the idea that men emitted their seed "faster" and in a "more sudden" manner than women is something that most people today would readily agree with![9] Building upon Arabic authorities, who in general were sympathetic to, and accepting of, the importance of sexual pleasure in overall human health, some Western authors, such as William of Saliceto, Pietro d'Abano, Antonio Guainerius, and Michael Savonarola, developed a greater appreciation of what produced pleasure in women, describing recommended foreplay such as kissing and fondling the breasts, as well as the mechanics of clitoral stimulation, namely, how the motion and rubbing of the penis stimulated the "nerves and veins" at the "mouth of the womb," which now represented a third "delight" that women had in intercourse, in addition to giving and receiving sperm. William even recommended that a man delay ejaculation until his female partner experienced orgasm, as this indicated her emission of seed.[10]

Nor can we rule out direct experience as the basis for these observations. When the thirteenth-century philosopher and theologian, Albertus Magnus, stated that "some women take the neck of a vessel in their vagina" for stimulation, or that black women "are sweetest for mounting, as the pimps say," he must, at the very least, have talked with people who had direct knowledge of such things, even if we suspect that what they told him indulged in hyperbole and misinformation.[11] On the whole, medical treatments of sexual pleasure in women, even though they hewed to the theological line that it should strictly serve the purposes of reproduction, were less moralistic and judgmental in tone, approaching the subject from a naturalistic point of view. It is even argued that at this time, an "art of love" or an "erotic science" developed in which "pleasure in itself was the subject of a train of thought quite independent of reproduction". In this view, sex as a natural act had no shame in it, since "nothing natural is shameful," and sex fulfilled a necessary function of releasing pent-up semen and thus restoring the balance of the humors, essential for both physical and mental health.[12]

All this contrasts with the "gloomy" view of Christian moralists and theologians, who since the early Middle Ages viewed sexual passion as "a threat to the welfare of the individual and society" which, especially if given free rein, could prove to be a "disruptive force" through "irrational and frenzied couplings that would disrupt the orderly creation of families and the management of household resources".[13] In this view, the sole purpose of sexual intercourse was for procreation.[14] However, if taken too far, a "rigorist" renunciation of sex could interfere with its reproductive purpose and veer dangerously close to the dualist heresies, which viewed all things of the flesh as evil. Especially in the early medieval Church, authorities' dim view of sex even within marriage—the ideal was virginity among married couples as well as maidens—threatened to be just as disruptive a force to society through lack of procreation and of perpetuation of the family name as sexual libertinage.[15]

A more clear-eyed view on medieval sex—one that perhaps was more likely to be held by "real" people and the common folk—is to be obtained from other sources generated outside the academy or the cloister, such as legal texts that recorded suits over the "debt of marriage," or the obligation to provide sexual intercourse to one's marriage partner, and popular literary works, such as the *fabliaux*. For example, the *fabliaux*, which were short tales in verse that usually revolved around a sexual theme, have been described as featuring characters that were "portrayed realistically, speaking an earthy dialogue, performing 'natural' acts, and exhibiting, uncensored, their needs and desires with grace, lust, and enjoyment".[16] These are the sorts of texts championed by those who would argue that medieval sex was all about the active/passive dichotomy—who was doing what to whom—as mentioned above.[17] But, even though such sources tend to be far less sophisticated and nuanced than medical works—some might even call them excessively "ribald" or obscene, the "raunchy comedy" of the Middle Ages[18]—interpreting them is far from straightforward.

Stories such as the "Fisherman of Pont-sur-Seine," the "Four Wishes of Saint Martin," the "Wife Who Insisted on Feeding Brownie," and the "Woman who Got Herself Fucked on her Husband's Grave," obviously did not flinch from being more than explicit about sex.[19] But what were they actually saying to contemporary medieval audiences who listened to them? The stories essentially portrayed women as obsessed with male penises and insatiable in their desire to be penetrated by them; yet even as the penetrated partner of intercourse, these women were by no means passive but were able to manipulate and, to some degree, control their husbands. Such behavior could even be seen as dangerous and threatening, as witnessed by the *Malleus Maleficarum* (Witches' Hammer) of 1486, which indulged in almost pornographic fantasies of how witches stole men's penises and "put them in a bird's nest, or shut them up in a box, where they move themselves like living members, and eat oats and corn, as has been seen by many and is a matter of common report".[20] On the other hand, was this the kind of behavior associated with only a certain class of women, namely the peasantry, who could not control their lust, as opposed to the exalted ladies who withheld their favors in courtly romances? Were the stories simply intended to entertain, and thus featured highly exaggerated characters, who bore little relation to reality? Since the stories were almost certainly composed by men (traveling *jongleurs* or minstrels), do they tell us more about men's fantasies about women than about the women themselves? Given that sex was far more closely associated with reproduction back then than in this day and age of widely-available contraceptives and birth control, is it possible that the women of these stories had a hidden agenda, namely, to secure the semen of their husbands for procreative purposes? So long as it was not done purely out of pleasure or lust, could this even be seen as a good thing, especially in the late Middle Ages, when society was seeking to recover from the excessive mortalities of the Black Death? These are simply some of the questions that make the subject of medieval sex a particularly challenging one, even when the sources seem rather obvious or crude.[21]

Sex within and outside marriage

Our clearest view onto the sexual practices of married couples during the Middle Ages come from the evidence of canon law, which mainly specified what men and women *could not* do in the bedroom. For example, by law, a spouse could not refuse a demand for sex from his or her married partner, as payment of the so-called "marriage debt" (an idea ultimately derived from St. Paul); this was justified by the Church as necessary for procreation and to prevent "incontinence," or loss of control over one's sexual urges.[22] Any breach of this obligation was grounds for divorce, as heard by the Church courts. Obviously this mostly worked to the advantage of the man, but at times the debt could also work the other way, in that a wife could lodge a complaint that she was not receiving requisite payment from her husband, which obviated her capacity to produce children.[23] (In Jewish law, the debt of marriage, or *onah*, only applied to the husband, not the wife.[24]) In 1433 the ecclesiastical court of the diocese of York heard a case in which it was alleged that one John, apparently an older man, was unable to pay his marriage debt to his younger wife. As part of the proceedings, John was tested by no less than seven women to see if he was truly impotent. Even after embraces, kisses, and rubbing of the penis and testicles, John's penis was said to remain "scarcely three inches long . . . without any increase or decrease".[25] Church law thus seems to have held that "sexual intercourse was an intrinsic and essential element in marriage," or in other words, without at least the possibility of sex (i.e., if either partner was impotent) then there was no marriage, unless both partners agreed to a chaste marriage.[26] What is equally revealing from this case is that sexual satisfaction was measured solely by the husband's ability to penetrate his wife, and no more.

On the other hand, sexual intercourse was not to be "excessive," however this was defined. A husband or wife who loved his or her spouse too passionately, demanding sex all the time, during the day and the night, was adjudged to transgress the bounds of "modest and decorous marital behavior".[27] If we take Church regulations literally, which forbade sex on all feast days, Sundays, and whenever a wife was deemed "unclean" (i.e., during menstruation and pregnancy), then this would have left married couples time to only have sex, on average, less than one day a week during the year.[28] The Church also prescribed only one really acceptable position for intercourse, namely, the "missionary" position, with the man on top; other practices, such as the "dorsal" position (with the woman on top), rear entry, oral and anal intercourse, etc., were condemned on various grounds, such as being contrary to human or to men's (but not women's) nature, or to the procreative purpose of sex.[29] There was no mention of the relation of any of these practices to sexual pleasure.

If married couples were practicing birth control, one can assume they were having sex for pleasure. Although condemned by the Church, knowledge of contraceptives and abortifacients were preserved in medical texts. These consisted mainly of plant lore, but also mechanical methods, such as monitoring menstrual cycles and *coitus interruptus*.[30] Alternative sexual positions (i.e., the woman on top), as well as oral and anal sex, could also be interpreted as attempts to prevent conception.[31] Much of this knowledge was inherited from ancient Latin and Arabic authors but also could include local traditions, with the saintly nun, Hildegard of Bingen, giving instructions for "menstrual regulators" using plant names given in German.[32] But how much of this reached the common folk? It is possible that much was passed on through oral tradition, while it is even hypothesized that parish priests conveyed such information to enquiring parishioners, although this seems rather far-fetched.[33] There are no legal records of anyone prosecuted for using contraception or abortifacients. Nonetheless, it is assumed by some scholars, based on denunciations of the practice by preachers and in pentitentials, that contraception was widespread and became of greater concern to clerical authorities in the wake of the depopulation caused by the Black Death.[34] Yet we lack any hard evidence of the use of such methods by the Christian laity, so that, to date, the question remains undecided, one way or the other.[35]

Then there was love or sex magic, which was used to restore or sustain love and enhance sexual pleasure between married partners. Unlike contraception, we know that this was not simply confined to the theoretical musings of natural philosophers, but was actually employed by real people, since alleged witches were prosecuted for dispensing such "marriage counseling" to their clients. While some of these aphrodisiacs required men to take the initiative, such as by smearing magical ointments on their penis, women could also initiate the ritual, such as by serving mashed earthworms, a hen's heart containing her pubic hair, or semen in her husband's food.[36]

Sex with a partner who was not one's spouse—no matter whether conducted by a single person or a married one—was a social taboo in the Middle Ages. However, "fornication" carried different consequences for men than it did for women. Men were allowed a lot more leeway when it came to sex outside marriage, provided that it did not compromise another man's honor (never mind the woman's), such as intercourse with his wife or daughter. Indulgence in sex was a man's privilege, at the expense of "normalized" violence against women (especially if they were of lower social status). Even though women were deemed the more lustful of the sexes, it was men who allegedly had an aggressive and "unstoppable" sex drive, which is one reason why prostitution was officially patronized in municipal brothels, and why rape was so little condemned or prosecuted.[37]

Adultery was a far more serious matter for a woman because it cast doubt on the paternity of existing and future heirs and was considered a violation of sacred marriage vows.[38] This was particularly so for women of the upper classes, where control of great estates could be at stake and where, even in the case of singlewomen, sexual activity was a family concern because it could affect the daughter's value in the marriage market and reflect upon family honor. Indeed, it seems that the more exalted the status of a medieval woman, "the more closely monitored" was her sexuality.[39] Just how serious this could be was demonstrated by the Tour de Nesle Affair, when two French princesses, Margaret of Burgundy and Blanche of Burgundy, married respectively to the future Louis X (r. 1314–16) and Charles IV (r. 1322–28), were tried and found guilty of adultery in 1314 and accordingly sentenced to life imprisonment, while their lovers were castrated and then executed. The scandal cast a shadow over the succession to the French throne, which eventually saw the Capetian line die out due to lack of surviving male heirs, leaving the way open to a disputed claim put forward by King Edward III of England (r. 1327–77), son of Philip IV's only surviving child, Isabella, which contributed to the start of the Hundred Years War between England and France in 1337.

At the same time, adultery among the upper classes seemed to be tacitly sanctioned by chivalrous and courtly romances, which extolled relationships between a married woman and her lover, usually of a lower social standing. In fact, the assumption was that true love and sexual fulfillment could only be found outside of marriage, which may have held a ring of truth for many medieval listeners owing to the prevalence of arranged marriages, particularly among the aristocracy.[40] Medieval aristocratic men tolerated their wives' adultery, it is argued, because they were not so much concerned about the potential illegitimacy of their heirs as with the security of their fiefs or feudal estates, in which they needed their wives' support as heiresses rather than as mothers.[41]

Heloise, whose relationship with Peter Abelard was the most famous love affair of the Middle Ages, wrote in one of her letters that she was extremely reluctant to marry her lover, precisely because she loved him. She feared that the burdens of marriage would interfere with his vocation as a philosopher (and perhaps with hers as well). But marriage also seems to have been equated with anything but romantic passion in the Middle Ages. As Heloise says, while the "name of wife seems holier and stronger, sweeter ever to me was the name of mistress, or if you can bear it, concubine or whore". Indeed, she expressed her preference to be Abelard's whore rather than Augustus' empress, even though, as a consequence of her "unbounded love" for him, she did consider Abelard bound to her by a debt greater than the one of marriage.[42] The "court of love" in romances invariably decided in favor of the lady granting her favors to a suitor who proved his worth, even if this meant cheating on a spouse. Scholars have debated how to interpret the adulterous message of the romances: Was this simply a "literary game," or did it mean that adultery was accepted, even common, among some medieval cultures, particularly in the *joie de vivre* atmosphere of the south of France? Did chivalric literature pay honor to the lady, or did it rather objectify her by placing her on a pedestal?[43] Based on the Nesle Affair, one suspects that, when it came down to the messy facts of real life, adultery was not a game, and was by no means tolerated, especially when a wealthy kingdom or lordship was at stake. Indeed, it is hypothesized that the Nesle Affair considerably dampened the enthusiasm for courtly romances, leading to their permanent decline.[44]

Among the lower classes, there may have been more wiggle room for adultery, but the popular literature, such as the *fabliaux*, provides conflicting evidence in this regard. Many of these stories, such as the "Bourgeoise of Orléans" or Boccaccio's eighth tale of day seven in the *Decameron*, make it clear that an adultery involved not just the couple themselves, but their relatives as well, on both the wife's and husband's side, whose honor was thereby implicated by a woman's adultery (but not a man's). A couple's sex life was not the private affair we assume it is today, but was everybody's business. The basic question scholars ask themselves is, with whom did the audience sympathize more in these stories, the woman or the man? Often, the husband was a jealous character who elicited little sympathy as he got his deserved comeuppance. But the wife who tricked him was not exactly a role model either for the medieval version of the "good wife". If any female character in these tales was rooted for by a medieval audience, it was likely the young wife married off to an older man who was unable to satisfy her sexual desires. This seems to reflect an attitude that women were "entitled to love," and would get it any way they could. We see this both in the courtly romances, such as the tale of *Yonec,* and in the more popular literature, such as the "Merchant's Tale" of May and January in Chaucer's *Canterbury Tales.*[45] This also jives with actual court cases where wives brought suit against their husbands over the debt of marriage, as mentioned above.

Unmarried women, particularly at the level of the peasantry, perhaps had more freedom than their married counterparts to engage in extramarital sex, which in this case was called "fornication" rather than adultery and was "reasonably common," based on the frequency with which *leyrwite,* i.e., a "fornication tax," was levied in manorial courts (almost always against women).[46] However, it can be debated whether something that was frequent necessarily meant that it was seen as acceptable.[47] One could argue that lords viewed *leyrwite* more as a "fiscal mechanism" or revenue stream to be exploited, rather than as a "penalty for sin," and even Church authorities apparently had a hard time convincing their flock that "simple fornication" was a sin, since "sexual relations between unmarried men and women seem to most people [to be] so natural and so inevitable".[48] But there was also a considerable double standard when it came to medieval opprobrium against fornication, with society far less forgiving of female transgressions than of men's.[49] Aside from a fine, adulterous women might have suffered whipping or banishment and ostracization, while some girls were apparently so shamed by giving birth out of wedlock that they killed their infants.[50] Even just being called a sexually loose woman (i.e., a "whore" or "harlot") could have consequences, as the suits of defamation brought in the Church courts make clear.[51] The social stigma that could attach itself to a young girl through fornication can also be adduced from the fifteenth-century ballads, "A Servant-Girl's Holiday" and "Jolly Jankin," where the shame of a swelling womb was the price of indulging in sex play in the dirt with Jack or with the merrily-singing priest, Jankin.[52] Indeed, the signs of pregnancy were the main means by which *leyrwite* or *childwite* was assessed upon singlewomen, even if it also uncovered clandestine marriages and adultery.[53]

Women who migrated to the towns to find work, typically as household servants or wage workers, may have enjoyed more latitude with respect to their pre-marital sex life, as they were away from the supervision of their parents (but not of employers, who acted in *loco parentis*). These women may have viewed fornication as "simply a prelude to marriage," to be contracted in the future when their economic situation was such that they could afford to marry.[54] But they were also more susceptible to rape and seduction, particularly from their employers, in such situations.[55] To become someone's "concubine," which in the Middle Ages comprised a "quasi-married" state akin to the modern terms of "mistress" or "girlfriend,"—i.e., someone whom one might marry, or just as easily might not— perhaps posed a third way for women to remain sexually active without facing the restrictions imposed either by a legal spouse or by the convent.[56] This seems to be what Heloise originally had in mind as her preferred relationship with Abelard, despite her dramatic invocation of "whore" to contrast with "empress". But as we move into the high and late Middle Ages, the term "concubine" itself became more vituperative as it became associated with the partner of a priest; this practice was more and more unacceptable as the Church pursued its reform program, such that "priest's concubine" became synonymous with "priest's whore".[57] Certainly, there were medieval women who managed to live a single life without being wedded to either a mortal man or as the handmaiden of Christ, as the life of Cecilia Penifader of Brigstock during the first half of the fourteenth century shows. But because this was so unusual a category for a woman in a medieval context—being "covered" in law by neither father nor husband—we know next to nothing about Cecilia's sex life, if she had any.[58]

The sodomites of medieval Gomorrah

Homosexuals in the Middle Ages present a conundrum: how to refer to them when the term, and arguably the sexual identity of, "homosexual," is itself a modern invention, a product of the nineteenth century, along with more recent terms, such as "gay" and "queer," that are commonly used in historical studies of the subject.[59] This is more than just a question of semantics. It gets at the heart of how we should approach the history of minorities: Should they be studied on their own terms, strictly within their local milieu, or can the experiences of "gay" people in the Middle Ages be made relevant to those of homosexuals in modern times? More to the point, can we actually speak of homosexual or gay people at all in a medieval context? Traditionally, this has been framed within the broader debate between the "essentialist" and "social constructionist" approaches to history, i.e., between those preferring to see the connections to be made across space and time, versus those who limit themselves to the unique circumstances that can be found in any given society.[60] These days, historians of medieval homosexuality have moved beyond such binary categorizations, which they regard as "artificial" and "barren," in favor of more modulated, flexible, and inclusive definitions.[61]

It is undeniably true that the terms, "homosexual," "gay," or "queer" were never used in the Middle Ages to designate a distinct culture or group of individuals with same-sex proclivities. Instead, those whom we today designate as homosexuals came under the broader category of "sodomites," and their sexual act was classified as "sodomy," a term that could include a whole range of sexual activities to include masturbation, fellatio, bestiality, intercrural sex, and, of course, anal intercourse (both male-male and male-female).[62] Collectively, these were the "sins against nature," so-called because they were viewed as non-procreative acts that allegedly violated God's command to humankind to "be fruitful and multiply" (Genesis 1:28).[63] The fact that "sodomites" immediately brought to mind another passage from Genesis, whereby the inhabitants of Sodom and Gomorrah were destroyed by God with "brimstone and fire" (Genesis 19:24), helps explain the extraordinary urgency and vehemence, especially when compared with other sex crimes, with which sodomy was punished throughout the Middle Ages.[64] Beginning with *Novella* 77 issued by the Emperor Justinian in 538, which explicitly referred back to examples from the Old Testament, sodomy was outlawed on the grounds that such a crime could result in disasters that affected all of society—such as pestilences, famines, and earthquakes—as opposed to sins that harmed the physical or spiritual well-being of individuals.[65] Real-life catastrophes that seemed to fulfill just such a prediction were not long in coming, as the First Pandemic of plague began in the emperor's capitol at Constantinople in 542.[66] Towards the end of the Middle Ages, this argument came full circle as the Black Death, or Second Pandemic of plague, arose in 1348 and returned regularly once a decade, giving new impetus to anti-sodomy laws enacted, and often brutally enforced, by secular governments throughout Europe.[67] These secular laws superseded the earlier jurisdiction of the Church over sodomy, which had generally adopted a more lenient, penitential approach.[68]

It's clear that, just from their use of different terms like sodomy, medieval people thought of homosexuality in different ways than we do. For the most part, the meaning and definition of sodomy was kept deliberately vague by medieval writers, the "unmentionable" vice that was not meant to be even spoken of. The closest medieval analogy to the modern-day homosexual—a "sodomite" who engaged in anal intercourse—must be clearly identified from the context. Only when this is possible can comparisons be attempted. This chapter will focus on male homosexuality, as the sources available for the study of lesbianism in the Middle Ages are rather limited. For medieval, mostly male, authors, same sex intercourse between women was "twice marginal" and therefore "twice invisible": first, because their sex was not conducive to procreation (as was also true of male homosexual intercourse); and second, because there was no penetration, or at least no perception of the possibility for penetration, which for medieval people was the *sine qua non* of sexual activity.[69]

The Boswell thesis

Any discussion of homosexuality in the Middle Ages is overshadowed by the seminal work of the Yale historian, John Boswell, who published his *Christianity, Social Tolerance, and Homosexuality* in 1980. Boswell's thesis is, at first glance, a surprising one: That gays (his preferred term) were relatively well tolerated by medieval society throughout the early and most of the high Middle Ages, until about the middle of the thirteenth century; only then, and during the subsequent late medieval period, were gays truly persecuted. For Boswell, tolerance of gay people in medieval Europe was synonymous with the rise of urban environments, with both reaching their apogee from about 1050 to 1150, when, Boswell claimed, there was an efflorescence of a gay subculture, including the emergence of a coherent canon of gay literature "for the first time since the decline of Rome".[70] This is precisely the same time as when a "persecuting society" was emerging in medieval Europe, according to Robert Moore, and thus Boswell's thesis represented a considerable challenge to Moore's.[71] By the time we get to the fourteenth century, according to Boswell, the persecution of gays was now in full swing, although the crucial turning point for him was the equation of sodomy with crimes "against nature," which Boswell saw as principally the work of thirteenth-century scholastic philosophers, such as Albertus Magnus (c.1200–1280) and, most especially, St. Thomas Aquinas (1225–74).[72]

Anyone perusing Boswell's book will notice almost immediately that, as a historian, he was prone to two main methodological flaws. One is that he tended to make *ex silentio* arguments, or inferences based on the silence of the historical record, as opposed to assertions based on positive evidence. This is especially evident in the chapter on the "Early Middle Ages," where Boswell attempted to show that the coming of Christianity to Europe did not disrupt a basic tolerance for gays that was prevalent in Roman times. For example, Boswell assumed that homosexuality was viewed as equivalent to masturbation and adultery, and thus viewed rather leniently, simply because these were all lumped together under the same category of sodomy. In his words, "homosexual acts were in effect demoted from the position of unique enormity to which a few influential early fathers had promoted them and joined the ranks of common failings with which almost anyone could empathize".[73] This is, in fact, quite a leap in assumption. Applying this same logic, the first Church penitentials and collections of canon law, such as the *Decretum* of Burchard of Worms from the early eleventh century, also evinced a tolerant attitude towards homosexuality on the grounds that penances assigned for the act were equivalent to those for sins that, by any measure, were rather minor. Thus, Boswell argued that Burchard viewed certain forms of homosexual intercourse as "about as serious as challenging a friend to a drinking bout or having intercourse with one's own spouse within two weeks of receiving communion," since the severity of the penances for all these acts were roughly the same.[74] However, the forms of "homosexual intercourse" that Burchard referred to did not involve anal penetration—with penetration of any sort being the *sine qua non* of medieval definitions of sex— but rather consisted of mutual masturbation and intercrural sex, exterior stimulations that were viewed as much less serious, perhaps rationalized as simply the "sexual rough-and-tumble of randy unmarried young men".[75] Moreover, Burchard, according to Boswell, "did not consider homosexual behavior between single persons sinful at all," since all of his penances assigned to homosexual acts "seem to apply only to married men".[76] This, too, is an argument from silence, since it assigns certain attitudes to an author based on what he *did not* say, rather than on what he did. (In other words, the fact that nowhere did Burchard say, "homosexual acts with single men are sinful," is *not* the same thing as Burchard saying, "homosexual acts with single men are not sinful").[77]

An alternative view is that the Christian Church was inherently hostile and intolerant towards homosexuality from its very beginnings, inheriting "homophobia" from Judaic traditions in the Old Testament and even from Greco-Roman attitudes towards "passive" or "gender discordant" behaviors. Early on, the Church fathers, beginning with St. Paul (c.5–c.67 A.D.), condemned homosexuality, and from the mid-fourth century such condemnations were bolstered with the full force of the law, as emperors decreed the death penalty for sodomy. With the fall of the Roman Empire and the advent of the early Middle Ages, Church penitentials took over the jurisdiction of sodomy, decreeing from 3 to 15 years' penance for anal intercourse, which were among the most severe of all penalties for the sodomite class of sins.[78] (Germanic laws, by contrast, in general had nothing to say on the subject.) From the mid-eleventh century, coinciding with the Gregorian reform movement, the Church inaugurated a new, more concerted phase in its persecution of homosexuality as part of its "moral purity crusade" against sexuality in general. Beginning in the thirteenth century, with the advent of the Inquisition, homosexuality was equated with heresy, and the "sodomy delusion," which saw homosexuals as an all-pervasive and demonic threat to Christian society, foreshadowing the coming persecution of witches, was in full swing.[79] It is only at this point that the more hard-nosed (some might say "clear eyed") view of the Church's history with homosexuality begins to coincide with the Boswell Thesis.[80]

Boswell could even be accused of "whitewashing" the long history of persecution and intolerance of gays on the part of the Church. Indeed, some of Boswell's severest critics in this regard were fellow members of the gay community, who regarded the long history of persecution by the medieval Church as comprising the very roots of homophobia.[81] As a gay Catholic, Boswell clearly had an agenda to find precedents for tolerance of gays within the Church. But for many of his critics, this was an oxymoronic exercise.

The other main weakness of the Boswell Thesis was its penchant for anachronism, or interpreting medieval evidence from a modern perspective. This was especially noticeable when Boswell tried to argue that a number of prominent figures—all churchmen—during the high Middle Ages were gay, which was part of his overall argument that medieval society, and the Church in particular, was generally tolerant of homosexuality. These supposedly gay churchmen included

St. Anselm of Canterbury (1033–1109), St. Aelred of Rievaulx (1110–67), Baldric of Dol (c.1050–1130), and Marbod of Rennes (1035–1123). It is true that in their letters and other writings, Anselm and Aelred used Latin words like *dilectio* and *amor*, which can mean "love" in the carnal sense, but this has to be established beyond any doubt from the context. Instead, the preponderance of evidence indicates that it was spiritual, or platonic, love and friendship that was meant. Nonetheless, such homosocial bonds in the Middle Ages were passionately felt, "erotically charged" even, but evidently were never allowed to transgress to the point of physical intimacy. Indeed, the line between platonic friendship and carnal love among medieval men could be a fine one. Aelred, for example, was criticized in his own time for the "too carnal" love he expressed for his friend, Simon, as evidenced by the "tears" he shed upon Simon's demise. The very fact that Aelred felt he had to defend himself in this matter, insisting that the "Lord" would see his tears and judge them accordingly, is evidence enough that he was dangerously close to transgressing into inappropriate territory, even in a medieval context where erotic expressions of friendship between two men were apparently normal. If Aelred did have carnal desires for his fellow monks—and it is quite possible, perhaps even likely, that he did—then he evidently was able to control them and never acted upon those desires.[82]

Baldric of Dol and Marbod of Rennes, who were also high churchmen, wrote love poetry that Boswell likewise interpreted as evidence of an openly gay lifestyle. But, as with any literature, it is hard to know how much was autobiographical, and how much was simply literary invention. In general, the convention of the times would again argue that it was platonic or spiritual friendships between members of the same sex that were intended to be extolled, while carnal desires were to be suppressed. In Marbod's case, he actually wrote a work called "An Argument against Copulation between People of Only One Sex" (*Dissuasio concubitus in uno tantum sexu*) that explicitly denounced gay intercourse, condemning any such "wretch" as a sodomite to the fires of hell, where "guilty hips and cock never cool".[83] This was fairly representative of a whole body of literature in the twelfth century, by such authors as Hildebert of Lavardin, Bernard of Cluny, and Alain of Lille, that complained of sodomy as the most prevalent of the vices, to the point that "Ganymedes" were taking over women's place at the hearth and in the bedroom, and transvestites were popping up everywhere (*ille fit illa*, or "he becomes a she").[84] One can certainly interpret this as evidence of a widespread gay culture that was generally tolerated by society, if sodomy was indeed being practiced openly with no attempt to hide it or to express remorse over this "sin," as the authors claimed. But it can also be interpreted as an example of literary hyperbole, which mainly expressed the extreme hostility towards gays that was evinced by the medieval Church. Perhaps Marbod felt compelled to write his invective out of peer pressure to conform with this anti-gay attitude, but if so, it speaks volumes to the fact that being gay in the Middle Ages meant something quite different—with different challenges and life experiences—compared to the situation of gays in modern times.

More recent historians have progressed beyond Boswell's easy assumptions with regard to such erotic language expressed by medieval writers, which now poses something of a "dilemma" of interpretation. Just as contemporary authors like Aelred did, modern scholars of homosexuality need to walk a fine line: This one between interpreting expressions of male love in the Middle Ages as evincing a "universal human nature," in which such love always contains an element of sexuality (à la Freud), and interpreting such expressions as uniquely medieval, part of a culture that can never be fully known or understood by modern students of homosexuality. There are, of course, pitfalls in both approaches: missing out on revealing differences in past social behaviors on the one hand, and missing out on essential and eternal truths across space and time on the other.[85] Should we, for example, hold determinations of whether someone in the Middle Ages was gay to a lower standard than in modern times, simply because the level of repression and societal opposition to any expressions of such a preference was that much higher? Or should we hold them to a higher standard, because expressions of erotic, but still essentially platonic, love between members of the same gender was apparently accepted practice? The consensus seems to be that any expressions of erotic love from one medieval man to another counts as evidence of homosexual desire, "even if the person involved would not have recognized it as such"; but, by the same token, "this does not mean that all such erotic desires, whether heterosexual or homosexual, were put into action," which today we commonly consider to be an essential part of any open acknowledgment of one's sexual orientation.[86] Of one thing we can be sure, homosexuality in modern times was not the same as in the Middle Ages, as Boswell assumed.

One aspect of Boswell's thesis that I find quite convincing, and that I personally admire very much, is his analysis of medieval philosophical treatments of sodomy as a "sin against nature," particularly in the *Summa Theologiae* of St. Thomas Aquinas.[87] Boswell was especially adept at pointing out the logical inconsistencies— indeed the philosophical contortions—that thirteenth-century scholastics like Aquinas were forced to make in order to have pagan logic conform to prevailing Christian ethics, which can be considered part of the nominalist/realist debate within medieval philosophy (Chapter 7). Although sodomy was classified as a "sin against nature" from the early Middle Ages, it fell to scholastic philosophers of the thirteenth century to try to justify this position on philosophical grounds. Boswell showed how Aquinas was utterly unable to do so, no matter how he defined what was "natural" to human beings "in relation to homosexuality". If what was natural to man was defined in terms of his use of reason, then homosexuality did not violate "nature," since it rose above the "physical compulsion of procreation" common to most animals. If, on the other hand, what was natural was defined as what man had in common with other animals, namely, the urge to procreate as a means of preserving his species, then homosexuality no more "diminished" the individual or interfered with the overall reproduction of the human race than virginity or chastity, which was praised in a Christian context. Finally, if natural was defined as only applying to certain individuals whose homosexuality constituted a "defect" in their nature, then this was no more evil than being a female, whose condition was considered by most male thinkers of the day as being a "defect" when compared to the "perfection" inherent in being male.[88] In the end, Aquinas was forced to resort to popular notions of homosexuality, which viewed it as a "sin against nature" simply because the "union of male and female" was what was "natural to all animals," which philosophically reduced humans to the level of mere beasts. Boswell's great achievement here was to reveal Christian prejudice for what it was (and still is, in many denominations): a nakedly irrational and unjustifiably intolerant attitude towards those with a different sexual orientation.

Gay subcultures in Florence, Venice, and Cologne

It is rather a shame that Boswell ended his survey of medieval homosexuality in the early fourteenth century, for he thereby missed out on the most voluminous, fascinating, and arguably most important, evidence available. These are the legal records that survive in a few city archives, mostly dating to the fifteenth century but also some to the fourteenth, of special magistracies or courts that were assigned the task of policing sodomy, more specifically, homosexuality. In Florence, where homosexuality seemed to be especially prevalent, the sodomy court was called the Office of the Night (*Ufficiali di Notte*) and was in operation from 1432 to 1502; the Venetian counterpart was called the Lords of the Night (*Signori di Notte*), whose records survive from 1348 until their functions were taken over by the Council of Ten in c. 1418; and in Cologne a Secret Committee of thirteen "gentlemen" was charged with investigating the "dumb" or "mute" (i.e., unmentionable) sin in June and July of 1484.[89] Together, these records provide our best window onto how homosexuality was actually viewed and practiced in medieval society, and the degree to which homosexuals were persecuted by state governments that had assumed jurisdiction over sodomy by the late Middle Ages. They reveal that the practice and persecution of homosexuality was by no means static, but could change over time; yet through it all there was an abiding theme, namely, that the medieval experience of homosexuality was fundamentally different from that in modern times.

The most obvious point to make from a perusal of the records, particularly those of Florence and Venice, is that medieval homosexuality conformed to the "pederasty" model, in contrast to modern homosexuality, which was "androphile". In other words, male same-sex love in the Middle Ages was highly asymmetrical age-wise, usually between an adult (over age of 18) and a younger "boy" (aged 12 to 18–20), with the former almost always taking the active, or "inserter," role, and the latter the passive, or "insertee," one.[90] This hierarchal model applied even when sexual relations were between two adolescents, i.e., the older boy always took the active role. It also seems to have been intimately bound up with contemporary notions of masculinity and rite of passage into adulthood: Even when boys who had formerly been a passive partner continued their homosexual activities into adulthood, they consistently transitioned into an active role with a younger boy. This is all quite different from the modern practice of homosexuality, in which androphilia, or same-sex love between adults of roughly equal age or status, is the norm.[91]

This obviously presents a huge obstacle to those, like Boswell, who have a polemical motive of validating modern practices of homosexuality in the medieval past. In the Florentine records of the Office of the Night, a handful of cases (22, to be exact) listed the passive partner as aged 6–12.[92] In modern Western culture, this would be viewed as pedophilia, a psychiatric disorder that was identified since the late nineteenth century. (Pedophiles are also classified as child molesters, or child sex offenders.) Such practices conjure up deep reserves of fear and loathing today, but these terms, including pederasty, had no meaning to medieval people, who had inherited positive views of age-symmetrical relationships from the cultural norms of ancient Greece and Rome.[93] But given the relative scarcity of this age group in the records (comprising just 5 percent of the sample), it seems that pedophilia was frowned upon in the Middle Ages as well, and was most likely the product of either rape or "boyhood sexual play and experimentation".[94] Of course, homosexual relations with adolescents even above the age of 12 but below the age of 16 (the age of consent in many Western countries) is not viewed favorably in this day and age, to say the least. (About 40 percent of all passive partners in medieval Florence were aged 15 or younger.[95])

There are other caveats to keep in mind before we rush to judgment on medieval homosexuality, at least as based upon impressions derived almost exclusively from Florentine practice. It has been pointed out, for example, that Florence was unique in terms of the prevalence of homosexuality, a reputation that the city acquired even among contemporaries, as evidenced by the fact that *florentzen* became a slang term in Germany for engaging in homosexual intercourse.[96] Florence, and Italy in general, had a distinctly asymmetrical marriage pattern—with women marrying typically in their "early to middle teens" while men married in their "late twenties to early thirties"—a gap of usually about a dozen years. [97] Not only was there a coincidental relationship between heterosexual and homosexual practices with regard to this age pattern, there may have been a causal one as well.[98] The age gap between men and women meant that men spent much of their formative years unattached and, presumably, in the company of other men, whether at work in the workshop or at play in the tavern. The age gap and practice of marriage by arrangement also may have meant that men had little in common with their wives, whereas at least they chose their partners in the case of boys. But this experience may not have been typical of the rest of Europe, particularly in the North and in England. There, it is argued, women married later—typically in their "early twenties"—while men married a little younger than in Italy, usually in their "mid-twenties," so that men and women were closer in age and thus more "companionate". In addition, couples in the North may have had greater freedom in choice of partners, at least among the lower classes, and women were more likely to be active in the job market owing to their later age at marriage, making the workplace "a less exclusively homosocial environment".[99]

Boswell's critic, the classical scholar, David Halperin, has argued that pederasty was one of four categories of "male sex and gender deviance" in pre-modern societies, which also included: "effeminancy," defined as someone "who spent too much time in the company of women rather than that of men"; erotic male friendship and love; and "gender inversion," or men who played the "passive role" in sex, usually associated with women.[100] As we have seen, erotic male friendship and effeminancy may not have always implied a homosexual identity. Nor did pederasty, or "active sodomy"—the older male playing the active role in sodomizing a younger boy—necessarily imply someone who had "an exclusive preference for men," since this was still seen as evincing "masculine" behavior within the medieval context of sexual relations. Not even men who played the "passive role" in homosexual encounters—which Halperin argued was the only category in which men displayed a "sexual inversion" of gender identity, in which there was "a wholesale surrender of masculinity in favor of femininity,"—can be classified as homosexuals in the modern sense of the term.[101] Since such passive partners, according to the Florentine evidence, were typically men in their teens, this may have constituted a temporary "phase" in their sexuality rather than a permanent "lifestyle choice".[102] Likewise, men who cross-dressed as women, whom we classify today as "transvestites" or "transgendered" rather than homosexuals, cannot always be said to have played the passive role.[103] Nor can we be sure if the active/passive model of homosexual relationships held true throughout Europe, since the asymmetrical age pattern was not universal, although the active/passive model *is* how medieval Europeans thought about sexuality in general, i.e., "as something that someone did to someone else".[104] Nonetheless, given modern views about the practice, it is not surprising that Boswell mentioned pederasty only once in his book, and that in an attempt to deny its importance for medieval homosexuality.[105]

It is quite correct to say that homosexuality was one of the most brutally punished "crimes" of the medieval period. Civil penalties enacted in various countries included burning alive, beheading, buried alive, castration and other mutilations, and exile.[106] Thus, in theory, homosexuals were quite heavily persecuted in the later Middle Ages, as Boswell maintained. But in practice, as the records from Florence and Venice show, this persecution could vary considerably depending on a variety of factors. Venice had a reputation of punishing sodomites severely, especially under the Council of Ten, which took up sodomy cases from 1418. But even here, penalties were substantially mitigated, or waived altogether, for passive partners, especially those of a young age; for those who engaged in mutual masturbation or external stimulation, as opposed to anal intercourse; and for heterosexual sodomy, which seems to have been practiced as a form of birth control.[107]

Florence prosecuted by far the most sodomites of any city in the fifteenth century: During the seventy years of its operation between 1432 and 1502, the Office of the Night is estimated to have prosecuted between 15,000 to 16,000 individuals, as compared to 411 individuals prosecuted in Venice during roughly the same period.[108] Yet, Florence seems to have been much more lenient in its penalties for sodomy. From 1459, the government enacted perhaps the lowest penalties for sodomy anywhere in Europe, set at 10 florins for the first offense. Partly, this was designed to encourage denunciations and the levying of penalties, which apparently the Night officers were loathe to do when they were too high, particularly in the case of poor artisans and laborers who made up a substantial portion of the accused. This indeed had the desired effect of drastically increasing prosecutions, which greatly increased the revenues of the Office of the Night.[109] But, in the words of Michael Rocke, it may also have reflected "a fair degree of popular and official accommodation, if not outright tolerance, of sodomy in Florence".[110] This was more likely to be the case when the accused were wealthy, powerful, and influential men, which included some former Night officers themselves.[111] But it also seems to have reflected the political fortunes and make-up of the Florentine government. Under the *de facto* rule of Lorenzo di Medici (r. 1469–92), sodomy was vigorously prosecuted during the early years of the regime in the 1470s, but then an abrupt change of policy occurred in the 1480s and early 90s, when prosecutions were at their most lax in the entire history of the Office of the Night, averaging just 6–7 convictions per year.[112] This relative lenience towards sodomy seems to have been a function of Lorenzo's ability to finally consolidate his hold on Florentine government. Somewhat counter-intuitively, as Lorenzo tightened his grip on power, he correspondingly loosened restrictions on a whole host of morally ambivalent activities that otherwise would have invited criticism of the regime.[113] This obviously argues against Moore's thesis that persecution of minorities necessarily followed a centralization of authority. It was only with the fall of the Medicean regime in 1494, and the rise of the supposedly more democratic Republic, that Florence entered its most persecuting phase against sodomy, particularly under the influence of the incendiary preacher, Girolamo Savonarola (1452–98).[114]

Did the sodomite communities in Florence, Venice, and Cologne constitute a gay "subculture" or underground in the Middle Ages? Once again, the evidence is mixed on this point. There are some indications that there was a unique demography and topography to sodomy, i.e., that it was largely confined to certain groups and to certain quarters of the city.[115] We've already noted that, in Florence at least, an age asymmetry characterized medieval sodomy, with passive partners typically being young boys, and active partners adults between the ages of 18 and 40.[116] In all three cities, the practitioners of sodomy tended to be tradesmen, which in effect mirrored the predominant make-up of the population.[117] In Florence, certain public streets, such as the Street of the Furriers, and certain taverns, such as the Buco and the Sant' Andrea, were known as the "haunt" of sodomites, but other popular venues included workshops, churches, dancing and fencing schools, and private homes, some of which gained the reputation of being "virtual brothels".[118] In Venice, sodomy became associated with schools, particularly those that taught music and singing, gymnastics, fencing, and the abacus; apothecary shops; pastry shops; dark, secluded public spaces; and private homes, particularly those that hosted large dinner or gambling parties.[119] Perhaps the most persuasive evidence of a sodomite underground comes from Cologne, where it was reported that those "besmirched" with the "dumb sin" made up a "bad company" of about 200 men; that they frequented certain areas of the city such as the Hay, Linen, and Butter Markets; and that they even developed their own "sexually specific language and communication". It was even said that sodomites arranged rendezvous in public toilets, anticipating the "bathhouse" culture of modern-day homosexuality.[120]

On the other hand, there is a compelling argument to be made, especially on the basis of evidence from Florence and Venice, that medieval homosexuality was more broadly practiced, and thus less confined to a self-identifying minority or subculture, when compared with the homosexuality of today. Rocke argued that in Florence, homosexuality was so much intertwined with male culture and masculine identity in general that it made no sense to talk of a "sodomitical sub-culture" at all. Instead, in his words, "there was only a single male sexual culture with a prominent homoerotic character".[121] Rocke also found that:

> Sodomy in Florence was not limited to any particular social group or to a distinctive and permanent "homosexual" minority. Rather, it was part of the whole fabric of Florentine society, attracting males of all ages, matrimonial condition, and social rank. Indeed, sodomy was so widespread, and the policing apparatus for unearthing it so effective in the later fifteenth century, that in this period probably the majority of local males, at one time or another, were officially incriminated.[122]

Thus, sodomy for medieval Florentine males seems to have been a temporary stage in their lives instead of a lifetime "avocation". As already mentioned, this was a function of a long period of bachelorhood before marriage, when men did not get married until typically in their thirties, perhaps mostly for economic reasons, and thus homosexual relations were a "temporary outlet for sexual gratification, diversion, and companionship".[123] In other parts of Europe, such as Cologne, where asymmetrical marriage patterns were less the norm, perhaps sodomy became more of a conscious sexual orientation and permanent lifestyle choice that is more akin to the modern culture of homosexuality. In Venice, there were indications that homosexuality transitioned from a limited or marginal "underground subculture" in the fourteenth century to a more widespread and more "socially diverse" phenomenon in the fifteenth century, which therefore became "more visible and threatening" to authorities and, as a consequence, was more vigorously prosecuted.[124]

Above all, one must admire the courage and tenacity of medieval homosexuals, who were willing to pursue their preferences in spite of sometimes quite virulent persecution. Even in Venice, despite the best efforts of the Council of Ten, "the homosexual subculture became a well-entrenched part of Venetian life at all social levels," while in Florence, sodomites even fought back against their persecutors and made a show of resistance during the puritanical regime of Savonarola.[125] This is probably the most heartening lesson for modern observers to take away from the medieval experience of homosexuality.

Medieval prostitution

Traditionally, the prostitute has been seen as a reviled figure in medieval society, who stood at the opposite end of the ideal of chastity—someone who embodied the sin of lust and unbridled sexual appetite. As such, the prostitute was a marginal, rather than mainstream, figure. Yet one also can make the case that many of the attitudes medieval people had towards prostitutes were no different than the ones they had towards female sexuality, and towards women, in general.[126] One can interpret this either as indicating that medieval attitudes towards prostitution were far more complex than previously thought, or that it simply affirms how misogynist the medieval patriarchy really was towards women and their sexuality.

The original Latin term for prostitute, *meretrix*—meaning "she who earns"—certainly conveys the idea that prostitutes had sex for money, but this was not the only or even the primary meaning of the term for medieval commentators.[127] Instead, their main criterion seems to have been that the prostitute was someone (almost always a woman) whose sexuality lay outside the norms of accepted behavior.[128] Therefore, prostitute in a medieval context could include: a woman guilty of adultery or fornication; a "common woman" who had many sexual partners or who denied herself to no man; a woman who was publicly known to engage in sex in exchange for money; a woman who enjoyed sexual intercourse in ways that avoided procreation; or simply a woman of "loose morals".[129] In this way, *meretrix* demonstrates how precarious and vulnerable was the social position of any singlewoman in the Middle Ages who indulged in sexual activity, i.e., sex outside of marriage. Any woman who was not married and who was sexually active could be labeled a whore.[130]

Medieval canon law defined a prostitute as not just one who sold her body for monetary gain (derived from Roman law) but also one who was publicly promiscuous, copulating "indifferently and indiscriminately" like a dog and who, in the words of St. Jerome, was "available for the lust of many men".[131] Use of the modern word, "prostitute," is problematic in much the same way as is "homosexual," in that it fails to convey the flexible and varied meanings that the concept had for medieval people. For these reasons, some scholars prefer to only use terms that occur in medieval records, such as "whore" or "bawd" (meaning "pimp"), even though these may have different meanings for modern readers.[132]

One of the main issues debated by historians with regard to medieval prostitution is whether to classify prostitutes as "marginal" or "deviant" figures in the Middle Ages (i.e., does this subject belong here or in the previous chapter)? On one level, it seems natural to argue that prostitutes lived at the margins of medieval society.[133] In many cities throughout England and the Continent, prostitutes were marginalized quite literally, in that they were physically constrained and segregated by regulations. In some cities, they could only operate within municipally-licensed brothels, or they were confined to certain "red-light" districts or streets or even outside the city walls altogether. They were also often required, like the Jews, to wear distinguishing clothing, such as a striped hood or a red knot on the left shoulder. Prostitutes had almost no recognized legal status: They could not bring an accusation for rape, for example, since they were already considered common property whose violation injured no man, and their testimony was rarely admissible in court owing to their "evil fame". Although they were allowed to keep the profits of their trade, they could inherit no property. While some might argue that prostitutes could earn more than men and evince an entrepreneurial spirit, they were generally among the poorest elements of society. Some contemporaries forbade prostitutes to give alms or pay tithes to the Church, on the grounds that their contributions were unacceptable as "ill-gotten gains". Authorities associated them with a criminal "subculture," especially theft, and with social disorder, and they were concerned about the possibility that, if allowed to intermingle with respectable citizens too freely, they might be a polluting and corrupting influence. This is why Avignon forbade prostitutes (together with Jews) from touching bread and fruit on display in market stalls, and why sumptuary regulations forbade them from wearing noble finery such as jewels, furs, and silks, in order that other women might not be tempted into prostitution.[134]

But some scholars have made the counter-argument that prostitutes were, in fact, central to medieval society and well-integrated in their local communities.[135] From a practical standpoint, the medieval experience of prostitution was so varied that it can be said to have reflected the diversity of life itself. Ruth Karras noted, for example, that "there was no single medieval attitude toward prostitution either as a cultural or as a commercial phenomenon".[136] Towns took varied approaches to prostitution, ranging from outlawing it outright; to *de facto* toleration, where fines acted as a sort of licensing fee that allowed prostitutes to continue to ply their trade while at the same time generating valuable income for the town; to "institutionalizing" it through officially licensed and supervised municipal brothels.[137] Enforcement of regulations against prostitutes could also be considerably mitigated or ignored, although some would argue that such regulations were flouted from their very inception.[138]

In addition, there was considerable variation in terms of the kinds of prostitutes that appeared in the medieval records. Some worked out of official or unofficial brothels; some out of their homes; some walked the streets; some had pimps or other go-betweens; some procured customers on their own behalf; some made a life-long career out of prostitution; some were more transient, only plying the trade as economic necessity demanded. The careers of some real-life prostitutes, such as Isabella Wakefield and Margaret Clay, who operated as prostitutes in York between, respectively, 1403–31 and 1449–66, indicate that they could become respectable members of their community, since both were able to purge themselves of the charge of fornication, which was only possible if a number of "compurgators," or fellow citizens willing to testify to the good name and reputation of the accused, were willing to come forward.[139] Prostitutes could also interact with society in other ways, such as by providing eligible women with "information about the sexual prowess of potential marriage partners," or by serving as witness in Church courts on cases of alleged impotence, as noted above.[140] They were even invited to family gatherings, festivals, weddings, etc., which perhaps indicates a degree of social acceptance by their peers.[141] Particularly in the case of prostitutes "who operated independently or on a more casual basis," Karras argued that they could easily integrate themselves into their communities since their sexual practices were less offensive or obtrusive than those of prostitutes who operated out of brothels.[142] If they operated on a part-time basis, prostitutes could also easily go back to more "respected" occupations. It has likewise been pointed out that, throughout the Middle Ages, there were consistent efforts to try to "reform" or "reclaim" the prostitute, such as by funding Magdalene houses that offered a refuge for prostitutes, or by providing a dowry fund to enable reformed prostitutes to get married. These efforts indicate that, to the medieval mind, prostitution was never a permanent, "fallen" state for women and that prostitutes should not be completely cut off from society.[143]

Another argument for prostitution's integration into medieval society is that it was seen by contemporaries as fulfilling a necessary function in order to maintain good moral and public order. While this may seem contradictory, since the practice of prostitution itself was considered immoral, many medieval commentators, beginning with St. Augustine (354–430), perceived prostitution as a "necessary evil" that had to be tolerated if, in fact, the social and sexual order was to be maintained and wives and maidens not threatened by the "hydraulic model of masculine sexuality," i.e., that unless men had some way to release their pent-up sexual demands, all hell would break loose.[144] An anonymous thirteenth-century author posed the issue in a very visceral way that most people can readily understand: The brothel was like a sewer in a palace; if you took away the sewer, the whole palace would be filled with shit.[145] Prostitution also was justified on the grounds that young men had to be lured away from sodomy if the birth rate was not to get too low, a concern of particular importance in the wake of the Black Death.[146] Nonetheless, there is no reason why prostitution might not have proven equally seductive as sodomy in terms of dissuading "men from marriage and family".[147] Moreover, the demographic argument—that acceptance of prostitution arose out of a concern to reverse declining population—fails to explain the continuity in policies towards prostitution despite sometimes abrupt fluctuations in population levels. Yet the fact that it was easier for women to get married in the aftermath of the plague may have resulted in a shortage of prostitutes, which would have made their services more valuable, assuming that demand held steady at this time.[148]

Leah Otis has documented how prostitution became "institutionalized"—meaning that towns established red-light districts and municipally-owned brothels, where prostitutes could operate legally but be closely monitored and controlled—in Languedoc in southern France beginning in the late thirteenth and fourteenth centuries.[149] She argued that this represented an innovation and reversal from previous policies that attempted to expel prostitutes from "scandalized" neighborhoods. Moreover, institutionalizing prostitution was by no means confined to Languedoc, but "was the rule in most regions of Europe in this period".[150] While this might seem, on one level, to indicate a normalization of prostitution such that it became a regular feature of medieval society, it is also clear that institutionalization reflected an ambivalent attitude that municipal authorities had towards prostitution, whereby prostitutes had to be "sealed off" from mainstream society as the "mistrusted pawns in the effort to hedge off sexual and social disorder," even as prostitution was regarded as "inevitable" owing to the natural urges of sexual desire. Otis compared this rationale to the medical remedy of quarantine used to combat the contagion of disease.[151] It is therefore no coincidence that institutionalization of prostitution took off in the late fourteenth century, the so-called "troubled decades of plague, war, and social disorder".[152]

Otis therefore viewed the main rationale behind the institutionalization of prostitution—based on her reading of charter documents authorizing municipal brothels or red-light districts—as a variation on the Augustinian argument that they were needed in order to avoid a "greater evil".[153] In a time of great insecurity and anxiety, officially-sanctioned prostitutes and brothels could help fulfill a rising demand for "public order, public utility, public good". Far from being a symptom of moral decadence and decline, institutionalized prostitution was instead a "sign of increasing concern" for, and of increasing moral rigor with regard to, the "problems of sexual morality," and of female sexuality in particular. Initially, institutionalized prostitution was a sort of compromise between, on the one hand, the desire of the Church to impose stricter sexual mores—in which divorce, adultery, and concubinage were seen as threats to the "sacred" institution of marriage—and on the other, a resistance among the laity who wished to maintain a "double standard of sexual morality, strict for women and lax for men". Prostitution allowed married and unmarried men to persist in quasi-sanctioned fornication and adultery—i.e., without fear of legal or social repercussions—while at the same time it kept these mortal sins within strictly-defined spatial boundaries. Eventually, by the fifteenth century, lay opinion caught up to the Church's more rigorous standards of sexual morality, as evidenced by the harsher punishment of concubines and of the men who kept them, the ending of privileged protection for men found within the red-light district from prosecution for adultery, and the growing disapproval of excessive fornication, such as men "who frequented brothels habitually". This laid the groundwork for the general closing of brothels by the mid-sixteenth century.[154]

The dismantling of institutionalized prostitution by the Early Modern period implies a great transformation in societal attitudes towards prostitution, whereby it moved from the tolerated and rationalized mainstream to become "a part of the history of criminality and marginality in the early modern period".[155] This naturally calls into question how tolerated and accepted prostitution was in the first place, and even Otis admitted that, at the height of the institutionalization of prostitution during the fourteenth and fifteenth centuries, municipal authorities were ambivalent about using prostitutes as an instrument of social order and were gradually moving towards greater moral rigor and control of sexual morality and of prostitutes, thereby anticipating complete repression.[156] Yet the switch from seeing prostitution as an inevitable and necessary evil to something intolerable and dispensable needs to be explained. Otis viewed the main motivating force behind this shift as the Protestant Reformation of the early sixteenth century, when religious figures like Luther and Calvin insisted upon higher standards of moral, particularly sexual, behavior, in which simple fornication and adultery were no longer seen as natural or inevitable. This did no more than systematize and carry to their logical conclusion "ideas and feelings existing already at the end of the Middle Ages".[157] But one can doubt whether this is actually the case, given the fundamental differences in theology and approaches to salvation between the Catholic and Protestant religions. Moreover, while Calvinism may have penetrated Languedoc, plenty of French towns, as well as towns in Italy, where brothels were closed during the Reformation remained staunchly Catholic. Otis tried to paper over this discrepancy by pointing to a similar "struggle against sexual immorality" in the Catholic Counter-Reformation, which already "found its roots in the late medieval period," thus making the "desire for reform of church and society" broader and deeper than simply "its manifestation in the Reformation".[158]

Yet, an alternative explanation offers itself that is independent of the geographical vagaries of the Reformation, namely, that "the closing of brothels was a reaction to the spread of venereal disease," which began to occur indiscriminately throughout Europe, perhaps after having been imported from the Americas, in the 1490s.[159] Otis rejected this theory on the grounds that it did not "explain the chronology of the closings," since most of these happened decades later, and did not accord with medieval people's imperfect understanding of disease contagion, whereby a disease "could be communicated by a look as well as by intercourse".[160] But this underestimates "the cumulative effect of disease" gradually reinforcing "the moral pressure building up on the brothels".[161] As Otis herself pointed out, brothels were already being closed temporarily in the fifteenth century during epidemics of plague.[162] Overall, the argument for an institutionalization, and thereby acceptance and toleration, of prostitution in the late Middle Ages is by no means a clear-cut one, since it has a hard time explaining the transition to dismantling of prostitution in the Early Modern period.

A more conventional variation on the prostitution as a lesser evil argument is made by Jacques Rossiaud, who studied prostitution's role in the Burgundian town of Dijon in east-central France. Just as Otis argued for Languedoc, Rossiaud viewed the municipal brothel of Dijon (the *Grande Maison*) as playing the role of guarantor of a "collective order," and the prostitutes as fulfilling a moral and social responsibility to the town. But, in the case of Dijon, the order that was being defended was more specific, namely, the "honor of the virtuous ladies of the town," or of the women "of estate," which had to be safeguarded against "aggressive gangs" of unruly youths, who went around breaking into houses and raping women.[163] Such sexual violence was apparently endemic to Dijon, where 125 cases of rape occurred between 1436 and 1486, or an average of over two a year.[164] Contrary to what was stated as the putative victims of rape without prostitution, the actual victims were almost all from the lower classes—i.e., servants and daughters or wives of day laborers or "waged textile workers"—who were in their teens to early thirties. Over half were unmarried, while about a quarter were married to husbands who sometimes journeyed away from home for days or weeks at a time.[165] The perpetrators came from roughly the same social class as the victims—mostly they were young, unmarried journeymen, artisans, day laborers, or penniless burghers' sons. Rossiaud estimated that half the city's youths participated in such attacks, perhaps as "a rite of passage to manhood and of admission to neighborhood gangs".[166]

Rossiaud argued that such rape gangs acted out a kind of age and sexual warfare, in which they were venting their frustrations at more elderly rivals (i.e., over 30 years of age) who had better advantages in the marriage market and were thus "siphoning off" marriageable girls. This is backed up by figures that point to a relatively mature average age at marriage for men (i.e., mid- to late-twenties) and a large average age gap (around 8 years) for the vast majority of couples. A large percentage of married men over 30 were 8–16 years older than their wives, choosing their companions "from an age group in which they competed with younger men".[167] Although the rapists might have been thumbing their noses at the social order, they were also playing the role of a self-styled moral police, expressing their disapproval—in brutal fashion—of "transgressive" marriages and relationships, such as servant girls with their masters, concubines with their priests, and young girls with older widowers marrying for the second time.[168] Perhaps for this reason, and the fact that most attacks targeted women from the lower classes, authorities (namely, the *échevins* of the city council) turned a blind eye to these "disturbances" or crimes, even if they were recorded for posterity by the *procureurs-syndics*.[169] In this vein, Rossiaud argued that prostitution functioned in Dijon as a kind of safety valve or "tranquillizing agency," in which the sexual outlet of "municipalized fornication" defended ladies' honor (at least among the upper classes) by tempering "the aggressive nature of adolescents," and, what is more, served as a mediator and "institution for harmony between age classes and social groups".[170]

But did this actually work, and did contemporaries really see it that way? There are indications, in fact, that prostitution may have had the opposite effect, in that it made life for women more violent and insecure, not less, by encouraging young men to see all women as whores. Rossiaud claimed that the "atmosphere of insecurity" created by the gangs was operative "only among certain groups in the female population," leaving most "respectable" women and girls untouched, with "no reason to fear rape". But at the same time, Rossiaud admitted that "sexual violence was an everyday dimension of city life," such that he estimated that "all the city's youth, from burgher's sons to kitchen boys," had both visited a whore and "raped a poor girl at least once during their young years without being rejected by the city".[171] The rapes, as the perpetrators probably intended in their self-assigned role as moral enforcers, ruined girls' prospects for marriage and wives' relationships with their husbands, perhaps forcing them into prostitution, since, in the eyes of neighbors and even of the victims' own, "the status of a raped woman was brought singularly closer to that of a common prostitute".[172] Moreover, even older, married men, according to Rossiaud, behaved sexually with their wives in the same way as they did with prostitutes, in accordance with the urgings of "nature".[173] If prostitutes were "far from being marginalized" in Dijon, then perhaps this was not because they "assumed a real function" in the town's efforts to maintain order, but because the lines were so blurred between themselves and the rest of women, with truly horrific results.[174]

It is, in fact, prostitution's relationship with female sexuality, and human sexuality in general, that has proven to be the most fruitful avenue of investigation with respect to the issue of prostitutes' marginality during the Middle Ages. In a strictly literal sense, one can say that prostitution was an aberrant or "deviant" form of sexual behavior, in that the prostitute had far more partners or practiced sex in ways (i.e., non-procreative) that were not typical of most members of medieval society. But Ruth Karras argued that prostitutes, "as women entirely defined by their sexuality, provide the extreme case that helps define views of feminine sexuality in general".[175] For Karras, prostitutes were emblematic of medieval (predominantly male) society's efforts and concerns to control female sexuality, in that prostitutes as independently-operating and sexually active women could threaten that control—hence the necessity of defining prostitutes as the "common" property of all men.[176] It also has been pointed out that the medieval idea of prostitution exposed the contradictory—one might say hypocritical—attitudes towards female sexuality in the Middle Ages, in that women were accorded greater sexual urges than men, yet at the same time, they were expected to live up to higher standards of chaste behavior. Thus, a woman, even if married and faithful, who had a healthy sexual appetite was regarded, at least unofficially, as a whore, while this same attitude in men was considered completely natural.[177] At the same time, the Church's "moral ambivalence" about tolerating prostitution as a necessary evil "was emblematic of the difficulties that medieval societies experienced in confronting the realities of human sexuality".[178]

In the end, Karras argued that prostitution was central to female sexuality, and thus was not marginal at all, because it illustrated how pervasive was the medieval view of sex as a commodity, even in the case of married women. This is almost the complete opposite of modern views of sexuality and marriage, which is why we define a prostitute as one who exchanges sex for money, but medieval people did not define it this way, or at least, did not confine themselves to such a definition, because it would then be harder for them to distinguish prostitutes from all other women. One can see this link between "feminine sexuality and financial exchange" in both marriage law and popular literature, such as the *fabliaux*. A dowry of some form was expected in exchange for marriage, as recorded by the courts registering financial negotiations, or rather disputes, over marriage contracts (Chapter 6). In Karras' view, medieval society did not object to prostitutes taking money for sex because this was how they conceptualized legitimate marriage contracts, although it also meant that the "line between a respectable woman and a whore was a vague one".[179] In the *fabliaux* and other literature, the exchange of money for sex at all levels of society was also made explicit. The prostitute who figured in such tales was simply a more exaggerated version of the wife, extreme both in her greed and her lust. Prostitution thus made obvious what was only hinted at by more "respectable" institutions, such as marriage: In the Middle Ages, all women were for sale, and all female sexuality had its price, both for women, and for men.[180]

Notes

1 This question is explored in more detail in the next chapter, in the section on "Maidens, wives, and widows".

2 Ruth Mazo Karras, *Sexuality in Medieval Europe: Doing unto Others*, 2nd edn. (London: Routledge, 2012), pp. 10–14; Jeffrey Richards, *Sex, Dissidence and Damnation: Minority Groups in the Middle Ages* (London: Routledge, 1991), p. 22.

3 Karras, *Sexuality in Medieval Europe*, 2nd edn., pp. 4, 27.

4 Karras, *Sexuality in Medieval Europe*, 2nd edn., pp. 4, 27; Anna Clark, *A History of European Sexuality* (New York and London: Routledge, 2008), p. 64. One area where modern attitudes may come very close to medieval ones is in the case of rape, where even today, the victim is usually assumed to be someone who has been penetrated, i.e., a female, rather than one who has done the penetrating, i.e., a male, even if he is underage. Certainly, the penalties for those convicted of rape vary enormously depending on these circumstances.

5 Joan Cadden, *Meanings of Sex Difference in the Middle Ages: Medicine, Science, and Culture* (Cambridge: Cambridge University Press, 1993), p. 165.

6 Cadden, *Meanings of Sex Difference*, pp. 2, 134–35, 162.

7 Cadden, *Meanings of Sex Difference*, p. 65; Helen Rodnite Lemay, "Sexuality in Twelfth-through Fifteenth-Century Scientific Writings," in *Sexual Practices and the Medieval Church*, eds. Vern L. Bullough and James Brundage (Buffalo, NY.: Prometheus Books, 1982), p. 204.

8 Cadden, *Meanings of Sex Difference*, pp. 95–99, 142–43; Katherine Park, "Medicine and Natural Philosophy: Naturalistic Traditions," in *The Oxford Handbook of Women and Gender in Medieval Europe*, eds. Judith M. Bennett and Ruth Mazo Karras (Oxford: Oxford University Press, 2013), p. 95.

9 Cadden, *Meanings of Sex Difference*, pp. 155–63.

10 Danielle Jacquart and Claude Thomasset, *Sexuality and Medicine in the Middle Ages*, trans. Matthew Adamson (Princeton, NJ.: Princeton University Press, 1988), pp. 130–33; Cadden, *Meanings of Sex Difference*, pp. 152, 160; Lemay, "Sexuality," pp. 202–4; Park, "Medicine and Natural Philosophy," pp. 89, 96.

11 Cadden, *Meanings of Sex Difference*, pp. 150, 163–64.

12 Jacquart and Thomasset, *Sexuality and Medicine*, pp. 94, 138; Cadden, *Meanings of Sex Difference*, pp. 98–99, 137–38; Lemay, "Sexuality," p. 188–89; Park, "Medicine and Natural Philosophy," p. 96; Monica Green, "Bodies, Gender, Health, Disease: Recent Work on Medieval Women's Medicine," *Studies in Medieval and Renaissance History*, 3rd ser., 2 (2005): 11–12.

13 James A. Brundage, *Law, Sex, and Christian Society in Medieval Europe* (Chicago, IL.: University of Chicago Press, 1990), pp. 152, 154.

14 Richards, *Sex, Dissidence, and Damnation*, p. 23; Clark, *History of European Sexuality*, p. 51.

15 Brundange, *Law, Sex, and Christian Society*, pp. 173–75; Karras, *Sexuality in Medieval Europe*, 2nd edn., pp. 37–44; Richards, *Sex, Dissidence and Damnation*, p. 27; Conor McCarthy, *Marriage in Medieval England: Law, Literature and Practice* (Woodbridge, UK: Boydell Press, 2004), pp. 107–12.

16 Sidney E. Berger, "Sex in the Literature of the Middle Ages: The Fabliaux," in *Sexual Practices and the Medieval Church*, p. 162.

17 Karras, *Sexuality in Medieval Europe*, 2nd edn., p. 12.

18 Anna Clark has characterized the *fabliaux* as embodying "sexual desire as comic excess". See Clark, *History of European Sexuality*, p. 63.

19 For the original French versions of these stories, see *Nouveau Recueil Complet des Fabliaux*, ed. W. Noomen, 10 vols. (Assen, Netherlands: Van Gorcum, 1983–2001). For an English translation, see John DuVal, *Fabliaux Fair and Foul* (Binghamton, NY.: Medieval and Renaissance Texts and Studies, 1992). For commentary, see Karras, *Sexuality in Medieval Europe*, 2nd edn., pp. 14–16, 102–3; Berger, "Sex in the Literature of the Middle Ages," pp. 162–75; Mary Jane Stearns Schenck, *The Fabliaux: Tales of Wit and Deception* (Purdue University Monographs in Romance Languages, 24, 1987).

20 Karras, *Sexuality in Medieval Europe*, 2nd edn., pp. 152–53.

21 Karras, *Sexuality in Medieval Europe*, 2nd edn., pp. 15–16. See also Clark, *History of European Sexuality*, pp. 62–64, for another take on some of these questions.

22 McCarthy, *Marriage in Medieval England*, p. 113; James A. Brundage, "Sex and Canon Law," in *Handbook of Medieval Sexuality*, eds. Vern L. Bullough and James A. Brundage (New York: Garland, 1996), p. 40; Richards, *Sex, Dissidence and Damnation*, p. 27.

23 James A. Brundage, "The Problem of Impotence," in *Sexual Practices and the Medieval Church*, pp. 135–36. In Chaucer's *Canterbury Tales*, the Wife of Bath declares that, "Why else the proverb written down and set/In books: 'A man must yield his wife her debt?'" This was not intended to be admirable, however, but as an example of the Wife's overly lusty nature. See Clark, *History of European Sexuality*, p. 62.

24 Karras, *Sexuality in Medieval Europe*, 2nd edn., p. 100.

25 R.H. Helmholz, *Marriage Litigation in Medieval England* (Cambridge: Cambridge University Press, 1974), p. 89 and n. 54.

26 Brundage, "Problem of Impotence," p. 140.

27 Richards, *Sex, Dissidence and Damnation*, p. 35; McCarthy, *Marriage in Medieval England*, p. 107–8; Jo Ann McNamara, "Chaste Marriage and Clerical Celibacy," in *Sexual Practices and the Medieval Church*, p. 24; Marty Newman Williams and Anne Echols, *Between Pit and Pedestal: Women in the Middle Ages* (New York: Markus Wiener, 1994), p. 85; Clark, *History of European Sexuality*, pp. 51–52. Indeed, St. Jerome judged a husband who loved his wife too passionately as an adulterer!

28 Richards, *Sex, Dissidence and Damnation*, p. 29; Williams and Echols, *Between Pit and Pedestal*, pp. 85–86; Brundage, *Law, Sex, and Christian Society*, pp. 155–56.

29 Richards, *Sex, Dissidence and Damnation*, p. 29; Williams and Echols, *Between Pit and Pedestal*, p. 85.

30 John M. Riddle, "Contraception and Early Abortion in the Middle Ages," in *Handbook of Medieval Sexuality*, pp. 261–73; Jacquart and Thomasset, *Sexuality and Medicine*, p. 96.

31 Karras, *Sexuality in Medieval Europe*, 2nd edn., p. 106.

32 Riddle, "Contraception," pp. 264–69.

33 P.P.A. Biller, "Birth-Control in the West in the Thirteenth and Early Fourteenth Centuries," *Past and Present* 94 (1982):19–20.

34 Richards, *Sex, Dissidence and Damnation*, pp. 32–33, 37–38.

35 Riddle declared confidently that "medieval peoples knew about and used contraceptives and birth control, and they employed them sufficiently well to limit births". However, he offered no hard evidence to support such a statement beyond the existence of medical texts that explained various methods of birth control. Biller was more cautious, suggesting merely the "possibility" of a "positive case" for medieval birth control. He concluded his article by admitting that the "body of evidence" for such a case was

"slender and patchy" and could be subject to future revision should new evidence come to light. See Riddle, "Contraception," p. 261; Biller, "Birth-Control," pp. 3, 26.

36 These include the trials of Gabrina degli Albeti in 1375 at Reggio and of Matteuccia Francisci in 1428 at Todi, both in Italy. See Richard Kieckhefer, "Erotic Magic in Medieval Europe," in *Sex in the Middle Ages: A Book of Essays*, ed. Joyce E. Salisbury (New York: Garland Publishing, 1991), pp. 30–37, 43–45.

37 Karras, *Sexuality in Medieval Europe*, 2nd edn., pp. 157–66.

38 Karras, *Sexuality in Medieval Europe*, 2nd edn., p. 114; Brundage, "Sex and Canon Law," p. 42; Ruth Mazo Karras, "Sex and the Singlewoman," in *Medieval Single Women: The Politics of Social Classification in Late Medieval England*, ed. Cordelia Beattie (Oxford: Oxford University Press, 2007), pp. 136–37; Tim North, "Legerwite in the Thirteenth and Fourteenth Centuries," *Past and Present* 111 (1986):11.

39 Karras, "Sex and the Singlewoman," pp. 135–36; Williams and Echols, *Between Pit and Pedestal*, pp. 92–93.

40 Georges Duby, *Love and Marriage in the Middle Ages*, trans. Jane Dunnett (Chicago, IL.: University of Chicago Press, 1994), p. 60; Clark, *History of European Sexuality*, pp. 54–56; Joan Kelly-Gadol, "Did Women Have a Renaissance?" in *Becoming Visible: Women in European History*, eds. Renate Bridenthal and Claudia Koonz (Boston, MA.: Houghton Mifflin, 1977), pp. 178–84.

41 Kelly-Gadol, "Did Women Have a Renaissance," p. 182. Kelly based her argument on the evidence of courtly love literature, which she claimed evinced a "marked lack of concern about illegitimacy". Women then supposedly lost this sexual freedom once Renaissance humanism imposed the more patriarchal values of classical antiquity. For a re-evaluation of Kelly's thesis, see Theresa Coletti, "'Did Women Have a Renaissance?' A Medievalist Reads Joan Kelly and Aemilia Lanyer," *Early Modern Women* 8 (2013):249–59.

42 Christopher N.L.Brooke, *The Medieval Idea of Marriage* (Oxford: Oxford University Press, 1989), pp. 111–12; M.T. Clanchy, *Abelard: A Medieval Life* (Oxford: Blackwell, 1999), pp. 164–68; Ruth Mazo Karras, "The Christianization of Medieval Marriage," in *Christianity and Culture in the Middle Ages: Essays to Honor John van Engen*, eds. David C. Mengel and Lisa Wolverton (Notre Dame, IN.: Notre Dame Univeristy Press, 2015), pp. 14–15.

43 Karras, *Sexuality in Medieval Europe*, 2nd edn., pp. 116–20; Karras, "Sex and the Single-woman," p. 136; C.N.L. Brooke, "Marriage and Society in the Central Middle Ages," in *Marriage and Society: Studies in the Social History of Marriage*, ed. R.B. Outhwaite (New York: St. Martin's Press, 1982), pp. 30–31; Duby, *Love and Marriage*, pp. 62–63. Duby suggested a third possibility, that the courtly romances were primarily about the love between two men, namely, between the young suitor and his prince, the husband of the wife to whom he (superficially) addressed his advances. This, then, would be a literature written by men, for men, leaving women altogether out of the equation.

44 Peggy McCracken, *The Romance of Adultery: Queenship and Sexual Transgression in Old French Literature* (Philadelphia, PA.: University of Pennsylvania Press, 1998), pp. 171–72.

45 Karras, *Sexuality in Medieval Europe*, 2nd edn., pp. 116, 120–22.

46 Karras, *Sexuality in Medieval Europe*, 2nd edn., p. 123; North, "Legerwite," pp. 10, 12; E.D. Jones, "The Medieval Leyrwite: A Historical Note on Female Fornication," *English Historical Review* 107 (1992):945–47; Judith Bennett, "Writing Fornication: Medieval Leyrwite and its Historians," *Transactions of the Royal Historical Society*, 6th ser., 13 (2003): 136–27. The Myntling Register of Spalding Priory recorded only 98 fines for leyrwite in 225 years (i.e., between 1253 and 1478), but Jones believed this vastly underestimated the level of "actual illicit sexual activity" on Spalding's manors. Judith Bennett commented that, even though "jurisdiction of leyrwite netted so few offenders and so little profit," we must conclude that "peasants either did not fornicate or did not get caught".

47 Karras, "Sex and the Singlewoman," p. 129; H.E. Hallam, *Rural England, 1066–1348* (Brighton, Sussex and Atlantic Highlands, N.J.: Harvester Press and Humanities Press,

1981), pp. 262–63. Another possible reason for imposing *leyrwite* was for demographic purposes, to control population growth prior to the Black Death, especially among the "poorer elements of society". See: Bennett, "Writing Fornication," pp. 142–43, 152; Mark Bailey, *The Decline of Serfdom in Late Medieval England: From Bondage to Freedom* (Woodbridge, UK: Boydell Press, 2014), p. 41.

48 Bennett, "Writing Fornication," p. 135–36, and n. 17; Karras, *Sexuality in Medieval Europe*, 2nd edn., p. 123; Karras, "Sex and the Singlewoman," p. 129; Ruth Mazo Karras, "Two Models, Two Standards: Moral Teaching and Sexual Mores," in *Bodies and Disciplines: Intersections of Literature and History in Fifteenth-Century England*, eds. Barbara Hanawalt and David Wallace (Minneapolis, MN.: University of Minnesota Press, 1996), p. 127; Brundage, "Sex and Canon Law," p. 41. E.D. Jones, however, concluded that Spaulding Priory made so little profit from *leyrwite* that it "did not levy the fine from primarily financial motives". See Jones, "Medieval Leyrwite," p. 947.

49 Karras, "Sex and the Singlewoman," p. 130; Karras, "Two Models, Two Standards," pp. 128–33; Bennett, "Writing Fornication," pp. 153–54. Bennett has also noted a double standard over fornication with respect to social status, with poor women much more likely to be charged and fined with *leyrwite* than those from well-off families, perhaps because the former were viewed as an additional charity burden on their communities. See Bennett, "Writing Fornication," pp. 142–44, 151–55.

50 Williams and Echols, *Between Pit and Pedestal*, pp. 91–92; Ann Julia Kettle, "Ruined Maids: Prostitutes and Servant Girls in Later Mediaeval England," in *Matrons and Marginal Women in Medieval Society*, eds. Robert R. Edwards and Vickie Ziegler (Woodbridge, UK: Boydell Press, 1995), pp. 25–27; Bennett, "Writing Fornication," p. 136; Paul B. Newman, *Growing Up in the Middle Ages* (Jefferson, NC.: McFarland and Co., 2007), p. 41. Men could also be prosecuted and sentenced to beatings for fornication, but only if they did so regularly, "as a man with his wife".

51 L.R. Poos, "Sex, Lies, and the Church Courts of Pre-Reformation England," *Journal of Interdisciplinary History* 25 (1995):593–600; Karras, "Two Models, Two Standards," pp. 131–32; Ruth Mazo Karras, "The Regulation of Sexuality in the Late Middle Ages: England and France," *Speculum* 86 (2011):1017–20. Most victims of defamation were women, but, interestingly enough, the defamers of women were fellow women, in about equal proportion to men. Karras found that more accusations of fornication were brought in the Church courts of London than in those of Paris in the late fifteenth century, which perhaps reflected local networks of gossip and rumor, even though many cases were dismissed as groundless.

52 Karras, *Sexuality in Medieval Europe*, 2nd edn., pp. 125–26.

53 Karras, *Sexuality in Medieval Europe*, 2nd edn., p. 123; Karras, "Sex and the Singlewoman," p. 130; North, "Legerwite," p. 9; Jones, "Medieval Leyrwite," pp. 945–53.

54 Karras, *Sexuality in Medieval Europe*, 2nd edn., pp. 123–25; Karras, "Regulation of Sexuality," pp. 1032–36; P.J.P. Goldberg, *Women, Work, and Life Cycle in a Medieval Economy: Women in York and Yorkshire, c.1300–1520* (Oxford: Clarendon Press, 1992), pp. 210, 232, 258–59, 263, 271–74, 327, 345, 352, 358, 361; Maryanne Kowaleski, "Singlewomen in Medieval and Early Modern Europe: the Demographic Perspective," in *Singlewomen in the European Past, 1250–1800*, eds. Judith M. Bennett and Amy M. Froide (Philadelphia, PA: University of Pennsylvania Press, 1999), pp. 40, 48; Bennett, "Writing Fornication," pp. 145–46; Mavis E. Mate, *Daughters, Wives and Widows after the Black Death: Women in Sussex, 1350–1535* (Woodbridge, UK: Boydell Press, 1998), pp. 31–37. If vows were exchanged *in futuro* or in the future tense, then the couple was considered married in the eyes of the Church immediately upon engaging in sexual intercourse; such "clandestine" marriages were, of course, one of the main reasons for matrimonial disputes being brought before the Church courts.

55 Karras, *Sexuality in Medieval Europe*, 2nd edn., p. 146; Ruth Mazo Karras, "'Because the Other is a Poor Woman She Shall be Called his Wench': Gender, Sexuality, and Social Status in Late Medieval England," in *Gender and Difference in the Middle Ages*, eds. Sharon

Farmer and Carol Braun Pasternack (Minneapolis, MN.: University of Minnesota Press, 2003), p. 216; Kettle, "Ruined Maids," pp. 21, 28, 30.

56 Karras, *Sexuality in Medieval Europe*, 2nd edn., p. 127; Karras, "Regulation of Sexuality," pp. 1023–26. "Concubinage," however, may not have been universally recognized across medieval Europe. Karras found it a fairly common "offense" in Church courts in Paris (20 percent of cases), perhaps signifying "a level of recognition for this type of union," even if a punitive one. By contrast, concubinage was not mentioned in London courts, since English common law did not recognize the status of "concubine," and instead the much more derogatory label of "common whore" (*meretrix comunis*) was used to refer to women engaged in long-term sexual relationships outside of marriage.

57 Karras, *Sexuality in Medieval Europe*, 2nd edn., pp. 128–32; Ruth Mazo Karras, *Common Women: Prostitution and Sexuality in Medieval England* (New York: Oxford University Press, 1996), p. 86; Leah Lydia Otis, *Prostitution in Medieval Society: The History of an Urban Institution in Languedoc* (Chicago, IL.: University of Chicago Press, 1985), p. 107.

58 Judith M. Bennett, *A Medieval Life: Cecilia Penifader of Brigstock, c. 1295–1344* (New York: Mcgraw-Hill, 1976), esp. pp. 114–27. For a time, Cecilia did form a joint household with her bachelor brother, Robert, perhaps for legal convenience.

59 Michel Foucault, *The History of Sexuality*, 3 vols., trans. Robert Hurley (New York: Pantheon Books, 1978–88), 1:43; David Halperin, *How to Do the History of Homosexuality* (Chicago, IL.: University of Chicago Press, 2002), pp. 24–47; Warren Johansson and William A. Percy, "Homosexuality," in *Handbook of Medieval Sexuality*, p. 155. "Gay" was the preferred term used by John Boswell in his pioneering work, *Christianity, Social Tolerance, and Homosexuality: Gay People in Western Europe from the Beginning of the Christian Era to the Fourteenth Century* (Chicago, IL.: University of Chicago Press, 1980). More recently, "queer" has also come into vogue among medieval scholars wishing to challenge the "heteronormative" discourse. See: Karma Lochrie, "Mystical Acts, Queer Tendencies," in *Constructing Medieval Sexuality*, eds. Karma Lochrie, Peggy McCracken, and James A. Schultz (Minneapolis, MN.: University of Minnesota Press, 1997), pp. 180–200; Karma Lochrie, "Response: Presidential Improprieties and Medieval Categories. The Absurdity of Homosexuality," in *Queering the Middle Ages*, eds. Glenn Burger and Steven F. Kruger (Minneapolis, MN.: University of Minnesota Press, 2001), pp. 87–96; Judith M. Bennett, "'Lesbian-Like' and the Social History of Lesbianisms," *Journal of the History of Sexuality* 9 (2000): 4–5; Bill Burgwinkle, "*État Présent*: Queer Theory and the Middle Ages," *French Studies* 60 (2006):79–88; Tison Pugh, *Sexuality and its Queer Discontents in Middle English Literature* (New York: Palgrave Macmillan, 2008), pp. 1–19, 145–50.

60 See the useful discussion by John Boswell, "Revolutions, Universals, and Sexual Categories," in *Hidden from History: Reclaiming the Gay and Lesbian Past*, eds. Martin Duberman, Martha Vicinus, and George Chauncey, Jr. (New York: Meridian, 1989), pp. 17–37. Boswell framed this debate within the context of the age-old dichotomy between realism and nominalism. Within the field of medieval gay studies, Boswell has been lumped in the essentialist camp, while his critic, David Halperin, presented the social constructionist point of view. Boswell himself denied that he was an "essentialist" (or that any other historian could be classified as one) and claimed that he was "agnostic" with respect to this debate. He did, however, believe that gays have always existed throughout history, if they are defined as "those whose erotic interest is predominately directed toward their own gender". Meanwhile, Halperin defended a "modified constructionist approach" to the history of homosexuality, an approach that he labeled "historicism," in which he acknowledged "the existence of transhistorical continuities" and reintegrated them into his analysis. See: Boswell, "Revolutions," p. 35; Boswell, *Christianity, Social Tolerance, and Homosexuality*, pp. 41–59; Halperin, *How to Do History of Homosexuality*, pp. 1–23, 104–37; David Halperin, *One Hundred Years of Homosexuality and Other Essays on Greek Love* (New York: Routledge, 1990), p. 46; Mathew Kuefler, "The Boswell Thesis," in *The Boswell Thesis: Essays on Christianity, Social Tolerance, and Homosexuality*, ed. Mathew Kuefler (Chicago, IL.: University of Chicago Press, 2006), pp. 8–12.

61 David Clark, *Between Medieval Men: Male Friendship and Desire in Early Medieval English Literature* (Oxford: Oxford University Press, 2009), pp. 9–13; C. Stephen Jaeger, *Ennobling Love: In Search of a Lost Sensibility* (Philadelphia, PA.: University of Pennsylvania Press, 1999), p. 17.

62 Michael Goodich, *The Unmentionable Vice* (Santa Barbara, CA.: ABC-Clio, 1979), p. 28; Brundage, *Law, Sex, and Christian Society*, p. 213; Mark D. Jordan, *The Invention of Sodomy in Christian Theology* (Chicago, IL.: University of Chicago Press, 1997), pp. 29–44; Bernd-Ulrich Hergemöller, *Sodom and Gomorrah: On the Everyday Reality and Persecution of Homosexuals in the Middle Ages*, trans. John Phillips (London and New York: Free Association Books, 2001), pp. 6–25; Richards, *Sex, Dissidence, and Damnation*, p. 135; Karras, *Sexuality in Medieval Europe*, 2nd edn., p. 173; Harry J. Kuster and Raymond J. Cormier, "Old Views and New Trends: Observations on the Problem of Homosexuality in the Middle Ages," *Studi Medievali*, 3rd ser., 25 (1984):590. Boswell deliberately avoided using the term "sodomy" because it was too "vague and ambiguous". See Boswell, *Christianity, Social Tolerance, and Homosexuality*, p. 93, n.2.

63 Vern L. Bullough, "The Sin against Nature and Homosexuality," in *Sexual Practices and the Medieval Church*, pp. 55–71; Brundage, *Law, Sex and Christian Society*, pp. 212–14; Kuster and Cormier, "Old Views and New Trends," pp. 590–91.

64 Goodich, *Unmentionable Vice*, pp. 35–36; Boswell, *Christianity, Social Tolerance, and Homosexuality*, pp. 92–98; Johansson and Percy, "Homosexuality," pp. 156–57; Guido Ruggiero, *The Boundaries of Eros: Sex Crime and Sexuality in Renaissance Venice* (New York: Oxford University Press, 1985), pp. 111–12, 135; Helmut Puff, *Sodomy in Reformation Germany and Switzerland, 1400–1600* (Chicago, IL.: University of Chicago Press, 2003), p. 26.

65 Derrick Sherwin Bailey, *Homosexuality and the Western Christian Tradition* (London: Longmans, Green, 1955), pp. 73–74; Goodich, *Unmentionable Vice*, pp. 75–76.

66 Just two years later, in 544, Justinian issued *Novella 141* that reiterated the threat of civil penalties for sodomy. In the *Novella*, Justinian referred explicitly to God's "just judgment upon those who lived in Sodom" and justified his actions as that, "by means of legislation we may avert such an untoward fate". See Bailey, *Homosexuality*, pp. 74–75.

67 Plague was a theme of preaching against sodomy in Florence, Venice, and Siena throughout the 15th Century. See: Ruggiero, *Boundaries of Eros*, pp. 112–13, 135; Michael Rocke, *Forbidden Friendships: Homosexuality and Male Culture in Renaissance Florence* (Oxford: Oxford University Press, 1996), pp. 28, 36–37.

68 Goodich, *Unmentionable Vice*, pp. 25–28; Brundage, *Law, Sex, and Christian Society*, pp. 166–69.

69 Jacqueline Murray, "Twice Marginal and Twice Invisible: Lesbians in the Middle Ages," in *Handbook of Medieval Sexuality*, pp. 191–222; Helmut Puff, "Same-Sex Possibilities," in *Oxford Handbook of Women and Gender*, pp. 379–95; Kim M. Phillips, *Medieval Maidens: Young Women and Gender in England, 1270–1540* (Manchester, UK: Manchester University Press, 2003), p. 145; Bennett, 'Lesbian-Like' ," pp. 5–6; Kuster and Cormier, "Old Views and New Trends," pp. 598–99. For examples of how lesbian meanings can be teased out of various sources, readers should consult the essay collection, *Same Sex Love and Desire among Women in the Middle Ages*, eds. Francesca Canadé Sautman and Pamela Sheingorn (Basingstoke, UK: Palgrave, 2001).

70 Boswell, *Christianity, Social Tolerance, and Homosexuality*, p. 243.

71 Moore's response was to co-opt much of Boswell's narrative of homosexual history, with the caveat that Boswell's thesis was the exception that proved the rule of the interdependence of oppressed minorities. See R.I. Moore, *The Formation of a Persecuting Society: Power and Deviance in Western Europe, 950–1250* (Oxford: Basil Blackwell, 1987), pp. 91–94.

72 Boswell, *Christianity, Social Tolerance, and Homosexuality*, pp. 303–32.

73 Boswell, *Christianity, Social Tolerance, and Homosexuality*, p. 204.

74 Boswell, *Christianity, Social Tolerance, and Homosexuality*, pp. 205–6.

75 Richards, *Sex, Dissidence, and Damnation*, p. 137; Brundage, *Law, Sex, and Christian Society*, p. 167; Puff, *Sodomy in Reformation Germany*, pp. 28–29.

76 Boswell, *Christianity, Social Tolerance, and Homosexuality*, p. 205.

77 Boswell was at least aware of the dangers of making an argument from silence here, since he admitted that "silence alone does not constitute proof that Burchard did not consider homosexual behavior between single persons sinful at all". But in the next sentence, he argued that it was "at least fair to infer that he was not sufficiently concerned about it to assign a specific penance for such activity". Helmut Puff, in a recent reassessment of Boswell's argument, was willing to grant this point, that the penitential handbooks demonstrated "the Church's relative lack of interest in homosexual behavior". At the same time, however, Puff warned against misinterpreting "lack of interest as signifying tolerance," which Boswell seemed to do. This lack of interest could be for any number of reasons aside from tacit approval of homosexuality, such as that Burchard did not consider homosexual activity prevalent enough to be worried about it. See: Boswell, *Christianity, Social Tolerance, and Homosexuality*, p. 206; Puff, *Sodomy in Reformation Germany*, p. 21.

78 Readers should consult table 4.2, containing a list of penances assigned by penitentials for sodomy, in Brundage, *Law, Sex, and Christian Society*, p. 174. As Brundage pointed out, the table does not bear out Boswell's conclusion that "penitentials treated homosexuality as a commonplace and not terribly serious matter".

79 Vern L. Bullough, "Heresy, Witchcraft, and Sexuality," *Journal of Homosexuality* 1 (1976):183–99; Vern L. Bullough, "Postscript: Heresy, Witchcraft, and Sexuality," in *Sexual Practices and the Medieval Church*, pp. 206–17; Brundage, *Law, Sex, and Christian Society*, p. 399, 473. Equations of sodomy with heresy also become prevalent in civic trials and records beginning in the late fourteenth century. See: Puff, *Sodomy in Reformation Germany*, pp. 23–25; Marc Boone, "State Power and Illicit Sexuality: The Persecution of Sodomy in Late Medieval Bruges," *Journal of Medieval History* 22 (1996):139.

80 Johansson and Percy, "Homosexuality," pp. 159–76.

81 Johansson and Percy, "Homosexuality," pp. 159–61.

82 Karras, *Sexuality in Medieval Europe*, 2nd edn., pp. 184–85; Bernd-Ulrich Hergemöller, "The Middle Ages," in *Gay Life and Culture: A World History*, ed. Robert Aldrich (London: Thomas and Hudson, 2006), pp. 60–62; Brian Patrick McGuire, *Brother and Lover: Aelred of Rievaulx* (New York: Crossroad, 1994), pp. 89, 142; Jaeger, *Ennobling Love*, pp. 110–14. McGuire concluded that Aelred was a homosexual and had sexual experiences in his youth, but that, upon entering the monastic life, he sublimated the physical into the spiritual and subordinated individual desire to the well-being of the community. However, some scholars contend that genital contact or penetration is not essential for a relationship to be considered homosexual, which they instead characterize as "homosocial" or "homoerotic," although medieval people themselves seem to have regarded penetration as the *sine qua non* of any sexual relationship. See: Clark, *Between Medieval Men*, pp. 15–18; Jaeger, *Ennobling Love*, pp. 14–17; Halperin, *How to Do History of Homosexuality*, pp. 117–21; Karras, *Sexuality in Medieval Europe*, 2nd edn., pp. 4, 27.

83 Gregory Woods, *A History of Gay Literature: The Male Tradition* (New Haven, CT.: Yale University Press, 1998), p. 46. Conspicuously, Boswell failed to even mention this work.

84 Woods, *History of Gay Literature*, p. 46.

85 Karras, *Sexuality in Medieval Europe*, 2nd edn., p. 192.

86 Karras, *Sexuality in Medieval Europe*, 2nd end., p. 192.

87 Boswell, *Christianity, Social Tolerance, and Homosexuality*, pp. 318–30. For other discussions of Aquinas' treatment of this topic, see: Goodich, *Unmentionable Vice*, pp. 62–63; Mark D. Jordan, "Homosexuality, *Luxuria*, and Textual Abuse," in *Constructing Medieval Sexuality*, eds. Karma Lochrie, Peggy McCracken, and James A. Schultz (Minneapolis, MN.: University of Minnesota Press, 1997), pp. 24–39; Jordan, *Invention of Sodomy*, pp. 136–58.

88 In the late Middle Ages, natural philosophers had developed a "science of sodomy" that explained same-sex preferences as a product of both nature and nurture: that "some men are born with anatomical defects that divert the semen from its proper path," while "others develop their sexual appetites as habits formed from experiences early in life". See Joan Cadden, *Nothing Natural is Shameful: Sodomy and Science in Late Medieval Europe* (Philadelphia, PA.: University of Pennsylvania Press, 2013), p. 3.

89 These records were analyzed and presented in: Rocke, *Forbidden Friendships*; Ruggiero, *Boundaries of Eros*; and Hergemöller, *Sodom and Gomorrah*. In general, the evidence indicates that sodomy was persecuted much more consistently and vigorously in Florence and Venice as opposed to north of the Alps, in Germany, Switzerland, and the Low Countries. See: Puff, *Sodomy in Reformation Germany*, p. 25; Boone, "State Power and Illicit Sexuality," pp. 135–53.

90 According to statistics compliled by Rocke, 84 percent of passive partners were aged 13 to 18 and 92 percent were aged 13 to 20. See Rocke, *Forbidden Friendships*, pp. 89–90.

91 Rocke, *Forbidden Friendships*, pp. 87–111; Johansson and Percy, "Homosexuality," pp. 158–59; Ruggiero, *Boundaries of Eros*, p. 124.

92 Rocke, *Forbidden Friendships*, p. 243. This is based on a survey of the records from 1478 to 1502.

93 Johansson and Percy, "Homosexuality," p. 158.

94 Rocke, *Forbidden Friendships*, pp. 116, 162–63.

95 Rocke, *Forbidden Friendships*, p. 243.

96 Karras, *Sexuality in Medieval Europe*, 2nd edn., p. 178.

97 David Herlihy and Christiane Klapisch-Zuber, *Tuscans and their Families: A Study of the Florentine Catasto of 1427* (New Haven, CT.: Yale University Press, 1985), pp. 203–11; Karras, *Sexuality in Medieval Europe*, 2nd edn., p. 182.

98 Herlihy and Klapisch-Zuber, *Tuscans and their Families*, pp. 222–23.

99 Karras, *Sexuality in Medieval Europe*, 2nd edn., pp. 182.

100 Halperin, *How to do the History of Homosexuality*, pp. 109–30; Karras, *Sexuality in Medieval Europe*, 2nd edn., p. 167.

101 Halperin, *How to do the History of Homosexuality*, pp. 121–30.

102 Rocke, *Forbidden Friendships*, p. 146.

103 Two examples are known from the Middle Ages: One was Rolandino/Rolandia, arrested in 1354 in Venice, who by his own account had the breasts and face of a woman but the penis and testicles of a man, who was married but never knew his wife carnally, and who worked as a female prostitute; the other was John/Eleanor Rykener, arrested in London in 1394, who also worked as a prostitute, in London, Oxford, and Burford. Rolandino/Rolandina always seems to have played the passive role, never achieving an erection, but John/Eleanor did have "sex as a man with many women," apparently not for pay. See: Karras, *Common Women*, pp. 70–71; Karras, *Sexuality in Medieval Europe*, 2nd edn., pp. 183–84.

104 Karras, *Sexuality in Medieval Europe*, 2nd edn., pp. 4, 27.

105 Boswell tried to argue that "age was not a consideration" to medieval gays, since terms like "boys" were used interchangeably for both young and older males, and that pederasty therefore "has no more relation to the age of the objects of desire than 'girl chasing.'" See Boswell, *Christianity, Social Tolerance, and Homosexuality*, p. 30; Boswell, "Revolutions," p. 30.

106 Hergemöller, "Middle Ages," pp. 70–71, 74–75; Brundage, *Law, Sex, and Christian Society*, p. 473, 534; Puff, *Sodomy in Reformation Germany*, pp. 23–27; Boone, "State Power and Illicit Sexuality," pp. 138–41. Tables indicating the frequency of various penalties levied by the Office of the Night and the Eight of Watch in Florence were given in Rocke, *Forbidden Friendships*, pp. 237–41.

107 Ruggiero, *Boundaries of Eros*, pp. 114–27. Cities north of the Alps, such as Bruges, seem to have adopted more severe and inflexible attitudes towards sodomy, which was seen as a threat to the social order. No less than 90 persons were executed for sodomy at

Bruges between 1385 and 1515, and Marc Boone noted that judges "seldom reduced sentences in the light of extenuating circumstances". See Boone, "State Power and Illicit Sexuality," pp. 145, 151.

108 Rocke, *Forbidden Friendships*, p. 47.
109 Rocke, *Forbidden Friendships*, pp. 63–64.
110 Rocke, *Forbidden Friendships*, p. 73.
111 Rocke, *Forbidden Friendships*, p. 74.
112 Rocke, *Forbidden Friendships*, pp. 198–201.
113 Rocke, *Forbidden Friendships*, p. 200.
114 Rocke, *Forbidden Friendships*, pp. 201–21.
115 Hergemöller, "Middle Ages," 71–73; Boone, "State Power and Illicit Sexuality," p. 149.
116 Rocke, *Forbidden Friendships*, p. 245.
117 In Florence, the predominant occupation of sodomites was in the textile and clothing trades, for which the city was famous. See Rocke, *Forbidden Friendships*, p. 249.
118 Rocke, *Forbidden Friendships*, pp. 153–61.
119 Ruggiero, *Boundaries of Eros*, pp. 138–40.
120 Hergemöller, *Sodom and Gomorrah*, pp. 104–5. Marc Boone presented similar, but perhaps less persuasive, evidence for the existence of a homosexual subculture in Bruges. See Boone, "State Power and Illicit Sexuality," pp. 148–49.
121 Rocke, *Forbidden Friendships*, p. 191.
122 Rocke, *Forbidden Friendships*, p. 146.
123 Rocke, *Forbidden Friendships*, p. 146.
124 Ruggiero, *Boundaries of Eros*, pp. 135–38.
125 Ruggiero, *Boundaries of Eros*, p. 145; Rocke, *Forbidden Friendships*, pp. 221–23.
126 This was particularly the case with poor women and urban women employed in certain trades, such as laundress, who were regarded as having ample opportunity and motive for sex work. See Karras, "Gender, Sexuality, and Social Status," pp. 215–16, 223.
127 Karras, *Common Women*, p. 10–11; Bullough, "The Prostitute in the Early Middle Ages," in *Sexual Practices and the Medieval Church*, p. 35.
128 The only male prostitutes known from the medieval records are Rolandino/Rolandina Ronchaia of Venice and John/Eleanor Rykener of London, who were arrested in 1354 and 1394, respectively, who were men posing as women (i.e., transvestites) in order to ply their trade. See: Karras, *Common Women*, pp. 70–71; Karras, *Sexuality in Medieval Europe*, 2nd edn., p. 183–84.
129 Karras, *Common Women*, pp. 3, 11–12; Karras, "Sex and the Singlewoman," pp. 130–31.
130 Karras, "Sex and the Singlewoman," pp. 128, 130–32.
131 James A. Brundage, "Prostitution in the Medieval Canon Law," in *Sexual Practices and the Medieval Church*, p. 150; Richards, *Sex, Dissidence and Damnation*, p. 118.
132 Karras, *Common Women*, pp. 10–12; Bullough, "Prostitute in the Early Middle Ages," p. 35. Contemporaries did know the Latin verb, *prostituo*—meaning "to expose publicly"—which certainly ties in with a modern definition of prostitute, but the word "prostitute" itself was apparently not used.
133 Ruth Mazo Karras, "Prostitution in Medieval Europe," in *Handbook of Medieval Sexuality*, pp. 249–51; Kettle, "Ruined Maids," pp. 22, 26–27; Bronislaw Geremek, *The Margins of Society in Late Medieval Paris*, trans. Jean Birrell (Cambridge: Cambridge University Press, 1987), pp. 239–41.
134 Brundage, "Prostitution in the Medieval Canon Law," pp. 154–56; Brundage, "Sex and Canon Law," p. 44; Vern L. Bullough, "Prostitution in the Later Middle Ages," in *Sexual Practices and the Medieval Church*, pp. 178–82; Richards, *Sex, Dissidence and Damnation*, pp. 119–29; Williams and Echols, *Between Pit and Pedestal*, pp. 95–96; Karras, *Common Women*, pp. 14–22, 95–100; Karras, "Prostitution in Medieval Europe," pp. 245–47; Kettle, "Ruined Maids," p. 22.
135 These arguments were chiefly made by: Karras, *Common Women*, pp. 84–101; Leah Lydia Otis, *Prostitution in Medieval Society: The History of an Urban Institution in Languedoc*

(Chicago, IL.: University of Chicago Press, 1985), pp. 15–39; and Jacques Rossiaud, *Medieval Prostitution*, trans. Lydia G. Cochrane (Oxford: Basil Blackwell, 1988), pp. 55–71.

136 Karras, "Prostitution in Medieval Europe," p. 244.

137 Karras, "Prostitution in Medieval Europe," p. 244; Karras, *Common Women*, pp. 32–43; Otis, *Prostitution in Medieval Society*, pp. 25–39; Rossiaud, *Medieval Prostitution*, pp. 59–61; Richard C. Trexler, "La Prostitution Florentine au XVᵉ Siècle: Patronages et Clientèles," *Annales. Histoire, Sciences Sociales* 36 (1981):983–1015; Kettle, "Ruined Maids," p. 21.

138 Rossiaud, *Medieval Prostitution*, pp. 62–66; Jacques Rossiaud, "Prostitution, Sex and Society in French Towns in the Fifteenth Century," in *Western Sexuality: Practice and Precept in Past and Present Times*, eds. Philippe Ariès and André Bèjin (Oxford: Basil Blackwell, 1985), p. 78; Richards, *Sex, Dissidence and Damnation*, p. 130. An exception was London, where Church courts regularly prosecuted prostitutes, in contrast to York and Paris, where prosecutions were rare. See: Karras, "Regulation of Sexuality," pp. 1027–28; Karras, *Common Women*, pp. 66–68, 138–39.

139 Karras, *Common Women*, pp. 65–76; Karras, "Gender, Sexuality, and Social Status," p. 221.

140 Karras, *Commen Women*, pp. 96–98; Karras, "Gender, Sexuality, and Social Status," p. 221.

141 Rossiaud, *Medieval Prostitution*, p. 69.

142 Karras, *Common Women*, p. 96. In her latest publication on this issue, however, Karras has moderated this view a bit, noting that even "though prostitutes were not ostracized from their communities, they were certainly degraded, so that accusations of whoredom would be an effective weapon against women who were resented for other reasons". See Karras, "Gender, Sexuality, and Social Status," pp. 221–22.

143 Bullough, "Prostitution in the Later Middle Ages," pp. 183–86; Brundage, "Sex and Canon Law," pp. 44–45; Karras, *Common Women*, pp. 34, 81–83; Karras, "Prostitution in Medieval Europe," p. 254; Leah Lydia Otis, "Prostitution and Repentence in Late Medieval Perpignan," in *Women of the Medieval World: Essays in Honor of John H. Mundy*, eds. Julius Kirshner and Suzannne F. Wemple (Oxford: Basil Blackwell, 1985), pp. 149–56.

144 Some scholars see justification for this hydraulic model in the fact that in some cities, such as Florence, social expectations demanded that men wait until their late 20s or early 30s to get married, thereby denying them "legitimate sexual outlets for as long as two decades after puberty" and raising "erotic tensions" to a high level. See Herlihy and Klapisch-Zuber, *Tuscans and their Families*, pp. 222–23.

145 This comment is often attributed to Thomas Aquinas, who repeated the analogy but apparently did not invent it. See: Richards, *Sex, Dissidence and Damnation*, pp. 118–19; Bullough, "Prostitute in the Early Middle Ages," p. 36; Brundage, "Sex and Canon Law," p. 43; Karras, *Common Women*, pp. 6, 133–34; Karras, "Prostitution in Medieval Europe," p. 245.

146 Florence, for example, set up the "Office of Honesty" in April 1403, which was charged with supervising public morality, more specifically, with eliminating the "sodomitical vice" by establishing the city's first municipally-run brothel, staffed by non-Florentine immigrants, in the hopes that this would turn men from sodomy towards marriage and procreation, via the lesser vice of prostitution. It was in this same year, 1403, that the Office of Decency was established to oversee public morals and promote marriage and childbirth. When two more municipal brothels were authorized in 1415, the stated aim was "to eliminate a worse evil by means of a lesser one", with sodomy implied as the "worse evil". See: Trexler, "Prostitution Florentine," pp. 983–84; Bullough, "Prostitution in the Later Middle Ages," p. 180; Karras, *Sexuality in Medieval Europe*, 2nd edn., pp. 87, 179; Karras, *Common Women*, pp. 32, 136; Karras, "Prostitution in Medieval Europe," p. 245; Richards, *Sex, Dissidence and Damnation*, pp. 126–27; Williams and Echols, *Between Pit and Pedestal*, p. 94.

147 Otis, *Prostitution in Medieval Society*, p. 101.

148 Otis, *Prostitution in Medieval Society*, pp. 101–3.

149 Otis, *Prostitution in Medieval Society*, pp. 25–39.

150 Otis, *Prostitution in Medieval Society*, pp. 38–39.

151 Otis, *Prostitution in Medieval Society*, p. 104.

152 Otis, *Prostitution in Medieval Society*, p. 31.

153 As noted above, a similar phrase was used by Florentine authorities in attempting to establish two more municipal brothels in 1415. But whereas Trexler interpreted the "greater evil" as sodomy, and Rossiaud interpreted it as rape of wives and daughters, Otis saw it in broader and deeper, if less precise, terms as referring to "sexual and social disorder". See: Otis, *Prostitution in Medieval Society*, pp. 103–4; Richards, *Sex, Dissidence and Damnation*, pp. 127–28.

154 Otis, *Prostitution in Medieval Society*, pp. 104–8.

155 Otis, *Prostitution in Medieval Society*, p. 45.

156 Otis, *Prostitution in Medieval Society*, pp. 104–10.

157 Otis, *Prostitution in Medieval Society*, pp. 43–45; Rossiaud, "Prostitution, Sex and Society," p. 94; Kettle, "Ruined Maids," p. 30.

158 Otis, *Prostitution in Medieval Society*, p. 44.

159 Otis, *Prostitution in Medieval Society*, p. 41; Rossiaud, *Medieval Prostitution*, p. 50; Ann G. Carmichael, *Plague and the Poor in Renaissance Florence* (Cambridge: Cambridge University Press, 1986), pp. 123–24.

160 Otis, *Prostitution in Medieval Society*, p. 41.

161 Richards, *Sex, Dissidence and Damnation*, pp. 130–31.

162 Otis, *Prostitution in Medieval Society*, p. 41; Rossiaud, "Prostitution, Sex and Society," p. 77.

163 Rossiaud, *Medieval Prostitution*, p. 43; Rossiaud, "Prostitution, Sex and Society," p. 87.

164 Rossiaud, *Medieval Prostitution*, pp. 11–12.

165 Rossiaud, *Medieval Prostitution*, pp. 27–28.

166 Rossiaud, *Medieval Prostitution*, pp. 13, 21.

167 Rossiaud, *Medieval Prostitution*, pp. 15–18; Rossiaud, "Prostitution, Sex and Society," p. 82.

168 Rossiaud, *Medieval Prostitution*, pp. 20–26.

169 Rossiaud, *Medieval Prostitution*, pp. 13–14; Rossiaud, "Prostitution, Sex and Society," p. 85.

170 Rossiaud, *Medieval Prostitution*, p. 48; Rossiaud, "Prostitution, Sex and Society," pp. 86–87.

171 Rossiaud, *Medieval Prostitution*, pp. 13–14, 48; Rossiaud, "Prostitution, Sex and Society," p. 85.

172 Rossiaud, *Medieval Prostitution*, pp. 29–30.

173 Rossiaud, *Medieval Prostitution*, p. 49; Rossiaud, "Prostitution, Sex and Society," p. 81.

174 Rossiaud, *Medieval Prostitution*, p. 37.

175 Karras, *Common Women*, p. 3.

176 Karras, *Common Women*, p. 3.

177 Brundage, "Prostitution in Medieval Canon Law," pp. 152–53, 159. The connection between prostitution and female heterosexual activity was even more strongly drawn in the case of singlewomen. See Karras, "Sex and the Singlewoman," pp. 127–40.

178 Brundage, "Sex and Canon Law," p. 45.

179 Karras, *Common Women*, pp. 87–88; Karras, "Sex and the Singlewoman," p. 135.

180 Karras, *Common Women*, pp. 88–95.

6

HAIL MARY AND EVE

Women in medieval society

On a balmy winter's day in 1999, I had a job interview as a finalist for a teaching position at a state university in the Pacific Northwest. The position was in the History Department, as an entry-level, assistant professor who was to instruct students in the history of his or her specialty (left unspecified). It was probably the worst interview I've ever had in my life.

As I faced a dozen or so of my colleagues who all interviewed me (simultaneously) for the position, one interrogator in particular stands out in my memory. She was a professor of modern U.S. women's, or gender, history, and when she learned that my specialty was the Middle Ages, her comment to me was: "I've always hated the Middle Ages. It was such a terrible, repressive time for women". At the time, I didn't know quite how to respond to such a blanket statement of dismissal. Needless to say, the rest of the interview did not go well.

Looking back on it now, I should have said this in reply: "The Middle Ages was not a terrible time for women. You just had a terrible teacher!" More specifically, I could have pointed out any number of examples of medieval women who achieved considerable power and prestige, and perhaps even equality, with men. During the twelfth century, a Benedictine nun, Hildegard of Bingen (1098–1179), founded no less than two nunneries, and her mystical visions were endorsed by the greatest churchmen of the age, St. Bernard of Clairvaux (1090–1153) and Pope Eugenius III (r. 1145–53). In the same century, the most powerful noblewoman in history, Eleanor of Aquitaine (1122–1204), who married successively the two most powerful rulers in Europe, Louis VII of France (r. 1137–80) and Henry II of England (r. 1154–89), managed singlehandedly to shift the balance of power between them through her dowry, the duchy of Aquitaine, which she held throughout her life in her own right. Towards the end of the Middle Ages, in the fifteenth century, a remarkable peasant girl, Joan of Arc (1412–31), led armies into battle and achieved what no Frenchman could do, to turn the tide of the Hundred Years War and make France victorious over England. At the same time, a widow, Christine de Pisan (1364–1430), was able to make a living for herself as an author, a considerable achievement for any person in any age. Composing 41 works in 30 years, Pisan aimed to counter the negative image of women in literature, and, in her last work, the *Song of Joan of Arc*, she celebrated the contemporary, and not just historical, achievements of her sex. To dismiss a whole era simply because it is perceived to be misogynist is to do a great injustice to medieval women and, I would argue, is not a particularly feminist way of studying history.[1]

The debate over medieval women's history

Needless to say, all of the above arguments I rehearsed in my head with hindsight. But I tell this story because it does epitomize much of the debate that, for the past few decades, has surrounded medieval women's history. At its heart, the debate essentially comes down to this: Was the Middle Ages, at any time in its history, a "golden age" for women, a "renaissance" or "paradise" that was then lost as we move into the modern era?[2] Did medieval women hold their own, or even improve their lot, achieving a "rough and ready equality" with men, as the *grand-dame* of medieval women's studies, Eileen Power, wrote three-quarters of a century ago?[3] Or instead, did medieval women remain beholden to the age-old patriarchy, continuing to labor under institutionally-enshrined disadvantages as second-class citizens to men?[4]

This debate can be, and has been, recast in many different forms. Some see it as a clash between optimism and pessimism, between seeing the glass half full or half empty with respect to women's status by the end of the Middle Ages.[5] In the former view, women played a valuable and important role in the transformational changes that occurred in medieval society at this time, through their own initiative and achievement in exploiting the largely economic opportunities that presented themselves.[6] In the latter view, women could not escape the oppressive patriarchy that consistently undervalued and demeaned their contributions to family and society and disempowered them by placing obstacles in their path "at every turn". Any gains women made were effectively nullified by the fact that society ensured men were rewarded more and better, thus maintaining women's subordinate position.[7] Indeed, proponents of the pessimistic interpretation of medieval women's history have gone so far as to claim that, in the medieval world view, "men were human and women were different".[8] To my mind, this is a quite remarkable statement—one that, in effect, charges medieval European society with treating women as less than human—and bespeaks of much hidden anger on the part of feminist scholars lying underneath the genteel surface of academic discourse.

The debate also can be posed as one between change, or transition, and continuity in the period from 1300 to 1700, encompassing the late Middle Ages and most of the Early Modern period.[9] Historiographically speaking, the alignment is rather an odd one, as transition to the era of the Renaissance and the Reformation usually implies some degree of progress in the human condition, but here is inter-preted in quite negative terms for women. Likewise, continuity implies a reassuring endurance of what is best in human culture, but here, in the form of an oppressive patriarchy, it is very much to be deplored.

This is also largely an argument about family: In the "golden age" view, the lot of women improved during the late Middle Ages, because the lot of most peasant households improved as a result of the more favorable economic climate in the aftermath of the Black Death.[10] Since women were in "partnership" with men in the family unit, they could not but help share in the bounty, and even as singlewomen they were able to take advantage of new economic opportunities opened up by the plague.[11] This golden age came to an end during the transition to the Early Modern period from the mid-fifteenth century onwards, as economic depression throughout northern Europe set in as a result of prolonged population loss and/or stagnation.[12] But in the continuity/patriarchy view, the family was simply another means to exploit women, placing a lower value on their labor, despite its multi-faceted nature (i.e., child-rearing, cooking, cleaning, sewing, etc.). Women could hardly share in post-plague economic benefits, since all land and goods, with some exceptions, were owned by men. Moreover, according to this view, the family was not even a natural state of human affairs, but, rather, was purely a socio-cultural "phenomenon," reflecting the "patriarchal authority of men in medieval society".[13]

It was many years ago that Eileen Power, in her pioneering study of medieval women, summed up medieval attitudes towards women as vacillating between the opposing poles of the Virgin Mary and Eve, symbolizing, respectively, the unattain-able ideal of religious purity and chivalry, on the one hand, and the admonitory figure of the "supreme temptress" and Devil's instrument, on the other.[14] These days, most scholars reject the Mary/Eve dichotomy as too crude to encompass the complexity of the female experience during the Middle Ages.[15] But now a similar dichotomy seems to have emerged around the "golden age"/patriarchal—which otherwise can be called the optimistic/pessimistic or change/continuity—inter-pretations of medieval women's history. Although much of this debate has focused on late medieval women in the aftermath of the Black Death, a similar divide has opened up around the significance of the year 1000 as a possible turning point for women.[16] Yet more nuanced alternatives offer a middle road between these two poles: neither seeing the medieval history of women's work as an unalloyed golden age, nor as one unrelievedly beholden to patriarchy. While the golden age thesis is criticized as painting too rosy a picture of women's employment opportunities and wage rates in the aftermath of the Black Death, the patriarchy thesis is also attacked for being too gloomy, in that it does not acknowledge the tangible gains that medieval women were able to achieve "in terms of the num-ber of jobs they had access to and in terms of their remuneration [relative to men]".[17] This is also an interpretation that emphasizes *both* continuity and change in women's economic roles. It acknowledges that women did face some funda-mental disadvantages and handicaps, such as their ability to access credit, that did not change with time; but it also recognizes that some women had opportunities to break out of the "low-skilled, low-status, low-paid" sectors of the economy to which they were normally confined, particularly in the brewing and textile trades.[18] Others warn against telling a "simple tale of benefit or loss" for medieval women, which fails to acknowledge that they were part of "the complexity of the response to changes taking place in society at large".[19] Some have argued that women's experience during the Middle Ages was too varied, particularly along class lines, and our knowledge too incomplete, even with an emerging plethora of local studies, for us to make any sort of generalizations about medieval women.[20]

It is undeniably true that gender or women's history has had a political/polemical element ever since its emergence as a distinct field in the 1970s, and some would insist that a feminist agenda be maintained in current scholarship.[21] For example, the historian, Judith Bennett, who has devoted much of her career to studying the women of Brigstock, England, during the first half of the fourteenth century, argued that a "patriarchal equilibrium" has dominated women's experience throughout history, so that, no matter whether one is talking about women's wages in 1315 or 2015, their value relative to men's has remained remarkably the same, at about a ratio of 3:4 (i.e., women were paid three-quarters of what men were paid). This, for Bennett, underlines the remarkable continuity throughout history in women's status within an entrenched patriarchal social order, whereby women were (and are) at a severe disadvantage in almost every conceivable way: legally, economically, politically, socially, and culturally. The overriding question for such feminist historians then becomes whether women in any given time and place made any headway against the dominant patriarchy, and thus achieved any progress towards the ultimate goal of gender equality with men.[22] If it is any consolation to such historians, one can say that, certainly within the field of medieval women's history, if not medieval history as a whole, a kind of matriarchy now rules, in which the vast majority of scholarly participants are women.[23] In perhaps a nice bit of irony, the more pessimistic assessments of women's history in the Middle Ages tend to come from the leading female scholars in the field, while the most optimistic views come from male commentators.[24]

I believe that the question of gender equality is certainly a legitimate one for modern historians to ask when reviewing the centuries-long history of Western society's treatment of women. But is it appropriate when we are seeking to understand medieval women on their own terms, within the context of their unique, contemporary perspectives? Indeed, one could argue that, to project modern, feminist expectations upon medieval women—whereby they are always judged based on standards relative to men—is almost setting them up for depressing failure and is perhaps treating them in almost as demeaning a fashion as the patriarchy itself. It is more than likely that women during the Middle Ages did not think in terms of gender equality and thus would not have measured their status and well-being in such a fashion. Granted, medieval women were trapped within the gender-biased circumstances of their time, but few historians writing on medieval women's history today would go so far as to say that the Middle Ages, as the whole, was a time of unrelieved misery and repression for women. If one could go back in time and ask them directly, medieval women—notwithstanding the male-oriented context in which they lived—may have thought that our questions were entirely irrelevant. Women could never be the equal of men, since the sexes were too different (regardless of who was better) and each moved within his or her own sphere.[25] Perhaps the ideal for them was to achieve a state—such as mystical union with God—that constituted a "third gender," or where gender did not matter.[26] Feminist historians may not like this answer, but it may be that we are asking the wrong questions about medieval women.

Trying to capture a woman's perspective during the Middle Ages is a difficult endeavor, as most of the sources that we have were written by men. A male-privileged, if not downright misogynist, perspective was sanctioned by all three religions to be found in medieval Europe—Christianity, Judaism, and Islam—and permeated the literature, both on a learned, philosophical level and in the more popular folktales and *fabliaux*.[27] Nevertheless, one can be skeptical as to how much "intellectual and literary discourses" about women reflect the reality of their actual condition within medieval society.[28] Even when women were portrayed in medieval art and literature as having the upper hand, looks could be deceptive. In Carlisle Cathedral in England, there is a fifteenth-century misericord carving (i.e., a carving made on the underside of the seats in the choir stall) of a wife beating her husband (Figure 6.1). The brutal dominance of the wife is made absolutely clear: She grabs her husband by the beard with her left hand and raises a square-headed club with her right. The message conveyed by the carving is almost certainly not a flattering one. This is the "world turned upside down," a reversal of the supposed natural order of things. In actual fact, medieval law generally sanctioned the beating of wives by their husbands, not the other way around. The fourteenth-century legal code of Aardenburg in Flanders went even further, allowing a husband to not only beat his wife, but slash her body from head to toe and "warm his feet in her blood," provided that he nursed her back to health.[29]

The "shrewish wife" was also the theme of many a medieval folktale. In the late medieval story of the "Three Wily Women"—about three German housewives who held a competition to see who could most trick her husband for the prize of the odd *haller* from selling their eggs at market—the victor, Mistress Mechtild, succeeded in literally emasculating her husband, Farmer Siegfried, by slicing off his testicles with a knife as he stood naked in church.[30] Giovanni Boccaccio, a writer who is thought to have been empathetic towards women—since he wrote the first biographical account devoted exclusively to them, the *De Mulieribus Claris* (On Famous Women), from 1374—nonetheless devoted the entire seventh chapter (or the seventh "day" of storytelling) of his famous *Decameron* to ten tales "in which wives play tricks on their husbands," usually by cuckolding them. In Geoffrey Chaucer's *Canterbury Tales*, the Wife of Bath was portrayed as a sexually rapacious, domineering wife, outlasting no less than five husbands, in which she was the master and held the "whippe" in the relationship. These tales were not

FIGURE 6.1 Fifteenth-century misericord carving of a wife beating her husband, Carlisle Cathedral

Courtesy of www.misericords.co.uk

meant to "empower" women, but to actually warn men of the need to keep their wives in check.

There were, however, some medieval works that seemed to be genuinely appreciative of women. The fifteenth-century English poem fragment, *A Woman is a Worthy Wight*, reminded listeners how the housewife "serveth a man bothe daye and night," for which all she got in return was "care and wo".[31] The similarly incomplete *Ballad of a Tyrannical Husband*, also dating to the fifteenth century, told a tale of how an abusive man became a "good howsbande" after he switched roles with his wife for the day and attempted to perform all the tasks she did around the house and grounds; in this way, the author hoped to make amends to women for the fact that "moche they ar blamyd and sometyme with wronge".[32] Yet, as one may have noticed, even these works were not entirely free of the patriarchal assumptions of their time. Perhaps the only, true "proto-feminist" from the Middle Ages was the fifteenth-century author, Christine de Pizan, who demonstrated a clear awareness of the misogynist tradition and attempted to combat it with her vigorous defense of women in the *City of Ladies*.[33] Pizan was also willing to champion women who defied traditional gender roles, as evidenced by her *Ditie de Jeanne d'Arc* (Song of Joan of Arc), written at the end of July 1429, shortly after Charles VII's coronation. But even Pizan clearly endorsed the conventional roles women were expected to play in medieval society and laid this out in her *Treasure of the City of Ladies*.[34]

Medieval women's studies must tread a fine line between the marginal and the mainstream. While medieval women certainly did labor under a bias that was "inherent in the system," they cannot really be described as constituting a minority in the Middle Ages, with a minority's handicaps.[35] In terms of numbers and presence, women played far too great a role in everyday medieval society for them to be considered marginal. As in all periods, their history during the Middle Ages defies easy stereotype or categorization.

Nevertheless, one can identify three main debates in the historiography of medieval women's history. One has to do with women's work, especially during the later Middle Ages, when women arguably benefitted from the high demand for labor of all kinds in the wake of the Black Death. How extensively did single and married women take advantage of employment opportunities, how long did these opportunities last, and how did they affect women's lives, especially in comparison with similar opportunities for men? A second subject for debate revolves around marriage patterns for medieval women, which have been studied and compared for different regions of Europe. Local customs, laws, Church definitions, and popular perceptions of marriage all play a role in historians' assessment of the married life for medieval women. Included in this debate are the decisions and preparations that singlewomen made prior to marriage, and their status and prospects after marriage, as widows. The third subject for debate, women's sexuality during the Middle Ages, already has been explored in the previous chapter.

I recognize that the terms of these debates are constantly changing: For example, feminist historians these days are said to focus more on women's "wealth" than on women's work, since the former term is more inclusive in terms of what women could contribute to the family and society.[36] I also acknowledge that I leave out many aspects of medieval women's history that are both fascinating and important. I have no room to comment, for example, on witches during the later Middle Ages, on the power and authority of queens, and on the religious lives of women, including nuns, anchoresses, and mystics. But the subjects I have chosen have been, for the better part of the historiography on medieval women, the most intensely argued and debated in the field, based on the amount of literature they have produced. They also tie in well with themes that are treated in Chapters 8 and 9, namely on the Black Death and the transition to the Early Modern period. Moreover, they remind us that, although women are by all means deserving of their own, separate field of enquiry, they are also an integral part of society and of the history of the entire human condition.

Women's work

Our view of what constitutes "women's work" is obviously quite different today compared to what it was in the Middle Ages. In this day and age, women are almost expected to go out and find a job or a career outside the home, and in most Western countries, paid maternity leave is provided by the government so that women do not have to make a choice between their family and their career. Implicit in this policy is that being a "stay-at-home" mom is not really a career proper or a category of employment, although this view might be changing. But even if a spouse does stay at home to take care of the kids, it can no longer be assumed that it will be the wife who does this; we can just as easily imagine a "house husband" or "house father" taking on this task, while the wife continues to work outside the home as the "breadwinner".

Nevertheless, the late Middle Ages may have seen the beginnings of our present attitudes towards women's work. For it was at this time, it is argued, that the definition of employment began to change with the greater professionalization and specialization of work, as the economy moved away from small, independent craft and artisanal production towards the more "formalized and impersonal systems" of organized commodity production and capitalism, such as the putting-out system.[37] Prior to this, market production was focused inside the home, where women, it is argued, could play the role of equal "working partners" in the family economy, since the line between market and subsistence production was blurred.[38] When market production shifted from the family unit to the individual, women were shut out of high-status work because they were then caught in a Catch 22: either they give up their former place in family businesses but continue to provide subsistence goods to support their partner in a "newly constructed partriarchal household," or they abandon their role as household managers to assume "the newly organized high-status work in market production". In truth, the latter alternative was not realistic, as it would entail a complete overthrow of the "patriarchal order of society," whereby women would "assume active political roles" as guild masters and leaders to complement their new economic status, while the household economy would be effectively destroyed without its managers, unless, of course, men assumed these roles.[39] Instead, it was men who "gained a monopoly over the high-status work outside the family production unit," since they alone had access to political clout (i.e., office-holding in guilds) and flexibility in order to compete in the new markets.[40] Because this new high-status work moved outside the home, the new definition of employment, and of male identities as the breadwinners of the family, moved with it.

There are at least two possible exceptions to this line of argument. One is that women always held weak work identities in the medieval economy, owing to several, long-term factors: their lack of formal training (i.e., underrepresentation in guilds); their relegation to low-status, low-paid work, both in terms of the trades they practiced (i.e., domestic service, huckstering, prostitution, etc.) and the work they performed within otherwise respectable trades (such as spinning, washing, carding, etc. within the cloth industry); the intermittent nature of their work; and, related to this, the fact that they often practiced more than one trade, all of them by necessity on a part-time basis (i.e., as "bye-industries"), which made it difficult to specialize in any one endeavor. Even if women contributed on an equal basis to the household economy, their contributions are "often hard to trace in the medieval documents" because their husbands represented the household in all legal records and because their work was so often of "the type of part-time, low-investment, household-related trade particularly suited for women juggling the demands on their time of household and family". Oftentimes, indeed, a woman's contribution as partner to her husband's trade only became clear upon the husband's death, when his widow was able to carry on his trade in his stead.[41] The other exception is the argument that women could take an independent, strong role in the economy only when the traditional family structure was weak. In Montpellier, France, for example, this held true even before the Black Death owing to various circumstances, such as immigration, overcrowding, disease, etc., all of which tended to disrupt or fragment family ties. Since women in Montpellier could not rely on family enterprises, they had to make do on their own, which meant they practiced trades on their own behalf. Women's economic involvement was thus in inverse proportion to their involvement in the family.[42]

It is true, however, that some trades experienced growing pains in the late Middle Ages, which made it substantially more difficult for women to continue to participate in them as they had done before. A prime example is the brewing of ale. This was a drink typically made by English housewives (i.e., "ale-wives") as part of their normal domestic duties, since water was not safely potable on its own. Ale was made in small batches and then quickly consumed or the excess sold to neighbors, since it spoiled easily and did not travel well. Ale-brewing seems to have been one of the many ways that medieval women could supplement the family income on an occasional, opportunistic basis. By the late fourteenth and fifteenth centuries, however, beer began to replace ale as a drink of preference throughout England. A new production process was introduced, originating in Germany and the Low Countries, in which hops were added to the fermenting process, giving beer its distinctive taste and prolonging the life of the product.[43] As a consequence, beer could be made in much larger batches and shipped in bulk in barrels, so that the professional "brewhouse" replaced the home as the center of production. When this happened, women rapidly began to fall away from the trade, shifting from alebrewers to alesellers, and production concentrated in fewer hands, even as consumption of beer and ale increased. Largely this was because women had little access to the credit that was necessary in order to invest in new equipment and ingredients that were needed for brewing beer.[44]

A similar scenario seems to have happened to women in other trades, such as cloth-making or weaving, where the new, larger looms became cost prohibitive for women.[45] In addition, women, in both the country and the city, were disadvantaged by being excluded from local political governance, such as village and guild offices and pledging systems, where men made many of the connections crucial to their success in business.[46] Women did belong to guilds, and in some trades, such as gold-spinning and silk and yarn manufacture, membership was almost entirely composed of women. Yet, in the case of mixed guild membership, one has to wonder if women and men were on equal footing, especially given that office-holders were restricted to men. Moreover, in many cases, women inherited their membership in guilds upon their husbands' demise, which implies that they were not really welcome on their own terms, as women. Even in the case of all-female guilds, it has been argued that men still ran them and that, by the end of the Middle Ages, men had frozen out women from membership as well.[47]

Various explanations are possible for declining fortunes in women's work. A popular argument is that economic depression after the mid-fifteenth century created greater competition for employment in the various trades, so that women were excluded in order to preserve the jobs of men. It is undeniable that around this time, cities in England, Germany, France, Italy, and the Low Countries recorded restrictions upon the daughters, wives, and widows of craftsmen from practicing their trades.[48] (Whether these restrictions in law were entirely enforced in practice is another matter.[49]) But examples of similar restrictions can be found in other time periods, although recent demographic evidence suggests that population recovery, and therefore population pressure for excluding women from the workforce, began to take effect in c. 1450 (see Chapter 8).[50]

One also can blame "the emergence of more rigidly patriarchal attitudes towards women" in the late Middle Ages, which objected to any sort of employment opportunities that might facilitate "female independence" (particularly for single women, who posed a threat to the "moral order of their communities").[51] Yet the most convincing case for the overriding influence of patriarchy on medieval women's experience argues that this was a constant, continuous force in history. In this view, women never broke out of their confinement to "low-skilled, low-status, low-paid" employment, even in the aftermath of the Black Death, and women of whatever rank were continually hampered by entrenched political and legal liabilities, all of which hardly gave men any reason to intensify their patriarchal attitudes.[52] Then again, it is entirely possible that women's exclusion from the workforce had really nothing to do with an explicit desire to exclude women at all, but was simply a result of the changing tastes in the market, where consumers could demand a better quality product and pay for it with the higher standards of living that working people enjoyed in the aftermath of the Black Death.[53] Since these products required higher capital investments, and a greater access to technology and training, than medieval women were ever allowed, women were inevitably excluded from these trades.

Nonetheless, in its heyday, women's work encompassed almost every conceivable trade, although certainly women predominated in the sorts of professions that were traditionally associated with their gender, such as domestic service, selling food and drink, and textile manufacture.[54] The degree of women's involvement in the medieval economy could, of course, vary by region: Generally, women seemed to have enjoyed greater freedom, independence, and opportunity in the north rather than in the south of Europe, with Florence and Ghent supplying contrasting examples. The difference largely owed to the later age at marriage for northern women as part of the "Northwest marriage pattern" (coined by the statistician, John Hajnal), giving girls a longer interval as singlewomen to develop skills in a trade (Chapter 8).[55] But there were also legal differences between the South and the North, with Germanic law being formative in the North and

Roman law influential in the South, while England went its own way with the common law. Culturally, the South seems to have placed a premium on an early, dowried marriage and on female chastity and "passivity"; consequently, young singlewomen were more generally expected to remain in their parents' household under parental control until marriage. Running off to the city to find work as a domestic servant was frowned upon in the South as a desperate last resort for the poor, since it exposed a girl to potential dangers to her sexual honor, and to the honor of her family.[56]

Women's work was quite different in a rural as opposed to an urban environment, reflecting differences in the gender division of labor, although one can argue that some degree of division of labor transcended individual circumstances.[57] At the same time, peasant women, whose work was characterized by a large degree of flexibility and variety, often were called out to the fields alongside their men, especially during busy seasons such as harvest time, when they performed tasks such as mowing or reaping, weeding, threshing, winnowing, binding sheaves and carrying grain, gleaning, goading and driving the plough beasts, etc.[58] Women also were traditionally associated with pastoral husbandry, particularly dairy work, which may have served them well in the aftermath of the Black Death when hired help was at a premium.[59]

Women's work also varied according to the stage in their life cycle. As maidens, women could generally expect to work only in low-status, low-paid trades such as domestic service, food and drink retail, spinning, brewing (usually in the employ of others), and prostitution.[60] Only with marriage did women sometimes gain access to capital to invest in an enterprise, or the opportunity to go into business with a male partner.[61] In some cities, such as London, wives even had the option to act as *femme soles*, or women operating a business alone, as if they were single, although it is not clear how often women took advantage of such opportunities or whether it gave them any substantial benefits, as opposed to acting in partnership with their husbands.[62] As widows, women had the opportunity in some cities to take over their husband's trade and to enter the guild on his behalf, although they never could become fully equal members with men.[63] Finally, women's work could vary according to urban locales, whereby different cities had different rules and craft traditions, and also according to certain time periods, when opportunities could vary depending on what was happening to the economy.[64] It is this last factor that has generated perhaps the most debate with regard to women's work in the Middle Ages.

The Black Death of the mid-fourteenth century supposedly inaugurated the "golden age of the laborer," when wages and employment opportunities increased for most categories of workers as the result of labor shortages caused by the mass death of the plague (Chapter 8). But did it result in a "golden age" for female workers as well? How much did women share in the economic windfall for Europe's working classes? Did it fundamentally change women's work in the late Middle Ages? Basically, the answers to these questions come down to whether women were able to find work outside the domestic sphere and engage in the kind of high-skilled, high-status, high-paid jobs that men typically enjoyed in the public sphere. If women did perform the same work as men, were they paid the same wages? A disturbing assumption of this debate is that any progress made by women is to be measured in terms of how much their work approximated that of men.[65] But is it right that women's work be judged in this way? Although women's work in the home has been described as an economy of "makeshifts," whereby housewives performed an assortment of tasks (i.e., cooking, cleaning, childrearing, sewing, brewing, etc.) that contemporaries did not view as a professional work identity, some scholars argue that this did not make it any less important or central to medieval society and therefore worthy of study.[66] Indeed, by holding women's work up to the standard of being high-skilled, high-status, and high-paid, does this not simply adopt the patriarchal values that demean women's work in the first place?

In assessing women's work, one could ignore men's work altogether, but this does not seem possible in current feminist scholarship. Some scholars have tried to expand the discussion of women's contribution to the medieval economy by examining the material wealth that wives could bring to a marriage, and thereby to a family business, and by seeing "wealth" in expansionary and unconventional terms, such as a bodily commodity that had value for being able to produce an heir.[67] To date, the debate has largely fallen along the lines of whether women were able to enter the traditional crafts and trades of the medieval urban economy, and whether they received the same wages as men for agricultural labor as recorded on the manor. But these definitions of women's "improvement" in their economic condition may change in future scholarship.

One aspect of the "golden age" argument is that women in the aftermath of the Black Death enjoyed greater employment and entrepreneurial opportunities that previously were open only to men, owing to the shortage of workers and manufacturers created by the plague.[68] This argument might be more convincing if it could be shown that plague showed a preferential mortality for men as opposed to women, but the evidence for sex differentials during plague epidemics is not conclusive.[69] In post-plague England, the end result was that men outnumbered women by some 10–15 percent on average, although women outnumbered men in towns, which could have been due to migration just as easily as plague mortality.[70] The main problem is that the evidence for improvement in women's work is very sketchy.[71] Undeniably, some women were able to go into business for themselves or practice a trade, but this seems to have been along the customary lines that already held true before the Black Death, namely, widows inheriting what their husband owned, or engaging in crafts such as silk manufacture that had always been dominated by women. In other words, the high-skilled, high-status jobs continued to be the preserve of married women, who gained access to them largely through their husbands.[72] This is also a matter of perception: Judith Bennett, for example, argued that, even at the height of their trade, brewsters "remained stuck in low-status, low-skilled, and poorly remunerated work" in comparison with the opportunities that arose for male brewers with the "late medieval expansion of the brewing trade" after the introduction of hops and methods for making beer.[73] But Marjorie McIntosh argued that brewing was considered a respectable trade for medieval women, based on her matching of husbands who were chief pledges of their town with wives who were listed as brewsters. Moreover, the additional income that brewsters brought to the family household was perhaps greatly appreciated by their husbands. When women did disappear from the trade by the sixteenth century, this seems to have been due not only to economic unfeasibility, but also out a "mounting sense that drink work was not suitable for respectable women".[74]

Opportunities for singlewomen were, again, largely confined to low-skilled, low-status, low-paid careers such as domestic service. Work as a servant was usually the preserve of young, singlewomen, as being unmarried was a requirement of service, although there were cases of older spinsters and widows employed in the trade.[75] While not particularly well paid, domestic service was perhaps attractive because it required no special skills and offered the security of a home environment, at least for those servants who "lived-in" with their masters.[76] Jeremy Goldberg has argued that, between the late fourteenth and mid-fifteenth centuries, many young singlewomen migrated to the cities in order to take advantage of increased employment opportunities, even delaying marriage prospects in order to do so. The main opportunities for these singlewomen were initially in "traditional" female trades such as domestic service, but as "demographic recession" coupled with economic expansion continued, women may have been drawn into other trades that were "formerly male economic niches". Thereafter, these opportunities became fewer as the economy contracted in the late fifteenth and early sixteenth centuries, when women were deliberately "excluded from the full range of occupations they had previously enjoyed so as to protect male employment".[77] Goldberg's argument, however, was based on a very small sample of some three dozen single female deponents in the York cause papers evidence, which seems hardly enough to be representative of the population at large.[78] Nor did Goldberg present any comparable evidence from before the Black Death in order to put women's post-plague employment opportunities in perspective. Others have questioned the attractiveness of domestic service to young singlewomen, given its nature as low-status and low-paid employment.[79] In addition, domestic service tied workers down to fixed, yearly contracts, as opposed to more flexible piece-work available in the agricultural labor market, and greater opportunities may have been available for marriage at this time, which would have allowed women to set up their own household rightaway and, if they so chose, continue to work outside the domestic sphere on a casual basis (perhaps in order to supplement the family income). Just because a medieval woman got married did not mean that she couldn't take advantage of the new labor market created by the Black Death.[80]

Perhaps the most concrete evidence that we have as to women's work in the late Middle Ages concerns wage rates that were paid to laborers on English manors and building sites in the aftermath of the Black Death. A reliable wage data series for English female laborers—comparable to that for male laborers—has now been constructed for the entire late Middle Ages and beyond.[81] Based on an impressive collection of sources, this wage series overcomes previous caveats raised regarding female wages being subsumed within mixed team work recorded as violations of English labor laws; that female wages present different comparative standards depending on whether women were paid by the day (i.e., "time-rates") or by the amount of work produced ("piece-rates"); and that wage rates must take into consideration not only cash remuneration but also payments in kind (i.e., food, clothing, lodging, etc.) typically included in annual contracts.[82] The new data series also "shatters stereotypes of women's work as purely domestic or less physically demanding," revealing that medieval women engaged in a wide array of occupations (even including building work) and that thus their wage rates, even if paid by the piece, were directly comparable to those of men.[83] The data relate solely to unskilled female labor, paid both on a casual basis (usually by the day) and on an annual contract, and drawn from across the country but excluding London (which arguably had artificially high wage rates) and excluding harvest and haymaking wages (when laborers were paid at extraordinarily high rates compared to the rest of the year).[84]

What this female wage series tells us is that women were indeed paid at substantially lower rates than men throughout the late Middle Ages, even when the wages of all categories of laborers improved exponentially in the aftermath of the "supply-side shocks" imposed by the Black Death. From 1260 to 1400, women earned wages that consistently were about 30 percent lower than those of men, even as average casual wage rates for both sexes doubled during the second half of the fourteenth century, when England's population was culled not only by the "Great Mortality" of plague in 1348–50 but by at least four more national outbreaks, albeit of lower virulence (Chapter 8). Moreover, this discrepancy between female and male wage rates only grew worse in the course of the fifteenth century as the Middle Ages came to a close. Between 1400 and 1450, casual female laborers were paid 42 percent less than men on average, while the gap increased to 53 percent between 1450 and 1500, so that men were now being paid fully half as much more as women. At the height of the wage gender gap, in the decades around 1450, men's casual and annual wages were nearly 5 times greater than women's. Put another way, men improved their casual wages by some 18 percent during the first half of the fifteenth century, with their gains holding steady during the second half; meanwhile, women's casual wages improved only by 10 percent in 1400–1450, while their gains were actually pared back to just 3 percent—i.e., nearly reverting back to what they had earned a century earlier—in 1450–1500.[85]

All of this bolsters the patriarchy argument, that even if women benefitted economically from the Black Death, they were still unable to overcome a structural disadvantage compared to men, and in fact seem to have lost ground.[86] In other words, employers' misogynistic "custom and prejudice" with regard to paying women trumped the gender-neutral laws of "supply and demand". Thus, the idea that economic gains accrued more to the low-status, low-skilled, low-paid sectors of employment, owing to the fact that plague mortality and its supply-side shocks were higher among the poorer classes of society, did not really apply to women.[87] On the other hand, women's consistently cheaper labor (a fact apparently acknowledged in farming manuals) would have made their work more attractive to employers whose incomes were being squeezed by the overall higher cost of labor in the aftermath of the Black Death. This doesn't square with assertions that women's work was used "reluctantly and sparingly" as a kind of "reserve labor force".[88]

This data also has "powerful implications" for the debate over the European marriage pattern.[89] Basically, it incentivized marriage, the complete opposite of the Northwest marriage pattern (in which significant numbers of women delayed marriage or never married at all). This is because casual labor—which garnered almost all the gains made by female workers in the late Middle Ages—was especially suited and available to married women, who sought to supplement family incomes and who could take advantage of husbands' contacts to find work and also fall back on other means of support when wage work was scarce.[90] By contrast, annual contract work—which was typically sought by single women entering domestic service or employment as manorial *famuli*—saw virtually no gains in the century and a half after the Black Death. For example, annual wages barely crept up by some nine percent in the second half of the fourteenth century, compared to the half century before the plague. But by the first half of the fifteenth century, annual wages actually went into reverse, declining by 27 percent to end up 20 percent lower than their pre-plague levels. Wages improved somewhat in the second half of the fifteenth century, increasing by 20 percent, but to a level that was still below what they had been in the half century before the plague. Basically, annual wages in the closing decades of the fifteenth century returned to what they had been in the decades just after the advent of the Black Death a century earlier.[91]

This hardly tempted single females in the country to migrate to the cities in order to find work as domestic servants. Of course, single as well as married women could engage in casual labor, which, nearly throughout this period between 1350 and 1500, required less than 200 days of work to match what was earned by annual contracts and, during its heyday from about 1400 to 1450, actually required 100 days or less to match annual incomes.[92] The problem is that rootless single females on the move looking for work and under no immediate paternal authority were definitely frowned upon in medieval society and may actually have been subject to arrest by the statute of laborers. Harsh enforcement of the laws (especially for women) and the uncertainties of finding casual labor probably combined to nudge most single women into annual contracts. Thus, how realistic an option it was for single women to take advantage of casual labor is open to question.[93] It was not until about 1550 that annual wage rates began to outpace those of casual labor and thereby look more attractive, which, by assuredly no coincidence, is also when Europe began to definitively evince the Northwest marriage pattern.[94] In the meantime, single women seem to have been almost entirely left out of the "golden age" of the wage laborer.[95] It was left up to married women to feel the "girl power" of earning higher wages (albeit still considerably lower than men's). In an optimistic world, such higher earnings would have allowed women to create more "social capital for themselves" and acquire "more independence and control over their lives," thereby fundamentally changing "the balance of power between men and women" and creating a new, mutually-reinforcing marriage pattern.[96]

Maidens, wives, and widows

A medieval woman was usually classified as belonging to one of three identities: a maiden, wife, or widow.[97] However, not much is known about the first category, since an adult, never-married woman was a relative anomaly in medieval society.[98] (A "low-pressure" marriage regime in Northwestern Europe was said to be defined by just 10 percent of women never marrying.) In English common law, a single woman was classed as a *femme sole* ("woman alone"), who was not "covered" by her father or husband or other male guardian but who acted on her own behalf, representing herself in court and owning land and goods in her own right. (Married women in London could also be classified as *femme soles* for legal purposes, usually in cases where they ran businesses independently of their husbands.) In Spain, a single woman might also be called a *muger soltera*, translated as spinster or "old maid," but without the "negative connotations" usually accorded these terms in both medieval and modern cultures.[99]

It is unlikely that remaining single was a desirable option in the minds of most medieval women: The status of *femme sole*, for example, was frequently used as a legal defense to "evoke sympathy" for the defendant who was portrayed as lacking in personal or financial support.[100] Therefore, remaining single throughout one's life must have been a daunting prospect for women—raising the specter of insecurity, poverty, and vulnerability—unless she was part of a community of some kind, such as a religious convent. Aristocratic women had perhaps the best chance of leading a comfortable single life; otherwise, spinsters had to rely on the charity of relatives and evidently led a precarious existence.[101] Moreover a single woman had to closely guard her chastity if she was not to raise suspicions among her peers, as virginity was held up as the ideal for such women, and sexual promiscuity, even if practiced more commonly than we know, made her in others' eyes no better than a whore. Indeed, this could become a self-fulfilling prophecy, as a woman with no marriage prospects could easily become destitute and fall into prostitution (Chapter 5).[102] Nonetheless, there were women in the Middle Ages who stayed single throughout their lives, such as Cecilia Penifader of Brigstock, who lived during the first half of the fourteenth century and whose life, such as it can be gleaned from the records, was documented by Judith Bennett.[103] Bennett has argued that young, singlewomen enjoyed access to public power and a degree of economic independence, such as being able to represent themselves in court and to own property in their own right, that they then lost when they got married, since their husbands assumed these rights and privileges on their behalf.[104]

It has been suggested that in the aftermath of the Black Death, during the late fourteenth and early fifteenth centuries, women may have chosen to remain single in order to migrate to towns and take advantage of employment opportunities opened up by the plague mortality. Statistics based on the English poll-tax returns of 1377 do show higher rates of single people in town as opposed to the country—40 percent to 30 percent.[105] Some scholars argue that these single people either never married at all or delayed marriage in order to enjoy "a greater degree of economic independence" or autonomy, thereby being free to choose whom and when they married and even to pay for their own marriage licenses (*merchet*). In this scenario, women waited to get married until their mid-twenties and formed more "companionate," even affectionate, marriages in which they were closer in age to their partners.[106] But others argue that women were single more out of necessity than by choice, either because no suitable marriage partners were available owing to skewed sex ratios in favor of women (a situation apparently common in many medieval towns), or because their families could not afford a dowry (although many confraternities had a dowry fund to help with just such a necessity).[107] A career-oriented mentality, where work is "a form of liberation," was no doubt anachronistic to the Middle Ages, when marriage was seen as a natural state for women (and was perhaps the reason women were working in the first place, to earn enough to afford a dowry).[108] Moreover, the "careers" that many medieval single women made in towns have been characterized as of the "low-status, low-skilled, low-paid" variety, such as domestic service, which were hardly attractive alternatives to marriage.[109]

The next stage in a medieval woman's life, getting married, has been described as more of a business proposition than as part of the process of falling in love that we take it to be today.[110] Admittedly, much of the medieval literature took a rather dim view on this score. A popular saying from the *fabliaux* tradition, for example, was that "no man marries without regretting it," while in many tales of courtly romance, true love was only attainable outside marriage.[111] Certainly, arranged marriages were much more common in medieval times than now, which must have affected how people related to each other within a marriage. But circumstances also could have varied by status: Ironically, the higher status you were, probably the less choice one had in marriage, since much more was at stake (i.e., in terms of property and wealth). Therefore, those of lower status, such as the peasantry, may have had more freedom to choose a companionate marriage partner, although even here financial expectations could have played a role.[112] However, one study of patrician marriage alliances in late medieval Venice found that the greater wealth enjoyed by wives in the form of bridal dowries made for more affectionate and loving relationships between husband and wife, as evidenced by the terms of endearments used in wills, and that this affection only became stronger as the fifteenth century wore on.[113] In this case, money really did buy marital bliss, because "the increase in married women's wealth led the menfolk to take their mates more seriously and to court their favor more assiduously".[114]

But other factors besides class played a role in determing whom one could marry. One limiting factor was the degree of blood relationship between two people: By the Fourth Lateran Council of 1215, the Church was successfully enforcing the rule that one could not marry within four degrees of relatedness, which prohibited one from marrying anyone with whom one shared a great-great-grandparent, or closer.[115] In a small village that saw few outsiders, this quickly could have become a major impediment. This must have impelled some people to look further afield for a marriage partner, although unfree serfs had to pay a fine for the privilege of marrying outside the manor.[116] Country girls who left home to work in the city (typically as domestic servants) were undoubtedly freer to choose their marriage partner than those who stayed at home under their parents' supervision.[117] Perhaps the most important development in terms of promoting equitable love between marriage partners was the Church's imposition of consent as a necessary condition for marriage, which seems to have become widespread by the mid-fifteenth century.[118] We also get a glimpse of companionable marital relations in the fact that husbands entrusted their wives as executors of their wills and guardians of their children.[119] Oftentimes, spousal love may have happened *after* the couple was married, as they got to know each other once they got past the awkward stage where they were introduced for the first time as part of an arranged union.[120] The fifteenth-century author, Christine de Pisan, says that her husband, Etienne de Castel, a French notary hand-picked by her father, was very considerate on their wedding night, giving her time to get to know him and winning her over with his affectionate ways.[121] The process of a medieval courtship can also be glimpsed in the fifteenth-century letters of the Stonor family, which testify to "the love and tenderness" that could emerge and grow between couples.[122]

Here, however, we will focus on the legal and economic considerations that went into making a marriage, since this is where there has been the most research and debate, and these also largely determined the kind of marriage that would ensue. Marriage law and contract negotiations revolved around two concepts: dower and dowry. The former emerged from both Roman law (*donatio propter nuptias*) and Germanic custom, in which the husband endowed his wife with a portion of his property (typically a third to a half) in order to ensure her support if she was widowed. This seems to have been separate from the Germanic customs of morning gift (*morgengabe*) and bride price, also payable by the husband to his wife or her family. Women's value in Germanic society, particularly their ability to bear children and heirs, is likewise attested by substantial *wergilds* that were assessed should she be killed.[123] In return, the bride's family gifted the dowry, a holdover from Roman law (the *dos* or *maritagium*), which was the bride's share of the family inheritance and supposedly went to help the couple set up a new household or family business but which was also expected to help maintain the bride in her widowhood.[124] The custom in most European countries was that the husband had the right to control or "manage" both the dower and dowry during his wife's lifetime, even though such property was legally held under joint ownership and the husband could not alienate or sell it without his wife's consent.[125]

Dowry and dower amounts could vary substantially by region. "Dowry inflation" became notorious in Madrid in Spain in the thirteenth century, when municipal authorities began imposing spending limits on dowries, while Italian cities such as Florence and Venice followed suit in the fifteenth century and at the same time set up state-sponsored savings accounts to help parents plan for such an expense upon the birth of a daughter.[126]

In the meantime, the Church began to assert its control over the ceremony of marriage itself.[127] By promoting marriage to a sacrament, the Church began insisting on the indissolubility of marriage and on the free consent of both parties as the defining condition of marriage. Both of these are seen as beneficial developments for women, because wives could no longer be set aside by their husbands for failing to produce an heir, and because women could now take a more "individualistic" approach to marriage, defying the wishes of parents or lords if need be in favor of a preferred partner.[128] At the same time, the Church was concerned to replace "clandestine" marriages—in which couples were considered legally married even if they only exchanged vows privately, uttered either in the present tense or as a future commitment that was then followed by sexual intercourse—with a public, formal ceremony presided by a priest "before the face of the church"; the main goal here was to avoid legal disputes and complications that were flooding Church courts.[129]

How successful the Church was in this effort is open to debate.[130] Although the Church was able to impose some kind of uniformity in the practice of canon law across Europe, the enforcement of marriage rules could vary based on local custom, and some courts continued to see abundant litigation, with the woman more often bringing suit to enforce a marriage, based on evidence from England and Spain.[131] Male testimony was, as a rule, privileged over female, but Church courts also tended to decide in favor of marriage formation rather than against it.[132] Another consideration was whether consent had been freely given or the party married out of "force and fear" (with both men and women claiming to be pressured by the bride's family into getting married); in the case of clandestine marriages, the party claiming that vows had been exchanged had the burden of proof, usually in the form of witness testimony.[133]

Although canon law is commonly perceived as having been detrimental to women, an argument also can be made that it promoted equality between the sexes. While the Church generally upheld the patriarchal principle that women should be subservient to their husbands, it also promoted the view that marriage was a partnership between two people equal in the eyes of God. Each surrendered their rights over their own bodies to the other, which was typically expressed in law as that both men and women had to pay the "marriage debt" (i.e., sex on demand by the other spouse). But there was also room for amendment of these obligations, such as seeking a vow of celibacy within marriage (provided the other spouse consented) and seeking a legal separation or annulment on legitimate grounds, such as impotence and adultery. Many scholars would argue that, in practice, these rules were not quite equal, particularly with regard to the marriage debt and adultery, where a man's sexuality was privileged over the woman's (i.e., men invariably demanded sex from their wives rather than the other way around, and men faced a much higher standard for being convicted of adultery than a woman). But conditions could change with time: By the fifteenth and sixteenth centuries, both the Church and secular society seem to have become much less tolerant of adultery, no matter whether committed by a man or a woman.[134]

Taken all together, how did these developments affect women? The answer really depends on when and where one is looking. In England, some historians contend that the common law, introduced gradually in the wake of the Norman Conquest of 1066 and which granted men complete control of a woman's assets and rights upon marriage, "crushed women more than any other western law has ever done".[135] More recent research has, however, yielded a more nuanced view, which claims that the "Conquest did not bring about any immediate change in women's rights or status".[136]

In Italy and the Mediterranean, the dotal regime that dominated the marriage market from the eleventh century onward is often portrayed as negatively affecting women, who were thereby excluded from inheriting in their own right and reduced to being mere pawns in a "gilded cage" for the transfer of wealth from one generation to the next.[137] However, not all scholars see late medieval dowries in this light. One study of patrician marriages in fifteenth-century Venice argued that dowries, albeit used primarily to promote family alliances, may at the same time have given women the leverage to impose a more affective and individualistic culture upon their men, since ultimately it was they who controlled dotal wealth upon the end of a marriage.[138] Through ever inflated dowries, daughters inherited more of the family patrimony than brothers, and women gained greater influence and status in a supposedly patriarchial society.[139] Quite simply, the wealth of wives meant that their men tried to keep them happy. This argument is, however, limited to the patrician class and is largely conjectural, based as it is on a subjective interpretation of the language used by spouses and parents in their wills.[140]

An alternative interpretation sees the earlier *morgengabe* or morning gift tradition inherited from Germanic law as giving women more control over their wealth. In Genoa, for example, where morning gifts persisted into the twelfth century even as other cities were switching to dowries, women played a prominent role in Genoa's rise to a maritime power, investing either their own money or that of their husbands in the city's rapidly expanding trade economy.[141] In southern France and Spain, the relatively high percentage of women appearing in charters as property owners from the ninth to the twelfth centuries seemed to be a holdover from Visigothic and Burgundian laws, which placed no "juridical restrictions" on a woman's "freedom to administer her own property". Not coincidentally, these are also the areas where the use of the matronymic, or adoption of the mother's family name by children, indicating the greater prominence and prestige of women, was most prevalent, since in these instances, the children were inheriting from the mother.[142]

Nevertheless, Italy's economic influence and the "social cachet" of its notoriously inflated dowries seem to have resulted in dotal regimes being widely adopted throughout Europe, while a trickle-down effect also spread dowry expectations to the lower classes, such that a woman who could not afford a dowry was condemned to spinsterhood or to being forced to work for a number of years in order to save up for one.[143] Some northern towns, such as Douai, enacted safeguards designed to protect the bride's interests in a dowry, chiefly by not separating the ownership and management of the dowry. Upon widowhood, a woman could demand an inventory of her deceased husband's assets in order to secure restitution of her dowry, while her immunity from prosecution for her husband's debts made her a popular repository for wealth that normally would have gone to sons or brothers-in-law.[144]

The Church's intervention in marriage, particularly the ruling from the time of Pope Alexander III (r. 1159–81) that consent of the couple alone made a marriage, may have given some women bargaining ammunition to assert their independence from parental and seigneurial pressure.[145] Indeed, the principle of consent has been characterized as having "by itself assured that the medieval family could never develop into a true patriarchy".[146] However, local custom could supersede the Church's ruling, while most girls of marriageable age were still largely dependent upon their parents for dowries and hence would have sought their approval.[147] Clandestine marriages represented another option whereby women could defy outside influences and exercise freedom of choice, since the Church felt itself obligated to recognize such marriages provided they were conducted according to the proper form.[148]

The onset of the Black Death in the mid-fourteenth century also may have struck a blow for women's greater freedom to form their own marriages, since it eventually did away with unfree peasant dues such as *merchet*, by means of which lords could influence potential marriages, and by creating employment opportunities that allowed singlewomen to escape from parental influence and migrate to the cities, where they might earn enough to pay for their own dowries and *merchets*, where these still applied. Inheritance rights also seem to have greatly improved for women, whereby daughters could inherit as well as sons, or the property could be divided equally among them; however, this still depended to some degree on what kind of land was being inherited and the local law or custom in this regard. Women seem to have had the best chance of inheriting in the case of town property held according to the terms of burgage tenure and in the case of land subject to partible inheritance. Freehold lands (which included most aristocratic estates) automatically went to the eldest male heir by right of primogeniture, but if there was no son, then daughters inherited in equal proportion. Land subject to military tenure was liable to knight service dues, which had to be performed by a man if a woman inherited. More likely, such land was held by a guardian until the woman came of age (14 years old), whereupon she was under great pressure to marry.[149]

The mortality from the plague undoubtedly created a windfall for women with respect to inheritances. An analysis of Inquisitions *post mortem* (records of the deaths, estates and heirs of the king's tenants-in-chief, for the purpose of assessing feudal dues) shows that among the English landed aristocracy, women's role in inheritances more than doubled in the 1370s compared to the decade just before the Black Death of 1348; their role was either in the form of direct heiresses (i.e., daughters), or in the form of providing either collateral heiresses or the only surviving line to produce a male heir (i.e., "male collaterals descended in the female line"). Despite inheritance strategies to bypass heiresses, such as use of the entail (i.e., settlements in the tail male), families were reluctant to disinherit daughters and were quite simply compelled to leave estates to the female line by the lack of direct or collateral male heirs, making the "later medieval period the last great age of the heiress".[150] Likewise, in Bologna in Italy, families that made their wills during the plague year of 1348 proved more than willing to make daughters the sole or joint heiresses, even to the point of disregarding tradition that excluded married daughters from inheriting, owing to their already possessing a dowry (*exclusio propter dotem*).[151] However, evidence indicates that peasant women were excluded from these trends: Their chances of owning land may actually have declined in the aftermath of the Black Death. This is in spite of the fact that land became cheaper at this time, which may have increased singlewomen's participation in the late medieval land market, although the evidence for this is still sparse.[152] The fact of the matter seems to be that, when fathers had both male and female heirs available and complete legal freedom in terms of to whom they could will their land, they mostly preferred to leave their daughters cash or goods rather than land, which was to serve as their marriage portion or dowry. Some might consider this a loss of inheritance rights for women, but there is also evidence that daughters were given a greater share of such goods than sons in order to make up for their lack of land.[153] But no matter how much they inherited, one can make the argument that, in the end, women were still no better off because, once they got married, they never controlled what they owned, since legally they ceased to exist as an independent entity once they got married (i.e., they became *femme couvert*, "covered" by their husbands).[154] In this sense, then, women were simply the conduit for the transfer of wealth from one generation to another.[155] Nonetheless, if the Northwest marriage regime holds true for much of Europe during the late Middle Ages as well as the Early Modern period, then this would indicate that late medieval women, by waiting longer to get married, exercised greater freedom of choice in whom they married and formed more companionate marriages in which they were closer in age to their partners.[156] This alone would represent a very real advance in women's prospects for happiness in marriage.

It seems to be a popular assumption that "the best years of a woman's life in the late middle ages were those of her widowhood".[157] Finally "liberated" or "emancipated" from their husbands' all-powerful control and influence, widows could now flourish "in their new-found freedom". Released from the legal and cultural restraints of marriage and from the "encumbrance of pregnancies," the widow could now assume full control over the family finances and property and make all the decisions regarding her own welfare and that of her children.[158] If she lived in the country, she might take over the running of her husband's estate or farm; if she lived in town, she might inherit her husband's trade or business, even becoming a member of his guild on his behalf. She was now, for perhaps the only time in a medieval woman's life, a fully-fledged, independent person, answerable to no man.

This is undoubtedly an appealing scenario for many historians of women's history. But not everyone buys into it. Judith Bennett, for example, denied that widows were truly "liberated" and emphasized the weighty responsibilities that widows faced as heads of households for the first time. About half of the widows of Brigstock, England, for example, participated in the public life of the village to such an extent that their "social horizons had more in common with the experience of male householders than with those of daughters or wives"; the other half, insofar as this can be traced from manorial court records, essentially withdrew from society, even though few widows shirked their household duties altogether. Overall, Bennett emphasized the variety and uniqueness of widows' experiences.[159] The fact that widowhood was the only time in a woman's life when she was free and independent of men's control was also a source of concern, not celebration, to contemporary moralists, who were concerned above all about widows' potential "wanton" behavior.[160] Once again, if we were able somehow to ask a medieval woman directly how she felt about her situation, in this case, widowhood, we might get a different answer from what most modern observers might expect. In the end, we can never know or predict the idiosyncrasies of individual affection and loss.[161] Christine de Pizan, who lost her husband to a plague epidemic in 1389, leaving her a young widow of 25 with three children to support, described how fickle Fortune, who had blessed her with a partner she loved "more than any other thing in this mortal world," then took him from her, leaving her a grieving widow afflicted with such a "deep sadness" that she became a recluse and, apparently, even contemplated suicide.[162]

Unlike their counterparts in modern Western societies, women in medieval Europe do not seem to have lived as long as men—due to a combination of biological, environmental, and cultural factors.[163] Nonetheless, within medieval marriages, women were still more likely to outlive their husbands rather than the other way around, largely because men were so much older than their wives, which is thought to have been the typical pattern for much of Europe for most of the Middle Ages.[164] It is estimated that among the aristocracy of fifteenth-century England, two out of three men left a widow and only one out of three became a widower.[165] Widowhood is therefore assumed to have been a "common experience" for most married medieval women.[166]

But this experience of widowhood could vary substantially, depending on the woman's status and circumstances during marriage. If she was counted among the aristocracy, then she could become a wealthy heiress through her dowry and dower estates, so that "widowhood was the the most powerful phase of an aristocratic woman's life-cycle".[167] Indeed, if she remarried multiple times without producing heirs, she could collect inheritances into one vast estate.[168] Some historians, adopting the perspective of a widow's heirs, pronounce a harsh judgment on these women, seeing them as a "drain on the patrimony" or a "blight" on their sons' fortunes.[169] But even aristocratic widows had limitations on what they might expect to receive. For example, by the common law of England, all widows had to vacate their primary residence within 40 days (which reverted back to her husband's family) and find a "dower residence," typically one "smaller and less well appointed". Likewise, in Spain, a widow was guaranteed possession of the marriage bed, but not necessarily the house it came in. If much land was at stake, a widow might be harassed—both legally and extra-legally—by stepsons or even natal sons and kinsmen, who typically forced the widow to accept a lifetime annuity, but even these arrangements were not always honored.[170] Though a widow's right to dower lands in England was guaranteed by Magna Carta, she still might have had to defend this right in court, which in itself can be considered as having "called forth an active and competent response by the women".[171] In Spain, it was the custom in many towns to put the guardianship of a minor up for "auction," in which control of inheritance was given to whoever could promise the highest return on assets, thereby potentially depriving the widow of her own children.[172] Typically, a widow's dower rights were challenged on the grounds that her husband had not legally owned the property that was assigned to the dower.[173] Even when a widow won her case, which seems to have been half the time, it might be years before she enjoyed full possession of her property owing to the lengthy legal process.[174]

Lower down the social scale, urban and gentry widows could lead a comfortable existence if they inherited their husband's manor or business and moveable goods, but they could experience a sharp drop in standard of living if they had relied on their husband's income from official positions or trades from which women were excluded. This was particularly hard on women who inherited properties that were rented instead of owned outright. Even when women were able to continue running their husbands' shops, towards the end of the Middle Ages they were allowed to do so only for a year or two after their husband's death, presumably to avoid competition with men. If admitted to a guild, women were still excluded from voting and holding official positions, which meant that they were shut out of political connections that could greatly further their business. If allowed to train apprentices, women were still at a great disadvantage in attacting good help and maintaining discipline.[175] Likewise, women in charge of a manor or estate might have found it difficult to run things especially in the aftermath of the Black Death, when labor was scarce and expensive and rental income was low.[176] Meanwhile, both urban and gentry widows faced the same court challenges to their dower lands as did aristocratic widows. Finally, towards the bottom of the social scale, widows of husbandmen, craftsmen, and laborers might have suffered a fatal blow to their household economy with the loss of their husband's wages. If they didn't fall into abject poverty or debt, they might have relied on the charity of friends and relatives, forced to lodge in a single chamber of another's household, or sought employment in whatever work was available, which was typically low-skilled and low-paid.[177]

A widow's position could also depend upon the inheritance laws that applied in different regions of Europe, and upon legal developments that were taking place at the time. Some places allowed a widow full ownership of her dower and dowry lands, in which she could bring these with her to a subsequent marriage (thus greatly increasing her attractiveness in the marriage market); others provided that she only had the use of this property during her lifetime, or until she remarried, whereupon it reverted to the heir or to the original grantor's family. (The latter was known in England as "free bench".) Husbands could likewise make such stipulations in their wills, forcing a widow to choose between a comfortable single life or an uncertain future with a new husband.[178] However, widows could also display considerable ingenuity in disposing of inherited lands, even when encumbered by "custodial restrictions". For example, they could lease the land; sell it covertly; secure free control from the land's eventual heirs (i.e., the widow's son); and dispose of the land via a "two-step transfer" (i.e., convey the land to a son, who then conveyed it to the originally intended third party).[179]

Much of the complexity in medieval widows' legal position arose from new developments in property transfers that supplemented or even replaced the traditional instruments of dowry and dower. From the thirteenth century, for example, the custom arose of jointure, or that married men and women could own property jointly. This device was used even by the lower classes, whereupon a newly-married couple could be regranted a tenancy by the lord under the new terms of jointure. This could greatly benefit a widow, as she did not need to go to court to claim an inheritance that she already owned. She was also allowed to carry jointure lands with her to a new marriage, and they were not affected by competing family claims, as might be the case with dower. For this reason, jointure seems to have replaced dower as the husband's provision for his wife, while dowries became money or goods rather than land, since the latter was now provided by the groom's side of the family. There was no limit to jointure grants, but they were usually no more than a third of the total estate. Then, in the next century, following the Black Death, the "enfeoffment to use" came into play, whereby the husband would appoint a trustee, known as a "feoffee," who was granted land to hold in trust after the husband's death. This generally bypassed a widow's right to dower and instead instructed the trustee to allow her use of a certain portion of land, usually under certain conditions, such as that the use lands would pass to the heir when he came of age (with the widow then receiving an annuity) or when she remarried. The use, therefore, could be generally considered detrimental to a widow's interests. Finally, there were *inter vivos* ("among the living") and deathbed transfers, which arose in manorial, as opposed to common law, courts. Land could be transferred during the lifetime of tenants (*inter vivos*), or the husband could summon a third party and witnesses to his deathbed in order to make last-minute, oral amendments to his will, which were then officially announced by the third party at the next meeting of the manor court. By these means, a husband could either make a special provision for his widow, or bypass her altogether.[180] Thus, by the late Middle Ages, husbands had many more options in terms of how they could dispose of their property and wealth, but not all of these benefitted widows.

Whether a widow remarried depended, of course, on many circumstances. Generally, however, remarriage seems to have been "fairly common" among widows in the late Middle Ages if the women were still young, i.e., 40 years or younger. Once they got past 40, women seem to have had far less opportunity, or choice, to remarry.[181] There were some strong inducements or circumstances that favored remarriage: the prospect of companionship (with a greater likelihood of the couple being age companionate); a higher standard of living from the new husband's income; the support of a man to run the estate or business and to raise children; better representation in court, especially to secure dower inheritances; greater protection and security from harassment, sexual or otherwise; and so on. Overall, medieval culture favored marriage as "the natural state for women," and a widow's remarriage set the seal on her "reintegration" into society.[182] At the same time, it can be argued that the fact that widows tended to remarry within the same status group but outside the husband's family line, thus dispersing wealth and connections "horizontally" rather than "vertically," may have helped undermine the patriarchy of medieval society.[183]

Of course, widows' remarriage could vary substantially by the circumstances of regional culture, the economy, individual preferences, etc. In late medieval London, widows faced "significant pressure" to remarry from their late husband's guild " in order to keep the tools of the trade and shops within the guild".[184] But in the English countryside, rates of widow remarriage varied greatly. At Brigstock, Northamptonshire, remarriage rates were only around 8 percent in the early fourteenth century, but at Halesowen in Worcestershire, they were more like 60 percent.[185] The remarriage rate was also low in Montpellier in southern France (only around 5 percent), because there widows had an incentive not to marry if they wanted to continue to enjoy the profits from husbands' estates.[186] In Spain during the Reconquest, remarriage of widows was encouraged by many towns through tax incentives, provided she waited the customary year of mourning for her deceased husband.[187] In Italy, there were apparently "immense familial and religious pressures" upon a widow *not* to remarry, particularly if children were involved, and, in any case, eligible bachelors and widowers seem to have had their pick of unmarried, teenage brides.[188] If widows found the greater independence and freedom of widowhood attractive, as some scholars claim, then this may have been balanced out by the difficulties widows faced in managing a business or farm alone, or in defending their reputation as "honest women".[189] Any "buoyancy" in employment, and in the economy overall, in the aftermath of the Black Death that encouraged widows to remain single largely disappeared after the mid-fifteenth century.[190] Some factors were more involuntary, in that they were mostly outside a widow's control. Thus, sex ratios may have been unfavorable for widow remarriage, particularly if more men than women succumbed to the Black Death; at the same time, the migration of young women to towns to take up job opportunities may have reversed this ratio in rural areas. Also, it seems that widows were more attractive as marriage partners before the Black Death, when there was a "land hunger" or shortage of opportunities for land ownership, as well as a greater competition for entering trades, owing to overpopulation. After the Black Death, however, land to rent or buy was far more plentiful, and opportunities to inherit or to enter a trade were far greater, which made widow endowments almost redundant.[191]

In the end, the decision of a widow to remarry must have been an intensely personal one. Christine de Pizan told of the no end of "troubles" and "obstacles" that faced her "from all sides" when she was widowed, having to contest numerous "lawsuits and legal disputes" over debts and land ownership, to the point that she faced bankruptcy and had her possessions confiscated. Nonetheless, Christine never remarried. Instead, she said that she "transformed" herself into a man, metaphorically speaking, so that she could have the strength to become the "master" of her family ship. In this way, she was able to make a life and a living for herself as a celebrated author, using her muse to enshrine the memory of her loving, and most beloved, husband.[192]

Notes

1 For the argument that feminism has had a big impact on medieval studies, see Judith M. Bennett, "Medievalism and Feminism," *Speculum* 68 (1993):309–31.
2 Caroline Barron, "The 'Golden Age' of Women in Medieval London," in *Medieval Women in Southern England* (Reading Medieval Studies, 15, 1989), pp. 35–58; P.J.P. Goldberg, *Women, Work, and Life Cycle in a Medieval Economy: Women in York and Yorkshire, c. 1300–1520* (Oxford: Clarendon Press, 1992). In addition to the late Middle Ages in the aftermath of the Black Death, another "golden age" for women has been argued for the early Middle Ages, particularly in terms of the power and authority accorded to queens, but which was then superseded after the year 1000 by the exalted status accorded to the "third gender" of celibate males, as part of the Church's reform movement. This "golden age" theory likewise has been challenged, this time on the grounds that even after 1000, aristocratic women could still have exerted considerable power and authority through their use of written documents and their support of industry and commerce in towns. Another alternative interpretation sees greater mobility among women at the turn of the millennium, leading to "more variety of options" and a greater "control over their own situations". See: Jo Ann McNamara and Suzanne Wemple, "The Power of Women through the Family in Medieval Europe: 500–1100," in *Women and Power in the Middle Ages*, eds. Mary Erler and Maryanne Kowaleski (Athens, GA.: University of Georgia Press, 1988), pp. 83–101; Jo Ann McNamara, "Women and Power Through the Family Revisited," in *Gendering the Master Narrative: Women and Power in the Middle Ages*, eds. Mary C. Erler and Maryanne Kowaleski (Ithaca, NY.: Cornell University Press, 2003), pp. 17–30; Constance H. Berman, "Gender at the Medieval Millennium," in *The Oxford Handbook of Women and Gender in Medieval Europe*, eds. Judith M. Bennett and Ruth Mazo Karras (Oxford: Oxford University Press, 2013), pp. 546–49; Lisa M. Bitel, *Women in Early Medieval Europe, 400–1100* (Cambridge: Cambridge University Press, 2002), p. 264.
3 Eileen Power, *Medieval Women*, ed. Michael Moissey Postan (Cambridge: Cambridge University Press, 1975), p. 34. These essays were collected and edited posthumously by

Power's husband, Michael Postan, after her death in 1940. The theme of a golden age of rough equality between working men and women in the pre-industrial age was perhaps first put forward by Alice Clark in *Working Life of Women in the Seventeenth Century*, first published in 1919. It has also been used by historians such as Doris Stenton to characterize Anglo-Saxon English society and to contrast it with what ensued in the aftermath of the Norman Conquest of 1066. For overviews of the historiography of medieval English women's history, see: Barbara A. Hanawalt, "Golden Ages for the History of Medieval English Women," in *Women in Medieval History and Historiography*, ed. Susan Mosher Stuard (Philadelphia, PA.: University of Pennsylvania Press, 1987), pp. 1–24; Mavis E. Mate, *Women in Medieval English Society* (Cambridge: Cambridge University Press, 1999), p. 5.

4 Judith M. Bennett, "Medieval Women, Modern Women: Across the Great Divide," in *Culture and History, 1350–1600: Essays on English Communities, Identities and Writing*, ed. David Aers (Detroit, MI.: Wayne State University Press, 1992), pp. 147–75; Judith M. Bennett, *History Matters: Patriarchy and the Challenge of Feminism* (Philadelphia, PA.: University of Pennsylvania Press, 2006); Mavis E. Mate, *Daughters, Wives and Widows after the Black Death: Women in Sussex, 1350–1535* (Woodbridge, UK: Boydell Press, 1998), pp. 3–8; Barbara A. Hanawalt, *The Wealth of Wives: Women, Law, and Economy in Late Medieval London* (Oxford: Oxford University Press, 2007), pp. 161–62, 183–84; Diane Hutton, "Women in Fourteenth Century Shrewsbury," in *Women and Work in Pre-Industrial England*, eds. Lindsey Charles and Lorna Duffin (London: Croom Helm, 1985), p. 96.

5 Bennett, "Medieval Women, Modern Women," p. 163; S.H. Rigby, "Gendering the Black Death: Women in Later Medieval England," *Gender and History* 12 (2000):748–49; Mate, *Women in Medieval English Society*, p. 3.

6 Rigby, "Gendering the Black Death," pp. 746–48.

7 Bennett, "Medieval Women, Modern Women," pp. 160–62; Judith M. Bennett, *Ale, Beer, and Brewsters in England: Women's Work in a Changing World, 1300–1600* (New York: Oxford University Press, 1996), pp. 152–57; Sandy Bardsley, "Women's Work Reconsidered: Gender and Wage Differentiation in Late Medieval England," *Past and Present* 165 (1999):4–5, 28–29; Maryanne Kowalski and Judith M. Bennett, "Crafts, Guilds, and Women in the Middle Ages: Fifty Years after Marian K. Dale," in *Sisters and Workers in the Middle Ages*, ed. Judith M. Bennett (Chicago, IL.: University of Chicago Press, 1989), pp. 11–38.

8 Judith M. Bennett and Ruth Mazo Karras, "Women, Gender, and Medieval Historians," in *Oxford Handbook of Women and Gender*, p. 14.

9 Bennett, "Medieval Women, Modern Women," pp. 149–51, 164–65; Rigby, "Gendering the Black Death," pp. 748–49; Edith Ennen, *The Medieval Woman*, trans. Edmund Jephcott (Oxford: Basil Blackwell, 1989), 267–82.

10 Politically, however, the fortunes of women, especially aristocratic and urban women, are thought to have suffered in the late Middle Ages owing to the separation of political power and authority from the family. See Martha C. Howell, "Citizenship and Gender: Women's Political Status in Northern Medieval Cities," and McNamara and Wemple, "Power of Women Through the Family," in *Women and Power in the Middle Ages*, pp. 53–53, 96–97.

11 Barbara A. Hanawalt, "Peasant Women's Contribution to the Home Economy in Late Medieval England," in *Women and Work in Preindustrial Europe*, ed. Barbara A. Hanawalt (Bloomington, IN.: University of Indiana Press, 1986), pp. 16–17; Barbara A. Hanawalt, *The Ties that Bound: Peasant Families in Medieval England* (Oxford: Oxford University Press, 1986), pp. 107–23; Martha C. Howell, *Women, Production, and Patriarchy in Late Medieval Cities* (Chicago, IL.: University of Chicago Press, 1990), pp. 9–10, 27–29, 43–46; Goldberg, *Women, Work, and Life Cycle*, pp. 336–37.

12 Goldberg, *Women, Work, and Life Cycle*, p. 337. Goldberg proposed a three-stage model for women's employment opportunities in the late Middle Ages, with the first two stages, extending from the late fourteenth to the mid-fifteenth centuries, marking a

"steady growth" and then a "high point" in women's employment opportunities in the medieval economy, followed thereafter by the third stage, in which women were confined to "marginal and poorly paid occupations" after the onset of urban economic depression.

13 Bennett, "Medieval Women, Modern Women," p. 152; Judith M. Bennett, "Medieval Peasant Marriage: An Examination of Marriage License Fines in *Liber Gersumarum*," in *Pathways to Medieval Peasants*, ed. J.A. Raftis (*Papers in Mediaeval Studies*, 2, 1981), pp. 212–13. Coming at the question from a different perspective, Goldberg also argued that "it is no longer appropriate to assume that woman's 'natural' role was always in home, marriage, and family," but he assumed this because he believed that greater economic opportunities for women that allowed them to delay marriage and household formation were opened up in the wake of the plague, an assumption with which Bennett disagreed. See Goldberg, *Women, Work, and Life Cycle*, p. 360.

14 Power, *Medieval Women*, pp. 1–26. Power, however, saw "no apparent sense of inconsistency" in the fact that both exemplars of Mary and Eve were held up for medieval women simultaneously.

15 Bennett and Karras, "Women, Gender, and Medieval Historians," p. 1; Marty Newman Williams and Anne Echols, *Between Pit and Pedestal: Women in the Middle Ages* (Princeton, NJ.: Markus Wiener Publishers, 1994), p. 3; Joan Cadden, *Meanings of Sex Difference in the Middle Ages: Medicine, Science, and Culture* (Cambridge: Cambridge University Press, 1993), p. 3.

16 Berman, "Gender at the Medieval Millennium," pp. 545–60.

17 Tine de Moor and Jan Luiten van Zanden, "Girl Power: The European Marriage Pattern and Labour Markets in the North Sea Region in the Late Medieval and Early Modern Period," *Economic History Review* 63 (2010):14; Marjorie Keniston McIntosh, *Working Women in English Society, 1300–1620* (Cambridge: Cambridge University Press, 2005), pp. 28–37; Hanawalt, "Golden Ages," pp. 17–18; Kathryn Reyerson, "Urban Economies," in *Oxford Handbook of Women and Gender*, p. 298.

18 McIntosh, *Working Women*, pp. 28–42; Bennett, "Medieval Women, Modern Women," p. 159.

19 Mate, *Daughters, Wives and Widows*, p. 9.

20 Rigby, "Gendering the Black Death," pp. 750–51.

21 Bennett, "Medievalism and Feminism," pp. 321–23. Bennett claimed that feminism "has promoted neither doctrinaire nor biased scholarship," nor that it has "undermined the fundamental disinterestedness of medieval research," in spite of the fact that she admitted that her own interpretation of history "necessarily reflects my feminist politics". But then, in Bennett's view, and apparently in the view of all feminist historians, there is no such thing as "truth" in history, and "the interpretations of *all* historians reflect their political views". Personally, I disagree with this relativist approach (although Bennett refused to call it that), but that is a topic for another book.

22 See, in particular, Bennett, *History Matters*. A related question is how do we define patriarchy, beyond the simplistic understandings of popular culture? See Bennett, *Ale, Beer, and Brewsters in England*, pp. 152–57.

23 In the *Oxford Handbook of Women and Gender*, just four out of 39 contributors are men, while in the essay collection, *Women in Medieval Western European Culture*, five out of 25 contributors are men.

24 The pessimistic view, for example, is well represented in the works of Judith Bennett, Mavis Mate, and Maryanne Kowaleski, while the optimistic view was championed by Jeremy Goldberg, John Hatcher, and Rodney Hilton. There are, of course, exceptions, notably, Caroline Barron, who batted for the optimistic team, and David Herlihy, who swung for the pessimists.

25 Medieval physicians and natural philosophers understood the differences between the sexes primarily in terms of complexion (i.e., men were generally hot and dry, women cold and wet), but also in terms of shape (i.e., anatomy), and disposition, or temperament. The view that male and female bodies were essentially alike can be found in the early

medieval work of Isidore of Seville, basing himself on the second-century physician, Soranus. Galen's theory of the "one-sex body" was taken up by some Greek and Arabic writers, but did not have much influence on the European medical tradition. In fact, medieval medical writers were clearly uncomfortable with ambiguously-gendered individuals, such as hermaphrodites, and tended to pass over in silence same-sex acts that violated the "binary construct" of the sexes. See: Katherine Park, "Medicine and Natural Philosophy: Naturalistic Traditions," in *Oxford Handbook of Women and Gender*, pp. 84–98; Cadden, *Meanings of Sex Difference*, pp. 170–218.

26 Jo Ann McNamara, "The Herrenfrage: The Restructuring of the Gender System, 1050–1150," in *Medieval Masculinities: Regarding Men in the Middle Ages*, ed. Clare A. Lees (Minneapolis, MN.: University of Minnesota Press, 1994), pp. 3–29; Berman, "Gender at the Medieval Millennium," pp. 546–48.

27 Bennett and Karras, "Women, Gender, and Medieval Historians," pp. 5–7.

28 Rigby, "Gendering the Black Death," p. 746.

29 Shulamith Shahar, *The Fourth Estate: A History of Women in the Middle Ages*, trans. Chaya Galai (London: Routledge, 1983), p. 90; Judith M. Bennett, *Women in the Medieval English Countryside: Gender and Household in Brigstock Before the Plague* (Oxford: Oxford University Press, 1987), p. 103.

30 *Medieval Comic Tales*, ed. Peter Rickard (Totowa, NJ.: Rowman and Littlefield, 1974), pp. 89–94.

31 Edward Bliss Reed, *English Lyrical Poetry from its Origins to the Present Time* (New Haven, CT.: Yale University Press, 1914), p. 90.

32 *Reliquae Antiquae: Scraps from Ancient Manuscripts, Illustrating Chiefly Early English Literature and the English Language*, eds. Thomas Wright and James Orchard Haliwell, 2 vols (London, 1841–42), 2:196–99.

33 Roberta L. Krueger, "Towards Feminism: Christine de Pizan, Female Advocacy, and Women's Textual Communities in the Late Middle Ages and Beyond," in *Oxford Handbook of Women and Gender*, pp. 593–96. Christine is also famous for her *Debate on the Romance of the Rose*, in which she responded to misogynist elements in Jean de Meun's poem.

34 See Krueger, "Towards Feminism," p. 596, n. 23, for scholarly works that criticize Christine as an ambiguous or contradictory feminist figure.

35 Barbara Hanawalt has argued that medieval women were marginalized in terms of their physical space, i.e., being confined to the home or allowed out in public only under certain conditions. But her proof of this, that coroners' inquests reveal greater percentages of women killed in private spaces such as houses compared to men, has been challenged on the grounds that such deaths only reflect the danger inherent in certain tasks, whether performed in public or private, and not the degree to which men or women spent time in such spaces. The extent of spatial marginalization of women also may have varied greatly by social status and regional customs. See: Barbara A. Hanawalt, "At the Margin of Women's Space in Medieval Europe," in *Matrons and Marginal Women in Medieval Society*, eds. Robert R. Edwards and Vickie Ziegler (Woodbridge, UK: Boydell and Brewer, 1995), pp. 8–9; Barbara A. Hanawalt, "Peasant Women's Contribution to the Home Economy in Late Medieval England," in *Women and Work in Preindustrial Europe*, pp. 7–10; P.J.P. Goldberg, "The Public and the Private: Women in the Pre-Plague Economy," in *Thirteenth Century England, III*, eds. P.R. Coss and S.D. Lloyd (Woodbridge, UK: Boydell Press, 1991), pp. 75–89; Mate, *Women in Medieval English Society*, pp. 31–32; Sarah Rees Jones, "Public and Private Space and Gender in Medieval Europe," in *Oxford Handbook of Women and Gender*, pp. 250–52.

36 Bennett and Karras, "Women, Gender, and Medieval Historians," p. 10. Much of what Bennett and Karras encompass in women's wealth, such as the dowries women brought to marriage and the sale of their bodies as prostitutes, are covered in this chapter and in Chapter 5.

37 Howell, *Women, Production, and Patriarchy*, pp. 24, 180; Martha C. Howell, "Women, the Family Economy, and the Structures of Market Production in Cities of Northern

Europe during the Late Middle Ages," in *Women and Work in Preindustrial Europe*, pp. 209–10; David Herlihy, *Opera Muliebra: Women and Work in Medieval Europe* (Philadelphia, PA.: Temple University Press, 1990), pp. 186–91.

38 Howell, *Women, Production, and Patriarchy*, pp. 9–10; Howell, "Women, Family Economy, and Structures of Market Production," pp. 198–216; Barron, "Golden Age of Women," p. 40; Maryanne Kowaleski, "Women's Work in a Market Town: Exeter in the Late Fourteenth Century," in *Women and Work in Preindustrial Europe*, p. 152; Kay E. Lacey, "Women and Work in Fourteenth and Fifteenth Century London," in *Women and Work in Preindustrial England*, p. 24. Although he agreed with the basic outlines of Howell's thesis that saw a decline in women's work with the greater specialization and professionalization of the late medieval economy, David Herlihy saw domestication and household production as contributing to this decline, rather than alleviating it, owing to the fact that all household members "worked under the supervision and for the benefit of the usually male household head". See Herlihy, *Opera Muliebra*, pp. 186–88.

39 Howell, *Women, Production, and Patriarchy*, p. 161; Howell, "Women, Family Economy, and Structures of Market Production," pp. 213, 215. In the end, women were given no choice in the matter, because they were either formally excluded from participation in guilds (or from positions of political power within guilds), or else formal work rules were imposed that "conflicted with women's obligations to their families".

40 Howell, *Women, Production, and Patriarchy*, pp. 178–79; Howell, "Women, Family Economy, and Structures of Market Production," pp. 209–10, 213, 215; Herlihy, *Opera Muliebra*, pp. 187, 190–91; Kowaleski, "Women's Work," pp. 145–46.

41 Kowaleski, "Women's Work," pp. 155–58; Goldberg, *Women, Work, and Life Cycle*, p. 336; Diane Hutton, "Women in Fourteenth Century Shrewsbury," in *Women and Work in Pre-Industrial England*, pp. 84–97.

42 Kathryn L. Reyerson, "Women in Business in Medieval Montpellier," in *Women and Work in Preindustrial Europe*, pp. 137–38.

43 R.W. Unger, "Technical Change in the Brewing Industry in Germany, the Low Countries and England in the Late Middle Ages," *Journal of European Economic History* 21 (1992):281–313.

44 Bennett, *Ale, Beer, and Brewsters in England*, pp. 37–59, 150; Judith M. Bennett, "The Village Ale-Wife: Women and Brewing in Fourteenth-Century England," in *Women and Work in Preindustrial Europe*, pp. 20–36; McIntosh, *Working Women*, pp. 145–56; Hanawalt, *Wealth of Wives*, pp. 181–82; Mate, *Women in Medieval English Society*, pp. 38–43; Howell, "Women, Family Economy, and Market Production," pp. 215–16.

45 Howell, *Women, Production, and Patriarchy*, pp. 70–94; Howell, "Women, Family Economy, and Market Production," pp. 215–16; McIntosh, *Working Women in English Society*, pp. 210–38; P.J.P. Goldberg, "Female Labour, Service and Marriage in the Late Medieval Urban North," *Northern History* 22 (1986):32–33; Herlihy, *Opera Muliebra*, p. 190; Benjamin R. McRee and Trisha K. Dent, "Working Women in the Medieval City," in *Women in Medieval Western European Culture*, pp. 252–54; Kowaleski, "Women's Work," pp. 149–50.

46 Judith M. Bennett, "Public Power and Authority in the Medieval English Countryside," and Howell, "Citizenship and Gender," in *Women and Power in the Middle Ages*, pp. 18–29, 37–54; Howell, *Women, Production, and Patriarchy*, pp. 178–79; Howell, "Women, Family Economy, and Structures of Market Production," pp. 210, 213, 215; Kowaleski, "Women's Work," pp. 150, 153–54; Ennen, *Medieval Woman*, p. 268; Goldberg, "Female Labour, Service and Marriage," p. 32. Howell argued that women's exclusion from city government and positions of public authority was a recent development in the late Middle Ages, owing to a "constitutional innovation" in which political power was separated from family units and reserved for individual men "in the interests of civic peace, unity, and independence".

47 Gervase Rosser, *The Art of Solidarity in the Middle Ages: Guilds in England, 1250–1550* (Oxford: Oxford University Press, 2015), pp. 110–11; Howell, *Women, Production, and*

Patriarchy, pp. 124–58; Howell, "Women, Family Economy, and Structures of Market Production," pp. 210–14; Hanawalt, *Wealth of Wives*, pp. 177–80; Mate, *Women in Medieval English Society*, pp. 52–53. Initially, women were not excluded from these guilds but were frozen out of political positions that controlled them. This was because many of their skills were still necessary to the production of these goods, which had "long been the preserve of women from 'good' families".

48 McRee and Dent, "Working Women in the Medieval City," p. 252; Goldberg, *Women, Work, and Life Cycle*, pp. 337, 347, 354; Goldberg, "Female Labour, Service and Marriage," pp. 34–36; Howell, "Women, Family Economy, and Structures of Market Production," p. 213; Herlihy, *Opera Muliebra*, pp. 177–80; Lacey, "Women and Work," p. 25. The typical example cited is the 1461 guild ordinance of Bristol weavers that excluded wives, daughters, and female servants from being employed in the trade, on the grounds that the "kings' men," i.e., the veterans of his wars, should not "lack employment". But even earlier examples are available, such as the regulations in Florence in the 1320s, Strasbourg in 1330, Ghent in 1374, Cologne in 1378 and 1397, and Paris in 1397 and 1428. By 1450, even the five all-female guilds in Paris were "absorbed into predominately male corporations".

49 Hutton, "Women in Fourteenth Century Shrewsbury," pp. 83–84. Hutton's conclusion was that "the most one can say about such regulations is that they represent a situation which the civic and craft elite would have liked to bring into existence".

50 McRee and Dent, "Working Women in the Medieval City," pp. 254–55; Bennett, "Medieval Women, Modern Women," p. 159; Herlihy, *Opera Muliebra*, p. 180. Herlihy, for example, pointed out that guilds began restricting membership to women even before the Black Death.

51 McRee and Dent, "Working Women in the Medieval City," pp. 253–54.

52 Bennett, "Medieval Women, Modern Women," pp. 163–65; Bennett, *Women in the Medieval English Countryside*, pp. 185–86, 197–98; Kowaleski, "Women's Work," pp. 150, 153–58; Howell, "Women, Family Economy, and Structures of Market Production," p. 212. This may be why women were not excluded from guilds when members of the *Gaffeln* took over the government of Cologne in 1396, because women could simply be excluded from positions of political power, rather than from economic activity altogether.

53 Christopher Dyer, *Standards of Living in the Later Middle Ages: Social Change in England, c. 1200–1520* (Cambridge: Cambridge University Press, 1989), pp. 151–87; Christopher Dyer, *An Age of Transition? Economy and Society in England in the Later Middle Ages* (Oxford: Clarendon Press, 2005), pp. 128–32.

54 McRee and Dent, "Working Women in the Medieval City," pp. 241–47; Reyerson, "Women in Business," pp. 119–37; McIntosh, *Working Women*, pp. 45–238; Herlihy, *Opera Muliebra*, pp. 142–77; Kowaleski, "Women's Work," pp. 147–54; Lacey, "Women and Work," pp. 49–57; Hutton, "Women in Fourteenth Century Shrewsbury," pp. 89–96; Williams and Echols, *Between Pit and Pedestal*, pp. 51–63. Women's participation seems to have been very limited in banking and lending, merchant trade and commerce; leather-, metal- and wood-working; butchery; baking; and real estate, even though they did sometimes have a presence.

55 However, there are some caveats to such a generalization. One is that women in Italy may have married at a later age than previously supposed, because tax surveys (such as the *Catasto* of Florence) recorded only what fathers reported of their daughters, namely, the ages at which women *should* marry (i.e., in their teenage years), rather than the ages at which they actually *were* married. Second, towards the end of the Middle Ages, i.e., the fifteenth century, parents in Italy may have favored a later age at which their daughters got married (based on such evidence as wills proved in Venice), out of a "new fatherly concern for daughters' vocational preferences". See: Anthony Molho, "Deception and Marriage Strategy in Renaissance Florence: The Case of Women's Ages," *Renaissance Quarterly* 41 (1988):204; Stanley Chojnacki, "The Power of Love: Wives and Husbands in Late Medieval Venice," in *Women and Power in the Middle Ages*, p. 133.

56 McRee and Dent, "Working Women in the Medieval City," pp. 250–51; Reyerson, "Urban Economies," pp. 299–301; De Moor and Van Zanden, "Girl Power," pp. 12–14; Christiane Klapisch-Zuber, "Women Servants in Florence during the Fourteenth and Fifteenth Centuries," in *Women and Work in Preindustrial Europe*, pp. 70–75; Goldberg, *Women, Work, and Life Cycle* , pp. 330, 333–45, 360–61; Maryanne Kowaleski, "Singlewomen in Medieval and Early Modern Europe: The Demographic Perspective," in *Singlewomen in the European Past*, eds. Judith M. Bennett and Amy M. Froide (Philadelphia, PA: University of Pennsylvania Press, 1999), pp. 41–45, 50–51, 63; R.M. Smith, "Geographical Diversity in the Resort to Marriage in Late Medieval Europe: Work, Reputation and Unmarried Females in the Household Formation Systems of Northern and Southern Europe," in *Woman is a Worthy Wight: Women in English Society, c. 1200–1500*, ed. P.J.P. Goldberg (Wolfeboro Falls, N.H.: Alan Sutton, 1992), pp. 16–59.

57 Hanawalt, "Peasant Women's Contribution," pp. 1–17; H. Graham, "A Woman's Work": Labour and Gender in the Late Medieval Countryside," in *Woman is a Worthy Wight*, pp. 126–48. Howell argued that in a more urban setting with a strong market economy, "so strict a division of labor was economically unnecessary, because the "family could buy what it did not produce," but Hutton found that much division of labor still held true in Shrewsbury. On the other hand, Miriam Müller argued that "there was no division of labour according to sex" in medieval peasant society, on the basis of manorial customs that detailed the labor services expected of tenants. See: Howell, *Women, Production, and Patriarchy*, p. 28; Hutton, "Women in Fourteenth Century Shrewsbury," pp. 84–97; Miriam Müller, "Peasant Women, Agency and Status in Mid-Thirteenth- to Late Fourteenth-Century England: Some Reconsiderations," in *Married Women and the Law in Premodern Northwest Europe*, eds. Cordelia Beattie and Matthew Frank Stevens (Woodbridge, UK: Boydell Press, 2013), p. 99. In general, one can say that, except for the work of Hanawalt and Bennett, most of the scholarly research on medieval women's work has naturally focused on towns, where municipal archives survive, to the detriment of our picture of women's work in the countryside.

58 R.H. Hilton, *The English Peasantry in the Later Middle Ages* (Oxford: Clarendon Press, 1975), pp. 101–2; Hanawalt, *Ties that Bound*, pp. 147–48; Mate, *Women in Medieval English Society*, pp. 16, 28; Bennett, *Women in the Medieval English Countryside*, pp. 115–19, 186; Jane Whittle, "Rural Economies," in *Oxford Handbook of Women and Gender*, pp. 316–20; Simon A.C. Penn, "Female Wage-Earners in Late Fourteenth-Century England," *Agricultural History Review* 35 (1987):2, 7, 13.

59 Hanawalt, "Peasant Women's Contribution," p. 10; McIntosh, *Working Women*, pp. 196–98; Reyerson, "Women in Business," p. 137.

60 McIntosh, *Working Women*, pp. 36–61, 130–32; Kowaleski, "Women's Work," pp. 153–54; Kim M. Phillips, *Medieval Maidens: Young Women and Gender in England, 1270–1540* (Manchester, UK: Manchester University Press, 2003), pp. 131–34. Young singlewomen could be apprenticed in trades, such as the silk industry in London, or the food, textile, and precious metalwork trades in Montpellier, but their numbers seem to have been small and usually outside the formal guild system. In late fourteenth-century Exeter, women rarely received formal training in any trade, since they could not enter the "freedom," an organization that controlled all apprenticed trades in town, although they could receive informal training, such as a wife might have received from her tradesman husband. See: Reyerson, "Women in Business," pp. 120–21; Kowaleski, "Women's Work," p. 155.

61 This was particularly true of the luxury trade, which required substantial capital investment. See Reyerson, "Women in Business," p. 122; Howell, "Women, Family Economy, and Structures of Market Production," pp. 210–12; Goldberg, "Female Labour, Service and Marriage," pp. 33–34.

62 The advantage of *femme sole* status seems to have been that it gave women access to credit and allowed them to hire their own apprentices, although it could also make them liable for debts. There are also indications that women may have adopted *femme sole* status

simply to avoid the debts of their husbands, or husbands the debts of their wives. See: Hanawalt, *Wealth of Wives*, pp. 169–73; Kowaleski, "Women's Work," p. 146; Lacey, "Women and Work," pp. 46–48; Marjorie K. McIntosh, "The Benefits and Drawbacks of *Femme Sole* Status in England, 1300–1630," *Journal of British Studies* 44 (2005):410–39.

63 Bennett, "Medieval Women, Modern Women," p. 160; Kowaleski, "Women's Work," p. 156; Lacey, "Women and Work," pp. 45–46, 57; Ennen, *Medieval Woman*, pp. 150–51; Barbara A. Hanawalt, "Remarriage as an Option for Urban and Rural Widows in Late Medieval England," in *Wife and Widow in Late Medieval England*, ed. Sue Sheridan Walker (Ann Arbor, MI.: Univeristy of Michigan Press, 1993), pp. 158–59. By the fifteenth century, however, widows' rights to continue in their husbands' businesses were being curtailed in many cities. See Howell, "Women, Family Economy, and Structures of Market Production," p. 213.

64 Ennen, *Medieval Woman*, p. 159; Goldberg, *Women, Work, and Life Cycle*, p. 355. For a detailed examination of one city's laws relating to women's work (in this case, London), see Lacey, "Women and Work," pp. 36–40, 42–45.

65 Hutton, "Women in Fourteenth Century Shrewsbury," p. 97.

66 Hanawalt, "Peasant Women's Contribution," pp. 3–17; Hanawalt, *Ties that Bound*, pp. 141–55; Hutton, "Women in Fourteenth Century Shrewsbury," p. 97; Müller, "Peasant Women, Agency and Status," pp. 98–99.

67 Bennett and Karras, "Women, Gender, and Medieval Historians," p. 10; Hanawalt, *Wealth of Wives*, pp. 70–82.

68 Goldberg, *Women, Work, and Life Cycle*, pp. 336–37, 345, 352, 361; Goldberg, "Female Labour, Service and Marriage," pp. 18–38; Barron, "Golden Age," pp. 35–58; Lacey, "Women and Work," p. 25; Müller, "Peasant Women, Agency and Status," p. 102; Jim Bolton, "'World Upside Down': Plague as an Agent of Economic and Social Change," in *The Black Death in England*, eds. W.M. Ormrod and P.G. Lindley (Donnington, UK: Shaun Tyas, 2003), pp. 70–77. Lacey's other possible explanation for women's greater participation in the economy after 1350 is that there simply was a "general increase in legal documentation" recording their work.

69 It is often assumed that plague was "gender-selective" for women on the grounds of their greater exposure to the domestic environment of rats and fleas and their frailer health, but both the archival and archaeological evidence for sex differentials is mixed: Evidence can be found that plague was selective for women, for men, or for neither. There is some solid evidence, however, that pregnant women were especially prone to the disease. See: Sandy Bardsley, "Missing Women: Sex Ratios in England, 1000–1500," *Journal of British Studies* 53 (2014):288–89; John Mullan, "Mortality, Gender, and the Plague of 1361–2 on the Estate of the Bishop of Winchester," *Cardiff Historical Papers* (Cardiff, 2007–8), pp. 22–33; Sharon N. DeWitte, "Sex Differentials in Frailty in Medieval England," *American Journal of Physical Anthropology* 143 (2010):285–97; Sharon N. DeWitte, "The Effect of Sex on Risk of Mortality During the Black Death in London, A.D. 1349–1350," *American Journal of Physical Anthropology* 139 (2009): 222–32; Michel Signoli, Isabelle Séguy, Jean-Noël Biraben, and Olivier Dutour, "Paleo-demography and Historical Demography in the Context of an Epidemic: Plague in Provence in the Eighteenth Century," *Population* 57 (2002):838–39; Stephen R. Ell, "Three Days in October of 1630: Detailed Examination of Mortality during an Early Modern Plague Epidemic in Venice," *Reviews of Infectious Diseases* 11 (1989):132–33, 135–37; Mary F. Hollingsworth and T.H. Hollingsworth, "Plague Mortality Rates by Age and Sex in the Parish of St. Botolph's without Bishopsgate, London, 1603," *Population Studies* 25 (1971):144–45; Ole J. Benedictow, *The Black Death, 1346–1353: The Complete History* (Woodbridge, UK: Boydell Press, 2004), pp. 266–67.

70 Maryanne Kowaleski, "Medieval People in Town and Country: New Perspectives from Demography and Bioarchaeology," *Speculum* 89 (2014):573–600; Bardsley, "Missing Women," pp. 278–82, 286–94; Mate, *Daughters, Wives, and Widows*, pp. 38–39; Goldberg, *Women, Work and Life Cycle*, p. 224; Goldberg, "Female Labour, Service and Marriage," pp. 19–20; Ruth Mazo Karras, "The Regulation of Sexuality in the Late

Middle Ages: England and France," *Speculum* 86 (2011): 1029. Bardsley calculated that men outnumbered women by a ratio of 1.13:1 based on the 1377 poll tax returns, and by 1.17–1.19:1 based on archaeological data from cemeteries, some of which predated the Black Death.

71 Hanawalt, *Wealth of Wives*, p. 162.

72 Howell, *Women, Production, and Patriarchy*, pp. 85–86; Howell, "Women, Family Economy, and Structures of Market Production," pp. 210–12.

73 Bennett, *Ale, Beer, and Brewsters*, pp. 147–48. Another factor may have been that women were frozen out of credit markets, access to which was required in order to upgrade to beer making. See Chris Briggs, "Empowered or Marginalized? Rural Women and Credit in Later Thirteenth- and Fourteenth-Century England," *Continuity and Change* 19 (2004):13–43.

74 McIntosh, *Working Women in English Society*, pp. 155–56.

75 In southern Europe, a much greater proportion of domestic servants were older women, perhaps owing to cultural taboos against young girls leaving home. For example, in Florence throughout the fifteenth and early sixteenth centuries, married and widowed women made up about half or more of all female domestics. See Klapisch-Zuber, "Women Servants in Florence," p. 63; Christiane Klapisch-Zuber, *Women, Family, and Ritual in Renaissance Italy*, trans. Lydia G. Cochrane (Chicago, IL.: University of Chicago Press, 1985), pp. 172–73.

76 McIntosh, *Working Women in English Society*, pp. 46–47. Based on poll-tax returns, between 20–30 percent of adult English men and women were servants, although this percentage was higher in towns and lower in the countryside. In the city of York, a third of all households employed servants, while at the manor of Halesowen in Worcestershire, as many as 40 percent of tenants had servants. See: Goldberg, "Female Labour, Service and Marriage," p. 21; Zvi Razi, "Family, Land and Village Community in Later Medieval England," *Past and Present* 93 (1981):31.

77 Goldberg, *Women, Work, and Life Cycle*, pp. 336–37; Goldberg, "Female Labour, Service and Marriage," pp. 21–36.

78 Goldberg, *Women, Work, and Life Cycle*, pp. 223, 230, 337–38, 355, 358; Goldberg, "Female Labour, Service and Marriage," pp. 22–23. In his article (published earlier than his book), Goldberg mentioned "deposition evidence relating to nearly 400 witnesses," but it is not clear if these were all single females. Goldberg himself acknowledged the "unsatisfactory" and "difficult" nature of his evidence, namely, its sample size, as well as that regional variations made the real picture more complex, such that he characterized his own analysis as "tentative," "impressionistic," and in the nature of a "hypothesis". Another historian who has studied the York cause papers evidence, Charles Donahue, concluded that they were biased in favor of "the wealthy, the powerful, and the persistent among the litigants". Others have commented on the "paucity of evidence for female domestic service" in the late Middle Ages. Kim Phillips' view was that country girls had plenty of work, including wage labor, to do around the farm to keep them employed at home, rather than migrate to the city to find work, if they so chose. See: Charles Donahue, Jr., "Female Plaintiffs in Marriage Cases in the Court of York in the Later Middle Ages: What Can We Learn from the Numbers?" in *Wife and Widow in Medieval England*, ed. Sue Sheridan Walker (Ann Arbor, MI.: Univeristy of Michigan Press, 1993), p. 185; Ann Julia Kettle, "Ruined Maids: Prostitutes and Servant Girls in Later Mediaeval England," in *Matrons and Marginal Women in Medieval Society*, eds. Robert R. Edwards and Vickie Ziegler (Woodbridge, UK: Boydell Press, 1995), p. 30; Phillips, *Medieval Maidens*, pp. 128–29; Mark Bailey, "Demographic Decline in Late Medieval England: Some Thoughts on Recent Research," *Economic History Review*, n.s., 49 (1996):7.

79 Phillips, *Medieval Maidens*, pp. 130–31; Mate, *Women in Medieval English Society*, pp. 57–59.

80 Bailey, "Demographic Decline," pp. 11–14; Simon A.C. Penn and Christopher Dyer, "Wages and Earnings in Late Medieval England; Evidence from the Enforcement of the Labour Laws," *Economic History Review*, 2nd ser., 43 (1990): 366–69, 375; Christopher

Dyer, *Making a Living in the Middle Ages: The People of Britain, 850–1520* (New Haven: Yale University Press, 2002), p. 277.

81 Jane Humphries and Jacob Weisdorf, "The Wages of Women in England, 1260–1850," *Journal of Economic History* 75 (2015):405–47.

82 Humphries and Weisdorf, "Wages of Women in England," pp. 407–19; Sandy Bardsley, "Women's Work Reconsidered: Gender and Wage Differentiation in Late Medieval England," *Past and Present* 165 (1999):11–22; John Hatcher, "Debate: Women's Work Reconsidered: Gender and Wage Differentiation in Late Medieval England," *Past and Present* 173 (2001):191–98; Sandy Bardsley, "Reply," *Past and Present* 173 (2001):199–202; Penn, "Female Wage-Earners," pp. 2–14; Mate, *Women in Medieval English Society*, pp. 28–31; Mavis E. Mate, "Work and Leisure," in *A Social History of England, 1200–1500*, eds. Rosemary Horrox and W. Mark Ormrod (Cambridge: Cambridge University Press, 2006), p. 282; Goldberg, *Women, Work and Life Cycle*, p. 337; Richard Britnell, *Britain and Ireland, 1050–1530: Economy and Society* (Oxford: Oxford University Press, 2004), p. 378; Hilton, *English Peasantry*, pp. 102–3.

83 Humphries and Weisdorf, "Wages of Women in England," p. 409; John Langdon, "Minimum Wages and Unemployment Rates in Medieval England: The Case of Old Woodstock, Oxfordshire, 1256–1357," in *Commercial Activity, Markets and Entrepreneurs in the Middle Ages: Essays in Honour of Richard Britnell*, eds. Ben Dodds and Christian D. Liddy (Woodbridge, UK: Boydell Press, 2011), pp. 35–40.

84 Humphries and Weisdorf, "Wages of Women in England," pp. 409–10.

85 Humphries and Weisdorf, "Wages of Women in England," pp. 424, 428, 431.

86 Humphries and Weisdorf, "Wages of Women in England," p. 419; Bennett, "Medieval Women, Modern Women," pp. 162–63; Bolton, "'World Upside Down'," pp. 76–77.

87 Hilton, *English Peasantry*, pp. 102–3; Benedictow, *Black Death*, pp. 382, 389–90; Klapisch-Zuber, "Women Servants in Florence," pp. 65–66; De Moor and Van Zanden, "Girl Power," p. 13; Penn, "Female Wage-Earners," p. 8. Some exceptions include salaries of female domestic servants in Florence, which more than doubled between 1348 and 1470, overtaking even those of male servants, while in England, wages of female thatcher assistants tripled between 1348 and 1400 (from 1 to 3d.), while those of male thatchers increased by only a third (from 3 to 4d.).

88 Hatcher, "Debate: Women's Work Reconsidered," pp. 191–98; Bardsley, "Reply," pp. 199–202; Mate, *Medieval Women in English Society*, pp. 28–31; Mate, "Work and Leisure," p. 282; Goldberg, *Women, Work and Life Cycle*, p. 337; Britnell, *Britain and Ireland*, p. 378. The attractiveness of women's cheap labor for employers apparently also held true in the urban trades, at least until the mid-fifteenth century.

89 Humphries and Weisdorf, "Wages of Women in England," pp. 424–26, 430.

90 Humphries and Weisdorf, "Wages of Women in England," pp. 425–26.

91 Humphries and Weisdorf, "Wages of Women in England," pp. 425, 431.

92 Humphries and Weisdorf, "Wages of Women in England," pp. 418, 420.

93 Humphries and Weisdorf, "Wages of Women in England," pp. 420–23.

94 Humphries and Weisdorf, "Wages of Women in England," pp. 418, 431.

95 Humphries and Weisdorf, "Wages of Women in England," p. 430.

96 De Moor and Van Zanden, "Girl Power," pp. 14–15; Humphries and Weisdorf, "Wages of Women in England," pp. 425–26; Bolton, "'World Upside Down'," pp. 76–77. Humphries and Weisdorf were decidedly more pessimistic as to the "'girl-powered' economic breakthrough" for women in the aftermath of the Black Death, as compared to De Moor and Van Zanden and Bolton.

97 Cordelia Beattie, *Medieval Single Women: The Politics of Social Classification in Late Medieval England* (Oxford: Oxford University Press, 2007), p. 15.

98 Scholarly works that focus on medieval single women include: Beattie, *Medieval Single Women*; Phillips, *Medieval Maidens*; and *Singlewomen in the European Past*. See also the comments of Mate, *Daughters, Wives and Widows*, p. 45.

99 Heath Dillard, *Daughters of the Reconquest: Women in Castilian Town Society, 1100–1300* (Cambridge: Cambridge University Press, 1984), p. 19.

100 Beattie, *Medieval Single Women*, pp. 24–31.

101 Mate, *Daughters, Wives and Widows*, pp. 37–38; Klapisch-Zuber, *Women, Family, and Ritual*, pp. 170–72. This is borne out by figures from the Florentine *Catasto*, which show that 10 percent of women from the ruling class remained unmarried, whereas just 3 percent of women from the lower classes did so.

102 Beattie, *Medieval Single Women*, p. 23; Ruth Mazo Karras, "Sex and the Singlewoman," in *Medieval Single Women: The Politics of Social Classification in Late Medieval England*, ed. Cordelia Beattie (Oxford: Oxford University Press, 2007), p. 127; Phillips, *Medieval Maidens*, pp. 146–62.

103 Judith M. Bennett, *A Medieval Life: Cecilia Penifader of Brigstock, c.1295–1344* (Boston, MA.: McGraw Hill College, 1999).

104 Bennett, "Public Power and Authority," pp. 21–23.

105 Kowaleski, "Medieval People in Town and Country," pp. 579–81. These figures include both women who never married and widows.

106 Goldberg, *Women, Work, and Life Cycle*, pp. 259, 262–63, 271, 273, 325–29, 339, 345, 352; Goldberg, "Female Labour, Service and Marriage," pp. 23–27; Bennett, "Medieval Peasant Marriage," pp. 197–208, 213–24; Kettle, "Ruined Maids," pp. 20–21. The assumption here is that women in urban settings, particularly those enrolled in domestic service to another family, were freer of parental influence and thus could have exercised greater independence and freedom with respect to marriage than rural women living at home. However, Bennett found that peasant women on the manors of Ramsey Abbey between 1398 and 1458 paid their own *merchets* in equal proportion to fathers, and that they were likely using their own financial resources to do so, perhaps from wage labor. However, there is evidence that women commonly paid their own *merchets* even before the Black Death. Also, there may be too little evidence on female domestic service to determine if singlewomen were indeed seeking out such work in order "to amass their own dowries, conduct their own courtships, and arrange their own marriages free of family pressures". See: E.D. Jones, "The Medieval Leyrwite: A Historical Note on Female Fornication," *English Historical Review* 107 (1992):949; Kettle, "Ruined Maids," p. 30.

107 Mate, *Daughters, Wives and Widows*, pp. 39–40; Mate, *Women in Medieval English Society*, pp. 57–59; Reyerson, "Women in Business," p. 137; Kowaleski, "Singlewomen in Medieval and Early Modern Europe," pp. 45–51; Bolton, "'World Upside Down,'" pp. 37–38. Marriage may not have been as crucial for young men in the city as opposed to the country, because a family was not as essential to running a trade as it was to running a farm. By contrast, a study of suits brought in the church court of York to enforce marriage contracts suggests that, during the fourteenth century, women especially valued marriage, certainly relative to men, since they made up most of the litigants (73 percent). By the fifteenth century, however, women seemed to have valued marriage less and remaining single more, since they now made up a lower percentage of litigants (61 percent). This was perhaps due to greater economic wealth and stability (i.e., rising real wages) that was especially pronounced between 1375 and 1450, which made it easier for women to live without a husband. See: Donahue, "Female Plaintiffs," pp. 195–205; Herlihy and Klapisch-Zuber, *Tuscans and their Families*, p. 221.

108 Phillips, *Medieval Maidens*, p. 122.

109 Mavis Mate has commented that, "A single woman, eking out a living, and faced with an offer of marriage, would surely have had to find the suitor very unattractive before she rejected him". The extremely low status of domestic service is also borne out by Maryanne Kowaleski's research on female workers in late fourteenth-century Exeter, where she found servants were mostly young, unmarried immigrants referred to only by their first name and that of their employer, and whose most common "alternative occupation" was prostitution. Mate and Kowaleski have also observed that singlewomen rarely were apprenticed to a trade. See Mate, *Daughters, Wives and Widows*, p. 39; Mate, *Women in Medieval English Society*, p. 57; Kowaleski, "Women's Work," pp. 153–55, Phillips, *Medieval Maidens*, p. 130.

110 Georges Duby, *Love and Marriage in the Middle Ages*, trans. Jane Dunnett (Chicago, IL.: University of Chicago Press, 1994), pp. 22–35; Williams and Echols, *Between Pit and Pedestal*, p. 70; H.E. Hallam, *Rural England, 1066–1348* (Brighton, Sussex, and Atlantic Highlands, NJ.: Harvester Press and Humanities Press, 1981), pp. 255–56. Duby concluded that: "Everything therefore conspired to prevent there being a passionate relationship between the married couple comparable to what we regard as conjugal love; instead there was a cold relationship of inequality which consisted at best in condescending love on the part of the husband, and at best timorous respect of the part of his wife" (p. 60). However, Duby seemed to restrict himself to marriages in an aristocratic milieu.

111 Duby, *Love and Marriage*, pp. 56–63; Bennett, *Women in the Medieval English Countryside*, p. 140; Williams and Echols, *Between Pit and Pedestal*, p. 85.

112 Hilton, *English Peasantry*, p. 105; Bennett, "Medieval Peasant Marriage," pp. 212–14; Goldberg, *Women, Work, and Life Cycle*, pp. 248–50; Williams and Echols, *Between Pit and Pedestal*, pp. 71–72. The picture of peasant society that we get from the inquisitorial register of Jacques Fournier, who investigated the villagers of Montaillou, shows both arranged marriages as well as love matches. See Emmanuel Le Roy Ladurie, *Montaillou: The Promised Land of Error*, trans. Barbara Bray (New York: Vintage Books, 1979), pp. 179–91.

113 Chojnacki, "Power of Love," pp. 134–38.

114 Chojnacki, "Power of Love," p. 132. See also Martha Howell, "The Properties of Marriage in Late Medieval Europe: Commercial Wealth and the Creation of Modern Marriage," in *Love, Marriage and Family Ties in the Later Middle Ages*, eds. Isabel Davis, Miriam Müller, and Sarah Rees Jones (Turnhout, Belgium: Brepols, 2003), pp. 17–61. Howell argued that the creation of the modern, companionate marriage went hand-in-hand with the "explosion of commercial wealth" in the late Middle Ages, whereby wealth was more "moveable" or flexible and could be shared and passed down between husbands and wives.

115 Ruth Mazo Karras, *Sexuality in Medieval Europe: Doing unto Others*, 2nd edn. (London and New York: Routledge, 2012) p. 78; Christopher N.L. Brooke, *The Medieval Idea of Marriage* (Oxford: Oxford University Press, 1989), p. 161.

116 Licenses to marry a husband from outside the village made up 26 percent of all *merchets* purchased on the manors of Ramsey Abbey between 1398 and 1458. See Bennett, "Medieval Peasant Marriage," pp. 197, 200.

117 Mate, *Women in Medieval English Society*, p. 60; Goldberg, *Women, Work, and Life Cycle*, pp. 243–51; Goldberg, "Female Labour, Service and Marriage," pp. 23–27; Karras, "Regulation of Sexuality," pp. 1029–39.

118 De Moor and Van Zanden, "Girl Power," pp. 5–6; Ruth Mazo Karras, "The Christianization of Medieval Marriage," in *Christianity and Culture in the Middle Ages: Essays to Honor John van Engen*, eds. David C. Mengel and Lisa Wolverton (Notre Dame, IN.: Notre Dame University Press, 2015), p. 12; J. Murray, "Individualism and Consensual Marriage: Some Evidence from Medieval England," in *Women, Marriage, and Family in Medieval Christendom: Essays in Memory of Michael M. Sheehan*, eds. C.M. Rousseau and J.T. Rosenthal (Kalamzaoo, MI.: Medieval Institute Publications, Western Michigan University, 1998), pp. 140–44; Dillard, *Daughters of the Reconquest*, pp. 37–41.

119 Bennett, *Women in the Medieval English Countryside*, p. 102; Hanawalt, "Peasant Women's Contribution," pp. 14–15; Barbara A. Hanawalt, "The Widow's Mite: Provisions for Medieval London Widows," in *Upon My Husband's Death: Widows in the Literature and Histories of Medieval Europe*, ed. Louise Mirrer (Ann Arbor, MI.: University of Michigan Press, 1992), p. 26; Chojnacki, "Power of Love," pp. 132–33. Hanawalt found that 86 percent of husbands making a will proved in the Husting Court of London during the fourteenth and fifteenth centuries named their wives as executors.

120 Chojnacki, "Power of Love," pp. 127–28.

121 This is from Ballad 26, available in *Oevres Poétiques de Christine de Pisan* (Paris: Firmin Didot, 1891), p. 237.
122 Hanawalt, *Wealth of Wives*, p. 82.
123 Ennen, *Medieval Woman*, pp. 27–28, 32; Helen M. Jewell, *Women in Dark Age and Early Medieval Europe, c.500–1200* (New York: Palgrave Macmillan, 2007), pp. 37–39; Helen M. Jewell, *Women in Late Medieval and Reformation Europe, 1200–1550* (New York: Palgrave Macmillan, 2007), pp. 31–32; McNamara and Wemple, "Power of Women Through the Family," pp. 86–87, 96.
124 Ennen, *Medieval Woman*, pp. 25–26; Jewell, *Women in Dark Age and Early Medieval Europe*, p. 38; Jewell, *Women in Late Medieval and Reformation Europe*, p. 33–34; Kathryn Reyerson and Thomas Kuehn, "Women and Law in France and Italy," in *Women in Medieval Western European Culture*, ed. Linda E. Mitchell (New York: Garland Publishing, 1999), pp. 132, 138.
125 Bennett, *Women in Medieval English Countryside*, pp. 110–14; Lacey, "Women and Work," p. 26; Julius Kirshner, "Materials for a Gilded Cage: Non-Dotal Assets in Florence, 1300–1500," in *The Family in Italy from Antiquity to the Present*, eds. David I. Kertzer and Richard P. Saller (New Haven, CT.: Yale University Press, 1991), pp. 184–85; Dillard, *Daughters of the Reconquest*, p. 77. In some places, such as northwestern Portugal, wives were allowed to retain control over their own personal property even after marriage, while in southern France, wives may have had "access to movables and to real property acquired after marriages" owing to laws of joint ownership. See: Reyerson and Kuehn, "Women and Law in France and Italy," p. 133; Kirshner, "Materials for a Gilded Cage," p. 206.
126 Jewell, *Women in Late Medieval and Reformation Europe*, p. 33; Susan Mosher Stuard, "Brideprice, Dowry, and Other Marital Assigns," in *Oxford Handbook of Women and Gender*, pp. 151–56; Herlihy and Klapisch-Zuber, *Tuscans and their Families*, pp. 223–26; Donald E. Queller and Thomas F. Madden, "Father of the Bride: Fathers, Daughters, and Dowries in Late Medieval and Early Renaissance Venice," *Renaissance Quarterly* 46 (1993):688–99, 706–7; Dillard, *Daughters of the Reconquest*, p. 53. This dowry inflation was largely driven by a shortage of eligible grooms and non-paternal bequests to the bride, largely made by female relatives motivated more by "affection rather than calculation" and which largely rendered legal limits to dowries ineffective.
127 This represented a turnaround from the position of early Church fathers, who often viewed marriage as a last resort for those unable to stomach virginity. In the words of St. Paul, "Better to marry than to burn". See: Brooke, *Medieval Idea of Marriage*, p. 49; Conor McCarthy, *Marriage in Medieval England: Law, Literature and Practice* (Woodbridge, UK: Boydell Press, 2004), p. 107–8; Jo Ann McNamara, "Chaste Marriage and Clerical Celibacy," in *Sexual Practices and the Medieval Church*, eds. Vern L. Bullough and James Brundage (Buffalo, NY.: Prometheus Books, 1982), pp. 23–24; Karras, "Christianization of Medieval Marriage," pp. 8–9.
128 Karras, "Christianization of Medieval Marriage," pp. 7, 11–13; Ennen, *Medieval Woman*, pp. 37–43, 105; Jewell, *Women in Dark Age and Early Medieval Europe*, pp. 34–36; Jewell, *Women in Late Medieval and Reformation Europe*, p. 29; Michael M. Sheehan, "The Formation and Stability of Marriage in Fourteenth-Century England: Evidence of an Ely Register," *Mediaeval Studies* 33 (1971):229–30; Christopher N.L. Brooke, "Marriage and Society in the Central Middle Ages," and Martin Ingram, "Spousals Litigation in the English Ecclesiastical Courts, c.1350–c.1640," in *Marriage and Society: Studies in the Social History of Marriage*, ed. R.B. Outhwaite (New York: St. Martin's Press, 1981), pp. 23–34, 37–39; Jack Goody, *The Development of the Family and Marriage in Europe* (Cambridge: Cambridge University Press, 1983), pp. 146–53; Linda E. Mitchell, "Women and Medieval Canon Law," in *Women in Medieval Western European Culture*, pp. 146–47; Sara McDougall, "Women and Gender in Canon Law," in *Oxford Handbook of Women and Gender*, p. 167; De Moor and Van Zanden, "Girl Power," p. 6. One dissenter is Jeremy Goldberg, who argued that women's "greater individualism in marriage" was due more to the institution of domestic service, which provided "for

a high degree of emotional and even economic independence from parents and family at an early age," rather than the Church's ruling on consent. See Goldberg, *Women, Work, and Life Cycle*, pp. 327, 344.

129 R.H. Helmholz, *Marriage Litigation in Medieval England* (Cambridge: Cambridge University Press, 1974), p. 25; Sheehan, "Formation and Stability of Marriage," p. 230, 234–56; McCarthy, *Marriage in Medieval England*, pp. 28–29; Goldberg, *Women, Work, and Life Cycle*, p. 235; P.J.P. Goldberg, "Women," in *Fifteenth-Century Attitudes: Perceptions of Society in Late Medieval England*, ed. Rosemary Horrox (Cambridge: Cambridge University Press, 1994), p. 126; Ingram, "Spousals Litigation," pp. 36, 39–42; L.R. Poos, *A Rural Society after the Black Death: Essex, 1350–1525* (Cambridge: Cambridge University Press, 1991), pp. 133–34; McDougall, "Women and Gender in Canon Law," p. 167; Donahue, "Female Plaintiffs," pp. 190, 199. For example, Donahue found that 95 percent of fourteenth-century marriage cases in the church court of York concerned attempts to enforce a "*de presenti* informal marriage," with a slightly lower percentage for fifteenth-century cases.

130 Karras, "Christianization of Medieval Marriage," p. 14; Goldberg, *Women, Work, and Life Cycle*, pp. 235–36, 253–54, 260–62, 339–40; Ingram, "Spousals Litigation," pp. 42–44; Richard M. Smith, "Marriage Processes in the English Past: Some Continuities," in *The World We Have Gained: Histories of Population and Social Structure*, eds. L. Bonfield, K. Wrightson, and R.M. Smith (Oxford: Blackwell, 1986), pp. 47–52, 69–78; Richard M. Smith, "Some Reflections on the Evidence for the Origins of the 'European Marriage Pattern' in England," in *The Sociology of the Family: New Directions for Britain*, ed. C. Harris (Keele, Staffordshire: University of Keele Press, 1979), pp. 88–90. Goldberg argued that the number of contract disputes at York declined by the latter half of the fifteenth century and attributed this to singlewomen's loss of "economic independence," and hence of their ability to "contest disputed contracts," even though women also evinced a greater urgency to contract marriages out of "economic necessity". But Ingram found that contract disputes at Ely and Canterbury were still heard in "significantly large numbers" in the fourteenth and fifteenth centuries, and only declined "to a trickle" by the seventeenth century. Ingram believed that this reflected a real decline in spousal lawsuits and the causal motivations behind them.

131 Charles Donahue, Jr., *Law, Marriage, and Society in the Later Middle Ages: Arguments about Marriage in Five Courts* (Cambridge: Cambridge University Press, 2007); Donahue, "Female Plaintiffs," p. 195; Ingram, "Spousals Litigation," pp. 42–44; McDougall, "Women and Gender in Canon Law," p. 168; Karras, "Regulation of Sexuality," pp. 1010–39; Dillard, *Daughters of the Reconquest*, p. 41. Donahue, for example, found that 73 percent of plaintiffs in fourteenth-century marriage cases in the Church court of York were female. Donahue and Karras have also found regional differences between England and the Continent (i.e., France and Belgium) in terms of how Church courts enforced marriages and disciplined fornication leading up to marriage. While England took a "dispute-resolution" approach and had a more rigid, "process" orientated view of marriage, based on *verba de presenti* or vows uttered in the present tense, France and Belgium adopted a "law-enforcement" model but recognized an intermediate stage between simple fornication and full marriage, i.e., long-term sexual relationships or "concubinage," based on *verba de futuro* or betrothals for marriage in the future. The former may indicate a more "individualistic" attitude towards marriage, while the latter was more "communitarian," in which marriages were typically arranged on behalf of younger spouses.

132 For example, plaintiffs who were endeavoring to enforce a marriage contract in the Church court of York were successful 80 percent of the time during the fourteenth century, and 78 percent of the time in the fifteenth. This led Donahue to declare that the York court consistently "indulged in a broad presumption in favor of marriage". This held true in spite of the fact that the sex ratios of plaintiffs changed over the course of the fourteenth and fifteenth centuries, with a higher proportion of female plaintiffs in the fourteenth century (73 percent) than in the 15th (61 percent). Thus, although

one can argue that the court's "pro-plaintiff pattern of judgments" may have helped "redress the imbalance of power between the sexes" in favor of women during the fourteenth century, overall, this pattern seems to have been gender neutral insofar as the court's application of principle was concerned. There is also some evidence that Church courts became more reluctant to confirm disputed marriage contracts in the Early Modern period. At the Church court of Ely, for example, success rates for the enforcement of marriage contracts declined from over 50 percent in the late fourteenth century to just 20 percent in the 1580s. Ingram, however, viewed this as evidence of "the Church's long-term success in securing recognition of its authority in matrimonial matters and in fostering the acceptance of ecclesiastical solemnization in church as the normal mode of entry into the married state". See: Donahue, "Female Plaintiffs," pp. 190–206; Ingram, "Spousals Litigation," pp. 52–53.

133 McDougall, "Women and Gender in Canon Law," p. 167; Sheehan, "Formation and Stability of Marriage," pp. 257–58. The fact that fewer women were suing to enforce a marriage in the Church court of York during the fifteenth century may help explain why female plaintiffs' success rate was roughly equal to males' at this time, as compared to their lower success ratio in the fourteenth century. See Donahue, "Female Plaintiffs," pp. 201–3.

134 McDougall, "Women and Gender in Canon Law," pp. 164–65, 170–75; Karras, "Christianization of Medieval Marriage," pp. 10–11.

135 Jouon des Longrais, "Statut de la femme en Angleterre," *La Femme, vol. 2* (Recueils de la société Jean Bodin, 1962), p. 140; Margaret Wade Labarge, *A Small Sound of the Trumpet: Women in Medieval Life* (Boston, MA.: Beacon Press, 1986), p. 34; Lacey, "Women and Work," p. 26.

136 Mate, *Women in Medieval English Society*, p. 20.

137 Kirshner, "Materials for a Gilded Cage," pp. 206–7; Stuard, "Brideprice, Dowry, and Other Marital Assigns," p. 155; Reyerson and Kuehn, "Women and Law in France and Italy," p. 137; McNamara and Wemple, "Power of Women Through the Family," p. 96; Dillard, *Daughters of the Reconquest*, pp. 70–73. The exception may be Castile in Spain, where the "society of acquisitions" acquired by the couple upon marriage has been described as an egalitarian partnership between the man and wife. Kirshner, however, argued that even non-dotal assets inherited by a bride upon marriage were controlled by the husband, at least in Italy, and thereby represented "a victory for patriarchy".

138 Chojnacki argued that, by this means, women called forth a more solicitous and sensitive gender identity from men and made them more responsive to personal and spousal ties, as opposed to natal ones based on family lineage. See Chojnacki, "Power of Love," pp. 130, 139–40.

139 One outlet through which women may have expressed this new-found social status and influence was in fashion, namely, the wearing of "sumptuous clothing". See Chojnacki, "Power of Love," pp. 130–32.

140 Chojnacki, for example, admitted that he was venturing "into psychological waters ill charted in the sources and the literature," and that he was offering no more than a "hypothesis" in need of "further study". See Chojnacki, "Power of Love," pp. 132, 140.

141 Stuard, "Brideprice, Dowry, and Other Marital Assigns," pp. 154–55; Mark Angelos, "Urban Women, Investment, and the Commercial Revolution of the Middle Ages," in *Women in Medieval Western European Culture*, pp. 263–66. But Genoa was not the only city where women invested in trade. At Montpellier, small numbers of women (18 in total) from all walks of life invested in partnership contracts, a form of investment credit for trading enterprises, mostly in the form of overland ventures, rather than maritime ones. At Cologne, women also were involved in commerce and the export-import trade, but only as members of a family business headed by a merchant husband. See: Reyerson, "Women in Business," pp. 129–32; Howell, "Women, Family Economy, and Structures of Market Production," p. 214.

142 David Herlihy, "Land, Family, and Women in Continental Europe, 701–1200," in *Women in Medieval Society*, ed. Susan Mosher Stuard (Philadelphia, PA.: University of Pennsylvania Press, 1976), pp. 16–32.

143 Stuard, "Brideprice, Dowry, and Other Marital Assigns," pp. 156–58.

144 Stuard, "Brideprice, Dowry, and other Marital Assigns," pp. 149–50, 155–58; Martha C. Howell, *The Marriage Exchange: Property, Social Place, and Gender in Cities of the Low Countries, 1300–1550* (Chicago, IL.: University of Chicago Press, 1998), pp. 212–17. By 1500, however, Roman law began to penetrate marriage property law in Flanders, with the result that women's control over their dowry may have suffered.

145 However, it is not until the fifteenth century that we have evidence from the Church courts that Alexander's ruling on consent received widespread acceptance in Christendom. See: Goldberg, *Women, Work, and Life Cycle*, p. 237; De Moor and Van Zanden, "Girl Power," pp. 5–6.

146 David Herlihy, *Medieval Households* (Cambridge, MA.: Harvard University Press, 1985), p. 81; De Moor and Van Zanden, "Girl Power," p. 6. Ingram's conclusions were considerably more restrained: He argued that, if parents arranged marriages, then they were obligated to respect the wishes of their children, while if young people did take the initiative themselves to seek out a potential mate and commence courtship, which "was apparently not uncommon at the social levels generally represented in contract suits," then parents had, in effect, a veto power over the match. See Ingram, "Spousals Litigation," p. 49.

147 Ingram, "Spousals Litigation," p. 51; Dillard, *Daughters of the Reconquest*, p. 41. For example, the *fueros* of Leon and Castile required that a daughter seek approval of her parents before marriage, even after the ruling of the Fourth Lateran Council in 1215.

148 Mate, *Women in Medieval English Society*, p. 87–88, 94–95; Sheehan, "Formation and Stability of Marriage," p 230; Ingram, "Spousals Litigation," p. 40; De Moor and Van Zanden, "Girl Power," p. 6; Donahue, "Female Plaintiffs," p. 191.

149 Mate, *Daughters, Wives and Widows*, pp. 80–81; Mate, *Women in Medieval English Society*, p. 91; Janet S. Loengard, "Common Law for Margery: Separate But Not Equal," and Reyerson and Kuehn, "Women and Law in France and Italy," in *Women in Medieval Western European Culture*, pp. 119–21, 132.

150 Simon J. Payling, "Social Mobility, Demographic Change, and Landed Society in Late Medieval England," *Economic History Review*, 45 (1992):54–62.

151 Shona Kelly Wray, "Women, Testaments, and Notarial Culture in Bologna's Contado (1348)," in *Across the Religious Divide: Women, Property, and Law in the Wider Mediterranean (ca. 1300–1800)*, eds. Jutta Gisela Sperling and Shona Kelly Wray (New York: Routledge, 2010), pp. 90–91.

152 Phillips, *Medieval Maidens*, pp. 125–28; Mate, *Women in Medieval English Society*, p. 90; Müller, "Peasant Women, Agency and Status," pp. 108–12. Müller argued that peasant women's participation in the land market largely varied from manor to manor, depending on the nature of lordship and its attitude towards such activity.

153 Mate, *Daughters, Wives and Widows*, p. 81; Mate, *Women in Medieval English Society*, p. 91; Amy Louise Erickson, *Women and Property in Early Modern England* (London: Routledge, 1993), p. 224. The exception may have been medieval peasants in agrarian societies, where land was the normal dowry endowment that would allow a new couple to set up their own household. See Bennett, "Medieval Peasant Marriage," pp. 209–11.

154 Bennett, *Women in the Medieval English Countryside*, pp. 104–14. For a discussion of the legal implications of coverture, see: Müller, "Peasant Women, Agency and Status," and Matthew Frank Stevens, "London's Married Women, Debt Litigation and Coverture in the Court of Common Pleas," in *Married Women and the Law*, pp. 92–94, 120–21.

155 Mate, *Daughters, Wives and Widows*, pp. 81–82.

156 The exception to the Northwest marriage pattern is typically taken to be Tuscany in Italy (right on the border of the "Hajnal line"), based on the *Catasto* for Florence of 1427–30, which pointed to an early age at marriage for women (in their teens), a large age gap (8 years on average) between the bride and her spouse, and her being subject

to the paternal authority of her in-laws, as well as to that of her husband, since the young couple often moved into the husband's natal household instead of forming their own. However, the ages at marriage for women as reported in the *Catasto* may not be entirely reliable, and women's age at first marriage may have risen to their early 20s by the latter half of the fifteenth century, although the age gap between spouses may also have widened. See: Klapisch-Zuber, *Women, Family, and Ritual*, pp. 18–20, 29, 170; Molho, "Deception and Marriage Strategy ," p. 204; Chojnacki, "The Power of Love," p. 133.

157 Rowene Archer, "Rich Old Ladies: The Problem of Late Medieval Dowagers," in *Property and Politics: Essays in Later Medieval English History*, ed. A.J. Pollard (Gloucester, UK: Stroud, 1984), p. 19.

158 Hanawalt, *Ties that Bound*, pp. 220, 223; Hanawalt, *Wealth of Wives*, p. 174; Hanawalt, "Widow's Mite," p. 35; Bennett, "Public Power and Authority," p. 23; Peter Franklin, "Peasant Widows' 'Liberation' and Remarriage before the Black Death," *Economic History Review* 39 (1986):196.

159 Judith M. Bennett, "Widows in the Medieval English Countryside," in *Upon My Husband's Death*, pp. 69–89, 96–103.

160 Barbara A. Hanawalt, "Remarriage as an Option for Urban and Rural Widows in Late Medieval England," in *Wife and Widow in Medieval England*, pp. 142–43. It should be noted that the evidence of *leyrwite*, such as on the manors of Spalding Priory, indicate that widows rarely engaged in sexual intercourse outside marriage. See Jones, "Medieval Leyrwite," p. 949.

161 Joel T. Rosenthal, "Fifteenth Century Widows and Widowhood: Bereavement, Reintegration, and Life Choices," in *Wife and Widow in Medieval England*, p. 36; Bennett, "Widows in the Medieval English Countryside," p. 103.

162 From Christine de Pizan's *The Book of the Path of Long Study*, in *The Selected Writings of Christine de Pizan: New Translations, Criticism*, trans. and ed. Renate Blumenfeld-Kosinski and Kevin Brownlee (New York: W.W. Norton and Co., 1997), p. 62.

163 Bardsley, "Missing Women," pp. 274–75, 294–305.

164 Hanawalt, "Widow's Mite," pp. 22–23; Hanawalt, "Remarriage as an Option," pp. 146–47. For the debate over the Northwest marriage pattern in late medieval Europe, see Chapter 8.

165 Joel T. Rosenthal, *Patriarchy and Families of Privilege in Fifteenth Century England* (Philadelphia, PA.: University of Pennsylvania Press, 1991), pp. 182–83; Mate, *Daughters, Wives and Widows*, p. 94.

166 Mate, *Daughters, Wives and Widows*, p. 94.

167 Mate, *Women in Medieval English Society*, p. 81.

168 The typical case cited here is of Thomasine Bonaventure, born to poor parents in Cornwall in 1450, who married three times and was so wealthy a widow in 1507 that King Henry VII fined her 1000 pounds on a trumped-up charge. See Hanawalt, "Remarriage as an Option," p. 157.

169 Eric Acheson, *A Gentry Community: Leicestershire in the Fifteenth Century, c.1422–c.1485* (Cambridge: Cambridge University Press, 1992), p. 153; Archer, "Rich Old Ladies," p. 26; Hanawalt, "Widow's Mite," p. 25.

170 Mate, *Daughters, Wives and Widows*, pp. 94–96, 99–100; Mate, *Women in Medieval English Society*, pp. 81–82; Lacey, "Women and Work," p. 37; Dillard, *Daughters of the Reconquest*, pp. 103–14.

171 Sue Sheridan Walker, "Litigation as Personal Quest: Suing for Dower in the Royal Courts, circa 1272–1350," in *Wife and Widow in Medieval England*, p. 81. For the impact of Magna Carta on women's dower rights, see Janet Senderowitz Loengard, "*Rationabilis Dos*: Magna Carta and the Widow's 'Fair Share' in the Earlier Thirteenth Century," in *Wife and Widow in Medieval England*, pp. 59–80.

172 Dillard, *Daughters of the Reconquest*, pp. 110–11.

173 Walker, "Litigation as Personal Quest," pp. 86–98; Hanawalt, "Widow's Mite," pp. 26–35. Other grounds for denying a widow's dower included that the husband was not really dead (i.e., missing in action in war); that the widow had not been legally married

to her husband; that the husband was a felon; and that the widow had been an adulterer. Quite often, the party contesting the widow's dower was her own, adult child or relatives of the dead husband, all of which must have added an "emotional intensity" to the litigation.

174 Hanawalt, "Widow's Mite," pp. 26–35; Walker, "Litigation as Personal Quest," p. 86; Mate, *Daughters, Wives and Widows*, pp. 94–95. Hanawalt found that the mean length of time for dower disputes in the Husting Court of London between 1301 and 1433 was about a year, with the longest case taking over five years to settle, but that disputes became less lengthy by the early fifteenth century. Over this same time period, out of 186 cases that achieved some kind of resolution, London widows won 53 percent of them, usually through the voluntary surrender or default of the defendant, winning outright in only 10 percent of cases. By the same token, widows typically lost their suits by default or by failing to present and by retracting their writs, losing outright in only 13 percent of cases.

175 Lacey, "Women and Work," pp. 45–48, 57; Goldberg, "Female Labour, Service and Marriage," pp 32–33.

176 Müller, "Peasant Women, Agency and Status," pp. 110–11. The decades just before the Black Death, on the other hand, are seen as a "time of considerable opportunity for widows' 'liberation,'" when widows, especially those holding gravel land, were more likely to choose to remain single and independent rather than remarry, since labor was cheap and readily available. See Franklin, "Peasant Widows' 'Liberation' and Remarriage," pp. 193, 202.

177 Mate, *Daughters, Wives and Widows*, pp. 118–21; Mate, *Women in Medieval English Society*, pp. 85–86; McRee and Dent, "Working Women in the Medieval City," p. 252; Hanawalt, *Wealth of Wives*, pp. 141–42; Goldberg, "Female Labour, Service and Marriage," p. 34.

178 Mate, *Daughters, Wives and Widows*, pp. 97–98; Mate, *Women in Medieval English Society*, p. 80; Chojnacki, "Power of Love," pp. 136–37; Bennett, "Widows in the Medieval English Countryside," pp. 100–2; Lacey, "Women and Work," pp. 34–30. As Bennett showed, inheritance and tenure customs for widows could vary even from town to town within the same country (in this case, between Brigstock, Northamptonshire, and Iver, Buckinghamshire), although she argued that all widows shared the same "essential responsibilities and opportunities".

179 Bennett, "Widows in the Medieval English Countryside," pp. 92–94.

180 Mate, *Women in Medieval English Society*, pp. 79–85; Hanawalt, "Widow's Mite," pp. 25–26; Hanawalt, "Remarriage as an Option," p. 145; Dillard, *Daughters of the Reconquest*, pp. 101–2. Hanawalt, based on the evidence of 1,743 wills proved in the Husting Court of London, concluded that "husbands were, on the whole, generous to their wives in providing for their widowhood," leaving them property with no strings attached, with some men even attempting to go beyond the law and leave their wives "real" property (i.e., property that widows could own outright, instead of just having a life interest in it), but that the court always objected to such provisions.

181 Mate estimated that two-thirds of "young or middle-aged widows" in fifteenth-century Sussex did remarry, which matches what figures are available from elsewhere in Europe, namely, Early Modern France. See: Mate, *Daughters, Wives and Widows*, pp. 126–27.

182 Mate, *Daughters, Wives and Widows*, pp. 130–31; Rosenthal, "Fifteenth Century Widows and Widowhood," pp. 36–41; Hanawalt, "Widow's Mite," p. 37; Hanawalt, "Remarriage as an Option," pp. 152–54.

183 Hanawalt, "Remarriage as an Option," pp. 141, 160.

184 Hanawalt, "Widow's Mite," pp. 37, 39.

185 Bennett, "Widows in the Medieval English Countryside," p. 74. According to Bennett, these rates largely depended on whether land in the open market was readily available, as opposed to being dependent on inheritance through a widow, while Müller also pointed out that some lords, such as the abbot of Glastonbury, placed pressure on

widows to remarry to ensure that labor services were fulfilled. Figures derived from sixteenth-century parish registers indicate that, on the whole, 25–30 percent of country widows remarried. See: Müller, "Peasant Women, Agency and Status," p. 110; Hanawalt, "Remarriage as an Option," pp. 147–48.

186 Reyerson, "Women in Business," p. 137.
187 Dillard, *Daughters of the Reconquest*, p. 98.
188 Reyerson and Kuehn, "Women and Law in France and Italy," pp. 138–39; Herlihy and Klapisch-Zuber, *Tuscans and their Families*, p. 217. The *Catasto* of Florence of 1427 revealed a high proportion of unmarried widows, who made up 1 in 4 of the female population. However, this proportion was much lower, 1 in 10, in the Florentine countryside.
189 Hanawalt, "Widow's Mite," p. 38; Hanawalt, *Ties that Bound*, p. 220; Hanawalt, "Remarriage as an Option," p. 159; Mate, *Daughters, Wives and Widows*, p. 129; Rosenthal, "Fifteenth Century Widows and Widowhood," p. 42; Müller, "Peasant Women, Agency and Status," pp. 110–11.
190 Goldberg, *Women, Work, and Life Cycle*, pp. 271–72. The evidence of *merchets* on the manors of Spalding Priory does indicate that widow remarriage, which seems to have been common in the decades before the Black Death (i.e., nearly 19 percent of all marriages between 1300–1349), then dropped off precipitously afterwards (i.e., comprising only 1.2 percent of marriages between 1400–49), perhaps indicating that, if given a choice, widows preferred not to remarry. See Jones, "Medieval Leyrwite," pp. 949–50.
191 Mate, *Daughters, Wives and Widows*, pp. 129, 131–33; Hanawalt, "Remarriage as an Option," pp. 148–49; Jack Ravensdale, "Population Change and the Transfer of Customary Land on a Cambridgeshire Manor in the Fourteenth Century," in *Land, Kinship and Life-Cycle*, ed. Richard M. Smith (Cambridge: Cambridge University Press, 1984), pp. 209, 218–19. This is not to say, however, that the well-endowed widow was no longer an attractive marriage partner. For example, 50–65 percent of London's wealthy widows remarried in the century and a half after the Black Death, while in Durham, remarriage of landed widows became so popular that the bishop issued a special marriage license to these "bishop's widows". See: Hanawalt, "Remarriage as an Option," pp. 150–51; Hanwalt, "Widow's Mite," pp. 36–37; P.L. Larson, *Conflict and Compromise in the Late Medieval Countryside: Lords and Peasants in Durham, 1349–1400* (New York: Routledge, 2006), pp. 94–97.
192 All this is told in Christine's *Book of Fortune's Transformation* and in her *Vision*, as translated in *The Selected Writings of Christine de Pizan*, pp. 106–7, 188–89.

7

THE MAN WHO TORE HIS EYES OUT OVER UNITY OF FORM

Intellectual and environmental history

"Thereafter he went to Bologna, where he returned to his old heresies; but there he fell into a very great madness and misery, so that, having torn out his eyes, he ended his life in despair".[1]

Thus died Richard Knapwell, a Dominican friar and theologian who taught at the University of Oxford and who, in 1288, became a martyr to philosophy. Even the Dunstaple chronicler who wrote the above obituary for Knapwell and was evidently less than sympathetic to his cause, acknowledged how much Knapwell suffered for his beliefs. The Latin word that the chronicler used here, *angustia*, is the root of "anguish," which in modern existentialist philosophy expresses fear of the unknown in a world without absolute truths. In Knapwell's case, his anguish was over his defense of the doctrine of unity of substantial form, the idea that in every living creature, there is only one "form"—or soul, if you like—that animates and gives existence to a body.[2] This is a position that can ultimately be attributed to the ancient philosopher, Aristotle (384–22 B.C.), but in the thirteenth century, it was championed and given new expression by the great theologian, St. Thomas Aquinas (1225–74), of whom Knapwell, a fellow Dominican, was a great admirer and defender.[3] Aquinas did not associate this unity of form with the universal "world soul" (*anima mundi*) of Plato; rather, each individual human, animal, or plant had his own substantial form, if a single one. Any other forms were merely "accidental," corresponding to one or another of the individual's attributes but not essential to his essence or existence. The opposing position was that a plurality of substantial forms or souls animated each individual, such as, in humans, an intellectual, animal, and vegetable soul that corresponded to man's reason, senses, and growth and nourishment. This position was championed by medieval neo-Platonists, among whom there numbered some prominent Franciscans in the thirteenth century. From the Thomist point of view, this was nonsense, because then it would mean that if a person lost any of his senses, by going blind for example, he would then lose one of his substantial forms and would no longer be the same person. For Aquinas, the single substantial form in each human corresponded to his rational soul that also controlled all his animal and vegetable functions.[4]

Where Aquinas, and also Knapwell, got into trouble was in trying to argue that the substantial form of humans continued to exist even after the death of the body, meaning that the dead body of the person was no longer to be identified with that same body in life, since all of one's being inhered in the substantial form, which was now separated from the body.[5] "Pluriformists" completely rejected this position, and not just on philosophical grounds, but theological ones as well. For if Christ had only one substantial form, this would mean that his dead body lying for three days in his tomb was not the same as his living one, and therefore should not be venerated by Christians.[6] By the same token, this called into question the eucharist, or the blessing of bread by the priest which was then believed to become the real body of Christ; if the body was that of Christ after his death, then the sacrament had no meaning, for it was not Christ at all, since it was devoid of his substantial form. This is precisely why Knapwell was excommunicated, and his opinions declared heretical, by the archbishop of Canterbury, John Pecham (formerly a Franciscan friar), in 1286.[7] Knapwell's appeal to the papal court in Rome was not heard until 1288, when "perpetual silence" was imposed upon him by Pope Nicholas IV (r. 1288–92). Much of Knapwell's misfortunes owed not just to philosophical differences, but also to the political rivalry between the mendicant orders, in that he was a Dominican being judged by Franciscans, namely, Pecham and Nicholas.[8]

Clearly, there was more at stake here than just a philosophical idea. It is hard for modern observers to understand just how passionately felt were the arcane issues debated by medieval thinkers; but evidently, even contemporaries like the Dunstaple chronicler were puzzled as to why Knapwell would tear out his eyes over such a "specialized matter," putting it down to his "madness and misery".[9] One suspects, however, that Knapwell was protesting something bigger than just a polemical attack on unity of form. Perhaps he was distraught over his exile from the rich and lively intellectual environment of Oxford. Or maybe he sensed, in his own plight, the coming decline of scholasticism at the hands of Franciscan skeptics.

Thomas Aquinas was, of course, famous for his ability to expound matters of faith with reason and justify even the most obscure Christian doctrine with logical argument. For some historians of philosophy, the "Thomistic synthesis" represents the pinnacle of achievement in medieval thought.[10] But already within a few years of Aquinas' death in 1274, his positions were being attacked for their overreliance on Aristotle, who postulated an eternal (i.e., uncreated) universe and the inseparability of the human soul from the body (i.e., that an individual soul is not immortal). Both positions were naturally deemed incompatible with fundamental tenets of the Catholic faith.[11] These issues were by no means new, but had already been debated a century or two earlier within Islamic philosophical schools, especially by al-Ghazali (1058–1111) and Averroes, or Ibn Rushd (1126–98). Nonetheless, the late-thirteenth century attack on Thomism opened the door for a new generation of philosophers around the turn of the fourteenth century at Oxford, namely, John Duns Scotus (c.1266–1308) and William of Ockham (1285–1347). These thinkers began to emphasize the separation of reason and faith and the unknowability of God, who was unbounded by human intellect or will (a doctrine known as "voluntarism"). For Ockham, in particular, the existence of God and other "higher truths" of Christian doctrine could only be known through faith, since human reason was fallible and not up to the task; instead, reason should be directed towards what it could actually prove, namely, phenomena in the natural world.[12] In contrast to the admirers of Aquinas, modern "Ockhamist" scholars see this critical or skeptical phase as inaugurating "one of the liveliest periods of medieval philosophy," in which the overly theoretical speculation of the scholastic schools was replaced with a new spirit of scientific empiricism at the universities.[13] Other critics of Aquinas take their cue from Ockham's skepticism to take a fresh look at Thomist philosophy, in which they claim that Aquinas' attempt to rationalize certain metaphysical issues, such as his attempt to explain the relationship between substantial form and matter or to prove the existence of God, were doomed exercises that descended into "confusion and obscurity" or into "sophistry and illusion".[14]

The challenge posed by Ockham to Thomism also can be cast as a debate over universals, or the age-old struggle between "realism" and "nominalism".[15] On a very simplistic level, realists believed in universal truths or "universals"—general categories or "groups" in which all individual examples participated—that not only could be known by the mind but had an "extra-mental" reality outside our thought processes. Nominalists denied the existence of universals in any physical reality, although they still deemed universals useful as mental categories in order to organize individual realities directly observed and experienced by the senses. This dualism in philosophy went all the way back to Plato (c.428-c.348 B.C.) and Aristotle, albeit in a more subtle form than simply that Plato was the original realist, and Aristotle the nominalist. Aristotle, for example, did believe in the reality of universals, which he called "essences," but he believed that their existence was only to be found as expressions in individual, concrete examples within the physical world (i.e., the "essence" of something was what all the real specimens in that category participated in). He denied any reality to transcendent, immaterial ideals, compared to which all things of this earth were mere shadowy reflections, which Plato called "forms". In this sense, Aristotle has been called a "moderate realist" as opposed to a nominalist, since he did accept that universals were real, but not in the same way or to the same degree as Plato.[16]

When we come to the "problem" of universals, as expounded by Scotus and Ockham, the debate can become very complex: Indeed, the question of universals has been described as "a problem that vexed almost every medieval philosopher and theologian," as well as being "one of the key debates in medieval philosophy".[17]

Even when modern scholars of philosophy weigh in on the matter, the debate can get so technical that "ambiguities and confusions" can occur, particularly with regard to the labels or definitions of the two positions and where Scotus and Ockham fit into them.[18] Both realists and nominalists were themselves divided into sub-camps. For example, realists were either "extreme realists," also known as "Platonic realists"—who believed that universals were "abstract entities" that existed outside the mind or individual examples—or else "moderate realists," also sometimes referred to as "immanent realists"—who believed that universals only existed within individuals "as a constituent or part of them" (i.e., Aristotle's position). Similarly, nominalists were either "moderate nominalists," who believed universals only existed as mental categories that were needed so that human beings could "bring order into the extra-mental world". Or they were "extreme nominalists," who did not believe in universals altogether, whether imagined or real. Then there was "trope theory," considered a form of nominalism, in which each "trope" was an individual variation on a single property (i.e., "forest green" is a trope of greenness).[19]

Where do Scotus and Ockham fit into this spectrum of realism and nominalism? Here is where much of the debate comes in. Some say Scotus was a moderate realist, some say Ockham was a moderate nominalist, while others say that both Scotus and Ockham were trope theorists.[20] But an argument also can be made that it is impossible, or at least very difficult, to determine from their writings what, exactly, Scotus and Ockham really were. Scotus, for example, stated that each individual had two metaphysical components: a "common nature" that he shared with all members of his species; and a unique quality that no other individual had, which Scotus called a *haecceity* (from the Latin, meaning "thisness"). With regard to "common nature," did Scotus mean by this: something that was "universal," here defined as an abstract, mental concept that was then applied to individual "instances" (i.e., "immanent realism"); did he mean something that was "particular" to each member of a species, like a trope (i.e., trope theory); or did he mean neither of these? With regard to *haecceity*, it seems that the only thing that can definitely be said is that Scotus believed it to be a unique, unrepeatable, and "essential component of each and every physical individual," but he never exactly defined what *haecceity* was, by means of which it "individuated" the individual. Nor is it clear how "common nature" and *haecceity* combined to make up an individual.[21]

Compared to Scotus, Ockham is placed more securely in the nominalist camp, because he criticized what he perceived as the "immanent realism" of Scotus. Ockham rejected both "immanent universals," or things that were present in several individuals at once, and "common natures," when these were supposed to be "particular" to each member of a species, since "common" and "particular" were contradictory concepts. But is it not clear that Ockham was reading Scotus right, and therefore that his criticisms were valid.[22] Moreover, when it comes to Ockham's own theory of universals, it is not clear exactly what he meant either. Ockham said that each extant entity was "individual" or "particular," so that nothing outside our minds in the physical world could be said to be "universal". But what did he mean by this? Did he mean that each extant entity was like a trope, a "non-universal particular" that nonetheless could be repeated into almost exact copies of each other (i.e., trope theory)? Or did he mean that each entity was unique and unrepeatable (i.e., similar to Scotus' *haecceity*), which would imply that universals were merely linguistic or conceptual "signs" that had absolutely no reality in the physical world, only in our minds (i.e., "predicate nominalism" or "conceptual nominalism")?[23] As one can see, there may have been a large degree of overlap between Scotus and Ockham, or there may have been genuine differences between them. If Scotus was a realist and Ockham was a nominalist, it is still not clear what kind of realist or nominalist each of them was. It is also not clear whether Scotus or Ockham made any kind of meaningful or intelligible contribution to the universals debate that can be applied to modern philosophical thinking.[24] Only further investigation, and coherent explication, of their writings can answer these questions.[25]

The debate over environmental history

Yet another example of how the persistence of the realist/nominalist divide among intellectuals extends even into modern times comes from the relatively new field of environmental history. Thought to have been born sometime in the 1970s, environmental history is a field that is growing rapidly and, some would say, is now reaching maturity.[26] Clearly, the "burgeoning beast" that is the field of environmental history is experiencing growing pains and, instead of welcoming all comers to its formerly "big tent," is now beginning a debate on who should practice environmental history, and what constitutes "true" environmental history. This is where the realist/nominalist divide comes in.

The historian of American environmental history, John McNeill, postulated three main "varieties" of environmental history, of which only two really apply to the pre-modern aspect of the field. One is a "material" approach to environmental history, which seeks to record changes in the "biological and physical environments and how those changes affect human societies"; the other is a cultural/intellectual approach that "emphasizes representations and images of nature in arts and letters, how these have changed, and what they reveal about the people and societies that produced them".[27] (A third approach, that of political environmental history, is mainly concerned with public policy debates that are only relevant to modern history.[28]) One might consider the material approach to be the "nominalist" wing of environmental history, since it is mainly concerned with accumulating scientific data on ancient flora and fauna, out of which it hopes to build a picture of the environment of the past. (Some call this, more properly, "ecological history" or "historical ecology," in order to indicate their "tighter alliance" with science.[29]) The cultural/intellectual approach is the "realist" wing, because it seeks a broad consensus or overview of widely-shared contemporary attitudes towards nature and the environment.[30]

Lately, it seems that environmental historians, including those working in pre-modern environmental history, are trying to make the case that the material (i.e., the nominalist) approach is the only one that can produce a true or "serious" work on environmental history.[31] Since this entails a specialist knowledge in scientific fields such as biology or chemistry in which many historians lack training, and in fact will never be comfortable, this implies a dramatic shift away from earlier attitudes in which the field "put up few to no formal barriers" or "restrictions" for entry, and whose borders were "porous" and "undefended," leaving the "doors open" for historians of different backgrounds who were all "invited to participate".[32] Now excluded would be "sojourners" in environmental history who come at the field from the perspective of other specializations, but which might help invigorate environmental history with an interdisciplinary approach that is often held up as one of the defining (and beneficial) hallmarks of the field.[33] The intellectual/cultural approach also has been compromised by out-sized claims for the uniquely destructive impact of the Judeo-Christian tradition upon the environment in the West. Such claims have been widely criticized, both on the grounds that other religio-cultural traditions can be shown to have been equally environmentally "rapacious" or exploitative, and on the grounds that extrapolating from an "abstract idea" (i.e., God's command to humans in Genesis 1:28 to "go forth and multiply" and have "dominion" over the earth) to demonstrable action and consequences for the environment is ultimately unprovable.[34]

Another way in which the realist/nominalist divide in pre-modern environmental history seems to express itself is in the approach to narrating this history. One method, which we may call the realist one, is to trace the influence of the environment as an "historical actor" or "protagonist" upon the stage of history, whose role has traditionally been neglected in most historical accounts of the Middle Ages. This approach basically seeks to unify the entire history of the Middle Ages with an environmental theme.[35] However, this is also an approach that is exceedingly difficult to execute, if only because the environment must interact with a whole range of other factors in order to produce history.[36] This means that, either one must tell a general history of the Middle Ages, with the environment playing only one of many roles in the story, or else one must attempt to isolate and separate the environment as an agent of historical change, which risks simplifying history.[37] Indeed, the same challenges would face any historian attempting to write history from strictly one point of view, such as an economic history, political history, etc. Nonetheless, it is true that, traditionally, historians have neglected the environment as a major player in history, preferring instead to relegate it to being a "backdrop" to the main action, perhaps because historians are naturally suspicious of any "exogenous" factor like climate, earthquakes, animal or insect vectors of disease, etc., that would seemingly diminish the human role in the story and turn us into mere "victims" of implacable natural forces.[38]

Traditionally, environmental influences were divided into factors that were either "exogenous" (i.e., outside of human experience or influence), or "endogenous" (i.e., intrinsic to human societies). These days, however, historians see any attempt to favor one or the other as setting up a "false dichotomy" between these two forces, since they are so inter-related.[39] Indeed, humans have proven that, even in pre-modern times, they were capable of altering their environment and other circumstances such that they affected the history of an exogenous agent like disease, rather than simply being a "plaything" at the mercy of microscopic pathogens.[40] But elevating the environment to an important place in medieval history is still a relatively "novel point of view" in the field.[41]

To take one example of the difficulties involved in the realist approach to narrating medieval environmental history, one can recite the Franco-Flemish war of 1315, which coincided with the advent of the Great Famine in northern Europe as a result of relentless, flooding rain. Due to the "ugly weather" of that year, the armies of King Louis X of France (r. 1314–16) on their way to fight the Flemings were bogged down in quagmires of roads, where cart horses transporting supplies had to wade through "mud up to their knees," making military logistics for the campaign impossible. This seems like a perfectly straightforward tale of the environment dictating the course of history, but is it? The rainy weather certainly frustrated Louis's desire for a quick resolution to the conflict through battle, but it doesn't seem to have altered the French monarchy's determination to eventually bring Flanders under its control (which it did through diplomacy in 1320). While the French certainly had a negative view of the environment in this case, the Flemings had quite another, seeing the rains as their deliverance from God. And the famine in Flanders of that year was affected not only by the weather, but also by Louis' policy of imposing a trade embargo on the region.[42]

Another example of the dangers of assuming a mono-causal environmental explanation of history is the theory that an atmospheric event, such as a meteor strike (causing gas-releasing earthquakes), or sea outgassing, may have caused the Black Death in the mid-fourteenth century. This is an intriguing theory, if for nothing else than the fact that it would give a scientific basis to seemingly fantastic, contemporary tales of reddish and yellow "vapors" seen on the horizon, "poisonous winds," rain of fire from the sky, trees covered in dust, and masses of dead fishes washing up on the shore. Heightened levels of CO_2 in the medieval atmosphere can, in fact, be measured through "proxy" data such as analysis of tree rings (dendrochronology), radiocarbon testing of peat bog samples, and measurements of the gaseous content of air bubbles trapped in ice cores.[43] But even if such data can be precisely dated, it can only provide an explanation for local events during the Black Death, and not the universal phenomenon which all historical records tell us it was.[44] Moreover, the outgassing theory has now been rendered obsolete by another field of scientific enquiry, that of paleomicrobiology, which has been able to isolate DNA fragments, and even reconstruct a complete genome, of *Yersinia pestis*, the bacterial agent of plague, from the remains of victims in mass graves (Chapter 8). Plague certainly provides more of an opening than outgassing for humans to play a role in the history of the Black Death, such as through their trade networks in grain (a favorite food of rats and their fleas), through sanitation and quarantine measures in towns, and through medical prophylactic measures against the disease.[45]

The "nominalist" alternative to narrating medieval environmental history is simply to approach each aspect of the medieval environment—such as soils, water, woods, animals, etc.—and to explain human interaction with, and attitudes towards, each of these aspects individually. This is perhaps a less than satisfactory approach in that it fails to stress the importance of the environment to the grand sweep of history. It also risks eliding regional differences between different climactic or geographical zones, presenting Europe's medieval ecology as too homogenous and predictable.[46] But it is one to which even narrative realists must, to some degree, resort.[47]

Then, there is theory. Some environmental historians seem to insist that, in order to do good environmental history, one must be conversant, and fully engage, with modern environmental theory. As John McNeill pointed out, historians are usually "thin on theory".[48] In the case of environmental history, one difficulty is that any theory faces the sheer chaotic and complex nature of natural forces.[49] Nevertheless, there are some interesting attempts to apply some kind of theory to pre-modern environmental history.[50]

One assumption made about the modern environment that is also applied to the past is that humans always have, and had, a role to play in nature. Indeed, for most environmental historians, "the mutual relations between humankind and the rest of nature" is the very definition of environmental history.[51] A variation on this theme was famously made by William Cronon, who argued that our notion of "wilderness"—a pristine place untouched by human intervention—was flawed, an invented construct that never corresponded to reality, a "state of mind [rather] than a fact of nature".[52] Although Cronon was primarily thinking of designated "wilderness" areas in the United States, one would expect that his argument would be even more true of pre-modern environments in Europe, where humans have had centuries' more opportunity to interact with nature.[53] But while I certainly agree that human involvement in nature is a historical fact that must be acknowledged by every modern historian of the environment, such an approach may not always help us to understand how medieval people themselves viewed their relationship with nature, which had a morally didactic/religious element that is often missing in modern secular outlooks.

It is true that the high Middle Ages marked a "collaborative" stage in medieval attitudes towards nature, when man was viewed as being more in harmony than in opposition to his natural surroundings, which was perhaps a product of Europeans' successful expansion in both population and agricultural production at this time.[54] But all this changed with the advent in the mid-fourteenth century of the Black Death, considered the greatest natural disaster in human history.[55] Then, medieval authors like Gabriele de Mussis could imagine God commanding the "Earth," an allegorical figure for all of creation (i.e., the planets, stars, elements, etc.) to "exterminate" the human race by means of the plague as a punishment for abundant human wickedness and sin.[56] This was more than just an "adversarial" or "hostile" relationship between humans and nature, which is a stereotype some have applied to early medieval attitudes towards the environment.[57] It was the total removal of humans from nature. Indeed, the incredible mortality of the first outbreak of the Black Death, wiping out an overall average of 50–60 percent of Europe's inhabitants (Chapter 8), means that this elimination of humans from the environment was nearly accomplished (or at least seemed to be so!).

Another variation of the distinctly modern outlook that sees humans as inevitably and invariably a part of nature is the effort to integrate urban history into environmental history, indeed, to elevate it to central importance in the field. Proponents of urban environmental history see it as a necessary and useful corrective to views that would look "at wilderness in isolation," and to the "declensionist" narrative that views humans "as agents of harmful physical change" who would be best taken out of nature.[58] Urban environmental historians also view pre-modern times as when urban dwellers in fact had a closer relationship with nature than their counterparts of today, and when nature was even more important "as a shaper of urbanization".[59]

However, the fact of the matter is that, even by the late Middle Ages, about 80 percent of the population of Europe, on average, still lived in the country rather than the city, although this of course varied by region and according to the definition of what constituted an urban environment.[60] Thus, when undertaking a broad survey of the environmental history of the Middle Ages, one can argue that it doesn't make sense to focus on urban environmental history, since this really applied to only a small percentage of the population. Nonetheless, urban medieval history has a long and distinguished pedigree, going back to the work of the Belgian medievalist, Henri Pirenne, in the early twentieth century. One can also argue that, by the fourteenth century at least, urban environments had become large and diffuse enough to form a web or network of trading links with rural hinterlands, such that their influence and impact extended far beyond their physical walls.[61] While many of these interconnections between city and country remain vague, their very existence is strongly implied by the mere fact that the Black Death of the mid-fourteenth century so successfully penetrated into even thinly inhabited places. At the same time, however, the Black Death undoubtedly reduced the "ecological footprint" of even Europe's largest cities substantially, simply by decimating their inhabitants (often by half or more).[62] The result of this urban decline in the late Middle Ages seems to have been a slight reduction in the number of towns by the early sixteenth century, compared to 1300 (i.e., before the plague), with the proportion of the population living in towns (around 20 percent) remaining the same.[63] Moreover, it doesn't seem that cities participated in the "critical transformations" taking place in European society during the transition from the late medieval to the Early Modern periods.[64]

There are some environmental historians, such as Donald Worster, who do not consider urban spaces to be really part of nature, or the environment properly speaking (i.e., the "nonhuman world"), since they are entirely man-made and consist of a "social environment" in which humans interact "only with each other in the absence of nature".[65] Urban environmentalists' response to this is to point out that cities draw upon natural resources far beyond their borders, and thus constitute an "urban system" that "is much larger and complex than a traditional view of a city within narrowly conceived political boundaries". At the same time, "cities are also major modifiers of the physical environment," which again reach far beyond their physical limits.[66] While all this is true of the medieval city as well, the scale is much smaller than in the modern example that is usually drawn upon by urban environmental historians.[67] One must also acknowledge that there is a long history of prejudice and antagonism between city and country that goes back to the very Middle Ages: For example, Italians (who were much more urbanized than other Europeans) had a saying: "The task of the town is to make good people; that of the village is to make good beasts".[68] (A famous *New Yorker* cover cartoon from March 29, 1976, by Saul Steinberg, "View of the World from Ninth Avenue," famously illustrates this perspective.) Since many academics are necessarily based in cities where universities and colleges (at least large ones) are based, this urban prejudice may, even subconsciously, seep its way into their writing.

Finally, there is theory as to how to approach medieval environmental sources. One theory, adopted by Richard Hoffmann, is the "interaction model," which was developed by two members of the Institute of Social Ecology in Vienna, Marina Fischer-Kowalski and Helga Weisz.[69] This model presumes that almost all sources of environmental history, whether written or artifactual (i.e., archaeological or material), are the product of the interaction between nature (the "natural sphere of causation") and human culture (the "cultural sphere of causation").[70] By contrast, a complete separation of these two spheres is deemed the "traditional" or outdated approach.[71] The advantage of the interaction model is that it can be endlessly elaborated upon in order to portray the various interactions between humans and nature which, after all, is a main theme of environmental history, and which

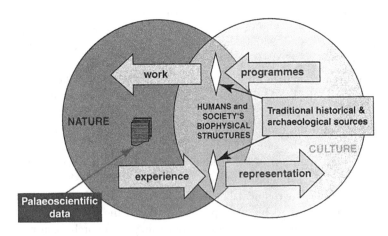

FIGURE 7.1 Venn diagram of the "Sources for environmental history"

Hoffmann developed to especially elaborate effect in order to portray the pre-industrial "agroecosystem".[72] But not all sources for medieval environmental history fit so neatly into this model; in actual fact, it is possible that the model can lead the historian astray.

One cautionary example is when environmental historians approach the disease event known as the Black Death.[73] According to the interaction model, medieval writers should have noted an abundance of rats dying from the plague, if the Black Death was indeed a disease that only spread to humans (in the bubonic form) when all the rats in a locality died (i.e., an epizootic), leaving their fleas to feed on the nearest hosts available.[74] But medieval authors generally did not mention rats, except as an environmental "sign" portending a coming plague, when they supposedly exited out of their holes in order to flee the corrupt air trapped in the earth.[75] Yet, just because there was an absence of rats from the cultural/artifactual sphere, does not mean they were absent from nature. Medieval observers were unlikely to observe sick or dying rats, since these tended to burrow deep underground or within existing structures in order to evade cannibalism from their own species (Chapter 8).[76]

By the same token, something that exists in the cultural sphere does not always intersect with natural reality. Going back to the Black Death, one cannot always trust medieval physicians' "detailed descriptions" of the symptoms of plague. While they may have been "well trained" to make such observations, they very often simply recycled ancient diagnoses, instead of making their own. A good example is how physicians described buboes, the classic symptom of bubonic plague, as appearing in a veritable rainbow of colors, including red, yellow, or green, a statement that was lifted from the *Prognostics* attributed to Hippocrates (460–370 B.C.), but for which there is no evidence that it was ever validated through empirical observation.[77] Nevertheless, this medieval testimony has been cited by some modern scholars in order to challenge the identification of the Black Death with plague, on the grounds that the two do not match in terms of their respective symptomology (Chapter 8).[78] In this case, a supposed natural or empirical phenomenon (the colorful appearance of Black Death symptoms) is purely a product of cultural assumptions made by medieval writers, with no evident basis in reality.[79] Although historians naturally look for the "sweet spot" where the designated sets or regions of theoretical diagrams overlap or intersect, in many cases, we must think outside the Venn.

Notes

1 *Annales Monastici*, ed. Henry Richards Luard, 5 vols. (London: Longmans et al., 1864–69), 3:341.

2 David A. Callus, "The Origin of the Problem of the Unity of Form," *The Thomist* 24 (1961):257–85; Anthony Kenny, *Aquinas* (Oxford: Oxford University Press, 1980), p. 44.

3 Knapwell contributed to the *Correctoria Corruptorii* (Corrections of the Corruptor), a reply to the original *Correctorium* published by William de la Mare, which listed 117 purported errors in Thomas Aquinas' writings. Knapwell's contribution, known as the

Correctorium "Quare," is available in vol. 1 of *Les Premières Polémiques Thomistes* (Le Saulchoir, France: Revue des Sciences Philosophiques et Théologiques, 1927).

4 Kenny, *Aquinas*, pp. 44–47.

5 This was apparently one of the 30 theses condemned by Archbishop Robert Kilwardby at Oxford in 1277, which coincided with the more famous condemnation by Bishop Etienne Tempier at the University of Paris. See Kenny, *Aquinas*, p. 47.

6 Kenny, *Aquinas*, p. 47.

7 *Annales Monastici*, 3:323–25.

8 See Francis E. Kelley's introduction to his edition of Richard Knapwell, *Quaestio Disputata de Unitate Formae* (Binghamton, NY.: State University of New York at Binghamton, 1982).

9 *Annales Monastici*, 3:323, 341.

10 C.J.F. Martin, *An Introduction to Medieval Philosophy* (Edinburgh: Edinburgh University Press, 1996), pp. 121–26; John Marenbon, *Medieval Philosophy: An Historical and Philosophical Introduction* (London: Routledge, 2007), pp. 245–46; Russell L. Friedman, "Latin Philosophy, 1200–1350," in *The Oxford Handbook of Medieval Philosophy*, ed. John Marenbon (Oxford: Oxford University Press, 2012), pp. 208–9. There is also debate as to whether Aquinas should be more properly classified as a philosopher or a theologian. See Brian Davies, "Thomas Aquinas," in *Routledge History of Philosophy. Volume 3: Medieval Philosophy*, ed. John Marenbon (London: Routledge, 2003), pp. 242–43, 262.

11 Wim Blockmans and Peter Hoppenbrouwers, *Introduction to Medieval Europe, 300–1550*, trans. Isola van den Hoven (London and New York: Routledge, 2007), pp. 259–60.

12 Jacques Le Goff, *Intellectuals in the Middle Ages*, trans. Teresa Lavender Fagan (Oxford: Blackwell, 1993), pp. 130–32; Blockmans and Hoppenbrouwers, *Introduction to Medieval Europe*, p. 260.

13 See, in particular, John Marenbon's review of C.J.F. Martin's *Introduction to Medieval Philosophy* in *Speculum* 73 (1998):869.

14 Kenny, *Aquinas*, pp. 32–60.

15 Claude Panaccio, "Universals," in *Oxford Handbook of Medieval Philosophy*, pp. 393–96.

16 Blockmans and Hoppenbrouwers, *Introduction to Medieval Europe*, pp. 260–61.

17 Blockmans and Hoppenbrouwers, *Introduction to Medieval Europe*, p. 260; J.T. Paasch, "Scotus and Ockham on Universals and Individuation," in *Debates in Medieval Philosophy: Essential Readings and Contemporary Responses*, ed. Jeffrey Hause (New York: Routledge, 2014), p. 371.

18 Paasch, "Scotus and Ockham," pp. 374, 392.

19 Paasch, "Scotus and Ockham," pp. 372–73; Blockmans and Hoppenbrouwers, *Introduction to Medieval Europe*, p. 261.

20 Paasch, "Scotus and Ockham," p. 374; Panaccio, "Universals," pp. 393, 395, 397; Blockmans and Hoppenbrouwers, *Introduction to Medieval Europe*, p. 261.

21 Paasch, "Scotus and Ockham," pp. 374–83; Marenbon, *Medieval Philosophy*, p. 284; Anthony Kenny, *Medieval Philosophy* (Oxford and New York: Clarendon Press and Oxford University Press, 2005), p. 87.

22 Paasch, "Scotus and Ockham," pp. 383–90; Panaccio, "Universals," pp. 396–97.

23 Paasch, "Scotus and Ockham," pp. 390–92; Marenbon, *Medieval Philosophy*, pp. 297–300; Kenny, *Medieval Philosophy*, p. 90–91; Panaccio, "Universals," pp. 397–99.

24 Some historians of medieval philosophy see the medieval universals debate as so rooted in its contemporary context that it is simply a curiosity that "has no direct relevance for current philosophical interests". Claude Panaccio, however, took a "moderately continuistic" view, in which he argued that at least some medieval arguments "are directly relevant to today's discussions," a case that he made in particular for Ockham's formulation of nominalism. See Panaccio, "Universals," pp. 385–86, 396–99.

25 Paasch, "Scotus and Ockham," p. 392.

26 J. Donald Hughes, *What is Environmental History?* (Cambridge: Polity Press, 2006), p. 124; J.R. McNeill, "Observations on the Nature and Culture of Environmental

History," *History and Theory* 42 (2003):11, 15; Richard W. Unger, "Introduction: Hoffmann in the Historiography of Environmental History," in *Ecologies and Economies in Medieval and Early Modern Europe: Studies in Environmental History for Richard C. Hoffmann* (Leiden, Netherlands: Brill, 2010), p. 1; Donald Worster, "Appendix: Doing Environmental History," in *The Ends of the Earth: Perspectives on Modern Environmental History*, ed. Donald Worster (Cambridge: Cambridge University Press, 1998), p. 290.

27 McNeill, "Observations," p. 6. There are, of course, other ways of organizing these themes. For example, Donald Hughes viewed the three themes of environmental history as encompassing: 1) "the influence of environmental factors on human history"; 2) "environmental changes caused by human actions"; and 3) "the history of human thought about the environment". One can consider Hughes' first and second themes to correspond with McNeill's first, while Hughes' third theme corresponds with McNeill's second. See Hughes, *Environmental History*, p. 3.

28 McNeill, "Observations," p. 8.

29 Worster, "Doing Environmental History," p. 294; Hughes, *Environmental History*, pp. 13–14.

30 Hughes, *Environmental History*, pp. 11–12. Hughes characterized the cultural approach to environmental history as "a subfield of intellectual history".

31 Unger, "Introduction," p. 14. Unger stated that historians who "are often driven from considering work on environmental topics because of their lack of scientific knowledge" but who have done so anyway should have followed their original instincts, because they "produce work that is of lower quality than it ought to be". The sentiment is, in my view, ungracious.

32 McNeill, "Observations," pp. 9, 11; Unger, "Introduction," pp. 13–14.

33 Hughes, *Environmental History*, pp. 124–25; McNeill, "Observations," pp. 7, 11 and n. 10; Unger, "Introduction," p. 5. This exclusion seems to be enforced by reviewers who declare that unacceptable works do "more harm than good" to the field, a judgment that I consider far in excess of what is called for by reasonable criticism.

34 Richard C. Hoffmann, *An Environmental History of Medieval Europe* (Cambridge: Cambridge University Press, 2014), pp. 87–91; John Aberth, *An Environmental History of the Middle Ages: The Crucible of Nature* (London: Routledge, 2013), p. 30; McNeill, "Observations," pp. 7–8. The main statement of the view that the Judeo-Christian tradition lies behind the West's environmentally exploitative attitudes is the famous article by Lynn White, Jr., "The Historical Roots of our Ecologic Crisis," *Science* 155 (1967):1203–7, which has generated a whole literature in response. Hoffmann, in *Environmental History of Medieval Europe*, pp. 110–12, called upon historians to explain or bridge the gap between medieval philosophical ideas of nature and their actual experiences with the environment.

35 Hoffmann, *Environmental History of Medieval Europe*, pp. 2–3; Bruce M.S. Campbell, "Nature as Historical Protagonist: Environment and Society in Pre-Industrial England," *Economic History Review* 63 (2010):310. In his textbook on medieval environmental history, Hoffmann summed up his work as "medieval history as if nature mattered".

36 For virtuoso examples of how this sort of interdisciplinary history can be done, see: Bruce M.S. Campbell, *The Great Transition: Climate, Disease and Society in the Late-Medieval World* (Cambridge: Cambridge University Press, 2016); Kyle Harper, *The Fate of Rome: Climate, Disease, and the End of an Empire* (Princeton, NJ.: Princeton University Press, 2017).

37 The latter has been done as a kind of whimsical "biography" of typhus and its role in human history, in Hans Zinsser, *Rats, Lice and History* (Boston, MA.: Little, Brown, and Co., 1935). In this kind of account, humans are relegated to playing a reactive role in forces—in this case, the *Rickettsia* bacteria and their vector, the human louse—which pre-modern societies little understood, let alone controlled. For a more serious effort that argues for the deterministic role of disease—in this case, yellow fever and malaria—in history, see J.R. McNeil, *Mosquito Empires: Ecology and War in the Greater Caribbean, 1620–1914* (Cambridge: Cambridge University Press, 2010). Also see Andrew

Cunningham, "Disease: Crisis or Transformation?" in *New Approaches to the History of Late Medieval and Early Modern Europe: Selected Proceedings of Two International Conferences at The Royal Danish Academy of Sciences and Letters in Copenhagen in 1997 and 1999*, eds. Troels Dahlerup and Per Ingesman (*Historisk-filosofiske Meddelelser*, 104, 2009), pp. 408–9.

38 Worster, "Doing Environmental History," p. 297; McNeill, "Observations," pp. 9, 36; Hughes, *Environmental History*, pp. 5, 15; Hoffmann, *Environmental History of Medieval Europe*, p. 3.

39 Campbell, *Great Transition*, pp. 22, 396; Campbell, "Nature as Historical Protagonist," p. 309.

40 Cunningham, "Disease," pp. 409–13; John Aberth, *Plagues in World History* (Lanham, MD.: Rowman and Littlefield, 2011), pp. 13–14.

41 Hoffmann, *Environmental History of Medieval Europe*, p. 3.

42 William Chester Jordan, *The Great Famine: Northern Europe in the Early Fourteenth Century* (Princeton, NJ: Princeton University Press, 1996), p. 20.

43 M.G.L. Baillie, *New Light on the Black Death: The Cosmic Connection* (Stroud, UK: Tempus, 2006); M.G.L. Baillie, "Putting Abrupt Environmental Change Back into Human History," in *Environments and Historical Change: The Linacre Lectures, 1998*, ed. Paul Slack (Oxford: Oxford University Press, 1999), pp. 60–72; Aberth, *Environmental History of the Middle Ages*, p. 4.

44 This objection was, in fact, recognized by contemporary authors at the time, such as Konrad of Megenberg. In his treatise on earthquakes as a scientific explanation for the Black Death, Megenberg acknowledged, and attempted to rebut, "doubts" as to whether the vapor released by an earthquake could explain the deaths of all people at all times and places during the plague. See Karl Sudhoff, "Pestschriften aus den ersten 150 Jahren nach der Epidemie des 'schwarzen Todes von 1348," *Archiv für Geschichte der Medizin* 11 (1919):47–51.

45 See John Aberth, *The Black Death: A New History of the Great Mortality*, forthcoming with Oxford University Press.

46 See Richard Keyser's review of Aberth, *Environmental History of the Middle Ages*, in the online journal, *The Medieval Review*, for 2013.

47 Hoffmann, *Environmental History of Medieval Europe*, esp. Chapters 5 and 6. Hoffmann did, to his credit, try to avoid some of the pitfalls noted above in the nominalist approach by addressing separately the respective "agroecosystems" in northern and Mediterranean Europe.

48 McNeill, "Observations," p. 36.

49 McNeill, "Observations," p. 38; Marina Fischer-Kowalski and Helga Weisz, "Society as Hybrid between Material and Symbolic Realms: Toward a Theoretical Framework of Society-Nature Interaction," in *New Developments in Environmental Sociology*, eds. Michael R. Redclift and Graham Woodgate (Cheltenham, UK: Edward Elgar, 2005), pp. 20–21.

50 McNeill, in "Observations," pp. 37–39, mentioned worlds systems theory and gender theory as two theoretical frameworks that have impacted environmental history, but I am not currently aware of any examples in pre-modern environmental history.

51 McNeill, "Observations," p. 6. See also: Worster, "Doing Environmental History," pp. 290–92, 297–98; Hughes, *Environmental History*, pp. 4–6, 10–11, 14–15.

52 William Cronon, "The Trouble with Wilderness, or, Getting Back to the Wrong Nature," in *Uncommon Ground: Rethinking the Human Place in Nature* (New York: W.W. Norton and Co., 1995), pp. 69–90.

53 Medieval designations of "wilderness," a term often used by monastic writers, referred to places that were desolate, otherworldly, and solitary, a refuge from material distractions, and did not necessarily designate areas previously untouched by human habitation. See: Aberth, *Environmental History of the Middle Ages*, p. 128; Hoffmann, *Environmental History of Medieval Europe*, p. 104.

54 David Herlihy, "Attitudes Toward the Environment in Medieval Society," in *Historical Ecology: Essays on Environment and Social Change*, ed. Lester J. Bilsky (Port Washington,

NY.: Kennikat Press, 1980), pp. 100–16; Hoffmann, *Environmental History of Medieval Europe*, pp. 101–8.

55 Charles R. Bowlus, "Ecological Crises in Fourteenth Century Europe," in *Historical Ecology*, pp. 86–99.

56 Aberth, *Environmental History of the Middle Ages*, pp. 1–2.

57 Herlihy, "Attitudes Toward the Environment," pp. 100–16; Hoffmann, *Environmental History of Medieval Europe*, pp. 94–97. For a more nuanced view of environmental attitudes during the early Middle Ages, see Ellen Arnold, *Negotiating the Landscape: Environment and Monastic Identity in the Medieval Ardennes* (Philadelphia, PA: University of Pennsylvania Press, 2013).

58 Martin V. Melosi, "Humans, Cities, and Nature: How Do Cities Fit in the Material World?" *Journal of Urban History* 36 (2010): 4, 7, 11.

59 Christine Mesiner Rosen and Joel Arthur Tarr, "The Importance of an Urban Perspective in Environmental History," *Journal of Urban History* 20 (1994):304.

60 If one considers an urban population as comprising, at minimum, 2000 souls, then urbanization in such localities could rise to 27–30 percent, even in primarily rural countries like England, Germany, and Russia. Such urbanization levels were also obtained in the heavily industrialized regions of Europe, such as northern and central Italy and the Low Countries. Nonetheless, a 20 percent urbanization of Europe by c. 1300, which represents a doubling from older estimates of around 10 percent, is probably the upper limit of what could be sustained by agricultural production and commodity markets in the rural hinterlands. See: Campbell, *Great Transition*, pp. 121–25; Christopher Dyer, "How Urbanised was Medieval England?" in *Peasants and Townsmen in Medival Europe: Studia in Honorem Adriaan Verhulst*, eds. J.-M. Duvosquel and E. Thoen (Ghent: Snoeck-Ducaju & Zoon, 1995), pp. 169–83; Christopher Dyer, *An Age of Transition? Economy and Society in England in the Later Middle Ages* (Oxford: Clarendon Press, 2005), pp. 14–25; S.R. Epstein, "Introduction. Town and Country in Europe, 1300–1800," in *Town and Country in Europe, 1300–1800*, ed. S.R. Epstein (Cambridge: Cambridge University Press, 2001), pp. 2–3; Hoffmann, *Environmental History of Medieval Europe*, p. 228; Ole J. Benedictow, *The Black Death, 1346–1353: The Complete History* (Woodbridge, UK: Boydell Press, 2004), pp. 32, 57; Paul Bairoch, Jean Batou, and Pierre Chèvre, *The Population of European Cities from 800 to 1850: Data Bank and Short Summary of Results* (Geneva: Publication du Centre d'histoire économique internationale de l'Université de Géneve, 1988), pp. 255, 271.

61 For example, London by the early fourteenth century imported one million bushels of grain produced from as far away as eastern Norfolk and coastal Sussex, which stimulated intensive farming practices there, while Florence imported 10,000 tonnes of grain from Sicily and Apulia, thus altering and perhaps "colonizing" their ecosystems. See: *Trade, Urban Hinterlands and Market Integration, c. 1300–1600*, ed. J. Galloway (Centre for Metropolitan History Working Papers Series, 3, 2000); Christopher Dyer, "Market Towns and the Countryside in Late Medieval England," *Canadian Journal of History* 31 (1996):17–35; Hoffmann, *Environmental History of Medieval Europe*, pp. 227–28, 231–37; John Hatcher and Mark Bailey, *Modelling the Middle Ages: The History and Theory of England's Economic Development* (Oxford: Oxford University Press, 2001), pp. 144–45; Campbell, *Great Transition*, p. 118; Bruce M.S. Campbell, James A. Galloway, Derek J. Keene, and Margaret Murphy, *A Medieval Capital and its Grain Supply: Agrarian Production and its Distribution in the London Region, c. 1300* (Historical Geography Research Series, 30, 1993).

62 R.H. Britnell, "The Black Death in English Towns," *Urban History* 21 (1994):195–210; Christopher Dyer, *Making a Living in the Middle Ages: The People of Britain, 850–1520* (New Haven: Yale University Press, 2002), pp. 300–1; J.L. Bolton, *The Medieval English Economy, 1150–1500* (London and Totowa, NJ.: J.M. Dent and Sons and Rowman and Littlefield, 1980), pp. 246–86. Counterintuitively, plague was less virulent in the city as opposed to the country, owing to the well-known inverse correlation between plague mortality and population density. However, one must also factor in migration or exodus

from cities as people attempted to flee the plague, as famously attested to in Boccaccio's *Decameron*. See Ole J. Benedictow, *What Disease was Plague? On the Controversy over the Microbiological Identity of Plague Epidemics of the Past* (Leiden, Netherlands: Brill, 2010), pp. 289–311; Benedictow, *Black Death*, pp. 31–34; Ole J. Benedictow, "Morbidity in Historical Plague Epidemics," *Population Studies* 41 (1987):401–31.

63 Dyer, *Age of Transition*, p. 21; Dyer, *Making a Living*, pp. 303, 312–13. Dyer estimated that the number of towns in Britain fell from 800 to 750 at this time; this is not to deny that there was some urban growth in the late medieval period, but, as Dyer emphasized, it "tended to be localized and small scale".

64 Christopher R. Friedrichs, "Urban Transformation? Some Constants and Continuities in the Crisis-Challenged City," in *New Approaches to the History of Late Medieval and Early Modern Europe*, pp. 253–54, 256–58, 269–70.

65 Worster, "Doing Environmental History," p. 292.

66 Melosi, "Humans, Cities, and Nature," p. 10.

67 Hoffmann, *Environmental History of Medieval Europe*, pp. 232–37.

68 Blockmans and Hoppenbrouwers, *Introduction to Medieval Europe*, p. 287.

69 Fischer-Kowalski and Weisz, "Society as Hybrid ," pp. 215–51; Hoffmann, *Environmental History of Medieval Europe*, pp. 7–15. Fischer-Kowalski and Weisz explained that they developed the interaction model from "modern systems theory," in particular from the models of Stephen Boyden, Maurice Godelier, and Rolf Peter Sieferle, in order to bridge the "epistemological dualism" between the natural and social sciences, or between the material and the symbolic. They claimed to do this through the identification of "two key processes of society-nature interactions: socioeconomic metabolism and colonization of natural processes".

70 Fischer-Kowalski and Weisz, "Society as Hybrid ," pp. 24–25; Hoffmann, *Environmental History of Medieval Europe*, pp. 14–15. The only sources that Hoffmann excluded from the intersection area of his Venn diagram were "paleoscientific data," such as "inferences from tree rings, ice cores, isotopic analysis of organic items, animal bones," and other such "proxy data," which he placed entirely in the Nature portion of his diagram. An even more complex Venn diagram to illustrate a "dynamic socio-ecological system" was produced by Bruce Campbell, comprising no less that six "core components" intersecting with each other, including: "Climate," "Society," "Ecosystems," "Biology," "Microbes," and "Humans". See Campbell, *Great Transition*, p. 22, figure 1.2.

71 Hoffmann, *Environmental History of Medieval Europe*, p. 7.

72 Hoffmann, *Environmental History of Medieval Europe*, pp. 9, 157–58.

73 Hoffmann, *Environmental History of Medieval Europe*, pp. 289–98. In this section, Hoffmann clearly favored the work of plague deniers like Samuel Cohn and gave no indication that he consulted the work of anti-revisionists, such as Ole Benedictow's *What Disease was Plague*, which was published by Brill in 2010. For example, Hoffman stated that Cohn's "gathering attack on received diagnostic opinion . . . has not yet been fully refuted" and that "unproven diagnoses provide no grounds for deeper explanations". But by favoring plague denial arguments, Hoffmann missed the opportunity to fully explore the environmental interconnectedness of humans, microbes, rodent hosts, and insect vectors, which is a defining feature of bubonic plague. See: Hoffmann, *Environmental History of Medieval Europe*, p. 292; Campbell, *Great Transition*, pp. 230–40; Kenneth L. Gage and Michael Y. Kosoy, "Natural History of Plague: Perspectives from More than a Century of Research," *Annual Review of Entomology* 50 (2005):505–28.

74 Hoffman, *Environmental History of Medieval Europe*, pp. 294–95; Anne Karin Hufthammer and Lars Walløe, "Rats Cannot Have Been Intermediate Hosts for *Yersinia pestis* during Medieval Plague Epidemics in Northern Europe," *Journal of Archaeological Science* 40 (2013):1753–56; G. Karlsson, "Plague Without Rats: The Case of Fifteenth-Century Iceland," *Journal of Medieval History* 22 (1996):263–65, 276–80; David E. Davis, "The Scarcity of Rats and the Black Death: An Ecological History," *Journal of Interdisciplinary History* 16 (1986):455–70; Samuel K. Cohn, Jr., *The Black Death Transformed: Disease and Culture in Early Renaissance Europe* (London and Oxford: Arnold and Oxford University

Press, 2003), pp. 1, 21–22, 81–82, 134; Graham Twigg, *The Black Death: A Biological Reappraisal* (New York: Schocken Books, 1984), pp. 111–12; J.F.D. Shrewsbury, *A History of Bubonic Plague in the British Isles* (Cambridge: Cambridge University Press, 1970), pp. 7, 23, 53; Susan Scott and Christopher J. Duncan, *Biology of Plagues: Evidence from Historical Populations* (Cambridge: Cambridge University Press, 2001), pp. 56–57. Such arguments from silence as to the non-existence of medieval rats have been effectively countered by: Michael McCormick, "Rats, Communications, and Plague: Toward an Ecological History," *Journal of Interdisciplinary History* 34 (2003):5–6, 14–15; Benedictow, *What Disease was Plague*, pp. 85–97, 140–41; Anton Ervynck, "Sedentism or Urbanism? On the Origin of the Commensal Black Rat (*Rattus rattus*)," in *Bones and the Man: Studies in Honour of Don Brothwell*, eds. Keith Dobney and Terry O'Connor (Oxford: Oxbow Books, 2002), pp. 95–96.

75 Benedictow, *What Disease was Plague*, pp. 81–82; Cohn, *Black Death Transformed*, p. 133. This sign was derived from Avicenna and was unlikely to have been actually observed in the field.

76 Benedictow, *What Disease was Plague*, pp. 92–97; L. Fabian Hirst, *The Conquest of Plague: A Study of the Evolution of Epidemiology* (Oxford: Clarendon Press, 1953), pp. 147–48. Even during the Third Pandemic, modern researchers, armed with a "rat intelligence staff" and with the epidemiological knowledge of exactly how bubonic plague was spread, had difficulty in finding rats while excavating plague-infested houses. See: W.B. Bannerman, "The Spread of Plague in India," *Journal of Hygiene* 6 (1906):183–84; Indian Plague Research Commission, Reports on Plague Investigations in India, XXIII: "Epidemiological Observations in the Villages of Sion, Wadhala, Parel and Worli in Bombay Villages," *Journal of Hygiene* 7 (1907):825, 836, 839, 845–46, 854, 869; Indian Plague Research Commission, Reports on Plague Investigations in India, XXXVI: "Observations of Plague in Belgaum, 1908–1909," *Journal of Hygiene* 10 (1910):453–54.

77 Karl Sudhoff, "Pestschriften aus den ersten 150 Jahren nach der Epidemie des 'schwarzen Todes' von 1348," *Archiv für Geschichte der Medizin* 11 (1919):151.

78 Cohn, *Black Death Transformed*, pp. 61–62.

79 See Hoffmann, *Environmental History of Medieval Europe*, pp. 14–15, 291, 297.

8

ASHES TO ASHES, WE ALL FALL DOWN

The Black Death

Ever since I can remember, I have been fascinated by the Black Death, a disease pandemic that, in just a few years in the mid-fourteenth century, wiped out at least half the population of Europe and which is often described as the greatest natural disaster in the history of humankind.[1] To a large degree, I believe my fascination is due to the fact that I myself have had a close brush with death. When I was five years old, I was diagnosed with a lung condition that required major surgery—a bilateral lobectomy, which in laymen's terms means a portion of the lungs, in my case, a quarter of them, was removed on both sides of the chest. I can still remember being wheeled to the operating room: the cold, crisp green of the bedsheets, the nauseating smell of antiseptic, and then my horizon filled by a black mask being lowered down onto my face as I heard it hissing gas that soon suffocated me into a vision of swirling spirals. When I woke up, my head was in an oxygen tent and I looked down to see tubes coming out of my chest, draining fluid. I was later told that I had a 25 percent chance of dying that day. While the operation did save my life, my time in hospital was also a nightmare that haunted me throughout my childhood.

Given this traumatic experience, it somehow (and rather perversely) gives me comfort to know that a whole society suffered equally, if not more, during the Black Death. Here was a time when death was everywhere, and virtually no one could escape death. My near-brush with death was the norm, and not so strange at all.

Obviously, the Black Death is fascinating to a lot of people, for a variety of reasons. It is probably fair to say that the Black Death has been one of the most hotly debated of historical topics, and that for a very long time, although this debate has become particularly heated in recent years. Indeed, the use of the term, "Black Death," in Danish, Icelandic, German, and English works beginning in the seventeenth century, already seems to mark the emergence of the subject as an academic industry.[2] (Contemporary commentators during the Middle Ages invariably referred to the event as the "plague," the "pestilence," or the "great mortality".) But really, what is so fascinating about the Black Death?

I believe that this has to do with more than just the fact that a lot of people died (about 50 million in Europe, according to best estimates[3]). It also has to do with the fact that many others *survived*. The Black Death is about as close (hopefully) as Western civilization will ever come to the Apocalypse, the end of everything. This is, in fact, what contemporaries believed in 1348. Did not the Sienese chronicler, Agnolo di Tura, who buried five of his children with his own hands, remark, "So many have died that everyone believes it is the end of the world"?[4] And was it not the humanist author, Francesco Petrarch, who said, "When will posterity believe this to have been a time in which nearly the whole world— not just this or that part of the earth—is bereft of inhabitants, without there having occurred a conflagration in the heavens or on land, without wars or other visible disasters"?[5] And yet, this was not the end. It was, rather, the beginning, the start of a rebirth, a transition to the Renaissance. In spite of the recurrence of plague throughout the latter half of the fourteenth and throughout the fifteenth centuries, Europe recovered and went on to forge a dynamic society, economy, and culture that was poised to extend itself across the globe by the very end of the Middle Ages. In this regard, the Black Death is actually quite an uplifting story, one full of hope and promise, which holds out the lesson that humans can be incredibly and profoundly resilient, even in the face of the worst that God and nature can throw at them. It is also a story that historians have struggled to explain ever since.

This chapter can only scratch the surface of the historiography surrounding the Black Death. My focus here will be on three hotly-debated topics: the identity of the disease with plague; the demographic scale of the mortality; and the socio-economic impact of plague. I realize that I am omitting many other topics on the Black Death that are important to scholars, including myself.[6] But I believe that these topics are not only central to Black Death studies but also illustrate some of the burning issues associated with the study of all historical occurrences of disease.

The great denial of plague

For nearly the past half century, a debate has been raging as to whether the Black Death is to be identified with the disease known as plague. Plague is caused by a bacterium, *Yersinia pestis*, which produces three forms of the disease depending on how it invades the human body. By far the most common form throughout history has been bubonic plague, so named because its characteristic symptom is the bubo, a lymphatic swelling at the nodular point closest to where the victim has become infected, in this case, by the subcutaneous bite of a flea. The flea, in turn, became infected by living on a rat whose bloodstream was swarming with the plague bacteria, as much as 100–200 million per cc of blood.

Absent antibiotics, an average of 80 percent of human victims die from bubonic plague in 3–5 days of infection.[7] In the second form, known as pneumonic plague, victims contract the disease directly from another victim by inhaling expectorated droplets containing the plague bacteria into the lungs. Pneumonic plague is 100 percent fatal without the timely administration of antibiotics, and victims typically die within two days as they cough up blood (but do not develop bubos). However, because pneumonic plague is harder to get than a viral infection, such as flu (bacteria are about 1000 times larger than viruses, and thus do not travel so easily through the air or down into the lungs), and because victims are typically infective for very short periods of time (19 hours on average, during which coughing symptoms emerge), pneumonic plague is not thought to have played a major role in most epidemic outbreaks in history.[8] Finally, there is septicemic plague, in which the bacteria have somehow managed to invade the victim's bloodstream directly, bypassing the lymphatic system that is the body's first line of defense against infections, and proliferate rapidly, invading nearly all the bodily organs and causing rapid death, again without emergence of the tell-tale bubos. Septicemic plague, while rare, is also 100 percent fatal and has been found to cause death in 15 hours on average, with some victims dying in just one hour from infection and others lasting, at most, 24 hours.[9]

It should be stated at the outset that the debate over whether the Black Death is to be identified with plague is now effectively over—with the verdict decisively in favor of the Black Death being plague. A definitive resolution of this debate was made possible by paleomicrobiology, the science of studying past disease epidemics by recovering the ancient DNA (aDNA) of pathogens from human remains.[10] Two decades ago, a French team pioneered the technique of extracting the dental pulp from the teeth of plague victims by splitting open the tooth longitudinally and then scraping out the pulp in the form of a brown or white powder.[11] Assuming that the plague victim developed bacterial septicemia (i.e., bacteremia), the plague bacteria, after migrating through the blood stream into the blood vessels (i.e., the dental pulp) of teeth, would then have been "encapsulated" by the tooth enamel after the death of the patient, preserving the sample for centuries.[12] Nonetheless, the initial findings of the French team were challenged, largely on the grounds that their ancient samples may have been contaminated by modern *Yersinia pestis* DNA in the laboratory, even though no proof was ever adduced of such contamination.[13] When an English team tried to replicate the results, they failed, although this was hardly surprising, given that they didn't use the same dental pulp extraction technique, nor did they sample hardly any subjects from confirmed plague pits.[14]

The years 2010–11 proved to be a turning point in the paleomicrobiological study of plague. Three studies published by two large, international teams of scientists confirmed the presence of *Yersinia pestis* aDNA at mid-fourteenth century plague pits in Hereford and East Smithfield, London, in England; at Bergen-op-Zoom in the Netherlands; and at Saint-Laurent-de-la-Cabrerisse in France.[15] Because the aDNA recovered from these plague pits show damage patterns consistent with aging in other ancient samples, we know that they are medieval and not contaminated by modern *Yersinia pestis* DNA.[16] The research team working on the East Smithfield site even was able to reconstruct a complete genome, or DNA sequence, as well as a complete plasmid, or DNA molecule, from ancient samples recovered from no less than 100 plague victims buried during the first outbreak of the Black Death in 1349.[17] Meanwhile, at least thirteen more studies published between 2002 and 2010, building upon the two pioneering French studies of 1998–2000, confirmed *Yersinia pestis* aDNA recovery from sites dating to both the First and Second Pandemics in England, France, Germany, and Italy.[18]

Based on the aDNA reported in 2010–11, as well as genetic mapping of modern global samples, scholars now believe that the Black Death was caused by new (albeit not necessarily more virulent) strains of *Yersinia pestis*—distinct from those that caused the First Pandemic, now extinct—that emerged during a genetic "big bang" in Asia sometime during the late thirteenth or early fourteenth century (perhaps 1268?), shortly before the advent of the Second Pandemic.[19] What is more, the aDNA of *Yersinia pestis* seems to have mutated during the first outbreak of the Black Death, resulting in different strains that afflicted the Netherlands as opposed to France and England, with the Netherlands strain now extinct.[20] Since the pivotal studies of 2010–11, at least six more have been published or conducted that confirm recovery of *Yersinia pestis* aDNA in sites dating to both the First and Second Pandemics in England, Italy, France, and Germany.[21] All told, I have counted at least 24 separate studies—representing 32 grave sites in five European countries—that have independently confirmed through paleomicrobiology that the Black Death was indeed plague.[22]

It was therefore the Black Death that introduced the world to the plague as we know it today. What is actually surprising is how few genetic changes have accrued to *Yersinia pestis* DNA since the Black Death, while a comparison of the plasmid responsible for virulence reveals that the Black Death and modern strains of plague are nearly identical in terms of their pathogenic effect on humans.[23] This means that, as a toxic organism, *Yersinia pestis* has barely changed for the past 670-odd years, remaining as deadly today as it was in the Middle Ages. This should really not be surprising, as *Yersinia pestis*, rather than selecting for lower virulence over time as is typical of most microorganisms, instead selects for *higher* virulence, and thus evolutionary stability, because its chief animal vector is the rat, not a human, and it must cause virulent septicemia in rats in order to saturate the bloodstream enough to infect more rodent fleas.[24] Perhaps the next stage in this genetic research is to use the reconstructed genome to resurrect a live *Yersinia pestis* bacterium from the Black Death and test its virulence in the laboratory, as has been done for the infamous H1N1 strain of the influenza virus that was responsible for the 1918–19 flu pandemic; needless to say, however, the ethics surrounding such an experiment are extremely controversial.[25]

Taken all together, the paleomicrobiological evidence is now overwhelmingly conclusive and should really end debate on the matter, since it constitutes scientific proof and cannot be refuted or explained away.[26] But for a hardcore group of "plague deniers," or skeptics, it hasn't ended the debate at all.[27] When presented with the facts, these scholars have responded in a variety of ways, including outright denial or even misrepresentation of the evidence.[28] Sometimes plague deniers contested the paleomicrobiological evidence pre-emptively, even before this presented itself. In their view, this stance was justified on the grounds that their interpretation of historical incongruities between the medieval and modern occurrences of plague trumped the scientific findings of paleomicrobiology.[29] Some historians also insisted that the "laboratory construction of plague" was irrelevant to pre-modern epidemics, on the assumption that the techniques of the laboratory could never be applied to diseases of the past, an assumption that was true until paleomicrobiology proved them wrong.[30]

Obviously, a position that believes it is so right that it cannot be gainsaid even by science, leaves little room for debate or testing of its hypothesis according to the scientific method.[31] Moreover, to claim unquestioning orthodoxy for plague denial comes off as rather hypocritical, in that it comes full circle to the position that most plague deniers were rebelling against in the first place, namely, the dogmatic assumption that the Black Death was plague! That diagnosis was originally made by a group of researchers in the early twentieth century, who had the advantage (from a strictly academic point of view) of having actual, personal experience out in the field with plague as a human disease during the Third Pandemic.[32] It is right and proper that, after a hiatus of about a half century or so, scholars should have taken a second look at the evidence and reviewed the case for the Black Death being plague. But it is also right and proper that, now that an almost equal amount of time has passed since plague deniers first made their case, it be the turn of plague denial to receive the scrutiny that had formerly been wielded against plague.[33]

This scrutiny might seem superfluous in light of the verdict of paleomicro-biology, but actually, the task of hearing out plague deniers on their own terms is more urgent now than ever. This is because plague deniers' objections continue to be cited, even by those who accept the paleomicrobiological evidence, as caveats to what otherwise would be a definitive end to debate.[34] Plague denial arguments are also used to revive long-established alternatives to the rat-based spread of bubonic plague, such as that most victims of the Black Death succumbed to pneumonic plague, or that the disease was spread person-to-person via the human flea, *Pulex irritans*, and perhaps the body louse, *Pediculus humanus humanus* (see below).[35] Is there really an "insoluble conundrum" between what the science of paleomicrobiology and the evidence of history say, or do both confirm that the Black Death was, indeed, bubonic plague?[36]

To some observers, the very fact that the opposing position has been proved by scientific evidence would indicate that something is terribly wrong with the arguments of plague denial. The counter-skeptics do indeed contend that plague denial is plagued (to pardon the pun) by so many logical fallacies that it is rendered quite invalid.[37] Added to this was the, at times, strident and confrontational tone in which some plague deniers made their case, which in hindsight now appears as overcompensation for an inherently weak argument.[38] Perhaps emboldened by the verdict of paleomicrobiology, counter-skeptics have only recently begun to challenge plague denial and push back against some of its claims.[39]

Plague denial rests on three main "pillars". Perhaps the "trump card" of plague deniers—since it seems to be one of the most popular and often-cited of their claims—is that, historically, the Black Death spread too fast across the continent of Europe to be the same disease as the slow-moving plague that spread gradually across the continent of India (and other continents, such as the United States) during the Third Pandemic.[40] A favorite expression is that the Black Death spread "almost as quickly" per day as plague spreads in a year, "despite the latter having the benefit of the railway and motorized transport".[41] If true, this would indeed be a remarkable circumstance that would make it almost impossible to reconcile the Black Death disease with plague. But counter-skeptics would argue that this is actually no more than an excellent illustration of the logical fallacy of the false analogy, or false equivalence, between two phenomena occurring in entirely different contexts.

The allegedly slow-moving spread of plague, which is characterized as occurring at a rate of anywhere between 4 to 20 miles a year, applies only to *panzootics*, or spread of disease across large regions among rats and wild rodents.[42] Here, plague does indeed progress slowly and gradually, as one infected colony must contaminate an adjacent one through *contiguous* spread.[43] But this does not apply to *zoonotics*, or disease outbreaks passing from rats to humans.[44] In this case, plague spreads by "metastatic" leaps, or spread at a distance, in which the rat hosts and flea vectors are transported, typically in grain cargos, by means of human-mediated methods, which in the Middle Ages would be by ship (at about 25 miles per day) or by cart- or pack-horse (12–30 miles per day).[45] These are well within the "astonishing" and fast spread rates claimed for the medieval Black Death (1–3.7 miles per day).[46] Once at their new location, the infected rats and fleas established new "epicenters" of infection, from which new animal and insect carriers were transported metastatically, and so on, spreading the plague in a multiplicative or exponential fashion.[47]

Obviously, plague deniers are here conflating two very different kinds of disease outbreaks, i.e, one among only rats and wild rodents (panzootics), and one among rats and humans (zoonotics and pandemics), each having a very different mechanism of spread. Given that plague failed to establish an enduring endemic focus in Europe, except in the Caucasus region between the Black and Caspian Seas, it is possible that plague never spread across the Continent by contiguous means, but always traveled via human-mediated transport of rats and fleas.[48] This means that, for the purposes of comparison with, or modeling of, the potential spread rate of the medieval Black Death, we should only use modern data that relates to human pandemics, specifically, the spread of plague by metastatic leaps.

There is plenty of evidence on the mechanism of metastatic leaps as the means of spreading plague during the Third Pandemic, which was gathered by the Indian Plague Research Commission under the heading of the phenomenon's Latin name, *per saltem* ("by leaps"). In reports from 1906, the Commission relied mainly on anecdotal evidence of plague spreading to distant villages by means of human-mediated transport of the clothing or bedding of infected victims.[49] But in the next year, 1907, the Commission was able to scientifically prove that plague was spread short- to intermediate-range distances by means of infected fleas concealed on travelers' clothing or in their bedding, and over longer distances by means of both infected rats and infected fleas transported in grain and other merchandise. The Commission traced victims or carriers who traveled between Mumbai and several outlying, isolated villages; sometimes researchers even took suspected clothing and bedding back to the laboratory, where guinea pigs that roamed free among the clothing came down with plague, but those protected from fleas by a mesh or gauze barrier were spared.[50] Spread of plague by metastatic leaps was also independently confirmed by additional studies and observations of the disease in Egypt, China, Indonesia, and South America.[51] Reflecting back on 40 years' worth of evidence during the Third Pandemic, L. Fabian Hirst concluded that transportation of merchandise, particularly grain, rather than of human persons, was the more important factor in the passive spread of plague by metastatic leaps, and that fleas traveling alone were of equal, if not greater, importance as rats as the carriers of infection in this merchandise.[52] Whatever the exact mechanism, the ability of plague to spread all around the world by metastatic leaps—namely, infected rats and fleas traveling on steamships—was demonstrated by the fact that within a few years, between 1894 and 1901, plague spread from the ports of Hong Kong and Mumbai to other ports of call in Madagascar, South Africa, Southeast Asia, South America, Russia, Australia, and the western United States.[53]

The haphazard spread of plague by metastatic leaps was noted not just by modern researchers. Medieval authors who lived through the first outbreak of the Black Death in 1348–49 observed it too.[54] Plague was observed to suddenly change direction, sometimes reversing course and retracing "its steps in places already visited," or else it raged "in two towns a long way from each other," but not "in places in between," only to hit the intermediate place later.[55] Some observers compared this to "a bodily form propelled by winds in the airy regions," or else to "a hail storm leaving one area intact while destroying another".[56] Others said it was like the leaping or skipping moves of a game of chess.[57] Such erratic or unpredictable movements no doubt contributed to the fear and terror with which plague was regarded by contemporaries, in that plague seemed to have a mind all its own, "as if [arbitrarily] choosing where it might rage [next]".[58] This seems to have been a general phenomenon, for similar observations were made by authors no matter if they were based in Germany, Italy, or France.[59]

Metastatic leaps are fully compatible with the chronicle and archival record of when and where plague made landfall in various localities throughout Europe.[60] They are also supported by paleomicrobiology, in that one study found two separate strains of *Yersinia pestis* (both presumably originating in central Asia): one occurring in southeastern France (Saint-Laurent-de-la-Cabrerisse) and southwestern England (Hereford); the other in southern Netherlands (Bergen op Zoom). This suggests that there were different routes of dissemination of the disease, one heading north from France to England, the other going south from Norway (and ultimately, England) and Friesland to the southern Netherlands.[61]

However, metastatic leaps are not amenable to mapping. By their very nature, maps convey a linear progression of the disease that belies any ambiguities and complexities in the historical record.[62] Even a map that uses "state-of-the-art" stochastic modeling in order to reveal the unique "spatio-temporal character" of the Black Death will be biased if it assumes a linear transmission of the disease involving "direct contact between infecteds and susceptibles," and it will only be as good as the historical figures that are plugged into it, which, given the vagaries of the medieval record, means that the starting and end points of any given "chain [of] transmission" cannot be known precisely.[63] Because plague spread by metastatic leaps can invade two places at the same time from different directions, it can give the *illusion* of very rapid spread in a straight line from point A to point B. To give one example, which can stand in for many, it traditionally has been assumed that the Black Death, having arrived in Marseilles at the end of December 1347, then traveled directly due north overland to Paris, where it arrived at the end of June 1348, covering a distance of about 482 miles in 182 days, or at a rate of 2.5 miles per day.[64] But, based on fuller records, it now appears that the Black Death came to Paris from the *north*, namely, from Rouen just inland from the Normandy coast, where it probably arrived at the end of April 1348 by ship. This would mean that the Black Death traveled the 75 miles from Rouen to Paris in 62 days, or at a rate of 1.2 miles per day, half the overland pace assumed from Marseilles to Paris.[65]

The default assumption is that a person-to-person transmission of the Black Death—whether in the form of pneumonic plague, a viral disease, or bubonic plague transmitted by the human flea (*Pulex irritans*) or by the body louse (*Pediculus humanus humanus*) —would solve this alleged problem of its too rapid spread.[66] But in actuality, a far and fast spread of the Black Death in medieval Europe would have been *less* likely, not more, if it was strictly a human-mediated disease. The fact of the matter is that human travelers communicating plague would have needed to travel in exactly the same way as rats and fleas, namely, by ship or horse transport. Presumably, the time saved in human contagion would be owing to the fact that a rat epizootic, or die-off, would not now be necessary before the disease made the jump to humans.[67]

However, it recently has been discovered that "early-phase transmission" can occur in rat flea vectors, including *Xenopsylla cheopis*, considered to be the main flea vector of the Black Death. Here, fleas can effectively transmit plague in less than 4 days, as opposed to 10–14 days in "blocked" transmission, meaning that the time required to ignite a zoonotic from rats to humans is now cut in half, from about 3–4 weeks on average to 1½–2 weeks.[68] If rats were spreading plague among each other by pneumonic means, then this might shave off a few more days, as the incubation and progression to death was much shorter than in bubonic plague.[69] By comparison, most deadly inter-human diseases, even viral ones like smallpox or hemorrhagic fever, still require close, prolonged contact for infection and in addition have long incubation periods in their human host, such as 9–12 days for smallpox and a similar period for hemorrhagic fever.[70] While presumably victims could still travel while incubating the disease, the window of opportunity for long-distance travel was short—a week at most—before incapacitating sickness set in.[71] Moreover, while early-phase transmission does make it more likely that *Pulex irritans*, which rarely blocks, could act as an effective vector of plague, there is still the insuperable obstacle that human victims rarely produced the high levels of bacteremia required to infect new flea vectors that could then transmit plague person-to-person.[72]

Perhaps the biggest obstacle to human-to-human spread of the Black Death is the fact that, if such a mode of transmission really did prevail, then medieval people would have had both the knowledge and the capacity to prevent so tragic a loss of life, but clearly were unable to do so. Doctor after doctor writing during the Black Death warned readers that plague was contagious, and, while they did not think of contagion in the same way as we do today—i.e., interpreting this in "miasmatic" terms rather than via germs—this would not have impeded their ability to prevent such contagion.[73] Medieval doctors like Gentile da Foligno, writing in 1347 just before plague arrived on mainland Italy, warned that plague was spread through "poisonous air" from "man to man, household to household, neighborhood to neighborhood, city to city," and also from "region to region".[74] Because, it was said, people got infected by means of "communication with other, infected people," Foligno advised that "no sick man from contaminated parts should be permitted to enter the city".[75] Plague doctors also warned readers of their treatises to be wary of approaching plague patients, or to simply flee from them, even if they be close family members, and to take other precautions, such as ventilating the room and turning one's face away from the patient in order not to be "infected by his fetid breath".[76] Moreover, one must avoid not only those obviously infected by the disease, such as people "covered with sores" or who gave off a bad stench, but even those "who appear in the best of health" but who came from infected places.[77]

We know that at least some of this advice was acted on: The city of Pistoia, whose ordinances from 1348 survive, ordered that no one from surrounding towns be allowed to enter the city (nor that any citizen be allowed to leave to travel to those towns), and this quarantine was extended even to foreigners' clothing and bedding.[78] By the fifteenth century and on into the Early Modern period, town health boards organized quite impressive plague control measures to be implemented at the first hint of an epidemic.[79] But while these efforts may have had some impact, they certainly didn't halt the persistent, and sometimes heavy, mortality of later plague outbreaks.[80] If the Black Death had truly been a person-to-person, airborne disease, the measures should have had an appreciable effect. During the Third Pandemic, the North Manchurian Plague Prevention Service, under Dr. Wu Liande, demonstrated how effective simple plague controls could be—even before the age of antibiotics—when it was able to reduce the tens of thousands of deaths from the first pneumonic plague outbreak in 1910–11 down to 9,300 during the second outbreak in 1920–21, a reduction of anywhere from

78 to 85 percent.[81] All this was accomplished by basic precautions that could have been easily adopted (and were) by medieval predecessors, such as isolation of plague victims and their contacts (in railway boxcars) and by avoiding the breath of victims (by wearing a cotton–gauze mask over the mouth).[82] By contrast, the very fact that rats and their fleas went unnoticed by most observers during the Black Death would, in this instance, be a point in their favor as candidates for a disease vector and host, since this would have enabled them to slip into human population centers with relative ease.

This brings us to the second pillar of plague denial, that there weren't enough rats in medieval Europe to spread bubonic plague, on the grounds that evidence is lacking for their existence.[83] This relies on the argument from silence, i.e., that if something is not mentioned in the historical record, then it does not exist.[84] The argument is a particularly weak one in this instance, as the method of looking for evidence of the presence of medieval rats has, until fairly recently, been so very flawed. Here, there are two types of evidence to consider: archaeological and written sources. Archaeologically, evidence of rat bones requires special techniques not normally employed by excavators armed only with the trowel and the naked eye: These include fine sieving (1–2 mm mesh or smaller) and examination of sieved residue under a microscope. They also require a more imaginative search for clues, such as evidence of gnawing on other animal bones, and presence of rat bones in owl pellets and the like.[85] Nonetheless, the presence of any rat bones underground must reflect only a fraction of the actual rat population that originally existed, as black rats not only like to burrow into earthen floors but also, being nimble climbers, nest in thatch or tile roofs, where their bones would have been dispersed once the roofs were replaced or the buildings fallen down.[86] Even so, the latest survey of medieval rat archaeological finds states that the new data "challenge the opinion that late medieval Europe had too few rats to have sustained bubonic plague during the Black Death". In fact, the most numerous rat finds have been found on sites dating to the thirteenth century or later, hinting at "hugely expanding rat populations" on the eve of the Black Death.[87]

The other difficulty is in identifying rats in medieval written sources. This is not as straightforward as it might seem, as, linguistically speaking, classical and medieval Latin did not distinguish between a rat and a mouse, using the term *mus* for both. (In fact, *mus* remained the scientific name for rat, as in *Mus rattus* rather than *Rattus rattus*, up until 1910.) Specific, vernacular terms for "rat" were only just coming into usage during the late Middle Ages.[88] More importantly, it is unrealistic, and anachronistic, to expect medieval chroniclers and other observers to mention rats or rat epizootics at all in connection with the Black Death.[89] The role played by rats and their fleas in the spread of plague to humans was not explicated until 1898 by the French researcher, Paul-Louis Simond, who was working in India during the Third Pandemic.[90] During the Middle Ages (and indeed, right up until the late nineteenth century), most natural philosophers and physicians assumed that plague was spread through the air, in what was known as the "miasmatic" theory of disease. The only notice taken of rats in this context would have been as one of many species of vermin, including flies, worms, snakes, frogs, etc., whose appearance above ground indicated that the corruption spreading through the air had originated in the earth.[91]

Urban authorities also tended to associate disease with pigs, owing to their perceived affinity for filth and refuse and their ubiquitous presence in city landscapes and slaughterhouses.[92] Otherwise, the standard position of most medieval thinkers was that humans and animals had different susceptibilities to disease owing to their different complexions, with men understood to be more prone to plague owing to their "finer" or "nobler" disposition.[93] It also seems to be the case that black rats, shy creatures by nature, become even less visible when, weakened and sick with plague, they hide down burrows and within walls in order to escape predation by other rats. Rats eating other rats was observed during the Third Pandemic, both out in the field and under laboratory conditions, and the difficulty of finding dead rats from a plague epizootic—even for modern researchers armed with the knowledge of a rat-plague connection and who employed a "rat intelligence staff" to excavate burrows and tear apart the walls and roofs of homes to find them— was testified by the experience of fighting plague in India, Australia, Egypt, Sri Lanka, and Java.[94]

Regardless of these caveats, there are, in fact, a number of chroniclers and other authors who mentioned rats in connection with the Black Death. Some of this testimony was apocryphal and thus unlikely to accord with any reality-based observations. Giovanni Villani of Florence, for example, wrote in 1348 that in Sivas in Anatolia, "it rained an immeasurable quantity of vermin [*vermi*], some as big as eight hands, all black and with tails".[95] The Greek chronicler, Nicephorus Gregoras, was perhaps more realistic when he stated that many domestic animals living with men were also killed by plague, including dogs, horses, all species of birds, and "the rats that happened to live within the walls of houses".[96] Many plague treatise authors paraphrased a passage from the *Canon* of the eleventh-century Persian physician, Avicenna (Ibn Sīnā), to the effect that during a pestilence, mice or rats (*mures*) and other "animals that dwell underground" fled to the surface and exited out of their holes.[97] This, also, cannot be taken at face value, since it was one of the environmental "signs" of plague that medieval doctors repeated verbatim from Avicenna, with no evidence that it had any basis in actual experience with the disease.[98]

There is, however, one testimonial that seems to be a genuine empirical observation of rats in connection with the medieval Black Death. The fifteenth-century Strasbourg physician, John of Saxony, related a personal anecdote by way of illustrating Avicenna's authoritative statement on rats issuing from holes in the ground. It so happened that a "certain neighbor" of his in Strasbourg lost eight of ten children in the space of eight days from bubonic plague, all of them coming down with a "pestilential swelling [*bocio pestilenciali*]". On the good doctor's advice, the surviving household transferred itself to another dwelling, whereupon it was cured of its infection "in fifteen days". Meanwhile, a horde of rats or mice (*mures*) "scurried into the same house so that the rest of the household that had stayed put could not fend them off," and the remaining occupants thereby decided to decamp, leaving "a lamp burning that is [still] there to the present [day]".[99] Saxony's advice to the poor survivors of this family ravaged by the plague was remarkably in sync with the native Indian response during the Third Pandemic, namely, to evacuate the plague-afflicted area, which the Plague Research Commission admitted was one of the few measures that proved successful in halting plague outbreaks (since it removed potential victims from the site of rat epizootics).[100] While, admittedly, Saxony did not witness a rat epizootic, namely, he had not seen any rodents dead from the plague, to dismiss this important piece of evidence on these grounds is absurd.[101] Saxony clearly described a rat infestation of a household overrun by the plague, and this alone is extremely significant.

The third pillar of plague denial argues that the appearance, number, and location of bubos and other skin manifestations of the disease as described by chroniclers and doctors during the Black Death does not accord with the symp-tomology of modern plague.[102] There is indeed an impressive marshalling of evidence in support of this argument.[103] On the other hand, counter-skeptics argue that no amount of evidence matters if the interpretation of it is method-ologically flawed. Plague deniers are charged once again with the logical fallacy of the false analogy, or false equivalence: in this case, that they expect the testimony of medieval doctors and chroniclers to live up to the same standards as those of modern, clinical diagnoses of plague, such as were made during the Third Pandemic in India.[104] It is perhaps true that plague doctors evinced a new-found empiricism as a direct result of their experience with the Black Death .[105] But this does not mean that plague doctors abandoned authorities; for many, marshaling *both* authority and experience—and somehow reconciling the two—in support of their assertions was the ideal.[106] Even those doctors, like John of Burgundy and Raymond Chalin de Vinario, who seemed to dismiss authority in favor of modern experience with the plague, nonetheless continued to rely on, and defer to, the ancients in support of their positions.[107] Not every statement, therefore, made by medieval doctors with regard to plague symptoms can be assumed to be a veridical one based on personal observation, even if they were no longer "slavishly" following the authority of the ancients.[108]

To take one example, medieval doctors are famous for describing plague boils in a veritable rainbow of colors, including red, yellow, green, and black.[109] This is obviously not a description that accords with any modern diagnosis of plague.[110] But it is also not one that we know any medieval doctor saw, either. It is lifted straight out of the *Book of Prognostics* attributed to Hippocrates (460–370 B.C.), one of the more frequently cited of that author's works.[111] I have never found any evidence that this was something actually witnessed by any plague doctor.[112] Medieval physicians typically made a clear distinction between the "apostemes," "bubos" or "glandular swellings" (*glandulae*) that arose on the emunctories of the neck, armpit, and groin, and other skin manifestations, such as carbuncles, *antraces*, and pustules, that appeared elsewhere on the body. The papal surgeon, Gui de Chauliac (1300–68), who contracted bubonic plague and survived, described the *antrax* as a "malignant carbuncle" that could be red, yellow, or black in color," the last of which was a most mortal sign from which "no one escapes".[113] His description was largely based on Avicenna and the thirteenth-century French surgeon, Henry de Mondeville, and his classifications were followed by later doctors in the fifteenth century, such as Bartholomew of Ferrara, Michael Boeti, Hermann Schedel, and Johannes Martzacaro of Mainz.[114] Another plague doctor with personal experience of bubos, Blasius of Barcelona, physician to King Martin of Aragon (r. 1396–1410), likewise distinguished between swellings that appeared on the emunctories and other symptoms, such as the *papula* or "pimple," a "blister-like swelling" that did not"cease to extend itself" over the members and was a mortal sign (perhaps of septicemic plague). Blasius, in fact, noted that the *papula*'s colors of red, blue, or black were "very rarely to be found in glandular swellings".[115]

Even if we were to take every symptom ever mentioned by plague doctors or by chroniclers at face value, this still would not disqualify identifying the Black Death as plague, because modern observers of the Third Pandemic did describe a variety of skin manifestations in addition to bubos that occurred on plague patients, usually on or near the flea bite that was the original source of infection: These included "boils," "carbuncles," "pustules," "ulcers," "abrasions," "vesicles," and in one instance, a "vesicular and pustular rash".[116] The petecchiae, or DIC (disseminated intravascular coagulation), of septicemic plague must have been observed fairly often, since complications of septicemia occur in 35–40 percent of primary bubonic plague victims.[117] A single occurrence of any one of these "unusual" symptoms of plague may have made enough of an impression for it to have been included in a plague treatise or a chronicler's account; we thus can have no idea of the frequency with which such symptoms occurred in the Middle Ages.[118] Moreover, given the messy and inexact nature of interpreting evidence from as long ago as the Middle Ages, one can question whether it is realistic to expect an exact correlation of symptoms between medieval and modern accounts of plague in every possible respect (i.e., the "nirvana" fallacy).[119] If, rather, a *preponderance* of the evidence favors the defining features of bubonic plague, as has long been argued to be the case, some would say that this should be considered sufficient.[120]

Leaving aside other arguments made by plague deniers,[121] one has to ask: Where does the debate go from here? I believe that plague denial—due to both the verdict of independently-produced, scientific evidence (i.e., paleomicrobiology) and deniers' employment of weak methodology (i.e., logical fallacies such as argument from silence, false analogy, etc.)—is now at an intellectual dead-end. Perhaps plague deniers still serve a purpose as conscientious objectors to historical complacency,[122] but they also risk being relegated to the status of cranks or fringe theorists, akin to those who claim that climate change is a hoax or that there is no such thing as evolution! I believe that we are indeed indebted to plague deniers for spurring on the exciting discoveries of paleomicrobiology, which have forever changed our approach to historical epidemiology and opened up new vistas on interdisciplinary research.[123] But I also believe that the door has now closed on this conversation, and that there is no longer any useful function served in continuing the debate. Doing so will only distract us from moving on to the next chapter in our history of the Black Death.

Late medieval demography: mortality vs. fertility

The contours of much of the debate over late medieval demography in the aftermath of the Black Death have changed considerably in the past few decades. For example, an earlier generation endlessly repeated the shibboleth that only a third of European population perished in the first outbreak of plague in 1347–53.[124] This was based almost entirely on a 1948 study of Inquisitions *post mortem*, which recorded the deaths of the royal tenants-in-chief, or feudal barons, of England, who numbered just 505 individuals, equivalent to a small village.[125] Now, a new consensus is emerging that at least 50–60 percent, or perhaps even higher, of Europeans died in these few years, which is based on a veritable avalanche of local studies derived from manorial records, bishops' registers, tax surveys, etc., which are far more representative of the population's experience with plague.[126]

Naturally, this revision upwards of the Black Death's initial, and greatest, mortality is also substantially changing the way the Black Death should be viewed in terms of its importance and role in history.[127] Nearly half a century ago, a collection of essays questioned whether the Black Death should be seen as a "turning point in history," simply through its question mark in the title.[128] Building on Malthusian and Marxist interpretations that preferred to see the Black Death as part of a *longue durée* of historical change, these historians assumed that the plague merely "aggravated a preexisting situation," namely, one of demographic decline already taking place in the first half of the fourteenth century, after Europe's population had reached a peak around 1300.[129] Such minimalist views of plague's impact were obviously facilitated by a low estimate of plague mortality of only around a third.[130]

Yet the assumption of pre-plague decline has also been recently challenged: Comprehensive demographic overviews of the half century before the Black Death conclude that the evidence, such as it is, is extraordinarily difficult to interpret and offers no clear trends.[131] An alternative view sees this half century as engaged in a demographic "deadlock" or "stalemate" that was only broken, for better or worse (mostly for the better), by the arrival of the Black Death.[132] This, then, restores the Black Death as a crucial turning point, or "watershed," in late medieval history, especially given that the mortality arrived with an unprecedently high percentage of deaths.[133] Some historians also argue that the Black Death was simply one of many "crises" in the late Middle Ages, which included the ravages of famine and war. But even though there was a Great Famine throughout northern Europe in 1315–22, famine basically disappeared from the landscape during the period of the Black Death, with perhaps one or two exceptions, such as dearths recorded in 1391–92 and the late 1430s.[134] And certainly, conflicts such as the Hundred Years War between England and France (1337–1453) could have devastating impacts on affected regions, such as Normandy, but these impacts were localized in both space and time, unlike the plague.[135] There is, indeed, nothing really to touch the Black Death in terms of its wide-ranging and long-lasting catastrophic impact. There is good reason why it is frequently described as one of the greatest natural disasters in the history of humankind, let alone of the Middle Ages.

In addition to the "Great Mortality" of the mid-fourteenth century, we now have a much better picture of mortality throughout the rest of the Middle Ages, which previously had received far less attention from historians.[136] This shows that plague kept European population at a low level throughout the late Middle Ages, until at least 1450, rather than allowing for any sort of population recovery, which some had claimed came as early as the late fourteenth century.[137] Evidence from the Continent—which includes wills, necrologies, and hearth tax records—shows unpredictable spikes in mortality during the second half of the fourteenth century that were certainly lower than that for 1347–53, but that really establish no clear, overall pattern.[138] In England—which has the best evidence in the form of manorial court rolls (including tithing lists) and episcopal registers—the demographic trend remains fairly flat until the end of the century, when death rates go up again dramatically.[139] Several English chronicles also reported that later epidemics, such as the ones in 1361, 1369, and 1378, were particularly fatal to the young or children.[140] Since plague has been found to be fairly indiscriminate with respect to age in terms of its mortality profile, this impression is probably owing to a greater proportion of children in the living population in the aftermath of the Black Death.[141]

The main debate concerns what was happening to population during the second half of the fifteenth century. During the first half, from 1400 to 1450, there seems broad consensus that English population continued its gradual decline, reaching a nadir in 1450 that was less than half what it had been before the plague and that, according to some estimates, approached levels that had not been seen since the Domesday Survey of 1086.[142] What happened to population trends after 1450 is where the real debate comes in.

In one view, "background" mortality in England rose to "savagely high levels" after 1450, owing to both increased virulence and number of epidemics of plague and other diseases.[143] The evidence for this rising mortality pattern in the second half of the fifteenth century largely consists of obituary lists and other data from three English monasteries—Christ Church Priory in Canterbury, Westminster Abbey in London, and Durham Priory in Durham.[144] All three monasteries yielded strikingly similar mortality patterns, despite their geographic variation at virtually opposite ends of the country. The detailed data on the monks allowed researchers to plot their life expectancies—described as "the purest measure of mortality"—which exhibited a relatively stable pattern in the first two or three decades of the fifteenth century but then a sharply falling decline in life expectancy until 1475–85, after which it began to slowly rise until, by the first decade of the sixteenth century, it finally returned to what it had been a century or more earlier.[145] If we take the life expectancy of monks at age 25 (a fair measure of their mortality, since monks were professed into the monastery at ages 18–21), then the life expectancy averaged for all three monasteries started from a high of around 30 years in total (i.e., they could expect to live five more years from the age of 25) at the start of the fifteenth century and fell to just 19 years by 1475, a decline of 11 years, or 36 percent. Not until three decades later did life expectancy recover somewhat, reaching just over 28 years by 1505.[146] In terms of crude death rates, all three monasteries suffered from recurring and severe epidemics of "crisis" mortality throughout the fifteenth century, with considerably higher annual and moving averages in the second half.[147]

Some evidence for lay mortality during the fifteenth century seems to confirm the monastic trends. For example, the sharp decline in life expectancies for the monks after 1450 is matched quite closely by that for tenants-in-chief based on Inquisitions *post mortem*.[148] Wills surviving from East Anglia, London, Hereford, and York, and court rolls from Worcester, point to many of the same years from the latter half of the fifteenth century—namely, 1451–52, 1457–59, 1464–65, 1467, 1471–73, 1478–80, and 1485—as those coinciding with mortality peaks at Christ Church, Westminster, and Durham and that also correspond well with what chronicles said were years of epidemic disease.[149] Evidence from tithing or frankpledge dues at the Essex manors of High Easter, Great Waltham, and Margaret Roding shows a long, stable flatlining of population throughout the fifteenth century, with a renewed population contraction taking place at High Easter in the century's last decades.[150]

What evidence there is for the Continent shows an opposite trend, namely, rising population, and likely lower mortality, after 1450. Tax records for Tuscany, Sicily, and Provence record that, although population did fall catastrophically until about the mid-fifteenth century, thereafter population made a steady recovery, growing at an annual rate of from .6 to well over 1 percent through to the mid-sixteenth century.[151] Wills proved at Lyon in south-eastern France bear evidence of a rise of between two-and-a-half to five times the replacement rate, or average number of children living per household, in the second half of the fifteenth century compared to the second half of the fourteenth.[152] Hearth tax records for eastern Normandy show population rising slowly in the latter half of the fifteenth century, although Hainaut and Catalonia post declines.[153]

Did England follow the Continent's example? Some say that it did. Based on probate evidence, Sylvia Thrupp pioneered the study of replacement rates, or the measure of how many surviving sons were being produced by each male testator to succeed him, being thereby a measure of fertility and potential population growth. She found replacement rates to be rising in Hertfordshire from the 1460s and in Essex from the 1470s and '80s, when, during the latter decade, replacement rates finally rose above unity (i.e., more than one male heir replacing the testator).[154] Thrupp's student, Robert Gottfried, conducted a similar study for Norfolk and Suffolk and found that replacement rates there were on the rise during the 1470s and '80s, even if these were not yet above unity, despite the fact that national and regional epidemics struck every other year throughout the decade.[155] Jeremy

Goldberg found that probate records for the diocese of York showed steep declines in mortality after 1483, while Pamela Nightingale claimed that her evidence of creditors' deaths in certificates of debt also showed steep mortality declines, in this case after 1470.[156] On a national level, replacement rates among tenants-in-chief of the crown, as measured from Inquisitions *post mortem*, turned a corner in 1450, surpassing unity and staying that way for the rest of the century, so that the annual growth rate of population based on these figures averaged .75 percent during these decades.[157]

Which was more truly representative of the demographic experience of the population at large, the rising replacement rates of feudal barons and will-makers, or the declining life expectancies of feudal barons and monks? As if this issue was not thorny and confusing enough, one notices that the same sources—such as Inquisitions *post mortem*—can be used to support both sides of the debate. Monks and feudal barons, but not necessarily all will-makers, were generally among the more privileged classes of society, being better fed, clothed, housed, and medically cared for than most, and thereforethe one can argue that they should have been *less* susceptible to disease than the general population.[158] On the other hand, one can argue that monks, by living a cloistered lifestyle, were exposed to *greater* communicability to disease than normal, a fact that was not lost on contemporary doctors, who commented on the susceptibility to plague of nuns and incarcerated persons.[159] For example, Nightingale has argued that the mortality patterns among all three monasteries of Christ Church, Westminster, and Durham were *too* uniform, in that this showed that the "overriding factor" in their mortality was simply the "nature of their common institutional life".[160] John Hatcher, who championed the monastic evidence as a true indicator of general mortality trends, responded that, if the monks' communal lifestyle uniformly exposed them to disease, this nevertheless does not explain why the life expectancies of the monks fluctuated over time, and that therefore their susceptibility to disease was "likely to have been driven in major part by the same forces which were determining the health of the population at large".[161]

It is entirely possible that both could be right, that there were mortality crises periodically recurring throughout the latter half of the fifteenth century, *and* that replacement rates were nonetheless on the rise. Gottfried explained this contradiction as due either to the fact that plague at this time was less deadly towards children, or that marriage and fertility rates responded to and overcame episodes of crisis mortality.[162] Goldberg and Nightingale argued that a change in seasonal patterns of epidemics from summer to spring indicated the prevalence of diseases less lethal than plague, and that epidemics perhaps became more localized and thus less severe in scope.[163] Urban environments, such as existed for the monks at Canterbury and Westminster, and among the scholars of Winchester and New College in Oxford, may have been more punishing for novices from the countryside, who had not been exposed to "crowd" diseases and therefore lacked natural immunity.[164] Regionally, the lesser populated South West, North West, and West Midlands of England were among the counties with the highest annual growth rates after 1377.[165] This would anticipate the Early Modern experience of plague, when epidemics because an urban phenomenon and the countryside was "significantly healthier than towns".[166] The consensus, if there is one, is that replacement rates of "materially privileged tenants-in-chief" are a more reliable demographic indicator than life expectancies of "cloistered communities of Benedictine monks," even if both samples are skewed, and that the former evidence was "a clear signal that the negative demographic pressures which had prevailed for a century following the Black Death were at least easing".[167]

In light of the fact that the century after 1450 represents a "dark age" in surviving manorial records, in contrast to the early stages of the Black Death when these records give us such a comprehensive picture of mortality, perhaps the best chance of definitively settling this debate is by reconstructing what was happening to England's population on either side of the fifteenth century divide.[168] Of crucial importance is to establish what the population was on the eve of the Black Death, which provides us with a baseline for all the changes that happened thereafter. Here, estimates have ranged widely, from 4.5 million to as high as 6.7 million.[169] Recently, however, it has been argued that England's population could have been no greater than 4.8 million—at the low end of the estimates—on the very cusp of the Black Death, in 1348.[170] This is based on a detailed analysis of England's agricultural capacity at this time, correlated with the population level that it could support.[171] It is likely that this now represents consensus opinion on the matter. The next sure measure of national population—based on the poll taxes first levied in 1377—gives us a figure of 2.5 million, representing a decline of some 50 percent, which is assumed to have sunk further to a nadir of 1.9 million by 1450, a decline from pre-Black Death levels of 60 percent and nearly reaching the population total recorded by the Domesday survey in 1086 of 1.7 million.[172]

The question then becomes, how did population reach the sure estimate of 2.83 million in 1541, which is based on the evidence of parish registers which were first established by Thomas Cromwell in 1538 and used in modern times by the Cambridge Group for the History of Population and Social Structure to conduct a national survey based on 404 parishes?[173] If we adopt Hatcher's argument that population stagnated until at least the 1520s due to excessive mortality crises, then this would have required a growth rate of over 2 percent a year in order to reach the 1541 figure of 2.8 million in less than 20 years.[174] Arguably, such a growth spurt is unrealistic, given that England's peak rate of growth before the twentieth century—i.e., during the first three decades of the nineteenth century—still averaged only 1.5 percent.[175] A more realistic trajectory would have English population turning a corner in 1450, growing at progressively higher, but still relatively modest, rates up until 1541. One projection has the nation starting out by growing at the snail's pace of just .1 percent a year from 1450 until 1475, with population adding just 100,000 persons as it went from 1.9 million to 2 million in that time; then, the annual growth rate trebled to .34 percent from 1475 until 1522, adding 350,000 persons to grow from 2 million to 2.35 million; finally, the growth rate trebled again, to 1 percent a year, going from 2.35 million to 2.8 million by 1541.[176]

Even if the declining or stagnating population trend of the post-Black Death world ended in 1450, instead of a century later in 1550 as Hatcher would have it, this still represents a seismic demographic shift that argues strongly for the late Middle Ages comprising its own demographic pattern distinct from that which ensued during the Early Modern period.[177] Thus, the late medieval demographic pattern is said to be characterized by low average life expectancies—in the low 20s or even below—and a high average mortality of 4–5 percent per year; this contrasts with the pattern for the Early Modern period, when life expectancies were in the low 30s and mortality averaged 3–3.5 percent per year.[178] These differences are significant (i.e., a 10-year gap in life expectancies) and indicate dramatically different demographic patterns, which would be justification enough for historians to draw a dividing line between when the Middle Ages end, and the Early Modern period begins (although settling on an exact date is still very much open to debate).[179] While plague strikes after 1348–49 were not as spectacular or impressive, they were, collectively, just as important as the "Great Mortality," because without them, European population would have reverted to the deadlock of the pre-plague period, instead of the first outbreak marking the transition to a new world.[180] But which factor, mortality or fertility, played the decisive role in this transition?

Traditionally, demographers have assumed that the late Middle Ages experienced a "high pressure" regime—namely, one in which high fertility rates (as indicated by low average ages at marriage and high rates of marrying) were balanced out by high mortality—whereas the Early Modern period in England experienced a "low pressure" regime—that is, low fertility (indicated by high ages at marriage and substantial portions of the population never marrying) but also low mortality.[181] In the course of this supposed transition from late medieval high pressure regime to Early Modern low pressure one, mortality was more likely to have been the prevailing factor: It had to be responsible for both the stagnant or declining population trend during the late Middle Ages and for the increasing one during the Early Modern period, since in both cases the fertility side of the equation was working against the trend.[182] But here a conundrum presents itself. If, as the consensus opinion seems to aver, mortality crises continued to recur until the mid-sixteenth century,[183] this would argue for a leading role for fertility, in order to overcome the mortality crises and set population on an upward trajectory by 1450.

The only way that fertility, rather than mortality, played a determining role in Europe's demographic trends was for a low fertility pattern to have persisted during the late Middle Ages, since only in this way could fertility have influenced the stagnant or slightly declining population arc established for this period.[184] And indeed, a low "replacement rate," i.e., one below unity, or a one-to-one replacement of a tenant with his heir, seems to have held true in England throughout the second half of the fourteenth and the first half of the fifteenth centuries.[185] This could, of course, reflect a conscious choice among couples not to have children, but a far more likely explanation is that it reflected extraordinarily high child mortality due to repeated outbreaks of plague.[186]

Usually, however, the preferred measure of fertility is the marriage rate, which is more easily and directly recovered from the medieval record than the replacement rate, on the assumption that there was a direct correlation between medieval marriages and births.[187] Basically, the argument here is that the Northwest European marriage pattern—i.e., high ages at marriage and large proportions never marrying at all—that has been established for Europe after 1541 on the basis of parish register data, should also hold true for the late medieval period.[188] This is in spite of the fact that the typical economic incentives for early and high rates of marriage—namely, easy availability of land and rising standards of living—held true for at least a century in the wake of the Black Death.[189] While this "mixed," low-high pressure regime of low fertility and high mortality may well explain Europe's "lagged" or "sluggish" demographic trend during the late Middle Ages, we must then assume that population suddenly shifted into a high fertility pattern (i.e., a pure high pressure regime) around 1450, and then just as suddenly downshifted to a pure low pressure regime of both low fertility and low mortality in 1550, in order to continue population growth into the Early Modern period. As yet, it has not been explained why such a dramatic shift in fertility should have occurred around 1450, given that England and probably the rest of Europe were in the midst of an economic depression, or "Great Slump".[190]

Yet the evidence for low fertility, i.e., a low marriage rate, in the late Middle Ages is not a slam dunk, as it is for high mortality. A favorite source in this regard is the poll tax returns for England, of which the most reliable are those levied in 1377. But even these are assumed to underenumerate women (for the purposes of tax evasion), and therefore must be "corrected" if they are to reflect a roughly equal proportion of men and women in medieval society.[191] However, it may be that the poll taxes do not need to be corrected after all. Archaeological evidence from cemeteries corroborates that there was a built-in sex ratio bias in medieval society in favor of men, on the order of 1.13–1.19:1. In other words, men generally outnumbered women in Europe during the Middle Ages, which did not reverse itself until the Early Modern era. Such a ratio argues for a high marriage/high fertility regime, as men tended to compete for available spouses. Medieval women seem to have suffered from both high infant and high adult mortalities owing to a combination of factors, including poor nutrition, mortality from childbirth, and exposure to environmental risk hazards, such as smoky and rat-infested homes.[192]

Nonetheless, evidence from the English returns, and from other tax surveys throughout continental Europe's Northwest region—which includes France, the Low Countries, Germany, and Switzerland—indicates that urban areas did see a high proportion of singlewomen, making up 30–40 percent of the adult female population, that was probably a function of the high proportion of domestic servants (i.e., 20–30 percent of taxpayers) typically employed and living in cities. In more rural areas, the English poll taxes yield an average of around 30 percent of women who were single (with just 10 percent in domestic service), but evidence for the Continent is more mixed, with some demographers favoring a relatively low percentage (20–30 percent), but others, a high one (35–40 percent).[193] Thus, while urban percentages could possibly fit into a definition of the Northwest European marriage pattern—i.e, at least 45 percent of adult women unmarried at a given point in time—rural percentages don't quite make it. Meanwhile, tax surveys for Tuscany and other Mediterranean regions such as southern France and Spain indicate a traditional, "non-European" or "medieval" marriage pattern (i.e., high rates of marriage and low ages at first marriage), even though these areas also experienced demographic decline or stagnation, at least until the mid-fifteenth century.[194]

If there is a consensus, it seems to be that both mortality and fertility, in roughly equal and synergistic fashion, contributed to Europe's transitional population trends during the late medieval and Early Modern periods, and that we will simply have to accept that both were of periodic or episodic character, too complex and volatile to be easily modeled or predicted beyond "a succession of sub-periods each with its own distinctive characteristics".[195] Granting this, I would still argue that mortality was the lead partner in this dance, on the grounds that, if we want to explain how fertility played a role in the failure of Europe's population to recover its numbers for at least a century in the aftermath of the Black Death, it is hard to escape the conclusion that fertility was a function of mortality, rather than being an independent factor of its own.[196] Marriage, for example, could be suppressed by lop-sided sex ratios due to the preferential mortality of a particular epidemic, or else from migration in response to an epidemic. Meanwhile, a number of motivational factors for suppressing marriage—such as elevated employment opportunities for women, social dislocations and rootlessness, even a climate of fear and uncertainty for the future—were only made possible by the high and repeated mortality of plague.[197] But perhaps the main reason why mortality influenced fertility is the fact that, in general, plague was indiscriminate in its virulence, afflicting all age groups in roughly equal proportions (ie., a "catastrophic" mortality pattern, as opposed to an "attritional" one). This means that not only could a community lose the children it needed to "replace" the older generation, it could also lose many of its couples of child-rearing age (i.e., aged 15–40) who could be expected to make more children.[198] Thus, even if marriage and fertility rates spiked in response to epidemics, there were not enough of such couples to make up for the losses that a population sustained.[199] Moreover, such catastrophic mortality would suppress marriage and fertility over the long-term. In other words, fertility, no matter whether high or low, was never allowed to play a decisive role in the wake of the indiscriminate mortality of plague.

If it is inescapable that mortality played the prevailing role in Europe's demographic transition sometime either in the fifteenth or sixteenth centuries, then this still requires an explanation for why the mortality pattern changed at this time to one that was less punishing for potential population recovery. One solution is that black rats (*Rattus rattus*), the main commensal rodent host of bubonic plague, developed immunity to the disease, thus obviating the necessity of fleas to seek human victims, since no major epizootics of rats would then have occurred.[200] The ability of rats to acquire immunity to plague was demonstrated by the Indian Plague Research Commission during the Third Pandemic, and more recent research has discovered genetic resistance to plague among gerbils and marmots in Central Asia and among mice and voles in the western United States.[201] However, rats can apparently lose their immunity to plague within as little as eight years from their last epizootic.[202] It is therefore believed that temporary rat immunity can only account for short-term intermissions in between epidemics, contributing to the periodicity of plague occurring at 10–20 year intervals in some towns.[203] This is assuming that plague persisted in Europe, at least in small-scale epidemics, by circulating among rodent reservoirs in ports, cities, and towns, leaving larger-scale epidemics—such as ones in 1360–63, 1400, 1438–39, and 1478/82—at the hands of periodic reintroductions of the bacillus from endemic centers outside the Continent.[204] Although it has been suggested that wild or sylvatic rodents also may have harbored plague in Europe, such as the Alpine marmots native to the Savoy, this is unlikely, given that no endemic centers of plague remain on the Continent (except in the Caucasus) to compare with those in Asia, Africa, or the Americas.[205] Likewise, even though humans are unable to "acquire" immunity to plague within their lifetimes, some human populations repeatedly exposed to the disease may, over generations of genetic evolution, have developed an innate, inherited immunity at the cellular level. This, however, remains a complex topic on which research is ongoing.[206]

Another solution is to assume that human intervention played a decisive role. Traditionally, it has been argued that plague control measures—such as quarantine —that were adopted in many port cities were responsible for the disappearance of plague from western Europe between 1656 and 1720. The main argument here is that plague control and the disappearance of plague matched each other in terms of their geographical and temporal timing: Because the "anti-plague measures" taken by governments were "irregular" and "incomplete" in terms of their adoption and success, so too was plague's disappearance from Europe in the late seventeenth and early eighteenth centuries. This argument can actually be demonstrated by matching aborted or lax quarantine measures with subsequent outbreaks of plague in a locale, or else effective and rigorous application of such measures with plague's absence, even while neighboring regions were being struck.[207]

But can this explanation be equally applied to the fifteenth or sixteenth centuries, to the time of transition to a new demographic regime? Some argue that it was not until the fifteenth century that contemporaries began to see plague as "a natural phenomenon, one that could be prevented, limited or halted by human countermeasures," or when town councils began to adopt measures, such as quarantine, designed to limit contact with the sick in line with contagionist ideas of spread of the disease.[208] However, this ignores the fact that plague control measures were tried from the very beginning of the Black Death in 1348, to apparently no effect, and measures designed to either control miasmatic "stenches" or limit contagion from person-to-person would have had no impact on bubonic plague, which was specifically spread by rats and fleas. At this point, it also behooves to remind ourselves that not everyone in the Middle Ages accepted the contagionist causation of the Black Death, even on empirical grounds. While contagion did have its champions in Islamic medicine, notably from the Moorish physicians, Ibn Khātima (d.1369) and Ibn al-Khatīb (1313–74), the fifteenth-century Egyptian scholar, Ibn Hajar al-'Asqalānī (1372–1449), denied contagion based on the observation that not everyone in the same household as a plague victim always came down with the disease.[209]

So far, scholars have been unable to establish a clear link between anti-contagionist responses and an effective reduction in the severity or occurrence of epidemics, which is admittedly difficult to prove.[210] Here, the application of a modern, "laboratory" definition of plague may actually help focus research and debate in a positive, productive direction. Since plague was spread by "metastatic leaps," mainly through trade in grain that harbored infected rats and fleas, one would expect that a quarantine on ship cargoes and other imports would effectively halt the epidemic. Such a strategy *does not* seem to have been followed in the early stages of the Black Death, when plague ordinances, such as the ones that survive from Pistoia from 1348, tended to focus on the movement of infected persons and trade in their personal effects, particularly clothing.[211] As a matter of fact, civic policies were counter-productive in this respect, as towns were concerned to secure adequate food supplies during an epidemic in order to avoid attendant famine, which contemporaries saw as a contributing factor to plague.[212]

The first true trade embargo or shipping quarantine against plague was apparently tried at Ragusa (modern-day Dubrovnik), opposite the Adriatic Sea from Italy, during the late fourteenth century. Adopted initially for political reasons, as a policy directed against the trading power of Venice, quarantine nonetheless would have been effective only if suspect cargoes and crews were truly kept isolated for the required forty days, which would have given any infection time to burn itself out. By 1400 shipping quarantine was in turn adopted by Venice in retaliation for Ragusa's policies, but a more sanitary-based and general quarantine with respect to commerce in plague-time does not seem to have been taken up until 1423.[213] From the mid-fifteenth century on, permanent health boards began to be generally established, first in Italy, and then later, extending into the sixteenth century, further north in France, England, and the Low Countries; it was not until such boards were armed with truly comprehensive powers of jurisdiction and enforcement that quarantine measures could become truly effective.[214]

But perhaps the most important development in plague controls was the creation of "conduits of communication," or an information-sharing network, whereby towns were given warning of where and when plague began to strike so that they could close their borders to trade and thus stop the chain of transmission (while at the same time allowing themselves to continue to be supplied from safe areas).[215] Indeed, this exact same strategy is what still proves most effective today and has been used by the WHO (World Health Organization) to successfully nip in the bud such emerging potential pandemics as SARS (Severe Acute Respiratory Syndrome), Avian Flu, MERS (Middle East Respiratory Syndrome), Ebola, and the Zika virus. This also must have taken much of the terror out of a disease like plague, which instilled such fear due to the uncertainty of its next strike. All this must have taken some time to develop and perfect, so that it may not have been until the latter half of the seventeenth century before Europe had a truly effective response to plague. It also may be that trade inadvertently changed in ways that favored a reduction in the occurrence and extent of plague epidemics. For example, demand for grain declined considerably throughout the late medieval period, due both to vastly fewer mouths to feed and changing food tastes among the peasantry, who could now afford more meat and fish in their diet.[216] This inevitably reduced the need for long-distance trade in grain in favor of more local sources of supply, which would naturally reduce the risk of importation of plague from abroad.[217] In addition, new international trade routes established by Early Modern explorers may have enabled Europe to bypass endemic centers of plague in Central Asia, which would be particularly important if plague had to be continually re-introduced to native rat colonies.

Overall, it is likely that a combination of factors, acting interdependently, led to a turning of the tide against plague and other epidemic diseases in the Early Modern period.[218] But a large degree of uncertainty remains, and probably will always do so into the foreseeable future, as to what exactly happened to make plague less of a menacing and mortal force in European life.[219] Whatever the reason, it is undoubtedly true that it was a reduction in the extent, severity, and frequency of plague that was primarily responsible for lower mortality rates, and rising populations, in Early Modern Europe.[220]

The plague economy

The fortunes of plague have waxed and waned in medieval historiography insofar as what kind of role it was assigned in the late medieval economy and society. In the early twentieth century, historians of manorial economies, such as Elizabeth Levett, who studied the estates of the bishop of Winchester in southern England, and Frances Page, who focused on the manors owned by Crowland Abbey in the East Midlands, were impressed by the resilience and recovery from the first outbreak of the Black Death in 1348–49.[221] On this basis, they concluded that the plague was not "revolutionary" in its effects nor had "any far-reaching influence upon subsequent events".[222] Later work on other estates scattered throughout the country tended to confirm this picture of a quick return to "normalcy" in the immediate aftermath of the first plague, with lords able to fill vacant tenancies on pretty much the same terms as before, i.e., at the same (high) level of rents and for the same dues and services, in the case of customary (villein) tenures.[223] This was perhaps aided by an excess reserve or surplus of labor and tenants—

the so-called "teeming" or "pullulating throng" of people on the eve of the Black Death—whose culling by the plague was supposedly "more purgative than toxic".[224]

Nevertheless, it seems to be a general rule in Black Death studies, that the more that research is conducted into the primary sources of the era, the more that evidence is found of the plague's importance in its demographic and economic impact. This was nicely antipated by John Saltmarsh, writing in the midst of World War II, who claimed that the late medieval economic crisis extending into the mid-fifteenth century could be explained by long-term population decline owing to a "permanent infection," or "succession of epidemics," of plague. But, since empirical data was still lacking, Saltmarsh was limited to expounding no more than an "unverified hypothesis".[225] Vindication, however, soon came from proliferating manorial studies, particularly those that focused on the Black Death in a specific location, which demonstrated that the plague *did* accomplish some far-reaching changes in medieval society, once a longer perspective, extending beyond the mid-fourteenth century through to the fifteenth century, was obtained.[226] This went hand-in-hand with accumulating evidence of plague's long-term demographic impact, which fundamentally revised John Bean's claim from the early 1960s that any population decline had been arrested and then reversed "by the end of the fourteenth century".[227] Indeed, the new demographic evidence showed that plague could "be elevated to the position of a constant economic force" throughout the late Middle Ages, which had previously been thought unlikely.[228] By 1994, John Hatcher declared that it was "time to rein back the exuberance with which historians have long sought to undermine the significance of the Black Death," arguing that "new directions" discerned in the late medieval economy would not "have been followed with the same force and for the same duration without the intervention of the Black Death and later epidemics".[229] Even so, some historians continue to view late medieval economic change as more "evolutionary" than "revolutionary" in its progress and development.[230]

What is more, a re-examination of the evidence for the immediate impact of the Black Death reveals that the disease was far more disruptive than previously thought, and that the picture of recovery is in many ways superficial and illusory. For example, the Winchester Pipe Rolls used by Levett were heavily edited accounts produced by the bishop's central administration, which recorded only the figures that auditors often substituted for crossed-out originals in each manorial account roll drawn up locally by the manor reeve. Thus, with respect to manorial incomes in particular, what we see in the Pipe Rolls is an *ideal*, or what the auditors and the lord wished to be true in the midst of a rapidly changing world, rather than what actually occurred.[231] Disruptions also could be concealed within the overall estate by moving around resources from less-heavily hit manors to those more in need, while various accounting devices could be used to conceal illegally high wage rates paid to laborers.[232] Overall, a more sensitive and penetrating reading of the original manorial account rolls shows that disruptions in the running of manors in the immediate aftermath of the Black Death—including slack performance of customary works, falls in grain and livestock production and sales, and outright neglect of arable and pastoral husbandry, all of which accords with the testimony of contemporary chroniclers—did indeed occur.[233] Even on a manor such as Inkpen in Berkshire, owned by Titchfield Abbey, that suffered less than 20 percent mortality of tenants in 1348–49, could still record vacant tenancies years later.[234] In a sense, our views have now come full circle to those of the late nineteenth century, which tended to emphasize the importance and scale of plague's impact, and which authors like Levett and Page were already denigrating as "old school".[235]

Another area of debate through the years has been whether the Black Death was an overall good or a bad influence upon the late medieval economy.[236] Again, going back to the late nineteenth century, the English economist, Thorold Rogers, was the first to christen the late Middle Ages as the "Golden Age of the Wage Labourer," based on his pioneering index of wage and price data that showed agricultural workers earning steadily higher wages as prices fell, substantially raising their real income and overall standard of living.[237] Further refinements of this index have only made these gains more impressive: The latest data show that farm laborers' wages tripled between c. 1300 and 1450, while, at the same time, their real wages (i.e., wages relative to prices) doubled.[238] By these measurements, the living standards of the late fifteenth-century English peasantry were not to be surpassed until four hundred years later, in the late nineteenth century, with the achievements of the Industrial Revolution.[239]

These arguments were then expanded during the 1950s and '60s by Friedrich Lütge and Anthony Bridbury. Lütge emphasized the favorable land-labor ratio brought about by the Black Death, by which survivors could now enjoy a surfeit of resources of all kinds, in addition to being able to command higher wages.[240] Similarly, Bridbury described how the Black Death mortality unleashed a land grab by the peasantry such that it could be compared to "a sort of Marshall Aid on a stupendous scale".[241] Responding to assertions of a "crisis" in the late medieval economy, Bridbury also argued that, because per capita agricultural and industrial production rose even as population declined—or at least that per capita production declined less steeply than population—the late fourteenth and fifteenth centuries were an age of economic expansion which benefitted everyone—the lords and urban middle classes as well as peasants—so that it made no sense to talk of a late medieval crisis at all.[242]

Carrying this optimistic view to its logical conclusion, scholars such as Christopher Dyer and Maryanne Kowaleski championed a "consumer revolution" that supposedly took hold in all sectors of the late medieval economy, which was the direct result of the rising real wages of the vast majority of the peasantry, effectively doubling their purchasing power and disposable income, while prices, owing to increased per capita production that counteracted increased per capita demand, remained stable or in some cases declined. The consumer revolution encompassed a wide variety of goods and services, including better food and drink, clothing, housing and lodging, religious charities, etc. This, in turn, stimulated trade and manufacturing (or, if you like, commerce and industry) in order to meet the new consumer demand, which only raised standards of living further.[243]

On the other hand, a more "gloomy" outlook on the late medieval economy was being put forward beginning in the 1930s by the Cambridge historian, Michael Moissey Postan. Postan argued that the economy of the late Middle Ages was in "crisis," which he defined as "a relative decline in the total volume of national wealth," owing to both a decline in agricultural production and a decline in urban trade, more specifically, in wool and cloth exports. For Postan, the fourteenth and fifteenth centuries were "a time of falling land values, declining rents, vacant holdings and dwindling profits of demesne cultivation".[244] Of course, this was a disaster from the perspective of the landlords or the landed aristocracy and gentry, but could be considered a boon and an economic blessing from the point of view of the peasantry and most tenants. This pessimistic line has been continued by Postan's student, John Hatcher, who argued that the "golden age" of the laborer "is in need of a severe dose of debasement". In Hatcher's view, not even the spectacularly rising wage rates of the late Middle Ages could be translated into rising living standards, since most wage labor was seasonal in nature, and it would therefore be hazardous to extrapolate day wages into yearly incomes. Hatcher also viewed the "consumer revolution" as rather limited, in that it included only basic goods and services rather than high-end, luxury items.[245] In addition, Hatcher has drawn attention to the "Great Slump," or economic depression, that prevailed in Europe during the middle decades of the fifteenth century, when practically all sectors of agricultural and industrial production experienced contraction. This had knock-on effects for land values, consumer consumption, employment, trade, etc., which affected nearly all classes of people, from landlords down to day laborers.[246]

Nevertheless, in spite of these criticisms, proponents of the optimistic view, like Dyer, still see the "golden age" as viable, if not quite so rosy as previously made out, in which "improved living conditions for the lower ranks of wage earners was a memorable characteristic of the late medieval economy".[247] While acknowledging that daily rates of pay cannot be equated with year-round earnings, proponents of the golden age nonetheless argue that a yearly income of £3–4— equivalent to a daily wage of at least 4 pence for 180–240 days, which was quadruple the rate generally obtained before the Black Death—was entirely achievable for an entire *household*. This would include income brought in not just by the adult male breadwinner, but also by his wife and children. In most cases, their recorded wages probably underestimated their true remuneration, since payments in kind, such as food, were left unmentioned; when food was listed as specifically *not* given, the money wage was substantially higher than average. Moreover, as landholding became common among even the formerly landless class of peasants, workers had the opportunity to lower their expenses by relying more on home-grown food. Higher landholding rates among the peasantry also created more employment opportunites, even in hard economic times, as each village now had a substantial number of tenants owning 30 acres or more, with an elite owning 50–100 acres, which inevitably required permanent hired help to farm.[248]

If we can talk of a "Plague Economy" in the aftermath of the Black Death, then this may not have been a bad thing, provided we view the plague has having had mostly beneficial economic effects for the vast majority of the population, i.e., the peasantry. By taking away not only vast numbers (50 percent or more) of the general population, but also those members of the population most eligible to work (i.e, those aged 15–40), the Black Death delivered "the greatest supply side shock to the labour market in recorded history," fundamentally changing the land-labor ratio to one that was now extremely favorable for tenants.[249] The main economic changes supposedly accomplished in the Plague Economy were threefold: a new, free market in labor and goods, resulting in substantially higher real wages for laborers; the demise of serfdom, resulting in the commutation of labor services and customary dues for unfree tenants; and a redistribution of land and widespread leasing of demesne farms, resulting in greater access to the "land market". Obviously, we don't have space to delve in great detail into each of these topics. All I can do here is outline the main contours of debate, particularly as these apply to the Black Death.

By the economic laws of supply and demand, a demand- and supply-side shock on the order of that generated by the Black Death should have meant substantially higher wages for laborers, and lower prices for at least basic goods, such as foodstuffs; this, in turn, should have translated into rising incomes (especially relative to cost of living) and rising living standards for most of the medieval peasantry, while doing the opposite for the lords and gentry (i.e., the agrarian "producers"), who had to pay higher labor costs and accept lower earnings for their products.[250] But the trend in wage rates could vary considerably by country. Both England and Italy registered almost immediate gains in the daily real wage rate for building workers after the Black Death, but while Italy's peaked in the 1370s and then fell back, England's continued to rise to reach a parity with Holland's in the mid-fifteenth century, when it was more than double what it had been before the Black Death. Towards the end of the century, England's rate fell back to Italy's, while Holland's stayed almost unchanged. Meanwhile, Spain's wage rate actually contracted to below what it had been before the Black Death until at least 1400, whereupon it rose slowly to reach its pre-plague peak before sagging again after 1450.[251]

All this indicates that there was by no means a simple correlation between demography and economic trends, but that the dynamics of the Plague Economy were more complex. A rather obvious point to make here is that the late Middle Ages was not yet a fully capitalistic society, but was, at best, in transition to one. The mere fact that country after country enacted labor legislation in the wake of the Black Death—designed to fix wages and working conditions (especially freedom of movement) to what had held true before the plague—should indicate that this was not yet a society that allowed the laws of supply and demand to operate freely.[252] Indications are that, in England, the wage laws of 1349 and 1351 were rigorously enforced during the 1350s, '60s, and '70s, at first by specially-appointed justices of laborers and then, after 1359, by regular justices of the peace.[253] An alternative explanation is that "wage stickiness"—i.e., the flatness of wages relative to prices—of these years was instead due to monetary trends, specifically, the easy availability of hard currency, or coin, which tended to promote inflation. This argument is strengthened by the fact that real wages were "sticky," i.e., relatively flat, in the Low Countries and for a longer period of time than in England, even though no labor laws were in force there.[254]

But these limitations on plague were not to last. Enforcement of the Statute of Laborers, first enacted in 1351, eventually waned in England, as evidenced by the perceived need to periodically re-issue legislation, a policy that had political ramifications even as it demonstrated the law's economic impotence.[255] Likewise, although a case has been made that "demographic forces can influence long-term price movements only by their interaction with other real economic forces," namely, with monetary trends, this argument is most persuasive for the early decades of the Black Death.[256] And while price movements do tend to parallel changes in the money supply, insofar as this can be determined (i.e., high prices when money was easy, low prices when it was tight), the same cannot be said of wages. Real wages, at least in England and Holland, inexorably rose even after c.1400, when the money supply eased and prices drifted upwards, which ordinarily should have depressed real wages.[257] Thus, in the long run, plague emerges as the prime mover of the inflationary arc of real wages, where this occurred, because it managed to maintain its demand- and supply-side shocks through continued and consistent suppression of population, even if this demographic pressure was initially countered by other factors.

Perhaps a more important question to ask is, how much of a difference did higher real wages make to the overall improvement in peasants' living standards as a result of the Black Death? If one extrapolates wages paid per day to a year's worth of income, then the improvement is very large indeed, perhaps unrealistically so, since it exceeds what was earned by members of the gentry, the very men paying these wages.[258] Hard data on how many days wage laborers worked in a year is very hard to come by and greatly depends on the kind of labor being performed.[259] Typically, wage labor was employed on farms for only a few weeks in the year, at harvest time, and was mostly employed by fellow peasant farmers, who were not inclined to pay the stratospheric rates recorded by institutional employers, such as bishoprics and monasteries, which make up the bulk of wage and price data.[260] Perhaps because it was so seasonal, wage labor is estimated to have made up only a fraction—a fifth or a quarter—of the total labor employed in the medieval economy.[261] On the other hand, very few peasants had the luxury of regular, full-time employment with an annual salary; if so, then they were typically hired as domestic servants, or *famuli*, on a year-long, contractual basis. Usually, they had to cobble together a living from self-sufficient farming, seasonal wage employment, and sales of other goods and services.[262] Real wages, it is argued, cannot be translated into an index of standard of living because they are based on what was paid to *famuli*, who represented no more than five percent of the rural population.

But there were plenty of other ways in which peasants could improve their quality of life in the aftermath of the Black Death besides earning higher wages. For example, the decline of serfdom at this time obviously freed many peasants from the burdens of performing customary labor services for their lords ("week work" and "boon work") and paying them customary dues, including merchet, heriot, chevage, millsuit, etc. Indeed, the effective end of villeinage between c.1380 and c.1450 is widely held to be the "single most important" economic and social development of the late Middle Ages.[263] The commutation of labor services and other customary dues, and the conversion of customary tenures to "copyhold" and "leasehold," is something that can be documented on a number of English manors throughout the fourteenth and fifteenth centuries.[264] A demographic explanation of this process is that the Black Death, having delivered "the greatest supply side shock to the labor market in recorded history," since it swept away "up to one half of prospective tenants and workers," then forced lords to compete with and outbid each other with respect to ameliorating, or eliminating altogether, servile obligations in order to attract and keep workers.[265] All in all, the demographic explanation is an extremely powerful one that commands many adherents.[266]

At the same time, there is an equally powerful argument that the demographic factor can't be the whole explanation, because, even in spite of universal forces such as the Black Death and its supply- and demand-side shocks, villeinage ended at different times in different places and generally extended its hold somewhere in England until the mid-fifteenth century.[267] Elsewhere in Europe, France presents an analagous situation to England's in that any surviving vestiges of serfdom seem to have disappeared through a long process of attrition in the wake of the plague, while in heavily urbanized regions, such as Italy and the Low Countries, serfdom was already a dead letter by the time of the arrival of the Black Death.[268] In Catalonia in Spain, lords were able to "tighten their control over tenants" in the aftermath of the Black Death by exercising a literal "right to mistreat" serfs (*ius maletractandi*) and by setting unrealistically high redemption prices for serfs to buy their freedom.[269] In Eastern Europe (i.e., Prussia, Poland, Bohemia, Hungary, the Baltic States, and Russia), lords were actually able to impose serfdom for the first time, even as the institution was dying out everywhere else, because they were able to increase their political and jurisdictional powers at the expense of monarchies, a reversal of the centralizing trend in the West.[270] All this indicates that political, social, and legal pressures, as well as economic and demographic ones, could be brought to bear upon the trajectory of villeinage's demise, where this occurred in Europe.[271]

However, the other factors in serfdom's decline, which include manumission or redemption, peasant resistance, and migration, still cannot topple King Death from his throne, largely because they are so intertwined and plague is still the prime mover of them all. Manumission, an expensive proposition for all but the wealthiest peasants, did not seem to have been especially common and thus "contributed little to the demise of serfdom".[272] In fact, lords may have been more inclined to manumit serfs or commute labor services prior to the Black Death, when it would have allowed them to charge higher rents than allowed by custom or else to raise cash and make formerly customary tenures more attractive.[273]

Peasant resistance seems to have reached a "crescendo" of activity in the aftermath of the Black Death, when, it is argued, only the "actions of countless individuals" to rebel, rather than the "impersonal action of the forces of supply and demand," can explain serfdom's demise.[274] The enactment of labor legislation and the occurrence of outright rebellion, such as the Peasants' Revolt in England of 1381, can be cited as evidence of intolerable seigniorial oppression. Obviously, local customs and conditions of tenure, as well as seigniorial attitudes and valuations of serfdom, determined "the pace and direction of change," which varied from manor to manor.[275] But it also can be argued that it was the Black Death, and its supply-side shocks, that made peasants realize the value of their labor—and the intolerability of their situation, especially when compared to that of their less shackled neighbors—in the first place.[276]

After the English government successfully quashed the Peasants' Revolt in 1381, renegotiation and commutation of labor services and dues nonetheless continued apace, evidently driven by the new "economic realism" of a demographic landscape permanently changed by the Black Death, and with small acts of defiance on the peasants' part setting the seal on the change.[277] Even as powerful a lord as the bishop of Durham, who enjoyed special palatine powers in his episcopate, was compelled by the prospect of hundreds of acres of his tenements lying waste to compromise and effectively commute all his labor services into rents by the 1380s; this was in spite of his vigorous and harsh efforts during the 1350s to attempt to maintain the manorial system, measures that included arrest and imprisonment, pledges for good behavior, and charging of vacant tenancies on remaining villagers.[278] Obviously, what had changed and made it easier for peasants to advance their demands, and more difficult for lords to resist them, was the continuance of a land-labor ratio in the peasants' favor, owing to persistent population harvests caused by the plague.[279] Moreover, the fact that only half of the peasants and land tenures in England were still of unfree status on the eve of the Black Death, and only a third still performed week work, calls into question the degree of importance—and resentment–that serfdom held in the overall peasant mindset.[280]

Finally, migration was undeniably a factor in serfdom's demise, since in this way, peasants could "vote with their feet" and simply leave the manor in search of better terms and conditions elsewhere, which they had been doing even before the Black Death. But the evidence clearly indicates that migration picked up significantly in the aftermath of the plague, beginning in the 1350s.[281] While it is undoubtedly true that the motivations for migration were complex and many, it can hardly be denied that the Black Death created a much more favorable market for peasants to hawk their labor to the highest bidder, simply by making that labor much more scarce. In almost every instance, therefore, plague emerges as the prime mover behind the causes of serfdom's decline.[282]

Land, being the main source of food, was perhaps the most highly valued commodity in the Middle Ages, and ownership of it usually provided the measurement of wealth.[283] The Black Death flooded the medieval land market, vastly relieving the human pressure on land that had been building up prior to the plague.[284] It did this in two ways. The most obvious was in making land available through inheritances and other *post-mortem* transfers, as large numbers of occupants or owners died in the plague, while the pool of potential inheritors was also reduced.[285] The second was through *inter-vivos* transfers (i.e., transfers accomplished during the owner's lifetime), as rules governing such transactions were greatly relaxed by landlords eager to see their tenancies occupied by any means possible.[286] This was a more gradual process, but one that eventually overtook *post-mortem* transfers and which culminated with landlords leasing out their demesnes, either in their entirety or piecemeal, as they abandoned direct farming, thus releasing hundreds of acres at a time on the local land market.[287] This also created a new hierarchical layer inbetween many tenants and their lord, thus further weakening the manorial system; indeed, sometimes the lessee was the entire village, i.e., a group of peasants acting collectively so that individuals could increase their landholdings.[288] Rents and entry fines also became cheaper for tenants, who generally had the upper hand and initiative in this new economic climate.[289] Overall, the most important developments in the late medieval land market were probably the demise of custom governing land transfers, in favor of a more free market, proto-capitalist approach, and the attendant process of land redistribution and consolidation, which marked an about-face from the previous trend towards fragmentation prior to 1348–49.[290]

Undoubtedly, it was the Black Death that was the prime mover behind these changes, as only "the postponement of any recovery in population" through to the mid-fifteenth century could have achieved the "decay of such customary institutions," while the plague also "maintained a sufficiently flexible supply of land to permit the build-up of substantial holdings by piecemeal acquisition".[291] Nevertheless, while the Black Death created unprecedented opportunities in land ownership, it was up to individual initiative and resources, as well as the conditions that prevailed in each locality, to determine whether these opportunities were acted upon.[292] There were also considerable social implications of the new land market, particularly in terms of customary inheritance and the traditional bond between families and the land. Customary inheritance patterns suffered, since sons no longer had to wait for patrimony in order to enter into their own land.[293] Turnover in some villages could be quite high, with three-quarters of families disappearing from the records every half century or so, so that the old, established families "were swept away to be replaced by a more mobile and transient community".[294] Yet other research indicates that land could still remain within the family, but taken up by more distant relatives, whose connections within an extended kinship network are simply harder to trace.[295]

The great debate over the late medieval land market concerns who benefitted the most from the spectacular availability of land, and how exactly they did so.

This is mainly a debate between those who favor an "economic promotion" interpretation, i.e., that the new land market created a relatively equal redistribution of land, and those who say that there was a "polarization" of land acquisition, as land fell into the hands of a few "peasant aristocrats" at the expense of those who became landless or were left with small holdings.[296] Both views, of course, may be right within the context of the evolution of the land market in the century and a half after the first outbreak of the plague.

In the immediate aftermath of the Black Death, one would expect that the landless class of peasants would be one of the greatest beneficiaries of the new availability of land, as they now had the opportunity to either inherit land or acquire land at low entry fines and rents.[297] In general, it is estimated that the landless—here defined as consisting of cottagers, wage laborers, and servants—went from making up over half of English households in 1300 to a third by 1524.[298] This may help explain the high rate of migration and tenant turnover on many manors, and it would have had the added economic impact of decreasing the supply of wage labor, thus making this even more expensive, while at the same time depressing the price of grain, since more people now had self-sufficient plots to feed themselves.[299] However, it is difficult to know what exactly happened to the landless, as they are generally omitted from manorial and tax records, except to say perhaps that they were noticeably absent from rolls in the wake of the Black Death.[300] It is counter-argued that the landless would not have been in a strong position to take advantage of newly-available units, especially as these were being offered in larger and larger parcels that required a reserve of capital in order to purchase and exploit them. The most likely beneficiaries were thereby existing landholders or immigrants seeking such opportunities. Smaller, more affordable parcels were available through subtenancies offered by fellow peasants, but these were likely to be on no more generous terms than those of the lord.[301]

Initially, the new land market created by the plague does not seem to have changed the tenurial structure of villages all that much. At the manor of Coltishall in Norfolk, for example, the size distribution of landholdings remained basically unchanged from 1300 to 1400, with no tenant holding more than 30 acres, and the vast majority of tenants, 85 percent, holding five acres or less. The volume of land transactions, measured both in total area exchanged and in number of transactions, did not spike until the late 1360s to the early 1390s, and then again in the first half of the first decade of the fifteenth century.[302] Likewise, it was not until the late fourteenth century that several manors in Berkshire experienced a high number of transactions and turnover of landholders.[303] Eventually, a new land market pattern did assert itself, one in which larger parcels and more "composite holdings" changed hands and at a much more rapid pace, so that even as the number of persons participating in the market declined, the "*per capita* transfer of land*" increased.[304] All this is seen as largely the result of the recurrence of plague and its "liberating effect upon the land market"; prior to the plague, transactions were typically conducted by a larger number of people selling smaller holdings as a way to raise needed cash to buy grain during periods of bad harvests and famine.[305] Many peasants may have been reluctant to participate in land acquisition simply because they lacked the capital resources needed to exploit large holdings.[306] It is estimated that, in order to cultivate a virgate, or 30 acres, of arable land plus perform customary services for the lord, a farmer would need either a large family or to hire labor, an expensive proposition in the aftermath of the Black Death.[307] Peasants were also reluctant to take up customary tenures that still retained the burden of dues and services, or whose rents were artificially higher than that of freeholds, which were allowed to fluctuate with the market (which was steadily trending downwards). This is why manorial court rolls recorded tenancies that were "thrown," or "imposed," upon recalcitrant tenants.[308]

It was not until the fifteenth century that land turnover and land accumulation, also known as "engrossing," reached "new heights" and an "unprecedented scale" at manors like Coltishall.[309] This coincided with a mass movement away from direct farming to leasing of demesnes by aristocratic landlords. However, this was an era of very challenging conditions for farmers, with low grain prices and high labor costs. Since landlords could not make a go of farming, either, under these conditions, one wonders how their lessees managed to do so.[310] The answer seems to lie in specialization, as farmers grew for a captive market, typically a local city or town, which contrasts with the typical manorial approach of mixed cultivation to achieve self-sufficiency.[311] Otherwise, farmers had a hard time of it, as indicated by their indebtedness and failure year after year to make rent.[312] This was especially the case when lords reserved for themselves the most productive and valuable land, which in the aftermath of the Black Death tended to be pasture, by means of which large flocks or herds could be maintained with little labor, especially when the land was enclosed. Lords who opted to go all in on such a strategy began what later became known as the enclosure movement, which was only made easier as tenants died or moved away (usually voluntarily).[313] But it is undoubtedly true that the late medieval land market allowed some to become the "agrarian capitalists" of the post-plague economy, and in general created a much more variegated hierarchy of tenantry than before.[314] Whether the new "peasant aristocracy" survived to become the yeomen families of the sixteenth century is something that is still open to debate.[315]

What, in the end, did come out of the Plague Economy? The most obvious measure of economic growth and activity that may have been impacted by the Black Death is a country's Gross Domestic Product (GDP). In historical terms, there are several ways of estimating GDP. One of the more common is based on daily wage rates of workers, often taken as proxies for living standards and, in turn, GDP per head, and for which there is good data from England going all the way back to the mid-thirteenth century.[316] The downside is that these wage-rates must be multiplied by the number of days worked in order to arrive at GDP, but establishing just how many days the average laborer worked is extremely difficult, and wage rate series take little account of "refinements of skill and advances in technology," of total household incomes, and of the seasonal nature of agricultural work that may skew the data.[317] Also, this measure of GDP is particularly narrow, based as it is entirely on income. Another way of estimating GDP is based on output, or the sum total of the value added to the economy of three main sectors, namely, agriculture, industry, and services. This, too, has its drawbacks, such as the necessity of relying on proxy data, particularly when estimating services output, which to date has received relatively little attention from historians. But at least this measure is more comprehensive than GDP based on wage-rates, and it seems to be the favored one among more recent studies of historical economies.[318]

GDP per head, which is the standard measure used today to rank countries around the world in terms of their wealth, did benefit greatly in some parts of Europe from the demographic shock of the Black Death. In England, where the greatest amount of data is available, GDP per head allegedly registered a gain of 30–35 percent in the immediate aftermath of the first outbreak of the Black Death in 1348–49, largely owing to the fact that the extraordinary mortality resolved the "intractable economic problem" of overpopulation and poverty that had existed prior to the plague. For the next half century, GDP per head then grew at a rate of .76 percent a year, which was not to be bettered until the second half of the seventeenth century. It then slowed considerably, to just .15 percent a year, or basically remaining flat, for the entirety of the fifteenth century. Even so, GDP per head, as almost a direct result of the Black Death, had risen to 50 percent above its pre-plague level, an impressive achievement in itself of economic growth.[319]

One can certainly explore the dimensions of this growth, in terms of the respective sectors of agriculture, industry, and services. Industry fared the best at this time, with growth per head exceeding one percent during the second half of the fourteenth century and output booming, particularly in textile production and tin-mining. The was the late medieval "golden age" of industry, before a "sag" ensued during the mid-fifteenth century, coinciding with the "Great Slump" in the overall economy, after which industrial production commenced more sustained growth in succeeding centuries.[320] Output in services peaked at the same time as industry, while agricultural output contracted during the late fourteenth and during the fifteenth centuries, owing to fewer mouths having to be fed, although livestock production expanded relative to that of grain due to changing tastes and access to more expensive food.[321] Overall, the share of the industry sector contributing to economic output expanded, and that of agriculture contracted, over the course of the late Middle Ages, a trend that was continue throughout the Early Modern period.[322]

It is undoubtedly true that most peasants improved their standards of living and quality of life in the aftermath of the Black Death as a result of these economic trends. Consumption of food in terms of kilocalories per head increased by a quarter by the 1380s compared to before the Black Death, with consumption of meat and dairy increasing by a half and that of grain by about a third, so that "diets at this time had more calories, were of superior quality, better balanced and contained more processed and refined foodstuffs than those of the early fourteenth century".[323] In terms of social distribution of income and households living in poverty, the number of families living below the poverty line more than halved by 1381 compared to 1290, while the purchasing power of the wages of unskilled and skilled laborers increased by 55 percent and 47 percent respectively, although the Gini coefficient, a measure of income inequality, increased slightly.[324] The Black Death thus substantially reduced the level of poverty in medieval society, even if it did not change the basic structure of income distribution.

What was the significance of the Black Death for modern economic development in an international, or European and even global, context? Basically, the Black Death set the stage for the emergence of northwest Europe, in particular England and the Netherlands, as industrial and trading powers, while the economic fortunes of Mediterranean counties, such as Italy and Spain, declined (the "Little Divergence"); at the same time, Europe as a whole pulled greatly ahead of Asia in terms of wealth and technology, a reversal of the situation that had prevailed for much of the Middle Ages (the "Great Divergence"). This is a story that took place over several centuries and which lies beyond the scope of this book. Suffice it to say that the structural changes to the economy inaugurated by the Black Death laid the foundation for these long-term trends and set them in motion.[325]

During the era of the Black Death itself, from about 1348 to 1500, England improved its GDP per head by 43 percent, while the Netherlands increased it by 69 percent, Italy by just 2 percent, and Spain's GDP actually contracted, by about 14 percent. England and Holland were therefore already positioning themselves to be the new economic powerhouses of Europe, taking over this role from Italy, with the economic epicenter shifting from southern to northern Europe. England's and Holland's economic gains from the Black Death proved to be more enduring, while Italy's was more ephemeral, based solely on an improvement in the population-to-resources ratio that evaporated once population began growing again in c.1450; Spain, with the least amount of people prior to the Black Death of these four countries, was unable to sustain its economy with a population reduction so great that commercial networks, specialization, and income per head all suffered.[326] Spain's experience was probably also true of large areas of eastern Europe that also were characterized by a "thinly peopled frontier economy," while for the more populated and urbanized regions, such as England, France, the Low Countries, Germany, and Italy, the Black Death was more of "an economic boon than a misfortune".[327] What data we have from Asia, specifically China, tells us that its GDP per head declined slightly, by about 10 percent, by 1400 as compared to what it had been during the twelfth century, to a level that was roughly comparable with Spain's. It then recovered somewhat by 1500, but then commenced a long, slow decline thereafter, much like what happened in Italy and Spain.[328]

By the eighteenth century, Holland had reached the peak of its growth, and by 1800, in the midst of the Industrial Revolution, England had surpassed the Netherlands in terms of GDP per head and was already a global trading and colonial power.[329] The structural changes in the economy brought about by the Black Death laid the groundwork for this transformation and set England on the path to growth.[330] By solving at a stroke the overburdening of population relative to resources, albeit in drastic fashion, the Black Death allowed England and other overly populated countries to break out of the Malthusian trap, or "economic stalemate".[331] In addition, the excessive mortality of the plague "relieved society of the heavy burden of poverty, reflated demand per head and initiated an immediate increase in incomes per head".[332] England's good fortune was to maintain GDP per head even when population began growing again after 1450.[333] It has been called one of the "great ironies" of history that, by the time Thomas Malthus published his *Essay on the Principle of Population* in 1798, England had already demonstrated that it could achieve strong economic output and prosperity even as population continued to grow.[334] This seemed to vindicate Adam Smith's view that population and the economy could grow hand-in-hand through specialization and division of labor.[335]

In addition, wage rates were allowed to rise, greater access to and engrossment of land occurred, and constraints upon the free movement of labor and goods were removed. The fact that English society allowed these changes to take their course, despite the enactment of labor laws, meant that the economy could prosper to the benefit of all, as opposed to a more repressive society, such as Egypt, where the economy stagnated.[336] Many would argue that the socio-economic changes set in motion by the Black Death were essential for the emergence of agrarian "entrepreneurs" and a transition from feudalism to a kind of agrarian capitalism by the end of the Middle Ages.[337] In particular, the free movement of labor, the loss of government control over prices and wages, and the sweeping away of ancient manorial customs could all be considered necessary prerequisites for true capitalism to take hold and for the agricultural and industrial revolutions to take place.[338] Moreover, as population began to rise again after the mid-fifteenth century, an "industrious" revolution seems to have taken place.[339] The immediate, post Black Death world was perhaps the most leisure-friendly society in history: Workers could labor for 150 days, or just three days out of the week, and still supply all their basic needs.[340] As wages fell with rising population after 1450, workers in England worked longer hours in order to maintain their accustomed standards of living. In this way, the gains in GDP and output inaugurated by the Black Death were retained even as population pressures were reinstated.[341]

The Plague Economy was therefore an integral part of the transition from the Middle Ages to the modern world.[342] In the wake of the plague, lords granted their economic concessions grudgingly, in the expectation that these would be temporary, only "until the world is restored".[343] But this was a stipulation for which they were to wait in vain.

Notes

1 Some such assessment, which seems to have only strengthened with time and additional research, is given by many historians. See, for example: Robert E. Lerner, "The Black Death and Western European Eschatological Mentalities," in *The Black Death: The Impact of the Fourteenth-Century Plague*, ed. D. Williman (Binghamton, N.Y.: Center for Medieval and Early Renaissance Studies, 1982), p. 77 ("one of the worst disasters on

record"); Paul Freedman, *The Origins of Peasant Servitude in Medieval Catalonia* (Cambridge: Cambridge University Press, 1991), p. 156 ("the most cataclysmic event in medieval European history"); D.G. Watts, "The Black Death in Dorset and Hampshire," in *The Black Death in Wessex* (*The Hatcher Review*, 5, 1998), p. 28 ("greatest human disaster in the recorded history of southern England"); Ole J. Benedictow, *The Black Death, 1346–1353: The Complete History* (Woodbridge, UK: Boydell Press, 2004), p. 3 ("greatest-ever demographic disaster"); Paula Arthur, "The Black Death and Mortality: A Reassessment," in *Fourteenth Century England, VI*, ed. Chris Given-Wilson (Woodbridge, UK: Boydell Press, 2010), p. 49 ("England's worst natural disaster in history"); Mark Bailey, "Introduction: England in the Age of the Black Death," in *Town and Countryside in the Age of the Black Death: Essays in Honour of John Hatcher*, eds. Mark Bailey and Stephen Rigby (Turnhout, Belgium: Brepols, 2012), p. xx ("the greatest disaster in documented human history"); David Stone, "The Black Death and its Immediate Aftermath: Crisis and Change in the Fenland Economy, 1346–1353," in *Town and Countryside*, p. 213 ("one of the most cataclysmic episodes in history"); Bruce M.S. Campbell, *The Great Transition: Climate, Disease and Society in the Late-Medieval World* (Cambridge: Cambridge University Press, 2016), pp. 307, 319 ("single greatest public health crisis in recorded European history").

2 Stephen D'Irsay, "Notes to the Origin of the Expression, 'Atra Mors'," *Isis* 8 (1926):328–32; Francis Aidan Gasquet, *The Great Pestilence* (London: Simpkin Marshall, Hamilton, Kent & Co., 1893), p. 7.

3 Benedictow, *Black Death*, p. 382.

4 John Aberth, *The Black Death: The Great Mortality of 1348–1350. A Brief History with Documents* (Boston, MA: Bedford/St. Martin's, 2005), p. 81.

5 John Aberth, *The Black Death: The Great Mortality of 1348–1350. A Brief History with Documents*, 2nd edn. (Boston, MA.: Bedford/St. Martin's, 2017), p. 60.

6 For a full survey of the Black Death, readers should consult my forthcoming book, *The Black Death: A New History of the Great Mortality*, with Oxford University Press. Also see John Aberth, *From the Brink of the Apocalypse: Confronting Famine, War, Plague, and Death in the Later Middle Ages*, 2nd edn. (London: Routledge, 2010), especially pp. 94–210.

7 Ole J. Benedictow, *Plague in the Late Medieval Nordic Countries: Epidemiological Studies* (Oslo, Norway: Middelalderforlaget, 1993), pp. 146–49; Ole J. Benedictow, *What Disease was Plague? On the Controversy over the Microbiological Identity of Plague Epidemics of the Past* (Leiden, Netherlands: Brill, 2010), pp. 6, 9; Benedictow, *Black Death*, p. 9. However, case fatality rates can range from 40–90 percent in any given epidemic. See: R. Pollitzer, *Plague* (Geneva: World Health Organization, 1954), p. 418; Kiersten J. Kugeler, et al., "Epidemiology of Human Plague in the United States, 1900–2012," *Emerging Infectious Diseases*, 21 (2015):18; Robert D. Perry and Jacqueline D. Fetherston, "Yersinia pestis—Etiologic Agent of Plague" *Clinical Microbiology Reviews* 10 (1997):58.

8 Wu Lien-Teh, *A Treatise on Pneumonic Plague* (Geneva: Publications of the League of Nations, 1926), pp. 247–50; Benedictow, *Plague in Late Medieval Nordic Countries*, pp. 23–32, 214–27; Benedictow, *Black Death*, pp. 27–31.

9 W. M. Philip and L.F. Hirst, "A Report on the Outbreak of the Plague in Colombo, 1914–1916," *Journal of Hygiene* 15 (1917):529–30, 534–35.

10 Paleomicrobiology can be considered a specialty of "paleopathology," which has been defined in general terms as an exploration of "the impact of disease in past human groups". There are some challenges that are specific to paleomicrobiology. See Donald J. Ortner, "Paleopathology in the Twenty-First Century," in *Bones and the Man: Studies in Honour of Don Brothwell*, ed. Keith Dobney and Terry O'Connor (Oxford: Oxbow Books, 2002), pp. 5, 9–11.

11 Michel Drancourt, et al., "Detection of 400-Year-Old *Yersinia pestis* DNA in Human Dental Pulp: An Approach to the Diagnosis of Ancient Septicemia," *Proceedings of the National Academy of Sciences* 95 (1998):12637–40; Didier Raoult, et al., "Molecular Identification by 'Suicide PCR' of *Yersinia pestis* as the Agent of Medieval Black Death," *Proceedings of the National Academy of Sciences* 97 (2000):12800–3. The 1998 study

examined victims of plague buried at Lambesc, France, in 1590 and at Marseilles in 1722, while the 2000 study used victims buried at Montpellier in the second half of the fourteenth century.

12 Based on the testing of human plague victims during the Third Pandemic in India and Vietnam, secondary septicemia seems to occur in humans in about 30–45 percent of bubonic plague cases, and nearly always in the case of pneumonic and septicemic plague. What this means, of course, is that we cannot expect every victim in a plague pit to test positive for *Yersinia pestis* aDNA in their dental pulp. See Ole J. Benedictow, *The Black Death and Later Plague Epidemics in the Scandinavian Countries: Perspectives and Controversies* (Warsaw, Poland: De Gruyter Open, 2016), pp. 21, 634–36, 639–49.

13 Samuel K. Cohn, Jr., *The Black Death Transformed: Disease and Culture in Early Renaissance Europe* (London and Oxford: Arnold and Oxford University Press, 2003), p. 248; Alan Cooper and Hendrik N. Poinar, "Ancient DNA: Do It Right or Not at All," *Science* 18 (2000):1139; J.W. Wood and S.N. DeWitte-Aviña, "Was the Black Death Yersinial Plague?" *The Lancet: Infectious Diseases* 3 (2003):327–28. The French team had relied on rigorous cleaning of teeth, use of specially-dedicated facilities, testing with "suicide PCR" primers that were used only once, and comparison with negative control samples in order to eliminate possible contamination with modern *Yersinia pestis*.

14 Thomas P. Gilbert, et al., "Absence of *Yersinia pestis*-Specific DNA in Human Teeth from Five European Excavations of Putative Plague Victims," *Microbiology* 150 (2004):341–54; Michel Drancourt and Didier Raoult, "Molecular Detection of *Yersinia pestis* in Dental Pulp," *Microbiology* 150 (2004):263–64; Thomas P. Gilbert, et al., "Response to Drancourt and Raoult," *Microbiology* 150 (2004):264–65. Drancourt and Raoult noted that the Gilbert team only used their dental pulp extraction technique in seven out of 108 samples, 5 of which came from a "probable" plague pit at Verdun, which also yielded negative results for Drancourt and Raoult. Thus, only 2 teeth were tested properly from a confirmed plague pit, located in Copenhagen from 1711–12. In the vast majority of instances, the Gilbert team used much cruder techniques of extraction, including grinding up the entire tooth into powder or lopping off the root tip and drilling out the insides, which mainly targeted dentine, the calcified tissue of the tooth lying just underneath enamel that could not possibly contain *Yersinia pestis* DNA, since it is not supplied by blood vessels. By 2014, Gilbert had retracted his earlier skepticism, stating that "great technological progress with regards to the extraction and analysis of degraded DNA has been made in recent years, extending the boundaries of what was thought possible". See Thomas Gilbert, "*Yersinia pestis*: One Pandemic, Two Pandemics, Three Pandemics, More?" *The Lancet: Infectious Diseases* 14 (2014):264–65.

15 Stephanie Haensch, et al., "Distinct Clones of *Yersinia pestis* Caused the Black Death," *PLoS Pathogens* 6 (2010):online, e1001134; Verena J. Schuenemann, et al., "Targeted Enrichment of Ancient Pathogens Yielding the pPCP1 Plasmid of *Yersinia pestis* from Victims of the Black Death," *Proceedings of the National Academy of Sciences* 108 (2011):746–52; and Kirsten I. Bos, et al., "A Draft Genome of *Yersinia pestis* from Victims of the Black Death," *Nature* 478 (2011):506–10.

16 Schuenemann, et al., "Targeted Enrichment of Ancient Pathogens," pp. 746–51; Bos, et al., "A Draft Genome of *Yersinia pestis*," p. 506. New protocols and assays for testing and assuring the authenticity of ancient DNA samples also improved upon previous methods, which invited skepticism. See: Lisa Siefert, et al., "Strategy for Sensitive and Specific Detection of *Yersinia pestis* in Skeletons of the Black Death Pandemic," *PloS One* 8 (2013): online, e75742; Alan Cooper and Hendrik N. Poinar, "Ancient DNA: Do It Right or Not at All," *Science* 18 (2000):1139.

17 Schuenemann, et al., "Targeted Enrichment of Ancient Pathogens," pp. 746–52; Bos, et al., "A Draft Genome of *Yersinia pestis*," pp. 506–10.

18 Michel Signoli, Isabelle Séguy, Jean-Noël Biraben, and Oliver Dutour, "Paleo-demography and Historical Demography in the Context of an Epidemic: Plague in Provence in the Eighteenth Century," *Population* 57 (2002):829–54; A. McKeough and T. Loy, "Ring-a-Ring-a-Rosy: DNA Analysis of the Plague Bacillus from Late Medieval

London," *Ancient Biomolecules* 4 (2002):145; Christina Garrelt and Ingrid Wiechmann, "Detection of *Yersinia pestis* DNA in Early and Late Medieval Bavarian Burials," in *Decyphering Ancient Bones: The Research Potential of Bioarchaeological Collections* (Documenta archaeobiologica, 1, 2003), pp. 247–54; Ingrid Wiechmann and Gisela Grupe, "Detection of *Yersinia pestis* DNA in Two Early Medieval Skeletal Finds from Aschheim (Upper Bavaria, 6th Century A.D.)," *American Journal of Physical Anthropology* 126 (2005):48–55; Michel Drancourt, et al., "Genotyping, Orientalis-like *Yersinia pestis*, and Plague Pandemics," *Emerging Infectious Diseases* 10 (2004):1585–92; Carsten M. Pusch, Lila Rahalison, Nikolaus Blin, Graeme J. Nicholson, and Alfred Czarnetzki, "Yersinial F-1 Antigen and the Cause of Black Death," *The Lancet: Infectious Diseases* 4 (2004):484–85; Michel Drancourt, et al., "*Yersinia pestis* Orientalis in Remains of Ancient Plague Patients," *Emerging Infectious Diseases*, 13 (2007):332–33; N. Cerutti, A. Marin, and Massa E. Rabino, "Plague in Ancient Remains: An Immunological Approach," in *Plague: Epidemics and Societies*, ed. Michel Signoli (Florence: Firenze University Press, 2007), pp. 238–41; Raffaella Bianucci, et al., "Technical Note: A Rapid Diagnostic Test Detects Plague in Ancient Human Remains: An Example of the Interaction between Archeological and Biological Approaches (Southeastern France,16th.–18th Centuries)," *American Journal of Physical Anthropology* 136 (2008):361–67; R. Donat, O. Passarius, G. Aboudharam, and M. Drancourt, "Les Sépultures Simultanées et l'Impact de le Peste," in *Vilarnu: Un Village du Moyen-Âge*, eds. O. Passarius, R. Donat, and A. Catafau (Trabucaire: Canet-en-Rousillon, 2008); D. Hadjouis, et al., "Thomas Craven, Noble Anglais Mort de la Peste en 1636 à Saint-Maurice (Val-De-Marne, France)," in *Identification et Détermination de la Cause de la Mort par l'ADN* (Biométrie humaine et anthropologie, 26, 2008), pp. 69–76; Raffaella Bianucci, et al., "Plague Immunodetection in Remains of Religious Exhumed from Burial Sites in Central France," *Journal of Archaeological Science* 36 (2009):616–21; Ingrid Weichmann, Michaela Harbeck, and Gisela Grupe, "*Yersinia pestis* DNA Sequences in Late Medieval Skeletal Finds, Bavaria," *Emerging Infectious Diseases* 16 (2010):1806–7.

19 Schuenemann, et al., "Targeted Enrichment of Ancient Pathogens," p. 751; Bos, et al., "A Draft Genome of *Yersinia pestis*," pp. 508–9; Kirsten I. Bos, et al., "*Yersinia pestis*: New Evidence for an Old Infection," *PLoS One* 7 (2012):on-line, e49803; Haensch, et al., "Distinct Clones," online, e1001134; David M. Wagner, et al., "*Yersinia pestis* and the Plague of Justinian," *The Lancet: Infectious Diseases* 14 (2014):323–25; Giovanna Morelli, et al., "*Yersinia pestis* Genome Sequencing Identifies Patterns of Global Phylogenetic Diversity," *Nature Genetics* 42 (2010):1140–42; Yujun Cui, et al., "Historical Variations in Mutation Rate in an Epidemic Pathogen, *Yersinia pestis*," *Proceedings of the National Academy of Sciences* 110 (2013):578–79; Campbell, *Great Transition*, pp. 246, 293–94. The discovery of these pre-Black Death strains has rendered obsolete the older classifications of *antiqua*, *medievalis*, and *orientalis* strains thought responsible for, respectively, the First, Second, and Third Pandemics, but which are now known to be all modern lineages of *Yersinia pestis* DNA.

20 Haensch, et al., "Distinct Clones of *Yersinia pestis*," online, e1001134.

21 Thi-Nguyen-Ny Tran, et al., "High Throughput, Multiplexed Pathogen Detection Authenticates Plague Waves in Medieval Venice, Italy," *PLoS One* 6 (2011):online, e16735; Michaela Harbeck, et al., "*Yersinia pestis* DNA from Skeletal Remains from the 6th Century A.D. Reveals Insights into Justinianic Plague," *PLoS Pathogens* 9 (2013):on-line, e1003349; Siefert, et al., "Strategy for Sensitive and Specific Detection of *Yersinia pestis*," online, e75742; Wagner, et al., "*Yersinia pestis* and the Plague of Justinian," pp. 319–26; Michal Feldman, et al., "A High-Coverage *Yersinia pestis* Genome from a Sixth-Century Justinianic Plague Victim," *Molecular Biology and Evolution* 33 (2016):2911–23. In early 2014, an English team also recovered *Yersinia pestis* aDNA from 4 out of 12 individuals at a site in Charterhouse Square, Clerkenwell, London, dated to 1349. However, these results have yet to be written up in a peer-reviewed scientific journal, but they were reported in various media outlets and were the subject of a Channel 4 documentary, *Secret History: The Return of the Black Death*, that aired on April 6, 2014.

22 Other overviews of paleomicrobiological research on *Yersinia pestis*, up until 2008–14, include: Benedictow, *Black Death and Later Plague Epidemics*, pp. 79–92; Benedictow, *What Disease was Plague*, pp. 381–95; Lester K. Little, "Plague Historians in Lab Coats," *Past and Present* 213 (2011):267–90; J.L. Bolton, "Looking for *Yersinia Pestis*: Scientists, Historians and the Black Death," in *The Fifteenth Century, XII: Society in an Age of Plague*, eds. Linda Clark and Carole Rawcliffe (Woodbridge, UK: Boydell Press, 2013), pp. 15–38.

23 Haensch, et al., "Distinct Clones of *Yersinia pestis*," online, e1001134; Schuenemann, et al., "Targeting Enrichment of Ancient Pathogens," pp. 746, 749, 751; Bos, et al., "A Draft Genome of *Yersinia pestis*," pp. 506–7, 509. Recent research suggests that plague's mutation rate is rather variable, remaining dormant during endemic and enzootic phases, but then picking up when the disease breaks out into epidemics and epizootics. These genetic changes or mutations are also thought to have occurred in *Yersinia pestis* DNA largely through neutral processes such as genetic drift, or random rearrangements and insertions of segments of DNA, resulting in inactivation of particular genes and the rapid fixing of single-nucleotide polymorphisms (SNPs), rather than through creation of new genetic material entirely. Research on three *Yersinia pestis* strains from the Former Soviet Union does, however, suggest that plague can vary in its virulence, and that the nature of this virulence is still poorly understood. See: Cui, et al., "Historical Variations," pp. 580–81; Chythanya Rajanna, et al., "Characterization of pPCP1 Plasmids in *Yersinia pestis* Strains Isolated from the Former Soviet Union," *International Journal of Microbiology* (2010):online, ID760819; Bolton, "Looking for *Yersinia Pestis*," p. 26; Campbell, *Great Transition*, pp. 246, 292.

24 Ellen A. Lorange, Brent L. Race, Florent Sebbane, and B. Joseph Hinnebusch, "Poor Vector Competence of Fleas and the Evolution of Hypervirulence in *Yersinia pestis*," *Journal of Infectious Diseases* 191 (2005): 1909–10; Benedictow, *Black Death*, pp. 21–22; Benedictow, *What Disease was Plague*, pp. 210–11. Whereas Benedictow assumed that the driving force behind plague's genetic stability was the need to cause "blockage in the ventricular system of fleas," Lorange and her colleagues instead argued that a high septicemia in rodent hosts is "mandated" precisely because the vector competence of blocked fleas, including *Xenopsylla cheopis*, is so poor. A high septicemia ensures that at least one or more resident fleas "will ingest an infectious blood meal" and thus become infective, even though the transmission time, i.e., the life span of infected rodents, is short.

25 John Aberth, *Plagues in World History* (Lanham, MD.: Rowman and Littlefield, 2011), pp. 118–19.

26 Little, "Plague Historians ," p. 280; Bolton, "Looking for *Yersinia Pestis*," pp. 25–26, 28, 36. While acknowledging the conclusiveness of the paleomicrobiological evidence in proving that *Yersinia pestis* was the cause of the Black Death, both authors nonetheless still acknowledged the validity of revisionist arguments such as made by Samuel Cohn, but without subjecting these to any critical analysis or review.

27 "Plague deniers" is a term coined by John Kelly in the Afterword of his popular book, *The Great Mortality: An Intimate History of the Black Death, the Most Devastating Plague of All Time* (New York: HarperCollins, 2005), pp. 295–304. Plague deniers do not carry the same moral or ideological baggage that "Holocaust deniers" do, but they are reminiscent of "Climate change deniers" and other fringe groups who refuse to accept majority scientific opinion on an issue.

28 In 2013, Samuel Cohn stated that the paleomicrobiological research extending over the decade from 1998 to 2008 produced "mixed" results, with "most" researchers coming up with "negative findings" as to identifying *Yersinia pestis* aDNA in human remains. (He made a similar claim in 2008, stating that "few have in fact corroborated the findings of the Marseilles team" from 1998.) This is simply not true. Out of 14 separate studies that I have been able to document for this time period, only one, by the British team led by Gilbert (who since reversed himself) that attempted in 2004 to duplicate the earlier, positive results of a French team, reported negative results. The other "negative"

finding that Cohn cited, by a German team that investigated the seventeenth-century cemetery of St. Germanus in Stuttgart, actually did positively identify *Yersinia pestis* aDNA and its F1 antigen in the sample; an opening statement attributed to the authors, alleging that they disagreed with the view that "*Yersinia pestis* was the cause of the Black Death," was apparently included owing to an editorial error. See: Samuel K. Cohn, Jr., "The Historian and the Laboratory: The Black Death Disease," in *The Fifteenth Century XII*, p. 196; Samuel K. Cohn, Jr., "Epidemiology of the Black Death and Successive Waves of Plague," in *Pestilential Complexities: Understanding Medieval Plague*, ed. Vivian Nutton (*Medical History Supplement*, 27, 2008), p. 100, n. 132; Gilbert, et al., "Absence of *Yersinia pestis*-Specific DNA," pp. 341–54; Pusch, Rahalison, Blin, Nicholson, and Czarnetzki, "Yersinial F-1 Antigen," pp. 484–85; Benedictow, *What Disease was Plague*, pp. 389, 392, and n. 28.

29 In 2004, the team of Susan Scott and Christopher Duncan declared the search for *Yersinia pestis* DNA in mass graves to be a "red herring" that was not going to derail them from their alternative theory, namely, that the Black Death was "haemorrhagic plague," a fictitious disease that Scott and Duncan made up themselves. Likewise, Samuel Cohn, in his article of 2008, announced his own intention of disputing results, "even if new advances in paleopathology should one day settle the question that *Yersinia pestis* was the agent of all three pandemics". This was on the grounds that only a "quick and radical genetic mutation in both humans and bacteria" occurring simultaneously and globally could explain why plague had lost its supposedly efficient, "person-to-person" spread, and why humans lost their supposed immunity to it. Then, in 2013, Cohn wrote that, "isolation of the pathogen alone cannot resolve what was the Black Death disease" owing to the allegedly "extreme" or "extraordinary" differences between the medieval and modern occurrences of plague that he himself identified. This was in spite of the fact that, at the beginning of his article, Cohn admitted that the results of 2010–11 have "given closure to the question of the Black Death's pathogen" in the minds of the "scientific community". See: Susan Scott and Christopher Duncan, *Return of the Black Death: The World's Greatest Serial Killer* (Chichester, UK: Wiley, 2004), pp. 185–90; Cohn, "Epidemiology of the Black Death," p. 100; Cohn, "Historian and the Laboratory," pp. 196–97, 212; Benedictow, *What Disease was Plague*, p. 637.

30 Andrew Cunningham, "Transforming Plague: The Laboratory and the Identity of Infectious Disease," in *The Laboratory Revolution in Medicine*, eds. Andrew Cunningham and Perry Williams (Cambridge: Cambridge University Press, 1992), pp. 216, 242.

31 Although Cohn has called for a new spirit of "cooperation between scientists and historians," this rings hollow given his previous rough treatment of paleomicrobiologists and their work. See: Samuel K. Cohn and L.T. Weaver, "The Black Death and AIDS: CCR5-Δ32 in Genetics and History," *Quarterly Journal of Medicine* 99 (2006):501; Cohn, "Epidemiology of the Black Death," p. 100; Samuel K. Cohn, Jr., "The Black Death: End of a Paradigm," *American Historical Review* 107 (2002):735 and nn. 132 and 133. For other, more apparently genuine calls for cooperation between scientists and historians to solve the mysteries of plague, see: Little, "Plague Historians," p. 286; Bolton, "Looking for *Yersinia pestis*," p. 36; Fabian Crespo and Matthew B. Lawrenz, "Heterogeneous Immunological Landscapes and Medieval Plague: An Invitation to a New Dialogue between Historians and Immunologists," in *Pandemic Disease in the Medieval World: Rethinking the Black Death*, ed. Monica Green (*The Medieval Globe*, 1, 2014), pp. 240, 242, 244, 251.

32 In India, research was conducted under the auspices of the Indian Plague Commission, which in 1905 became the Indian Plague Research Commission and which came out with articles every year in the *Journal of Hygiene* from 1906 to 1937. These articles are now available online at the website of the National Center for Biotechnology Information, a division of the U.S. National Library of Medicine at the National Institutes of Health: www.ncbi.nlm.nih.gov/pmc/journals/336, accessed June 14, 2018. Another important body of evidence was compiled by the North Manchurian Plague Prevention Service, headed by Dr. Wu Liande, which published a series of *Reports* in five volumes

covering the years 1911 to 1926. Dr. Wu, under the name Wu Lien-Teh, also published *A Treatise on Pneumonic Plague* and two articles in the *Journal of Hygiene*: "First Report of the North Manchurian Plague Prevention Service," *Journal of Hygiene* 13 (1913):237–90; and "Plague in Manchuria," *Journal of Hygiene* 21 (1923):307–58. Readers also will want to consult: L. Fabian Hirst, *The Conquest of Plague: A Study of the Evolution of Epidemiology* (Oxford: Clarendon Press, 1953); Pollitzer, *Plague*; Thomas Butler, *Plague and Other Yersinia Infections* (New York: Plenum Medical Book Co., 1983).

33 The first work that can be counted in the plague denial camp is J.F.D. Shrewsbury, *A History of Bubonic Plague in the British Isles* (Cambridge: Cambridge University Press, 1970), which didn't so much deny the historical existence of bubonic plague as deny it as a significant historical event, claiming that it killed no more than five percent of Britain's population. This was then followed up by Graham Twigg, *The Black Death: A Biological Reappraisal* (New York: Schocken Books, 1984); Twigg was the first to reject plague altogether as the disease behind the Black Death, proposing instead an alternative theory, namely, that anthrax (also a bacterial disease) was the cause. Other main contributions to plague denial include: Scott and Duncan, *Biology of Plagues*, and Cohn, *Black Death Transformed*. For a detailed critique of the alternative theories of each of these authors, see Benedictow, *What Disease was Plague*, pp. 489–672.

34 Little, "Plague Historians," p. 273; Bolton, "Looking for *Yersinia Pestis*," pp. 26–28; Richard Hoffmann, *An Environmental History of Medieval Europe* (Cambridge: Cambridge University Press, 2014), pp. 294–97; Vivian Nutton, "Introduction," in *Pestilential Complexities*, p. 12; Campbell, *Great Transition*, pp. 239–40.

35 For a review of these alternative theories, see Benedictow, *Black Death and Later Plague Epidemics*, pp. 355–624. Recently, researchers mathematically modeled out spread of plague by a human ectoparasite transmission (i.e., via the human flea or the body louse), as well as by pneumonic transmission and transmission via rats and their fleas, and matched these to mortality data from nine historical epidemics, dating from 1348 to 1813. Although the researchers concluded that the human ectoparasite model was the best fit for all but two of the historical outbreaks, the Achilles heel of the study was the assumption in the human ectoparasite model that "moribund humans transmit plague at a high rate to vectors". Epidemiologically speaking, this is far from being the case, given the low rate of septicemia emerging in human cases (30–45 percent) and the insufficient concentration of bacteria in the blood to reliably infect vectors when it does occur. This can be considered an exercise in the logical fallacy of reification, or treating a model or hypothesis as real before it is actually demonstated to have a basis in reality. See Katharine Dean, et al., "Human Ectoparasites and the Spread of Plague in Europe during the Second Pandemic," *Proceedings of the National Academy of Sciences* 115 (2018):1304–9.

36 Bolton, "Looking for *Yersinia pestis*," p. 28. Of course, historical evidence, and even paleomicrobiological data, can be interpreted differently to suit a given agenda. But I would suggest that Bolton accepted too uncritically the arguments made by Cohn and other plague deniers.

37 Some of the most glaring logical fallacies charged against plague denial include the false analogy or equivalence, and the argument from silence (*argumentum ex silentio*), which are discussed below.

38 For example, Cohn included in his book, *Black Death Transformed*, chapters entitled, "Scientists square the circle" (Chapter 1) and "Historians square the circle" (Chapter 3). According to Ole Benedictow, in these pages Cohn clearly implied that those who championed the Black Death as plague were "intellectually incompetent or dishonest or both". See: Cohn, *Black Death Transformed*, pp. 7–24, 41–54; Benedictow, *What Disease was Plague*, pp. 26–34, 54–62.

39 By far the most detailed critical examination (running to nearly 750 pages!) of plague denial is that by Benedictow, *What Disease was Plague*, published in 2010. But see also: Lars Walløe, "Medieval and Modern Bubonic Plague: Some Clinical Continuities," in

Pestilential Complexities, pp. 59–73 (2008); and John Theilmann and Frances Cate, "A Plague of Plagues: The Problem of Plague Diagnosis in Medieval England," *Journal of Interdisciplinary History* 37 (2007):371–93. Both these articles, however, provide qualified critiques: Walløe accepted revisionist arguments that rats and their fleas could not have been the main vectors of bubonic plague, owing to lack of evidentiary support for their existence and adverse climactic conditions in medieval Europe, while Theilmann and Cate argued that plague did not act alone in any of its outbreaks, but did so in conjunction with other diseases.

40 Twigg, *Black Death*, pp. 131–46; Scott and Duncan, *Biology of Plagues*, p. 358; Cohn, *Black Death Transformed*, pp. 109–11; Cohn, "Epidemiology of the Black Death," pp. 78–79, 83; Bolton, "Looking for *Yersinia Pestis*," pp. 27–28; George Christakos, Ricardo A. Olea, Marc L. Serre, Hwa-Lung Yu, and Lin-Lin Wang, *Interdisciplinary Public Health Reasoning and Epidemic Modelling: The Case of the Black Death* (Berlin: Springer, 2005); G. Christakos, R.A. Olea, and H.-L. Yu, "Recent Results on the Spatiotemporal Modelling and Comparative Analysis of Black Death and Bubonic Plague Epidemics," *Public Health* 121 (2007):700–20; Campbell, *Great Transition*, pp. 240, 298–99. The teams of Scott and Duncan and Christakos et al. use as the basis of their research the "Reed-Frost" model of epidemiology, which assumes a viral disease spread by cross-infection, or person-to-person spread via airborne droplets, which naturally is a preconceived notion biased against bubonic plague, spread by a rat host and insect vector. See: Benedictow, *What Disease was Plague*, pp. 633–36; Benedictow, *Black Death and Later Plague Epidemics*, pp. 45–47.

41 Cohn, "Black Death: End of a Paradigm," p. 712; Cohn, "Epidemiology of the Black Death," p. 78; Cohn, "Historian and the Laboratory," pp. 201–2.

42 Cohn, "Black Death: End of a Paradigm," p. 712, n. 52; Cohn, "Historian and the Laboratory," p. 201; Twigg, *Black Death*, p. 139. Originally, in 2002, Cohn derived his spread rate for plague from table 10 on p. 139 of Twigg, which listed a spread rate of 8–12 miles per year in South Africa between 1899–1924 for *murine* plague (i.e., plague among rats or mice only) and c. 20 miles per year for *sylvatic* plague (i.e., plague among wild rodents, which can include rats but also prairie dogs, marmots, gerbils, etc.). It also listed a spread rate of 8 miles a year for sylvatic plague in India and North America between 1901–40, and 4 miles per year for murine plague in Suffolk, England, between 1906–10. These were derived from reports such as J. Alexander Mitchell's "Plague in South Africa: Historical Summary" for the *Publications of the South African Institute for Medical Research* for 1927, and C.R. Eskey and V.H. Hass' "Plague in the Western Part of the United States" for the *Public Health Bulletin* of the United States Public Health Service for 1940. In 2013, Cohn claimed a spread rate of as low as 6.5 km, or 4 miles, per year for the overland spread of rat plague in New Orleans, based on Hirst, *Conquest of Plague*, p. 304, who in turn derived this information from a *Public Health Report* by R.H. Creel in 1915. However, Creel's original study in New Orleans was on the movements of healthy brown rats, who were found to travel as much as four miles within the city limits when released from the city center, and had nothing to do with plague in its panzootic form. For a review of how Twigg propagated the "myth" of contiguous spread of plague, see Benedictow, *Black Death and Later Plague Epidemics*, pp. 464–68.

43 The Indian Plague Research Commission found that plague spread among adjacent rat colonies at a rate of 300 feet in six weeks, which is equivalent to about 2600 feet in a year. Jim Bolton hypothesized that medieval plague could have spread "across the countryside from colony to colony of wild animals," i.e., in panzootic fashion, and then given rise to epidemics when the plague infected "household and barnyard animals". But since rats are mainly sedentary animals, venturing no more than 200 meters, or 656 feet, during their entire lifetimes, it seems unlikely that rat colonies in human households would have had much contact with wild, wider-ranging animal carriers. See: Indian Plague Research Commission (IPRC), Reports on Plague Investigations in India, XXIII: "Epidemiological Observations in the Villages of Sion, Wadhala, Parel and

Worli in Bombay Villages," *Journal of Hygiene* 7 (1907):839; Jim Bolton, "'The World Upside Down': Plague as an Agent of Economic and Social Change," in *The Black Death in England*, eds. W.M. Ormrod and P.G. Lindley (Donington, UK: Shaun Tyas, 2003), p. 25; Michael McCormick, "Rats, Communications, and Plague: Toward an Ecological History," *Journal of Interdisciplinary History* 24 (2003):10.

44 Campbell, *Great Transition*, p. 236.

45 Benedictow, *Black Death*, pp. 229–31; Benedictow, *What Disease was Plague*, pp. 173, 187; Wendy R. Childs, "Moving Around," in *A Social History of England, 1200–1500*, eds. Rosemary Horrox and W. Mark Ormrod (Cambridge: Cambridge University Press, 2006), p. 261. Benedictow estimated that the Black Death spread at an average pace of 1.2 miles (2 km) per day along main roads, but this seems to be an extremely conservative estimate for cart- and pack-horse travel.

46 Cohn, "Epidemiology of the Black Death," p. 78; Cohn, "Historian and the Laboratory," p. 202. Any such assertions as to the exact spread rate of the medieval Black Death are complete nonsense, because: 1) we can never know the precise chronology of this spread, since when an epidemic was recognized by human records was not the same as when it actually arrived in the form of infected rats and fleas; and 2) we can never know how it spread geographically, owing to the haphazard pattern of metastatic leaps. Benedictow regularly adjusted his assumptions of when plague actually arrived in a town by backdating 1½–2 months from when humans recognized the disease, based on his calculations of the incubation period for an epidemic (*Black Death*, pp. 18, 57–59), which may now be shorter owing to early-phase transmission. To make calculations or to map the spread of the Black Death based on assumptions that human records give an accurate picture of the timing of the Black Death, and that it had a straightforward, linear progression, is to make the a priori assumption that the Black Death was not plague but rather a human-mediated disease.

47 Benedictow, *What Disease was Plague*, p. 173.

48 There is some debate over whether subsequent outbreaks of plague after the Great Mortality of 1348 were the product of reintroductions of the bacillus from outside Europe, or the result of the disease circulating between endemic foci, among either wild or domestic rodents in cities and their hinterlands, that have since died out. See: Boris V. Schmid, et al., "Climate-Driven Introduction of the Black Death and Successive Plague Reintroductions into Europe," *Proceedings of the National Academy of Sciences* 112 (2015):3022–23; Ann G. Carmichael, "Plague Persistence in Western Europe: A Hypothesis," in *Pandemic Disease in the Medieval World*, pp. 177–80.

49 W.B. Bannerman, "The Spread of Plague in India," *Journal of Hygiene* 6 (1906):189–195; J. Ashburton Thompson, "On the Epidemiology of Plague," *Journal of Hygiene* 6 (1906):542–43; Benedictow, *What Disease was Plague*, pp. 153–55.

50 IPRC, Reports on Plague Investigations in India, XXIV: "General Considerations Regarding the Spread of Infection, Infectivity of Houses, etc. in Bombay City and Island," *Journal of Hygiene* 7 (1907):886–91. The Commission also tested its hypothesis by introducing guinea pigs into the homes of travelers who had died of plague. See IPRC, "Epidemiological Observations," pp. 869–71; Benedictow, *What Disease was Plague*, pp. 157–65.

51 Benedictow, *What Disease was Plague*, pp. 166–69.

52 Hirst, *Conquest of Plague*, pp. 303–31. The migration of plague epidemics following the migration of rats and their fleas, which in turn follow movement of grain after being harvested, has more recently been confirmed by the experience of plague during the 1990s in Madagascar. Although Cohn did admit that plague could be spread over long distances by means of "plague-ridden rats" traveling with grain cargoes, he denied that this could be done through plague-infected fleas travelling alone and living on grain dust, on the grounds that fleas "rarely live more than five days" away from their rat host. Yet, it was already demonstrated in the first half of the twentieth century that infected rat fleas can survive "at least fifty days" without a blood meal, while more recent research shows that infected but unblocked fleas can survive for a year or more and still

infect new hosts. See: Hirst, *Conquest of Plague*, pp. 324, 330; Kenneth L. Gage and Michael Y. Kosoy, "Natural History of Plague: Perspectives from More than a Century of Research," *Annual Review of Entomology* 50 (2005):517–18; Cohn, *Black Death Transformed*, pp. 28–29; Suzanne Chanteau, et al., "Current Epidemiology of Human Plague in Madagascar," *Microbes and Infection*, 2 (2000):29.

53 Myron Echenberg, *Plague Ports: The Global Urban Impact of Bubonic Plague, 1894–1901* (New York: New York University Press, 2007). A simple calculation will show that, if we take the flight distance between Hong Kong and San Francisco—11,092 km, or 6892 miles—and divide this by the time that it took for plague to reach San Francisco from Hong Kong—i.e., a total of six years (1894–1900), or 2190 days—then plague traveled in this instance (by ship) at a rate of about 5 km, or 3 miles, per day, which is at the upper end of the "astonishing" spread rate that Cohn hypothesized for the Black Death!

54 This contradicts the revisionist claim that medieval chroniclers universally observed the terrifying swiftness of the spread of the Black Death. Such remarks, like Giovanni Boccaccio's famous dictum that plague spread "with the speed of a fire racing through dry or oily substances that happened to be placed within its reach," were usually made within the context of perceived contagion from one person to another and were not used to describe the geographical spread of the disease from city to city or region to region. In the latter regard, what was so terrifying about plague to contemporaries was the *unpredictability*, rather than the speed, of plague's spread, so that they did not know where it would strike next. See: Cohn, *Black Death Transformed*, pp. 111–12; Aberth, *Black Death*, pp. 32; Aberth, *From the Brink of the Apocalypse*, pp. 85–86.

55 Karl Sudhoff, "Pestschriften aus den ersten 150 Jahren nach der Epidemie des 'schwarzen Todes' von 1348,'" *Archiv für Geschichte der Medizin (AGM)* 11 (1919):47; *Documents Inédits sur la Grande Peste de 1348*, ed. L.-A. Joseph Michon (Paris, 1860), p. 81; Henricus de Hervordia, *Liber de Rebus Memorabilioribus sive Chronicon*, ed. Augustus Potthast (Göttingen, Germany, 1859), p. 280.

56 Sudhoff, "Pestschriften," *AGM* 11 (1919):47; Cohn, *Black Death Transformed*, pp. 137–38.

57 Hervordia, *Liber de Rebus Memorabilioribus*, p. 280; "Gesta Archiepiscoporum Magdeburgensium," in *Monumenta Germaniae Historica (MGH)*, *Scriptores in folio (SS)*, 14:435; Konrad von Halberstadt, *Chronographia Interminata, 1277–1355/59*, ed. Rainer Leng (Wissensliteratur im Mittelalter, 23, 1996), p. 208.

58 Hervordia, *Liber de Rebus Memorabilioribus*, p. 280.

59 Of these authors, Giovanni Villani was based in Florence; Heinrich of Herford at Minden in northwestern Germany; Konrad of Halberstadt and an anonymous author from Magdeburg in north central Germany; and the anonymous medical practitioner of Montpellier in southern France. Konrad of Megenberg seems to have been based in Avignon at the time he was writing, but evidently "gathered" his information from various merchant informants. See Dagmar Gottschall, "Conrad of Megenberg and the Causes of the Plague: A Latin Treatise on the Black Death Composed ca. 1350 for the Papal Court in Avignon," in *La vie culturelle, intellectuelle et scientifique à la cour des papes d'Avignon*, ed. Jacqueline Hamesse (Turnhout, Belgium: Brepols, 2006), pp. 321–22.

60 Benedictow, *Black Death*, pp. 57–226.

61 Haensch, et al., "Distinct Clones of *Yersinia pestis*," online, e1001134; Benedictow, *Black Death and Later Plague Epidemics*, pp. 113–14.

62 David C. Mengel, "A Plague on Bohemia? Mapping the Black Death," *Past and Present* 211 (2011):8. ; Christoph Cluse, "Zur Chronologie der Verfolgungen zur Zeit des 'Schwarzen Todes'," in *Geschichte der Juden im Mittelalter von der Nordsee bis zu den Südalpen*, ed. Alfred Haverkamp (*Forschungen zur Geschichte der Juden*, 14/1, 2002), p. 240, n. 87. Perhaps the most influential map of the Black Death has been that produced by Élisabeth Carpentier in 1962, even though it is by now badly outdated. The only map that attempts to show metastatic leaps is by Ole Benedictow, produced in 2004. See: Élisabeth Carpentier, "Autour de la peste noire: famines et épidémies dans l'histoire

du XIVe siècle," *Annales: Economies, Sociétés, Civilisation* 17 (1962): map opposite pp. 1070–71; Benedictow, *Black Death*, map 1, opposite p. xvi.

63 Christakos, et al., *Interdisciplinary Public Health Reasoning*, pp. 204–7, 217; Christakos, Olea, and Yu, "Recent Results on the Spatiotemporal Modelling," pp. 700–20. Christakos' geographical mapping of the spread of the Black Death in half-year intervals assumed a "wave" pattern that was really no different from Carpentier's 1962 map. By contrast, his mapping of the spread of bubonic plague in India during the Third Pandemic assumed a "cloud" pattern that was more akin to metastatic leaps, in which "the disease disappeared and reappeared several times at certain locations". It is little wonder, then, that Christakos concluded that "the two epidemics exhibited some differences in their spatiotemporal characteristics". Recently, Samuel Cohn has seized on Christakos' data to claim that the Black Death spread across Europe "to the 4th power of time," or twice the rate of plague's spread across India during the Third Pandemic; while Christakos himself claimed that, based on geographical spread, the mortality of the Black Death was "two orders of magnitude" higher than bubonic plague in India. Meanwhile, John Hatcher and Mark Bailey stressed the pitfalls of making imprecise historical figures fit into the straitjacket of a scientifically precise, theoretical model. See: Cohn, "Epidemiology of the Black Death," p. 78; Cohn, "Historian and the Laboratory," pp. 201–2; Benedictow, *Black Death*, pp. 227–31; John Hatcher and Mark Bailey, *Modelling the Middle Ages: The History and Theory of England's Economic Development* (Oxford: Oxford University Press, 2001), pp. 15–17.

64 Twigg, *Black Death*, p. 139.

65 This is precisely the average pace that Benedictow estimated the Black Death traveled by land. See Benedictow, *Black Death*, p. 107.

66 Bolton, "Looking for *Yersinia Pestis*," pp. 29–32; Campbell, *Great Transition*, pp. 239–40, 305. Although Cohn claimed to offer "no alternatives" to plague as the culprit behind the Black Death, he clearly had in mind a viral-type disease spread "person-to-person" that produced immunity in adults such that it became a childhood disease. See: Cohn, "Black Death: End of a Paradigm," pp. 712–13; Cohn, *Black Death Transformed*, p. 247; Cohn, "Epidemiology of the Black Death," pp. 78, 100; Cohn, "Historian and the Laboratory," p. 208. For a review of the modern-day evidence for the human flea, *Pulex irritans*, as a vector in plague epidemics, see: Rebecca J. Eisen, David T. Dennis, and Kenneth L. Gage, "The Role of Early-Phase Transmission in the Spread of *Yersinia pestis*," *Journal of Medical Entomology*, 52 (2015): 1188–90. The case for the role of *Pulex irritans* in the Black Death was made by: G. Blanc and M. Baltazard, "Recherches sur le mode de transmission naturelle de la pest bubonique et septicémique," *Archives de l'Institut Pasteur du Maroc* 3 (1945): 173–354; G. Blanc, "Une opinion nonconformiste sur le mode de transmission de la peste," *Revue d'Hygiene et de Médicine Sociale* 4 (1956): 535–62; Walløe, "Medieval and Modern Bubonic Plague," pp. 71–72; Anne Karin Hufthammer and Lars Walløe, "Rats Cannot Have Been Intermediate Hosts for *Yersinia pestis* during Medieval Plague Epidemics in Northern Europe," *Journal of Archaeological Science* 40 (2013): 1756–58. The case for pneumonic plague was made by: Christopher Morris, "Plague in Britain," in *The Plague Reconsidered: A New Look at Its Origins and Effects in 16th and 17th Century England* (Local Population Studies Supplement, 1977), pp. 37–47; G. Karlsson, "Plague Without Rats: The Case of Fifteenth-Century Iceland," *Journal of Medieval History* 22 (1996):263–84; Theilmann and Cate, "Plague of Plagues," pp. 383–86. Some lab experiments and field testing of lice as a possible vector of plague have been done, but the results are far from conclusive. See: Michel Drancourt, Linda Houhamdi, and Didier Raoult, "*Yersinia pestis* as a telluric, human ectoparasite-borne organism," *The Lancet: Infectious Diseases* 6 (2006):237–40; Linda Houhamdi, et al., "Experimental Model to Evaluate the Human Louse as a Vector of Plague," *Journal of Infectious Diseases* 6 (2006):1589–96; Saravanan Ayyaduri, et al., "Body Lice, *Yersinia pestis Orientalis* and Black Death," *Emerging Infectious Diseases*, 16 (2010):892–93; Renaud Piarroux, et al., "Plague Epidemics and Lice, Democratic Republic of Congo," *Emerging Infectious Diseases* 19 (2013):505–6. Each of these theories is critiqued in more detail in

Benedictow, *What Disease was Plague*, pp. 9–16, 491–552, 664; Benedictow, *Black Death and Later Plague Epidemics*, 355–94, 593–624.

67 Guido Alfani and Samuel K. Cohn, Jr., "Catching the Plague: New Insights into the Transmission of Early Modern Plague," *Princeton Working Papers*, 2009, available online at http://iussp2009.princeton.edu/papers/90564, accessed June 14, 2018.

68 Eisen, Dennis, and Gage, "Role of Early-Phase Transmission ," pp. 1184–85; Rebecca J. Eisen, A.P. Wilder, S.W. Bearden, J.A. Montenieri, and K.L. Gage, "Early-Phase Transmission of *Yersinia pestis* by Unblocked *Xenopsylla cheopis* (Siphonaptera: Pulicidae) is as Efficient as Transmission by Blocked Fleas," *Journal of Medical Entomology* 44 (2007):680–82; Rebecca J. Eisen, et al., "Early-Phase Transmission of *Yersinia pestis* by Unblocked Fleas as a Mechanism Explaining Rapidly Spreading Plague Epizootics," *Proceedings of the National Academy of Sciences* 103 (2006):15380–81; Benedictow, *Black Death*, p. 18; Benedictow, *What Disease was Plague*, p. 6; Campbell, *Great Transition*, p. 296. "Blocked" transmission means that *Yersinia pestis* bacteria multiply and gel together into a mass that obstructs the flea's upper stomach, or *proventriculus*. Freshly-ingested blood becomes mixed in with some of the bacterial mass extending into the esophagus, and the whole is then regurgitated or flushed by "elastic recoil" of the distended esophagus back into the bite wound of the host once the flea has relaxed its pharyngeal muscles. Benedictow, in his latest publication, rejected early-phase transmission on the grounds that its precise mechanisms have yet to be explained to his satisfaction. See Benedictow, *Black Death and Later Plague Epidemics*, pp. 443–46, 627–34.

69 During the second pneumonic plague outbreak in Manchuria in 1920–21, Dr. Wu Liande conducted laboratory experiments on captured marmots that demonstrated that they were "easily susceptible" to primary pneumonic plague when the bacteria were sprayed in aerosol form directly into their faces, and that they then were able to communicate pneumonic plague to each other. Similar results were reported in 2009 from lab experiments on brown Norway rats, who were infected by "intranasal instillation" and then progressed to fatal pneumonia within 2–4 days. See: Wu Lien-Teh, Chun Wing Han, and Robert Pollitzer, "Plague in Manchuria: II. The Role of the Tarabagan in the Epidemiology of Plague," *Journal of Hygiene* 21 (1923):329–41; Deborah M. Anderson, et al., "Pneumonic Plague Pathogenesis and Immunity in Brown Norway Rats," *American Journal of Pathology* 174 (2009):910–21.

70 Aberth, *Plagues in World History*, p. 75; Benedictow, *What Disease was Plague*, p. 649. Scott and Duncan argued for a latency period of 10–12 days, followed by an actively infectious stage without signs of 20–22 days, for their alternative disease of "haemhorragic plague". This would certainly allow infected people to travel and mix with others, but with a month-long incubation period that would hardly spread the disease faster than bubonic plague. Cohn has criticized Scott and Duncan's theory as unproven, since the parish registers from which they derived their data recorded only the date of burial of victims, and even in households where two or more family members died, the interval between burials cannot be taken as indicating the absolute time of infection, sickness, and death of one member by another. Cohn's own household reconstructions of late fifteenth–early sixteenth century plague cases from Milan point to the majority of victims dying within 1–4 days of infection, which hardly gave them enough time to travel and spread the disease, especially if they were coming down with such early, debilitating symptoms as "continuous fever, headaches, and vomiting". See: Scott and Duncan, *Biology of Plagues*, pp. 128–29; Samuel K. Cohn, Jr. and Guido Alfani, "Households and Plague in Early Modern Italy," *Journal of Interdisciplinary History* 38 (2007):180–86.

71 Campbell, *Great Transition*, p. 299. The latest assessment of human travel in the late Middle Ages concluded that it was "frequent and not too difficult". Thus, the worldwide transmission of diseases spread human-to-human was not inconceivable in the pre-modern period. But, in order to achieve the massive mortalities on the scale of the Black Death, such diseases required massive numbers of contacts (in addition to other factors), which was only attained by smallpox and measles over the course of several centuries during the European voyages of discovery to the Americas, and by the Influenza

Pandemic of 1918–19 through the unprecedented mobilization of troops and other personnel during World War I. There is no indication that human traffic on such a scale occurred during the Black Death. See: Wendy R. Childs, "Moving Around," in *Social History of England*, p. 275; Cohn and Alfani, "Households and Plague," pp. 184–85.

72 Eisen, et al., "Early-Phase Transmission," p. 15383; Benedictow, *Black Death*, pp. 14–17; Benedictow, *What Disease was Plague*, pp. 9–16; Benedictow, *Black Death and Later Plague Epidemics*, pp. 639–49. As mentioned, the percentage of human bubonic plague cases developing secondary septicemia is 30–45 percent, based on data collected in India and Vietnam during the Third Pandemic. An even smaller percentage, 10 percent or less, developed a high enough bacteremia sufficient to infect a flea.

73 John Aberth, *Doctoring the Black Death: Europe's Late Medieval Medical Response to Epidemic Disease*, forthcoming with Rowman and Littlefield; Vivian Nutton, "The Seeds of Disease: An Explanation of Contagion and Infection from the Greeks to the Renaissance," *Medical History* 27 (1983):1–34; John Henderson, "The Black Death in Florence: Medical and Communal Responses," in *Death in Towns: Urban Responses to the Dying and the Dead, 100–1600*, ed. Steven Bassett (London and New York: Leicester University Press, 1992), pp. 139–41.

74 Gentile da Foligno, *Consilium contra pestilentiam* (Colle di Valdelsa, c. 1479), pp. 3, 5.

75 Sudhoff, "Pestschriften," *AGM* 5 (1912):338, forthcoming.

76 Foligno, *Consilium contra pestilentiam*, p. 38; Sudhoff, "Pestschriften," *AGM* 6 (1913): 338; *AGM* 9 (1916):130; *AGM* 14 (1922–23):145; *AGM* 17 (1925):42. For other examples and further discussion of this issue, see Aberth, *Doctoring the Black Death*, forthcoming.

77 Sudhoff, "Pestschriften," *AGM* 14 (1922–23):93; Foligno, *Consilium contra pestilentiam*, p. 5.

78 *The Black Death*, trans. and ed. Rosemary Horrox (Manchester, UK: Manchester University Press, 1994), pp. 195–96; Ann G. Carmichael, *Plague and the Poor in Renaissance Florence* (Cambridge: Cambridge University Press, 1986), pp. 108–9; Cohn, "Epidemiology of the Black Death," p. 98.

79 Carlo M. Cipolla, *Public Health and the Medical Profession in the Renaissance* (Cambridge: Cambridge University Press, 1976), pp. 11–66; Carlo M. Cipolla, *Faith, Reason, and the Plague in Seventeenth-Century Tuscany*, trans. M. Kittel (Ithaca, NY.: Cornell University Press, 1979), pp. 1–14; Carmichael, *Plague and the Poor*, pp. 98–126; C. de Backer, "Maatregelen Tegen de Pest te Diest in de Vijftiende en Zestiende Eeuw," *Koninklijke Academie voor Geneeskunde van Belgie* 61 (1999):273–99; Neil Murphy, "Plague Ordinances and the Management of Infectious Diseases in Northern French Towns, c.1450–c.1560," in *The Fifteenth Century XII*, pp. 139–59; Carole Rawcliffe, *Urban Bodies: Communal Health in Late Medieval English Towns and Cities* (Woodbridge, UK: Boydell Press, 2013); Kristy Wilson Bowers, *Plague and Public Health in Early Modern Seville* (Rochester, NY.: University of Rochester Press, 2013), pp. 30–88.

80 Undoubtedly the reason for this was that medieval and Early Modern plague ordinances focused on inter-human contagion as the mechanism for spread of the disease, rather than on what we now know to be the true one, namely, transport of infected rats and fleas via grain shipments. Quite the contrary, urban centers in particular were concerned to maintain their food supplies during plague epidemics, in order to avoid starvation among their poorer citizens and the risk of famine, which they believed could be a concurrent cause of plague. See: Murphy, "Plague Ordinances in Northern French Towns," p. 144; Aberth, *From the Brink of the Apocalypse*, pp. 37–42.

81 Mark Gamsa, "The Epidemic of Pneumonic Plague in Manchuria, 1910–1911," *Past and Present* 190 (2006): 154, 162 and nn. 13, 38. Estimates of those dying in the first outbreak of 1910–11 range from 42,000 to 60,000. Dr. Wu clearly favored figures that boosted the effectiveness of his North Manchurian Plague Prevention Service, but even at the most conservative estimates, the reduction in deaths is still impressive.

82 John Aberth, *The First Horseman: Disease in Human History* (Upper Saddle River, NJ.: Pearson/Prentice Hall, 2007), pp. 103–5, 109.

83 The main arguments in this regard have been made by: Hufthammer and Walløe, "Rats Cannot have been Intermediate Hosts," pp. 1753–56; Karlsson, "Plague without Rats," pp. 263–65, 276–80; and David E. Davis, "The Scarcity of Rats and the Black Death: An Ecological History," *Journal of Interdisciplinary History* 16 (1986):455–70. But see also: Cohn, *Black Death Transformed*, pp. 1, 21–22, 81–82, 134; Twigg, *Black Death*, pp. 111–12; Shrewsbury, *Bubonic Plague*, pp. 7, 23, 53; Scott and Duncan, *Biology of Plagues*, pp. 56–57.

84 Benedictow, *What Disease was Plague*, pp. 85–91; Benedictow, *Black Death and Later Plague Epidemics*, pp. 47–55, 395–443; Theilmann and Cate, "Plague of Plagues," pp. 379, 388. Benedictow summed up his criticisms of the argument from silence with the catchy phrase, "Absence of evidence is not evidence of absence".

85 McCormick, "Rats, Communications, and Plague," pp. 5–6; Anton Ervynk, "Sedentism or Urbanism? On the Origin of the Commensal Black Rat (*Rattus rattus*)," in *Bones and the Man*, pp. 95–96.

86 Benedictow, *What Disease was Plague*, p. 124.

87 McCormick, "Rats, Communications, and Plague," p. 14. For other surveys of rat archaeology relating to the Black Death, see: F. Audoin-Rouzeau and J.-F. Vigne, "La colonization de l'Europe par le Rat noir (*Rattus rattus*)," *Revue de Paléobiologie* 13 (1994):125–45; F. Audoin-Rouzeau, "Le rat noir (Rattus rattus) et la peste dans l'occident antique et medieval," *Bulletin de la Société de pathologie exotique* 92 (1999):422–26; F. Audoin-Rouzeau, *Les chemins de la peste: Le rat, la puce et l'homme* (Rennes: Presses Universitaires de Rennes, 2003), pp. 115–24.

88 McCormick, "Rats, Communications, and Plague," p. 4; Benedictow, *What Disease was Plague*, p. 134; Benedictow, *Black Death*, p. 24.

89 Benedictow, *What Disease was Plague*, pp. 78–84.

90 Paul-Louis Simond, "La propagation de la peste," *Annales de l'Institut Pasteur* 12 (1898): 625–87.

91 Aberth, *Doctoring the Black Death*, forthcoming; Benedictow, *What Disease was Plague*, pp. 81–82; Cohn, *Black Death Transformed*, p. 133.

92 Thus, Boccaccio famously described how, during the 1348 epidemic in Florence, he personally witnessed two pigs "mauling" the rags of a plague victim that had been thrown out into the street, until they dropped dead within a short time "spread-eagled upon the rags that had brought about their undoing". Benedictow has called this "an anecdotal story made up or repeated by Boccaccio and related in the I-form in order to dramatize the introduction to his novel"; in modern epidemiological terms, pigs are known to be "refractory" to plague. See: Murphy, "Plague Ordinances in Northern French Towns," p. 143; Aberth, *Black Death*, p. 32; Benedictow, *What Disease was Plague*, p. 361.

93 Konrad of Megenberg, writing in c. 1350, and Saladin Ferro de Esculo, writing in 1448, provided the classic expositions of this position. See: Sudhoff, "Pestschriften," *AGM* 11 (1919):49–50; Universitätsbibliothek Leipzig, MS 1227, fol. 147v.

94 Benedictow, *What Disease was Plague*, pp. 92–97; Benedictow, *Black Death and Later Plague Epidemics*, pp. 54–55; Stefan Monecke, Hannelore Monecke, and Jochen Monecke, "Modelling the Black Death: A Historical Case Study and Implications for the Epidemiology of Bubonic Plague," *International Journal of Medical Microbiology* 299 (2009):590; Hirst, *Conquest of Plague*, pp. 147–48. Although heresay evidence of dead and dying rats being found in plague-infested houses was reported at the turn of the 20th century in Calcutta and the Punjab, the later, more scientific researches of the Indian Plague Research Commission, such as conducted at four villages near Mumbai in 1907 and at Belgaum in 1908–9, reported difficulty in obtaining rat carcasses for research purposes even when employing a "rat-catching staff". Cohn's claim that contemporary observers of the Black Death should have seen thousands, millions, or even billions of dead or dying rats "falling from rafters, littering buildings, streets, and lanes" is the product of fantasy perhaps inspired by the Pied Piper of Hamlin, rather than any actual experience during the Third Pandemic in India. He set up the same unrealistic

expectations with regard to descriptions of fleas on humans, which Cohn claimed should have been seen to be "popping out of bedding and clothing like popcorn". See: Bannerman, "Spread of Plague in India," pp. 183–84; IPRC, "Epidemiological Observations," pp. 825, 836, 839, 845–46, 854, 869; IPRC, Reports on Plague Investigations in India, XXXVI: "Observations of Plague in Belgaum, 1908–1909," *Journal of Hygiene* 10 (1910):453–54; Cohn, "Epidemiology of the Black Death," p. 76, n. 11, and p. 98; Cohn, "Historian and the Laboratory," p. 208.

95 Aberth, *Black Death*, 1st edn., p. 20.

96 Aberth, *Black Death*, 1st edn., pp. 15–16; Benedictow, *What Disease was Plague*, p. 82.

97 Avicenna, *Liber Canonis* (Hildesheim: Georg Olms, 1964), fol. 416v.

98 Cohn does a curious double-take with this evidence. On the one hand, he admitted that it was purely "theoretical" and not based on "true observations," but, on the other hand, he wanted to take it as evidence that no one observed rat epizootics in the Middle Ages, since all these animals were seen as issuing from their holes alive, and were even captured as such. See Cohn, *Black Death Transformed*, pp. 22, 133–34; Cohn, "Epidemiology of the Black Death," p. 78.

99 Universitäts- und Forschungsbibliothek Gotha, Codex Chart. A 501, fols. 279r.-v.; Sudhoff, "Pestschriften," *AGM* 16 (1924–25):25. The remarkable death toll of eight children in eight days undoubtedly inspired Saxony to list this as his "eighth sign".

100 Bannerman, "Spread of Plague," pp. 185–86; IPRC, "Epidemiological Observations," pp. 828–29; IPRC, "Observations on Rat and Human Plague in Belgaum," p. 452; Aberth, *First Horseman*, pp. 81–82. In the fifteenth century, the bishop of Brescia, Dominico Amanti, defended the right of humans to flee plague by reading animal signs such as those given by Avicenna, and many plague doctors recommended flight from a plague-infested region as the "best" remedy against the disease. Medieval Europeans were therefore not so "blind" and "ignorant" in this regard compared to modern Indians, as Cohn claimed. See: Cohn, "Epidemiology of the Black Death," p. 76, n. 11; Cohn, "Historian and the Laboratory," p. 208; Aberth, *From the Brink of the Apocalypse*, p. 196.

101 Although he mentioned Saxony's account as possible evidence "of rats associated with plague," Cohn was still skeptical because there was "no description of an epizootic of rodents; the mice were still alive". But this test of validity is completely unrealistic, since, as mentioned above, finding dead rats was difficult even for modern observers of the Third Pandemic, who were actively looking for a rat-plague connection. Cohn adopted this same, ridiculously extreme conditional response to medieval observations of fleas on victims: Even though contemporary observers like Eustache Deschamps did note various insects on persons dead from the plague, Cohn dismissed the evidence on the grounds that no one observed fleas "on those stricken by the disease while they were still alive". Although medieval people did believe that plague could be communicated through victims' clothing, this was understood in miasmatic terms "as due to the trapping of corrupt air within the folds of fabric," rather than transmitted by flea bites. See: Cohn, *Black Death Transformed*, p. 134; Cohn, "Epidemiology of the Black Death," pp. 98–99, n. 126; Benedictow, *What Disease was Plague*, p. 86; *Black Death*, trans. and ed. Horrox, p. 195, n. 38; Murphy, "Plague Ordinances in Northern French Towns," p. 155.

102 Cohn, *Black Death Transformed*, pp. 57–95; Cohn, "Historian and the Laboratory," pp. 206–8.

103 Cohn boasted that his assessment of medieval descriptions of bubonic plague symptoms was based on "407 chronicles, calendars, and 'necrologies' covering the plague years from 1347 to 1450" consulted in "various libraries in Britain, France, and Italy". In addition, his bibliography listed over 100 plague treatises, although only 30–55 of these related to bubonic plague symptoms. See Cohn, *Black Death Transformed*, pp. 68–95, 274–79; Benedictow, *What Disease was Plague*, pp. 341, 356–58.

104 Cohn, *Black Death Transformed*, pp. 77–78; Benedictow, *What Disease was Plague*, pp. 340–80.

105 Cohn, *Black Death Transformed*, pp. 67–68; Cohn, "Black Death: End of a Paradigm," pp. 707–10. See also the criticisims made in this regard by Benedictow, *What Disease was Plague*, pp. 340–41, 346–48, 351, 358–59, 362, 365.

106 In my own survey of 240 plague treatises between 1347 and c. 1450, I would say that nearly all of them cite at least one name out of the 61 famous doctors or philosophers cited from ancient to medieval times. References to some sort of eyewitness testimony or personal observation on the author's part—such as this was what "I have seen," or this was what was proven "by experience"—occur in about a quarter of the treatises, which is on a par with the frequency with which the most popular authorities, such as Avicenna or Galen, were cited. See my forthcoming, *Doctoring the Black Death* with Rowman and Littlefield.

107 *The Black Death*, trans. and ed. Horrox, p. 192; Robert Hoeniger, *Der Schwarze Tod in Deutschland* (Berlin, 1882), pp. 160, 165. The position of both these doctors was that "practical" experience with plague must be grounded in a thorough knowledge of astrology, which hardly qualifies as giving up "stargazing" for "practical lessons" about the plague, as Cohn would have it. See Cohn, "Black Death: End of a Paradigm," p. 710.

108 Cohn, *Black Death Transformed*, p. 68.

109 Cohn, *Black Death Transformed*, pp. 61–62.

110 In his report on plague patients admitted to Grant Road Hospital in Mumbai in the spring of 1897, Dr. A. McCabe Dallas described the appearance of bubos as being usually of a red color, but which could change to a "purple or livid aspect" as a result of internal hemorrhaging, which indicated a poor prognosis. See W.F. Gatacre, *Report on the Bubonic Plague in Bombay, 1896–97* (Mumbai, India: Times of India Steam Press, 1897), p. 97.

111 As cited by an anonymous doctor from Lübeck, Germany, writing in 1411. See Sudhoff, "Pestschriften," *AGM* 11 (1919):151.

112 To my mind, the author with the most convincing testimony about the Black Death symptoms is the Moorish physician from Almería in Spain, Ibn Khātima, who observed the plague from the beginning of June 1348 until February 1349. Khātima, who allegedly treated "countless" victims and who even provided case histories of his patients, listed three "kinds" of the disease that read like a classic textbook description of plague. The "first kind" was characterized by "hard, bloody knots" known as "bubos" that formed "behind the ears, on the underarms, and the groin"; the second was blood spitting brought up from the lungs, for which there was no treatment and from which symptom alone Khātima had seen many patients die; the third was "black bubos" that appeared like "blisters" or "burns on the body," which were accompanied by "inflammation and heat" and exuded a "little watery liquid" when opened. This last seems to be the DIC (disseminated intravascular coagulation) of septicemic plague. Cohn virtually ignored this valuable evidence, even though he was clearly aware of its existence. See: Aberth, *Black Death*, 2nd edn., pp. 37–39; Cohn, *Black Death Transformed*, pp. 115, 234.

113 Gui de Chauliac, *Inventarium, sive Chirurgia Magna. Volume One: Text*, ed. Michael R. McVauh (Leiden, Netherlands: Brill, 1997), pp. 71–73.

114 Vienna National Library, Codex Latin 5289, fol. 13v.; Universitätsbibliothek Leipzig, MS 1162, fols. 356v.–357v.; Sudhoff, "Pestschriften," *AGM* 14 (1922–23):95; Berlin MS 746, fols. 1v.–2v.

115 Sudhoff, "Pestschriften," *AGM* 17 (1925):113, 116. Blasius reminisced how, when he was a medical student at the University of Toulouse, he came down with no less than two "glandular swellings" on either side of his groin, probably during the second pestilence of 1361–63.

116 Gatacre, *Report on the Bubonic Plague*, pp. 36, 57–58, 67, 83, 109, 223; Llewellyn J. Legters, Andrew J. Cottingham, Jr., and Donald H. Hunter, "Clinical and Epidemiologic Notes on a Defined Outbreak of Plague in Vietnam," *American Journal of Tropical Medicine and Hygiene*, 19 (1970):645, 647, 651–52; Benedictow, *What Disease*

was Plague, pp. 373–77. A similar argument could be made with respect to the location or number of bubos on a patient. The fact that medieval doctors gave prominence to neck boils, for example, may simply have been due to their being good "Galenists," in that they were following the famous Roman physician, Galen, who claimed that the brain was the most important organ in the body (as opposed to the heart, in the view of Aristotle), and therefore any symptom appearing on the emunctory of the brain, namely on the neck or behind the ears, should likewise have been accorded more importance. Observers of the Third Pandemic noted a small percentage of cases where bubos occurred on the arm, the back of the knee, the back, and the breast, while in as many as ten percent of cases, multiple bubos occurred on the patient. See: Cohn, *Black Death Transformed*, pp. 64–65, 68–71, 77–81; Cohn, "Black Death: End of a Paradigm," pp. 716–17; Benedictow, *What Disease was Plague*, p. 367; Gatacre, *Report on the Bubonic Plague*, pp. 27, 36–38, 43–44, 49, 109, 123, 128, 140; William Hunter, "Buboes and their Significance in Plague," *The Lancet* 168 (1906): 83.

117 Gatacre, *Report on the Bubonic Plague*, p. 223; Benedictow, *Black Death and Later Plague Epidemics*, pp. 21, 639–49; Benedictow, *What Disease was Plague*, pp. 7, 18; Benedictow, *Black Death*, p. 26. In J.S. Wilkins' report on the plague epidemic in Cutch-Mandvi, contained within Gatacre's general report for Mumbai, he noted that the "petechiae [i.e., DIC] distributed generally over the body are often observed usually preceding a fatal issue" of bubonic plague. Benedictow adduced plenty of other testimony to the same effect from later observers of the Third Pandemic, which he claimed Cohn ignored. See Benedictow, *What Disease was Plague*, pp. 372–78.

118 Benedictow, *What Disease was Plague*, pp. 322–34.

119 Scott and Duncan, for instance, insisted that the Black Death should be diagnosed as plague as if one were a modern doctor making a diagnosis of a disease in a patient; they then used this argument to reject bubos as a clinical feature that could identity historical plague cases, on the grounds that, "No doctor would make a diagnosis on the basis of a single symptom: instead he would examine his patient carefully". By contrast, both Benedictow and Walløe, after reviewing the evidence, concluded that medieval chronicle descriptions of plague matched reasonably well with modern symptomology. See: Scott and Duncan, *Return of the Black Death*, p. 167; Benedictow, *What Disease was Plague*, pp. 322–34, 359–80; Walløe, "Medieval and Modern Bubonic Plague," pp. 63–67.

120 This is precisely the argument made in 1926 by Wu Liande: "The fact that the Black Death does not quite correspond to the form of infection as it is known today cannot eliminate the ample evidence that it was plague". Dr. Wu was referring specifically to the symptoms of the Black Death and to the fact that some of these "are not frequently encountered in modern outbreaks of plague, while others are altogether absent". More recently, in 2008, Elisabeth Carniel made much the same argument as Dr. Wu: "it should be emphasized that it is not possible to reject the plague aetiology of the Black Death simply because certain symptoms and epidemiological features do not match those found today". See: Lien-Teh, *Treatise on Pneumonic Plague*, p. 3; Elisabeth Carniel, "Plague Today," in *Pestilential Complexities*, p. 122.

121 Other arguments advanced by plague deniers include that the long-term mortality pattern of the Black Death after its first outbreak differs from that of modern plague, in that it evinces a "steep and steady" decline in mortality, indicating that survivors of the Black Death became immune to the disease, which is not possible in modern plague; that the Black Death struck with much higher death rates, especially in urban, heavily-populated areas, as compared to modern plague; and that the seasonality and pattern of recurrence of the Black Death does not match those of bubonic plague. See: Scott and Duncan, *Biology of Plagues*, pp. 97–114, 356–81; Cohn, *Black Death Transformed*, pp. 140–219; Cohn, "Black Death: End of a Paradigm," pp. 718–37; Cohn, "Epidemiology of the Black Death," pp. 83–87; Cohn, "Historian and the Laboratory," pp. 200–205. For counter-arguments, see: Stephen R. Ell, "Immunity as Factor in the Epidemiology of Medieval Plague," *Reviews of Infectious Diseases*, 6

(1984):871–76; Benedictow, *What Disease was Plague*, pp. 218–68, 675–79; Walløe, "Medieval and Modern Bubonic Plague," pp. 67–68; Aberth, *From the Brink of the Apocalypse*, pp. 10–12, 94–96; Crespo and Lawrenz, "Heterogeneous Immunological Landscapes and Medieval Plague," pp. 238–40; Bei Li, et al., "Humoral and Cellular Immune Responses to *Yersinia pestis* Infection in Long-Term Recovered Plague Patients," *Clinical Vaccine Immunology* 19 (2012):228–34; Schmid, et al., "Climate-Driven Introduction of the Black Death," pp. 3020–24; Tamara Ben Ari, et al., "Plague and Climate: Scales Matter," *PLoS Pathogens* 7 (2011): online, e1002160.

122 Bolton, "Looking for *Yersinia Pestis*," pp. 26–27, 36.

123 Many of those commenting on the plague denial debate have called for more collaboration and cooperation between scientists and historians. See: Little, "Plague Historians," p. 286; Bolton, "Looking for *Yersinia Pestis*," p. 36; Crespo and Lawrenz, "Heterogeneous Immunological Landscapes and Medieval Plague," pp. 240, 242, 244, 251; Cohn and Weaver, "The Black Death and AIDS," p. 501; Cohn, "Epidemiology of the Black Death," p. 100.

124 As far as I am aware, the first scholar to suggest the one-third rule for Black Death mortality was the Cambridge historian, G.G. Coulton, in 1929, but the rule has since been endlessly repeated in textbooks, perhaps the most influential of which was that on the *Black Death* by Philip Ziegler. Some medieval chroniclers, such as Gilles li Muisis of Tournai and John of Fordun of Aberdeen, also estimated that "a third of the population died". See: G.G. Coulton, *The Black Death* (New York: J. Cape & H. Smith, 1930), p. 103; Philip Ziegler, *The Black Death* (New York: Harper and Row, 1969), pp. 227–31; *Black Death*, trans. and ed. Horrox, pp. 49, 84.

125 Josiah Cox Russell, *British Medieval Population* (Albuquerque, NM.: University of New Mexico Press, 1948), p. 216. Based on Inquisitions *post mortem* for 1348–50, Russell came up with a mortality figure of 27.3 percent. For criticisms of Russell's methodology, see: Goran Ohlin, "No Safety in Numbers: Some Pitfalls of Historical Statistics," in *Industrialization in Two Systems: Essays in Honor of Alexander Gerschenkron*, ed. H. Rosovsky (New York: Wiley, 1966), pp. 77–81; J.Z. Titow, *English Rural Society, 1200–1350* (London: George Allen and Unwin, 1969), pp. 68–71; John Hatcher, *Plague, Population and the English Economy, 1348–1530* (London and Basingstoke, UK: Macmillan, 1977), pp. 23–24; Zvi Razi, *Life, Marriage and Death in a Medieval Parish: Economy, Society and Demography in Halesowen, 1270–1400* (Cambridge: Cambridge University Press, 1980), p. 100; Benedictow, *Black Death*, p. 342; Benedictow, *What Disease was Plague*, pp. 421, 424–25.

126 Benedictow, *Black Death*, pp. 245–384; Paula Arthur, "The Black Death and Mortality: A Reassessment," in *Fourteenth Century England, VI*, ed. Chris Given-Wilson (Woodbridge, UK: Boydell Press, 2010), pp. 49–72. Benedictow regularly "corrected" or adjusted his mortality figures, such as by adding 2.5 percentage points in order to account for the unrecorded "supermortality" of the poor. See Benedictow, *Black Death*, pp. 259–66.

127 Benedictow, *Black Death*, pp. 387–94.

128 *The Black Death: A Turning Point in History?* ed. William M. Bowsky (New York: Holt, Rinhart, and Winston, 1971).

129 Élisabeth Carpentier, "Orvieto: Institutional Stability and Moral Change," in *The Black Death: A Turning Point in History*, p. 118; Guy Bois, *The Crisis of Feudalism: Economy and Society in Eastern Normandy, c. 1300–1550* (Cambridge and Paris: Cambridge University Press and Editions de la Maison des Sciences de l'Homme, 1984), p. 53; Andrew Hinde, *England's Population: A History Since the Domesday Survey* (London and New York: Arnold and Oxford University Press, 2003), pp. 22–37. The main exponent of the Malthusian interpretation of late medieval history was Michael Moissey Postan, whose collected works are most accessible in: M.M. Postan, *Essays on Medieval Agriculture and General Problems of the Medieval Economy* (Cambridge: Cambridge University Press, 1973). The main exponent of the Marxist approach was Robert Brenner, on whom readers should consult: *The Brenner Debate: Agrarian Class Structure and Economic*

Development in Pre-industrial Europe, eds. T.H. Aston and C.H.E. Philpin (Cambridge: Cambridge University Press, 1985).

130 Such a low estimate of death during the first outbreak of the Black Death has recently been revived by Pamela Nightingale, "Some New Evidence of Crises and Trends of Mortality in Late Medieval England," *Past and Present* 187 (2005): 46–47, 55. Nightingale's figures were based on certificates of debt that recorded deaths of creditors, as mandated by the Statute Merchant of 1285. The mortality rate of creditors was only 13.7 percent in 1349, the year of the Black Death in most of England, and only rose to 21.8 percent in 1350. In fact, Nightingale's peak average mortality for the five-year period of 1350–54 is still *lower* than that for 1320–24! Nightingale only succeeded in exceeding Russell's mortality of 27 percent for tenants-in-chief by backdating to 1349 all the "surplus deaths" of creditors above 2.4 percent from 1350 to 1354—yielding 34 percent mortality in 1349—on the assumption that their deaths were not recorded until years later owing to the chaotic conditions created by the plague itself. Her assertion of a "close conveyance" between creditor mortality and the mortality of "other groups in the population," including the poor, is largely based on a "test" comparison with heriot evidence from the first half of the fourteenth century. But, as Nightingale herself admitted, heriots are a notoriously difficult source to use accurately, and others have found serious flaws in their use for mortality estimates. To my mind, Nightingale's evidence, like Russell's, is simply too focused on an elite sliver of the population to be representative of the population at large—the average base population of creditors at risk from which she derived mortality percentages at five-year intervals from 1305 to 1529 is just 309 individuals! This is hardly worthy of the "confidence" that Nightingale claimed to place in her evidence. See: Nightingale, "New Evidence,", pp. 37, 41–46, 49, 53; Barbara Harvey, "Introduction: The 'Crisis' of the Early Fourteenth Century," in *Before the Black Death: Studies in the "Crisis" of the Early Fourteenth Century*, ed. Bruce M.S. Campbell (Manchester, UK: Manchester University Press, 1991), pp. 8–9; Martin Ecclestone, "Mortality of Rural Landless Men before the Black Death: The Glastonbury Head-Tax Lists," *Local Population Studies* 63 (1999): 24.

131 Richard M. Smith, "Demographic Developments in Rural England, 1300–48: A Survey," in *Before the Black Death*, pp. 25–77; Richard M. Smith, "Human Resources," in *The Countryside of Medieval England*, eds. G. Astill and A. Grant (Oxford: Blackwell, 1988), pp. 192–95; Nightingale, "New Evidence," pp. 40–46, 52–56, 61–62, 67. While Nightingale did claim that disease reached crisis proportions (i.e., 8 percent mortality or higher) in the first quarter of the fourteenth century, echoing the Malthusian line that she debunked at the beginning of her article, she also claimed that the second quarter of the fourteenth century was, by contrast, "a period of relative recovery based on lower mortality and a more prosperous economy". The difficulties of interpretation involve not just intractable sources, such as heriots or Statute Merchant certificates of debt, but also the fact that there is much regional and temporal variation in the evidence.

132 David Herlihy, *The Black Death and the Transformation of the West*, ed. Samuel K. Cohn, Jr. (Cambridge, MA.: Harvard University Press, 1997), pp. 4, 81. This book was based on Herlihy's lectures at the University of Maine in 1985 and was published after Herlihy's death in 1991.

133 David Herlihy, *Medieval and Renaissance Pistoia: The Social History of an Italian Town, 1200–1430* (New Haven, CT.: Yale University Press, 1967), pp. 65–66.

134 D.L. Farmer, "Prices and Wages," in *Agrarian History of England and Wales: Volume 3, 1348–1500*, ed. Edward Miller (Cambridge: Cambridge University Press, 1991), pp. 439–40, 455; Christopher Dyer, *An Age of Transition? Economy and Society in England in the Later Middle Ages* (Oxford: Clarendon Press, 2005), p. 14; Christopher Dyer, "Did the Peasants Really Starve in Medieval England?" in *Food and Eating in Medieval Europe*, eds. Martha Carlin and Joel T. Rosenthal (London: Hambledon Press, 1998), pp. 53–72. Even though low grain yields were recorded for some years of the Black Death, such as between 1349–52, famine and food shortages seem to have been avoided owing to far fewer mouths to feed thanks to the plague. Even the Great

Famine of 1315–22, which recorded mortalities of 10–15 percent, is judged not to have been a "watershed" event since population was able to quickly recover. See: Campbell, *Great Transition*, pp. 258, 287–88; William Chester Jordan, *The Great Famine: Northern Europe in the Early Fourteenth Century* (Princeton, NJ.: Princeton University Press, 1996), pp. 184–85.

135 Guy Bois has chronicled impressive population declines in Normandy, which was so frequently in the path of English soldiers, from 1348 to 1442, on the basis of *monnéage* hearth tax records. But here it is almost impossible to separate out what losses were due to plague and what to war and famine. See Bois, *Crisis of Feudalism*, pp. 53–55, 65.

136 Hatcher, *Plague, Population and the English Economy*, pp. 11–30; Bolton, "'World Upside Down'," pp. 29–33; Hinde, *England's Population*, pp. 38–64. For example, statistical estimates based on hard empirical evidence, such as monastic obituary lists, has now replaced anecdotal impressions based on chronicle accounts.

137 J.M.W. Bean, "Population and Economic Decline in England in the Later Middle Ages," *Economic History Review*, n.s., 15 (1963):430–32, 435. Bean argued that late medieval plague had become strictly an urban phenomenon that spared rural areas, which is no longer borne out by the evidence and goes against the known epidemiology of plague (i.e., an inverse correlation between mortality and population density).

138 Cohn, *Black Death Transformed*, pp. 191–203; Cohn, "Black Death: End of a Paradigm," pp. 724, 728–29; Bois, *Crisis of Feudalism*, pp. 53–59. Although Cohn wished to argue that "late-medieval wills, obituaries, and burials show a sharp and progressive decline in plague mortalities," the evidence does not bear him out. For example, the necrology of San Domenico in Siena shows the number of lay burials being higher in 1383 than for 1374, higher in 1400 than 1390, and higher in 1424 than 1411 and 1390, while the necrology for the Dominican friars of Florence shows burials in 1400 as nearly as high as those in 1363, and much higher than numbers in 1374 and 1383. Bois estimated that, after an initial drop of 30 percent during the first outbreak of plague in 1348, population in eastern Normandy declined by a further 20 percent between 1357 and 1374, but that then population recovered by some 35 percent between 1380 and 1413. When it comes to the fifteenth century, evidence such as the monastic obituaries becomes even more problematic for Cohn, as it shows a pattern of more frequent and more deadly mortality crises, as discussed below.

139 Aberth, *From the Brink of the Apocalypse*, 2nd edn., pp. 283–84; Alexander Hamilton Thompson, "The Pestilences of the Fourteenth Century in the Diocese of York," *Archaeological Journal* 71 (1914):132–34; Ransom Pickard, *The Population and Epidemics of Exeter in Pre-Census Times* (Exeter: James Townsend & Sons, 1947), pp. 24–26; Razi, *Life, Marriage and Death*, pp. 125–28; Titow, *English Rural Society*, p. 70; Richard Lomas, "The Black Death in County Durham," *Journal of Medieval History* 15 (1989):134; L.R. Poos, *A Rural Society after the Black Death: Essex, 1350–1525* (Cambridge: Cambridge University Press, 1991), pp. 96–103, 107–9; L.R. Poos, "The Rural Population of Essex in the Later Middle Ages," *Economic History Review*, n.s., 38 (1985):524–25; L.R. Poos, "Historical Demography of Northern Europe, 1400–1650," in *New Approaches to the History of Late Medieval and Early Modern Europe: Selected Proceedings of Two International Conferences at The Royal Danish Academy of Sciences and Letters in Copenhagen in 1997 and 1999*, eds. Troels Dahlerup and Per Ingesman (*Historisk-filosofiske Meddelelser*, 104, 2009), p. 373; Smith, "Human Resources," pp. 192–93; Richard M. Smith, "Measuring Adult Mortality in an Age of Plague: England, 1349–1540," in *Town and Countryside*, p. 46; Edward Miller, "Introduction: Land and People," in *Agrarian History of England and Wales: Volume 3*, pp. 5–8; Russell, *British Medieval Population*, pp. 217–18.

140 *Black Death*, trans. and ed. Horrox, pp. 85–86, 88.

141 Benedictow, *What Disease was Plague*, pp. 218–35.

142 Stephen Broadberry, Bruce M.S. Campbell, Alexander Klein, Mark Overton, and Bas Van Leeuwen, *British Economic Growth, 1270–1870* (Cambridge: Cambridge University Press, 2015), pp. 6–8, 20–22.

143 Mark Bailey, "Demographic Decline in Late Medieval England: Some Thoughts on Recent Research," *Economic History Review*, n.s., 49 (1996): 15; Bolton, "'World Upside Down'," pp. 30–33; Hatcher, "Understanding the Population History of England, 1450–1750," *Past and Present* 180 (2003): 95–98.

144 The three studies of each monastery's mortality are: John Hatcher, "Mortality in the Fifteenth Century: Some New Evidence," *Economic History Review*, 2nd ser. 39 (1986):19–38; Barbara Harvey, *Living and Dying in England, 1100–1540: The Monastic Experience* (Oxford: Clarendon Press, 1993), pp. 112–45; John Hatcher, A.J. Piper, and David Stone, "Monastic Mortality: Durham Priory, 1395–1529," *Economic History Review* 59 (2006):667–87. Nightingale criticized this evidence as untypical of the general population, on the grounds that the monks' communal lifestyle made them especially susceptible to "crowd" diseases, such as tuberculosis. Hatcher admitted this point, but at the same time, he pointed out that "there were no changes in monastic life sufficient to account for the massive deterioration in longevity, or for its subsequent partial recovery in the early sixteenth century". He argued that these life expectancy "fluctuations," replicated at all three monasteries, "were likely to have been driven in major part by the same forces which were determining the health of the population at large". On the other hand, if a wealthy urban elite such as the creditors were able to flee to country estates and escape local epidemics, as Nightingale claimed, then their mortality was hardly representative of that of the general population, especially of the "poorer manorial tenants," as she also claimed. See: Nightingale, "New Evidence," pp. 49–50, 57–59; Hatcher, "Understanding the Population History," pp. 97–98.

145 Hatcher, Piper, and Stone, "Monastic Mortality," pp. 674–76; Smith, "Measuring Adult Mortality," pp. 62–63.

146 Hatcher, Piper, and Stone, "Monastic Mortality," p. 674.

147 Hatcher, "Mortality in the Fifteenth Century," pp. 25–27; Hatcher, Piper, and Stone, "Monastic Mortality," pp. 676–78; Smith, "Measuring Adult Mortality," pp. 58–62. Christ Church, a community of between 75–95 monks, suffered the worst, experiencing no less than 27 years of "crisis" mortality—defined in this case as a death rate of 40 per thousand or more—which averages to more than one crisis every four years, with a greater frequency (17 years) during the first half of the fifteenth century, but with more severe "spikes" of mortality in the second half. Westminster suffered nine crises—here defined as 100 deaths per thousand, while Durham had 14 crisis years where there were at least 60 deaths per thousand. See: Harvey, *Living and Dying in England*," pp. 122–27; Hatcher, Piper, and Stone, "Monastic Mortality," pp. 676–78; Smith, "Measuring Adult Mortality," pp. 58–62.

148 Smith, "Measuring Adult Mortality," pp. 79–81.

149 Robert S. Gottfried, *Epidemic Disease in Fifteenth Century England: The Medical Response and the Demographic Consequences* (New Brunswick, N.J.: Rutgers University Press, 1978), pp. 35–52, 84–107, 204–22, 225–30; Paul D. Glennie, "A Commercializing Agrarian Region: Late Medieval and Early Modern Hertfordshire" (Ph.D. dissertation, University of Cambridge, 1983), pp. 53–59; M.A. Faraday, "Mortality in the Diocese of Hereford, 1442–1541," *Transactions of the Woolhope Naturalists' Field Club* 42 (1977):163–74; Christopher Dyer, *Lords and Peasants in a Changing Society: The Estates of the Bishopric of Worcester, 680–1540* (Cambridge: Cambridge University Press, 1980), p. 223; Paul Slack, *The Impact of Plague in Tudor and Stuart England* (Oxford, 1985); D.M. Palliser, "Epidemics in Tudor York," *Northern History* 8 (1973):45–63; P.J.P. Goldberg, "Mortality and Economic Change in the Diocese of York, 1390–1514," *Northern History* 24 (1933):38–55; Smith, "Measuring Adult Mortality," pp. 53–55; Hatcher, "Understanding the Population History," p. 96; Hatcher, *Plague Population and the English Economy*, p. 57.

150 Poos, *A Rural Society after the Black Death*, pp. 96–98, 109; Poos, "Rural Population of Essex," p. 525; Poos, "Historical Demography of Northern Europe," p. 373; Smith, "Human Resources," pp. 192–93; Smith, "Measuring Adult Mortality," p. 46. Other manorial demographic evidence, such as from Kibworth Harcourt in Leicestershire or

Holywell and Warboys in Huntingdonshire, which shows population decline during the first half of the fifteenth century, nonetheless ends at or before 1450. See David Postles, "Demographic Change in Kibworth Harcourt, Leicestershire, in the Later Middle Ages," *Local Population Studies* 48 (1992):45–46; Edwin Brezette DeWindt, *Land and People in Holywell-cum-Needingworth: Structures of Tenure and Patterns of Social Organization in an East Midlands Village, 1252–1457* (Toronto: Pontifical Institute of Mediaeval Studies, 1972), pp. 166–71; J.A. Raftis, *Warboys: Two Hundred Years in the Life of an English Mediaeval Village* (Toronto: Pontifical Institute of Mediaeval Studies, 1974), p. 68.

151 Smith, "Measuring Adult Mortality," p. 51; Stephen R. Epstein, "Cities, Regions and the Late Medieval Crisis: Sicily and Tuscany Compared," *Past and Present* 130 (1991):3–50.

152 Marie-Thérèse Lorcin, *Vivre et Mourir en Lyonnais à la Fin du Moyen Âge* (Paris, 1981), p. 529; Guy Bois, *La grande dépression médiévale: XIVᵉ-XVᵉ siècles* (Paris: Presses Universitaires de France, 2000), p. 68.

153 Bois, *Crisis of Feudalism*; Poos, "Historical Demography of Northern Europe," p. 373; Smith, "Measuring Adult Mortality," p. 50; Freedman, *Origins of Peasant Servitude*, p. 163.

154 Sylvia L. Thrupp, "The Problem of Replacement Rates in Late Medieval English Population," *Economic History Review* 18 (1965):114–16.

155 Gottfried, *Epidemic Disease*, pp. 204–24. Hatcher specifically criticized Gottfried's conclusions, arguing that his probate series, which ended in 1487, itself showed "a marked increase in both the frequency and severity of mortality crises after mid century," while other probate series from Herefordshire, London, and York "revealed that mortality crises remained common between 1487 and 1518, and were of unusual severity in the 1520s". See Hatcher, "Understanding the Population History," p. 96.

156 Goldberg, "Mortality and Economic Change," pp. 42, 48–49; Nightingale, " New Evidence," pp. 55, 60–61, 67.

157 T.H. Hollingsworth, *Historical Demography* (London: Hodder and Stoughton, 1969), p. 379; Broadberry, et al., *British Economic Growth*, pp. 17–18.

158 Thrupp claimed that her will-makers of Hertfordshire and Essex were relatively "humble people," since some made donations to the local parish church in amounts "only of a few pence, so that they do not make for any obvious bias towards the more prosperous". See Thrupp, "Problem of Replacement Rates," p. 114.

159 Hatcher, "Mortality in the Fifteenth Century," pp. 36–38; Harvey, *Living and Dying in England*, pp. 142–44; Hatcher, Piper, and Stone, "Monastic Mortality," pp. 682–83. Hatcher himself has gone back and forth on this question. In 1986, he argued that the Christ Church experience *underestimated* general mortality, on the basis of a comparison with data from the seventeenth–eighteenth century Benedictine monastery of Saint-Maur, which had both better life expectancies that those of contemporary Frenchmen and "enormously better expectations of life" than the fifteenth-century Benedictines of Christ Church. In 2006, however, he changed his mind, arguing that the Christ Church monks, owing to their communal lifestyle, suffered an "enhanced exposure to infectious disease" and that "the vast majority of people living outside the cloister enjoyed somewhat more favourable conditions". This was based on a new comparison with studies of Dutch monks from the nineteenth and early twentieth centuries.

160 Nightingale, "New Evidence," pp. 58–59.

161 Hatcher, "Understanding the Population History," pp. 97–98.

162 Gottfried, *Epidemic Disease*, pp. 213–22.

163 Goldberg, "Mortality and Economic Change," pp. 48–49; Nightingale, "New Evidence," p. 60; Dyer, *Lords and Peasants*, p. 225.

164 Hatcher, "Mortality in the Fifteenth Century," p. 36; Harvey, *Living and Dying in England*, pp. 73–77; Hatcher, Piper, and Stone, "Monastic Mortality," p. 682; Smith, "Measuring Adult Mortality," p. 81; Thrupp, "Problem of Replacement Rates," p. 116; Nightingale, "New Evidence," pp. 57–58.

165 Broadberry, et al., *British Economic Growth*, pp. 18–19.
166 Slack, *Impact of Plague* ; Broadberry, et al., *British Economic Growth*, pp. 19–20.
167 Broadberry, et al., *British Economic Growth*, p. 17.
168 Broadberry, *et al.*, *British Economic Growth*, pp. 16, 33. The reason for the dearth in manorial records after 1450 seems to owe to the fact that estate owners by this time were leasing out their demesnes wholesale, and manorial dues and services had largely fallen by the wayside.
169 Hinde, *England's Population*, pp. 23–26; Edward Miller and John Hatcher, *Medieval England: Towns, Commerce and Crafts, 1086–1348* (New York: Longman, 1995), p. 393; Miller, "Introduction: Land and People," p. 6; Hatcher and Bailey, *Modelling the Middle Ages*, pp. 31, 178; Hatcher, *Plague, Population and the English Economy*, pp. 14, 68–69; Bailey, "Demographic Decline," p. 15; Smith, "Human Resources," pp. 190–91; Smith, "Demographic Developments in Rural England," p. 49; Smith, "Measuring Adult Mortality," pp. 49–50; Poos, "Rural Population of Essex," pp. 529–30; M.M. Postan, *Medieval Economy and Society: An Economic History of Britain in the Middle Ages* (London: Weidenfeld and Nicolson, 1972), pp. 27–31; H.E. Hallam, *Rural England, 1066–1348* (Brighton, Sussex and Atlantic Highlands, NJ.: Harvester Press and Humanities Press, 1981), p. 246; Bruce M.S. Campbell, "The Land," in *A Social History of England*, 1200–1500, ed. Rosemary Horrox (Cambridge: Cambridge University Press, 2006), pp. 184, 186, 234; Bruce M.S. Campbell, *English Seignorial Agriculture, 1250–1450* (Cambridge: Cambridge University Press, 2006), p. 403; Gregory Clark, "The Long March of History: Farm Wages, Population, and Economic Growth, England, 1209–1869," *Economic History Review* 60 (2007):98–99, 120.
170 Broadberry, et al., *British Economic Growth*, p. 20. The figure for 1348 represents a return to the high figure of 1290—4.75 million—after a decline of about half a million in 1325 owing largely to the Great Famine.
171 Broadberry, et al., *British Economic Growth*, pp. 80–129. England is assumed to have been running at 100 percent capacity in terms of both crop and livestock production in the early 1300s. At this time, England was averaging nearly 8 bushels per acre of wheat, 9 bushels per acre of rye, 12 bushels per acre of barley and more than 8.5 bushels per acre of oats, with nearly 13 million acres devoted to arable production. The country was also supporting more than 1.5 million milk, beef and veal cattle, nearly 16 million sheep and 1 million pigs. Hallam, who argued that England had a population of as much as 7.2 million in 1295, before declining to 6.7 million after the Great Famine, provided a rough and ready calculation that the 37 million acres in England and Wales, divided by 7.2 million, supplied each household of 4.75 members with 24 acres to support itself. See Hallam, *Rural England*, pp. 247–47.
172 Broadberry, et al., *British Economic Growth*, pp. 20–22. I disagree with the authors' estimate of 46 percent mortality rate for England during the Black Death of 1348–49 (p. 14), which I argue should be more like 50 percent. This would then have the population basically remaining flat from 1351 to 1377, instead of declining slightly by 4 percent.
173 E.A. Wrigley and R.S. Schofield, *The Population History of England, 1541–1871: A Reconstruction*, rev. edn. (Cambridge: Cambridge University Press, 1989); Broadberry, et al., *British Economic Growth*, p. 28.
174 Hatcher, "Understanding the Population History," p. 26; Broadberry, et al., *British Economic Growth*, pp. 16, 21; Bruce M.S. Campbell, "The Population of Early Tudor England: A Re-Evaluation of the 1522 Muster Returns and 1524 and 1525 Lay Subsidies," *Journal of Historical Geography* 7 (1981):145–54. This is based on Campbell's estimate of 1.84 million people in 1522.
175 Broadberry, et al., *British Economic Growth*, pp. 16, 32.
176 Broadberry, et al., *British Economic Growth*, pp. 16, 20–21. By 1541, the annual growth rate evidently subsided to a still healthy .64 percent.
177 Ole Benedictow, "New Perspectives in Medieval Demography: The Medieval Demographic System," in *Town and Countryside*, pp. 20, 28

178 Benedictow, "New Perspectives in Medieval Demography," pp. 8, 27; Sandy Bardsley, "Missing Women: Sex Ratios in England, 1000–1500," *Journal of British Studies* 53 (2014):275–77.

179 Benedictow, "New Perspectives in Medieval Demography," pp. 32–36; Benedictow, *The Black Death*, pp. 387–94. Some historians, like John Hatcher, made the case for pushing the end of the late medieval demographic system back even further, well past the mid-sixteenth century. See Hatcher, "Understanding the Population History of England," pp. 102–4.

180 Bruce M.S. Campbell, "Population Pressure, Inheritance and the Land Market in a Fourteenth-Century Peasant Community," in *Land, Kinship and Life-Cycle*, ed. Richard M. Smith (Cambridge: Cambridge University Press, 1984), p. 126; Campbell, *Great Transition*, pp. 326–27, 351; Harvey, "Introduction: The 'Crisis' of the Early Fourteenth Century,", p. 24.

181 In the high-pressure fertility pattern, men and women typically married in their teens to early 20s, and over 80 percent married. In the low-pressure pattern, men and women married in their mid-20s or above and between 10–20 percent (30–45 percent of women) were single or chose never to marry at all. See: John Hajnal, "European Marriage Patterns in Perspective," in *Population in History: Essays in Historical Demography*, ed. D.V. Glass and D.E.C. Eversley (Chicago, IL.: Aldine Publishing, 1965), pp. 117–20; Benedictow, "New Perspectives in Medieval Demography," pp. 10–13, 34; Poos, "Historical Demography of Northern Europe," pp. 380, 390; R.M. Smith, "Some Reflections on the Evidence for the Origins of the 'European Marriage Pattern' in England," in *The Sociology of the Family: New Directions for Britain*, ed. Chris Harris (Sociological Review Monograph, 28, 1979), p. 74; Maryanne Kowaleski, "Singlewomen in Medieval and Early Modern Europe: The Demographic Perspective," in *Singlewomen in the European Past, 1250–1800*, eds. Judith M. Bennett and Amy M. Froide (Philadelphia, PA.: University of Pennsylvania Press, 1999), pp. 39–40, 45–46, 50–51; Bailey, "Introduction: England in the Age of the Black Death," p xxi.

182 This is particularly the case when starting out with a high-pressure regime, since then the mean age of marriage was already low and could not go any lower in order to improve fertility relative to mortality. If the end of the Middle Ages was "at the lower end of a high pressure" regime, and the beginning of the Early Modern period "at the upper end of a low-pressure regime," then the transition would require only a "small adjustment" downwards in mortality. Fertility, on the other hand, would in this scenario either go slightly downwards or remain constant, which would still be working against the transitional trend, namely, one of increasing population. See: Hatcher, *Plague, Population and the English Economy*, pp. 55, 72; Hatcher, "Understanding the Population History," pp. 95–98; Benedictow, "New Perspectives in Medieval Demography," pp. 14, 17–18; Bailey, "Demographic Decline," pp. 3, 17; Poos, "Historical Demography," p. 375; Smith, "Some Reflections," p. 90.

183 Hollingsworth, *Historical Demography*, p. 379; Hatcher, "Understanding the Population History," pp. 99–104; Wrigley and Schofield, *Population History of England*, pp. 335, 650; Smith, "Measuring Adult Mortality," pp. 56–57; Sandy Bardsley, "Missing Women: Sex Ratios in England, 1000–1500," *Journal of British Studies* 53 (2014):275–77. Hatcher argued that fertility and mortality rates were still highly volatile in the middle decades of the sixteenth century, with both spiking at this time, so that a "low pressure" regime consonant with rising population "was not in place before the 1580s at the earliest". Even Wrigley and Schofield concluded that mortality remained at crisis levels throughout the 1540s and '50s, leading them to remark that this "may have been the last throes of a late medieval regime of widespread epidemic mortality". It was not until 1565, according to their data, that mortality rates came down substantially.

184 This is the position adopted by the "Cambridge Group" of demographic historians, led by Richard M. Smith and his students, Larry Poos and Jeremy Goldberg.

185 Thrupp, "Problem of Replacement-Rates," pp. 109–11; Hollingsworth, *Historical Demography*, pp. 375–80; Hatcher, *Plague, Population and the English Economy*, pp. 26–30;

Campbell, "Population Pressure," pp. 98–99; Campbell, *Great Transition*, pp. 352–53. Thrupp's calculations based on manorial court rolls and wills are deemed by many scholars to be unreliable or unrealistically low, while Hollingsworth's, based on Inquisitions *post mortem*, are more trustworthy but based on a very limited sample population. It should be noted that the replacement rate is not the same as the birth rate, but merely tells us the number of children who survived the death of the father; more children could have been born but died before their parents. We seem to have no statistics that can directly tell us the birth rate of medieval populations; the closest are probably the churching records that survive in the fifteenth-century churchwarden accounts for Walden, Essex. But these recorded aggregate payments that must then be converted into individual churchings (i.e., births) based on a widely varying fee schedule. Poos' conclusion from this evidence was that Walden's fertility rate remained unchanged over the course of the fifteenth century, and that a comparision with Walden's parish records from the sixteenth century indicates that the same fertility pattern held true between the late medieval and Early Modern eras. See: Poos, *Rural Society after the Black Death*, pp. 121–27; Bolton, "'The World Upside Down'," pp. 35–39.

186 Campbell, *Great Transition*, p. 352.

187 Nonetheless, it could be argued that a high marriage rate was no guarantee of high fertility: Many marriages could involve older widows, especially in the wake of epidemics, and even in Mediterranean regions such as Italy, the average size of a household as deduced from tax records was a mere four individuals or less. See: Benedictow, *Black Death*, pp. 288–90; Christopher Dyer, "Changes in the Size of Peasant Holdings in Some West Midland Villages, 1400–1540," in *Land, Kinship and Life-Cycle*, p. 281.

188 Poos, *Rural Society after the Black Death*, p. 120; Poos, "Historical Demography," pp. 803–4; Smith, "Some Reflections," pp. 92, 100–1. Nevertheless, other northwestern European countries, such as the Netherlands and Switzerland, may not have adhered to the Northwest marriage pattern, and England may have entered its low fertility pattern slightly later than 1541: Crude marriage and birth rates, for example, based on parish register data remained stubbornly high between 1541 and 1565, and the proportion of adults who never married remained low—between 4.2 to 8.4 percent. Parish register data have also been criticized as being far too volatile to be predicative, especially in the case of women. See: Hatcher, "Understanding the Population History," pp. 100–1; Smith, "Some Reflections," pp. 84–85; Poos, "Historical Demography," p. 804.

189 Hatcher, "Understanding the Population History," pp. 94–95; Hatcher, *Plague, Population and the English Economy*, pp. 56–57; Bolton, "'World Upside Down'," p. 33. As Hatcher pointed out, Jeremy Goldberg got around this "incentives" conundrum by arguing that economic opportunities created by the Black Death actually encouraged single women to *delay* marriage, by migrating to towns to find work, typically as domestic servants. This favorable economic trend finally came to an end with the "Great Slump" or depression of the mid-fifteenth century, which Goldberg argued then worked to exclude women from employment and probably forced them into more and earlier marriages, thus raising the birth rate, and "from this followed the demographic recovery of the sixteenth century". Nightingale, however, still adhered to the more traditional model first put forward by Wrigley and Schofield, namely, that marriage and fertility rates rose with living standards, and consequently she assumed that higher fertility had to wait until 1500, when the "economy was sufficiently buoyant to encourage many more and earlier marriages". Presumably, this high fertility regime ended by 1541, when Wrigley and Schofield adduced their evidence from parish registers for a long-term, low fertility trend. See: Goldberg, *Women, Work, and Life Cycle*, pp. 336–37, 347; Nightingale, "New Evidence," pp. 66–67; John Hatcher, "The Great Slump of the Mid-Fifteenth Century," in *Progress and Problems in Medieval England: Essays in Honour of Edward Miller*, eds. Richard Britnell and John Hatcher (Cambridge: Cambridge University Press, 2002), pp. 237–72.

190 Wrigley and Schofield, *Population History of England*, pp. 402–84; Smith, "Some Reflections,", p. 96; Poos, *Rural Society after the Black Death*, pp. 120–29, 145–58; Poos, "Historical Demography," p. 387; Bailey, "Demographic Decline," p. 3; Hatcher, "Understanding the Population History ," pp. 84–92.

191 Hinde, *England's Population*, pp. 68–73; Carolyn Fenwick, "The English Poll Taxes of 1377, 1379, and 1381: A Critical Examination of the Returns (Ph.D. diss., London School of Economics and Political Science, University of London, 1983), pp. 167–96; Poos, *Rural Society after the Black Death*, pp. 152–53. For example, Poos "corrected" the raw Poll Tax data for Essex that showed 82.5 percent of women married (and just 17.5 percent unmarried) to 63.5 percent married (and 36.5 percent unmarried), on the grounds that more women must be added to bring the sex ratio up to 94.3 (a ratio based on the Princeton Model West tables), and moreover he assumed that all of these added women were single. Some might be forgiven for regarding these "corrections" as unacceptably large and based on random assumptions that water the raw figures down to a "thought experiment". See: Hatcher, "Understanding the Population History," pp. 94–95; Bailey, "Demographic Decline," p. 17; Smith, "Some Reflections," pp. 83–84.

192 Bardsley, "Missing Women," pp. 273–309.

193 Maryanne Kowalski, "Medieval People in Town and Country: New Perspectives from Demography and Bioarchaeology," *Speculum* 89 (2014):579–82; Kowaleski, "Single-women in Medieval and Early Modern Europe," pp. 46, 51; Tine de Moor and Jan Luiten van Zanden, "Girl Power: The European Marriage Pattern and Labour Markets in the North Sea Region in the Late Medieval and Early Modern Period," *Economic History Review* 63 (2010):16–17; Poos, *Rural Society after the Black Death*, pp. 153, 156; Smith, "Human Resources," pp. 210–11; Mavis E. Mate, *Daughters, Wives and Widows after the Black Death: Women in Sussex, 1350–1535* (Woodbridge, UK: Boydell Press, 1998), p. 49.

194 David Herlihy and Christiane Klapisch-Zuber, *Tuscans and their Families: A Study of the Florentine Catasto of 1427* (New Haven, CT.: Yale University Press, 1985), pp. 203–15; Kowaleski, "Singlewomen in Medieval and Early Modern Europe," p. 50.

195 Nightingale, "New Evidence," p. 68; Hatcher, "Understanding the Population History," pp. 88–89; Hatcher, "Great Slump," p. 239; Smith, "Measuring Adult Mortality," p. 82; Smith, "Human Resources," pp. 209–12.

196 Hatcher and Bailey, *Modelling the Middle Ages*, p. 178, n. 4.

197 Goldberg, *Women, Work and Life Cycle*, pp. 336–37; De Moor and Van Zanden, "Girl Power," pp. 14–15; Kowaleski, "Singlewomen in Medieval and Early Modern Europe," p. 58; Christopher Dyer, *Making a Living in the Middle Ages: The People of Britain, 850–1520* (New Haven: Yale University Press, 2002), p. 277.

198 This would be even more the case if, as numerous English chroniclers reported, epidemics, particularly those during the second half of the fourteenth century, targeted the young, who would have been the most fertile members of society. See Hatcher, *Plague, Population and the English Economy*, pp. 58–61.

199 In the opinion of Christopher Dyer, it is "overly-optimistic to think that every mortality peak was followed by a compensatory baby boom," since the pattern of frequent epidemics "cannot have created the confidence and optimism to encourage early and universal marriage," even in spite of generally improving living standards. See Dyer, *Making a Living*, pp. 235, 276.

200 Andrew B. Appleby, "The Disappearance of Plague: A Continuing Puzzle," *Economic History Review* 33 (1980):169–73; Massimo Livi Bacci, *The Population of Europe: A History*, trans. Cynthia De Nardi Ipsen and Carl Ipsen (Oxford: Blackwell, 2000), p. 76; Edward A. Eckert, "The Retreat of Plague from Central Europe, 1640–1720: A Geomedical Approach," *Bulletin of the History of Medicine* 74 (2000):25; Monecke, et al., "Modelling the Black Death," p. 591.

201 IPRC, Reports on Plague Investigations in India, V: "On the Effect upon Virulence of Passage of *B. pestis* through Rats by Cutaneous Inoculation without Intermediate Culture," and VI: "A Note on the Immunity of Bombay Rats to the

Subcutaneous Injection of Plague Cultures," *Journal of Hygiene* 6 (1906):505–8; IPRC "Observations on Plague in Belgaum,"pp. 458–59; Appleby, "Disappearance of Plague," p. 170; Pollitzer, *Plague*, pp. 273–74; Gage and Kosoy, "Natural History of Plague," pp. 513–14. From 1907 to 1937, the IPRC periodically tested rats in Mumbai for plague and found that their susceptibility fell from 45 percent to 10 percent.

202 Appleby, "Disappearance of Plague," pp. 170, 172–73; Paul Slack, "The Disappearance of Plague: An Alternative View," *Economic History Review* 34 (1981):470–71. Slack also argued that the disappearance of plague from Europe in the seventeenth and eighteenth centuries was "irregular" and gradual, as opposed to Appleby's hypothesis of a big "flame out" in which "most of the non-resistant rats may have died, leaving mainly resistant rats".

203 Slack, "Disappearance of Plague," p. 471.

204 Campbell, *Great Transition*, pp. 314, 321; Schmid, et al., "Climate-Driven Introduction of the Black Death," pp. 3020–25; Ell, "Immunity as a Factor," pp. 868–71. It should be noted, however, that, aside from the first outbreak in 1346, the only medieval sample years Schmid used in his reintroduction model were 1408–9, which do not stand out in the records as major plague epidemics.

205 Ann G. Carmichael, "Plague Persistence in Western Europe: A Hypothesis," in *Pandemic Disease in the Medieval World*, pp. 177–80; Schmid, *et al.*, "Climate-Driven Introduction of the Black Death," p. 3022; Ell, "Immunity as a Factor," pp. 868–69. Plague never became endemic among Europe's urban rodent populations perhaps because the climate or environment was not suitable. This would be especially likely if plague persistence depends on it surviving in the soil of wild rodent burrows in arid regions. See Rebecca J. Eisen, et al., "Persistence of *Yersinia pestis* in Soil under Natural Conditions," *Emerging Infectious Diseases* 14 (2008):941–43.

206 Crespo and Lawrenz, "Heterogeneous Immunological Landscapes and Medieval Plague," pp. 238–45; Li, et al., "Humoral and Cellular Immune Responses to *Yersinia pestis* Infection," pp. 228–34; H. Laayouni, et al., "Convergent Evolution in European and Rroma Populations Reveals Pressure Exerted by Plague on Toll-like Receptors," *Proceedings of the National Academy of Sciences* 111 (2014):2668–73. At the moment, human immunity to plague has been studied only through genetic sampling of modern populations, but paleomicrobiology may make it feasible to do so for medieval populations as well. Meanwhile, paleomicrobiology has ruled out genetic changes to the aDNA of *Yersinia pestis* that would have made it less virulent over time, since the pPCP1 plasmid responsible for virulence is nearly identical to that of modern samples. See: Haensch, et al., "Distinct Clones of *Yersinia pestis*," online, e1001134; Schuenemann, et al., "Targeting Enrichment of Ancient Pathogens," pp. 746, 749, 751; Bos, et al., "A Draft Genome of *Yersinia pestis*," pp. 506–7, 509.

207 Slack, "Disappearance of Plague," pp. 473–75; Livi Bacci, *Population of Europe*, pp. 77–80; Eckert, "Retreat of Plague," pp. 25–27. Blocking plague from establishing a foothold in port cities also prevented them from becoming epicenters, whereby the disease would then spread from there to more rural areas inland. Naturally, this argument would be considerably strengthened by the theory that plague was not endemic to Europe, but had to be periodically re-introduced from Central Asia, where plague is endemic among giant gerbils, as mentioned above (Schmid, *et al.*, "Climate-Driven Introduction of the Black Death," pp. 3020–25). For further examples from England, see Slack, *Impact of Plague in Tudor and Stuart England*.

208 Benedictow, "New Perspectives in Medieval Demography," p. 33; Murphy, "Plague Ordinances," and Jane Stevens Crawshaw, "The Renaissance Invention of Quarantine," in *The Fifteenth Century, XII*, pp. 150–51, 162. The earlier, more miasmatic approach to plague control focused on cleanliness with respect to city streets, sewers, and especially the air, i.e., anything that could give rise to a bad stench that could spread the disease.

209 Justin K. Stearns, *Infectious Ideas: Contagion in Premodern Islamic and Christian Thought in the Western Mediterranean* (Baltimore, MD.: Johns Hopkins University Press, 2011), p. 87. Al-'Asqalānī's argument finds an echo even among Christian plague doctors,

such as Gentile da Foligno, who heartily endorsed contagion. See Foligno, *Consilium contra pestilentiam*, p. 38.

210 Murphy, "Plague Ordinances," p. 158.
211 *Black Death*, trans. and ed. Horrox, pp. 195–96.
212 Murphy, "Plague Ordinances," p. 144.
213 Zlata Tomić Blažina and Vesna Blažina, *Expelling the Plague: The Health Office and the Implementation of Quarantine in Dubrovnik, 1377–1533* (Montreal: McGill-Queen's University Press, 2015); Crawshaw, "Renaissance Invention of Quarantine," p. 164.
214 Murphy, "Plague Ordinances," pp. 150–58; Cipolla, *Public Health and the Medical Profession*, pp. 36–44; Cipolla, *Faith, Reason, and the Plague*, pp. 1–14; Carmichael, *Plague and the Poor*, pp. 110–21; De Backer, "Maatregelen Tegen de Pest," pp. 273–99.
215 Cipolla, *Public Health and the Medical Profession*, pp. 11–66; Carmichael, *Plague and the Poor*, pp. 98–126.
216 Christopher Dyer, *Standards of Living in the Later Middle Ages: Social Change in England, 1200–1520* (Cambridge: Cambridge University Press, 1989), pp. 151–60; Christopher Dyer, *Everyday Life in Medieval England* (London: Hambledon Press, 2000), pp. 77–100; Christopher Dyer, "English Diet in the Later Middle Ages," in *Social Relations and Ideas: Essays in Honour of R.H. Hilton*, eds. T.H. Aston, P.R. Coss, Christopher Dyer, and Joan Thirsk (Cambridge: Cambridge University Press, 1983), pp. 213–14.
217 Richard Britnell, *Britain and Ireland, 1050–1530: Economy and Society* (Oxford: Oxford University Press, 2004), p. 395.
218 Slack, "Disappearance of Plague," p. 476; Bruce M.S. Campbell, "Nature as Historical Protagonist: Environment and Society in Pre-Industrial England," *Economic History Review* 63 (2010):309.
219 Slack, "Disappearance of Plague," p. 476.
220 Poos, "Historical Demography of Northern Europe," p. 376.
221 Ada Elizabeth Levett and A. Ballard, *The Black Death on the Estates of the See of Winchester*, ed. Paul Vinogradoff (Oxford: Oxford Studies in Social and Legal History, 5, 1916), pp. 142–60; Frances M. Page, *The Estates of Crowland Abbey: A Study in Manorial Organisation* (Cambridge: Cambridge University Press, 1934), pp. 120–25.
222 Page, *Estates of Crowland Abbey*, p. 125; Levett and Ballard, *Black Death*, p. 142. See also commentary by: Nils Hybel, *Crisis or Change: The Concept of Crisis in the Light of Agrarian Structural Reorganization in Late Medieval England* (Aarhus: Aarhus University Press, 1989), pp. 111–14; Tom Beaumont James, *The Black Death in Hampshire* (Hampshire County Council, UK: Hampshire Papers, 18, 1999), pp. 13–14; and Stone, "Black Death and its Immediate Aftermath,", p. 214. Although Levett did acknowledge that economic change, such as commutation, did occur on English manors from the 1360s onwards, she attributed this to other factors besides the Black Death.
223 George Holmes, *The Estates of the Higher Nobility in Fourteenth-Century England* (Cambridge: Cambridge University Press, 1957), pp. 114–15; J.A. Raftis, *The Estates of Ramsey Abbey: A Study in Economic Growth and Organization* (Toronto: Pontifical Institute of Mediaeval Studies, 1957), p. 252, n.4; Raftis, *Warboys*, p. 173; J.A. Raftis, "Peasants and the Collapse of the Manorial Economy on Some Ramsey Abbey Estates," in *Progress and Problems in Medieval England*, p. 193; J.A. Brent, "Alicston Manor in the Later Middle Ages," *Sussex Archaeological Collections*, 106 (1968):95; J.Z. Titow, *English Rural Society, 1200–1350* (London: Allen and Unwin, 1969), pp. 69–70; John Hatcher, *Rural Economy and Society in the Duchy of Cornwall, 1300–1500* (Cambridge: Cambridge University Press, 1970), pp. 102–21; John Hatcher, "England in the Aftermath of the Black Death," *Past and Present* 144 (1994):6; Barbara Harvey, *Westminster Abbey and its Estates in the Middle Ages* (Oxford: Clarendon Press, 1977), pp. 244–46; Dyer, *Lords and Peasants*, p. 239; Razi, *Life, Marriage and Death*, p. 110; J.L. Bolton, *The Medieval English Economy, 1150–1500* (London and Totowa, N.J.: J.M. Dent and Sons and Rowman and Littlefield, 1980), pp. 209–13; Cicely Howell, *Land, Family and Inheritance in Transition: Kibworth Harcourt, 1280–1700* (Cambridge: Cambridge University Press, 1983), p.43; T. Lomas, "South-east Durham: Late

Fourteenth and Fifteenth Centuries," in *The Peasant Land Market in Medieval England*, ed. P.D.A. Harvey (Oxford: Clarendon Press, 1984), pp. 260, 305; P.D.A. Harvey, "The Home Counties," Mavis Mate, "Kent and Sussex," and Edward Miller, "The Southern Counties," in *Agrarian History of England and Wales: Volume 3*, pp. 109, 119, 140–41; Ray Lock, "The Black Death in Walsham-le-Willows," *Proceedings of the Suffolk Institute of Archaeology and History* 37 (1992):323–24; Tom Beaumont James, "The Black Death in Berkshire and Wiltshire," in *The Black Death in Wessex*, ed. Tom Beaumont James (*The Hatcher Review*, 5, 1998), p. 19; Mark Bailey, *Decline of Serfdom: From Bondage to Freedom* (Woodbridge, UK: Boydell Press, 2014), pp. 105, 131, 199, 220; Mark Bailey, *Medieval Suffolk: An Economic and Social History, 1200–1500* (Woodbridge, UK: Boydell Press, 2007), pp. 180–82; Stone, "Black Death and its Immediate Aftermath," pp. 229–30, 239–40.

224 A.R. Bridbury, "The Black Death," *Economic History Review*, n.s., 26 (1973):588, 590–91; Lomas, "South-east Durham," p. 260.

225 John Saltmarsh, "Plague and Economic Decline in England in the Later Middle Ages," *Cambridge Historical Journal* 7 (1941):23–41; Hybel, *Crisis or Change*, pp. 154–56; Bean, "Plague, Population, and Economic Decline," p. 423; Hinde, *England's Population*, p. 56.

226 This indicates that what recovery did occur was fragile and easily undone by later epidemics, although, as Hatcher demonstrated, a well-run estate like the duchy of Cornwall could considerably mitigate some of these effects. See: Eleanor Searle, *Battle Abbey and its Banlieu, 1066–1538* (Toronto: Pontifical Institute of Mediaeval Studies, 1974), pp. 257–66; Hatcher, *Rural Economy and Society*, pp. 122–256; Harvey, *Westminster Abbey*, pp. 246–93; Dyer, *Lords and Peasants*, pp. 113–49; Howell, *Land, Family and Inheritance*, pp. 43–44; Lomas, "South-east Durham,", pp. 268–90; Harvey, "Home Counties," pp. 109–10; Mate, "Kent and Sussex," pp. 120–24; Miller, "Southern Counties," pp. 140–43; Lock, "Black Death in Walsham-le-Willows," pp. 323–26; James, "Black Death in Berkshire and Wiltshire," and D.G. Watts, "Inkpen: A Berkshire Manor and the Plague," in *Black Death in Wessex*, pp. 13–14, 29–31; James, *Black Death in Hampshire*, pp. 9–12; Bailey, *Medieval Suffolk*, pp. 183–203.

227 Bean, "Plague, Population and Economic Decline," pp. 432, 435; Hinde, *England's Population*, pp. 56–57.

228 Levett and Ballard, "Black Death," p. 143.

229 Hatcher, "England in the Aftermath of the Black Death," pp. 32–33.

230 Campbell, "The Land," p. 237; Hybel, *Crisis or Change*, pp. 109–11, 116.

231 Stone, "Black Death and its Immediate Aftermath," pp. 216–17. See also Bruce M.S. Campbell, "A Unique Estate and a Unique Source: The Winchester Pipe Rolls in Perspective," in *The Winchester Pipe Rolls and Medieval English Society* (Woodbridge, UK: Boydell Press, 2003), pp. 21–43.

232 Stone, "Black Death and its Immediate Aftermath," pp. 230–31, 237–39; Hatcher, "England in the Aftermath of the Black Death," pp. 19–25.

233 Stone, "Black Death and its Immediate Aftermath," pp. 215, 226–29, 236–37, 240–41.

234 Watts, "Inkpen," p. 30.

235 Levett and Ballard, *Black Death*, p. 143; Page, *Estates of Crowland Abbey*, p. 122. Nineteenth-century views of plague as an "overmighty" actor on the stage of history were represented, in England, by the work of Frederic Seebohm and Thorold Rogers and, in Germany, by Justin Hecker. Rogers, however, was more "ambivalent" than Seebohm, in that he viewed the Black Deeath as accelerating already existing trends. For good summaries of these authors' views, see: Hybel, *Crisis or Change*, pp. 1–19; Faye Marie Getz, "Black Death and the Silver Lining: Meaning, Continuity, and Revolutionary Change in Histories of Medieval Plague," *Journal of the History of Biology* 24 (1991): 275–281.

236 Hinde, *England's Population*, pp. 47–48.

237 James E. Thorold Rogers, *Six Centuries of Work and Wages: The History of English Labour* (London: T.F. Unwin, 1919), p. 326.

238 G. Clark, "The Long March of History: Farm Wages, Population, and Economic Growth, England, 1209–1869," *Economic History Review* 60 (2007):109; Britnell, *Britain and Ireland*, pp. 376–77; John Hatcher, "Unreal Wages: Long-Run Living Standards and the 'Golden Age' of the Fifteenth Century," in *Commercial Activity, Markets and Entrepreneurs in the Middle Ages: Essays in Honour of Richard Britnell*, eds. Ben Dodds and Christian D. Liddy (Woodbridge, UK: Boydell Press, 2011), pp. 3–5; Simon A.C. Penn and Christopher Dyer, "Wages and Earnings in Late Medieval England: Evidence from the Enforcement of the Labour Laws," *Economic History Review*, 2nd ser., 43 (1990):356, 373; Campbell, "The Land," p. 216.

239 Hatcher, "Unreal Wages," pp. 3–5.

240 Friedrich Lütge, "Das 14/15. Jahrhundert in der Sozial- und Wirtschaftsgeschichte," *Jahrbücher für Nationalökonomie und Statistik* 162 (1950):161–213; Howard Kaminsky, "From Lateness to Waning to Crisis: The Burden of the Later Middle Ages," *Journal of Early Modern History* 4 (2000):116–17.

241 A.R. Bridbury, *Economic Growth: England in the Later Middle Ages* (London: G. Allen and Unwin, 1962), p. 91.

242 Bridbury, "Black Death," pp. 577–92, and reprinted in A.R. Bridbury, *The English Economy from Bede to the Reformation* (Woodbridge, UK: Boydell Press, 1992), pp. 200–17. For example, it is estimated that the population of England declined by 44 percent between 1300 and 1380, while at the same time, the total cultivated area of England declined by 31 percent. Even though Richard Britnell agreed that agricultural output increased per head during the later Middle Ages, he argued that this was entirely due to population decline rather than increased productivity. In line with the commercialization model, Britnell viewed productivity suffering from reduced labor inputs (which was now much more expensive to employ), countering any improved practices such as abandonment of less productive soils and greater access to manure from higher pasture to arable ratios. See Britnell, *Britain and Ireland*, pp. 389, 395–401.

243 Dyer, *Age of Transition*, pp. 126–57; Dyer, *Making a Living*, pp. 322–37; Maryanne Kowaleski, "A Consumer Economy," in *Social History of England*, pp. 238–59. On a more cultural level, the optimistic view of plague's impact has been expressed as the "silver lining" thesis. See Getz, "Black Death and the Silver Lining," pp. 275–281.

244 M.M. Postan, "Revisions in Economic History—The Fifteenth Century," *Economic History Review* 9 (1938–39):160–67; Hybel, *Crisis or Change*, pp. 139–45.

245 Hatcher, "Unreal Wages," pp. 6–8, 20–22.

246 Hatcher, "Great Slump," pp. 237–72. Hatcher also preferred to explain late medieval economic history as "a succession of subperiods each with its own distinctive characteristics," rather than as one, long, monolithic trend, whether of growth or decline.

247 Christopher Dyer, "A Golden Age Rediscovered: Labourers' Wages in the Fifteenth Century," in *Money, Prices and Wages: Essays in Honour of Professor Nicholas Mayhew*, eds. Martin Allen and D'Maris Coffmann (Basingstoke, UK: Palgrave Macmillan, 2015), p. 195.

248 Dyer, "Golden Age Rediscovered," pp. 184–90; Dyer, *Age of Transition*, pp. 128–29; P.J.P. Goldberg, *Medieval England: A Social History, 1250–1550* (London: Arnold, 2004), pp. 170–71; Robert C. Allen, *Enclosure and the Yeoman* (Oxford: Clarendon Press, 1992), pp. 62–63; Britnell, *Britain and Ireland*, pp. 375, 431–32, 496. The acquisition of land and opting for more leisure time by wage laborers would also have had the effect of pushing up wage rates even higher, since fewer workers would have entered the wage labor market. Dyer argued that skilled craftsmen could earn even higher wages, at 6–8 pence per day, or £6–8 per year, and that even peasants owning just 15 acres, who comprised a "poor minority" in the fifteenth century, would still have needed to hire labor on a seasonal basis, such as at harvest time, although this was disputed by Allen.

249 Bailey, *Decline of Serfdom*, p. 65; Bailey, "Introduction: England in the Age of the Black Death," p. xxxv.

250 Dyer, *Making a Living*, p. 268.
251 Campbell, *Great Transition*, pp. 361, 374–76; Campbell, "The Land," p. 217; Dyer, *Making a Living*, p. 293; D.L. Farmer, "Prices and Wages," in *Agrarian History of England and Wales, Volume 3*, p. 444; Clark, "Long March of History," pp. 132–34; John Munro, "The Late Medieval Decline of English Demesne Agriculture: Demographic, Monetary, and Political-Fiscal Factors," in *Town and Countryside*, pp. 310, 312, 314, 317; John H. Munro, "Wage-Stickiness, Monetary Changes, and Real Incomes in Late-Medieval England and the Low Countries, 1300–1500: Did Money Matter?" in *Research in Economic History, vol. 21*, eds. Alexander J. Field, Gregory Clark, and William A. Sundstrom (Amsterdam, Netherlands: Elsevier Science, 2003), pp. 243–44; Britnell, *Britain and Ireland*, p. 377. For wage and price data on the Continent, in Italy, Spain and the Low Countries, see: C. Alvarez-Nogal and L. Prados de la Escosura, "The Rise and Fall of Spain (1270–1850)," *Economic History Review* 66 (2013):1–37; Paolo Malanima, "The Long Decline of a Leading Economy: GDP in Central and Northern Italy, 1300–1913," *European Review of Economic History* 15 (2011):173–78; Richard A. Goldthwaite, *The Economy of Renaissance Florence* (Baltimore, MD.: Johns Hopkins University Press, 2009), pp. 263–65; Munro, "Wage-Stickiness," p. 252; Earl J. Hamilton, *Money, Prices, and Wages in Valencia, Aragon, and Navarre, 1351–1500* (Cambridge, MA.: Harvard University Press, 1936), pp. 180, 186. See also the data set at http://gpih.ucdavis.edu/Datafilelist.htm, accessed January 3, 2018.
252 Samuel K. Cohn, Jr., "After the Black Death: Labour Legislation and Attitudes Towards Labour in Late-Medieval Western Europe," *Economic History Review* 60 (2007):457–85. Cohn mainly compared labor legislation in England, France, Spain, and Italy. He concluded that there was "a great variety of legal responses to perceived labour shortages and soaring prices after the Black Death," and that these responses were less determined by the demographic and economic logic of the supply and demand for labor, and more by the elite's fear and anxiety over political and social upheaval unleashed by "the Black Death's new horrors of mass mortality and destruction". At least with regard to England, I disagree with Cohn, because such unrest did not manifest itself until the Peasants' Revolt of 1381, which, one can argue, was the result, rather than the cause, of the labor laws themselves and peasants' frustrations arising out of their "rising expectations" in the wake of the plague. See Christopher Dyer, "The Social and Economic Background to the Rural Revolt of 1381," in *The English Rising of 1381*, eds. R.H. Hilton and T.H. Aston (Cambridge: Cambridge University Press, 1984), pp. 9–10.
253 B.H. Putnam, *The Enforcement of the Statutes of Labourers during the First Decade after the Black Death, 1349–1359* (New York: Columbia University Press, 1908); L.R. Poos, "The Social Context of Statute of Labourers Enforcement," *Law and History Review* 1 (1983):27–52; Farmer, "Prices and Wages," pp. 483–90; Penn and Dyer, "Wages and Earnings in Late Medieval England," pp. 357–59; E.B. Fryde, *Peasants and Landlords in Later Medieval England* (New York: St. Martin's Press, 1996), pp. 33–38. Penn and Dyer's assertion that the Statute of Labourers "was broken each year by hundreds of thousands of workers" does indicate widespread disregard of the law, but also, at the same time, its vigorous enforcement.
254 Munro, "Wage-Stickiness," pp. 186–88; John Munro, "Before and After the Black Death: Money, Prices, and Wages in Fourteenth-Century England," in *New Approaches to the History of Late Medieval and Early Modern Europe*, pp. 335–64; Munro, "Late Medieval Decline," pp. 300–23; John Day, *The Medieval Market Economy* (Oxford: Basil Blackwell, 1987), pp. 90–107; N.J. Mayhew, "Numismatic Evidence and Falling Prices in the Fourteenth Century," *Economic History Review*, 2nd ser., 27 (1974): 1–15. For a more detailed summary and critique of the monetary argument, see Hatcher and Bailey, *Modelling the Middle Ages*, pp. 186–92.
255 Chris Given-Wilson, "Service, Serfdom and English Labour Legislation, 1350–1500," in *Concepts and Patterns of Service in the Later Middle Ages*, eds. A. Curry and E. Matthew (Woodbridge, UK: Boydell Press, 2000), pp. 21–37; Chris Given-Wilson,

"The Problem of Labour in the Context of English Government," in *The Problem of Labour in Fourteenth-Century England*, eds. J. Bothwell, P.J.P. Goldberg, and W.M. Ormrod (Woodbridge, UK: Boydell Press, 2000), pp. 85–100; Britnell, *Britain and Ireland*, pp. 375–76. It is argued that medieval labor legislation foreshadowed the poor laws that were adopted in England under the Tudors.

256 Munro, "Wage-Stickiness," p. 193.

257 Hatcher and Bailey, *Modelling the Middle Ages*, pp. 190–91; Campbell, "The Land," p. 218; Campbell, *Great Transition*, pp. 361, 368, 374–76.

258 Hatcher, "Unreal Wages," pp. 11–12.

259 Munro, "Wage-Stickiness," p. 201; Penn and Dyer, "Wages and Earnings," p. 357. The data on number of days worked per year that Munro cited applies only to building workers in the Antwerp-Liers region.

260 Hatcher, "Unreal Wages," pp. 8–10; Penn and Dyer, "Wages and Earnings," p. 362.

261 R.H. Britnell, "Commerce and Capitalism in Late Medieval England: Problems of Description and Theory," *Journal of Historical Sociology* 6 (1993):364. There is some debate as to whether short-term wage labor vs. year-long domestic service increased proportionally in the overall labor force during the late Middle Ages. Some argue that employers preferred to hire servants and therefore drove up demand for them, while others point out that short-term wage labor was preferred by the employees themselves because it paid better by the day and allowed them the freedom to "shop around for the best rates". See: Smith, "Human Resources," p. 210; Penn and Dyer, "Wages and Earnings," pp. 366–70.

262 Christopher Dyer, "The Hidden Trade of the Middle Ages: Evidence from the West Midlands," in *Everyday Life in Medieval England*, p. 285; Penn and Dyer, "Wages and Earnings," p. 373.

263 Bailey, *Decline of Serfdom*, p. 5. See also: Dyer, *Age of Transition*, p. 6; Britnell, *Britain and Ireland*, pp. 495–97; Given-Wilson, "Service, Serfdom and English Labour Legislation," p. 24; Robert Brenner, "Agrarian Class Structure and Economic Development in Pre-Industrial Europe," in *Brenner Debate*, pp. 35–36; Rodney H. Hilton, *The Decline of Serfdom in Medieval England* (London: Macmillan, 1986), pp. 33–44.

264 Bailey, *Decline of Serfdom*, pp. 87–282; Bailey, *Medieval Suffolk*, pp. 193–201; Mark Bailey, "The Transformation of Customary Tenures in Southern England, c.1350–c.1500," *Agricultural History Review* 62 (2014):210–30; Dyer, *Lords and Peasants*, pp. 283–97; Harvey, *Westminster Abbey*, pp. 256–61, 269–73, 276–85; Hilton, *Decline of Serfdom*, pp. 44–51. Conversion of customary tenures to copyhold and leasehold also facilitated land transfers and land accumulation.

265 Bailey, *Decline of Serfdom*, p. 65; Campbell, "The Land," p. 233.

266 Bailey, *Decline of Serfdom*, pp. 65–66.

267 Brenner, "Agrarian Class Structure," pp. 21–23; Hatcher and Bailey, *Modelling the Middle Ages*, pp. 108–9; Bailey, *Decline of Serfdom*, pp. 7–8, 60–61; Dyer, *Lords and Peasants*, p. 264. Even though they conceded Brenner's argument that serfdom experienced different fates in different regions of Europe despite the universal impact of the Black Death, Hatcher and Bailey contended that this still did not mitigate the major role that population trends played in serfdom's decline, nor did it elevate class conflict to the status of being the "sole significant dynamic variable".

268 Patricia Croot and David Parker, "Agrarian Class Structure and the Development of Capitalism: France and England Compared," in *Brenner Debate*, pp. 79–90; Jerome Blum, "The Rise of Serfdom in Eastern Europe," *American Historical Review*, 62 (1957):811.

269 Paul Freedman, *The Origins of Peasant Servitude in Medieval Catalonia* (Cambridge: Cambridge University Press, 1991), pp. 154–202. Peasants in Catalonia were only able to make significant gains at the conclusion of the *Remença* civil wars from 1462–86.

270 Blum, "Rise of Serfdom," pp. 819–35; William W. Hagen, "How Mighty the Junkers? Peasant Rents and Seigneurial Profits in Sixteenth-Century Brandenburg," *Past and Present*, 108 (1985):80–116; Heide Wunder, "Peasant Organization and Class Conflict

in Eastern and Western Germany," in *Brenner Debate*, p. 100. Other factors in serfdom's rise in eastern Europe include the decline of cities and of the urban middle classes, and a substantial increase in direct farming of demesnes owing to the profitability of grain exports, all of which again ran counter to trends in the West.

271 Bailey, *Decline of Serfdom*, p. 68; Hatcher and Bailey, *Modelling the Middle Ages*, p. 96.

272 Bailey, *Decline of Serfdom*, pp. 62–65.

273 John Hatcher, "English Serfdom and Villeinage: Towards a Reassessment," *Past and Present*, 90 (1981)," pp. 253–54, 258–65; Bolton, *Medieval English Economy*, pp. 185–86; Jack Ravensdale, "Population Changes and the Transfer of Customary Land on a Cambridgeshire Manor in the Fourteenth Century," in *Land, Kinship and Life-Cycle*, pp. 223–24; John Mullan and Richard Britnell, *Land and Family: Trends and Local Variations in the Peasant Land Market on the Winchester Bishopric Estates, 1263–1415* (University of Hertfordshire Press, Studies in Regional and Local History, 8, 2010), pp. 57–58.

274 Bailey, *Decline of Serfdom*, p. 69.

275 Harvey, *Westminster Abbey*, p. 257.

276 Campbell, "The Land," pp. 224–25; Dyer, "Social and Economic Background," p. 27; Hatcher, "England in the Aftermath of the Black Death," pp. 34–35; Bolton, "'World Upside Down'," pp. 45–47.

277 R.H. Britnell, "Feudal Reaction after the Black Death in the Palatinate of Durham," *Past and Present* 128 (1990):47; Mullan and Britnell, *Land and Family*, pp. 58–64; Dyer, *Lords and Peasants*, pp. 275–81.

278 Britnell, "Feudal Reaction after the Black Death," pp. 32–47; Britnell, *Britain and Ireland*, p. 432.

279 Hatcher and Bailey, *Modelling the Middle Ages*, p. 109.

280 Bailey, *Decline of Serfdom*, p. 62; Hatcher, "English Serfdom and Villeinage," pp. 254–56.

281 Bailey, *Decline of Serfdom*, pp. 75–80; J. Ambrose Raftis, *Tenure and Mobility: Studies in the Social History of the Medieval English Village* (Toronto: Pontifical Institute of Mediaeval Studies, 1964), pp. 153–66; Razi, *Life, Marriage and Death*, pp. 117–19; Hilton, *Decline of Serfdom*, pp 33–35. A note of caution was, however, sounded by Larry Poos, based on his evidence from Essex, in that higher migration rates recorded in manorial accounts may simply have reflected greater concern by landlords over tenant mobility. Poos found that turnover rates in several Essex communities during the first half of the fourteenth century, prior to the plague, were comparable to those recorded 300 years later, in the seventeenth century. Evidence also indicates that when people migrated, they did not travel very far, typically within 10 miles of their native villages. See: Poos, *Rural Society after the Black Death*, pp. 160–62; Dyer, "Changes in the Size of Peasant Holdings," p. 281; Penn and Dyer, "Wages and Earnings," pp. 363–64; Bolton, "'World Upside Down'," p. 51.

282 Campbell, "The Land," p. 227; Hatcher, "England in the Aftermath of the Black Death," pp. 32–33.

283 Campbell, "The Land," p. 179; Lomas, "South-east Durham," , p. 317.

284 R. Faith, "Berkshire: Fourteenth and Fifteenth Centuries," in *Peasant Land Market*, pp. 116, 132.

285 Campbell, "Population Pressure," p. 121; Britnell, *Britain and Ireland*, p. 444.

286 Faith, "Berkshire," pp. 110–11; Miller, "Introduction: Land and People," p. 19. Rather than keeping tenancies intact, lords now had an interest in allowing land transfers, so long as they could profit by it, namely through fees such as entry fines. One landlord who was "heroically indifferent" to the trend of piecemeal fragmentation and sale of holdings were the monks of Westminster Abbey. See Harvey, *Westminster Abbey*, pp. 264–66.

287 Dyer, *Age of Transition*, p. 195; Dyer, *Making a Living*, pp. 332–33; Campbell, "The Land," pp. 201, 207; Campbell, "Population Pressure," p. 103; Lomas, "South-east Durham,", p. 302. This process seems to have begun in the latter half half of 1370s,

when the plague first began to really "bite hard into the traditional manorial economy," i.e., prices and rents fell while wages increased, thus squeezing manorial incomes. Leasing then accelerated in the 1390s and was pretty much complete by 1450. See: Bolton, *Medieval English Economy*, p. 214; Britnell, *Britain and Ireland*, pp. 401, 430–31.

288 Faith, "Berkshire,"p. 109; Lomas, "South-east Durham,"p. 303; Dyer, *Making a Living*, pp. 346–47; Dyer, *Age of Transition*, pp. 196, 208; Britnell, *Britain and Ireland*, p. 403. However, lords who leased demesnes generally retained the right to collect rents and other dues from their tenants. Dyer has also found that, although many lessees were of "peasant origin," nevertheless a "gulf" of social and economic inequality soon opened up between such entrepreneurial farmers and their fellow tenants, which was perhaps inevitable given that they were controlling as much as 10 times more acreage than other villagers.

289 Campbell, "The Land," pp. 207–8; Dyer, *Making a Living*, p. 336; Lomas, "South-east Durham," pp. 307–8; Britnell, *Britain and Ireland*, pp.439–44.

290 Campbell, "The Land," pp. 206–7; Faith, "Berkshire," pp. 118, 120–21; Mavis E. Mate, "The East Sussex Land Market and Agrarian Class Structure in the Late Middle Ages," *Past and Present* 139 (1993):46–65.

291 Campbell, "Population Pressure," pp. 100–1, 126–27. Migration also could have contributed to the slack land market, although this was a two-edged sword, in that tenants migrated *to* somewhere as well as away, and it was somewhat dependent on opportunities created by the plague. Campbell found that at Coltishall in Norfolk, migration only contributed to post-plague decline "until some time after the downward trend in numbers had become firmly established," i.e., sometime in the late fourteenth century.

292 Lomas, "South-east Durham," p. 326; Bailey, *Medieval Suffolk*, p. 242.

293 Faith, "Berkshire," pp. 114, 120–21, 129, 132, 136, 139, 151, 158; Lomas, "South-east Durham," pp. 296–99, 316, 354; Dyer, *Lords and Peasants*, pp. 302–3. Tim Lomas found that, on average, 70 percent of properties in the century and a half after the Black Death were transferred *inter vivos* outside the family on four manors owned by Durham Cathedral Priory, while this averaged 53 percent on four manors owned by the bishop of Durham. However, Lomas also found that stability and continuity in family land-holdings re-emerged towards the end of the fifteenth century. Dyer found that *inter vivos* transfers outside the family on four manors owned by the bishop of Worcester averaged 22 percent from the late fourteenth throughout the fifteenth centuries.

294 Dyer, "Changes in the Size of Peasant Holdings," pp. 281–94; Phillipp R. Schofield, "Tenurial Developments and the Availability of Customary Land in a Later Medieval Community," *Economic History Review*, n.s., 49 (1996), p. 265; Campbell, "The Land," p. 233; J. Whittle, "Individualism and the Family-Land Bond: A Reassessment of Land Transfer Patterns among the English Peasantry, c.1270–1580," *Past and Present* 160 (1998):63. Some spectacular examples of village turnover in the wake of the Black Death include the disappearance of more than two-thirds of tenant families at Durrington in Wiltshire by 1359, with a complete turnover by 1441, and a nearly three-fold increase in turnover at Kibworth Harcourt in Leicestershire between 1352–72; by the early 15th century, turnover at Kibworth "was so rapid that it becomes impossible to trace the descent of all but a handful of holdings". Of course, it is almost impossible to determine how much of this turnover was due to plague, and how much to other factors, particularly migration. See: J.N. Hare, "Durrington: A Chalkland Village in the Later Middle Ages," *Wiltshire Archaeological Magazine* 74/75 (1981):144; Howell, *Land, Family and Inheritance*, p. 48.

295 Zvi Razi, "The Erosion of the Family-Land Bond in the Late Fourteenth and Fifteenth Centuries: A Methodological Note," in *Land, Kinship and Life-Cycle*, pp. 295–304; Zvi Razi, "The Myth of the Immutable English Family," *Past and Present* 140 (1993):3–44.

296 Campbell, "Population Pressure," and Christopher Dyer, "Changes in the Size of Peasant Holdings," in *Land, Kinship and Life-Cycle*, pp. 130, 277; Campbell, "The Land," pp. 207–8; Dyer, *Lords and Peasants*, p. 298; Lomas, "South-east Durham,"

pp. 341–43; Miller, "Introduction: Land and People," pp. 30–32; Bolton, "'World Upside Down'," pp. 53–58; Bolton, *Medieval English Economy*, pp. 238–42; Bailey, *Medieval Suffolk*, p. 246.

297 Dyer provided one example, of a landless wage laborer named Edmund, servant of the rector of Ingatestone in Essex, who in 1359 joined the ranks of the tenantry by assuming a 7-acre holding for a term of 7 years. See Dyer, "Social and Economic Background," p. 21.

298 Britnell, *Britain and Ireland*, pp. 374, 431–32. Moving further up the scale, cottagers are believed to have increased their holdings from .5–1 acre to 5–6 acres; smallholders from 5–10 acres to 30 acres; and wealthy peasant elites, or yeomen, up to 60 or even 100 acres. See: Mavis E. Mate, "Work and Leisure," in *A Social History of England*, p. 286; Bolton, *Medieval English Economy*, p. 238; Britnell, *Britain and Ireland*, pp. 403, 445.

299 Campbell, "The Land," pp. 219–21; Britnell, *Britain and Ireland*, pp. 375, 432.

300 Faith, "Berkshire,", p. 162; Benedictow, *Black Death*, pp. 264–66. Benedictow estimated a 45–55 percent underestimation of poor and destitute persons in tax rolls prior to the Black Death. One tax roll that did record the landless were the head-tax lists kept by Glastonbury Abbey, which recorded the "garciones" or men who owned no property and therefore paid no rent, but who were still liable to the tax. See Ecclestone, "Mortality of Rural Landless Men before the Black Death," pp. 6–29.

301 Harvey, *Westminster Abbey*, p. 266; Schofield, "Tenurial Developments," p. 260; Campbell, "The Land," p. 230; Faith, "Berkshire,"p. 166; Lomas, "South-east Durham," pp. 314, 339–40; Bolton, *Medieval English Economy*, pp. 238–42; Miller, "Introduction: Land and People," pp. 25–26.

302 Campbell, "Population Pressure," pp. 103–4, 108–9. The persistence of smallholdings among the majority of tenantry into the late fourteenth century is likewise documented in the county of Suffolk and in Cornwall. See Bailey, *Medieval Suffolk*, p. 245; Hatcher, *Rural Economy*, p. 139.

303 Faith, "Berkshire," pp. 128, 133, 143, 150, 153–55. In County Durham, land transfers were particularly active immediately after the first outbreak of the Black Death and at the very beginning of the fifteenth century. See Lomas, "South-east Durham," pp. 304–5.

304 Campbell, "Population Pressure," p. 123; Faith, "Berkshire," pp. 119–20, 128, 139; Lomas, "South-east Durham," pp. 309–13. At Durham, much of the rapid turnover seems to have been due to a trend towards shorter-term leases, which ran contrary to what was usually demanded by lessees.

305 Campbell, "Population Pressure," pp. 112–13, 122.

306 Lomas, "South-east Durham," p. 350.

307 Campbell, "The Land," pp. 212, 220.

308 Mullan and Britnell, *Land and Family*, p. 59; Lomas, "South-east Durham," p. 305; Britnell, "Feudal Reaction," pp. 31–33.

309 Campbell, "Population Pressure," pp. 124–25; Dyer, *Lords and Peasants*, pp. 299–303; Harvey, *Westminster Abbey*, pp. 285–90; Hatcher, *Rural Economy*, pp. 229–31.

310 See: Dyer, *Age of Transition*, p. 200, and Hatcher, "Great Slump," p. 261, for some examples of tenant farmers' reluctance to take up leases. For examples of successful tenant farmers, on the other hand, see Bolton, *Medieval English Economy*, pp. 234–36.

311 Faith, "Berkshire," p. 165; Dyer, *Age of Transition*, pp 204–5; Britnell, *Britain and Ireland*, pp. 401–4; Bolton, "'World Upside Down'," pp. 66–70.

312 Dyer, *Making a Living*, pp. 335–37; Dyer, *Age of Transition*, p. 201. Farmers were rarely evicted, however, even when heavily in debt, owing to the difficulty of finding replacement tenants.

313 Campbell, "The Land," pp. 208, 224, 233; Faith, "Berkshire," pp. 167–73; Dyer, *Making a Living*, pp. 333, 350; Dyer, *Age of Transition*, pp. 196, 206–7; C.C. Dyer, "The West Midlands," and Harvey, "Home Counties," in *Agrarian History of England and Wales: Volume 3*, pp. 88–92, 113–15. Of course, pastoral husbandry was practiced by the new tenant farmers as well.

314 Faith, "Berkshire," pp. 128–29; Bailey, *Medieval Suffolk*, pp. 246–49; Hatcher, *Rural Economy*, p. 231.

315 Campbell, "The Land," p. 207; Campbell, "Population Pressure," pp. 103, 127, 130; Faith, "Berkshire," pp. 145, 157–58, 166–68, 173–77; Lomas, "South-east Durham," p. 316; Britnell, *Britain and Ireland*, p. 445; Bolton, "'World Upside Down'," p. 58; Bolton, *Medieval English Economy*, pp. 238–39. Rosamund Faith declared that the peasant aristocracy of Berkshire "came to nothing," as hardly any families identified in the fifteenth century survived to become the "prosperous yeomen" of the sixteenth century. Yet Tim Lomas asserted that at Durham, "some of the landed families of the later fifteenth century do seem to have prospered in later centuries". Bruce Campbell claimed that at Coltishall in Norfolk, "an incipient yeomanry was firmly established" by the end of the fifteenth century; indeed, he argued that the "process of class differentiation" between "capitalist farmer/landless wage labourer" was "irreversible" and essential to the later emergence of the agricultural revolution in the seventeenth and eighteenth centuries.

316 Clark, "Long March of History," pp. 97–135; Broadberry, et al., *British Economic Growth*, pp. 247–48.

317 Broadberry, et al., *British Economic Growth*, p. 249; Campbell, *Great Transition*, p. 374; Hatcher, "Unreal Wages," pp. 6–8.

318 Broadberry, et al., *British Economic Growth*, pp. xxxi–xxxix.

319 Broadberry, et al., *British Economic Growth*, pp. 206–9, 403–5. Estimates of GDP per head based on income reveal a larger and longer increase after the Black Death than GDP per head based on output (until c.1420), but the former ends up lower by the eighteenth and nineteenth centuries as compared to the latter, indicating less enduring, long-term growth. Thus, GDP per head based on income supports a "Malthusian stagnation" view of the history of the English economy, while GDP per head based on output chimes with one that sees the Early Modern centuries as an era of Smithian "efflorescence". See Broadberry, et al., *British Economic Growth*, pp. 250–52, 276–78.

320 Broadberry, *et al.*, *British Economic Growth*, pp. 178–82, 208–9.

321 Broadberry, et al., *British Economic Growth*, pp. 125–27, 178–79.

322 Broadberry, et al., *British Economic Growth*, p. 194. At this same time the share of the labor force in each sector also began to see a shift towards industry, which was to become more pronounced in the Early Modern period. See Broadberry, et al., *British Economic Growth*, p. 344.

323 Broadberry, et al., *British Economic Growth*, pp. 289, 416; Campbell, *Great Transition*, pp. 382–83.

324 Broadberry, et al., *British Economic Growth*, pp. 320–21, 329–30; Campbell, *Great Transition*, p. 373.

325 Broadberry, *et al.*, *British Economic Growth*, pp. 371–401, 422–28.

326 Broadberry, et al., *British Economic Growth*, pp. 375–79, 377.

327 Broadberry, et al., *British Economic Growth*, pp. 377–79; Campbell, *Great Transition*, pp. 377–79.

328 Broadberry, et al., *British Economic Growth*, pp. 375–76, 384–87.

329 Broadberry, et al., *British Economic Growth*, pp. 381–83, 395–401, 425–27.

330 Broadberry, et al., *British Economic Growth*, pp. 387, 405.

331 Broadberry, et al., *British Economic Growth*, pp. 266–70, 273, 320, 405, 424.

332 Broadberry, et al., *British Economic Growth*, p. 273.

333 Broadberry, et al., *British Economic Growth*, pp. 377, 405.

334 Broadberry, et al., *British Economic Growth*, p. 275.

335 Broadberry, et al., *British Economic Growth*, pp. 270–76.

336 Stuart J. Borsch, *The Black Death in Egypt and England: A Comparative Study* (Austin, TX.: University of Texas Press, 2005), pp. 24–112.

337 Dyer, *Age of Transition*, pp. 40–45; Campbell, "Population Pressure," p. 130; Bailey, *Decline of Serfdom*, pp. 6–7; Ellen Meiksins Wood, *The Origin of Capitalism: A Longer View* (London: Verso, 2002), pp. 95–105; Jane Whittle, *The Development of Agrarian*

Capitalism: Land and Labour in Norfolk, 1440–1580 (Oxford: Oxford University Press, 2000), pp. 5–27, 173–77; R.J. Holton, *The Transition from Feudalism to Capitalism* (New York: St. Martin's Press, 1985), pp. 206–18. Nonetheless, Jim Bolton argued that the gains made by peasant yeomen and gentry that may have paved the way for "the emergence of capitalist attitudes" in the Early Modern period were often transitory, since these were based on a favorable land-labor ratio that disappeared once population growth resumed. See Bolton, "'World Upside Down'," pp. 58–63; Bolton, *Medieval English Economy*, p. 245.

338 Campbell, "The Land," p. 237; Bailey, *Decline of Serfdom*, pp. 6–7; Christopher Dyer, "Were There Any Capitalists in Fifteenth-Century England?" in *Everyday Life*, pp. 305–28; Robert C. Allen and Jacob L. Weisdorf, "Was There an 'Industrious Revolution' Before the Industrial Revolution? An Empirical Exercise for England, c.1300–1830," *Economic History Review* 66 (2011):715–29.

339 J. de Vries, "The Industrial Revolution and the Industrious Revolution," *Journal of Economic History* 54 (1984):249–70; Broadberry, et al., *British Economic Growth*, pp. 263–65, 276, 381, 405.

340 Broadberry, et al., *British Economic Growth*, pp. 274, 320; Campbell, *Great Transition*, pp. 374, 380.

341 Broadberry, et al., *British Economic Growth*, pp. 274–78, 377, 381, 405.

342 Dyer, *Age of Transition*, pp. 1–6.

343 Dyer, *Making a Living*, p. 332. The phrase was used by the earl of Warwick's officials when commuting labor services to money rents on one manor in c.1400.

9

ALWAYS LOOK ON THE BRIGHT SIDE OF DEATH

A waning of the Middle Ages?

At the Cloisters museum in Fort Tryon Park in New York City, there is a gift shop where one can buy all sorts of trinkets and souvenirs having to do with the medieval theme of the museum's collection. On the back wall are displayed books for sale, and one book in particular is featured prominently: *The Waning of the Middle Ages*, by the Dutch scholar, Johan Huizinga.[1] The last time I was at the Cloisters, I must confess that I was sorely tempted to give vent to a scream worthy of Edvard Munch as soon as I caught sight of Huizinga's book on display. Out of all the medieval history books in all the world, they had to pick this one to peddle to unsuspecting tourists!

In truth, I have mixed feelings about Huizinga's *Waning of the Middle* Ages (now also referred to as *The Autumn of the Middle* Ages, based on a new English translation of 1996), which is often considered a "classic" among historical studies, but one that, I would argue, became a classic for all the wrong reasons.[2] It has indelibly stamped the late Middle Ages as a time of waning or decline of society and culture: Even Huizinga's staunchest defenders must admit that he cast a pall of darkness, melancholy, and pessimism over the age. To use his "harvest" imagery, Huizinga saw late medieval thought and culture as the "overripe fruits" of a civilization in its death throes, where anything fresh and new was suffocated by a rigid and ossified formalism.[3] Somehow, this gloomy portrait has struck a chord in the popular imagination and continues to sell the book quite successfully, as evidenced by its presence in the Cloisters' gift shop. Perhaps this is because people simply delight in bad news and like to hear tales of how people before them were miserable, since it makes their own times appear not so bad. So it is, that for nearly a century now, Huizinga's "waning" thesis has dominated both popular and academic discourse on late medieval Europe. Barbara Tuchman's *A Distant Mirror* (1978) can be considered simply a variation on Huizinga's theme of decline.[4]

Personally, I believe that this picture of late medieval society in terminal decline is utterly wrong. But I am by no means the only one to have reservations about a "waning" or "autumnal" late Middle Ages.[5] Textbooks on medieval history that address this question tend to eschew Huizinga's pessimistic model and instead prefer value-neutral terms such as "transitions" or "transformations" to describe what they see as an almost arbitrary demarcation of the late medieval period from the Early Modern one.[6] No one now talks about the "waning of the Middle Ages" except as a horribly stereotyped notion that must be avoided if one is to seriously study and understand either medieval or Early Modern history. A large part of the reason for this is that Huizinga's waning thesis goes against much of what we now know actually happened in European society towards the end of the Middle Ages. For example, it is hard to imagine a people anxious and depressed whose living standards—including diet and other measures of material comfort—were improving so vastly in the aftermath of the Black Death.[7] But this goes back to a criticism of Huizinga's *Waning* that was made almost as soon as the book appeared, namely, that it is extremely impressionistic, based on a few literary and artistic works from the Low Countries and Burgundy, and thus has little to no foundation in actual archival or documentary (i.e., "positivist") research and is rather limited in temporal and geographical scope.[8] Huizinga can also be considered an elitist, in that he focused almost exclusively on aristocratic court culture (such as chivalry) and thereby gave little sense of what life was actually like for the vast majority of people who lived at that time, whether in the country or the city.[9] Even in the cultural aspect that was his forte, Huizinga posed a contradictory dilemma, in that a society that was supposedly becoming stale in its excessively symbolic and formalist expressions was at the same time giving birth to a "Renaissance" or renewal in all forms of literary and artistic endeavors. Huizinga himself, especially in his other writings on the Renaissance, seemed to acknowledge this contradiction.[10] As he stated at the very end of the *Waning*: "A high and strong culture is declining, but at the same time and in the same sphere new things are being born. The tide is turning, the tone of life is about to change".[11]

But in spite of the almost universal dismissal of Huizinga's *Waning* thesis by scholars, it still retains a stranglehold on the popular imagination. Part of the reason for this is the "postimpressionist skill" with which Huizinga painted his subject. Even though the novelistic tone of the *Waning* has been heavily criticized, it is also its greatest strength, and why it has exerted such a popular appeal. No one can deny that Huizinga was a consummate raconteur. Like a magician, or, to use a comparison he perhaps would have preferred, a jester, Huizinga with his "sensuous," seductive prose cast an indefinable but definite spell on his readers.[12] This is indeed one aspect of the book that I personally admire very much and would dearly like to imitate, although it must drive a lot of academics crazy, in that Huizinga's place in popular culture is what ensures his continued relevance in academia. I also believe that Huizinga's success is largely due to the fact that he was very much in tune with his own times. Indeed, one might say that the *Waning*'s dark tone is a more accurate reflection of the interwar period, the "Lost

Generation" that became disillusioned and culturally adrift in the wake of the First World War, than of its ostensible subject, the late Middle Ages.[13]

Huizinga's defenders find plenty of other reasons to excuse his work. They point out that his ideas changed over time (a fourth Dutch edition of the *Waning* appeared in 1935) and that the complexity of his ideas are often lost in translation from the original Dutch.[14] Even though he cultivated an image of himself as the "avant-garde outsider," many of Huizinga's ideas were not out of the mainstream.[15] And even if he did not found a historical "school," Huizinga did inspire many imitators and enthusiasts in his wake, such as Tuchman.[16] And it is argued that the geographical scope of his purview should be extended to at least southeast England, thereby encompassing almost the whole of northwestern Europe.[17] I myself must confess that I have only read the *Waning* in a popular, 1954 paperback edition of Fritz Hopman's original English translation of 1924 (done in consultation with Huizinga himself), which in turn was based on an "unpublished French abbreviation" that the French historian, Jacques Le Goff, characterized as *"une trahison,"* or "a betrayal".[18] The very title of the first English translation—*Waning*— has been criticized as too bleak compared to more nuanced possibilities such as *Autumn* and *Harvest*, which, it is argued, at least make room for possibilities of positive outcomes and renewal.[19] Indeed, I have come around to the notion that the late Middle Ages did mark the end of something, largely owing to the influence of the Black Death, even if I don't view this in the same negative light as Huizinga.

Given all of this, there are two (out of the many) themes from Huizinga's work that I would like to re-examine in the pages that follow, which I feel is essential for any critical assessment of the end of the Middle Ages. One is the notion of "crisis" in late medieval society. The other concerns the "obsession" with death, or a "death culture," that is assumed to have prevailed in the wake of the Black Death. Finally, we will address what should replace "waning" as a historical narrative of the late Middle Ages.

The "crisis" of the late Middle Ages

In the opening chapter of the *Waning of the Middle Ages*, Huizinga declared that, "A general feeling of impending calamity hangs over all".[20] Huizinga seemed to be referring here to a "crisis" mentality in late medieval Europe, the vague sense that a "continuous insecurity" reigned over "the lives of great and small alike". This is, again, a largely impressionistic comment based on strictly anecdotal evidence, such as the *Testament* of François Villon, or the diary of the Burgher of Paris. Although Huizinga did not open the "crisis" debate among medieval scholars, since the concept seems to have been already in use in the previous century by such writers as the Swiss historian, Jacob Burckhardt, he did popularize the notion of crisis in connection with a putative collapse in European society and culture in the late Middle Ages.[21]

"Crisis" comes from the Greek word for "decision," which presumes that this is the culmination of long-standing developments.[22] In its origins, the concept is closely related to that of a medical crisis in a diseased body, which, according to Hippocrates (460–370 B.C.), signified the point at which the patient either fought off his illness, or succumbed to it.[23] In historical terms, Buckhardt saw a "crisis" as referring to a sudden acceleration of the historical process in "terrifying fashion," one that presaged structural transformations in society, even if the underlying political or social systems remained intact.[24]

As applied to the late Middle Ages, historians have characterized the fourteenth and/or fifteenth centuries as an "age of crisis," since there certainly were no shortage of catastrophic events heralding at least the potential for significant change.[25] These included: periodic outbreaks of plague, beginning with the Black Death of 1347–53; periodic outbreaks of famine, or "subsistence crises," starting with the Great Famine of 1315–22; violent conflicts between nation-states and other powers, such as the Hundred Years War between England and France from 1337–1453; and peasant and urban uprisings, such as the Jacquerie revolt in France of 1358, the Ciompi revolt in Florence of 1378, the Peasants' Revolt in England of 1381, and the War of the Remences in Catalonia beginning in 1462.[26] In addition, scholars also point to a "religious crisis" or "crisis in the Church" at this time, which included the "Babylonian Captivity" from 1309 to 1378, when the papacy resided in Avignon rather than its usual seat in Rome; the Great Schism between rival popes in Avignon and Rome (and, from 1409, at Pisa) that lasted from 1378 until 1417; new conflicts between papal and secular authorities, particularly the rising nation-states such as France and England that were forming "national churches"; challenges from new heresies such as the Lollards in England and the Hussites in Bohemia; and renewed calls for reform of the Church which, at their most extreme, called for the complete separation and removal of the Church from temporal affairs.[27] One also can point to a periodic "monetary crisis," triggered by violent fluctuations in the supply of hard currency or bullion in silver and gold, when either a glut or shortage of money in circulation caused inflation or deflation of prices, which in turn affected international trade and even simple, everyday business transactions and economic activities.[28] Then there was supposedly an "urban crisis," in which cities faced catastrophic declines in population and economic vitality, as well as loss of political autonomy due to the rising power of nation-states and conflicts among various citizen groups.[29]

But, did all this collectively result in a "crisis mentality," or an "age of anxiety," that prevailed in the late Middle Ages? Characterizations of late medieval society as experiencing a "crisis" remain very popular in textbooks.[30] In its general sense, crisis still seems to mean something very close to what Huizinga originally proposed, namely, a time of insecurity, fear, confusion, uncertainty, unrest, and a general questioning of the "normal" way of doing things. As the Czech historian, František Graus, put it, "Insecurity and fear became phenomena that ruled the minds and characterized a whole period and which could lead to both passiveness as well as radicalization".[31] But, as Graus also pointed out, simply to enumerate all the individual "crises" that go to make up a general "consciousness" or "feeling" of crisis among the population at large, or to explain this as simply an "accident" of history, is not sufficient. Historians, naturally, seek to find some meaning, some rationale or reason, behind the crisis or all the crises.[32]

This is where theory comes into play. Many historians see "structural" causes behind the crisis or crises that have their roots as far back as the "good times" during the high Middle Ages.[33] Two of the most influential historical models that employ the concept of crisis are the neo-Malthusian and neo-Marxist theories. The neo-Malthusian model, for example, enlists the concepts of "mortality crisis," "subsistence crisis," "agrarian crisis," and "economic crisis" in its attempt to explicate the relationship between human population growth and natural resources, particularly food. For example, "crisis mortality" refers to the fact that, particularly during the era of the Black Death, the death rate—owing to periodic outbreaks of plague—regularly exceeded the moving average number of deaths in the population in non-crisis years; usually, a mortality crisis is deemed to have occurred when mortality exceeded the average by 10 percent or more.[34] A subsistence crisis, i.e., a famine, rarely resulted directly in a mortality crisis through starvation (with the Great Famine perhaps being an exception), but nonetheless some historians see a link between them in that malnutrition suffered especially by children during subsistence crises is held to have made them more susceptible to later outbreaks of plague.[35]

The "agrarian crisis" can refer either to the inability of medieval agriculture to feed and sustain Europe's growing numbers of people in the half century or so before the Black Death, or else to a contraction of arable production and acreage in the aftermath of the plague.[36] An "economic crisis" was caused by an overall contraction in trade and manufacturing in the wake of the Black Death, which reached its peak during the "Great Slump" of the mid-fifteenth century.[37] An alternative interpretation, put forth by the neo-Marxist model, is that late medieval Europe suffered a "crisis in feudalism". In this view, lords and peasants were caught in a vicious circle, whereby lords, by attempting to oppressively appropriate all the "surplus" income and labor from their peasants, prevented that surplus from being re-invested in land productivity, which not only harmed their serfs but also themselves, since it could have raised their own incomes. This, in turn, forced lords to impose ever more burdensome services and dues upon their serfs in order to make up the difference, and so on, until a breaking point was reached when peasants revolted or otherwise resisted in various ways to bring serfdom to an end.[38]

Both the neo-Malthusian and neo-Marxist models have been criticized to such an extent and so effectively that they are now essentially defunct as operating paradigms of historical enquiry.[39] In particular, it is argued that they forecast a crisis, where in fact none occurred.[40] Even those historians who chronicle a crisis or crises in late medieval society must admit that the patient effected a remarkable recovery given the prognosis, in that this society was able to create "a new and dynamic civilization" that emerged "out of the ruins of successive disasters".[41] For this reason, some prefer more neutral terms than "crisis" to refer to the challenging situation facing Europe in the late Middle Ages, ones that are less associated with pessimism or contain less of an assumption of decline in the wake of crisis. Alternatives include "catastrophe," which was first used by the English historian of the Black Death, Francis Aidan Gasquet, at the turn of the twentieth century, while others now prefer "contraction" to "crisis".[42]

Then again, one can ponder the compulsion behind historians' need to have an explanation for a crisis or crises. Must there always be one? It is quite possible that crises simply emerged out of a chaotic and entirely unpredictable "kaleidoscope" of causes whose interaction was unique and would never be replicated again.[43] In that case, one might question why study history at all? This is especially the case if one believes that the main function of history is to learn the lessons of the past. Strangely enough, this would return us to a medieval explanation of events, that such things happen according to an inscrutable and inexorable design.[44] In the words of Prof. John Hatcher, whose lectures on the Black Death I attended at Cambridge University—a crisis is nothing more than that God with his great hammer put a great "whack" on medieval society.

Yet Hatcher himself was not satisfied with this response. He and Mark Bailey wrote that, "the great questions in history demand that answers to them continue to be sought, however misguided or partial these might eventually turn out to be".[45] But if there are answers, then they are not so simple as in the past. These days, "interaction" models see crises emerge out of the intersection of numerous factors, rather than relying on linear or moncausal "supermodels" that depend on one or two "prime movers," such as population and resources (Malthusian) or class conflict (Marxist).[46] Moreover, crises such as the Black Death or the Great Famine are no longer believed to be entirely due to "exogenous" factors, or influences external to the internal mechanisms of human society; rather, they are now understood to have had more direct links to human influences and decisions.[47] This necessarily implies that humans can still influence the outcome of events and change the course of history, and that therefore history is still very much worth studying.

A society "obsessed" with death?

Huizinga famously opened his chapter on "The Vision of Death" with the following words: "No other epoch has laid so much stress as the expiring Middle Ages on the thought of death. An everlasting call of *memento mori* resounds through life".[48] The Latin phrase, *memento mori*, is perhaps best translated as, "remember, you will die". This stark and brutal sentiment is, for Huizinga, the single, endlessly repeated theme of the late medieval obsession, or one might also call it fascination, with death. It was expressed, according to Huizinga, in three main variations: the *ubi sunt?* or "where are they now?" theme, usually expressed as an elegiac lament or meditation on the passing glory of the world; the *contemptus mundi* (contempt for the world) or "triumph of death" theme, usually expressed in the form of stern reminders that all human beauty would end in dust and worms and decay; and the *danse macabre*, or dance of death motif in literature and art, in which the figure of death led away various representatives of society in a dance to the otherworld.[49] One gets the impression that Huizinga did not really admire this aspect of late medieval culture. He seems to have viewed it as too stereotyped and overblown, a sterile and rigid from of expression hardly admitting of any nuance of feeling. His conclusion at the end of this chapter was that: "All that lay between—pity, resignation, longing, consolation—remained unexpressed and was, so to say, absorbed by the too much accentuated and too vivid representation of Death hideous and threatening. Living emotion stiffens amid the abused imagery of skeletons and worms".[50]

Some more recent scholars of late medieval death culture have followed Huizinga's lead in seeing the artistic and literary motif revolving around the skeleton or cadaver as expressing an unhealthy obsession or fascination with death, or what has also been called a "necromania". For these scholars, the imagery that is collectively described as "macabre" expressed "a strong sense of anxiety about the fate of the soul," as well as an excessive humility in terms of the attitude towards the physical body.[51] This "age of anxiety" was tied up with plenty of other pessimistic and melancholic emotions, such as "misery, angst, guilt, fear and an overwhelming sense of apocalyptical doom".[52] It is also assumed to be narcissistic, an individualized desire to save the soul from Purgatory through an obsessive-compulsive repetition of pious acts of devotion that focused on the dead body, in what has been described as a neurotic, fetishistic, voyeuristic fashion.[53] The main artistic expressions of the macabre that carry the weight of this interpretation include the *transi* tombs, the motif of the Three Living and Three Dead, and the Dance of Death.[54] In all three motifs—but particularly in the *transi* tomb (from the Latin verb *transire*, meaning to "pass away"), in which the patron had him- or herself portrayed as a decomposing cadaver or complete skeleton, often juxtaposed with a life-like but idealized image on the same tomb—the macabre was an almost surreal mirror-image of the individual as he or she would look in the future, in death. This is seen as expressing, once again, a "psychology of anxiety" or, in the case of the Dance of Death, a "new anxiety of social control," an extreme form of art, or rather, anti-art, in which "the grotesque, the bizarre and the morbid" were gleefully disgorged and put on display for all to see.[55] It also stands in high contrast to Renaissance art, which supposedly sought a cool, classical balance and a portrayal of the body in all its beauty and perfection, and which also conveyed a "new spirit" of the "triumph of worldly glory".[56]

An alternative interpretation of the macabre was offered up by the French historian of death culture, Philippe Ariès. Ariès also viewed macabre art as individualistic, but, rather than evincing a morbid anxiety and fear for the soul, he saw it as expressing a "passionate love of life," or *avaritia*, in the sense of an attachment to—but not necessarily accumulation of—worldly things and an extreme reluctance to let go of the things of this world, whether they be one's spouse or relatives and friends, as well as material wealth and possessions.[57] Nonetheless, Ariès did not necessarily consider his interpretation to differ from Huizinga's, since "Huizinga clearly understood the relationship between the passionate love of life and the images of death," and it was, in fact, people's deep "sense of disillusionment and discouragement" at not being able to take the world with them to the tomb that was at "the heart of the matter" of the macabre.[58] It was also Ariès who noticed that many forms of the macabre, such as the *transi* tomb, were prevalent in northern Europe but absent in the South, particularly in Italy, Spain, and Mediterranean France. (Italy did, however, indulge in the Triumph of Death and Three Living and Three Dead themes, the most famous example being the fresco in the Camposanto of Pisa.) Ariès attributed this difference to varying cultural norms between the two regions, such as whether the face was exposed or concealed in funeral displays, even though Italy was the heartland of Renaissance individualistic culture, which Ariès saw as the motivating force behind the macabre.[59]

Other French historians of death culture, such as Jacques Chiffoleau, Jean Pierre Deregnaucourt, and Michel Lauwers, have followed in Ariès footsteps in terms of chronicling a "new individualism" with respect to a focus on "one's own death" through a reading of last wills and testaments from Avignon, Douai, and Liège. But in this case, the individualism towards death expressed a "Great Melancholy," since will-makers seemed to evince an alienation and isolation from ancestors and other family members as they indulged in "profoundly narcissistic" funerals and masses and intercessory prayers for their souls. This is much closer to Huizinga's view of the age as marked by despair and pessimism as opposed to the Renaissance theme of revival and renewal as propounded by Jacob Burckhardt.[60] But an entirely different reading of such wills is argued by Samuel Cohn. Although he did notice that testators at Douai suddenly abandoned mention of their ancestors in 1400, which coincided with a major occurrence of plague in the city, they nonetheless continued to remember their parents, spouses, and other relatives and friends, which argues against the notion of them as "narcissistic egomaniacs" or "deracinated" individualists. Moreover, in Tuscany at around this same time, will-makers opted for burial crypts to house their entire familial lineage, suggesting, in fact, a renewed interest in ancestral remembrance in Italy.[61]

Another interpretation of the macabre that challenged Huizinga was offered up by the historian of late medieval English religion, Eamon Duffy. Duffy did admit that the "cult of the dead was ubiquitous" during the late Middle Ages, but he argued that it did not therefore follow that it was "morbid or doom-laden". Instead, Duffy proposed that the late medieval response to death was "more complex and more humane than Huizinga's stark polarities suggest". Specifically, the Church's "cult of intercession for the dead" posed an interdependent relationship between the living and the dead, in which the dead were comforted with the assurance of being remembered and prayed for in the afterlife, while the living benefitted by being able to make elaborate preparations for death that considerably mitigated the mental anguish of facing one's own demise. This obfuscation of the dividing line between the realms of the living and the dead owed more to an "ascetic ethos" in medieval piety that dated all the way back to early Christianity and did not represent a nihilistic innovation. Moreover, Duffy viewed the mentality of late medieval Englishmen and Englishwomen as evincing an impulse that was more inclusive than narcissistic or individualistic, one that encompassed the entire Christian community, both the living and the dead.[62]

The evidence for all this is adduced from a rich evocation of the last rites and other preparations for death that were part of the still-vital sacramental ritual of the late medieval Church. This included, of course, the *Ordo visitandi*, or the last rites administered by the priest at the victim's deathbed, which began with the priest holding up a crucifix as a reminder of Christ's passion and thereby the Church's empathy with the sufferings of the dying man, and continued with hearing confession and granting the all-important absolution as an assurance of eventual salvation. This was complemented by the *Ars moriendi*, or the art of dying manuals, which instructed laymen on the proper conduct at the deathbed; far from being a morbid description of the "agony of death," as Huizinga would have it, the art of dying, in Duffy's view, sought to remove the "needless terror about death itself, by preparing the Christian for the struggles against the Devil which characterized the last moments of all," which included the five temptations of unbelief, despair, impatience, pride, and avarice.[63] There were plenty of other ways to combat one's fear of death by preparing for it: This could include specifying funeral preparations in one's will, constructing memorials, and leaving bequests to the local church and priests, all of which were designed to elicit prayers for the departed (especially on the anniversary of their deaths) and ensure that they would not be forgotten, such as by being included in the General Mind, or list of benefactors that was read out on the parish bede-roll at an annual obit or requiem service. This was, again, a communal enterprise, in which requests for prayers often included others beyond the individual and his immediate family, in return for benefactions that profited the entire parish; even private chantry chapels employed priests who were expected to serve not just the chapel but participate in the worship of the entire church.[64]

Given Huizinga's assumption that late medieval people were obsessed or fascinated with death, it is rather surprising that he did not mention the Black Death, since one would think that the rampant mortality it caused would naturally have given rise to such a mindset.[65] But other scholars of the macabre actually denied the Black Death's importance in terms of the formation of medieval cultural attitudes towards death. Philippe Ariès and other French historians of death culture located the formative phase of the "new individualism" found in wills to the high Middle Ages, although others also saw an important shift in attitudes during the eighteenth century, at the time of the French Revolution.[66] One naturally expects this of the *Annales* school of interpretation, which prefers to explain historical change as the product of a *longue durée*, or long, drawn-out process extending over centuries, rather than the product of abrupt, dramatic events such as the Black Death.

Other historians of medieval death culture argued that it was impossible to trace the influence of the Black Death across time and space, since specific examples of macabre art—such as the Triumph of Death fresco in the Camposanto of Pisa—

could not be precisely dated and different areas of Europe responded to the plague in different ways.[67] But some historians, such as Samuel Cohn, viewed the Black Death as having an important impact upon late medieval attitudes towards death, as exemplified by an emerging "cult of remembrance" that could be traced in wills of the post-plague period. Evidence for this emerges from 1348 and the 1360s—coinciding with the first and second outbreaks of plague—in Tuscany, and from 1400 in Douai in Flanders. Testators evinced a much greater desire to specify their place of burial and to make arrangements for funerals and annual remembrances in order to avoid the ignominy of a nameless, mass burial that they may have witnessed during epidemics of plague.[68] This tied in very well with the social commentary of contemporaries, such as Giovanni Boccaccio, who noted widespread abandonment of plague victims by even close family members out of fear of contracting the disease.[69] This should not be surprising given the almost universal advice of plague doctors to flee the plague due to the disease's well-known contagiousness (even though bubonic plague is not actually spread person-to-person), and in fact a cardinal of the Church, Domenico de Dominicis, wrote an entire treatise dedicated to defending an individual's right to flight from the plague, even by priests who supposedly had the duty of administering last rites to the dying.[70]

I personally do not believe we can ever fully know the late medieval attitude towards death. The gulf in outlook between those times and our own is simply too wide to ever be spanned successfully. I say this because, the more I study late medieval death culture, the more it becomes clear to me how much has been irrevocably lost. Medieval people—specifically, the inhabitants of medieval Catholic Europe—had one of the most articulated and developed concepts of the afterlife of perhaps any other culture in history. The imaginative power of the medieval topography of the afterlife should be self-evident to anyone who has read Dante's *Divine Comedy*. In particular, the realm of Purgatory—a way-station for not-too-sinful souls who had to be purified before their final ascent towards heaven—was a concept that can be considered unique to Catholic Europe in the latter part of the Middle Ages. Although prayers for the dead are certainly to be found in other cultures, including Judaic, Islamic, and Buddhist religions, the emergence of Purgatory as a fully imagined and real place only seems to have occurred in Europe during the twelfth and thirteenth centuries.[71] It was specifically rejected by the Eastern Orthodox Church, and by Protestant reformers such as Martin Luther beginning in the sixteenth century. Nonetheless, Purgatory allowed late medieval Catholics to maintain a living relationship with their dearly departed dead through remembrances and prayers.

These days, in the modern, twenty-first century world, the afterlife doesn't seem to command much belief, at least in the West. When I ask my students how many believe in an afterlife, typically less than half the class will raise their hands. Most don't believe there is anything after death (i.e., we simply become nothing) or are not sure. But nihilism as a prevailing element to Western culture is rather new (perhaps dating to the nineteenth century?) and is utterly foreign to medieval thinking. In the nihilistic view, death does command a lot of attention and respect, because it is the actual end of all things. But for medieval people, death was only the beginning, the start of another, longer journey in the afterlife. In this scheme of things, death became a lot less important, and terrifying. I have argued previously that the skeletal figure or cadaver of late medieval macabre art should be considered a transitional figure, a marker towards the resurrection and reassemblage of the dead body, which medieval people believed would be rejoined with their souls at the end of time. In this way, the skeleton can be viewed as a hopeful and optimistic symbol, just as much as a morbid and gloomy one.[72] But in no way can it be viewed as expressing the finality of death, at least in a medieval context. If there is anyone who is obsessed or fascinated with death, it is ourselves.

When to end the Middle Ages?

Some people don't want the Middle Ages to end. By this I don't mean that they never want to stop studying medieval history, although I can understand that sentiment entirely. Rather, they literally don't want it to end. There has been a movement afoot (for some time now) to replace the old divisions between the medieval and Early Modern eras with a different periodization, one that is called "Old Europe," which would extend continuously from the eleventh to the eighteenth centuries. The argument for this is that there were many more continuities than discontinuities across the medieval/Early Modern divide, such as stability in political structures, social hierarchies, basic religious beliefs, etc.[73] This also seems to accord with the prevailing sentiment in most medieval history textbooks, which these days end on a note of continuity and gradual transition or transformation to the modern era, rather than abrupt change.[74]

At one time, I agreed with this outlook. I even proposed a new term, "transcendence," to describe the span from the late medieval to the Early Modern periods, in preference to "transition" or "transformation," because I did not believe there was really anything to transition or transform to! Instead, I argued that Europe "transcended" its late medieval crises without having to fundamentally alter its core culture and values.[75]

However, a strong case has recently been made by the medieval demographic historian, Ole Benedictow, that the division between the late medieval and Early Modern periods "is not arbitrary or simply a matter of expediency arising from historians' need for manageable chronological units," but emerges organically from distinctive demographic systems that, in turn, imply distinctive "social formations" in terms of economy, technology, politics, religion, social classes, etc.[76] In other words, there is a reason why historians write about and teach in their textbooks and college courses about the Middle Ages as a distinct historical era from modern times. It is fitting that this is the last debate mentioned in this book, for it bookends nicely with a similar debate we explored in Chapter 1 about the transition from Late Antiquity to the early Middle Ages and whether there really was a decline and fall of the Roman Empire. In similar fashion, the trend of the latest scholarship seems to be towards seeing a more sharply defined, abrupt transition rather than a continuous, gradual one.

The case for the late Middle Ages, roughly, the century or two centuries between 1350 and 1450/1550, comprising its own demographic system goes back to the mortality evidence which we explored in the previous chapter.[77] In addition, there were a number of societal transformations during this "long fifteenth century" which, it can be argued, also made for a clear-cut transition from medieval to modern culture and which marks this period as its own distinctive era. These transformations include: a political transition from feudalism to absolutism, or from local governing structures to a centralized state system; the religious fragmentation of Europe into Catholic and various Protestant "confessions" of faith; European expansion and contact with new worlds or continents, both west and east; and an economic transition from a feudalized, command economy to an open, market-orientated, "proto-capitalist" approach.[78] At least some of these transformations, particularly in the economic sphere, can be linked to the new demographic regime imposed by the Black Death.

I now think I was wrong to characterize the late medieval transition to Early Modern times as "transcendence". In fact, I've come to the completely opposite conclusion, that a new term is needed to convey the *discontinuity*, rather than continuity, that marks this transition. Perhaps, borrowing from the *Harry Potter* series of books, "transfiguration" (from the Latin word, *transfigurare*) is a good candidate, since it does convey transformation or transition in which a completely new form is assumed, as in a metamorphosis.[79] Whatever the term used, it is clear that there is no going back now from the persistently high mortality regime, owing to the Black Death, that has been assigned to the late Middle Ages, which is virtually undeniable based on the evidence. It is also undeniable, based on the evidence, that this plague mortality had very large impacts upon late medieval society and economy. And if we are to define the Middle Ages by such readily recognizable social systems as "feudalism," then it is, again, undeniable that the Middle Ages really did come to an end by about 1500. Our challenge is to bring closure to the Middle Ages, without having to resort to such value-laden terms as "waning" or "decline" that were so popularized by Huizinga. I think perhaps the best way out of this conundrum is to emphasize the unintentionally positive impacts—the "silver lining"—that the Black Death had upon late medieval society, and to admit that this society responded rather well, or at least better than expected, to what by all rights should have been an apocalyptic meltdown—a crisis that never came.[80] Maybe in this way we can acknowledge that the Middle Ages came to end, but that this was not necessarily a bad thing, nor that it signifies that a tragic tale must be told.

Notes

1 Johan Huizinga, *The Waning of the Middle Ages: A Study of the Forms of Life, Thought and Art in France and the Netherlands in the XIVth and XVth Centuries*, trans. Frederik Jan Hopman (London: E. Arnold and Co., 1924). Another book featured prominently in

the Cloisters' gift shop is the *Waning* knockoff, *A Distant Mirror: The Calamitous 14th Century*, by Barbara Tuchman, published by Alfred A. Knopf in 1978.

2 Edward Peters and Walter P. Simons, "The New Huizinga and the Old Middle Ages," *Speculum* 74 (1999):587. The authors clearly considered the *Waning* to be a classic that became so for the "right reasons," even though I think that their definition of the "wrong reasons" precisely fits Huizinga's work.

3 Peters and Simons, "New Huizinga," pp. 606–7.

4 Charles Wood provided a perceptive review of *A Distant Mirror* in *Speculum* 54 (1979):430–35. Based on her bibliography, Tuchman used the 1968 Penguin edition of Hopman's original 1924 English translation.

5 See especially H. Kaminsky, "From Lateness to Waning to Crisis: The Burden of the Later Middle Ages," *Journal of Early Modern History* 4 (2000):85–125.

6 Wim Blockmans and Peter Hoppenbrouwers, *Introduction to Medieval Europe, 300–1550*, trans. Isola van den Hoven (London: Routledge, 2007), pp. 3–4; John M. Riddle, *A History of the Middle Ages, 300–1500* (Lanham, MD.: Rowman and Littlefield Publishers, 2008), pp. 463–64; A. Daniel Frankforter, *The Medieval Millennium: An Introduction*, 2nd edn. (Upper Saddle River, NJ.: Prentice Hall, 2003), pp. 327–28; Robin W. Winks and Teofilo F. Ruiz, *Medieval Europe and the World: From Late Antiquity to Modernity, 400–1500* (New York: Oxford University Press, 2005), p. 238. An exception is František Graus, who viewed "transition" as essentially a meaningless term, since it could be used to describe almost any period. See František Graus, *Pest-Geissler-Judenmorde*, 2nd edn. (Göttingen, Germany: Vandenhoeck and Ruprecht, 1988), p. 553.

7 Christopher Dyer, *Standards of Living in the Later Middle Ages: Social Change in England, c. 1200–1520* (Cambridge: Cambridge University Press, 1989), pp. 109–50; Christopher Dyer, *Everyday Life in Medieval England* (London: Hambledon Press, 1994), pp. 77–100.

8 Peters and Simons, "New Huizinga," p. 601; Wessel Krul, "In the Mirror of van Eyck: Johan Huizinga's *Autumn of the Middle Ages*," *Journal of Medieval and Early Modern Studies* 27 (1997):372. Huizinga's distaste for "scientific" history is evident from the opening chapter of the *Waning*, where he wrote, "A scientific historian of the Middle Ages, relying first and foremost on official documents . . . occasionally runs the risk of neglecting the difference of tone between the life of the expiring Middle Ages and that of our own days". See Huizinga, *Waning of the Middle Ages*, p. 15.

9 Pieter Geyl, "Huizinga as Accuser of His Age," *History and Theory* 2 (1963):235, 260.

10 Johan Huizinga, *Men and Ideas: History, the Middle Ages, the Renaissance*, trans. Verzamelde Werken (New York: Meridian Books, 1959), pp. 243–87.

11 Huizinga, *Waning of the Middle Ages*, p. 335.

12 Peters and Simons, "New Huizinga," p. 592.

13 Geyl, "Huizinga as Accuser of His Age," pp. 231–62.

14 Peters and Simons, "New Huizinga," pp. 589–96.

15 Peters and Simons, "New Huizinga," pp. 596–604.

16 R.L. Colie, "Johan Huizinga and the Task of Cultural History," *American Historical Review* 69 (1964):621–22.

17 Peters and Simons, "New Huizinga," p. 618.

18 Peters and Simons, "New Huizinga," p. 590, n. 13.

19 Peters and Simons, "New Huizinga," pp. 604–5.

20 Huizinga, *Waning of the Middle Ages*, p. 29. The phrase perhaps inspired Barbara Tuchman's subtitle for *A Distant Mirror*, namely, *The Calamitous 14th Century*.

21 Graus, *Pest-Geissler-Judenmorde*, 2nd edn. p. 536.

22 Bernd Roeck, "Religious Crisis, 1400–1700: Some Considerations," in *New Approaches to the History of Late Medieval and Early Modern Europe: Selected Proceedings of Two International Conferences at The Royal Danish Academy of Sciences and Letters in Copenhagen in 1997 and 1999*, eds. Troels Dahlerup and Per Ingesman (*Historisk-filosofiske Meddelelser*, 104, 2009), p. 446.

23 Rudolf Vierhaus, "Zum Problem historischer Krisen," in *Historische Prozesse*, eds. K.G. Faber and C. Meir (Munich: Deutscher Taschenbuch-Verlag, 1978), p. 314; Roeck, "Religious Crisis," p. 445.

24 Jacob Burckhardt, *Force and Freedom: Reflections on History*, trans. James Hastings Nichols (New York: Pantheon Books, 1943), pp. 257, 267; Roeck, "Religious Crisis," pp. 445–47.

25 There is a similar debate among historians of ancient Rome as to whether to apply the concept of "crisis" to the late Roman Empire. See Wolf Liebescheutz, "Was There a Crisis of the Third Century?" in *Crises and the Roman Empire: Proceedings of the Seventh Workshop of the International Network, Impact of Empire, (Nijmegen, June 20–24, 2006)*, eds. Olivier Hekster, Gerda de Kleijn, and Daniëlle Slootjes (Leiden, Netherlands: Brill, 2007), pp. 11–20.

26 Blockmans and Hoppenbrouwers, *Introduction to Medieval Europe*, pp. 271–82, 287–91; Winks and Ruiz, *Medieval Europe*, pp. 241–52; Christopher Dyer, *An Age of Transition? Economy and Society in England in the Later Middle Ages* (Oxford: Clarendon Press, 2005), pp. 29–30; Christopher Dyer, *Making a Living in the Middle Ages: The People of Britain, 850–1520* (New Haven, CT.: Yale University Press, 2002), pp. 228–97; Bruce M.S. Campbell, "Physical Shocks, Biological Hazards, and Human Impacts: The Crisis of the Fourteenth Century Revisited," in *Le Interazioni fra Economia e Ambiente Biologico nell'Europa Preindustriale secc. XIII-XVIII*, ed. Simonetta Cavaciocchi (Florence: Firenze University Press, 2010), pp. 13–32; James L. Goldsmith, "The Crisis of the Late Middle Ages: The Case of France," *French History* 9 (1995):417, 446; J.L. Bolton, *The Medieval English Economy, 1150–1500* (London and Totowa, N.J.: J.M. Dent and Sons and Rowman and Littlefield, 1980), pp. 180–245.

27 Blockmans and Hoppenbrouwers, *Introduction to Medieval Europe*, pp. 328–43; Roeck, "Religious Crisis," pp. 447–51.

28 This is also sometimes called an "integration crisis" due to the integrated nature of the international monetary and commercial systems. England is thought to have avoided much of the effects of this crisis owing to their limited use of coinage and reliance instead on credit and account book entries. See Ian Blanchard, "The Late Medieval European 'Integration Crisis,' 1340–1540," in *New Approaches to the History of Late Medieval and Early Modern Europe*, pp. 316–28; S.R. Epstein, "The Late Medieval Crisis as an 'Integration Crisis'" (London School of Economics and Political Science: Working Papers in Economic History, No. 46/98, December 1998); Jim Bolton, "Was There a 'Crisis of Credit' in Fifteenth-Century England?" *British Numismatic Journal* 81 (2011):144–64; Jim Bolton, "'The World Upside Down': Plague as an Agent of Economic and Social Change," in *The Black Death in England*, eds. W.M. Ormrod and P.G. Lindley (Donington, UK: Shaun Tyas, 2003), pp. 40–43; Pamela Nightingale, "Money Contraction and Credit in Later Medieval England," *Economic History Review* 43 (1990):560–75; John Day, *The Medieval Market Economy* (Oxford: Basil Blackwell, 1987), pp. 1–54.

29 David M. Palliser, *Towns and Local Communities in Medieval and Early Modern England* (Aldershot, UK: Ashgate, 2006); David M. Palliser, "Urban Decay Revisited," in *Towns and Townspeople in the Fifteenth Century*, ed. J.A.F. Thompson (Gloucester, UK: Alan Sutton, 1988), pp. 1–21; Christopher R. Friedrichs, "Urban Transformation? Some Constants and Continuities in the Crisis-Challenged City," in *New Approaches to the History of Late Medieval and Early Modern Europe*, pp. 258–64; Richard Britnell, *Britain and Ireland, 1050–1530: Economy and Society* (Oxford: Oxford University Press, 2004), pp. 347–61; John Hatcher, "The Great Slump of the Mid-Fifteenth Century," in *Progress and Problems in Medieval England: Essays in Honour of Edward Miller*, eds. Richard Britnell and John Hatcher (Cambridge: Cambridge University Press, 1996), pp. 266–70; Dyer, *Age of Transition*, pp. 190–94; Dyer, *Making a Living*, pp. 298–313; Bolton, "'World Upside Down'," pp. 64–66; Bolton, *Medieval English Economy*, pp. 246–86; R.H. Britnell, "The Black Death in English Towns," *Urban History* 21 (1994): 195–210; Alan Dyer, *Decline and Growth in English Towns, 1400–1640* (Cambridge: Cambridge

University Press, 1991); Stephen R. Epstein, "Cities, Regions and the Late Medieval Crisis: Sicily and Tuscany Compared," *Past and Present* 130 (1991):3–50; Charles Phythian-Adams, "Urban Decay in Late Medieval England," in *Towns and Societies*, eds. P. Adams and E.A. Wrigley (Cambridge: Cambridge University Press, 1978), pp. 159–85; R.B. Dobson, "Urban Decline in Late Medieval England," *Transactions of the Royal Historical Society* 27 (1977): 1–22. For studies of individual towns in the context of urban crisis and decline, see: David M. Palliser, "A Crisis in English Towns? The Case of York, 1460–1640," *Northern History* 14 (1978):108–25; Charles Phythian-Adams, *Desolation of a City: Coventry and the Urban Crisis in the Late Middle Ages* (Cambridge: Cambridge University Press, 1979); Robert S. Gottfried, *Bury St. Edmunds and the Urban Crisis: 1290–1539* (Princeton, NJ.: Princeton University Press, 1982); R.H. Britnell, *Growth and Decline in Colchester, 1300–1525* (Cambridge: Cambridge University Press, 1986); S.H. Rigby, *Medieval Grimsby: Growth and Decline* (Hull, UK: University of Hull Press, 1993), pp. 113–35.

30 Blockmans and Hoppenbrouwers, *Introduction to Medieval Europe*, p. 282; Winks and Ruiz, *Medieval Europe*, pp. 238–39; Frankforter, *Medieval Millennium*, pp. 300–3.

31 Graus, *Pest-Geissler-Judenmorde*, 2nd edn., p. 529.

32 Graus, *Pest-Geissler-Judenmorde*, 2nd edn., pp. 536–38; Winks and Ruiz, *Medieval Europe*, p. 239.

33 Winks and Ruiz, *Medieval Europe*, p. 239.

34 E.A. Wrigley and R.S. Schofield, *The Population History of England, 1541–1871: A Reconstruction*, 2nd edn. (Cambridge: Cambridge University Press, 1989), p. 332; R.S. Schofield, "Crisis Mortality," in *Population Studies from Parish Registers: A Selection of Readings from "Local Population Studies,"* ed. Michael Drake (Matlock, UK: Local Population Studies, 1982), pp. 97–110. Other demographic historians have adopted different definitions of crisis mortality based on their sources. Christopher Dyer, using the manorial accounts of the bishopric of Worcester, set it at 6 percent, while Pamela Nightingale, basing herself on the Statue Merchant certificates of debt, raised it to 8 percent. John Hatcher defined crisis mortality based on fifteenth-century obituary lists for the monks of Christ Church, Canterbury, as 40 deaths per thousand (i.e., 4 percent), while Barbara Harvey, using similar records at Westminster Abbey, set it at 100 per thousand (10 percent). See: Christopher Dyer, *Lords and Peasants in a Changing Society: The Estates of the Bishopric of Worcester, 680–1540* (Cambridge: Cambridge University Press, 1980), p. 223; Pamela Nightingale, "Some New Evidence of Crises and Trends of Mortality in Late Medieval England," *Past and Present* 187 (2005): 41; John Hatcher, "Mortality in the Fifteenth Century: Some New Evidence," *Economic History Review*, 2nd ser., 39 (1986):27; Barbara Harvey, *Living and Dying in England, 1100–1540: The Monastic Experience* (Oxford: Clarendon Press, 1993), p. 122.

35 Josiah C. Russell, "Effects of Pestilence and Plague, 1315–1385," *Comparative Studies in Society and History* 8 (1966):464–73; William Chester Jordan, *The Great Famine: Northern Europe in the Early Fourteenth Century* (Princeton, NJ.: Princeton University Press, 1996), pp 185–87; Daniel Antoine and Simon Hillson, "Famine, Black Death and Health in Fourteenth-Century London," *Archaeology International* 8 (2004):26–28; Sharon DeWitte and Philip Slavin, "Between Famine and Death: England on the Eve of the Black Death—Evidence from Paleoepidemiology and Manorial Accounts," *Journal of Interdisciplinary History* 44 (2013):37–60.

36 This contraction in arable production was chronicled, region by region, for England and Wales in *The Agrarian History of England and Wales: Volume 3, 1348–1500*, ed. Edward Miller (Cambridge: Cambridge University Press, 1991), pp. 34–174. While Postan saw the post-plague contraction of arable as holding back population recovery, most scholars see the opposite, namely, that it was reduced labor inputs, owing to fewer people and higher costs, that resulted in lower agricultural outputs. Of course, many see this contraction as not a crisis at all, since population decline outpaced arable contraction, thus maintaining a food supply per head that was more than sufficient. See John Hatcher and Mark Bailey, *Modelling the Middle Ages: The History and Theory of England's Economic*

Development (Oxford: Oxford University Press, 2001), p. 58; Britnell, *Britain and Ireland*, pp. 389–95. For an exhaustive historiographical survey of the topic of agrarian crisis in late medieval England, see Nils Hybel, *Crisis or Change: The Concept of Crisis in the Light of Agrarian Structural Reorganization in Late Medieval England* (Aarhus: Aarhus University Press, 1989).

37 Hatcher, " Great Slump ," pp. 237–72; Hatcher and Bailey, *Modelling the Middle Ages*, pp. 49–52; Blockmans and Hoppenbrouwers, *Introduction to Medieval Europe*, pp. 278–82.

38 Hatcher and Bailey, *Modelling the Middle Ages*, pp. 21–43; *The Brenner Debate: Agrarian Class Structure and Economic Development in Pre-Industrial Europe*, eds. T.H. Aston and C.H.E. Philpin (Cambridge: Cambridge University Press, 1985).

39 For summaries of this criticism, see: Barbara F. Harvey, "Introduction: The 'Crisis' of the Early Fourteenth Century," in *Before the Black Death: Studies in the "Crisis" of the Early Fourteenth Century*, ed. Bruce M.S. Campbell (Manchester, UK: Manchester University Press, 1991), pp. 4–11, 16–19; Hatcher and Bailey, *Modelling the Middle Ages*, pp. 52–65, 95–120. Focus is now shifting to the environmental context and interactions with plague and famine that resulted in the late medieval crises. See: Bruce M.S. Campbell, "Nature as Historical Protagonist: Environment and Society in Pre-Industrial England," *Economic History Review* 63 (2010):310; Campbell, "Physical Shocks," pp. 30–31; Bruce M.S. Campbell, *The Great Transition: Climate, Disease and Society in the Late-Medieval World* (Cambridge: Cambridge University Press, 2016), p. 27.

40 Kaminsky, "From Lateness to Waning to Crisis," pp. 97–120; Harvey, "Introduction: The 'Crisis' of the Early Fourteenth Century," pp. 19–24.

41 Winks and Ruiz, *Medieval Europe*, p. 239.

42 Francis Aidan Gasquet, *The Great Pestilence* (London: Simpkin Marshall, Hamilton, Kent and Co., 1893); Blockmans and Hoppenbrouwers, *Introduction to Medieval Europe*, p. 282; Kaminsky, "From Lateness to Waning to Crisis," pp. 106, 116; Dyer, *Age of Transition*, p. 8; Britnell, *Britain and Ireland*, p. 368. Blockmans and Hoppenbrouwers explicitly explained that they preferred "contraction" to "crisis," because the latter term obscured the fact that many social groups, such as peasant wage earners, actually improved their standard of living, even as population and economic production shrank.

43 Bruce M.S. Campbell, "Panzootics, Pandemics and Climatic Anomalies in the Fourteenth Century," in *Beiträge zum Göttinger Umwelthistorischen Kolloquium, 2010–2011*, ed. Bernd Herrmann (Göttingen, Germany: Universitätsverlag Göttingen, 2011), p. 205. Hatcher and Bailey characterized this approach to history as "Chaos Theory". See Hatcher and Bailey, *Modelling the Middle Ages*, pp. 213–15.

44 Hatcher and Bailey, *Modelling the Middle Ages*, p. 215.

45 Hatcher and Bailey, *Modelling the Middle Ages*, p. 219.

46 Hatcher and Bailey, *Modelling the Middle Ages*, p. 215; Campbell, *Great Transition*, pp. 21–22; Campbell, "Panzootics, Pandemics and Climatic Anomalies," p. 183, 204–5.

47 Campbell, "Nature as Historical Protagonist," p. 309; Campbell, "Physical Shocks," pp. 31–32; Campbell, *Great Transition*, p. 396; Campbell, "Panzootics, Pandemics and Climatic Anomalies," pp. 177, 204–5; Harvey, "Introduction: The 'Crisis' of the Early Fourteenth Century," pp. 2–3; John Hatcher, "England in the Aftermath of the Black Death," *Past and Present* 144 (1994):5–6; Hatcher and Bailey, *Modelling the Middle Ages*, p. 57. Campbell eschewed the terms "exogenous" and "endogenous," because they created a "false dichotomy" with respect to the complex and interdependent environmental variables that impacted late medieval history. He was wrong, however, to assert that the Black Death was dependent on "threshold levels of population density" for its spread, since a defining feature of bubonic plague is its inverse correlation between mortality and population density. See Ole J. Benedictow, *What Disease was Plague? On the Controversy over the Microbiological Identity of Plague Epidemics of the Past* (Leiden, Netherlands: Brill, 2010), pp. 289–311.

48 Huizinga, *Waning of the Middle Ages*, p. 138.

49 Huizinga, *Waning of the Middle Ages*, p. 139.

50 Huizinga, *Waning of the Middle Ages*, p. 151.
51 Paul Binski, *Medieval Death* (Ithaca, NY.: Cornell University Press, 1996), p. 130; K. Cohen, *Metamorphosis of a Death Symbol: The Transi Tomb in the Later Middle Ages and the Renaissance* (Berkeley, CA.: University of California Press, 1973), p. 48.
52 Samuel K. Cohn, Jr., "The Place of the Dead in Flanders and Tuscany: Towards a Comparative History of the Black Death," in *The Place of the Dead: Death and Remembrance in Late Medieval and Early Modern Europe*, eds. Bruce Gordon and Peter Marshall (Cambridge: Cambridge University Press, 2000), p. 19; Jean Delumeau, *Sin and Fear: The Emergence of a Western Guilt Culture, 13th–18th Centuries* (New York: St. Martin's Press, 1990), pp. 35–85.
53 Binski, *Medieval Death*, pp. 125–26.
54 Binski, *Medieval Death*, pp. 134–59; Delumeau, *Sin and Fear*, pp. 66–85; Cohen, *Metamorphosis of a Death Symbol*, pp. 120–81.
55 Binski, *Medieval Death*, pp. 138,149–52, 158.
56 Binski, *Medieval Death*, p. 152; Cohen, *Metamorphosis of a Death Symbol*.
57 Philippe Ariès, *The Hour of our Death*, trans. Helen Weaver (Oxford: Oxford University Press, 1981), pp. 128–32.
58 Ariès, *Hour of our Death*, p. 137. I personally think this view is far-fetched, as Huizinga would have associated the "passionate love for life" with Jacob Burckhardt's interpretation of the Renaissance, to which Huizinga set himself up in opposition.
59 Ariès, *Hour of our Death*, p. 114; Binski, *Medieval Death*, pp. 130–31.
60 Jacques Chiffoleau, *La comptabilité de l'au'delà: Les hommes, la mort et la religion dans la région d'Avignon à la fin du Moyen Âge, vers 1320-vers 1480* (Rome: École française de Rome, 1980); Jean Pierre Deregnaucourt, *Autour de la mort à Douai: Attitudes, pratiques et croyances, 1250–1500* (Ph.D. dissertation, Université Charles de Gaulle-Lille, 1993); Michel Lauwers, *La mémoire des ancêtres, le souci des morts: morts, rites et société au Moyen Âge, diocèse de Liège, XIe-XIIIe siècles* (Paris, EHESS, 1997); Cohn, "Place of the Dead in Flanders and Tuscany," pp. 19–20.
61 Cohn, "Place of the Dead in Flanders and Tuscany," pp. 34–38.
62 Eamon Duffy, *Stripping of the Altars: Traditional Religion in England, 1400–1580* (New Haven: Yale University Press, 1992), pp. 301–5.
63 Duffy, *Stripping of the Altars*, pp. 314–16; Huizinga, *Waning of the Middle Ages*, p. 147; Binski, *Medieval Death*, pp. 40–41.
64 Duffy, *Stripping of the Altars*, pp. 327–37; Clive Burgess, "'Longing to be Prayed For': Death and Commemoration in an English Parish in the Later Middle Ages," in *The Place of the Dead*, pp. 44–65; Clive Burgess, "'For the Increase of Divine Service': Chantries in the Parish in Late Medieval Bristol," *Journal of Ecclesiastical History* 36 (1985):46–65; B.A. Hanawalt, "Keepers of the Lights: Late Medieval English Parish Guilds," *Journal of Medieval and Renaissance Studies* 14 (1984):21–37.
65 Huizinga's omission was noted by other scholars: See Binski, *Medieval Death*, p. 130.
66 Ariès, *Hour of our Death*, pp. 124–26; Lauwers, *Mémoire des ancêtres*, pp. 499–500; Chiffoleau, *La comptabilité*, p. 207; Cohn, "Place of the Dead in Flanders and Tuscany," p. 20.
67 Binski, *Medieval Death*, pp. 126–29. Binski was responding in particular to the thesis of Millard Meiss in *Painting in Florence and Siena after the Black Death* (New York: Harper and Row, 1951), which argued for the Black Death as a formative influence (a largely negative one) upon late medieval Italian painting. The Triumph of Death fresco in the Camposanto of Pisa is now dated to the 1330s or '40s, just before the advent of the Black Death. See: H.W. Van Os, "The Black Death and Sienese Painting: A Problem of Interpretation," *Art History* 4 (1981):237–49; J. Polzer, "Aspects of the Fourteenth-Century Iconography of Death and the Plague," in *The Black Death: The Impact of the Fourteenth-Century Plague*, ed. D. Williman (Binghamton, NY.: Center for Medieval and Early Renaissance Studies, 1982), pp. 107–30; Christine M. Boeckl, "The Pisan *Triumph of Death* and the Papal Constitution *Benedictus Deus*," *Artibus et Historiae* 18 (1997): 55–61; Phillip Lindley, "The Black Death and English Art: A Debate and Some

Assumptions," in *The Black Death in England*, eds. W.M. Ormrod and Phillip Lindley (Stamford, UK: Paul Watkins, 1996), pp. 131–32.

68 Cohn, "Place of the Dead in Flanders and Tuscany," p. 29; Samuel K. Cohn, Jr., *The Cult of Remembrance and the Black Death: Six Renaissance Cities in Central Italy* (Baltimore, MD: Johns Hopkins University Press, 1992).

69 John Aberth, *The Black Death: The Great Mortality of 1348–1350. A Brief History with Documents*, 2nd edn. (Boston, MA.: Bedford/St. Martin's, 2017), p. 65.

70 John Aberth, *From the Brink of the Apocalypse: Confronting Famine, War, Plague, and Death in the Later Middle Ages*, 2nd edn. (London: Routledge, 2010), pp. 109, 195–98. See also John Aberth, *Doctoring the Black Death: Europe's Late Medieval Medical Response to Epidemic Disease*, forthcoming with Rowman and Littlefield.

71 Jacques Le Goff, *The Birth of Purgatory* (Chicago, IL.: University of Chicago Press, 1984); Binski, *Medieval Death*, pp. 181–88; Duffy, *Stripping of the Altars*, pp. 338–76.

72 Aberth, *From the Brink of the Apocalypse*, 2nd edn., p. 269.

73 Dietrich Gerhard, *Old Europe: A Study of Continuity, 1000–1800* (New York: Academic Press, 1981); Kaminsky, "From Lateness to Waning to Crisis," pp. 123–25. Nearly a century ago, Charles Homer Haskins was making similar points in his *The Renaissance of the Twelfth Century* (Cambridge, MA.: Harvard University Press, 1927), pp. 5–6.

74 Frankforter, *Medieval Millennium*, pp. 327–28; Winks and Ruiz, *Medieval Europe*, p. 257.

75 Aberth, *From the Brink of the Apocalypse*, 2nd edn., pp. 274–75.

76 Ole Benedictow, "New Perspectives in Medieval Demography: The Medieval Demographic System," in *Town and Countryside in the Age of the Black Death: Essays in Honour of John Hatcher*, eds. Mark Bailey and Stephen Rigby (Turnhout, Belgium: Brepols, 2012), pp. 3–4.

77 Benedictow, "New Perspectives," pp. 20, 28.

78 Friedrichs, "Urban Transformation," pp. 254–55; *Handbook of European History, 1400–1600: Late Middle Ages, Renaissance and Reformation*, eds. Thomas A. Brady, Jr., Heiko A. Oberman, and James D. Tracy, 2 vols. (Leiden, Netherlands: Brill 1994–95), 1:xiii–xxiv. The period under consideration here is actually 1400 to 1600 or to 1660; by shifting the limits back fifty years at either end, I don't think I've changed the validity of any of the transformations, simply the extent of their development.

79 Ironically for Harry Potter, transfiguration has historically been used in a Christian religious context, as in the "transfiguration of Jesus".

80 F.M. Getz, "Black Death and the Silver Lining: Meaning, Continuity, and Revolutionary Change in Histories of Medieval Plague," *Journal of the History of Biology* 24 (1991):265–89; David Herlihy, *The Black Death and the Transformation of the West*, ed. Samuel K. Cohn, Jr. (Cambridge, MA.: Harvard University Press, 1997); Samuel K. Cohn, Jr., "Triumph over Plague: Culture and Memory after the Black Death," in *Care for the Here and the Hereafter: Memoria, Art and Ritual in the Middle Ages*, ed. T. van Bueren (Turnhout, Belgium: Brepols, 2005); Aberth, *From the Brink of the Apocalypse*, 2nd edn., pp. 206–10.

CONCLUSION

My only regret in finishing this book is that I know it will be outdated as soon as it appears in print. But such is the nature of any controversy—it seems to elude our grasp as soon as we attempt to pin it down. And with the ever- accelerating nature of academic publishing, it is certain that more books will appear on any given topic than we can ever hope to keep up with.[1] Besides, my editor has grown impatient.

Nonetheless, historical debates can seem to have a life span all their own, as some historians have argued for historical periods themselves (i.e., that there is a "birth" and a "waning" to the Middle Ages). For example, I would argue that there are some debates, or at least some aspects of them, that are reaching "senility," or, if you like, "closure". Thus, the debate over whether the Black Death is to be identified with plague has been effectively ended by paleomicrobiological research on this issue, while a consensus has emerged on the demographic and socio-economic impacts of the Black Death, based on a plethora of recent research (Chapter 8). While this certainly does not end all debate on the Black Death, it does, I would argue, redirect future research efforts into more productive areas. In similar fashion, research into eleventh-century charters and other documents has settled debate on the motivation for the First Crusade, deciding this in favor of a religious, as opposed to the more traditional "mercenary," interpretation. This has probably helped redirect research focus towards the later crusades and crusades within Europe, thus expanding the geographical, temporal, and definitional scope of crusading studies (Chapter 3).

Then there are some subjects in medieval history that are approaching "maturity," having experienced considerable and exciting growth. This seems to be the case for medieval environmental history, as indeed for the field of environmental history in general. The practitioners of this history must now decide in which direction to take future research, which I have argued is divided between realist/nominalist, or material/cultural, approaches (Chapter 7). Likewise, the histories of medieval sexuality and of marginal groups are experiencing their own growing pains. Historians of medieval homosexuality, for example, must decide how to advance their field in the wake of the controversy over the "Boswell Thesis," which consumed much of the early focus in the 1980s and '90s. Instead of debating the definition of "homosexual" or "gay" in pre-modern times, a more promising direction seems to be towards chronicling same-sex practices and communities in medieval cities, such as Florence, Venice, and Cologne. In this way, we seem to gain an appreciation, from the ground up, of what being a "homosexual" actual meant in the Middle Ages, and how this was similar, and how it was different, from the modern experience of being gay (Chapter 5).

Some debates probably will never be settled. I feel this to be true with regard to the decline and fall of the Roman Empire, one of the oldest historical debates covered in this book (Chapter 1). Although the idea of a long transition from "Late Antiquity" to the early Middle Ages has become something of an entrenched position in academia (as is also true with the concept of continuity across the late medieval to the Early Modern periods), recent scholarship, particularly with regard to the Late Antique environment, has also shown that it is not immune to challenge. Thus, a reset to earlier positions, with debate starting all over again, seems entirely possible. But then again, perhaps there are not enough sources from this early, and generally chaotic, time period to easily settle the matter.

Indeed, there are some debates that may never be truly decided, simply because sufficient sources do not exist to get a fully rounded, complete picture of the subject. This may be the case with medieval Jews, about whom much survives from the Christian perspective, but considerably less from the Jewish one, owing to the very persecution from which Jews suffered (Chapter 4).[2] The same is true with respect to the Vikings, whose image as fearsome pillagers and raiders has largely been shaped by Christian monastic writers, at the expense of the Vikings' many other, more peaceful activities, such as trading, exploration, religious worship, etc. (Chapter 2).

What is certain is that debates over medieval history will continue, and hopefully, will continue to be spirited and contentious (preferably in a respectful and mutually tolerant way). This would be a sure sign that our field remains vigorous and healthy. Long may it be so.

Notes

1   The historian John McNeil estimated in 2003 that the number of books published in his field of environmental history had grown a hundred-fold since 1985 and would therefore require "a century of summers" in order to read it all. J.R. McNeil, "Observations on the Nature and Culture of Environmental History," *History and Theory* 42 (2003):5.

2   A notable exception to this rule can be found in Robert Chazan, *Daggers of Faith: Thirteenth-Century Missionizing and Jewish Response* (Berkeley, CA.: University of California Press, 1989).

INDEX